Bob Ray
MODX: The Official Guide

"No components should EVER alter core tables or files. That's all I'm gonna say on that one."
Jason Coward (OpenGeek) March 28, 2010

"The mantra we must remember in Open Source is that you get what you give."
Shaun McCormick (splittingred) July 21, 2010

"Unequivocably, there's no way anyone can now claim the documentation for MODX isn't up to snuff."
Ryan Thrash (rthrash) August 3, 2011

Publisher: MODX Press
Editor: Haven Stephens
Technical Editor: Shaun McCormick
Cover Design: äkta
Interior Design: Ryan Thrash
Production Coordinator: Michael Hickey
Indexer: Bob Ray

ISBN: 978-0-9836194-0-6

MODX, LLC
25 Highland Park Village, Ste 100-413
Dallas, TX 75205-2789
http://modx.com/press/

42 11 04 10 9 8 7 6 5 3 2 1

D0907713

Table of Contents

Acknowledgments

Countless people have been invaluable in the production of this book. First and foremost, I owe a debt of gratitude to the founders and core developers of MODX: Ryan Thrash (rthrash), Jason Coward (OpenGeek), and Shaun McCormick (splittingred). They have developed a first-class Open Source CMS, and this book would not have been possible without their support and patience. Shaun served as the book's technical editor and deserves special credit for ensuring its accuracy. Haven Stephens, the book's editor, played a critical role in eliminating countless errors and making sure that the explanations in the book were as clear as possible.

I would also like to thank the many users of the MODX Forums, both those whose answers have taught me almost everything I know about MODX and those whose questions led to the creation of this book. In particular, I'd like to thank the following people (MODX Forum usernames in parentheses):

Susan Ottwell (sottwell), Jelle Jager (TobyL), (ganeshXL), David Molliere (davidm), (kongondo), (doze), (ZAP), Zaigham Rana (Zi), Andreas Wettainen (mrhaw), Jay Gilmore (smashingred), Shane Sponagle (dev_cw), (coroico), Kyle Jaebker (kylej), Garry Nutting (garryn), Jeff Whitfield (Bravado), (Everett), (flinx), Mike Reid (pixelchutes), Jared Carlow (jaredc), (Dr. Scotty Delicious), (Carsten), Steve Hamblett (shamblett), (NetProphET), Adam Crownoble (aNoble), (netnoise), (sirlancelot), Aaron Wardle (Onesmarthost), (Photowebmax), Erik Bjorn (Sylvaticus), (snop), (mademyday), Keith Penton (kp52), (charliez), (bob1000), (Chuck), (therebechips), Dimitri Hilverda (Dimmy), (Soshite), Adrian Lawley (Taff), (sinbad), Bruno Perner (Bruno17), (Breezer), (mmjaeger), (AMDbuilder), (sharkbait), (chinesedream) (cipa), (ChuckTrukk), (Paprikas), David Bunker (bunk58), (samba), (paulp), (Byzantium), (SandersDesign), (virtualgadjo), James Ehly (devtrench), Mark Hamstra (Mark H.), (treigh), (hotdiggity), (ottogal), (anso), (pleth), (lossendae), (mconsidine), (Jul), (xdom), Luca Reghellin, (microcipcip), (Pandy06269), Helen Warner (Muggins), Ivan Salcedo (odeclass), Stefan Moser (stefan), Rob Backus (robb), John Hughes, Zuriel Andrusyshyn (zurie).

My apologies to the many others whose names I've omitted either from lack of space or memory lapse.

I'd also like to thank my cat, Cosmo, who spent many hours each day for over two years curled up next to me as I worked on the book at my computer. His comments on the book were invaluable.

Disclaimer of Warranty (Legal Mumbo Jumbo)

Introduction

MODX is an advanced Open Source Content Management System (CMS). If you are not familiar with the term CMS, think of a word processor for web sites, but on steroids. A CMS will usually provide you with a graphical view of your web site, a database that stores the site's content, and one or more editors for creating web pages and populating them with links, lists, headings, and formatted text.

Every CMS tries to provide a convenient and powerful user interface for creating and maintaining web sites, but to some extent, convenience and power are in opposition to one another. Some CMS platforms, like WordPress, put convenience above power. If you want a standard blog with a ready-made look and feel, WordPress provides a surprisingly friendly and intuitive user interface for creating and maintaining one.

MODX, on the other hand, leans more toward the power side of the equation. The learning curve is a little steeper, but MODX allows you much more freedom in the design of your web site, more powerful tools you can use to make the web site unique, and the ability to customize the CMS itself.

MODX is also a powerful Content Management Framework (CMF). This means that the building blocks of MODX can actually be used to create any number of different CMS platforms. We will cover customizing the MODX user interface in later chapters. For the most part, however, the use of MODX as a CMF is beyond the scope of this book, which is mainly about MODX the CMS.

One guiding principle of MODX is to put as few restrictions on the web developer as possible. MODX puts no limits on the CSS and HTML code you use to build your site, and you can easily add PHP or JavaScript code to meet any need. One illustration of this flexibility is that you can take virtually any existing web site and make a MODX web site out of it that looks exactly the same to a front-end visitor. Trying that with many other CMS platforms will leave you cursing and tearing your hair out.

By the time you've finished reading this book, you should be able to use MODX to create new web sites or to port existing web sites to MODX. It was my goal in writing this book to provide all the information you need to use the basic building blocks of MODX to meet your needs as a web designer/developer.

About This Book

Before we dive into MODX, we need to discuss a few things about this book. In the following sections, we'll look at who the book is for, how it is organized, and how the typography of the book can help you understand what you're looking at.

Audience

This book is for anyone who wants to use MODX for web site design, development, and maintenance. In order to get the most out of this book, you should have a basic familiarity with (X)HTML, CSS, and how the two interact in the rendering of web pages.

You will also see some PHP code in the book. You can do a lot with MODX without knowing PHP, but to get the most out of MODX, you really should have at least some knowledge of PHP. If you don't, never fear. PHP is a relatively easy computer language, and the PHP Primer in this book's Appendix will help you get started.

There are many excellent PHP tutorials on the Web, and lots of expert MODX users knew no PHP when they started out. Often, they created a web site with no PHP, and then learned PHP, a little bit at a time, as they began to make their web site more and more interesting and easier to maintain.

This book is perfectly suitable for MODX beginners but contains plenty of in-depth information for power users as well. If you are brand new to MODX, some parts of the book may go over your head the first time you read them. Over time, however, you will grow more familiar with how MODX works, and they will gradually begin to make sense to you.

At first, I tried to put material for beginners at the beginning of the book and save the more advanced information for later. Because of the way MODX works, however, it just wasn't possible. As a result, you'll see things that may confuse you on the first pass. You should be able to ignore them and create a perfectly good web site using the things you do understand. Later, as things make more sense to you, you'll be able to refine your site to take advantage of MODX's more advanced features. The book is also meant to serve as a reference manual for both beginners and experts.

Organization of The Book

Generally, the book is organized on the basis of MODX objects, such as resources, chunks, snippets, plugins, placeholders, etc. If you are new to MODX, you won't be familiar with these at first. After reading Chapter 1, however, you should have a fair idea of what they are and how they work together. Later in the book, we'll look at each MODX object in depth. Because the objects constantly interact with each other, you'll be learning about them all bit-by-bit as we go along.

Conventions

A number of typographical conventions are used throughout the book to make it easier to understand what you're looking at. There are two main typefaces for content in the book: The regular font (used for this sentence) and the code font. The code font looks like this when it appears in a regular font paragraph: `This is the inline code font.` When it appears in a separate paragraph, it looks like this:

```
This is the code snippet font.
```

The code font is used for all (X)HTML, CSS, and JavaScript code and for all MODX tags and their contents. It is also used for file and directory names and for path names and for text to be entered in a field in the MODX Manager.

MODX internal variables such as system event names, settings, and resource/template variable field names will also be in the code font, but to make them distinguishable, they will be in boldface type wherever they appear:

```
OnManagerFormSave, site_start, pagetitle.
```

Key terms will generally be in the regular font in italics when they first appear. Terms referring to MODX objects (snippets, template variables, chunks, plugins, categories, placeholders, etc.) will be in lowercase when they appear in text except at the beginning of a sentence.

Names of resources or elements that you will be creating and editing yourself, will be in italics in the code font when they first appear, then in the regular font in roman type, usually in CamelCase:

Create a chunk called *FooterChunk*. The FooterChunk will contain code for the page footer.

Terms referring to specific areas of the MODX Manager or to form fields in the Manager will generally be in initial caps and in the regular font:

Create/Edit Resource panel, Long Title, Alias, Package Manager

Shorthand references to Manager commands that use menus for navigation will be in bold and have arrows between them:

Go to **Tools → Package Management**

Longer descriptions of Manager actions in the text will use initial caps and quotation marks around buttons and menu choices that you are meant to select:

Select "System" on the Top Menu, then click on "Package Management."

Field names and tab names used in the MODX Manager will be in initial caps when referring to the specific area of the Manager, but in lowercase when discussing them as general objects. They will be enclosed in quotation marks when they are included in directions to click or select them, but used without the quotation marks in general discussion:

Click on the "Elements" tab.

Chunks are listed on the Elements tab.

Chunks are classified as elements.

The names of specific resources and elements will generally be in CamelCase in the text. They will usually be in the code font and italics when they first appear (especially in directions to create them):

Create a resource called *News*.

Let's create our *ShowList* snippet.

Later references to them will be in the regular font in CamelCase:

The FooterChunk contains all the elements shown in the footer of the page.

They will be enclosed in quotation marks in instructions to click or select them in the Manager:

Click on the "ShowList" snippet on the "Elements" tab.

Variable names (including snippet properties) will generally start with a lowercase letter and have the first letter of each following word capitalized. They will be in the code font: `$wordLength`, `$fontColor`, `$textHeight`, though there are some exceptions to this rule. Property names, MODX settings, and placeholder names, for example, are often in all lowercase with an underscore character between words: **site_start**, **blocked_until**. MODX system event names are in CamelCase and begin with a capital letter. All start with "**On**": **OnManagerFormSave**. Resource field names are in all lowercase, and a few have underscores while most don't: **pagetitle**, **longtitle**, **pub_date**, **unpub_date**.

As mentioned earlier, MODX settings and system event names will be in the code font in bold. For resource field names, the caption used in the Manager will be in initial caps in the regular font (e.g., Page Title, Publish Date). The actual field names used internally by MODX (and by users in tags and snippets) will be in the code font and bold (e.g., **pagetitle**, **pub_date**).

When a MODX tag or example contains a name that the user will supply, the term will be in italics:

```
[[SnippetName? &property1=`value1` &property2=`value2`]]
```

In the above example, the user is expected to replace all the words in italics. This is important because new users sometimes type in the example exactly as it is written and are surprised when it doesn't work.

I've tried to be as faithful to these conventions as possible, but this is a long book with many complicated references. I hope the reader will forgive the inevitable errors in typography.

 Because the page width of this book is limited, some lines of PHP and HTML code that should be on a single line are broken into two or more lines. I tried to break them in a way that doesn't harm the user's understanding of what the code does, but it wasn't always possible. The extra lines of code created will always be indented.

The only time the lines must be combined is for Input Option Values of template variables. Here's an example:

```
Red==Red as a rose||Blue==Blue as the sky||
    Green==Green as the grass
```

The lines above must be entered as a single line, but MODX won't let you use a carriage return for Input Option Values anyway, so the need to combine them should be obvious.

In all other cases that I'm aware of, the code can be entered as written and no harm will be done — the PHP and HTML parsers are very forgiving about formatting — but you should feel free to combine the split lines to fit your coding style. Generally, the only negative effect of the split lines will be on the formatting of some raw HTML code you'll see if you select "View Source" in your browser.

About MODX

In the following sections, we'll look at whether MODX is a good choice for you, learn a little bit about the history of MODX, and discuss the various versions of MODX. We'll also take a look at the architecture and key features of MODX.

Is MODX for you?

MODX is designed to be useful to everyone from beginning web designers to advanced Content Management System developers, but it is somewhat difficult for the former. If you are looking for a system that will do everything you want out-of-the-box and let you produce a finished web site without getting your hands dirty, MODX is probably not for you. For a standard blog, for example, WordPress might be a better choice. You install it, select a theme (or use the default one), and begin entering your posts.

Where MODX shines is in cases where you want a unique web site with active pages that you design yourself. Its flexibility and power are unequalled in the CMS world. If you can describe what you want your web site to do, the odds are good that you can do it in MODX.

My first MODX web site, for example, was a site I designed for a local political organization. The site had the usual pages: a page describing the organization's officers, a volunteer page, a page for the local elected officials with links to their web sites, a page containing the organization's bylaws, a page where users could download issues of the organization's newsletter, etc. The site also had a front page with excerpts from news posts, each with a link to the full post.

Next, I added a series of photo galleries for various events and put a random photo from one of the galleries under the menu on the front page that served as a link to the photo's gallery. Then came a fundraising thermometer that showed the current level of contributions.

I set up one user as the photo editor who could easily create new galleries and upload photos in the front end. I set up a news editor who could write new articles that would automatically show up in the news section and be excerpted on the front page. I set up a newsletter editor who could upload new newsletters in .PDF format. Each editor had access to only his or her own section of the site.

I learned MODX, created the site, and wrote simple instructions for each user in a surprisingly short time — less than a week. The site has been rock-solid ever since with almost no intervention on my part.

On one of my next MODX sites, the client wanted a page with seasonal photos and a discount coupon that changed automatically four times a year, with the seasons. I was able to add this in MODX using a simple custom snippet in about an hour. Doing this on most other CMS platforms would have taken much, much longer and would have been extremely frustrating.

In order to use MODX at all, you'll need some basic familiarity with CSS and (X)HTML. It's best if you have created a few web sites before diving into MODX. You don't need to know PHP to use MODX, but it definitely helps. Many MODX users end up learning PHP a little bit at a time as they attempt to get the most out of the CMS.

If you don't know any PHP at all, don't be put off by the examples of PHP code in the book. They are there for advanced users, and you can still do quite a lot with MODX without knowing PHP. The odds are that you will pick it up as you develop your MODX skills and can then go back and read over any sections that confused you at first. There is a PHP Primer in the Appendix at the end of the book that will help get you started.

A Brief History of MODX

In 2004, Ryan Thrash and Raymond Irving started working on what was later to become MODX. The initial MODX project was a combination of the DocVars add-on for the Etomite CMS and Raymond's web-user add-on. There was resistance to the MODX project at Etomite, and the two eventually left that community to work on MODX as a separate CMS.

MODX 0.9.0 began as a fork of Etomite but has developed into an independent CMS platform, and as of the release of MODX 2.0 Revolution, all references to Etomite are gone from the MODX code.

In May of 2005, Jason Coward joined the project, and in 2007, Raymond Irving left (amicably). Jason became the principle architect of the MODX core code. In 2008, Shaun McCormick joined the project and is now primarily responsible for the MODX Manager interface. MODX has an extremely creative and responsive user community, and countless MODX users have contributed to the development process over the last few years.

In 2009, MODX Version 0.9.6 was supplanted by two new versions. The 0.9.6 designation was misleading — by that time, MODX was a very robust and mature product. As of this writing, MODX exists in two forms: MODX 1.x.x Evolution and MODX 2.x.x Revolution.

Versions of MODX

In 2009, both MODX 1.0.0 Evolution and MODX 2.0.0 Revolution were released. If you visit the MODX Forums, you may see them referred to as "Evo" and "Revo" for short.

There are many similarities between the two, especially from the point of view of the user. Under the hood, the two are quite different. We'll look at some of the similarities and differences in the following sections. For now, we'll say that the main components of MODX discussed in this book (chunks, snippets, templates, template variables, plugins, resources, settings, and tags) exist in both versions and play the same role in each.

The MODX Manager user interface has been redesigned for MODX Revolution but is similar enough that most users have little or no trouble making the transition from one to the other.

This book is written primarily from the perspective of MODX Revolution since that is the future of MODX. That said, most of the content in the book will apply equally well to either version, and there is a section at the end of each chapter describing how the content of that chapter applies in MODX Evolution.

MODX Evolution

MODX 1.0.0 Evolution is a mature, stable release of the original MODX codebase with a set of standard add-ons for things like menus, photo galleries, user management, and content aggregation. It provides a fairly seamless upgrade for all legacy MODX sites.

The version numbers of earlier versions of MODX (e.g., 0.9.2, 0.9.6) are somewhat misleading. The version numbers imply that they were beta versions. In fact, they were (and still are) very mature and used in thousands of production web sites.

MODX Evolution has been around longer, and as of this writing, is more familiar to most MODX users than Revolution and has more available add-ons. Evolution also has a smaller footprint and takes somewhat less memory to install and use. Revolution, however, is more robust and more secure. Revolution is a significant technical advance compared to Evolution and represents the future of MODX.

MODX Revolution

MODX 2.0.0 Revolution (which appeared briefly as version 0.9.7) is a complete re-write of the MODX core code and Manager with a new tag syntax and many revolutionary features (hence the name). The Manager is somewhat easier to navigate and has a number of extremely convenient features like drag-and-drop editing and the ability to create new elements and resources and clear the cache in pop-up windows without leaving your current work. Revolution also introduces convenient grids for editing language strings, system settings, and snippet properties.

By far the most "revolutionary" feature in Revolution from the average user's perspective is the Package Management system. In Revolution, add-ons can be downloaded from the

MODX repository and installed with a few clicks in the Package Manager. In Evolution, you have to download a .ZIP file for each add-on, unzip it, and cut and paste code into MODX elements and resources you create yourself — a much more time-consuming and error-prone process.

There is also much for the developer/web programmer to love in MODX Revolution. There is a completely new database API based on xPDO, which provides an efficient and easy-to-use way to read, create, and update all MODX objects. It also allows you to easily pull data from multiple MODX tables (with one query) in a single, elegant line of code.

Which Version Should I Use?

If you are upgrading an existing site that you don't work on very often, MODX Evolution may be a better choice for you. Evolution is also a better choice if you need to install and run your web site with limited memory. As I write this, Revolution needs at least 32M of memory to install (although there are plans to remedy this), so if your web host restricts you to 8M or 16M of memory and you are not allowed to change that, Evolution is the better choice. Most web hosts have higher limits, and many allow you to modify the amount of available memory.

 Many of the concepts described in this book are relevant for either version. If you will be working through the examples in the book, however, MODX Revolution is really your only choice. All of the tags and much of the code presented in the book's examples will only work as written in MODX Revolution.

In other situations, the key to making the choice is the available add-ons. At this writing, some of the add-ons available for MODX Evolution have not been ported to Revolution — though most of the important ones have. By the time you read this, there will certainly be more of them available in Revolution, but some less-popular third-party components may still not be available. Many of the standard MODX snippets and plugins have been replaced by faster and better versions for Revolution, and some have also been integrated into the MODX Manager. You should assess your needs and examine the available components (ask in the MODX Forums, if necessary) before making your decision.

Another consideration is the permissions system. MODX Revolution offers much more sophisticated and find-grained control over what users can do and see in the MODX Manager. The price of that control, however, is a steeper learning curve. Once the permissions for Revolution are set correctly, you can usually forget about them, but the initial process can be somewhat frustrating and time-consuming. If you will be the only user of the site, Revolution's default settings will be fine for you. If you have several users with different access rights and the permission system is relatively simple, Evolution may be a better choice. If you need to have users who will belong to more than one user groups and want them to have different capabilities for each group's documents, then Revolution is the better choice.

Assuming that the add-ons you need are available in Revolution (or you are capable of developing or adapting them yourself) and the Revolution permission system meets your needs, I would recommend it for everyone, including beginning MODX users. Revolution is a robust CMS platform and has many features that make it a superior choice.

Architecture and Key Features

The overriding principle in the design of MODX is freedom for the user. To the best of the designers' abilities, MODX puts no restrictions on what you can put in your web site. MODX users are free to use any (X)HTML, CSS, PHP, or JavaScript code to meet their needs.

You could port most existing web sites to MODX simply by pasting the code from each page into a MODX template, moving any PHP code into snippets, and creating an empty document for each page that uses that page's template. Doing this would be a horrible misuse of MODX's power, but the fact that it's possible shows how few restrictions MODX places on the user.

If you are not a power user/developer, you probably won't care what's under the hood in MODX. For those who do care, here is some information about the structure and design of MODX. Don't be put off if some of the following material goes over your head. You can create very impressive MODX web sites without knowing any of it.

xPDO

MODX's data handling is based on xPDO. Created by MODX core developer Jason Coward, xPDO is a PHP-based object-relational bridge that is designed to provide object-oriented access to a variety of underlying database platforms such as MySQL, SQLite, and PostgreSQL.

Both lightweight and robust, xPDO now requires PHP 5.1.1 or higher. It is significantly faster now that it no longer has to support PHP 4. It allows simple file-based result-set caching and custom cache implementations that can be optimized for particular needs. It also supports JSON caching for optimizing Ajax applications.

Using xPDO allows advanced MODX web site developers to easily integrate custom databases into a MODX install using built-in MODX methods. It also provides a relatively simple API that developers can use to obtain information from the MODX database.

At this writing, xPDO supports MySQL and Microsoft SQL databases, with more to follow.

User Interface

The MODX Manager is an Ajax-based user interface implemented with Smarty and ExtJS. In the Manager, users can create and edit content as well as perform a wide variety of administrative tasks like user management, publication scheduling, generating reports, installing add-on components, and adding user-created custom snippets and plugins. The MODX Manager is designed to be productive and intuitive.

In MODX Revolution, (unlike Evolution) many Manager tasks can be performed in pop-up windows, so users can create and update resources and elements and clear the MODX cache without leaving their current location in the Manager. Drag-and-drop functionality also increases productivity and reduces potential errors in the Manager.

Because the Manager is a web-based application, users can manage their MODX site from anywhere they have web access using no tools other than a web browser. MODX supports a wide variety of web browsers.

The Manager can be easily customized, and it can look very different for different users. Users can be restricted to certain areas of the Manager, and the areas they see can be customized for their particular needs and abilities. Multiple editors can be easily plugged into the Manager for use in creating and editing content as well as for managing various kinds of code.

Design Philosophy

MODX is designed around several basic principles. These include security, robustness, speed and efficiency, object-oriented design, core independence, and fine-grained cache control and user management.

Security

MODX is designed to be as secure as possible. All user input is analyzed for potential hazards, and no PHP code is allowed or executed in most MODX resources and elements. PHP code can only appear in snippets and plugins, and its execution is carefully regulated. All PHP code in the system can be contained in the database or in the MODX core, which can be shielded from web access. The user security system is also extremely tight and prevents unauthorized users from accessing sensitive areas of the Manager.

Robustness

MODX is designed from the core outward to be solid and fault-tolerant. Changes are evaluated and tested to ensure that they cause no problems in the operation of the system. MODX sites are generally rock-solid with virtually no downtime due to errors in MODX.

Speed and Efficiency

The developers of MODX are constantly profiling and refactoring MODX objects and their methods to make MODX as fast and efficient as possible. The caching process ensures that frequently accessed content and code are cached for maximum performance.

MODX is also designed to be a lightweight platform. Users install only the components they need for a particular site, and components are designed to be flexible and powerful enough that users can meet their needs with a small number of add-on components.

Object-oriented Design

MODX Revolution is object-oriented from the ground up. Every MODX object is a true PHP object, and all use of objects is through their properties and methods. Chunks, snippets, templates, and template variables, for example, are all subclasses of the `modElement` class. The MODX parser makes full use of the object methods available through the basic class. This makes the MODX core both efficient and easily extendable.

MODX also makes it easy to adhere to the principles of the model-view-controller (MVC) design philosophy by facilitating the separation of content, logic, and presentation.

Core Independence

Another principle is the complete separation of the MODX core from the content of the site. The core can be located in a directory that is not accessible from the Web for security. One MODX core can also support more than one web site.

Central to the separation of the core is a wide variety of built-in ways to extend and tap into the core processes. There is a well-developed API for accessing core methods and a comprehensive list of system events that fire at various points in the operation of the core.

Users can create PHP snippets that use the API to get information from the core and the database. They can also create PHP plugins that listen for the appropriate system event and step in to alter the processing at that point. The main purpose of these capabilities is to give the user the ability to do anything he or she can think of in MODX without touching the core code. When users upgrade to a new version of MODX, none of their custom work has to be done over again. Advanced developers can even create a custom parser class to override or extend the behavior of the MODX parser. Custom elements and resources are also a possibility for users with particular needs.

Fine-grained Cache Control

Another key principle is granular control of the MODX cache. Parts of the core are cached as needed, and various parts of each front-end page can easily be designated as cached or uncached by the user. In MODX Revolution, any element or resource can be designated as cached or uncached. As a result, nothing is cached but content and code that needs to be rapidly accessible. Because of MODX's xPDO base, database result-sets are also cached on an as-needed basis. In addition, there are a number of system settings that control whether certain MODX objects are cached and for how long.

Fine-Grained User Management

Like the caching process, user management is extremely granular in MODX Revolution. Since resources such as documents are in a hierarchical structure on the Resources tab, users can be limited to particular branches of the Resource tree shown on the Resources tab. In addition, individual resources can be placed in resource groups and individual elements can be placed in categories. Specific resource groups and categories can be made accessible only to members of specific user groups. Users can have designated roles that restrict them to specific actions in the Manager such as viewing, saving, editing, publishing, and unpublishing documents. Finally, the MODX Manager can be customized so that each user sees a completely different version of the Manager.

Chapter 1

How MODX Works

Using a Content Management System (CMS) is quite a bit different from just creating web pages and linking them together to make a site. A CMS takes a while to learn (and one as flexible and powerful as MODX takes a little longer). The time you spend getting familiar with MODX, however, will pay off many times over. It will make maintaining web sites easier and faster. It will also allow you to easily create web-site features that would be extremely difficult and time-consuming to produce without a CMS backing you up.

While many CMS platforms make life easy by severely restricting what you can do (with structured templates, built-in and add-on components that are hard to modify, hard-coded entity and directory names, etc.), MODX does just the opposite. Letting users do whatever they want is a primary goal of the MODX development team. The flexibility and freedom of MODX come with a price, however. Because there are fewer rules, it's harder to know how to solve any given problem. It's also a little easier to shoot yourself in the foot.

In this chapter, we'll touch on the various parts of MODX and how they work together to let you manage web sites. In later chapters, we'll cover the mechanics of using the MODX Manager, and the details of the various parts of MODX such as web resources, content elements, and files. This chapter is just to get your feet wet, introduce these elements, and give you an overall sense of how MODX does its job.

The MODX Database

If you are coming to MODX from another *Content Management System* (*CMS*) such as Drupal or Joomla!, you probably already have some sense of how such systems work. If, instead, you're used to working in straight (X)HTML and CSS, you may not be aware of how a CMS like MODX stores and presents the site's content. New users of MODX sometimes install the MODX sample site then look (unsuccessfully) for the HTML page files.

The reason they don't find the HTML files is that MODX, like most other CMS platforms, stores the page content in a MySQL or Microsoft SQL database (although future versions of MODX will be able to use a variety of other database platforms and will allow you to store web resources and content elements in files rather than the database if you wish).

When a user visits one of your pages, MODX goes to the MODX database, gets the information it needs for the requested page, assembles it, and sends it off to the user's browser for display. This all happens behind the scenes. Many MODX users create sites without ever dealing with the database or the process of saving and retrieving the information. To really make MODX sing, however, you'll eventually want to learn about how some of the behind-the-scenes processes work. For now, we'll just say that you create *web resources* (most of which will be *documents*) in the *MODX Manager* (also called the *back end*) and save them. When a user visits a particular web page at your site, MODX retrieves the appropriate content and sends it off to the user's browser for display. A lot can happen to that content before the user sees it, but we'll get to that later. First, let's look at the differences between MODX and its add-on components and between the back end and the front end of a MODX site.

MODX vs. Third-Party Components

In MODX Revolution, there has been a very determined effort to separate *MODX* itself from *components* contributed by others that extend or add to the functionality of MODX. A number of *third-party components* (also called *add-ons*, *3PC*s, *extras*, *add-on components*, or just *components*) were distributed and installed with earlier versions of MODX as a convenience to users. They added functions like custom menus, aggregated content display, text editors, photo galleries, etc. People often assumed that these were part of MODX itself, and when problems occurred, people complained about bugs in MODX. The MODX core developers would have to explain, over and over, that these were not part of MODX.

With MODX Revolution and future versions, only MODX is installed to begin with. It includes just three directories: **/core**, **/connectors**, and **/manager** (a **setup/** directory is present at first but is usually removed after a successful install). Users are also free to move and rename those three directories if they wish or even to install a different or customized manager to administer their sites.

Once you've completed the MODX base install, you can then easily add whatever third-party components meet your needs. This helps keep your MODX site from being loaded down with components you don't need. The download and install process for components is all done in the Manager, and it allows you to browse through the available components, download them, and install them with a few mouse clicks.

If you find you need more components later, new components become available, or new versions of existing components are released, it's a simple matter to browse the package repository and install them. Another advantage of this separation of the base install from third-party components is that the base install can remain "pure." It is unaffected by the installation and upgrading of components, and conversely, updating the base install to a new version of MODX is unlikely to affect any installed components.

Although the base MODX install contains no third-party components, by the time you read this, there may be additional distribution versions of MODX available that include various third-party components tailored to a specific purpose, such as a blog site, a photo gallery site, etc.

MODX Itself

The heart of MODX is in the **/core** directory (although you are free to rename and/or relocate that directory during the install, this is not recommended for new users). The **/core** directory contains the essential parts of the MODX content management engine. You could create a working web site with the tools available in the initial install, but it would have no dynamic menus, no WYSIWYG editor, no content aggregators — none of the things that really make MODX worthwhile for users. In order to gain those features, users need to add third-party components.

MODX Third-Party Components

The official term for anything added to the base MODX install is ***third-party component***. "Third-party component" is kind of a mouthful, so they are often referred to as ***3PCs***, ***extras***, or just ***components*** for short. At this writing, "components" is the more common term, but "extras" is gaining ground. Components are usually installed with a few mouse clicks in the Package Management section of the MODX Manager.

Components are divided into two groups: add-ons and core extensions. ***Add-ons*** do not modify or extend the MODX core but provide extra functionality for MODX. ***Core extensions*** (sometimes referred to as just "***extensions***") actually change or extend the MODX Core.

An extension might, for example, replace the MODX user class with a class that contains the same methods and member variables but adds some new ones (e.g., the user's astrological sign or income level). Another way to think about add-ons and extensions is that add-ons work with MODX and extensions change MODX. Most of the components you might install are add-ons. MODX is designed to make use of a wide variety of add-ons that can use a combination of ***chunks***, ***snippets***, and ***plugins*** (more on these later in this chapter) to do almost anything you want without altering MODX itself.

For most MODX users, the difference between add-ons and core extensions is not important. Users install components that meet their needs and don't really care about what goes on under the hood. For advanced MODX developers, however, the difference is an important one.

Even beginning users of MODX should know that components of all kinds are not officially part of MODX. Third-party components are contributed by volunteers of varying abilities. Some are carefully constructed and highly robust while others are less so. You should also be aware of the term "Sponsored Extras." ***Sponsored Extras*** are third-party components that have been created, edited, or reviewed by the MODX core programmers to assure that they adhere to MODX coding standards and will not interfere with the MODX core.

The Back End vs. the Front End

MODX is divided into two basic parts: the back end and the front end. The ***back end*** is another name for the MODX Manager. The ***front end*** is what visitors to your site see in their browsers.

The Back End

The ***MODX Manager*** (or ***back end***) is where you do the main work of building and managing your site. In the ***Manager***, you can create and edit content. You can also perform a whole array of administrative tasks such as creating users and controlling what those users can do and see at the site. You can create administrative users who can share the workload with you. You can also create and edit any of the various MODX objects such as resources (including documents), templates, template variables, snippets, chunks, plugins, lexicons, namespaces, categories, property sets, system settings, etc.

This list of MODX objects is often daunting for newcomers to MODX, but each of them has a useful part to play in the development of your site, and together, they'll let you do things with your site that you never thought possible. They'll also make your life as a web developer much easier and more productive (trust me). We'll cover each of them in depth, and by the time you finish the book, you should be comfortable with all the ones you need for your site.

The Front End

The ***front end*** is the part that visitors to your site see. There may be parts of your site that only logged-in users can see, but after logging in, they're still in the front end of the site. Depending on how you set things up, front-end users may still be able to add or edit site content and perform specific administrative tasks, but the key difference is that they are not in the ***MODX Manager*** — they are in the ***front end*** of the site. Because they are not in the Manager, what they can do is strictly limited (unless you create and implement code that bypasses the restrictions). This protects the security of your site. It also lets users contribute without learning the Manager interface.

If you have naïve users who need to perform administrative tasks but would be intimidated by the MODX Manager, you have two options. You can customize the MODX Manager to simplify and/or hide the intimidating parts, or you can install or create add-on components that let them perform their administrative tasks in the front end of the site.

Basic Building Blocks

The basic building blocks of a MODX site are web resources, content elements, and files. *Web resources* include documents, weblinks, symlinks, and static resources. ***Content elements*** include templates, template variables, chunks, snippets, and plugins. ***Files*** are just plain old files. We'll look at how to manage these things in more depth later in the book, but first, let's take a brief look now at what they are.

Web Resources

Web resources (usually referred to as just ***resources***) are the easiest to define of the MODX objects: They're simply things that can be accessed via a URL. The most commonly used resources, by far, in MODX are documents. In fact, the document is the default resource type. Many MODX users never create a symlink, weblink, or static resource, but everyone creates lots of documents. The most convenient way to create a resource is to right-click somewhere in the Resource tree (on the Resources tab at the left side of the Manager) and hover over Create. This will open a flyout with four choices:

- Create a Document Here
- Create a Weblink Here
- Create a Symlink Here
- Create a Static Resource Here

Clicking on one of the choices will open the Create/Edit Resource panel. On the right side, you'll see the Create/Edit Resource panel showing some of the various resource fields for the resource and several tabs at the top for accessing others. We'll discuss these in more detail later.

You can also create new resources by clicking on "Site" in the Top Menu and selecting the type of resource you want to create. There is also a small icon at the top of the Resource tree that will do the same thing. Doing this will create the resource at the top level of the Resource tree (under the web context icon). Usually, you'll want to put new resources at a particular place in the Resource tree, so right-clicking on the resource or folder that you want as the parent of your new resource is often a better method.

Documents

Before getting into the details of documents, let's take a moment to look at an important distinction that trips up some new MODX users: the difference between a *document* and a *web page*. In MODX, a *web page* is what the user sees in the browser window at any given time when visiting your site. The web page is rendered by the browser, which bases the rendering on the information sent to it by MODX. That web page may involve any and all of the basic building blocks we listed above, although the visitors won't know that because all they see is the final rendering.

A *document*, on the other hand, is a specific MODX object created in the MODX Manager. If you have used a word-processing program such as Microsoft Word, you've already created documents. Those documents had a title, some content, a creation date, an author, etc. Documents in MODX are very similar but are adapted for use in web pages. For example, they have more than one title. There is a short title (Title), a longer title often used as a page heading (Long Title), a title for use in menus (Menu Title), and a title for use in URLs that link to the document (Alias).

These characteristics of a MODX document are called "resource fields" (formerly "*document attributes*"), and they also include a Template, a Publish and/or Unpublish date, a Description, a Summary, etc. Some of these resource fields may be blank, but the document still has them.

There is another distinction we should mention. Many of the resource fields are known by two names. One is the actual name of the field in the MODX database. This is the name that must be used in code or in MODX tags (more on those later). The other is the general name for the field, usually taken from the Create/Edit Resource panel in the Manager where you actually fill in the values for the resource fields. One field, for example, is referred to on the Create/Edit Resource panel as "Summary," but it sets the **introtext** field in the MODX database. When we're talking about the general name for the field, we'll use the regular font and capitalize the first letter of each word in the field name (Summary, Menu Title, Long Title). When we're talking about the specific field in the database, we'll use bold type, lowercase, and a different font (**introtext**, **menutitle**, **longtitle**). There are no capital letters in any field name. This difference is not that important now, but will be critical when we talk about setting these fields in later chapters.

 In the book, we'll often refer to documents as resources (which they are). The document is the default type of resource and the most often used, but it is not the only one — weblinks, symlinks, and static resources are also resources. So all documents are resources, but not all resources are documents.

When users visit a web page at your site, the URL they are visiting is associated with a single document. The web page does more than just display the document's content, however. It will usually also show the document's content embedded in the template associated with that document (we'll discuss templates in the section below). It may also show the document's Title or some of the other resource fields. If the document is not currently published, the browser may not show it at all.

To complicate things slightly, a web page may be associated in various ways with more than one document. It might show a document that contains the summary fields of a number of other documents with links that will send the viewer to a full version of each document. A blog web page in MODX, for example, might show several different blog posts, each listing the author and date. Each of those posts is the **content** field of a separate document, and the author and date come from the **createdby** and **createdon** resource fields of that particular document. The summary presented for each item normally comes from the **introtext** resource field.

Given the complex relationships possible here, you can see why it's important to understand that web pages and documents are very different things in MODX. When we talk about documents in the book, we're always referring to the MODX document object created in the Manager, not to a web page viewed by a site visitor. We'll always refer to a single page displayed in a browser as a "web page."

Weblinks, Symlinks, and Static Resources

A *weblink* is a MODX Resource that contains a URL (also called a *link*) in its **content** field. With a weblink, the URL can be to a page at the MODX site or any other site on the Web.

In MODX, a *link* can be expressed as a full URL like this:

```
http://yoursite.com/home.html
```

If, instead, it is a link to a page on your own MODX site, it can be expressed as a *link tag* (e.g., [[~1]]). If your Home page is resource 1 on your site (in other words, its Resource ID number is 1), MODX will replace the link tag with a full URL that will take users to your Home page.

You should use link tags whenever you can because they will take you to the same page even if the title of the page changes or it is moved to another location in the Resource tree.

A *symlink* is also a MODX resource that refers to another document, but the Symlink field contains only the Resource ID of the document being referred to, and it must refer to a page on the MODX site.

The main use of weblinks and symlinks is to serve as links in a MODX menu. This is a somewhat advanced topic, and we'll cover it in more detail later in the book.

Static resources are resources that contain a file path in their **content** field. Most MODX pages have dynamic content because they contain elements, such as snippets and chunks, which may change over time. That means that the content of the page will be created on the fly before being seen by the site visitor. When you have content that you know won't change unless you edit it yourself, however, you can save it as a file and use a *static resource* to display it. The page will display faster and will put less strain on MODX and the Database.

Static Resources may also contain links to files you want to deliver to the visitor such as .PDF files or .DOC files for display or download. You can even use PHP code to create dynamic .PDF files, for example, that the user can view or download by following a link to the static resource. This also allows you to control access to the files so that some users can reach them and others can't.

Content Elements

Content elements (usually referred to as just "elements") in MODX are just what their name suggests: they are MODX objects that create, control, format, organize, and/or contain content. The phrase "content element" is somewhat flexible, and as MODX evolves, new elements are created, and sometimes things that were formerly resource fields may become elements. Sometimes elements can lose that status and be reclassified as something else. The best working definition of content elements is: "things that appear in the Element tree on the Elements tab at the left side of the MODX Manager."

The section below discusses the elements that existed at the time this book was written: templates, template variables, chunks, snippets, plugins, and categories. You should be aware, however, that a few of them may not be found in the Element tree in your version of MODX.

Templates

Most businesses have a standard letterhead they use when sending letters. It gives every letter the same look and saves time since the letter writer doesn't have to type the company name, address, and telephone/fax numbers on each letter. A MODX *template* performs the same function. It contains the basic information that will appear on a number of different web pages. It will usually contain the basic (X)HTML for a web page (DOCTYPE, <head>, <body>, etc.) as well as the banner at the top of the page and the footer at the bottom. It may also contain other MODX objects, as we'll see in the section below.

Like the company letterhead, the template will probably contain a header and footer (possibly with images) that will appear on every page that uses the template. Unlike a letterhead, however, a MODX template can also contain other MODX objects. It might contain a document's Title (and/or Long Title) and a menu. These will change on every page, but they will always appear in the same place and with the same styling for every page that uses that template.

When MODX receives a request for a web page from a browser, it finds the appropriate resource (usually a document), then checks to see what template is attached to that resource. The template contains (X)HTML code interspersed with MODX tags. MODX retrieves the template from the database and begins filling it with the appropriate content (by replacing the MODX tags) as the first step in preparing the web page to be returned to the browser.

Beginning MODX users sometimes create more templates than they need because they don't fully understand how flexible MODX templates can be. Some MODX sites (but not all) can get by with a single template even though there are things that will appear on some pages but not others. We'll look at templates in more detail later in the book.

Template Variables

"Template variable" is a confusing phrase for some users because it hasn't always been used consistently. Sometimes, the resource fields we discussed above (Title, Menu Title, Alias, etc.) have been referred to as template variables, even in the official MODX documentation. This is incorrect, however. Those things should be called "resource fields." *Template variables* are always created by a user who needs additional resource fields.

Template variables (often called *TV*s for short) provide a way of extending the list of resource fields. Imagine that you let registered users create some content on your site. When a page created by a user is displayed, you could show the document's Title and the date it was posted by using the document's **pagetitle** and **createdon** resource fields. What if you also wanted to show the author's astrological sign? You need another resource field. Luckily, you can easily add a TV called "Sign" to hold that information (we'll talk about exactly how to do this in a later chapter). Now, when someone edits the document in the MODX Manager, they'll see an extra field labeled "Sign" with a blank space for entering the user's astrological sign.

Template Variables are very flexible and can be used to hold many things such as text, images, (X)HTML code, dates, directory contents, etc. In fact, we could easily present our "Sign" TV as a drop-down list of the twelve astrological signs or as twelve radio buttons. This is quite easy to do in MODX, and we'll discuss how later in the book.

At this point, you might be wondering how the content of the "Sign" TV gets on the web page. The easiest way is just to place a *resource tag* in the template associated with that document (we'll discuss tags in more detail later in this chapter). A resource tag looks like this: [[*Field/TvName]]. Both template variables and resource fields can be displayed using resource tags. The following code in the template would display the title, date, and sign, on the page:

```
<p>Post Title: [[*pagetitle]]<br />
Created on: [[*createdon]]<br />
Author's sign: [[*sign]]</p>
```

Template variables are a powerful and underused part of MODX. They can hold strings of text, such as a person's sign, but they can also hold other objects you might want to put on a web page such as drop-down lists, date pickers, and even the content from other documents on the site. We'll talk about how to create them and use them in more detail later in the book.

Chunks

A MODX *chunk* is just a piece of reusable content. The key thing to remember about chunks is that they can't contain raw PHP code (that's the job of snippets). Many chunks are just bits of content embedded in (X)HTML code that you want to appear on multiple pages. The banner at the top of a page, the footer at the bottom, and the menu are often contained in chunks. That way, if you edit the chunk, it changes things on every page.

Special-purpose chunks called Tpl chunks are used as mini-templates. They usually contain text and placeholder tags (more on those later) and are used format output. Here is a simple example that could be used to display the name of the current president and vice-president of a company:

```
<h3>Officers</h3>
<p>President: [[+president]]</p>
<p>Vice-president: [[+vice-president]]</p>
```

Typically, code in a snippet would set the values for the two placeholder tags above so that the appropriate names would appear when the chunk is rendered.

Tpl chunks are also used for web forms and as mini-templates for the output of standard add-on components. Tpl chunks are sometimes referred to as "templates," but this is incorrect.

The content of a chunk makes it into a page in various ways. The most common method for displaying chunks is to put a *chunk tag* in the template or the **content** field of a document. A chunk tag looks like this: [[*$ChunkName*]]. We'll see some other methods of injecting chunk content later in the book, and we'll discuss tags in general a little later in this chapter.

Snippets

A *snippet* is simply a piece of executable PHP code. If your users can submit content (such as blog comments) that immediately appears on the site, what happens if a malicious user puts PHP code that erases your hard disk in a comment? In an unprotected site, the first time someone visits the page that shows that comment, it's goodbye site. In MODX, however, nothing happens at all because PHP code in a page's content is stripped out. To be executed, the code must be in a snippet. What appears in the page content, then, is the *snippet tag* (sometimes called a *snippet call*). A snippet tag looks like this:

[[*SnippetName*]]

or

[[*SnippetName*? **&firstName**=`John` **&lastName**=`Doe`]]

In the second example above **&firstName** and **&lastName** are just pieces of information called *snippet properties* (formerly called parameters) that we want to send to the snippet being called. Whatever is returned or printed by the snippet will replace the snippet tag in the page sent to the browser for display.

Important: Note that the values of the snippet properties are enclosed in back-ticks, not single-quotes. This allows you to use single- and double-quotes in your snippet properties (e.g., **&lastName=**`O'Connor`). The back-tick is under the ~ at the upper-left on most keyboards.

Using single-quotes, double-quotes, or nothing at all around snippet properties is the most common error made by new users of MODX. If you do that, your snippet simply won't work. Other common errors are forgetting the question mark after the snippet name or the ampersand before every snippet property, and misspelling the name of the snippet or a snippet property (the names are case-sensitive, so type carefully). One last common snippet error to check for is that a Rich Text Editor like TinyMCE may be changing the ampersands in your snippet tags to the "&" entity every time you save your work. To fix this, click on the "HTML" button in the editor and convert & or && to a single ampersand character inside snippet tags.

 Although we often put spaces around equal signs in PHP code to improve readability, we don't do it with snippet tags because it can confuse the parser in some older versions of MODX Evolution.

We'll discuss snippets and snippet tags in detail later in the book. If you don't know PHP, you won't be writing or editing snippets, but you'll still need to understand a little bit about how snippets do their jobs and how to work with snippet properties.

Many beginning MODX users know no PHP at all and have no intention of learning it. Some of them are able to create very sophisticated MODX sites without using PHP code. Many others, however, learn PHP gradually as they continue to use MODX, and some become quite good at it and begin writing their own snippets and plugins. As we said earlier, PHP is not a difficult language, and there is a short MODX PHP Primer at the end of the book to get you started. One of the great things about MODX is that no matter how much you know, there's always more to learn.

Plugins

Plugins are kind of an anomaly among the MODX elements. They often alter content, but you don't display them on a web page using tags. Plugins are used to interrupt the processing of the MODX engine and add custom functions.

There are a number of hooks into the MODX engine (called system events) that let you perform just about any kind of operation at key points in the processing. As MODX goes about its job, it periodically "fires" one of a number of system events. There are events that fire just before a page is rendered in the browser, just after a user attempts to log in, and just before a document or user is saved in the Manager, for example. Each system event has a name, and MODX plugins can listen for a particular system event and act when it fires.

A *plugin*, then, is just a bit of PHP code that listens for a particular *system event*. When that event "fires," the plugin's code executes. For example, a plugin can give you access to a document's content just before it is rendered as a web page by having it listen for the `OnWebPagePrerender` event. You could translate the document's content, emphasize key words, strip out HTML comments, turn some items into hyperlinks, etc.

You can also use a plugin to process documents before they're saved in the Manager, process a user's information during the process of logging in, or do any number of other transformations. Plugins are written in PHP code, and you can do anything with them that you can write code for.

The beauty of plugins is that they allow you to put custom processing in place without hacking the MODX core. That means your work will be unaffected by upgrading to newer versions of MODX. Because of the many built-in ways of expanding and extending MODX, you can do almost anything you can think of without touching the MODX core code.

Categories

Categories are basically just labels that you can apply to elements to help you organize them and control access to them. When you create or edit a snippet, plugin, chunk, template, or template variable, you can assign it to an existing category or create a new category for it. When that element is shown in the Element tree in the Manager, it will appear below its category name.

In MODX Revolution, you can assign elements to categories by dragging and dropping them onto the category folder at the bottom of the Element tree.

Note that categorized elements will not show in the Category section of the tree (even though that's where you dragged them). Instead, they'll show under a category folder in their respective sections. For example, a snippet added to the category MyCategory will appear in the Element tree in a MyCategory folder that appears in the Snippet section of the tree.

 Resources and files don't have categories. Resources in the Resource tree are organized into a hierarchy under their respective parents and files are organized by the physical directories in which they are stored.

You can have as many categories as you like, and you can have categories within categories. You might, for example, have a category called *MyChunks* to keep the chunks you create separate from the ones used by various MODX components. If you create a lot of chunks, you might have subcategories under MyChunks.

Once elements are placed in a category, you can hide them or control what users can do with them by creating Element Category Access ACL entries in the Manager (see Chapter 10 for more details on MODX security).

If you don't use categories to control access to elements, they are just there for your convenience in organizing your elements and making them easier for you to find when you want to edit them. Categories are completely optional. Some people don't use them at all. Others, especially those with very complex sites, use lots of them. As with so many things in MODX, it's up to you.

Other Elements

The following elements are not found in the Element tree, but they serve to store and present content on your site. They include placeholders, links, settings, tags, and files.

Placeholders, Links, and Settings

Placeholders are not shown in the Element tree in the Manager, but they qualify as elements because they hold content and can be displayed using resource tags. The reason they don't show in the Element tree is that their value is always set in snippets or plugins rather than being entered in the Manager. A snippet or plugin sets a placeholder by using the following bit of PHP code:

```
$modx->setPlaceholder('placeholderName','value');
```

Once the placeholder has been set, its value will replace any instance of the corresponding *placeholder tag*:

```
[[+placeholderName]]
```

Many MODX snippets set placeholders. You can display the values set for those placeholders with placeholder tags. The tags can go in a resource's content field, in a chunk, or in a template variable or template. If you have a snippet (let's call it *SetAuthor*), for example, that sets a placeholder called author_name to the name of the author of the current document, you could put the following snippet tag in your template: [[SetAuthor]]. The snippet tag would produce no output because your snippet neither prints anything nor returns anything — it just sets the placeholder. Anywhere in the content of your document, then, you could insert a placeholder that would be replaced by the author's name:

```
The author of this document is [[+author_name]].
```

Note that for the [[+author_name]] tag to work, the snippet tag must come before it in the code so that the placeholder will be set.

MODX does set a couple of placeholders for you on every page request that you can use to display the ID or username of the currently logged-in user (if any).

```
ID of the current user: [[+modx.user.id]]
Username of the current user: [[+modx.user.username]]
```

Links are a MODX shorthand for a URL to a page at the site and are based on one of the resource fields — the ***Resource ID***. Most of the time, links are used to refer to documents. The Resource ID of a document is sometimes called the document ID or document identifier, but the correct term is "Resource ID." The ID is shown in parentheses in the Resource tree in the Manager following the resource's name. You can place a link pretty much anywhere by using the ***link tag***:

```
[[~##]]
```

In the code above, you would replace ## with the Resource ID of the resource (document) you want a link to. That may sound complicated, but it's really pretty simple. Let's look at an example. Suppose you have a page about aardvarks that has a Resource ID of 12. You would see the number 12 in parentheses next to the name of the document in the Resource tree (on the Resources tab) in the Manager. Anywhere you would put `http://mysite.com/aardvark.html`, you could put [[~12]] instead. The name of the document might change, and its location on your site might change, but [[~12]] will always provide a reliable link to it because its Resource ID will never change. You should always use a link tag when creating a link to any page at your site.

Like placeholders, settings don't show in the Element tree but can be displayed using tags (*setting tags*, to be precise). A *setting* is essentially a variable whose value is available across the MODX site. They include system settings, context settings, and user settings (more on these later in this chapter). All are displayed with a setting tag:

`[[++setting_name]]`

You can use setting tags freely to display or use the values of any system, context, or user settings. Some system settings are critical to the operation of MODX, however, so don't change a system setting unless you're sure of what it does.

Tags

We've already seen some MODX *tags* in this chapter, but let's look at them a little more closely. All MODX tags are replaced by the object they represent. Here is a quick list showing what each tag will be replaced by:

- **Chunk tag** — Contents of the chunk
- **Resource tag** — Value of the resource field or template variable it represents
- **Snippet tag** — Output or return value of the PHP code in the snippet
- **Link tag** — The URL of the resource it refers to
- **Placeholder tag** — The value of the placeholder (often set in a snippet or plugin)
- **Setting tag** — The value of the context, user, or system setting
- **Language tag** — A particular language string from the current lexicon

In MODX Revolution and beyond, all tags begin with [[and end with]]. We've discussed most of the tags, but Table 1-1 gives a summary of the new tag style used in MODX Revolution and later and the tags used in earlier versions of MODX:

Table 1-1: Old and New Tag Styles

Tag Type	MODX Evolution (old)	MODX Revolution
Resource	`[*ResourceField/TvName*]`	`[[*ResourceField/TvName]]`
Chunk	`{{ChunkName}}`	`[[$ChunkName]]`
Snippet	`[[SnippetName]]`	`[[SnippetName]]`
Setting	`[(SettingName)]`	`[[++SettingName]]`
Placeholder	`[+PlaceholderName+]`	`[[+PlaceholderName]]`
Link	`[~ResourceId~]`	`[[~ResourceId]]`
Language	No Tag	`[[%LanguageStringKey]]`

Note that those symbols after the opening braces ($, +, ++, *, ~, and %) are called *tokens* in MODX. They tell MODX what kind of tag is being processed.

New users of MODX often don't realize that tags can be used almost anywhere in MODX and that you can nest them. A snippet tag can contain a chunk tag as a property, and the chunk could contain resource tags that might contain link tags.

Here's an example of a setting tag nested inside a link tag. It will display a link to the site's Home page:

```
[[~[[++site_start]]]]
```

Let's break that down and look first at the outer tag, which is a link tag.

`[[~X]]` is a link tag where *X* is the Resource ID of the document you want to link to. It will be replaced by the URL associated with that document. In other words, the tag `[[~12]]` will be replaced by the URL of the document whose Resource ID is 12.

 There is nothing special about the Home page of a MODX site. The `site_start` system setting can point to any page on the site and MODX treats the page like any other when it is rendered.

`[[++site_start]]` is a setting tag that will be replaced by the Resource ID of your site's Home page. So if the Resource ID of your site's Home resource is 1 (and it often is), this tag will be replaced by the number 1.

So `[[~[[++site_start]]]]` will be replaced by `[[~1]]` which will be replaced by something like **http://yoursite.com/home.html**. For an actual link to your Home page, you'd want something like the following (X)HTML code:

```
<a href="[[~[[++site_start]]]]">Home</a>
```

 When creating nested tags in MODX, always count the number of left and right brackets. The two numbers must be equal, and in MODX Revolution, each must be an even number.

For the more technically minded, here is a specification of the MODX tag syntax:

[[— opening brackets.

! — (optional) do-not-cache flag.

elementToken — token identifying the element type if it's not a snippet:

> **no token** — snippet.
> **$** — chunk.
> ***** — resource field/template variable (TV).
> **+** — placeholder.
> **++** — setting.
> **~** — link.
> **%** — language.

elementName — name of element (e.g., Wayfinder, MyChunk).

@propertysetName — (optional) property set identifier.

:modifierName=`modifierData`:... — (optional) one or more output modifiers.

? — indicates that properties are coming; required if there are properties.

&propertyName=`propertyValue` *&...* — properties prefixed with &

]] — closing brackets.

Here is a complex tag example with every possible type of tag element:

```
[[!getResources@propset1:default=`No resources found.`? &parents=`1`
&sortby=`RAND()`]]
```

The tag above tells MODX to process the getResources snippet uncached specifying `propset1` to override the default properties. The `:default` output modifier will produce a message if getResources returns nothing. Two properties, **&parents** and **&sortby** will be sent to the snippet and will override any other properties with the same names.

Files

In MODX, *files* are simply files that exist within the MODX site. As we've seen in the sections above, much of the content and format of a MODX web site is contained in documents, chunks, templates, and other MODX objects that exist in the MODX database. Files still play a role, however. You will probably have some files of your own. You might have image files, CSS files, JavaScript files, or other files that are used in your site. In addition, many MODX components have **readme.txt** files, class files, CSS files, example files, etc.

The files used by components are generally found in one of two places. Files that need to be web-accessible are located below this directory (where *component_name* is the name of the component):

`assets/components/`*component_name*

Files that don't need to be web-accessible are located below this directory:

`core/components/`*component_name*

The files for the Wayfinder snippet, for example, will be in these two directories:

```
assets/components/wayfinder/
core/components/wayfinder/
```

In MODX Revolution, the **/core** directory containing all of the critical MODX PHP files can be located outside of the **public_html** directory so that its files can't be accessed directly from the Web. This makes MODX much more secure. A good security principle for files is that files containing executable code (e.g., executable PHP files) or sensitive material like Social Security Numbers should go under the relocated **/core** directory so they can't be reached directly via the Web.

New users of MODX are often confused about where to put their own files. The official MODX answer is an emphatic, but somewhat unhelpful, "anywhere you want." It is a guiding principle of MODX not to restrict users in any way unless it's absolutely necessary for MODX to function correctly (and MODX is designed so that there are very few restrictions). As long as you know where the files are and you tell MODX where they are, anything goes.

Some users like to put the files in, or just under, the root directory for faster loading in **/images**, **/css**, **/js**, etc. Another good place to put them is somewhere under the MODX **/assets** directory (i.e., **assets/images**, **assets/css**, **assets/js**). Properly written third-party components always refer to the assets directory by the MODX_ASSETS_PATH setting, which you can set.

The **/assets** directory is never used directly by the MODX core. Because of the way the **/assets** directory is handled by MODX, you can be confident that it won't be touched when you upgrade your MODX installation to a new version. If all of your personal files are below the **/assets** directory, you can be certain that they won't be touched by an upgrade. Placing them there also makes it possible to rename, relocate, or re-upload the other MODX directories without worrying about your own files.

How MODX Delivers a Web Page

Now that you have some sense of the basic building blocks MODX uses to create a web page, let's look briefly at how MODX does the job.

When a user's browser requests a web page from the site, MODX first checks to make sure that the page exists. If it does not, the user is forwarded to the site's Error (page not found) page. Next, MODX checks to make sure that there are no security restrictions that would prevent the current user from viewing the page. If there are, the user is forwarded to either the Error page, or the site's Unauthorized page (depending on the security settings) and processing stops.

Assuming that there are no security restrictions that would prevent the user from seeing the page, MODX retrieves the document associated with that URL and checks to see what template is associated with that document. It then gets the template, and the MODX *document parser* goes to work.

The document parser loads the template into its own internal text editor. The template will contain tags identifying the various building blocks. The document parser replaces those tags with the things they represent. For example, a chunk tag will be replaced by the contents of the chunk and a snippet tag will be replaced by the output of the snippet. Once that replacement has been made, there may be some tags left in the page (the chunk might contain some tags, or the snippet might put some tags in the output it returns). The snippet might also pull content from another snippet or chunk or from a file and insert it into the output it returns.

The parser continues replacing tags until there are no more left. If any plugins are listening for the events that fire during this process, they may also alter the page content at various points in the process. In addition, if some of the content is cached, the parser will get the content from the MODX cache instead of the database. When the process is complete and there are no more tags to process, MODX delivers the page to the web browser for display. If the resulting page contains a reference to a file to be included (such as a CSS file, a JavaScript file, or an image file), the browser will handle that appropriately and then, finally, show the page to the user.

Transport Packages

Transport packages are new in MODX Revolution and are one of the best reasons to upgrade to the new version. A ***transport package*** is a .ZIP file that can contain files, MODX objects, and PHP scripts packaged for automatic installation in a MODX site. The most common transport package is used to install a specific third-party component, but transport packages can contain core extensions, updates, templates, simple collections of files, or even an entire MODX site.

In earlier versions of MODX, in order to install a third-party component, you needed to download the component, unzip the files in the appropriate directory at the MODX site, create elements, and cut-and-paste code from the component files into the elements. Sometimes the process was not very well-documented and it was easy to make mistakes that would make the component unusable. With Transport packages, you go to Package Management in the MODX Manager, search for available packages, download them, and click on "Install." All the work is done for you and done without errors.

Even better, Transport packages can interact with the user during the install process, so you can often set configurations and preferences during the install. The SPForm package, for example, creates a simple, spam-proof contact form for your site. During the install, you're asked for your return email address and you specify whether you want the sample `Contact` page installed. If you say yes, the package automatically installs all the necessary resources, elements, and files. It creates a `Contact Us` page and a `Thank You` page. At the end of the installation, you have a working contact form on your site that automatically appears in your menu.

The downside of Transport packages is that they are more work for developers who have to learn how to create them. This means that it may be a while before some of the existing components for MODX are available as Transport packages. Fortunately, the old installation method will still work as long as the component has been rewritten to work with MODX Revolution.

If you try to install a MODX add-on component in Revolution the old-fashioned way by downloading and cutting and pasting, make sure it has been rewritten to work with MODX Revolution.

Other MODX Concepts

In this section, we'll look at some other MODX objects: namespaces, the lexicon, topics, settings, workspaces, properties, and the MODX cache. With the exception of properties, they are less likely to be used by beginning users than the topics we discussed earlier in the chapter, but it's still useful to know a little bit about them.

Namespaces

A *namespace* is like a category tag for MODX components. It allows component developers to identify the various MODX objects that go with their component, such as topics in the MODX lexicon, resources, elements, and transport packages. The namespace also contains the path where the component can be found. For low-level development, the most important use of namespaces is with the MODX lexicon. We'll explain that when we discuss the lexicon in the next section.

If you are not developing components for distribution to other users, you probably won't need to know anything about namespaces. We'll discuss namespaces in more detail in later chapters.

The MODX Lexicon, Namespaces, and Topics

In MODX, the *lexicon* is just a dictionary of words and phrases that can be used in the MODX Manager or in web pages at your site. Entries in the lexicon (called *language strings*) are read from *language files*. Each language string has a key (used to retrieve it), a namespace, a language, and a topic. That way, third-party components can load the language strings they need into the lexicon and their keys can be used to retrieve them.

The term "language" is somewhat misleading since what constitutes a language in MODX is actually based on a particular culture rather than a language. That is, you could specify British English or American English as the language to be loaded into the lexicon. You could even have a "beginning user" language and an "advanced user" language if you wanted to. In some cases, you will see the word "culture" instead of "language." The system setting that controls the lexicon strings used in the front end of a MODX site, for example, is called `culture_key`.

As you might imagine, the lexicon is a great tool for internationalizing your site. You can change the language used in the MODX manager just by changing the lexicon used without directly altering the content of any panels, forms, or menus.

When you are using some part of the Manager, each word or phrase on the screen has its own lexicon entry. They all come from the language specified by the `manager_language` setting in the System Settings grid. If you change this system setting and the appropriate language is available, all the text in the Manager will change to the new language (you may have to log out and log back in to have this take effect).

 Note that using the lexicon doesn't mean that MODX will translate your site for you. It will just replace language tags on a web page or Manager page with the appropriate content from the language currently loaded in the lexicon.

A namespace, when used with the lexicon, is just a group of language strings used for a specific purpose. All the strings used with a particular add-on component, for example, will usually be in their own namespace. A *topic* is just a subdivision of a namespace.

The MODX *core* namespace contains all the language strings used in the Manager. The core namespace has a different topic for each part of the Manager (e.g., a snippet topic, a chunk topic, etc.). Language strings from the snippet topic, for example, are used as prompts when you are creating or editing a snippet in the Manager.

MODX Revolution only loads the topics it needs for a specific page to make things faster and more efficient. When you are editing a chunk in the Manager, for example, MODX loads the chunk topic and knows that it only has to search that topic for the language strings on the page.

If you don't like the wording of any string printed in the Manager or by a component, you can go to the lexicon grid in the Lexicon Management section of the Manager and change it. Your changes will survive upgrades to MODX or to any add-on components.

We'll discuss the lexicon in more detail later in the book.

System Settings

A *system setting* is a site-wide variable available across a particular MODX site. Sometimes a system setting contains a string of text such as the site name (contained in the `site_name` system setting). Others contain a value that controls some aspect of MODX such as the number of times a user can enter incorrect login information before being blocked (`failed_login_attempts`) or for how many minutes the user will be blocked after exceeding the number of failed attempts (`blocked_minutes`). System settings are divided into areas for your convenience in finding them.

Every system setting has a description that explains what it does and what the acceptable values are, and you can search for system settings by any key word in their names or descriptions. All system settings can be changed in the System Setting grid in the Manager. As you might guess, if you have no idea what a system setting does, it's best not to modify it. System settings are overridden by context settings and context settings are overridden by user settings — more on those later.

If you go to **System → System Settings** in the Manager Top Menu, you will see the System Settings grid. You can also edit any of the system settings there. Sometimes, you want to show a system setting on a web page. To do that, you simply put a setting tag on the page where you want the information to appear:

```
[[++site_name]]
```

The setting tag above would be replaced by the value of the `site_name` setting in the System Settings grid.

Context Settings and Workspaces

Contexts are a new concept in MODX Revolution. Many MODX users will not deal with contexts at all. Contexts are somewhat difficult to explain but are very useful in certain situations. The main thing to understand about contexts is that a context has its own resources and settings. If you want to host two different sites within one MODX site that share the same MODX database, you could create a new context for the second site. The second site could use a different language, for example, but would still be able to use the MODX core and any installed components. It could also have the same users but with different privileges and settings (e.g., the same user could have a different personal Home page in each context).

When you are using the MODX Manager, you are in the mgr context. The default front-end context is called web in MODX Revolution, and you can see it at the top of the Resource tree. All resources in that context will appear below web. For many sites, this is the only context you need.

If you are using an early release of MODX Revolution, you probably won't see workspaces at all. In later releases, each *workspace* will provide an area where you can work on the settings, lexicons, components, and resources for a particular context. MODX Revolution has a "core workspace," but since there is only one, you probably won't know it's there.

To modify or create context settings for a particular context, go to **System → Contexts**, then either click on "Create New" or right-click on an existing context and select "Update Context," then click on the "Context Settings" tab. Any context settings you create here will override any system settings with the same key (name). Creating new contexts complicates things in many ways, so be sure you really need a new context before creating one.

User Settings

User settings are just system settings that only apply to a particular user. When you create a new user at your site, that user has no user settings. All the site's system settings apply to that user (unless overridden by context settings). If you add user settings for that user that have the same names as system settings, those user settings will override both system settings and context settings for that user alone. To create user settings for a particular user, go to **Security → Manage Users**, right-click on a user and select "Update User," then click on the "Settings" tab.

Suppose that the Manager Language system setting (`manager_language`) is set to *en* in the System Settings grid. All the strings used in the Manager will be in English. If you have a user that speaks German, though, you can create a user setting for that user called `manager_language` and set it to *de* so that user will see nothing but German in the Manager. The user setting will override the system setting.

A user could also have a particular Home page on the site. If you create a `site_start` user setting and set its value to the Resource ID of a particular page on the site, when a user is logged in, any page that contains a MODX tag with a link to the Home page of the site will show a link to that user's particular Home page:

```
[[~[[++site_start]]]]
```

User Setting names don't have to match any of the system settings. You can add any settings you need. You could add user settings that stored a user's height and weight, for example, and they could be displayed on any page that the user visited at the site using a standard setting tag. For that particular example, though, it is more likely that you would put that information in an extended field of the user profile.

Properties

Most of the elements described earlier in this chapter can have properties. *Properties* are a lot like the settings we described in the three previous sections. They are a collection of variables each with a name (technically called the *key*), a value, and a description. Like settings, they can be created and edited in a grid in the Manager. Properties are most often used with snippets, but are also used with plugins, chunks, templates, and template variables.

This might make properties sound redundant, but there is an important difference between properties and settings. Settings are available to every page in the site. Properties, in contrast, are attached to individual MODX elements (chunks, snippets, plugins, templates, and template variables), so their scope is limited to the element they are attached to. This makes them a more efficient choice when you want a value available in a single element or a group of elements but not across the whole site.

When properties are attached to a snippet or plugin, the property values can contain information used in the element. When properties are attached to another element, the values are available in that element via placeholder tags.

Properties exist in three forms. They can be defined in an element tag, in the element's default properties, or in a property set. In all three cases, the properties serve the same function: to provide a set of key/value pairs that can be used with specific elements.

When sent in a tag, properties are always preceded by an ampersand character and their values are surrounded with back-ticks. The following example shows two properties sent in a snippet tag:

```
[[SnippetName? &color=`red` &size=`large`]]
```

In the example above, the value of the `color` property is set to "red" and the value of the `size` property is set to "large." Many standard MODX snippets use properties to provide information the snippet needs to do its job and to control the actions of the snippet.

A snippet like Wayfinder that produces a menu, for example, might have a property that determines whether the menu shows unpublished resources. That property might look like this in the snippet tag:

```
&showUnpublished=`1`
```

In addition to being sent in tags, properties can be created and edited in the **Tools → Property Sets** section of the Manager. They can also be created and edited on the Properties tab of any element they are attached to. The second method is usually a much better choice if you intend to use the property set with a particular element. If you just want to override a few default properties, it's easiest just to send them as properties in the element tag.

 In earlier versions of MODX, properties sent in a tag were referred to as *parameters*. You may still see that term used in older documentation and MODX forum posts.

We'll discuss properties and all their uses in much more detail later in the book.

The MODX Cache

MODX keeps much of the content of a site in the *MODX cache*. This makes web page access much faster because MODX doesn't have to query the database for the content. Very few users will deal with the MODX cache directly, but you still need to know a little about it because you can control what content is cached.

The rule for what to cache is simple: Let MODX cache content that doesn't change often. If you have a web page that shows the current time and the page is cached, every visitor to the site will see the time that the page was first visited instead of the current time. This will continue until the MODX cache is cleared. Then a new time will be cached until the next time the cache is cleared.

Caching is controlled in two ways. The caching of MODX resources is controlled by two checkboxes on the Page Settings tab of the Create/Edit Resource panel in the Manager. If you uncheck the "Cacheable" checkbox, MODX will get a new version of the page every time someone visits it. If the "Empty Cache" checkbox is checked (which it is by default), the cache will be cleared when you save the page.

For all MODX tags (including those for snippets, chunks, and template variables), the format of the tag controls whether caching will be in effect. Putting an exclamation point after the opening braces of the tag will make the object uncached; leaving it out will make it cached. The exclamation point means "get me a fresh version of this." If the contents of a chunk seldom change, for example, you can let MODX cache it by using this tag:

```
[[$ChunkName]]
```

You can clear the MODX cache manually whenever you change the chunk's content. Snippets often produce different output at different times. In those cases, you'll want to have them uncached:

```
[[!SnippetName]]
```

Remember that the caching of different things in MODX Revolution is independent. For our example above about a page that shows the current time, the time would probably be calculated, formatted, and displayed by a snippet (let's call it *ShowTime*). If the rest of the page never changed, you could leave the page itself cached but call the snippet with this tag:

```
[[!ShowTime]]
```

That way, the page content would be cached, but the snippet's output would always be fresh because the snippet is called uncached.

The cache is also a source of confusion for some users because if the content is cached, changes they make may not show up when they view the site. MODX may be showing you the old cached content. Remember, too, that your browser may be showing you a cached version of a page you have visited before. When you make changes and can't see them, or correct a problem but still see it, clear the MODX site cache and your browser cache and check again.

Summary

By now you should have a basic idea of how MODX stores the information for a web site and transforms that information into finished web pages. Don't worry if some of the details aren't completely clear. We'll be covering all the topics in more detail later in the book.

Although you could create a fairly polished site using the techniques described in this chapter, we've only just scratched the surface of the power and flexibility MODX brings to web design.

Once users master the basic techniques involved in creating a MODX web site, they soon discover that they want more. They begin thinking about their site (or sites) in new ways and considering things like allowing subsets of users to access certain parts of the site (or certain functions in the Manager), letting users create and edit pages in the front end without logging in to the Manager, customizing pages for individual users, or automatically highlighting certain key terms on various pages. They wonder if what they're thinking of is possible in MODX, and the answer is almost always "yes."

MODX Evolution Notes

If you are using a pre 2.0.0 version of MODX, most of the sections of this chapter will still apply. The core of MODX has been completely rewritten for MODX Revolution. From the user's point of view, however, it still has much in common with previous versions. There have been a few minor changes in the database, but the table names and structures of the tables are unchanged for the most part.

General Differences

MODX Evolution and earlier versions still store information in the database and still have a front end and a back end (MODX Manager). The Manager interface is different, but most of the same functions are there and most users switching from one to the other have little trouble finding the familiar areas of the Manager.

As we mentioned earlier in this chapter, there is still a distinction between MODX itself and the third-party components that extend and expand it. In MODX Evolution, however, the distinction is somewhat blurred by the fact that a number of third-party components are included in the base install. There is also an option to install a complete sample MODX site, which includes a template, user permissions, user logins, and a working blog.

Terminology

If you are using a version of MODX prior to Version 1.0.0 (e.g., MODX 0.9.6), there is also a difference in the terminology used for various resources and components between the two versions (in fact, the meanings of the terms "resource" and "element" are different).

In earlier versions of MODX, documents were historically called "documents" and elements such as snippets, chunks, and files were referred to as "resources." That terminology has shifted to match that of MODX Revolution, but not all the documentation has caught up.

In current versions of MODX (both Evolution and Revolution), documents are classified as resources; chunks, snippets, plugins, templates, and template variables are classified as elements; and files are just files.

The new terminology does a better job of matching the way the resources and elements are actually used and how they exist in the database and in the MODX code. This switch sounds confusing, but in practice, people have little trouble making the transition.

Navigation

Navigation in the Manager is a little more cumbersome in Evolution. In order to edit a chunk, for example, you have to go to **Elements → Manage Elements → Chunks** and then select the chunk name. In Revolution, you simply expose the Element tree (by clicking on the "Elements" tab) and click on the chunk you want to edit.

Content Elements

As for the elements themselves, they are largely unchanged. Chunks, snippets, plugins, placeholders, links, and system settings are essentially the same, although there are minor changes in the tags used to insert them (see the table earlier in this chapter), and there is no language tag in Evolution.

Core Code

The code that MODX uses to deliver a document has been revamped in Revolution, but on the surface, the process is much the same. The Evolution parser still cycles through the content replacing the tags until they're all replaced. One change is that all tags can be cached or uncached in Revolution. In Evolution, only snippets can be designated as cached or uncached. In addition, the caching process has been made much more consistent in Revolution.

Language

MODX Evolution has no lexicon or topics. It simply has language files that are pulled in explicitly in the code of components or the Manager. Loading of these files is not automatic as it is in Revolution, and creating and changing language strings in Evolution involves editing the physical language files in a text editor — there is no option to override the strings in the Manager. Evolution also has no namespaces.

System Settings

System settings are essentially the same in Evolution, but editing them is more cumbersome. In Revolution, they all appear in the System Settings grid, organized by areas, and can be searched for using key terms. In Evolution, they are spread across five different tabs with no search function. Individual settings can sometimes be difficult to find. The system settings in Evolution are reached by going to **Tools → Configuration** on the Top Menu.

Context, Settings, Workspaces, and Add-ons

Evolution has no context settings, user settings, or workspaces, and probably the most important difference in terms of convenience, no transport packages. In Evolution, you must install third-party components by manually copying files to the correct locations, creating new chunks, snippets, and documents, and pasting the code from the source files directly into them. Usually, the third-party component will come with a `readme.txt` file explaining how to perform the installation. It's easy to make a mistake during this process, and it's often difficult to discover what mistake you have made.

In Revolution, you can install any third-party component that has a transport package by selecting it in the Repository, waiting a few seconds for it to download, and then clicking on the "Install" button. All this is done without leaving the Manager. In Revolution, transport packages can automatically create any necessary elements, tags, resources, system settings, etc. Transport packages can also interact with the user to allow you to set configuration options during the install.

Properties and Caching

There are properties in Evolution, but in practice, they are only used with snippets. They are almost always sent in snippet tags. Snippets can have default properties in Evolution, but they are somewhat cumbersome and are seldom used.

The MODX cache performs the same function in both Evolution and Revolution. The only differences are that in Revolution more elements can be designated as cached or uncached, the tag usage for caching varies slightly, and the Revolution cache is more consistent.

Chapter 2

Installing MODX

MODX has a browser-based graphical user interface (GUI) for installing the platform. Installing it is a relatively simple process. You need to put the files in place and run the installation script (Setup).

In this chapter, we'll cover installing and configuring the current stable release of either of the two main flavors of MODX, installing add-on components, configuring Friendly URLs, installing MODX on your local machine using XAMPP, moving your local site to a remote server, and installing and upgrading the Development version of MODX. Near the end of the chapter, we'll also take a quick look at how to port an existing web site to MODX.

Installing the Current Stable Release

Before installing MODX, you first need to verify that you have the minimum requirements for MODX to work properly. Then, you'll need to download a copy of MODX and run the Setup script.

Requirements for MODX

The requirements for MODX change occasionally and some particular versions of PHP or MySQL have bugs that interfere with the operation of MODX. It's a good idea to check the current requirements on the MODX documentation web site before installing it. In addition, some web hosts are friendlier to MODX than others. MODX can almost always be installed at a host, but on MODX-friendly hosts, no extra steps are required. You can check the MODX Forums for hosting recommendations. As of this writing, these are the requirements for MODX Revolution:

Supported Operating Systems

- Linux x86, x86-64
- Mac OS X
- Windows XP, Server

Supported Web Servers

- Apache 1.3.x - 2.2.x (uses htaccess for Friendly URLs by default)
- IIS 6.0
- lighttpd
- Zeus

PHP Compatibility

* 5.1.1 and above (excluding 5.1.6 and 5.2.0 due to bugs)
* Required extensions:
    * zlib
    * JSON (or PECL library)
    * mod_rewrite (for Friendly URLs/.htaccess)
    * GD and FreeType libs (required for captcha and file browser)
    * PDO, specifically pdo_mysql (for xPDO)
    * SimpleXML
* Safe_mode off
* Register_globals off
* PHP memory_limit 24MB or more, depending on your server

MySQL Database Requirements

* 4.1.20 or newer, excluding versions 5.0.51 and 5.0.51a (serious bugs), with the following permissions:
    * SELECT, INSERT, UPDATE, DELETE are required for normal operation
    * CREATE, ALTER, INDEX, DROP are required for installation/upgrades and potentially for various add-ons (DROP may not actually be required for upgrades, but it potentially could be used)
    * CREATE DATABASE will allow new installs to create the database for you with the proper charset/collation.
    * CREATE TEMPORARY TABLES may be used by some third-party add-ons
* InnoDB storage engine
* MyISAM storage engine
* Microsoft SQL database

Supported Browsers (for Back End Manager Interface)

* Mozilla Firefox 3.0 and above
* Apple Safari 3.1.2 and above
* Microsoft Internet Explorer 8 and above

Installing any version of MODX involves downloading the files, putting them in place, configuring things, and running the install script. On some platforms, you may also have to create the MODX database.

Let's look at these steps in more detail.

Downloading the Current Version

The current stable release of MODX should be available at `http://modx.com/download`.

You will have to decide which major flavor of MODX you want to install — MODX Evolution or MODX Revolution. See the discussion of the two versions in the Introduction of this book to help you make your decision.

Download the current version's `.ZIP` file. There are two available distributions of MODX Revolution, called "Traditional" and "Advanced." The MODX code is the same for both, but the Advanced distribution allows you to set the names and locations of the various MODX directories during the install (for greater security). The Advanced version is also a much smaller download because it builds the MODX files in place. In order to use the Advanced distribution, you need to have the ability to set the correct folder permissions on your server. Most hosts allow this, but some don't. The Advanced distribution also requires more available PHP memory during Setup. The remainder of this chapter assumes that you are using the Traditional distribution.

Putting the Files in Place

Your ultimate goal is to have the following four directories and three individual files in the MODX Revolution site's root directory (we'll discuss the Evolution files and directories at the end of this chapter):

* `connectors/`
* `core/`
* `manager/`
* `setup/`
* `config.core.php`
* `ht.access`
* `index.php`

If you are using XAMPP on your local machine with Windows, the MODX site root will typically be something like this:

`c:/xampp/htdocs/`*`name_of_your_site`*`/`

Or like this on a Mac:

`Applications/xampp/htdocs/`*`name_of_your_site`*`/`

If you prefer, you can extract the directories and files somewhere else and just copy them to the root of your site.

On a remote server, the directories and files typically go here:

`public_html/`*`name_of_your_site`*`/`

For installation on a remote server, you'll need to put the files on the server with an FTP program or upload them using your host's upload utility. You can either extract the files to a directory on your local machine and then move them to the remote site, or upload the compressed archive file to the remote site and extract the files there. The latter is generally faster and more reliable.

The file you download from `http://modx.com/download` is a compressed archive containing all the necessary files to install MODX. How you put the files in place depends, to some extent, on the program you use to unzip the downloaded archive. Generally, you can extract all files in the archive to the root of your MODX site and end up with the directories listed above. If that doesn't put the files where you want them, you can always extract the files somewhere else and move them into place.

In order for the install to execute, the following directories need to be writable:

* The MODX root directory
* `/manager`
* `/connectors`.
* `/core/packages`
* `/core/cache`
* `/core/export`

Creating the MODX Database

If you skip this step, MODX will attempt to create the database for you. You'll need to know the username and password of a database user with full rights to your MySQL database.

If you don't have the proper permissions, the MODX Setup program will fail to create the database and you will get a warning telling you to create the database manually. It may also fail if your web host adds a prefix to the database name in the creation process, as many do, and you don't include that prefix when you specify the database name.

 If you create the MODX database yourself, don't add any tables. The Setup program will do that for you. All that's necessary is for the empty database to exist and have a user with full access to it.

I generally find it more convenient to create the MODX database myself ahead of time. The method for creating the database varies from host to host, but here are some general steps:

- Using the host's Control Panel, go to the area where you can create a database. Often, this is labeled "MySQL Databases." On some hosts (and on your local computer with XAMPP), you may have to use phpMyAdmin.

- If you have the option to set the MySQL Character Set and MySQL Collation Connection, the recommended value is utf-8 (utf8_unicode_ci).

- Create the database and give it a name. Many hosts add a prefix (usually involving your username), so the name you enter when you create the database may not be its actual name. Be sure to write down the full name of your newly created database. You'll need it to complete the install.

- Assign a user to the database and give the user full rights. Often this can be done on the same screen where you create the database. In phpMyAdmin, you can often create a new user on the Privileges tab of the database (once it exists). When there is more than one MODX install on a web server, some people prefer to create a new user for each MODX install to make their sites more secure.

- The database username may also get a prefix on some hosts. Write down the actual name of the user and the user's password.

- Before continuing with the install process, make sure you know the database name, the username, the user's password, and the character set used. Remember that you want the username and password of the database user, not the username and password you use to log in to your host's control panel.

Editing the Config file

You can skip this step if all goes well. If the **/core/config/config.inc.php** file is writable, MODX will do this for you. The MODX Revolution Setup program will attempt to create the following file:

/core/config/config.inc.php.

 The MODX Evolution config file is here:

/manager/includes/config.inc.php.

If it fails at this, you'll need to create an empty file called **config.inc.php** in the **/core/config/** directory. Make sure the file is writable by using File Manager in the host's Control Panel and setting the permissions for the file to 666. If that doesn't work, try 777. If your host is using suPHP or suExec, you may need to set the permissions to 644 and the directory permissions to 755. On your local machine using XAMPP, you'll just want to make sure the file is not set to read-only.

MODX Setup will write the contents of the file for you, but you'll want to check the contents yourself if there is any problem with the install to make sure that the database name, username, password, and character set are correct.

 After a successful install, it's important to secure your **config.inc.php** file by making it read-only. MODX will remind you to do this when you log in to the Manager.

Running Setup

Once you have the directories and files in the right place, type the URL of your MODX site into your browser's address window followed by **/setup**.

For remote hosts, the full URL will look something like this:

`http://`*`yoursite`*`.com/setup`

For XAMPP on your local machine, it will look something like this:

`http://localhost/`*`yoursite`*`/setup`

 The MODX Evolution installation directory is called **/install**, so replace the word "setup" with "install" in the URL to install MODX Evolution.

That should launch the MODX Setup script. If it doesn't, you should get an error message telling you what's wrong. If you simply get a "page not found" error, you'll need to review the steps above to get the files and directories in the proper place.

Once you see the MODX Setup screen, select your language. Then click "Select" and "Next" until you see the "Install Options Screen." If this is your first install, "New Installation" should be checked. If you know your host is using suPHP or suExec, change the permissions to 755 for folders and 644 for files. If you're not sure, leave the settings at the default values. Click on "Next."

Connection Information

The Connection Information screen is where you enter the information you wrote down earlier. The default database host is "localhost," and this is almost always correct unless you or your web host have configured the server to use a different host name.

Carefully enter the username in the Database Login Name field, and then enter the password for the database user.

The default database name is modx but this may not be the name of the database you created. In fact it shouldn't be if you will have more than one MODX install on the server. Note also that some hosts will add a prefix to any database name for databases you create. Fill in the true name of the database in the first field.

The next field is the MODX table prefix. This prefix will be added to the beginning of every table in the database. The default is modx_ and it can be used even if there will be more than one MODX install on the server unless they will be sharing the same database.

Note that this is not the prefix that your host may (or may not) have added to the database name or username. It is the prefix that MODX uses for the names of tables in the database.

If you will have more than one MODX install on the server, it's not a bad idea to use a different table prefix for each one so that the databases won't be corrupted if you accidentally connect a MODX install to the wrong database (it happens).

Now, click on the "Test Server Connection" link to make sure your entries are correct. Then click on the "Create or Test" link. You won't see the "Next" button until you've clicked on both links and the tests are successful.

If either of the tests isn't successful, it means that MODX can't connect to the server or the database. Check the host name and make sure that MySQL and PDO are installed and enabled on the server.

Once the Server Connection Test is successful, MODX will fill in the character collation, but check to make sure it's what you set if you created the database ahead of time. Then click on the "Create or Test" link to have MODX create or test your MODX database.

If the test is unsuccessful and you've double-checked the entries for the database name, host name, username, and password, you probably need to create the database manually as described above. There's no point in going on with the install until the Connection Test is successful.

If this is a fresh install, you'll be asked to enter the administrator username, email address, and password. Important: Make a note of the username and password — this will be your last chance to do so. Both are case-sensitive, so be sure to get them right.

If this is a remote install of a production site, use a strong password, preferably one that is at least 8 characters long, mixes numbers and letters, and contains no dictionary words or content related to you (e.g., your phone number, address, pet names, etc.)

Installation Summary

Click on "Next" to go to the Installation Summary screen. All the entries should have a green "OK!" next to them. If not, correct any problems noted and try again. If there are messages about files or directories that are not writable, change the permissions on those files/directories to 777 using an FTP program or your host's Control Panel File Manager. (If your host uses suPHP or suExec, you may need to set them to 755.) If this is a localhost install, just make sure those files/directories are not set to read-only.

Setting the proper permissions can be more complex when installing on a Windows IIS platform. Consult the IIS hosting forum on the MODX Forums at **http://modx.com/forums**.

When everything is correct, click on "Install" and wait for the installation to finish.

Installation

Be patient, but if it doesn't finish in 5 or 10 minutes, something is probably wrong. If you have all the files in the right places, the most likely problem is a missing or corrupted file resulting from a bad download or upload. There are many, many files in a MODX install, and this happens more often than you might think. The only solution is to re-download/ upload MODX and start over.

Once the install has finished, you should see the Installation Summary screen. If there are no messages in red, you should be good to go. Resist the temptation to click on the "Toggle Warnings" link — the warnings are usually irrelevant, and viewing them will just make you nervous. Click on "Continue" to go to the next screen.

At this point, you'll be offered a chance to delete the **setup/** directory. This is an important step if your site is on a remote server. If the **setup/** directory remains in place, anyone can run Setup the same way you did and cause untold damage to your site (and lock you out of it).

Some MODX users like to leave the **setup/** directory in place until they have successfully logged in to the Manager, but it is safer to delete it now and re-upload it if necessary. If you don't delete the **setup/** directory in this step, you may or may not be able to delete it on the Files tab in the MODX Manager. If not, you'll have to delete it via FTP or your host's Control Panel (or re-run Setup in Upgrade mode).

When the Setup script has finished, you should be able to log in to the MODX Manager by clicking on the "Login" button. Normally, you'll get to the Manager by typing this URL in your browser's address window:

`http://yoursite.com/manager`

Once you're successfully logged in to the MODX Manager, you can begin creating your web site. You should see a pop-up welcome screen with some information about MODX and some links to useful MODX sites.

Once you're finished with the welcome screen, you should deal with any issues that show up in the Configuration Check on the Manager home page.

Configuration Check

The first time you log in to the MODX Manager, it is normal to see a number of errors and warning messages. Most of the messages are reminders about things you haven't had a chance to do yet. Here is a list of the possible messages and suggestions about how to deal with them. MODX only shows a message if there is a problem, so you only need to deal with the ones you see in the configuration check.

Config File Still Writable

The MODX Revolution config file is found here:

`/core/config/config.inc.php`

It contains your username, password, and other sensitive information about your site, so it's critical on remote sites that you set it to read-only after the install is completed so that it can't be altered.

Using either an FTP program or your host's Control Panel File Manager, change the permissions to 444. Clear the MODX Cache (**Site → Clear Cache** on the Top Menu), and reload the main screen. If the message is still there, recheck to make sure the permissions have really changed.

 If you need to run Setup again to complete your install or to upgrade MODX in the future, you'll need to change the permissions of this file to make it writable again:

`core/config/config.inc.php`

Important: Be sure to flush permissions, flush sessions, and clear your browser's cache and cookies before re-running Setup.

Warning: register_globals is on

With `register_globals` on, PHP will inject your scripts with all sorts of variables, including request variables from any HTML forms on the site. Combined with the fact that PHP doesn't require variable initialization, this means your whole site is less secure (whether using MODX or not). Unfortunately, many web hosts still have `register_globals` turned on by default.

The whole register_globals problem can be avoided if you select a good hosting service to begin with. Go to the following URL to see a list of recommended MODX hosting services:

http://modx.com/partners/hosting-saas/

If you're lucky and have a good hosting service, register_globals will be off by default and you won't see this warning. If not, there are several methods of turning register_globals off.

The best first step is usually to go to your host's support forum and do a search for register_globals. It's very likely that there will be information there on whether it's possible to turn register_globals off and the best method for doing so. If not, here are some common methods that may work.

There may be a utility in your host's Control Panel that will let you set the value of register_globals.

Another method involves creating an **.htaccess** file in the MODX root containing the following line:

php_flag register_globals off

There are two important issues with using **.htaccess** in this way. First, on some hosts, putting a PHP directive in the **.htaccess** file will generate a server 500 error when you try to access your MODX site. Second, you will probably want to implement Friendly URLs in MODX at some point. When you do that, the normal method is to rename the MODX **ht.access** file to **.htaccess**, but you'll already have an **.htaccess** file.

If you decide to turn on Friendly URLs later, the solution (assuming that using php_flag works) is to delete your one-line **.htaccess** file, rename **ht.access** to **.htaccess**, and add that line anywhere in the file.

If using an `.htaccess` file doesn't work for you, another method is to create a `php.ini` file in the MODX root containing the following line:

```
register_globals = 0
```

If this method doesn't cause any problems (and it usually won't), but `register_globals` is still on (after clearing the Cache), your host may be using suPHP, in which case you'll also need an `.htaccess` file with a line like the following one that tells suPHP where the `php.ini` file is:

```
suPHP_ConfigPath /home/username/public_html/yoursite
```

Unfortunately, on some hosting services, none of these methods will work. If that's the case, you can either ask your host to turn `register_globals` off or change hosts. Running a public site with `register_globals` on is asking for trouble.

Installer Still Present

This message is reminding you that you haven't deleted the **setup/** directory. This is a critical security hole. Delete that directory at once. There are automated hacker- bots searching for MODX installs and attempting to run Setup, so it's important to delete the directory before they find you.

You can use an FTP program or the File Manager in your host's Control Panel to delete the directory. If you delete it in the File Manager and don't empty the trash, you can put it back by simply undeleting it.

 If you delete the **setup/** directory and find that you need to run Setup again, you can extract that directory from the archive and upload it to the root of your MODX site as long as the archive is the same version as the site.

Home, Unauthorized, and Error Pages

Now that you have a fully installed site, you should see a minimal Home page (with no content) listed in the Resource tree at the left of the MODX Manager. If you click on the "Elements" tab and expand the Template folder by clicking on it, you should also see the minimal template MODX has created for you called BaseTemplate. MODX also sets the Unauthorized page and the Error page to the Home page. Let's modify the Home page and create real Unauthorized and Error pages. Along the way, we'll learn a little more about creating and editing resources and elements. We'll also see how to change MODX system settings.

Editing the Home Page

Click on the "Resources" tab at the left of the Manager to see the Resource tree. Right-click on the "Home" resource and select "Edit Resource." This will open the Create/Edit Resource panel. Fill in the following fields in the panel (feel free to use different values):

Title: *Home*

Long Title: *My Home Page*

Description: *Site's Home Page*

Resource Alias: *home*

Menu Title: *Home*

Menu Index: *0*

Resource Content: *Welcome to my site.*

Make sure the "Published" checkbox is checked and click on the "Save" button at the upper right.

Now right-click on the "Home" resource in the Resource tree at the left side of the Manager and select "Preview Resource." You should see your home page in a new browser window.

 At this point, your Home page won't look like much if you preview it because the template is quite minimal and there is no CSS to style it. You can download some more sophisticated templates from the MODX repository (using the Package Manager — more on this in a bit). You can also use an existing template from a site you want to port to MODX or you can create a new template that meets your needs.

Editing the Template

Let's make a minor change to the minimal BaseTemplate that MODX has installed just to see how it's done. Click on the "Elements" tab, click on the Templates folder (if necessary) so the BaseTemplate is visible. Right-click on the BaseTemplate and select "Edit Template." The BaseTemplate should appear in the Create/Edit Template panel at the right. It should look something like this:

```
/* BaseTemplate Code */
<html>
<head>
<title>[[++site_name]] - [[*pagetitle]]</title>
<base href="[[!++site_url]]" />
</head>
<body>
[[*content]]
</body>
</html>
```

Notice that there are several MODX tags in the template — two system setting tags ([[++site_name]] and [[!++site_url]]) and two resource field tags ([[*pagetitle]] and [[*content]]. MODX will replace these with the appropriate values when any page using that template is rendered. The exclamation point in [[!++site_url]] makes the tag uncached so that it will reflect the URL that each user entered the site through. Let's add a line to the template to display the Long Title field as a heading. Put the following line between the <body> tag and the [[*content]] tag:

```
<h2>[[*longtitle]]</h2>
```

Now preview your Home page (by right-clicking on it in the Resource tree and selecting "Preview Resource"). You should see the Long Title ("My Home Page") rendered as a heading.

Changing the Site Name

MODX has already set the site name system setting to "MODX Revolution." Let's change that. On the Top Menu, go to **System → System Settings**. You should see the System Setting grid on the right side of the Manager. We could search for the setting by putting site_name in the "Search by Key" box at the upper right, but let's do it another way. Find the "Search by Area" box at the upper right. Click on the down arrow to drop down the menu and select "Site." You should see all the site system settings.

Find the site_name setting. Double click on the value ("MODX Revolution") and change it to "My MODX Site" (or whatever you like). If double-clicking doesn't work, right-click on the setting and select "Update Setting," then change the value (be careful not to change anything else). Notice the other settings in the grid. You can see a description of what each one does by clicking on the little plus sign next to it. The publish_default setting is another one you might want to change. It determines whether the Published checkbox is checked in newly created resources (e.g. documents). If you'd like new resources to be published by default, double-click on the "No" value and change it to "Yes." This is recommended for working on the examples in the book. If you leave it set to "No" and forget to check the Published checkbox when creating a new resource, it won't appear in the front end of the site.

Now, if you preview your Home page again, you should see the new value that you entered for the site_name setting at the top of your browser window.

Creating Real Unauthorized and Error Pages

As MODX has set things up, any user who tries to access an unauthorized, nonexistent, or unpublished page will simply be sent to the site's Home page with no error message. If this is what you want, you can leave things alone.

If, instead, you'd like your site to handle those events by sending the user to a page with an appropriate message, you can create the two pages and set the appropriate MODX system settings to point at them. The following section describes how to create those two pages and assign their roles.

One logical place for the two pages is below the Home resource in the tree. To create them there, right-click on the "Home" resource in the Resource tree at the left, and select **Create → Create a Document Here** (you'll do this once for each page). Fill in the fields on the Create/Edit Resource panel as we did above with the Home page (using values appropriate to each page).

You'll want to put something like, "Sorry, you're not authorized to visit that page," and "Sorry, we couldn't find the page you asked for" in the Resource Content fields of the Unauthorized page and Error page respectively.

You probably don't want these pages to show in any menu, so check the "Hide From Menus" checkbox. You can leave the Menu Index field blank since it will never be used.

Check the "Published" checkbox and click on the "Save" button. Do this for each of the two documents. They should now appear in the Resource tree under the Home resource. It's very important that these resources be published. If they're not, a user asking for a non-existent page will be forwarded to the Error page. If it's not published, MODX won't find it and will forward the user to the Error page again — over and over.

Double-check to make sure that the two pages are published. A quick way to do this is to right-click on them in the Resource tree. You should see the "Unpublish Resource" option. That means they are published.

Telling MODX Where the Pages Are

We've created our two resources, but MODX is still using the Home resource for both documents because we haven't told it where the new pages are. Make a note of the Resource ID for each page (in parentheses next to the page title in the Resource tree at the left). Go to **System → System Settings** on the Top Menu. You'll see a grid with all of MODX's System Settings. The settings for the two pages are in the Site area, but you can also search for them.

Let's set the Unauthorized page first. In the filter box at the upper right (next to the "Clear Filter" button), type *Unauthorized* and press Enter. In a moment, you should see the System Setting for the Unauthorized page. Double-click on the "Value" field. (If that doesn't work, right-click on it and select "Update Setting.") In the value field, change the value from 1 to the Resource ID of the Unauthorized page you just created. Click on the "Save" button.

 When you set the System Settings for the Unauthorized and Error pages (or any other System Settings), be very careful not to change any fields other than the Value field. Never edit the Name field of a MODX System Setting.

Follow the same procedure for the Error page by typing *Error* in the filter box and pressing Enter. Set the value for the Error Page system setting to the Resource ID of your Error (page not found) page.

Clear the Site Cache (**Site → Clear Cache**). Now, users who try to visit an unauthorized, missing, or unpublished page should get a more informative message.

Installing Add-on Components

At this writing, when you first install MODX Revolution (unlike earlier versions) there is not much of a web site in the install — just a minimal template, a minimal Home page, and no snippets or plugins.

You'll need to go to the MODX repository and download some "Extras" to help you build the site.

If you plan to use the MODX BaseTemplate, you should add a DOCTYPE at the top if there is not one there already. Without a DOCTYPE, some MODX extras may not render properly because of the way browsers respond to pages without a DOCTYPE

Viewing Available Packages

To see what packages are available for MODX Revolution, go to **System → Package Management** and click on the "Download Extras" button. That will take you to the MODX repository where you'll see the available packages. Once you download a package, it will appear, ready for installation, in the Package Management grid.

In order to see packages in the grid, you'll need cURL or sockets enabled (MODX recommends cURL). This is usually no problem on a public server, but if you are using XAMPP on your local machine, you can modify this file:

xampp\php\php.ini

Uncomment this line (remove the semicolon) to enable cURL:

;extension=php_curl.dll

You'll probably want a Rich Text editor such as TinyMCE, and you'll definitely want the Wayfinder snippet, a powerful tool for displaying menus on the site. If you want an FAQ page on your site, the EZfaq snippet provides an easy way to build one. The SPForm snippet creates a simple, spam-proof contact form. Look over the packages and select the ones you like. You can always come back later and get more.

Although there are MODX templates to download, it's recommended that you use the minimal BaseTemplate (or a template of your own from a site you are porting to MODX) until you get things working the way you want. Some of the MODX templates can create confusing displays when used with certain add-on packages and using the minimal template can avoid confusion while you are developing your site.

Downloading Packages

For each package you want to download, click on the "Download" button. Wait for the button to change to "Downloaded" before proceeding. Once downloaded the packages you want, click on the "Finish" button. The packages you've selected have been downloaded to your site and they should show up in the Package Manager grid.

In order to understand the options in installing, updating, and removing packages, it helps to know how MODX handles packages.

The physical packages are downloaded to the **core/packages** directory. The Package Manager grid, however, doesn't show that directory. Instead, it shows the content of the **transport_packages** table in the MODX database. When a package is downloaded from a MODX Provider, it automatically goes to both places. In other words, the file is saved to **core/packages**, and a record is created in the **transport_packages** table.

Packages can also be downloaded manually via FTP and placed directly in the **core/packages** directory. In that case, there is no record yet in the **transport_packages** table, so the package does not show up in the grid (and can't be installed). To get the package in the database and grid, simply click on "Add New Package", and select "Search Locally for Packages." MODX will then look in the **core/packages** directory and add any packages to the database that aren't there already. They will then show up in the grid.

Having packages listed in the Package Manager does not mean that they are installed. Installed packages will have the installation date in the Installed column of the grid. Uninstalled packages will have "Not Installed" in the Installed field. You can have more than one version of a package in the grid at one time, but only one should be installed.

 Always handle packages in the Package Manager. Never delete or rename packages manually in the **core/packages** directory.

Installing and Uninstalling Packages

Once a package appears in the grid in Package Manager, you can install it by simply right-clicking on it and selecting "Install Package" or by clicking on the "Install" button at the right of the grid. Packages have to be installed one at a time.

If you would like to learn more about a package before installing it, click on the plus sign at the left side of the grid next to the package name. This will show more information about the package and may provide a link to a support page.

For most packages, you'll see the **readme.txt** screen and a license screen during the install. You may also see a changelog showing changes in the various versions of the package and/or a screen that lets you set options and values related to the install.

As a package is installed, the console will pop up and give you feedback about the install. When packages are under development, you may see warnings or error messages in the console during the install. If you see the "Successfully installed" message at the bottom of the console, however, the chances are that the package is installed and usable.

Reinstalling and Updating Packages

Once a package is installed, right-clicking on it will show the option to reinstall it. If you have changed or deleted settings or properties for an add-on, reinstalling it will usually return everything to its default state. It's up to the package author to make sure this happens, so you can't absolutely count on it, but it's true for almost all packages.

If you have installed a package downloaded from the MODX repository, the Provider field will show the MODX site URL. For those packages, you can also see if an update is available for the package. There is no way to check for updates with packages placed in the **core/packages** directory manually before installation because they have no provider to check with.

Uninstalling and Removing Packages

The easiest method for uninstalling a package is to click on the "Uninstall" button in the Package Management grid. You will be given the choice of reverting to a previously installed version of the package (if there is one) with your new settings intact, reverting to the previous version and its settings, or uninstalling all versions of the package. None of these options will remove the package from the grid, and the actual transport package will remain in the **/core/packages** directory. This allows you to re-install the package at any time.

If you would like to completely remove a package, you can right-click on the package name and select the "Remove Package" option. This will uninstall the package from the site and remove it from the grid and from the **/core/packages** directory. If you check the "Force Package Removal" checkbox, the package will be removed from the grid and the disk even if uninstalling it from the site fails. After removing a package, you can always download the package again using the "Download Extras" button and re-install it.

Always remove transport packages through the Package Manager. If you physically delete the .ZIP file yourself from the **/core/packages** directory, the package will remain in the grid, but attempting to do anything with it will result in an error. Information about the package will remain in the database and the component may be corrupted if you try to install a newer version of it.

Sometimes, especially when a transport package is under development, the uninstall process will fail. When that happens, right-click on the package in the Package Manager grid and select "Remove Package" with the "Force Removal" checkbox checked. Then, you may need to uninstall the individual components of the add-on manually in the MODX Manager and remove its files by deleting the following two directories:

core/components/componentName

assets/components/componentName

Friendly URLs, Friendly Aliases

Friendly URLs (*FURLs*) is actually short for SEO-friendly URLs. SEO, as you probably know, is an acronym for Search Engine Optimization. Since "Search-engine-optimization-friendly-URLs" is quite a mouthful, they're usually referred to as FURLs in MODX.

In MODX, the `index.php` file is actually a kind of dispatcher module. All browser requests for web pages go through the `index.php` file. With FURLs off (as they are after you first install MODX), MODX refers to documents by their Resource ID numbers. So if the browser request is for the resource with the ID of 12, the URL will look something like this:

```
http://yoursite.com/index.php?id=12
```

If you have FURLs turned on, however, and resource 12 has an Alias of "support," the URL can look more like this:

```
http://yoursite.com/support.html
```

Why Use FURLs and Friendly Aliases?

Search engines, like Google, look for key words in indexing sites. They look at the page title, headings, and page content, but they also look at the URL of the page. Without FURLs, search engines will ignore the ID in the URL. They'll see any key words in the site's domain name, but they'll see the same thing for every page. The only other potential keyword a search engine will find in the URLs will be "`index.php`," which will also be ignored. So, turning on FURLs will make your site much better from an SEO standpoint.

 Before messing with FURLs, make sure that your site is properly installed and that you can perform all common Manager functions, such as creating and saving resources and elements, and browsing the file system. Make sure also that you can access the front end of the site in a separate browser where you are not logged in to the Manager. Back up the `ht.access` file in the site root and keep careful track of any changes you make in implementing FURLs so that you can undo them if you run into trouble.

System Settings for FURLs

There are basically two parts to implementing FURLs: Setting the FURL System Settings, and creating and editing the `.htaccess` file in the site root.

We'll discuss the System Settings first, then we'll deal with the .htaccess file. To see the system settings for FURLs, go to **System → System Settings**. In the "Search by key ..." window at the upper right, you could type *friendly* and press "Enter." A better method, in this case, would be to use the "Filter by Area" drop-down and select "Friendly URL."

You can click on the plus sign at the left of any setting to learn more about it. If you double-click on the value field, you can change the setting in most browsers. If that doesn't work, right-click on the setting and select "Update Setting."

Prefixes and Suffixes

In MODX Evolution, two system settings determined the prefix and suffix used with a FURL. These settings are gone in MODX Revolution. No prefix is used, and the suffix (e.g., "html") is generated automatically for web pages in the front end based on the Content Type field (on the Page Settings tab). Standard content types are shown in the drop-down menu, but you can create new content types by going to **System → Content Types**. Any new content types you create will show up on the Page Settings drop-down list. You can specify or alter the suffixes for all content types. You can also leave the suffix blank for content types that you don't want to have a suffix.

A new system setting in Revolution, **container_suffix**, determines the suffix for resources designated as containers when FURLs are on. In Revolution (unlike Evolution) resources can have children without being containers and can be containers without having children. This suffix is given to resources that have the "Container" checkbox checked, regardless of whether they have children. The default is '/'.

Use Friendly URLs

This is the setting that turns FURLs on and off. If this setting is set to No, all the other settings will be ignored. Remember that turning FURLs on won't give you the URL you want until you also deal with the .htaccess file.

Friendly Alias Path

This setting determines whether the FURL will show the whole path to the page or not. Say you have a Resource tree that looks like this:

```
fiction
    authors
        stephenking
```

With this setting set to Yes, the URL for the Stephen King page would look like this:

http://*yoursite*.com/fiction/authors/stephenking.html

With the setting set to No, the URL would look like this:

http://*yoursite*.com/stephenking.html

How you set the Friendly Alias Path setting is largely a matter of personal preference and your needs for a particular site. Turning it on provides more key words for search engines. On the other hand, it shows the structure of your site (which may be confusing), and it provides long (sometimes very long) URLs that may be difficult for users to type.

If you want to show users where they are in the site but don't want long URLs, you can leave this set to No and use the Breadcrumbs snippet to put the full path somewhere else on the page.

Use Friendly Aliases

This setting determines whether the FURL will contain the resource's Alias or not. If you set it to *No*, the Resource ID will be used in the FURL instead of the Alias. If you set it to *Yes*, the Alias will be used. In other words, if a resource has an ID of 12 and an alias of StephenKing, setting Use Friendly Aliases to *No* (with a suffix of .html) will give a URL like this:

http://*yoursite*.com/12.html

With the setting set to Yes, the URL will look like this:

http://*yoursite*.com/stephenking.html

Generally, this should be set to Yes when you use FURLs unless there's some reason you want to make your URLs uninformative (in which case, you'd probably leave FURLs off).

If the Use Friendly Aliases setting is set to Yes and a resource has no Alias, the Resource ID will be used instead (it will still get the prefix and suffix). If you want to use Friendly Aliases, make sure every resource has an alias.

Configuring the .htaccess File

Servers look for an `.htaccess` file, which sets a wide variety of settings that control how the server works. You can have an `.htaccess` file in any directory, but the one we're concerned about here is the one in the MODX root directory.

If you have located your MODX site in the `public_html` directory on a remote host, the first thing to check is whether the hosting service (or anyone else) has already put an `.htaccess` file in that directory. The odds are against it, but if there is one there, you should add the MODX FURL code into the existing file. Important: If there is an existing `.htaccess` file, back it up before making any changes!

During Setup, MODX places a file called `ht.access` in the root directory. This is not an `.htaccess` file. The `ht.access` file does nothing, but it serves as an example of the `.htaccess` file needed for MODX FURLs to work. If there is no existing `.htaccess` file, copy your `ht.access` file to `ht.access.bak` so that you'll have a backup. Next, create an `.htaccess` file by renaming `ht.access` to `.htaccess`.

 On some Windows platforms, Windows won't allow you to rename a file to `.htaccess` (Windows thinks of that as an extension because of the initial period and helpfully tells you that you've forgotten the filename). The solution is to load the `ht.access` file in a text editor, such as Notepad, and use "Save As" to save it as the `.htaccess` file.

Once you have created your `.htaccess` file, make sure Use Friendly URLs and Use Friendly Aliases are set to Yes in the MODX System Settings grid, and clear the MODX cache (**Site → Clear Cache**). If you have placed the MODX install in the `public_html` directory (or the `htdocs` directory with XAMPP on localhost), FURLs may already work for you. See the section below to test them. If they work, you're done.

With some versions of XAMPP, mod_rewrite is disabled by default and FURLs won't work. On Windows machines, check this file:

xampp/apache/conf/httpd.conf

For the Mac, it's this file:

Applications/xampp/etc/httpd.cnf

Make sure that the following two lines are uncommented (remove the semi-colon at the beginning of the line):

LoadModule rewrite_module

modules/mod_rewrite.so

If you have placed the MODX install in a subdirectory, you may need to edit the `RewriteBase` line in the `.htaccess` file to include the name of the subdirectory. For example, if you have placed the MODX install in a subdirectory called **modx**, the line might need to be changed to this:

RewriteBase /modx/

At this point, FURLs should be working for you. If not, one possibility is that your hosting service doesn't allow `.htaccess` files or doesn't allow mod_rewrite. Check with your host, and if this is the case and the host won't change the policy for you, you'll have to do without FURLs or change hosting services.

Testing FURLs

FURLs generally won't work with your Home page at first, and it won't get the suffix (e.g., `.html`). To test them, you need to create another resource (call it *Test*) in the Manager and make sure it is published and has an Alias (use *FURL-Test* for the Alias).

Put some arbitrary text in the Resource Content field. Check the "Published" checkbox, and click on the "Save" button.

Make sure you've followed the instructions above related to creating a Site Start page (Home page) for your site and turning on FURLs and Friendly Aliases. Then preview your site in another browser. You should see the Home page.

Now edit your site's Home page (Site Start page) to add a link to the second resource. Assuming that the second page has a Resource ID of 2 (the number in parentheses next to the name of the Test page in the Resource tree), add this line to the Resource Content field of the Test page:

```
<a href="[[~2]]">My Test Page</a>
```

If your Test page has a different Resource ID, use that in the tag above instead of 2. Once you have saved the Home page, look at your site in the other browser. You should see your Home page with the new link. When you hover the mouse over the link, you should see the FURL version of the URL at the bottom of your browser screen. When you click on the link, it should take you to the Test page and you should see something like this in the browser's address window at the top of the screen:

```
http://mysite.com/FURL-Test.html
```

If, instead, you see something like this,

```
http://mysite.com/index.php?id=2
```

FURLs are not working yet (but remember to check in another browser).

FURLs are somewhat complicated, and it often takes a few tries to get them to work the way you want them to. Once they work, however, they generally work for good and you never need to worry about them again. If you have trouble, ask for help in the MODX Forums at **http://modx.com/forums**.

Installing MODX on Your Local Machine

It's nice to have a local install of MODX on your machine. Copying files is faster, and there are fewer security considerations. You can leave the **setup/** directory in place and generally install and play with MODX without having to worry about file and directory permissions, and you won't have to deal with a host's Control Panel.

Many MODX users create new sites locally and then upload the finished site to a remote location.

Before you can install MODX locally, you need a local install of a server, PHP, and MySQL. Luckily, packages that include all three in a single install are now available for most platforms. XAMPP is the most popular system for Windows platforms and is available for both Linux and Mac OS X.

Downloading a Server Package

To download XAMPP, do a web search for *XAMPP* and look for "Apache Friends." XAMPP includes an Apache server, MySQL, PHP, and the FileZilla mail server.

Download the appropriate XAMPP package for your platform and follow the install instructions. By default, XAMPP installs to **c:/xampp/** (**Applications/xampp/** on the Mac), and there is no reason to change that. Once XAMPP is installed, you'll want to follow the suggested security recommendations.

To configure XAMPP, you can access the XAMPP configuration screen by entering the following line in you browser's address window:

```
localhost/xampp
```

After XAMPP is installed and configured, the root of your web site is in the **C://xampp/htdocs** directory in Windows and **Applications/xampp/htdocs** on a Mac. Try putting a simple HTML file called **index.html** in the **htdocs** directory and accessing it in your browser by entering **localhost/htdocs** in the browser's address window. You should see the content of the **index.html** file in the browser. If so, your XAMPP install was successful.

To access PhpMyAdmin under XAMPP and work with your MySQL database directly, just enter the following line in your browser's address window:

`localhost/phpmyadmin`

 As soon as you've successfully installed XAMPP (or any other server package), go into phpMyAdmin and set the default collation to utf-8 (utf8_unicode_ci).

Using that collation character set for all databases will save you many headaches later on.

The following lists contain the locations of critical files in the XAMPP package for both Windows and Mac.

Windows XAMPP Files

Type	Location
Apache configuration	`C:\xampp\apache\conf\httpd.conf,` `C:\xampp\apache\conf\extra\*.conf`
Apache logs	`C:\xampp\apache\logs\access.log,` `C:\xampp\apache\logs\error.log`
PHP configuration	`C:\xampp\php\php.ini`
MySQL configuration	`C:\xampp\mysql\bin\my.cnf`

Mac XAMPP Files

Type	Location
Apache configuration	`/Applications/xampp/etc/httpd.conf,` `/Applications/xampp/etc/*.conf`
Apache logs	`/Applications/xampp/xamppfiles/logs/access_log,` `/Applications/xampp/xamppfiles/logs/error_log`
PHP configuration	`/Applications/xampp/etc/php.ini`
MySQL configuration	`/Applications/xampp/etc/my.cnf`

Installing MODX on localhost

Once your server package is in place and configured, installing MODX is just like installing it anywhere. It's quite possible that you will ultimately want more than one MODX install. If so, you will want to put MODX in a subdirectory below the **htdocs** directory. Simply create the subdirectory and copy the MODX files to it as described earlier in this chapter. Then, point your browser at the **setup/** directory and install as described earlier in this chapter. If your subdirectory is named **modx**, for example, type this in your browser's address window:

```
localhost/modx/setup
```

From this point on, the installation process is exactly the same as it is for a remote server.

Moving Your Local Site to a Remote Server

At some point, you may want to move a local site you have created to a remote server. The process is fairly straightforward. By the time you read this, there may be a utility available that will help you transfer a MODX site — if not, here are the basic steps:

- Clear the MODX logs, cache, and flush permissions and sessions.
- Dump the MODX database to an .SQL file using PhpMyAdmin.
- Create the new database on the remote server and import the .SQL file into it.
- Edit the config.inc.php and .htaccess files.
- Copy all the files in the site to the new location.
- Set file and directory permissions and memory limits at the remote site (if necessary).
- Run Setup on the new site in Upgrade mode.

Let's look at the steps in more detail.

Clearing MODX

This step isn't strictly necessary, but it helps prevent transferring useless information and puts MODX in a relatively "clean" state before the transfer. Be sure to do the steps in the following order:

* Go to **Reports → Error Log** on the Top Menu and click on the "Clear" button
* Select **Security → Flush Permissions**
* Select **Site → Clear Cache**
* Select **Security → Flush All Sessions** (this will log you out — don't log back in)
* Turn off FURLs and rename `.htaccess` to `ht.access`.

Dumping the Database

Since much of the MODX site is contained in the database, it's not enough to just move the files. You also have to transfer the contents of the database.

Do this in phpMyAdmin. Enter the following line in your browser's address window:

```
localhost/phpMyAdmin
```

You should see the phpMyAdmin home screen. Follow these steps to export the data:

* Select the MODX database for your site from the list at the left.
* Before exporting, it's a good idea to empty a couple of tables that you don't need. Click on the "Structure" tab. Select the *modx_manager_log* and the *modx_event_log* by checking the checkbox next to each of them. Make sure only those two tables are se-

lected. At the bottom of the grid, find "With Selected" and set it to "Empty." Click on the "Go" button at the lower right and confirm that you want to truncate these tables.

- On the top menu for the database, select "Export."

- On the left side of the Export window, all the files in the database should be highlighted, so don't click in that area.

- Make sure that the SQL radio button is checked below the file list.

- In the "Structure" section, everything should be checked except the last item (Add CREATE PROCEDURE / FUNCTION / EVENT). Make sure that all the other boxes in the Structure section are checked.

- Near the bottom of the screen, check the "Save as File" box.

- Some people like to select a compression method here, but others don't, usually because they like to take a look in the file in a text editor after the dump.

- At the bottom right, click on the "Go" button.

- You should see a file download dialog that lets you specify the name and location of the .SQL file (make a note of where it is).

Importing the Database

Now that you have exported the contents of the database, you need to import them into the new site. First (on the new site), you need to create a database and assign a user to it with full rights. The process for this varies depending on your platform and hosting service. Important: be sure you specify the same character set/collation in the new database as the one used in your local database.

Once you have the database created, you need to run phpMyAdmin at the new site (usually via the host's Control Panel) to import the MODX data. On some versions of cPanel, you have to click on "MySQL Databases" then scroll down to the bottom to see a small link to phpMyAdmin.

In phpMyAdmin, select the database you've created for your new site. Then, on the top menu, select "Import." There's no need to FTP the .SQL file to the remote site — it will be read from your local machine.

At the top of the import screen, you'll see a field for the file name followed by a "Browse" button. Make a note of the maximum file size next to the "Browse" button and make sure your .SQL file is not too big — if it is, you'll have to repeat the export using compression.

It's a good idea to look in your SQL file and check the character set for the database and each table (assuming that you didn't choose to use a compressed file).

The database character set should be listed near the beginning of the file, and the character set for each table should be at the beginning of the section for each table. If you've followed the tip above, everything will be set to utf-8.

If the character sets don't match what's in the "Character Set" field on the Import page, you can change the field on the Import page to match the file's character sets, then later set the collation of the database and the MODX character set to match the file, but it's much better if they match to begin with.

A little safer method is to create a new database (and delete the older one) using a character set and collation that match the file and then import the file. Don't forget to add your database user to the new database before running Setup. Don't attempt to change the character set during this process. If you do that, the data in your tables will not match the character set used by the database.

Leave all the rest of the fields on the page as they are. Click on the "Browse" button and browse to the .SQL file you created on your local machine. Once you have selected the file, click on the "Go" button at the lower right. After the Import is finished, you should see the MODX tables listed in the database. Close phpMyAdmin.

 It doesn't happen often, but in some cases you may have a problem downloading extras through Package Manager after moving your site. If you can't find any extras at the repository, make sure cURL is enabled on your server. If the packages are there, but you can't download them, make sure your core/packages directory is writable. If cURL is enabled but you still have trouble downloading packages, you may have to go into PhpMyAdmin and edit the modx_workspaces table. It may still contain paths from your local site.

Editing the config.inc.php and .htaccess files

If your local MODX install has an .htaccess file in the root directory, copy it to a file called .htaccess.local so you can restore it later to make your local site work again. Leave the .htaccess file in the Manager directory alone.

Edit the .htaccess file in the root for the remote values. Usually, this means just changing the RewriteBase line to reflect the new site location. See the section earlier in this chapter on FURLs for what that line should look like.

I generally turn FURLs off and rename **.htaccess** to **ht.access** before moving a site. It's one less thing to worry about. I turn FURLs back on after the site is up and working.

Now, make a backup copy of this file:

core/config/config.inc.php

Call it:

config.inc.php.local

That way you can restore it after the transfer.

Transferring the Files

Using an FTP program, transfer all the files in the local MODX install to the parallel locations at the remote site. You can skip the two **.local** files you created if you like, although it won't hurt to transfer them (and it will give you an off-site backup of the files).

Some people like to put all the files in a compressed archive (e.g., a .ZIP file), transfer the compressed file, and extract the files on the remote server.

Restoring the config.inc.php and .htaccess Files

This step isn't a part of transferring the site, but it's required to make your local site work again. It also saves the new config and **.htaccess** files in case you need them later.

Make a backup copy of the **.htaccess** file in the root called **.htaccess.remote**. Copy the **.htaccess.local** file to **.htaccess**

Make a copy of this file:

`/core/config/config.inc.php`

Call it:

`config.inc.php.remote`

Now copy this file:

`config.inc.php.local`

Call the copy:

`config.inc.php`

At this point, your local site should be back to normal.

Setting Permissions and Memory Limits

The remote site will usually have permission requirements that are not necessary on the localhost install. See the permissions section earlier in this chapter, and set the permissions as suggested there.

You may also have to increase the memory limits on the remote site to install MODX. Consult your hosting service to find out how to do that. If Setup appears to work with no errors but you can't log in, you get a blank page, or the site doesn't work properly, the most likely cause is running short of memory during the Setup process.

Running Setup

Run Setup as you did earlier by putting something like the following in your browser's address window:

`http://your_new_site.com/setup`

Follow the steps described earlier in this chapter for completing the Setup, with one exception: the "Upgrade Existing Install" checkbox should be checked. That will preserve the data in the database from your local site. If you can't check the "Upgrade Existing Install" checkbox, don't continue. It means you haven't followed one of the steps above properly. Usually, it means that this file doesn't exist:

`/core/config/config.inc.php`

Doing a "New" install at this point will wipe out the content of your site.

 Users are often nervous about doing an upgrade install on a site they've put a lot of work into. As long as the "Upgrade Existing Install" box is checked, however, MODX is very good about respecting existing content. I've performed hundreds of upgrade installs of MODX and never lost a bit of my work.

The only exception would be if you have modified any of the MODX core code. That code could be overwritten during the install.

Once Setup has completed its work, follow the advice earlier in the chapter for securing the site (e.g., making **config.inc.php** read-only and removing the **setup/** directory).

At this point, your new site should look just like your old one. If you used MODX link tags for all the links and made any links to CSS files and links in Snippets relative to the site root, all links should work as they did before. If not, you may have to do a little editing.

 Don't panic if the front end of your new remote site looks like a complete mess at first. The chances are that it's just because the CSS file(s) aren't referenced correctly. Check any references to CSS files in your templates.

Installing the Development Version of MODX

If you would like to work with the "bleeding edge" version of MODX (or just keep your version up-to-date with the latest bug-fixes), you can install a development version of MODX from GitHub. The install process is different, and MODX will be less stable. You should only do this if you're willing to put up with some bugs and contribute to the development process by reporting them.

At this writing, the current release version of MODX Revolution can be downloaded from `http://modx.com/revolution/download/`. There will also be several branches of MODX at GitHub. If you want to use any of the development branches at GitHub, it's important to understand a little bit about both Git and the MODX development process.

The MODX Revolution GitHub repository is a set of "branches" of MODX. There are two permanent branches, `master` and `develop`, and there may also be release branches and hotfix branches. Each branch represents a complete, installable version of MODX. Each *branch* is made up of a series of commits. Every *commit* is a "snapshot" of MODX at a given point in its development. The commit includes all the changes to the MODX files since the previous commit. Collectively, the commits show every change that has ever been made to the code — every change to every file and every file that has been added or deleted. The most recent commit on each branch shows the state of that branch of MODX after all the changes have been applied. It is called the *HEAD commit*, or just `HEAD` for short. In Git commands, if no particular commit is specified, the `HEAD` commit is assumed.

In Git each commit has a kind of ID number called an *SHA1*. The `SHA1` is a 40-digit hexadecimal number. Here's an example:

```
5ef87c4634181e439762b791c83a3bbb5f2279a3
```

The `SHA1` is actually a hash value computed from the contents of every file in the commit, and it is guaranteed to be unique. If you need to specify a particular commit using its `SHA1` (and you rarely do), you only need to enter the first part of it — just enough to distinguish it from the other commits in your repository. Five or six characters are usually enough.

The `master` branch at GitHub will generally correspond to the current release branch. In other words, it matches the files in the .ZIP file available at the main MODX repository. There will also be a branch called `develop`. In the current development process (which could change), `master` and `develop` are the only two permanent branches. The `develop` branch is where both new features and regular bug-fixes are added. The `HEAD` of the `develop` branch, then, is the "bleeding edge" version of MODX. You definitely don't want to be using this branch on a client's site or any important site of your own.

If a critical bug is discovered in the current release version, a *hotfix branch* may be created where work will be done to fix the bug. The branch will be named after the bug. Once the bug is fixed, the changes in the hotfix branch will generally be merged into both the `develop` and `master` branches, and once it's clear that the fix worked, the hotfix branch will be deleted.

There may also be *feature branches* (named after the new feature). If a new Top Menu item, for example, were being added to MODX, the work on it would be done in a feature branch so that any serious bugs it caused would not interfere with other developers. Once the feature is mature, the feature branch will be merged into the `develop` branch and the feature branch will be deleted.

When the `develop` branch is ready for a new release of MODX, a new branch, called a *release branch*, will be created from it. The new branch will be named for the upcoming release version (e.g., `release-2.0.6-pl`). No new features or improvements will be added to the release version. The only changes will be fixes for newly discovered bugs. Any new features or improvements will be added to the `develop` branch or a feature branch. When it's time to actually release the new version, a .ZIP file will be created and made available at the main MODX repository. Then, the changes in the release branch will be merged into both the `master` and `develop` branches. At that point, the release branch will be frozen and no more changes will be made to it.

You'll find the MODX Revolution Git repository at:

`http://github.com/modxcms/revolution/`

If you go there, you'll see a "Switch Branches" drop-down menu that will show you all the current branches. If you select one of them, you can look at the most recent commits and see what's been going on with that branch. If you click on the SHA1 of a particular commit, you'll see the changes between that commit and the previous commit on that branch. You can download the files for a particular branch directly from GitHub, but it's much faster to get the files using a Git client, and doing so will allow you to contribute to the development of MODX.

Getting a Git Client

Git is a version-control system that lets developers store incremental changes in project files in a Git repository. MODX core developers use Git for all work on MODX. Unlike the stable versions available at **http://modx.com/download**, the development version of MODX is constantly changing, and the current version is always available in the public Git repository. If you're not familiar with Git, you'll probably want to read up on it. Do a web search for *understanding git*. You should find a number of helpful resources. If you'd rather learn from a book, Version Control with Git by John Loeliger is an excellent introduction to Git.

In order to check out the latest version of MODX, you'll need a Git client such as msysgit. Do a web search for *git client*. Then, download and install a Git client that's appropriate for your platform.

For Windows machines, *msysgit* is probably the most popular tool. It includes both a Git command-line tool called Git Bash and a graphical user interface tool called Git Gui. We'll use msysgit with Git Bash for our examples here because it is the most widely available. If you use another command-line client, the examples below should still work. If you use a GUI client, you'll have to find out how to use it to perform the actions below (or you can use a command-line client to perform the steps below then switch to a GUI client). *TortoiseGit* is another popular GUI client for Git.

Download the msysgit project installer. Make sure you get the one labeled "Full installer for official Git" — not the portable one, the net one, or the one for hacking on Git. Launch the installer to install msysgit on your local machine. Use the checkboxes to select the options for Git Bash, Git Gui, and adding shortcuts to your desktop.

Most people who work with the development version of MODX do so on their local machines using XAMPP rather than a remote server. Installing the development version of MODX on a public server (especially in shared-hosting situations) is not recommended.

In the following sections, we'll see how to use Git to download the development version of MODX from GitHub and keep it current with the latest changes and bug-fixes. We'll also discuss how you can work on the development version yourself and contribute your work back to the MODX repository at GitHub.

Cloning the Development Version of MODX

If all you want to do is keep up with the latest bug-fixes for MODX and report bugs you find, you don't actually need a GitHub account. You'll need a Git client, such as msysgit, and a place to put your local version of MODX (e.g., in **XAMPP/htdocs**). See the section earlier in this chapter on installing XAMPP on your local machine. Because MODX is a collective project, it depends on people like you to contribute to its development. The method we describe here sets things up so that you can do that. You could contribute a major new feature or an add-on component that will be used by thousands of MODX users. If your skills are more modest, you could just contribute a tiny change that makes MODX easier to use, such as a change in the wording of an error message. Every little bit helps. If you're absolutely certain that you'll never contribute, you can skip the sections on creating and configuring a GitHub account and just clone the MODX repository. The section below describes how to do that. If you think you might contribute, however, skip down to the section on Contributing to MODX Development.

Let's assume that you want to create a local copy of the development version of MODX in your **XAMPP/htdocs/modx/** directory. Open up the Git Bash command-line tool and navigate to the **htdocs/** directory with a command like this:

```
cd c:/xampp/htdocs
```

You should see the path to the **htdocs/** directory on the right side of the command prompt. Now, enter this line to clone the contents of the MODX repository in the **modx/** directory:

```
git clone http://github.com/modxcms/revolution.git modx
```

The clone command will duplicate the MODX Revolution repository on your local disk in a directory called **modx**. You can use a different directory name instead of **modx** if you wish by changing the last word in the line above. Git will give you progress messages while cloning the MODX repository. Because of the way the repository is configured, you have a full version of MODX when the clone process has finished, but there are a few more steps to complete before you can run Setup. First, you need to get the development branch of MODX and switch to it.

Type the following command in Git Bash to move to the MODX directory:

```
cd modx
```

Now enter this command:

```
git pull
```

You should see a message telling you that everything is up-to-date. Type:

```
git branch
```

That will show you the current branches in your local repository. There will probably be just one: master. It has an asterisk next to it to show you that it's the branch you are currently on. You should also see (master) at the end of the path Git shows you.

To get the proper development branch, use this command:

```
git checkout -b develop origin/develop
```

That will make all the local MODX files consistent with the develop branch of the MODX repository. The term origin, by the way, is just an alias for the remote repository we cloned our local copy from. The command creates and switches to a local branch called develop based on the remote develop branch. You should now see (develop) in Git Bash instead of (master). If you type git branch, you should see both master and develop with an asterisk next to develop to show that it is the current branch. As long as you don't issue another checkout command, you should remain on the develop branch, and you'll automatically be there every time you launch Git Bash to go to the **modx** directory.

At this point, you have the current development version of MODX. You now need to build it and run Setup. See the sections below on Building the Transport Package and Running Setup. Once you've done the build and run Setup, you'll have a working copy of the development version. You can log in to your MODX site by putting the following URL in your browser's address bar:

```
http://localhost/modx/manager
```

Of course changes will be made at the MODX remote repository as more bug-fixes come in, and you'll want to update your copy of MODX. You can update your local files with:

```
git fetch origin develop
git merge origin/develop
```

Occasionally, you will see [ReUp] or [Rebuild/Upgrade Required] in a commit message when you pull changes from the MODX repository. That means that you need to re-run the build and re-run Setup. This is an important step. If you skip it, your MODX install may not work properly.

The steps above will work fine if you never make any local changes of your own or if you make them in or under the **assets/** or **docs/** directories — your Git clone is configured to ignore those directories. Installing or upgrading MODX add-on components is also fine because all well-behaved components will only make changes in directories that Git ignores. If you need to add image, CSS, or JS files of your own, always remember to put them under the **assets/** directory.

Contributing to MODX Development

One way to contribute to MODX is to report bugs that you find. Report the bugs (or feature requests) using the bug-reporting tool you'll find in the "Support" section of the Manager's Top Menu. The current tool is called "Redmine," but that may change by the time you read this. When you report a bug, try to be as clear as possible about what's happening, and if possible, list the steps necessary to reproduce the problem. The MODX developers can't fix a problem that they can't reproduce. Be sure to provide as much information as you can about your environment (e.g., MODX version, MySQL version, Apache version, PHP version, available memory, etc.).

If it's even remotely possible that you might want to contribute some code of your own to MODX, you'll want to use a different process than the one described in the previous section. You may not consider yourself a potential contributor, but you never know. Your contribution could be as simple as changing the prompt on a form in the Manager to make it clearer or as complicated as a major new feature for MODX, such as a front-end editing system.

The basic workflow for potential contributors is a little more complicated than simply getting and updating the development version, but many of the steps only need to be done once.

The process is to create your own account at GitHub, fork the development version into your own repository at GitHub, and clone your fork to the local disk. You then `commit` changes locally in branches you create and push them to your own remote repository. Then you issue a "pull request" to tell MODX core developers that you have some code for them. They review the code, and if it is acceptable, they merge it into the main development branch. Let's look at those steps in more detail.

Creating a GitHub Account and SSH Key

In order to work at GitHub, you'll need an account. You'll also need to create an SSH key so that Git knows it's you when you push changes to your GitHub account. The following section is based on the current structure of the GitHub site, but be aware that it may have changed by the time you read this.

Go to `github.com` and click on the "Plans, Pricing, and Signup" button. On the next page, click on the "Create a Free Account" button. Enter your information and click on the "Create a New Account" button. Now click on the "Create Repository" button. The only required field is the name of the project. You can call it anything you like, but *Revolution* is a good choice, and we'll use that in our examples.

On the next page at GitHub, you'll see some directions, but we'll be ignoring some of them. Don't close the browser window, though, because we'll need to complete a step on it later.

Open up your Git Bash window by clicking on the Git shortcut on your local machine, and type the following commands very carefully:

```
git config --global user.name "YourGitUserName"
git config --global user.email you@yourdomain.com
```

Be sure to use the same username and email address you used to create the GitHub account. The username is case-sensitive.

Generating the SSH key

If the GitHub screen is still loaded in your browser, you should see a link that says, "Add another public key." If not, click on "Account Settings" and look for it there. You may have to click on "SSH Public Keys." Don't click on it yet. You need to generate the key pair first. The full details of generating a key pair can currently be found at **http://help.github. com/linux-key-setup/**, but here are the basic steps:

In the Git Bash window, type:

```
cd ~/.ssh
```

That should take you to the root of your user directory. Be sure the path shown by Git Bash ends in **.ssh**. Type ls to see the contents of the directory. If you see two files that start with **id_rsa**, you already have a key pair and you should skip the following steps for generating them.

We'll generate the key pair in a moment, but first you need to decide if you will have a passphrase or not. If your personal computer is fairly secure and you won't be using the key pair for anything other than GitHub access, you may choose not to have one. If you do have a passphrase, GitHub will ask you for it each time you do anything unless you set things up to launch ssh-agent in your profile. See **http://help.github.com/working-with-key-passphrases** for directions. If you don't want a passphrase, just press enter three times during the following step.

To generate a key pair, enter the following command in Git Bash (substituting the email address you used to register at GitHub in place of *you@yourdomain.com*):

```
ssh-keygen -t rsa -C "you@yourdomain.com"
```

When you see the prompts, press enter once. Then, either press it twice more (for no passphrase) or enter a passphrase twice.

If you type ls again, you should see the two **id_rsa** files. The id_rsa.pub file contains your public key. You'll need to paste the contents of that file into the public key field at GitHub. Unfortunately, Git Bash doesn't support cut and paste operations, so you'll want to open the file in another editor. On Windows machines, the file is in the **c:\users** *your_user_name***\.ssh** directory. At GitHub, click on "Add another public key." Leave the Title field blank and paste the entire contents of the **id_rsa.pub** file into the "key" field. Don't enter any white space or carriage returns in the window. Your key should look something like this:

```
ssh-rsa
AAAAB3NzaC1yc2EAAAABINQYg3PDyHhD+lDaO2rhC65BLV8JygEwAAAQEAxFZ4/
WCRU4vjXLf6v8v36UD03DozKd3Uvl44nYp5rALZ+WGp6xe/
xA1Yq4pz5aSLv08qcGTMDP55YPF2GYE2z5usIzKYEB0Zp1Cun95JDhgiSDrG/
6XqnRTIaIvtrMCloGZXtE7xr5RcqInyDaz6EYIr0F839azuAxXVBd1HzMJDhCZ
jbZ2hES4+TPPhCl8dfVMuOPeKWf1XVQb/M6oYjexEegez2Q8z4OXDNpeoxzS0
9/DZpL0V4OOLWLJRzf+DtlIw4id+HUsWZxla4AFH7P2wi75wMZl/
VsYHSwqYgpnPGeZLvSWmrjTS== you@yourdomain.com
```

Once you've pasted the key, click on the "Add Key" button. You can see if you were successful by typing the following command in the Git Bash window:

```
ssh git@github.com
```

You should see the following message (the "Error" is normal):

```
ERROR: Hi Username! You've successfully authenticated, but GitHub does not
provide shell access
Connection to github.com closed.
```

If you don't see that message, look for a link to the SSH key troubleshooting section on the GitHub web site.

Creating and Cloning a Fork

To create your fork of the MODX repository, go to GitHub and log in (if necessary). Once you are logged in, type **http://github.com/modxcms/revolution** in the browser's address window. That should take you to the MODX Revolution repository. Once there, click on the "Fork" button. GitHub will create a personal copy of the MODX repository (called a "fork").

When the fork process has finished, you'll be back at your own repository and you should see your own username in the upper left followed by /Revolution. Hover the mouse over the "Switch Branches" menu item to see the current branches in the repository. Switch to the `develop` branch. You might be tempted to download the source now from the GitHub page, but don't do it. We'll use the Git Bash window to clone your fork so that the files will be under Git control.

We'll assume that you want to create a local copy of the development version of MODX in your **XAMPP/htdocs/modx/** directory. Open up the Git Bash command-line tool and navigate to the **htdocs/** directory with a command like this:

```
cd c:/xampp/htdocs
```

Be sure you see the path to the **htdocs/** directory on the right side of the command prompt before proceeding.

If (and only if) you are on a Windows machine, type the following command in the Git Bash window:

```
git config --global core.autocrlf true
```

That will set up the proper line-ending operations so that your files won't cause trouble when merged with those of users on different platforms. This is very important because the line endings will affect the SHA1 values for every commit. If they are not correct, it can create serious problems for the core developers.

Next, make sure you are in the directory above the directory were you want to install MODX (**htdocs/** for most `localhost` installs). Enter the following command to clone the contents of the MODX repository to the **modx/** directory:

```
git clone git@github.com:yourGitUsernameHere/revolution.git modx
```

The cloning will take a while, and you should see progress messages along the way. If you're denied access, make sure your username is spelled exactly as it was in the `Hello Username` message you saw when testing with the SSH command earlier — the username is case-sensitive. When the process is finished, switch to the **modx/** directory with this command:

```
cd modx
```

You should see a prompt for the **modx/** directory showing that you are on the `(master)` branch. Type `git status` in the Git Bash window. You should see a message telling you that your working directory is clean.

Now, set up a remote that points to the MODX repository:

```
git remote add upstream http://github.com/modxcms/revolution.git
```

A remote is simply a reference to a repository somewhere else. It saves having to type in the whole URL every time you interact with the remote repository. The line above sets up a remote called `upstream` that points to the MODX repository. There is already a remote called `origin` that points to your fork (which was created automatically when you cloned the fork). If you type this command:

```
git remote -v
```

you should see your two remotes: `origin` (your fork) and `upstream` (the MODX repository) and the paths to them. The `-v` switch tells Git to give you a "verbose" response.

Your local files now match the latest stable version of MODX (the `master` branch of the MODX repository). You need to make your files match the `develop` branch. Make sure you are in the **modx/** directory and issue these commands in the Git Bash window:

```
git fetch upstream
git checkout -b develop upstream/develop
```

The first line above fetches all the branches from the MODX repository and creates what's called a local *tracking branch* for each of them. The tracking branches simply track the branches at the `upstream` repository. They always have a slash in their names, and the part after the slash is the name of the `upstream` branch. Whenever you "fetch" from the `upstream` repository, they will be updated to match the current state of the `upstream` branches. Never checkout (switch to) a tracking branch or make any changes to it except by fetching from the `upstream` repository.

The second line in the code above tells Git that you want to create and switch to a new branch called `develop` based on the files in the `upstream/develop` tracking branch.

You should see messages telling you that Git is now aware of some new branches after the first command. It will list all the tracking branches created from the branches at the upstream repository. After the second command, it should tell you that it has created a `develop` branch (a local branch) for you that tracks changes at the MODX repository's `develop` branch and has switched you to that branch:

```
Branch develop set up to track remote branch develop from upstream.
Switched to a new branch: 'develop'
```

Be sure to read the information in the following section on Git Contributor Workflow so that you don't accidentally revert your local files to a non-development version or make undesired changes to them.

 If you look at the local files on your computer, you might expect to see all the branches Git just created. In fact, none of them will be visible. You'll just see one set of the MODX files. That's because you can only have one branch checked out at a time. The other branches exist, and Git knows about them, but you'll only see the files from the branch you currently have checked out. When you check out a branch, Git changes all the files to match those of that branch. The set of files you see is usually referred to as the "working directory." Be careful not to switch branches while you have unsaved files in your editor or else you can end up with a real mess.

Now, update your local files from the MODX repository (`upstream`) just in case any commits have come in since you created your `develop` branch:

```
git fetch upstream develop
git merge --ff-only upstream/develop
```

The first command above updates the `upstream/develop` tracking branch. The second command above tells Git to merge any changes in the `upstream/develop` tracking branch into the current branch (`develop`). Note that the `--ff-only` option has two hyphens at the beginning. It tells Git to use a "fast forward" merge, which will automatically abort the merge if there are any merge conflicts. Conflicts will only occur if you modify tracked files in the local `develop` branch — something you should never do.

At this point, you can build and install a working version of MODX. See the sections below on how to do that.

Your local `master` branch is no longer of any use to you if you intend to work from the `develop` branch. You may want to keep it there for reference, but you may also want to delete it to prevent you from accidentally using it. To delete it, make sure you are on your `develop` branch (`git checkout develop`) and then issue this command in Git Bash:

```
git branch -D master
```

To prevent other kinds of confusion, you may also want to remove the rest of the local branches except develop, upstream/develop, and some of the branches at your fork. You can see the local branches with this command:

```
git branch
```

You can delete them as you did the master branch. You can see the branches at the remote repositories with this command:

```
git branch -r
```

That will show you the branches at the MODX repository (`upstream`) and the branches at your fork (`origin`). To delete a remote branch at your fork, issue this somewhat cryptic command:

```
git push origin :branchName
```

The colon in this command separates the source from the destination (`source:destination`). Since there is nothing on the left side of the colon, it tells Git to push "nothing" to the remote branch, which deletes the remote branch.

You can actually delete all of the branches at your fork (although GitHub will refuse to delete the current branch there — usually the `master` branch) since you should never be fetching anything from your fork. You'll do your work in a local branch you create just for a specific bug-fix or feature, and you'll push that branch to your fork. None of the other branches there are necessary. The only reason the fork exists is to hold branches that you issue pull requests for so that the MODX team can merge your changes into the MODX repository.

 You might expect that your fork at GitHub will be updated automatically to match the MODX repository you forked it from. This is not the case, however. That means that your fork will quickly be completely out of date, which is why you never want to fetch from it. The only reason the fork is there is so that you can push changes to it that you want to contribute to MODX.

At this point, your local `develop` branch matches the MODX repository's `develop` branch. You can now build and install MODX using the steps outlined in the sections below on Building the Transport Package and Running Setup, but be sure that you are on your `develop` branch (`git checkout develop`) before doing so.

Working in the MODX Manager won't affect any of the files that Git tracks in your local installation, so feel free to do anything you want in the Manager as long as you don't go to the Files tab and edit any of the MODX core files — something you should only do if you want to fix a bug in the core and contribute it to MODX.

Git Contributor Workflow

You now have a local copy of the development version of MODX. You can use Git fetch and Git merge as we did just above to get changes other people make to the MODX repository into your local copy to keep it up-to-date. When you make changes locally to fix bugs in MODX, you can use Git push to send them to your fork, but always be sure that you make your changes in a local branch you create just for your own work. You want to make sure your local `develop` branch always matches the MODX repository's `develop` branch, so never edit, delete, or rename files while on your `develop` branch.

The following guidelines are critical in order to keep things from blowing up in your face. They are especially important if your understanding of Git is less than perfect:

- Always fetch from the `develop` branch of the MODX repository at GitHub while on your `develop` branch. In other words, whenever you want to get updates from the MODX repository (and you should do this often), make sure you are in your `develop` branch. To update, use the following commands:

```
git checkout develop
git fetch upstream develop
git merge --ff-only upstream/develop
```

- Avoid typing `git fetch` by itself or else you'll get back all the branches you deleted. This won't hurt anything, but it wastes disk space.
- When you fetch changes, you may see [ReUp] or [Rebuild Upgrade] in the commit messages (always look to see if one of these appears). That message means that you need to re-run the build and Setup steps described in the following sections before logging

in to your MODX install. Failing to do so can trash your MODX install. I generally run a build and Setup whenever I update just to be on the safe side.

- Never modify any local files in your develop branch. It should always match the develop branch at the MODX repository (upstream).

- When you make changes in a local branch you've created, never merge them into the develop branch. If you submit a pull request and it is accepted, you'll get the changes when you update from the MODX repository.

- Always push your local bug-fix branches to the origin remote (your fork). Pushes to the MODX repository (upstream) will be rejected automatically. There is no need to keep the develop branch (or any other branches) at your fork up-to-date.

Let's work through an example that shows how to contribute a bug-fix or minor improvement to MODX. When you want to fix a bug in MODX and contribute your fix to the project, always follow these steps:

1. Update your develop branch just before creating a new work branch:

```
git checkout develop
git fetch upstream develop
git merge --ff-only upstream/develop
```

2. Create a branch to work in. We'll use the name bugfix in our examples, but you should use a descriptive name for your branch so that you and the MODX core developers will know which bug it fixes:

```
git checkout -b bugfix
```

3. Edit files and fix the bug. Then commit your changes to your bugfix branch. Be sure to enter a brief but clear commit message describing what you've done:

```
git commit -a -m "Your Commit Message"
```

4. When you are ready to submit your code, always update your bugfix branch from the MODX repository just before pushing it to your fork with these commands (while on your bugfix branch):

```
git fetch upstream develop
git rebase upstream/develop
```

The rebase command, which we haven't seen before, is a special kind of merge that tacks your local changes onto the end of all the other changes in the merge. In the rare case that the rebase fails, it means that someone else has modified at least one of the files you changed since you created your bugfix branch. If this happens, you need to save your changes somewhere outside the working directory, delete your bugfix branch, and start over from step 1.

5. Push your changes to a bugfix branch at your fork:

```
git push origin bugfix
```

6. Now, go to your repository at GitHub and switch to your bugfix branch by clicking on the "Switch Branches" menu item. Click on the "Pull Request" button. Notice that the message there says that you're asking for your commit to be pulled into the modxcms:master branch from your bugfix branch. You don't want that because all pull requests for the MODX master branch are ignored. Click on "modxcms:master" and on the left side of the screen, change master to develop. Click on the "Update Commit Range" message. Make sure that modxcms:develop appears in the top line and that the commit will be pulled from your bugfix branch. Now enter a message describing what your change does in the empty form field and click on the "Send Pull Request" button.

 When you perform a commit in Git Bash, you can use -m "message" to specify the commit message. If you leave it out, Git Bash will launch the Vim editor by default. Beginners usually feel trapped in Vim because it's not at all obvious what to do. If you find yourself in Vim, this should help:

Type the letter *i* to go into insert mode.

Type your message.

Press the *escape* key to go into command mode.

Type *:wq* to save and exit.

You can also configure Git to use the editor of your choice by editing the **users/your username/.gitconfig** file. Add a line like the following one containing the path to your editor in the [core] section of the file:

```
editor = "'c:/Program Files/Windows NT/accessories/wordpad.exe'"
```

Create a new branch for each bug you want to fix, fix a single bug on each branch, and never merge changes from one branch to another. If you need to make local changes to your MODX files that you don't intend to share, you can make them in a separate branch and never issue a pull request for that branch. Branching is "cheap" in Git, and you can create a new branch for everything you want to try. Pull changes at the MODX repository into your branch the same way you did it for your develop branch:

```
git fetch upstream develop
git merge --ff-only upstream/develop
```

If your changes on a branch don't work out, it's easy to delete the branch. Be sure you're not on the branch that you intend to delete. (If you try to delete a branch you are currently on, Git will tell you that can't do it.) Use these commands:

```
git checkout develop
git branch -D branchName
```

To delete a branch on your remote fork of MODX, use the command we describe earlier:

```
git push origin :branchName
```

Important: Never delete a branch at your fork while there is an open pull request for commits on that branch.

Although it's easy enough to work in separate branches in Git, some people prefer to keep a separate copy of MODX in a different directory for changes that they never intend to share. This prevents any possibility of accidentally merging changes.

As we mentioned earlier, you should never merge your own changes into your develop branch. The reason is that the next time you fetch from the MODX repository, Git will undo all your changes. If your pull request is honored, the changes will appear in the MODX repository and you'll get them when you fetch from it.

Contributing a New Feature

Rather than fixing a bug, you might want to add a whole new feature to the MODX core, such as a version-control system for MODX resources and elements. You should be aware, though, that most new features are best created as add-on components. Before doing a lot of work, you should ask about your proposed feature on the MODX forums. If creating an add-on component is more appropriate, see Chapter 13, which describes how to create a transport package. Contributing a feature is exactly like contributing a bug-fix or minor improvement. Follow the same steps we used above.

Building the Transport Package

Unlike the release versions of MODX that you download from the MODX main repository, any versions pulled from GitHub require you to perform a build step before running Setup. You need to "build" the transport package for MODX before Setup can install it. You also need to edit the config file that controls the build.

Go to the **_build** directory in your checked-out copy of MODX. Load the following file into a text editor:

```
build.config.sample.php
```

Edit the last four lines to match the settings for your MODX database. Save the file as **build.config.php**.

In that same directory, execute the file **transport.core.php**. You can usually double-click on it and have it execute in your web browser (assuming that there is a file-type association between the browser and PHP files). If you have a programming editor, such as NetBeans, you can execute it in the editor. If not, you can execute it by typing the following on the command line:

```
php transport.core.php
```

If the PHP executable file is not in your path, you may need to give the full path to the **php.exe** file like this (in Windows):

```
c:/xampp/php/php.exe transport.core.php
```

Or, for a Mac:

```
Applications/xampp/php/php.exe transport.core.php
```

You should see some progress messages as the build proceeds. It can take a while, so be patient. Once the build has been completed, you are ready to install the Development version.

Running Setup

After a successful build, you install MODX by putting the following line in the browser's address window (assuming that you've placed the MODX files in the **htdocs/modx/** directory):

```
localhost/modx/setup
```

Setup should run as it does on any MODX install with a few small differences. You'll see two extra checkboxes: "Core Package has been manually unpacked" and "Files are already in place." Leave them at their defaults.

On the following page (Connection Information), fill in the fields there with the name of the database and the database user/password. Click on the "Test Database" link, then on the "Create or Test" link. If this step fails, you'll need to create the database manually in PhpMyAdmin and re-run Setup. Once this step is successful, you should see the fields for the admin Super User's username, email, and password. Fill those in and click on the "Next" button.

On the next page (Context Installation), you'll see a lot of new fields. These allow you to move and/or rename the main MODX directories. Leave these alone. Altering them will make it impossible to submit a useful pull request. The rest of the Setup process should proceed as described earlier in this chapter.

Updating the Development Version

If you are using the Development version of MODX, you'll almost certainly want to update it when bugs are fixed or new features are added. We described that process earlier, but let's review it and add a couple of extra steps to make the upgrade faster and more reliable.

Before updating the MODX install, log in to the Manager, clear the cache, then go to Security on the Top Menu and select "Flush Permissions" and "Flush All Sessions" (in that order). That will log you out — don't log back in. Then close any instances of browsers connected to the MODX site. It's also a good idea to clear your browser cache and cookies at this point.

Open the Git Bash window and type these commands:

```
git checkout develop
git fetch upstream develop
git merge --ff-only upstream/develop
```

If you look at the commit messages Git shows for the update, you'll see [REBUILD/UPGRADE REQUIRED] or [RE/UP] for versions that require a build and Setup. Use the up arrow in Git Bash to see any that have scrolled off the screen. Important: If any version since the last one you installed is marked with this message, you need to do a build and an upgrade install. If you don't see either of those messages, you can skip the following steps, but it never hurts to run a build and Setup just to be on the safe side.

Before running **transport.core.php** on Windows, it's a good idea to delete the following directory:

core/packages/core

Delete this file as well:

core/packages/core.transport.zip.

The build will go faster and will be more reliable. Important: Be careful not to delete the **/core** directory by mistake!

Once you have updated the files (and optionally run **transport.core.php** and Setup), your site should be fully upgraded to the latest version.

Porting an Existing Site to MODX

The following sections describe the steps involved in taking an existing site and making it a MODX site — a logical next step after installing MODX if you already have a web site. It's difficult to create an exact tutorial because sites vary so much, so think of this as a general guide to moving a site to MODX. Even if you don't have a site you want to convert to MODX, many new users of MODX have commented that learning about porting a site to MODX really helped them to understand how MODX works.

If you have been playing with MODX and have turned on Friendly URLs (FURLs), turn them off and rename **.htaccess** to **ht.access** in the site root until after you have finished porting your site. It will give you one less thing to worry about during the process. Once the site is working properly, you can turn them back on.

Porting your Template

If you have an existing site that you are porting to MODX, you'll want to create a site template based on the look of your existing site. Before you do that, though, you can go to **System → Package Management**, click on the "Download Extras" button, and download a few sample templates. Take a look at them to see some of the things that should be in a MODX template.

Except for the MODX tags, the templates are standard (X)HTML code like you'd see for any web site. One of the things that developers like the most about MODX is that there are literally no restrictions on the template format. It's simply regular (X)HTML code with MODX tags in it. Look for the MODX tags in the template. The tags will all be surrounded by double brackets: [[*Tag*]]. One of the best methods for creating your own MODX template for an existing site is to duplicate one of the existing MODX templates and modify it. Here are the basic steps for creating your own from one of the sample ones (this assumes that you have installed at least one of the existing templates using the Package Manager):

- Click on the Elements tab
- Click on "Templates" in the tree at the left.
- Right-click on a template and select "Duplicate Template."
- Change the name to whatever you like (e.g., *MyTemplate*) and save it.
- Edit the description and save the template.

Now it's time to create your own page. Here's one way to do it. Make sure not to skip any steps. It's not a bad idea to print out one of the sample MODX templates to use as a reference. For the later steps, it's a good idea to look at the page in a browser after making the changes. If you mess up a page, sometimes the browser will show a blank page, and it's nice to know which step caused the problem.

Step 1: Copy your site's CSS file to the new MODX site and make a note of where it is. There's no right place to put it. Some MODX users create an **assets/css** folder. That's where the files should go if you are using the development version of MODX from Git. The **assets** folder is kind of an all-purpose holding area for files that need to be accessible via URL. Other users like to put CSS files in the site root (where **index.php** is) so they will load a little faster.

Step 2: Paste the code from the <body> section of your home page into the new template's <body> section (later, you'll remove the stuff that doesn't belong there).

Step 3: In the head section of the template, edit the reference to the CSS file so it points to the place where you put your CSS file in Step 1:

```
<link rel="stylesheet" href="assets/css/yourcssfile.css" type="text/css" />
```

Notice that we're using a relative URL here rather than an absolute one. Using a relative URL will make the site more portable in case you ever want to move it.

Step 4: Remove the main content of the page (basically, the material that is unique to that page). Save it somewhere (e.g., another text editor or a text file — do not use MS Word or any other full-featured editor unless it saves files as straight text). You can also cut it to the clipboard. Remove all the content as a single block. If there are sections in it that will appear on multiple pages, you can deal with those later.

Step 5: Where the content appeared in the page, add the following MODX resource tag:

```
[[*content]]
```

Step 6: Save your new template.

Porting Your Content

We've created a template that will serve as a shell for displaying the content, but we haven't created any content yet.

Step 7: Before proceeding, make sure the "Rich Text" editor is OFF before pasting any code (by unchecking the "Rich Text" checkbox and saving the resource). Go to the "Page Settings" tab. Uncheck the Rich Text checkbox. Save the document. The rich text editor will now be off and will not try to be "intelligent" about saving your code.

You can turn the Rich Text editor back on (assuming that you've installed one) after you're done porting your page by checking the "Rich Text" checkbox and saving the document.

Step 8: In the MODX Manager, create a new document by right-clicking on the "web" context icon in the Resource tree and selecting "Create" then "Create a Document Here." That will open up the Create/Edit Resource panel on the right where you can put the document's content.

Step 9: Paste the content you saved earlier when you created your template into the Resource Content field of the new document. If there is any PHP code on the page, you'll need to remove it. It will have to go in a snippet (or snippets if there's more than one section) to be created later. On the Element tree, you can use "Quick Create Snippet" to create the snippets without leaving the resource you are editing. Put a snippet tag for that snippet in place of each piece of the removed PHP code:

```
[[SnippetName]]
```

If the PHP code creates dynamic content (i.e., content that will not be the same each time the page is visited) use the ! token to make the snippet uncached:

```
[[!SnippetName]]
```

If you see PHP errors when you preview the page, it means that one or more of the snippets will have to be modified to work on the new site. At this point, it's best to just disable the snippets for now. The easiest way to do that is to add a space between the first two brackets of the snippet tag:

```
[ [!SnippetName]]
```

MODX will not see the tag as a tag and will simply print the tag itself. You can test each tag (by removing the space) to see which ones need to be modified.

Step 10: If there is a menu on the page, save it somewhere for future reference and replace it with the following snippet tag:

```
[[!Wayfinder? &startId=`0`]]
```

Step 11: If there are images in the page content, you'll have to move the image files to the MODX site. They can go anywhere, but the **assets/images** directory is a common place for them. If you have many images, you may want to create multiple subdirectories under **assets/images**. You'll also have to correct the links in the page content to point to wherever you put them.

Step 12: If there are links on the page to other pages on the site, wait to correct them until you have created the documents they point to. Then use link tags for the links to those documents. Make a note of their resource ID numbers (in parentheses in the Resource tree at the left side of the Manager screen), and change the links to look like this (using the actual document ID numbers instead of "*12*"):

```
<a href="[[~12]]">My Link</a>
```

Step 13: Save the new document. Right-click on the document in the Resource tree at the left of the screen and select Preview Document. You should see your original page, more or less, but with an abbreviated, unstyled Wayfinder menu. The page may be styled strangely, but you should see your content and at least some of your own styling from the CSS file.

Now go back and edit the template you created earlier. In the head section, replace the title code with two tags like these:

```
<title>[[++site_name]] | [[*pagetitle]]</title>
```

Preview the page again to make sure this worked. You should see your site name and page title in the title bar at the very top of the browser window. Feel free to alter the code to meet your needs, but use MODX tags for the parts. You may prefer to use the **alias**, **longtitle**, or **menutitle** of a document for the <title> code.

Step 14: At the top of the section where your main content goes (just above the [[*content]] tag), insert a longtitle resource tag like this one:

```
<h2>[[*longtitle]]</h2>
```

Preview the page again. You should see the content from the Long Title field of the document (if you've entered it) as a heading above your content.

You'll probably have some cleaning up and styling to do, but you should now have the beginnings of a MODX site. The Wayfinder menu is infinitely styleable (with drop-downs, fly-outs, etc.), but that is beyond the scope of this section.

To port the rest of your pages, you should be able to just create new documents in MODX, assign them to the template you created, and repeat the appropriate steps above — pasting their unique content into the Resource Content field. They will automatically show up in the Wayfinder menu as long as they are published.

If there is still content in your pages that will appear verbatim on multiple pages (e.g., a privacy statement or a copyright notice), move it into a chunk and replace it with a chunk tag:

```
[[$ChunkName]]
```

If your site has a "tree" structure or a hierarchy of documents, you will want to duplicate that on the MODX site. Make sure that any document that will have children is designated as a "container" by checking the "Container" checkbox on the document's Create/Edit Resource panel (reached by right-clicking on the document and selecting "Edit Resource").

To create a child document, you can right-click on the parent in the Resource tree and select "Create" and "Create a Document Here." If you forget or you want to reorganize the structure later, you can drag and drop the resources in the tree.

Don't forget to save each document after making any changes on the Create/Edit Resource page. If you edit your CSS file, be sure to clear the site cache before previewing the site.

Summary

The current version of MODX can be downloaded from **http://modx.com/download**. It's relatively easy to install MODX within the graphical user interface of the Setup script (**http://yoursite.com/setup**). MODX will attempt to create the database for you, but it's often easier to do it yourself ahead of time. If you've made the **/core/config** directory writable, you shouldn't need to edit the **config.inc.php** file.

When you first log in to the MODX Manager, you should correct any problems that appear on the Configuration Check panel, especially if it's a live site.

Add-on components are installed in Revolution with the Package Manager, which automatically downloads and installs them from the MODX repository. Friendly URLs (FURLs) are relatively easy to implement in MODX and can help make the pages of your site much easier to find with common search engines.

Many MODX users install MODX on their local machines and upload it to a remote site later. Users who want to help develop or test MODX can download the current (bleeding edge) development version using Git.

Porting sites to MODX is a relatively straightforward process because MODX templates contain nothing but standard (X)HTML and MODX tags.

MODX Evolution Notes

Downloading the current stable version of MODX is essentially the same for MODX Evolution, except that the main directories in the Evolution root are called **/assets**, **/install**, and **/manager**. Creating the database is the same for either version.

Config File

The Config file is similar and generally needs no editing before the install in Evolution, but its name and location are different:

/manager/includes/config.inc.php

The file is missing from the downloaded, but you should put a writable, blank file with that name in place. Go to this directory:

/manager/includes

Rename the following file:

config.inc.php.blank

Call it:

config.inc.php

Permissions

To set the proper permissions on Linux/Unix platforms, make sure that MODX can write to the following directories:

/assets/cache (and its files)
/assets/export
/assets/images
/manager/includes/config.inc.php

Install Script

Running the install script is very similar, but the name of the install script is different ("install" rather than "setup"). To run the script, put something like this in your browser's address line:

```
http://yoursite.com/install
```

For a localhost/XAMPP install, the line will look like this:

```
http://localhost/yoursite/install
```

In MODX Evolution, you will have the option to install the sample site and a number of add-ons during the install process.

Configuration Check

Once you log in to the Manager, you'll see the same Configuration Check. Remember that the Config file in Evolution is here:

/manager/includes/config.inc.php

The install directory is here:

/install/

The register_globals setting and the Unauthorized and Error pages work the same in Evolution except that the system settings for the two pages are found by going to **Tools → Configuration** on the Top Menu and selecting the "Site" tab.

Installing Add-ons

Installing add-on components is quite different in MODX Evolution because there is no Package Manager. Add-ons must be downloaded from the MODX repository at **http://modx.com/extras** and installed manually by following the instructions that come with the add-on. The instructions may be in a **readme.txt** file, in the **/docs** directory, or in comments in the main **.php** file.

Friendly URLs

Friendly URLs work the same in MODX Evolution except that there is no **container_suffix** system setting. The system settings that control FURLs are found by going to **Tools → Configuration** and clicking on the "Friendly URLs" tab. In some versions of Evolution, Friendly URLs will generally not appear to be working if you preview from the Manager. In that case, you will need to test them in another browser where you are not logged in to the Manager.

XAMPP

Installing XAMPP is exactly the same for MODX Evolution.

Moving Your Site

Moving your site to a remote server works almost the same way in MODX Evolution. The tables you want to clear in the database before exporting the data are called modx_event_log, modx_error_log, and modx_manager_log. The installation directory is called **install** rather than **setup**. Otherwise, the steps for moving your site to a remote server are the same.

Development Version

There is a Development version of MODX Evolution, but you can skip the build step in installing it. Simply check out the files and install as you would the regular version.

Chapter 3

The MODX Manager

Almost all the work you do on a MODX site will be within the MODX Manager. You launch the Manager by entering `http://yoursite.com/manager` in your browser's address bar. That will take you to the Manager login screen where you can enter the credentials that will get you into the Manager. Note that the username and password necessary for Manager login are the ones you created during the MODX Setup process, not the ones you use for cPanel access or the ones you created for the MODX database user.

In this chapter, we'll discuss the various parts of the MODX Manager. We'll see what they are for, and when and how to use them. A full discussion of the functions available in the MODX Manager would make this chapter hundreds of pages long, so this will just be an overview. Later chapters will go into more detail about how to perform the various tasks available in the Manager.

Because MODX is constantly evolving, the Manager may not be exactly as it is described here. Don't be surprised if there are some minor changes to the names and locations of the various parts of the Manager or if additional features have been added. With a little effort, you should still be able to find all the functional areas described below.

The Resource, Element, and File Trees

Before we start working our way through the various items in the Manager's Top Menu, let's take a look at the *Tree* at the left side of the screen. What we often call "the Tree" is actually three trees, one on each of the three tabs: Resources, Elements, and Files. We'll refer to them as the Resource tree, the Element tree, and the File tree. The Tree section will be visible in most parts of the Manager unless you have hidden it by clicking on the little left-arrow between the Tree section and the right panel. When the Tree is hidden, you can make it reappear by clicking on the little right-arrow at the left of the screen.

Assuming that you are an administrator with full access, the three trees show all of the resources, elements, and files on the site. The various sections of the tree can be expanded and contracted by clicking on the little triangle next to the parent item.

In the following sections, we'll look at working with each of the three tabs.

 It's fairly easy to make resources disappear from the Resource tree, even for the admin Super User, when messing with MODX security permissions. The missing items aren't gone; you've just created a situation where the admin Super User can't see them.

You can see them again if you modify the user groups that have access to the missing items either by adding the admin Super User to the group or by changing the Access Control rules.

Using the Resource Tree

The Resource tree shows all the resources (documents, weblinks, symlinks, and static resources) on the site. When you create, edit, publish, unpublish, or delete resources, you will almost always do it through the Resource tree. Clicking on a resource will load the resource into the Create/Edit Resource panel on the right side of the screen for editing.

In MODX Revolution, the Resource tree will be empty (except for the Home page) until you create some resources or install an add-on component that creates one or more resources.

Resources that have children in the Tree will show as folders. It's important to realize, however, that they are in all other ways normal resources. They can be edited in the MODX Manager and they can be viewed as web pages in the front end.

When editing a resource, you will see a container checkbox that designates whether or not the resource is a container.

In MODX Evolution, any resource with children is automatically a container, and the checkbox cannot be permanently unchecked.

In MODX Revolution, however, resources with children can be designated as non-containers using the checkbox. In snippets, the **isfolder** field tells you if the resource is designated as a container, and the resource's hasChildren() method tells you if it has children. The two are independent, and **isfolder** can be used by snippets to control display characteristics regardless of whether the resource has children or not. Similarly, hasChildren() can be used regardless of whether the resource is designated as a container.

Each resource in the Resource tree will have a number next to it in parentheses. This is its Resource ID, and it is very important. The Resource ID is how MODX refers to all resources. When you create a link to a resource on your site, always use the Resource ID (in a MODX link tag) to refer to it. Similarly, any reference to a resource in a snippet or plugin should be by its Resource ID. The resource's Title may change, but its Resource ID never will.

Resource tree Icons

The small icons at the top of the tree can control its behavior.

The up and down arrows expand and contract the tree (try it).

The next four icons will create a document, weblink, symlink, or static resource in the site root (although most experienced MODX users seldom use them).

The double-arrow icon refreshes the tree though it is seldom necessary since MODX will usually refresh the tree whenever it changes. Next to the refresh icon, there are four icons that let you create a new document, weblink, symlink, or static resource. When using these icons, the new resource will be created at the top level of the tree.

The next icon (a little folder with a down arrow) lets you control how the tree is sorted. If you click on the icon, the drop-down sort menu will appear. If you click it again, the menu will disappear.

The default method is to sort the tree by menu index, which shows the tree as it would be shown by a menu or aggregation snippet such as Wayfinder or getResources. If your documents have no menu index settings, they will generally be displayed in the order that you created them.

Other sort options are resource title (alphabetical), publish date (the date the resource last changed from unpublished to published), creation date (the date the resource was first saved), and edit date (the date the resource was last edited).

You can change the order of the items in the Resource tree by clicking and dragging them up and down, but this will only change the view if the tree is being sorted by Menu Index.

Note, too, that dragging them up and down actually changes the Menu Index numbers for individual resources. (Menu Index numbers are visible when editing a resource; they are often used by menu snippets, such as Wayfinder, to order the items on a menu.) Dragging the top item to the very bottom of the tree, for example, will change the Menu Index number for every document in the tree.

The little trashcan icon purges deleted resources. When you delete resources, they appear in the tree with a line through their names. They can be undeleted at any time. Many MODX users leave deleted resources in the tree and reuse them rather than creating new resources. It's a way of keeping your Resource ID numbers from growing too large.

When you purge deleted resources by clicking on the trashcan icon, they will be deleted permanently. Once you do that, there is no way to recover them.

Resource Tree Style

The style of an item in the Resource tree indicates the value of the following settings for the resource:

- Published — Roman type
- Unpublished — Italic Type
- Hide from Menus — gray
- Show in Menus — black

You can tell which resources are published and which will be shown in menus by looking at the style of the listing in the Resource tree.

Resource Tree Right-click Menu

If you right-click on an entry in the Resource tree, you'll see the right-click menu. This is where you'll most often select items for editing, publishing, or deletion and where you'll create new resources in MODX Revolution. Let's look at the choices on the right-click menu:

View Resource — Enables the user to see details about the resource without the ability to change anything. Low-level users may be given "view" rights but not "edit" rights.

Edit Resource — Loads the resource into the Create/Edit Resource panel on the right side of the screen for editing.

Quick Update Resource — Loads the resource into a pop-up editor. This is extremely useful for editing resources, elements, or files without leaving your place in the Manager. Not all fields can be edited in Quick Update (Template Variables, for example, are not available in Quick Update at this writing).

Duplicate Resource — Creates a duplicate of the resource and loads it into the Create/Edit Resource panel for editing.

Refresh Resource — Refreshes the local area of the tree around the resource but is seldom needed since the tree almost always auto-refreshes when appropriate.

Create — Displays the following submenu:

* **Create a Document Here** — Creates a document with the current resource as its parent.

* **Create a Weblink Here** — Creates a weblink with the current resource as its parent.

* **Create a Symlink Here** — Creates a symlink with the current resource as its parent.

* **Create a Static Resource Here** — Creates a static resource with the current resource as its parent.

* **Quick Create** — Is the same as Create, but loads the new item in a pop-up window with some fields unavailable for editing.

* **Publish/Unpublish Resource** — Shows only the appropriate option (e.g., Publish for unpublished resources, Unpublish for published resources) and allows instant publishing or unpublishing of resources.

* **Delete/Undelete Resource** — Delete Resource puts the resource in the trash so that it is no longer available in the front end. Users with the proper authority can still edit the resource. It can be undeleted unless the trash has been emptied.

* **Preview Resource** — Shows a preview of the resource in the front end.

Previewing resources via the tree is not always the same as viewing them as an anonymous user. For example, the URL may not appear as it would to an anonymous user.

For a true preview, it's helpful to view the page in another browser where the user is not logged in to the Manager.

Using the Element Tree

The Element tree is visible when you click on the "Elements" tab at the top of the Tree. It shows all templates, template variables, chunks, snippets, plugins, and categories on the site. Like the Resource tree, it will be empty in MODX Revolution (except for the BaseTemplate) until you either create elements or install an add-on component that creates them.

Clicking on an element will load it into the Create/Edit element panel on the right side of the screen for editing.

Unlike the Resource tree, elements can't be moved in the Tree by clicking and dragging. They are always displayed in alphabetical order, although you can drag an element into a category. This doesn't move the element, however. It just assigns the element to that category.

 If you are creating a number of elements that will be assigned to one or more categories, it's usually faster to just create them all, create the categories, and then drag the elements into them.

Element tree Icons

The down and up arrow icons will expand and collapse the Element tree. The double-arrow icon will refresh the tree. Refreshing the tree is seldom necessary because the tree will almost always auto-refresh when appropriate. Next to the refresh icon, you'll find icons for creating a new template, TV, chunk, snippet, or plugin. As with the Resource tree, clicking on the little triangle next to a section of the Element tree will expand or collapse that section.

Element Categories

Elements can be organized into categories as we described above. MODX uses the categories for organizing the Element tree display, but they have other uses as well. Using the MODX security permission system, you can hide elements from certain users by putting them in categories. You can also control what users can do with the elements in a particular category. You could, for example, create an AdminOnly category that is invisible to some users in the MODX Manager. You could also create a ReadOnly category that allows users to see but not modify elements in that category. See the section on controlling access to elements in Chapter 10. Elements can only be placed in existing categories, so you need to create a category before assigning any elements to it.

Categories can also be used in snippets and plugins. A snippet, for example, could randomly select a chunk in a particular category for display. The TV-based Chunks method will create a template variable that shows the user the chunks in a particular category in a drop-down list, as a series of radio options, or with a series of checkboxes. See the TV-based chunks section in Chapter 6 for more information.

To place an element in a category, simply right-click anywhere in the Element tree, and select "New Category." Give the category a name (and a parent if you want to place it below an existing category), and save it. Then you can drag and drop elements into (and out of) any existing category.

Another, (slower) method to assign elements to categories is to right-click on the element, select Quick Update Element, set the category with the drop-down in the right panel, and save the element.

Note that categories will show as folders in the Tree. Unlike the folders in the Resource tree, these are virtual folders and cannot be edited, though they can be renamed by right-clicking on them in the Categories section at the bottom of the tree.

Also, unlike the folders in the Resource tree, when you delete a category, you won't lose any of the elements under it. They'll just become uncategorized.

Element tree Right-click Menu

The contents of the right-click menu in the Element tree will depend on what you right-click on: an element type (e.g., "snippet" or "chunk"), a category, a categorized element, or an uncategorized element. Here are the possibilities (only the appropriate ones will show):

New *element*— Creates a new element of the type contained in the part of the tree you clicked in and loads it into the Create/Edit element panel for editing. The element will automatically be given the category you clicked on, though this can be changed on the editing panel.

Quick Create — Allows you to create any kind of element, which will automatically be given the category you clicked on. The creation will take place in a pop-up window without leaving your current location or work. Some functions available on the Create/Edit element panel will not be available in the pop-up.

Create Category — Creates a new category, to which any kind of element can then be assigned.

Remove Category — Removes the category you clicked on. All elements of any kind assigned to that category will then have no category. The elements in the category will not be deleted.

Edit *element* — Loads the element into the Create/Edit element panel for editing and saving.

Quick Update *element* — Loads the element into a pop-up editor for editing and saving without leaving your current location or work. Some functions available on the Create/Edit element panel will not be available in the pop-up.

Duplicate *element* — Creates a duplicate copy of the element. You can set the name of the new element during the duplication process.

Remove *element* — Deletes the element permanently. There is no way to undelete a removed element.

New Category — Creates a new category, but assigns no elements to it.

Using the File Tree

The File tree is visible when you click on the "Files" tab at the top of the Tree. It shows the files in your MODX install. Using the File tree, you can upload new files from any location. You can also create or remove directories; rename, edit, and delete files; and change file and directory permissions.

File tree Icons

The down and up arrow icons will expand and collapse the File tree. The double-arrow icon will refresh the tree. This is seldom necessary because the tree will almost always auto-refresh when appropriate. In addition, clicking on the little triangle next to a directory will expand or collapse that directory. There are also icons for creating a new folder and for uploading files. It's generally better to use the right-click menu for creating directories and uploading files because it allows you to place the new item or items where you want them in the tree.

File tree Right-click Menu

When you right-click on a directory, you will see the following menu:

Create Directory Here — Opens a dialog to create a new directory. The default location is beneath the directory you clicked on, but this can be changed in the dialog.

Chmod Directory — Opens a dialog to change the permissions on the directory you clicked on. Use this with care. In a successful install, the permissions are usually correct to begin with. The current permissions of the directory are shown in the input box. All entries should be 4 digits and should start with 0.

 The values used in setting directory permissions are actually octal numbers. The three digits following the leading 0 each represent the sum of the permissions for either the owner, the group the owner is a member of, or the world (everyone else).

The permissions are as follows:

    1 — execute
    2 — write
    3 — read

A value of 4 gives read-only access. A value of 6 (2 + 4) gives read and write permission. A value of 7 (1 + 2 + 4) gives full permissions.

Examples:

    0600 — read/write for the owner, nothing for the group or world
    0644 — read/write for the owner, read for the group and world
    0755 — Everything for the owner, read/write for the group and world

---

Rename — Opens a dialog in which the directory can be renamed.

Refresh Directory — Refreshes the directory to reflect any changes.

Upload Files — This will open a file upload dialog. Click on the "Add" button to select a file, browse to the file, and select it. Once you are done adding files to the list, click on the "Upload" button to upload them. The "Remove" button removes a file from the list. The "Reset" button removes all files from the list.

Remove Directory — Permanently removes the directory, which then can't be undeleted.

If you click on an individual file, you'll see the following right-click menu:

Edit File — Loads the file into a file editor for editing and saving.

Rename — Opens a dialog for renaming the file.

Remove File — Removes the file permanently from the server. After this operation, it can't be undeleted.

The Top Menu

As of this writing, the Top Menu contains the following items: Home, Site, Components, Security, Tools, Reports, System, User, and Support. The locations may have moved, and the menu choices under each one may have been renamed or moved by the time you read this, but the basic choices should be the same. Note that the Components menu choice won't show up unless you have at least one component installed. We'll look at each of these in turn in the following sections.

Home

The Manager's Home screen is the one you see right after logging in. You can return to the Home screen at any time by clicking on the "Home" choice at the left of the Top Menu. There are several panels on the right side of the screen. The left panel shows whichever Tree tab is currently selected. The various panels on the right can be collapsed or expanded by clicking on the bar at the top of each panel.

At the top of the Home Screen, just above the Top Menu, you'll see the current name of the site (something like My MODX Site). This is set in a System Setting called `site_name`. We'll discuss how to change it later when we cover System Settings. You'll also see the MODX version name, number, and rev. (revision) number. When you ask a question on the MODX forums, you should always give the version number (e.g., MODX 2.0.8) of your MODX installation.

Configuration Check

When you first log in to the Manager, you will usually see the Configuration Check displayed in the right-hand panel of the Home screen, just below the site name. The Configuration Check only appears when MODX detects a problem with your site. As soon as the problems are all solved, the Configuration Check section will disappear.

Common Configuration Check messages warn you about `register_globals` being on, the config file being writable, the installer still being present, and/or the `Error` and `Unauthorized` pages being missing or unpublished. If you don't see a warning about one of these, it's because MODX didn't find a problem with it.

Details about how to deal with these warnings can be found in Chapter 2.

MODX News and Security Panels

The MODX News panel contains an RSS feed that shows news from the MODX community. It is mostly concerned with announcements about new releases of MODX and MODX components. The Security panel alerts you to any serious security issues that have been identified and how to deal with them.

In some installations, these two news feeds can slow down the manager significantly. They may, for example, have trouble getting past a firewall or proxy setup. Ultimately, you'll probably want to fix these problems so that you can see the two feeds. In the meantime, however, you can turn them off by changing the two System Settings that control them. If you go to **System → System Settings** and type *feed* in the "Search by key ..." window at the upper right, you should see the two "Enable" settings as well as the two feed URLs.

You can double-click on the "Yes" next to each enable setting, and set the value to "No" to disable the news feeds. You can enable them again by doing the opposite.

Recent Documents

The Recent Documents panel, when expanded, will show the documents at the site that have been recently created or edited by you. The most recently edited will be at the top. The grid shows the Resource ID of the document, its title, description, published status, and deleted status.

The Recent Documents panel can be handy if you were recently working on a document and need to go back to it but can't remember the title.

Info

The Info panel, when expanded, shows your username, last login, and total number of logins.

Online

The Online panel, when expanded, shows all the users that are currently online at the site along with their user IDs, IP numbers, and the last action they performed in the Manager.

Site

The Site menu contains some general actions that affect the whole site as well as the opportunity to create new resources and log out. The following section contains details on each of the choices.

View

This option opens the site's Home page (as defined by the **site_start** System Setting) in a new window. Remember that this preview will not always show you the site as an anonymous viewer will see it because MODX may still consider you logged in to the Manager during the preview.

For a true preview, open the Home page in a separate browser where you are not logged in to the Manager. Note that using another window in the same browser is not reliable. You will not see pages using this message unless they are published.

Clear Cache

This option clears the entire MODX cache. When you make certain changes to the site, they may not be reflected in the site preview until the cache is cleared. Saving changes to resources and elements will usually clear the cache (unless you uncheck the "Clear Cache" checkbox), but other changes, such as alterations of included files, CSS files, JS files, etc., won't clear the cache, and your changes may not show up until the cache is cleared.

Remember, too, that your browser also has a cache that may prevent you from seeing changes to the site. When you've made a change that doesn't show up in the Manager or the Front end, try clearing the MODX cache and your browser cache.

If you have changed any security settings, you'll also have to flush permissions (on the Security menu). If everything else fails, flush sessions (on the Security Menu), clear the cache and cookies in your browser, and log in again.

Remove Locks

When files are loaded into an editor, they are locked to prevent other users from simultaneously changing the same file. If a user closes the browser without logging off, the files may remain locked and uneditable by other users. This option clears all the locks on all files at the site. If you have multiple users who can edit resources and elements, it's a good idea to check the Online panel on the Home screen before selecting this option to make sure that you don't unlock a file that is currently being edited.

Search

This option provides a sophisticated search of all the resources at the site. It opens up a search panel on the right side of the screen with a series of fields to search. The grid below the form will show all the resources on the site when you first open it. After you have set search criteria, it will show only the resources that match the criteria.

To search for a resource or resources, you can fill in one or more of the fields then click outside any of the fields or press Enter. The grid will reload and show only the resources that meet your criteria. The criteria for any field may be partial. For example, putting *hello* in the Content field will show all resources that contain that word in their **content** field. A common mistake by new users of MODX is to think that all fields in the search form must be filled. In fact, you will usually fill only one or two fields.

Clearing all the fields and clicking outside any field will again show all the resources on the site. The checkboxes below the input fields allow you to restrict the search to published or unpublished resources or deleted or not deleted resources. If you have a site with many resources, this feature can be tremendously helpful in finding the ones you want to work on. You could, for example, see a list of all resources containing a key word or phrase. In the grid showing the results of the search, you can right-click on a resource, then click on the "Edit Resource" button to edit it.

New Document, etc.

These four options — New Document, New Weblink, New Symlink, and New Static Resource — open the Create/Edit resource panel to allow you to create a new resource of the type selected. The new resource will be in the root of the site. See the chapter on resources (Chapter 4) for more information on each of the choices.

Most experienced MODX users seldom use these options. They create new resources by right-clicking in the Resource tree as described earlier in this chapter.

Logout

This option logs you out of the Manager. It is identical in function to the Logout button at the upper right of the Manager (which is easier to get to).

Components

This menu will be empty when you first install MODX Revolution. In fact, it won't show up in the Top Menu at all until at least one component has been created or installed. Third-party Components that extend the Manager will appear as menu items here after you install them through the Package Manager. Custom Manager Pages (CMPs) can also be added here.

Two commonly used components are Batcher and PackMan. Batcher allows you to perform bulk actions on groups of resources. With Batcher, for example, you can easily change the template, published status, parent, publish or unpublish dates, or author of any group of resources. PackMan allows you to create MODX transport packages from add-on components you have created for your site so you can share them with other users or move them to other sites of your own.

Security

The Security menu contains a number of items that relate to users, user groups, resource groups, security permissions, and customizing the manager. In the section below, we'll give a brief overview of the options. See the chapters on security (Chapter 10) and customizing the MODX Manager (Chapter 11) for more information.

Manage Users

This section allows you to create, edit, and delete users and to set their user attributes (such as username, password, email address, country, phone number, etc.).

This is not where you control the roles users are assigned to or what each user can do at the site. The only thing you can do to control a user's actions here is to block or unblock the user's ability to log in to the site. This action is usually used to block undesirable users (or users who enter the wrong credentials too many times), not for general access control.

 For security purposes, user passwords are not stored in the database. Instead, a one-way hash of the password is stored there. There is no easy way to decode the stored hash to get the password. Even if your database is compromised, user passwords will still be relatively safe. As of MODX 2.1, the very strong PBKDF2 algorithm is used for the password hash value. Earlier versions of MODX use the somewhat weaker MD5 algorithm.

Because the hashing is a one-way process, there is no way to convert stored MD5 password hashes directly to PBKDF2 format, but there is a plugin called pbkdf2Convert written by Jason Coward (OpenGeek) that will convert user password hashes from MD5 encoding to PBKDF2 encoding as each user logs in.

To update a user's information, right-click on the user in the grid and select "Update User" from the drop-down list. This will take you to the Create/Edit User panel which has four tabs:

General Information — Contains the username, password, and all user attributes for the user.

Settings — Allows you to create and set user settings, which will override system settings of the same name.

Access Permissions — Allows you to add users to user groups, although it's usually easier to manage user groups in the Access Controls section.

Extended Fields — Allows you to add extra fields for the user to contain information that is not on the General Information tab.

Access Controls

This section is the heart of the MODX security system. Here you can determine which resources and elements users can see in the Manager and what they are allowed to do with them. You can also control their ability to perform actions in the Manager (such as clearing the cache or removing locks) and whether they can see and edit various elements. This section contains a quick overview of the Access Controls area. The MODX Security chapter (Chapter 10), later in the book, goes into much more detail.

There are three tabs in the Access Controls section:

User Groups — This tab is where you create user groups and assign users to them (by right-clicking on the user group). When you right-click on a user group and select "Update User Group" a new screen (described below) will open where you can actually create the Access Control Lists (ACLs) that determine what users can and can't do at the site.

Roles — The roles tab is where you create user roles (by clicking on the "New Role" button) and assign authority numbers to them. You do not assign users to roles here (that happens when you assign users to user groups). A user can have more than one role, and you may have users with different roles in the same user group.

Access Policies — Access policies are simply lists of specific security permissions that allow users to perform specific actions on the site. Each permission has a checkbox that lets you enable or disable it. Several policies, including an Administrator policy, a Resource policy, and an Element policy, are provided to get you started. In general, these standard policies should not be edited. Rather than change them, you should duplicate them and edit the duplicates.

Policy Templates — The policy templates determine which permissions will appear in the policy. To add a new permission to a policy, you add the permission to the Policy Template attached to that policy, then edit the policy and make sure that the checkbox for that permission is checked. Adding permissions to a template is only necessary if you are creating custom permissions. Custom permissions can be used to hide Top Menu items from specific user groups. They can also be used by snippets and add-on components.

The Update User Group panel

As described above, this panel is reached when you right-click on a user group in the User Group tab of Access Controls and select "Update User Group" from the drop-down menu. This option deserves its own section here because it is where you create Access Control

Lists that actually determine what specific users in a group can and can't do. It's recommended that you not perform any of the following tasks until you have some understanding of MODX security permissions. The panel has the following five tabs:

General Information — Identifies the name and parent group of the user group. The parent group is for organizational purposes and does not affect security permissions. Note that future versions of MODX are likely to include inheritance of permissions from parent groups.

Users — Lists the users in the group and the roles they each have in the group. Users can be added or removed from the group, and their roles can be changed by right-clicking on their entries.

Context Access — Contains a grid with the Access Control List (ACL) that determines what Manager actions users in the group can perform. Each ACL entry assigns a context that the user group has access to, a minimum authority, and an Access Policy. Users in the group that have an authority number (role) equal to or less than the number here are granted the security permissions in the specified policy in the named context. The policies here should be based on the standard Administrator policy. You can have as many entries in the ACL grid as you want. You can also use this section to completely hide specified contexts from certain users.

Resource Group Access — Contains a grid with the Access Control List (ACL) that determines what users in the group can do with the resources in specific resource groups. Each ACL entry contains a resource group name, a minimum role, an access policy, and a context. Users in the group with an authority number (role) equal to or less than the specified minimum can perform the actions permitted in the named policy on resources in the named resource group in the named context. The policies here should be based on the standard Resource policy. You can have as many entries in the ACL as you want. In addition to controlling what users can do with specific resources, this section can also be used to hide resources from some users. Only resources that belong to resource groups are affected by the ACL entries on this tab.

Element Category Access — Contains a grid like the one above except that instead of a resource group, you specify an element category. Each ACL entry contains a category name, a minimum role, an access policy, and a context. Users in the group with an authority number (role) equal to or less than the specified minimum can perform the actions permitted in the named policy on elements (chunks, snippets, plugins, templates, and template variables) in the named category. The policies here should be based on the standard Element policy. You can have as many entries in the ACL as you want. In addition to controlling what users can do with specific elements, this section can also be used to hide categories and the elements under them from some users. Only elements that are in a category are affected by the ACL entries on this tab.

Resource Groups

This section allows you to create resource groups and assign resources to them. You create the groups by clicking on the "Create Resource Group" button. You assign resources to them by clicking and dragging the resources from the tree on the right (which shows all resources on the site) to the resource group on the left. You can expand or contract parts of either tree by clicking on the little triangles.

Form Customization

This option allows you to customize the Manager so that various functions and panels can be hidden from users in specific user groups. This can be done for security purposes or simply to make the Manager less intimidating for certain users. See the Form Customization section of Chapter 11 for more information on how to use this section.

Flush Permissions

When you make changes in any of the sections listed above, the changes won't take effect until you clear the current permission structure by selecting this option. This will affect current users (as soon as they move to another page or perform some action), but it won't force them to log in again.

Flush All Sessions

Because login status is contained in various session variables, selecting this option will log off all current users (including you) and force them to log in again.

It's a good idea to check the Online panel of the Home screen to see who will be affected before selecting this option.

It's also a good practice to flush permissions and flush all sessions before updating the site to a new version of MODX.

Tools

The Tools menu includes utilities for importing pages into a MODX site and for working with property sets.

Import Resources

You may have a set of files that you would like to import into your MODX site as static resources or as documents. If there are not very many of them, you can cut and paste their content or simply recreate them on the MODX site. If there are a lot of them, however, you may want to simply import them using this tool (or the Import HTML tool described below).

On this panel, you can specify the directory containing the files you wish to import and the parent container you would like them to appear under in the tree. To specify the parent, click once in the parent field, and click on the desired parent in the tree below the form. If you don't select a parent, the resources will be created in the root of the Resource tree.

In the path field, give the full path (not the URL) to the files. Be sure to include a final backslash on the end of the path.

To import static resources, put *modStaticResource* in the **modResource** field. MODX will create static resources for each file with the path to the file in the resource's Static Resource field (which is actually the **content** field). The filename (without the extension) will be placed in the **pagetitle** and **alias** fields.

To import the files as documents into the MODX site, put *modDocument* in the **modResource** field. MODX will create a new document for each file and place the file's contents in the resource's **content** field. For (X)HTML files, only the <body> section of the file will be imported. The filename (without the extension) will be placed in the **pagetitle** and **alias** fields.

To limit the import to files with certain extensions, put a comma-delimited list of extensions (without the period) in the Extensions field (e.g., *htm,html*).

In the root HTML element field, you can specify the part of the file to import. For (X)HTML files, you almost always want the <body> section, but you can choose to import just the <head> or <html> sections as well. If you have text files that you would like to import part of the content from, simply edit the files in a text editor and surround the part you want with <body></body> tags.

Click on the "Import Resources" button at the upper right to import the resources. If you refresh the Resource tree at the left of the screen, you should see your imported resources.

Import HTML

If you have a number of files with the same extension in a single directory and you only want to import some, but not all of them, this panel provides an easy way to do so. Simply copy the files you want to the **core/import** directory (make sure it's empty first). Then set the HTML root element and parent as described in the section above, and click on the "Import HTML" button at the upper right. The files will be imported as documents just like in the previous section, but only files in the **core/import** directory will be imported.

Property Sets

See Chapter 6 to learn what properties and property sets are and how they are used. Property sets that are attached to snippets serve the same purpose as properties passed in the snippet tag (although any properties passed in the snippet tag will override those in any attached property set).

For snippets, you can create and edit property sets on the Properties tab when editing the snippet. MODX Revolution, however, also allows you to create free-floating property sets that can be attached to chunks and other elements.

Because these property sets are not attached to any particular element, this option was created as another way to create and edit property sets and to attach them to elements.

 Snippets have default properties that are permanently attached to a single snippet and stored with the snippet code. These cannot be edited here. This section is only for creating, editing, and attaching property sets.

Generally, default properties for add-on components should not be edited at all because they may be overwritten when the add-on is updated to a new version. Instead, you should either use snippet properties in the tag to override the default values, or create a property set.

When creating a property set for a snippet, it's best to use the "Add Property Set" button on the snippet's Properties tab rather than creating them here.

If you click on "New Property Set," a dialog where you can specify the name of the property set, an optional category, and an optional description of the set will open. Be sure to click on the "Save" button in the pop-up dialog to save the new property set.

To work on a particular property set, you can either click on it in the tree or use the drop-down in the grid at the right. Once you have selected a property set, its properties (if any) will show in the grid at the right. To modify a property, you can right-click on it and select "Update Property" (or double-click on the Value field). To add a new property to the set, click on "Create Property." Be sure to click on the "Save Property Set" button when you're finished.

You can use the "Import Properties" and "Export Properties" buttons to save or load a property set that is stored as a text file. This can be handy if you want to move a property set from one site to another.

In order for an element to use a property set, you need to do two things. First, you need to attach the property set to the element. Do that by right-clicking on the property set's name in the tree and selecting "Attach Element to Property Set." Select the element type (Class Name) and element name (Element) using the drop-downs, and click on the "Save" button. Second, you need to tell MODX which property set to use with the element by specifying the property set in the element tag with the @ token. For a chunk, that would look like this:

```
[[$ChunkName@PropertySetName]]
```

Be sure not to leave any spaces between the element name, the @ token, and the property set name.

Reports

The Reports section provides general information about the site, including upcoming events, recent activity in the Manager, errors, information about the server, and information about MODX itself.

Site Schedule

This section shows information about upcoming publication and unpublication of resources. It shows only resources that have a Publish Date and/or an Unpublish Date. The report includes the Resource ID, the Resource's Title, and the dates. The button at the top of the grid toggles the display between upcoming publications and upcoming unpublications.

Manager Actions

The Manager Actions grid shows all the events that have taken place in the Manager. Each event shows the date, the action taken, and the object (e.g., resource or element) involved in the action.

By using the form above the grid, the events can be filtered by action, user, or date range.

Error Log

This panel shows the contents of the MODX error log. The log shows only errors logged by MODX itself, so many PHP and MySQL errors and other server errors will not appear here.

Some errors can be repeated very often, and the log may grow large enough to slow down the site, so it's important to look at it periodically and fix any reported errors. It's also a good idea to clear the log periodically using the "Clear" button at the bottom of the grid.

System Info

The System Info section has three tabs: System Info, Database Tables, and Recent Documents.

System Info — Shows information about MODX and about the MySQL server. You can see the MODX version and the server time, local time, and server offset settings. In the MySQL section, you can see the database charset, the database name, database server name, and MODX table prefix.

Notice the PhpInfo() "View" link on the first line. This link is easy to miss but very important. It shows the results of the PHP phpinfo() function, which provides a wealth of information about your server and how it is configured. You will have to scroll down to see the full results. When posting questions on the MODX forums, it is often critical to provide information from this screen, especially the PHP version and MySQL Client API version. Be careful, however, to remove any information that might be of use to hackers when posting, such as the paths to various important files on your site or the name of your database.

Database Tables — Shows all the tables in the MODX database along with some statistics for each table. For tables with significant overhead, the overhead column shows the overhead number as a link. If you click on the link, MODX will optimize the table. After you click on the link, the overhead column should show a zero, and the site should run a little faster. It's a good idea to visit this page every so often and optimize the tables that show significant overhead.

Recent Documents — Shows the documents that have most recently been created or edited. It shows the Resource ID, the Title, the User who made the change, and the date. You can alter the sort column and sort order by clicking on the drop-down next to each column heading. This grid may have multiple pages. If so, you can browse through them using the buttons at the bottom of the grid.

About

The About section provides information and links relating to MODX itself on three tabs: About MODX, Help, and Credits.

About MODX — Provides a link to information about MODX itself (and the MODX documentation) and to the GNU General Public License (GPL) under which MODX is released.

Help — Provides links to the MODX Forums and the MODX Revolution Online Documentation. It also provides a link to the system used to report bugs in MODX.

Credits — Contains information on the many people who have contributed (and continue to contribute) to the MODX development project.

It also has links at the top to the PHP, MySQL, and xPDO projects without which MODX could not function.

System

The System Top Menu choice provides links to a number of areas where you can control important aspects of the site.

Package Management

The Package Management section is where you install MODX third-party components (3PCs) that are available as transport packages.

In Package Management, you'll see a grid of available packages that have been downloaded and are installed or are ready to install.

To see a list of the packages available for download, click in the "Download Extras" button. This will take you to the MODX repository. Select a category in the tree at the left, and the packages will show in a grid at the right. If you don't see any packages, see the note about enabling cURL in the chapter on installing MODX (Chapter 2).

Clicking on the plus sign next to each package will show more information about the package. Click on the "Download" button for any packages you want. You can download as many packages as you like. Before proceeding to another package, wait for the button to change to "Downloaded."

When you're done downloading packages, click on the "Finish" button at the lower left to take you back to the Package Management grid. The packages you downloaded should show up there.

To install a package, click on the "Install" button next to it in the grid.

If you see a message at the end of package installation that says "Package Successfully Installed," the odds are that things are fine even if you see some error messages before that.

If you don't see the "success" message and you get errors that start out with "could not copy . . .," you could have a permissions problem. You might need to adjust the permissions on the **core/packages** directory and change the new_file_permissions and new_folder_permissions system settings.

For packages that are not in the repository but are in the form of a transport package (they will have **transport.zip** in the file name), download the package to your **core/packages** directory. Then click on the "Add New Package" button at the top of the Package Management grid, select "Search Locally for Packages," and click on the "Next" button. This will load any packages into the grid that aren't already there.

For a component that doesn't have a transport package, you'll need to download the file and expand it locally, then install the parts manually as you would in MODX Evolution. You can usually (though not always) find instructions in the **readme.txt** file or as comments in the code of the component.

If the component is for MODX Evolution, you will usually have to modify it to work in MODX Revolution.

System Settings

The System Settings grid contains all the settings for the site. Each setting has a Name (description), a key, and a value.

The system settings are divided into areas to make them easier to find. You can also use the "Search" box at the upper right, which will search the Name, Value, and Key fields for whatever you enter (click in the grid after entering the search value). Or, you can use the Area drop-down menu to search for system settings that relate to a particular area (e.g., Friendly URLs).

If you click on the plus sign next to a system setting, you can see a description of what it does.

You can change any system setting by double-clicking on the "Value" field or by right-clicking on the entry and selecting "Update Setting." You can also remove settings, but it is almost never a good idea to do so.

You can create a new system setting by clicking on the "Create New Setting" button at the top of the grid. This should only be done for values that you want to be available throughout the site.

System setting values (including ones you create) are available pretty much anywhere in HTML code, snippet tags, and chunk and resource content with a setting tag: [[++**SettingName**]]. In snippet and plugin code, they are available with:

```
$modx->getOption('SettingName');
```

They should be used wherever possible to make the site more portable and easier to maintain.

A link to the site's Home page, for example, should look like this:

```
<a href="[[~[[++site_start]]]]">Home</a>
```

In snippet code, included files should be referenced like this:

```
$path = $modx->getOption('core_path') .
    'components/mycomponent/myclass.inc.php';
include_once $path;
```

Note that all MODX path and URL settings end with a trailing slash.

Lexicon Management

The *Lexicon Management* section is used to override the language strings contained in the language files for both the MODX Manager and any add-on components. Many users will never have to deal with the lexicon directly.

Each entry in the lexicon has a key (Name) and a value. The key is how the entry is referred to in language tags and in snippet or plugin code. The value is what is displayed when the key is used.

Every bit of language used in the MODX Manager or in a well-written snippet or plugin has a language key in the MODX lexicon. This makes it possible to internationalize the Manager and add-on components without touching the core code.

Entries also have a namespace, topic, and language. The namespace is an identifier that helps MODX organize the entries. The core namespace includes all the language strings used by

MODX itself (mostly in the Manager). Other namespaces are linked to a particular add-on component. When a component loads the lexicon entries it will use, having a namespace makes their retrieval from the database more efficient.

Namespaces are divided into topics. The `core` namespace has many topics. Each part of the Manager has its own topic so that MODX can load only the lexicon entries it needs at the time. Most third-party components have only a `default` topic.

If you want to modify a particular language string, you can edit it in the grid at **System → Lexicon Management**. Just double-click on the language string and change it. Any changed entries will show in green. Be sure to select the correct namespace and topic before creating the new entry. Your changes won't be overwritten when you upgrade MODX or a component, but changes to the core entries will be lost if you click on the "Revert All Core Entries" button.

Content Types

The Content Types section is another area that most users will never need. It shows the MODX default MIME types for resources. If you need to add another MIME type (e.g., application, audio, or video), you can do it here.

Contexts

The Contexts section allows you to create and modify contexts (you can also modify them by right-clicking on the context's icon in the Resource tree).

When installed, MODX has two default contexts: `mgr` and `web`. The `mgr` context is the MODX manager itself. It is a special context allowing access to the Manager and should not be renamed or deleted. The `web` context contains the resources that will be available in the front end of the site.

See the Site Organization and Contexts chapter (Chapter 9) for more information on using contexts to organize your site. Many MODX sites have only the `mgr` and `web` contexts.

Actions

Actions are essentially menu choices in the Manager. Using this section, you can create custom manager pages and add new menu choices. You can also hide choices from specific users, rename menu choices, or reorganize Top-Menu items either for security or to make the Manager less intimidating for specific users.

See Chapter 11 for information on how to create custom Manager pages, create new menu items, or redesign the Manager's menus.

Namespaces

Many users will never need this section. It shows the existing namespaces and allows you to create new ones.

If you are creating a new add-on component, you can create a namespace for it here, but this is usually done automatically when creating a transport package (see Chapter 13).

The only time you might need to create a namespace here is if you are creating a complex component that will not be distributed in a transport package.

Each namespace must have a path associated with it. The standard form for a component's path is:

{core_path}components/*mycomponent***/**

Don't forget the trailing slash. One function of the namespace path is to allow MODX to find a component's lexicon (language) files, which will always be located in the **lexicon/** directory just below the namespace path. With the namespace path above and a core path of **core/**, for example, the lexicon directory would be located at the standard location for component lexicon files:

core/components/*mycomponent***/lexicon/**

Another use of the namespace path is to allow MODX to find the files used by Custom Manager Pages (CMPs).

User

The User choice on the Top Menu allows individual Manager users to update part of their user profiles, change their own passwords, see statistics about their actions on the site, and send and receive messages from other users.

This section allows limited access to user information. It does not show the user's full profile, and it doesn't allow the creation or deletion of users or any modification of their security permissions. Those tasks are in the Manage Users option of the Security menu (which some users may not have access to).

Profile

This section shows a limited version of the user profile on the General Information tab. Users can alter their profile information and save it.

The Reset Password tab allows the user to change his or her password. The Recent Resources tab shows a list of the resources the user has worked on and the publication status of each resource. You can publish or unpublish resources here by double-clicking on the "Published" field in the grid.

You can also right-click on a document to view, edit, or preview the resource. Clicking on "Edit" takes you to the Create/Edit Resource panel for that resource.

Messages

In the Messages section, users can see any messages sent to them by other users. They can also create messages for other users by clicking on the "New Message" button.

Support

The "Support" Top Menu option provides links to various support sites for MODX Revolution. Each choice on the Support menu opens a new browser window and takes you to the support site.

Forums

The Forums link takes the user to the MODX Forums. The forums are probably the most valuable resource for MODX. The MODX community uses the forums extensively and has traditionally been extremely friendly to new users and very generous in answering their questions.

Before asking for help, be sure to try finding the answer on your own with a web search, a search of the MODX documentation, and a search of the MODX Forums.

The Forum search itself is notoriously bad. Often, using a search engine (e.g., Google) and searching for something like `modx revolution yourtopic` or `modx revolution forums yourtopic` will get better results. If you know where you want to look, an even better way is to Google `site:modx.com yourtopic` to search for documentation or `site:modx.com/forums yourtopic` to search the MODX Forums.

If you post to the Forums, make your question as clear as you can and be sure that the subject of your post tells what the problem is so that people with expertise in that aspect of MODX are more likely to respond to it. Always indicate what version of MODX you are using, and if they might be relevant, list the type of server you're on and the version of PHP and MySQL installed there.

Remember that you paid nothing for MODX. Posts that demand help or imply that something is wrong with MODX or the people who created it are less likely to receive helpful answers. People who show a willingness to contribute to the MODX project get better results on the Forums.

Bear in mind that most of the people who created MODX and its add-ons are volunteers. None of them get paid for answering your questions. They are doing it because they are generous and helpful.

Asking questions in emails or personal messages to individual members of the MODX team is strongly discouraged because others can't benefit from the answers and the team members end up answering the same questions over and over (rather than working to improve MODX).

If you find a solution to your problem, it's good form to report the solution back to the Forum for others to see, to thank the people who helped you, and to put [Solved] in the subject line of your post.

Wiki

The name of this option may have changed by the time you read this. This link takes you to the official MODX documentation site. As with any open-source project, the documentation is a work in progress. It always lags behind the project because fixing known bugs and adding new features to MODX takes up most of the team members' time (and most have to make a living in addition to working on MODX).

It's a fact of life in the open-source world that the documentation is sometimes out of date and may contain errors. It's important to point this out in the appropriate Forum topic, but try to be polite about it.

Bugs

This link is for submitting bug reports and suggestions for improving MODX. If you have a feature request or a suggestion for improving any part of MODX (including add-on components), this is the place to report it. To avoid spam in the system, users need to register a free account there and log in each time they visit.

When reporting bugs, it's usually a good idea to search the Forums first, and if you don't find an answer, ask a question there. What you think is a bug may be due to a misunderstanding of how MODX works or a misconfiguration of your MODX install (or the server it runs on).

API Documentation

The API documentation is mainly for the use of programmers writing MODX add-on components. Even for them, the documentation usually has better information. The API documentation is compiled automatically from comments in the MODX code. If you can't find an answer in the documentation and you have a code editor that will search all of the MODX code itself, you can often find what you want faster that way.

Summary

Most work on a MODX site is done in the MODX Manager, and the various parts of the Manager are reached through the Manager's Top Menu.

The Resource tree, Element tree, and File tree are shown on tabs at the left side of the Manager screen. The Resource tree shows documents, weblinks, symlinks, and static resources. The Element tree shows templates, template variables, chunks, snippets, plugins, and categories. The File tree shows physical files on the site (though almost all of the site content is in the database rather than disk files).

The actual work done in the Manager is most often done in the right panel, which will vary depending on what section of the Manager you are in. All parts of the Manager can be reached through the Top Menu.

MODX Evolution Notes

The MODX Evolution Manager is very similar to the Revolution Manager, though with fewer features and menu choices. The Menu choices that are present in both usually perform the same function, though often in a slightly different way. In Evolution, there are no grids and usually no dragging and dropping. There are also no pop-up windows to create and edit resources and elements.

In Evolution, the Resource tree shows at the left of the Manager at all times. It has an abbreviated version of the Revolution right-click menu.

Elements in Evolution are found by going to **Elements → Manage Elements** on the Top Menu, which is composed of tabs. Each element has its own tab. If you go to **Elements → Manage Files** on the Top Menu, the File tree will be displayed in the right panel.

Evolution Top Menu

Here is the basic layout of the Evolution Top Menu with some notes on the differences:

Site Menu

Home — Return to the Manager home screen.

Preview — Preview the front end of the site.

Clear Cache — Clear the MODX site cache.

Search — Search the site's resources.

New Resource — Create a new resource (document) in the root of the tree.

New Weblink — Create a new weblink in the root of the tree.

Elements

Manage ElementsTemplates — Create/Edit templates

    Template Variables — Create/Edit template variables

    Chunks — Create/Edit chunks

    Snippets — Create/Edit snippets

    Plugins — Create/Edit plugins

    Combined View — Create/Edit all elements.

Manage Files — Display the File tree.

Manage META tags and Keywords — Deprecated, use template variables for these.

Modules

Manage Modules — Create or Configure a module.

Doc Manager — Perform bulk operations on site resources. Many of these operations can be done with drag-and-drop in Revolution or with the Batcher package.

> **Change Template** — Change the template of multiple documents at once
>
> **Template Variables** — Assign TVs to multiple templates.
>
> **Document Permissions** — Add documents to resource groups.
>
> **Sort Menu Items** — Set menu index numbers for part of the resource tree.
>
> **Other Properties** — Set various document settings (e.g., published status, publish date, createdby, editedby, etc.) for multiple documents.

QuickEdit — View the QuickEdit front-end editor documentation.

Security

Manager Users — Create/Edit Manager users, and set their profiles and roles.

Web Users — Create/Edit Web users and their profiles.

Roles — Create/Edit roles, and specify what security permissions are associated with them.

Manager Permissions — Create/Edit Manager user and Manager resource groups, and establish links between them.

Web Permissions — Create/Edit Web user and Web resource groups, and establish links between them.

Tools

Backup — Back up the MODX site.

Remove Locks — Unlock resources and elements that are locked to prevent editing.

Import HTML — Import existing HTML pages into the site as resources.

Export Static HTML — Export resources to static HTML files.

Configuration — Set the values of MODX system settings. Note that there is no method here for creating new settings.

Site — Edit general site system settings.

Friendly URLs — Edit system settings that control SEO-friendly URLs.

User — Edit system settings that control the user's interaction with the Manager

Interface & Features — Edit system settings that control the layout and function of the Manager for all users.

File Manager — Edit settings that configure and control the MODX File Manager.

Reports

Schedule — Show the schedule for upcoming publications and unpublications of resources on the site.

System Events — Show the log of system events and errors.

Manager Actions — Show successful actions taken in the Manager.

System Info — Report on the site configuration, `phpinfo()`, recently edited resources, tables in the database, and users currently online.

Other Functions

At the upper right of the Evolution Manager are four links to perform other functions.

Change Password — Allows Manager users to change their passwords.

Messages — Exchange messages with other Manager users.

Help — Show links to help resources.

Logout — Log out from the Manager.

Most of the material earlier in this chapter applies to the menu functions that appear in both Evolution and Revolution. Many of the methods for performing actions may differ because Evolution does not have the extensive JS infrastructure that forms the basis of the Revolution Manager. In most cases, however, you should have little or no trouble figuring out how to do things in Evolution. For more detail (especially on MODX security permissions) refer to the MODX Evolution notes in the other chapters of this book.

Missing Functions in MODX Evolution

The following basic functions are simply missing in the MODX Evolution Manager:

- Double-click editing of Manager fields
- Drag-and-drop for objects in the Manager
- Pop-up windows for clearing the cache and editing resources and elements
- Symlinks and Static Resources
- Access Control Lists
- Property Sets
- Adding System Settings
- Contexts and Context settings
- Custom User Settings
- Custom Permissions
- Package Management
- Lexicon Management
- Custom Content Types
- Namespaces
- Form Customization
- Manager Menu Customization

You can customize the Evolution Manager to some extent with the ManagerManager add-on component, but the ability to customize the Manager is not built into the Manager itself as it is in MODX Revolution.

Chapter 4

Resources

In this chapter, you'll learn more about how to create and use basic MODX resources like documents, weblinks, symlinks, and static resources and about the resource fields that are associated with them. We'll also discuss how to use MODX tags with resources.

Documents

In many ways, the document object is at the heart of MODX. Each URL at your site is associated with a particular document. When a browser requests that URL, MODX combines information from the template associated with that document and the document itself to create the finished web page. Technically speaking, a *document* is a MODX object that has a number of *resource fields* such as **pagetitle**, **longtitle**, **alias**, etc. A document may also have one or more template variables, which are extra resource fields that you create. Documents are usually created in the MODX Manager, but they can also be created by snippets or plugins. Occasionally, a third-party component will create a document or two when it is installed.

Creating Documents

When you want to add a web page to your site, you usually begin by creating a new document. There are a number of ways to create a document in MODX, but the best method in most cases is to right-click on a resource in the Resource tree in the Manager. Right-click on the object in the tree that you want to be the parent of the new document. If you want the document to be at the top level, right-click on the "Web" folder. Then select **Create → Create a Document Here**. That will open the Create/Edit Resource panel. Fill in the resource fields in the form on the right and any *Page Settings* you want in the *Page Settings tab*, and then click on the "Save" button at the upper right. That's all there is to it. You should see the new document in the Resource tree at the left. There are a lot of things to fill in, but none of them are required except for the Title field and the Uses Template field — although no content will show up when you preview your document if the Resource Content field is empty.

You'll almost certainly want a Title and a Long Title for your document as well as an Alias and Menu Title. You should also select a template for the document in the Uses Template field. You'll want some content in the Resource Content field, and you'll want to specify whether the document is published or not. The other fields are there if you need them but can be left blank if you don't. We'll discuss what each field is for in the next section.

Another method of creating a document is to click **Site → New Document** on the Top Menu. This second method will always create the document at the top level of the tree (directly under the web context icon). You can move the document later either by dragging and dropping it in the tree or by setting its Parent Resource in the Create/Edit Resource panel.

You can also create documents using PHP Code in a snippet or plugin (or in a transport package), but most MODX users will never use these methods. We'll discuss them later in the book.

Resource fields

Technically, the *resource fields* of a document include every field in the **site_content** table of the MODX database. Most MODX users don't need to know that, however, because the resource fields are available to you in several other ways. Here is a list of all the resource fields you are likely to use. The terms at the left refer to the actual field names in the **site_content** table in the MODX Database. These are the names that you will use in any *resource tags* referring to these fields. The word or phrase in parentheses is the term used in the MODX Manager (and on the MODX Forums) to refer to the field. If we are referring to the field as it is used in code, we'll generally use the term on the left. If we are referring to it in reference to the Manager user interface, we'll usually use the term in parentheses. Not all of these fields are editable in the Manager.

Because the following list is for reference purposes, the actual field name in the database is listed first (followed by the term used in the Manager in parentheses), and the list is alphabetical. In the section that follows, however, we'll discuss setting the fields in the Manager on the Create/Edit Resource panel. In that section, the term used in the Manager will come first, and we'll describe them in the order they appear on the Manager screen.

Resource fields

- **alias** (text — Alias)
- **cacheable** (int 0/1 — Cacheable)
- **class_key** (int — Class Key of the Resource)
- **content** (text — Resource Content)
- **content_type** (int — Content Type)
- **createdon** (date — Created On date)
- **createdby** (int — Created By User ID Number)
- **deleted** (int 0/1 — Deleted)
- **deletedby** (int — Deleted By User ID Number)
- **deletedon** (date — Date of Deletions)
- **description** (text — Description)
- **editedon** (date — Edited On date).
- **editedby** (int — Edited By User ID number)
- **hidemenu** (text — Hide From Menus)
- **id** (int — Resource ID)
- **introtext** (text — Summary)
- **isfolder** (int 0/1 — Container)
- **link_attributes** (text — Link attributes)
- **longtitle** (text — Long Title)
- **menuindex** (int — Menu Index)
- **menutitle** (text — Menu Title)
- **pagetitle** (text — Page Title)
- **parent** (int — Parent Resource)
- **pub_date** (date —Publish Date)
- **published** (int 0/1 — Published)
- **publishedby** (int — Published By User ID Number)
- **publishedon** (date — Published On)
- **richtext** (int 0/1 — Rich Text)
- **searchable** (int 0/1 — Searchable)
- **template** (int — Template ID number)
- **unpub_date** (date — Unpublish Date)
- **uri_override** (int 0/1 — Freeze URI)
- **uri** (string — URI)

In the following sections, we'll refer to the fields by the prompts on the *Create/Edit Resource panel* in the Manager because that's what you'll see when you enter the field values in the Manager. We'll put the actual field name in parentheses at the top of each section. For the `pagetitle` field, for example, the prompt in the Manager is simply "Title" even though `pagetitle` is the actual field name.

You set the values of some of the fields in the form on the right side of the Create/Edit Resource panel. You set others in the *Page Settings* tab. Some are created automatically when you perform actions on the resource (e.g., `createdon`). They are all resource fields, however, and all of the ones on the list above are available by using *resource tags*.

Remember that when you refer to a field in code or in a MODX tag, you need to refer to the actual database field name rather than the label used in the Manager.

 Although the field captions in the Manager begin with uppercase letters, all the actual field names are in lowercase. If you capitalize a letter in a resource tag, MODX won't recognize the tag and nothing will appear in place of the tag.

Let's look at the fields in more detail. As we mentioned above, the headings in this section are reversed from the list above. They have the Manager term for the field first, and then (in parentheses), the actual name of the database field. The term in parentheses is what you must use to refer to the field in code or in MODX tags. We'll start with the fields that are set on the Create/Edit Resource panel:

Resource ID (id)

We discussed the Resource ID (`id` field) earlier. A *Resource ID* is a unique number that identifies a resource in MODX. The Resource ID is shown in parentheses next to the resource's name in the Resource tree of the MODX Manager. It also shows at the top of the Create/Edit Resource panel. It is sometimes referred to as the *document identifier* or the *document ID*, but *Resource ID* is the correct term for it because it also is used for *Weblinks*, *Symlinks*, and *Static Resources*. When used to refer specifically to a document, though, especially on older documentation or MODX Forum posts, you may still see it called a document ID.

MODX automatically assigns Resource IDs when you create a new resource. Users sometimes ask how they can change them because after a while, the numbers can get large and out of sequence. If you are a MySQL wizard, you could change them directly in the database, but MODX strongly recommends that you never change Resource ID numbers because doing so will almost always lead to serious problems. Some MODX components, for example, assume that these numbers will never change, and altering the IDs could cause problems that would be hard to spot and even harder to fix. Most MODX users just get used to the numbers being arbitrary, and front-end users will never see them.

If you really care about the numbering sequence, you can build your site structure on paper and create the documents in order. That way, the Resource ID numbers will be in sequence. Remember, too, that you can reuse Resource IDs by unpublishing obsolete documents rather than deleting them (or deleting them but not emptying the trash) and just editing their resource fields rather than creating a new document. That will keep your Resource ID numbers lower. Generally, though, it's a lot easier just to live with the IDs that MODX assigns.

Uses Template (template)

The *Uses Template* field determines the MODX template associated with each document. When a document is requested by a browser, MODX checks to see what template is associated with that document. It then gets the template and processes it by replacing any MODX tags in the document before sending the page out to the browser for display. See the Templates section of Chapter 5 for more information.

Each document will have one, and only one, template. You can change the template associated with a document at any time by editing this value on the Create/Edit Resource panel and saving the document. When you change a document's template, you will be warned that the template variable associations will be lost. If the document has no template variables, you can ignore this warning.

When you create a new document, its Uses Template field will be set to the default template for the site. MODX gets the template to use from the `default_template` system setting, which is set to the ID of the BaseTemplate (1) created during the install. If you would like to change the default template, you can go to **System → System Settings** and put "template" in the Search by Key box at the upper right of the grid. You'll need the ID of the template you want to use. You can find that by clicking on the "Elements" tab and expanding the "Templates" section. The ID of each template is listed in parentheses next to its name. Change the "Value" of the `default_template` system setting to the ID of the template you want for your new default.

There is a plugin that sets the template of a new document to the template of the document's parent that may be available for Revolution in the MODX repository by the time you read this. You can also set the default template for specific groups of documents using form customization rules. See Chapter 11 for more information on form customization.

The [[*template]] resource tag is seldom, if ever, used in web page content. If used, it displays the ID number of the template rather than its name.

Published (published)

The *Published* checkbox determines whether a resource (document, weblink, symlink, or static resource) is available to site visitors. An unpublished resource isn't available to anyone except admin users who are using the "preview" function. To publish a resource, you simply check the Published checkbox and save the document. Doing the reverse will unpublish the resource. Using the Published checkbox makes the change take effect immediately (as long as the *site cache* is cleared or the page is uncached). If you would like to publish or unpublish a resource at some time in the future, you can use the optional Publish Date and/or Unpublish Date resource field settings (described in a bit).

Title (pagetitle)

The *Title* resource field contains whatever you put in the Title field in the Create/Edit Resource panel in the Manager, and you can edit it there whenever you like. Because documents are always referred to in MODX by their Resource IDs, you can change a document's Title without having to edit any links to it. As long as all your links use a proper link tag, the links will still work. If you want to put a link to document 12 anywhere in MODX, for example, the following code will always link to that document no matter what its Title or location is:

```
<a href = "[[~12]]">My Page</a>
```

As we mentioned earlier, the Title field is usually used in the `<title>` tag of a template:

```
<title>[[*pagetitle]]</title>
```

When the document is displayed in the browser, the [[*pagetitle]] resource tag will be replaced by the contents of the Title field set on the Create/Edit Resource panel.

Be careful not to use a title that matches any directory name at your MODX site (e.g., assets). Doing so can cause problems with the rewrite rules for Friendly URLs.

Long Title (longtitle)

Long Title is just a longer version of the Title. Many users use the Long Title for the main heading of their documents by putting something like the following line at or near the top of the <body> section of their templates:

```
<h2>[[*longtitle]]</h2>
```

You are free to use the Long Title field for anything you want, however (or not use it at all).

Description (description)

The *Description* resource field is usually used to hold a description of the document's purpose and/or short instructions for people who will be editing the document. The EZfaq Snippet, for example, uses an unpublished document to hold the FAQ content, so it would make sense to put this in the description field: `FAQ Content (leave unpublished)`. Although the description field is not often used via a resource tag, it is certainly available that way, and you are free to use it to hold any information you wish and to display that information on a page by using the `[[*description]]` resource tag. The description field is limited to 255 characters, and you are free to leave it blank if you don't need it.

Resource Alias (alias)

The *Resource Alias* is almost never used directly in page content, but it should always be filled in. Its purpose is to provide a name for the document that will be shown in the web page's URL (i.e., in the browser address window) when using MODX's *Friendly URLs (FURLs)*. With FURLs turned off, a document's URL will look like this:

```
http://yoursite.com/index.php?id=12
```

With FURLs on, however, the URL will be shown in this form:

```
http://yoursite.com/mypage.html
```

In the URL above, `yoursite.com` is the actual name of your domain, and *mypage* is the Alias set on the Create/Edit Resource panel. If you leave the Alias field blank and FURLs are turned on, MODX will use the document's Resource ID as the alias. The Alias field allows you to have an alias that is different from the Title if you want to, although there's no problem with having them match. There's no requirement to fill in the Alias field, but it's generally a good practice. If you have no special use for it, make it the same as the Title, but either make it all one word or replace the spaces with hyphens.

There is also a handy system setting called `automatic_alias`. If you go to **System → System Settings** on the MODX Top Menu and type automatic in the Search by key box at the upper right, you should see the setting in the grid. If you change its value to "Yes" (double-click on "No" and select "Yes") MODX will create an alias from the document's Title when you save it. The automatic alias will be in all lowercase letters and spaces in the title will be replaced by hyphens.

Link attributes (link_attributes)

When you specify a link in (X)HTML using the `<link>` or `<a>` tag, you are pointing to another document. You can specify the nature of the relationship between the current document and the one you are linking or describe characteristics of the current tag by setting a *link attribute* in the `<link>` or `<a>` tag. There are too many attributes to describe here, but some common examples are `rel="next"`, `rel="prev"`, `name="name"`, `charset="charset"`. You can do a web search for *html link attributes* if you want to learn more about them. If you fill in the Link Attributes field, MODX snippets can use that field to create specific kinds of links or anchors in a document. This field is often left blank and is almost never used in web page content via a resource tag.

Summary (introtext)

The *Summary* field is most often used to provide a brief summary of the document's content. A common use is on sites that have a News page with short "teasers" as links to the full articles. The getResources snippet, given the appropriate properties, will do this for you automatically.

 In MODX Revolution, getResources is a replacement for Ditto. Ditto is no longer being supported in Revolution, and getResources, along with getPage, can do almost everything that users could do with Ditto.

The Summary field can also be used at the top or bottom of a document as a preview or recap of the document's content (or for any other purpose — there are no restrictions on how you use it). The Summary field is limited to 255 characters. You can change this by modifying the `introtext` field in the MODX Database (e.g., by using phpMyAdmin), but this is not recommended. You are free to leave this field blank.

The following tag in a document's Resource Content field will be replaced with whatever is in the Summary field set on the Create/Edit Resource panel:

```
[[*introtext]]
```

Parent Resource (parent)

The *Parent Resource* field is almost never used in web page content, but it is required for each document. The Parent Resource field determines where the document will appear in the Resource tree at the left side of the Manager. It contains the Resource ID of the parent document. If you create the document by right-clicking on the desired parent and selecting **Create → Create Document Here**, the Parent Resource field will be set automatically. Snippets like Wayfinder (which creates dynamic menus) use the organization of the Resource tree to structure their output, so you should always think about the menu structure of your site when setting a resource's parent, though you can easily change the parent of a resource later.

If you create a document using the Top Menu (with **Site → New Document**), it will have the default parent, which is 0. A parent of 0 puts it at the top level of the Resource tree. If you need to change the parent later, you can edit the Parent Resource field on the Create/Edit Resource panel by clicking on the drop-down arrow next to the field and then clicking on the desired parent in the "Resources" tree at the left. You can also move the document in the Resource tree directly using drag-and-drop, which many users prefer because it will automatically reorder the menu index values.

Menu Title (menutitle)

Sometimes, neither the Title nor Long Title resource fields are appropriate for use in a menu. As you might guess, the *Menu Title* field is an optional resource field that is usually used to hold the menu entry for that document. It can be the same as the title or alias. This field is almost always used by code (usually in a snippet) that produces a menu. The Wayfinder snippet uses this field automatically when creating a menu. You can certainly use it in a document if you want to by using the [[*menutitle]] resource tag, but this is seldom done.

Menu Index (menuindex)

The *Menu Index* field is not used directly by MODX itself, except to order the Resource tree. It is there mainly for third-party components that build menus and navigation aids (such as the Wayfinder snippet), which can use it to sort the menus they produce. If the Menu Index field is blank, the menu items will usually appear in the order that they appear in the Resource tree. If you haven't moved them in the tree, they will normally be in the order in which they were created.

The Menu Index numbers do not have to be in sequence. If there is a resource that you want to always appear at the end of your menus, you can give it a high Menu Index (e.g., 999), so it will always come last. Note that if you drag and drop items in the Resource tree, the menu index numbers will be reordered and the number will change.

 There is a serious bug in MySQL Version 5.0.51 that can interfere with sorting. If Wayfinder is ignoring your Menu Index numbers, check to see if your server is using that version of MySQL.

Version 5.0.51 and 5.0.51a are notoriously buggy, so the best solution is to get your host to do an update of MySQL.

Hide From Menus (hidemenu)

You may have a number of pages that should not appear in any menu. Checking the *Hide From Menus* checkbox on the Create/Edit Resource panel sets this field. The Wayfinder snippet, and most other menu-building snippets, will then skip the document when creating a menu. The `hidemenu` field is available to any code that wants to use it to see whether a document should be included. A snippet that produces a sitemap, for example, will usually skip any documents that have this field set (although it's not required to do so).

Resource Content (content)

In many ways, the *Resource Content field* (the big window at the bottom of the panel) is the most important of the resource fields because it is where you put the main content of the document you are creating (the content the user sees when visiting the web page). The text you place in the Resource Content field will appear wherever the [[*content]] tag is placed in a template. If you would like the text in the Resource Content field to appear six times on a web page, you can just put six [[*content]] tags in the page template.

The Resource Content field can't contain any raw PHP code (neither can any other resource fields). Anything between <?php . . . ?> tags will be stripped out by MODX and discarded. This is important to know if you are trying to port a site to MODX that contains inline PHP code in the pages. The solution is to move the PHP code into snippets (replacing it with a snippet tag: [[*SnippetName*]]). This not only helps make your site more secure, but also helps you separate code from content, which will make your site much easier to maintain in the long run.

In addition to snippet tags that will add the results of PHP code to your page, you can add any of the other MODX tags (chunk tags, resource tags, link tags, language tags, etc.). We'll discuss these in more detail in the tags section later in this chapter. Be sure, however, not to put the specific tag [[*content*]] in the Resource Content field of a document. When the document is parsed, the tag will be replaced with the text in the Resource Content Field, which contains that tag again. MODX is smart enough to keep this from being an infinite loop, but your document's content will appear twice. Unless you have something unusual in mind, the [[*content*]] tag should go in a template.

We've been discussing the resource fields that are set on the Create/Edit Resource panel. Now let's look at the ones that are set on the **Page Settings** tab.

Container (isfolder)

The value of the **Container** checkbox determines whether a document should be treated as a folder in the Resource tree. It is used by some MODX components to help them process the tree itself. In fact, the MODX Manager uses it when it displays the tree. It is also used by menu snippets like Wayfinder, which not only process the tree, but can also use the information to create the menu.

 When a container has children, for example, Wayfinder can produce a fly-out or drop-down menu with links to the child documents. Links to container documents can also be given a different style.

 By default, Wayfinder ignores this field and looks instead at whether the document actually has children. In MODX Revolution, this field is independent of whether the document has children or not. If you turn on Friendly URLs, this field will affect the URL of a document. If the Container checkbox is checked, the Friendly URL will end with whatever the **container_suffix** System Setting is set to (usually '/'). If the checkbox is not checked, the URL will end with the extension setting for its content type (e.g., .html).

Rich Text (richtext)

The *Rich Text* resource field determines whether a *Rich Text Editor* (often called an RTE) will be used to edit the document's Resource Content field. The TinyMCE Editor is the RTE most often used with MODX, but other RTEs can be installed. If the Rich Text checkbox is checked (and there is an RTE installed in MODX) you can edit your documents in WYSIWYG mode with buttons to insert links and images and formatting controls. If the box is unchecked, you will edit your documents in raw (X)HTML.

Although TinyMCE is an excellent editor and provides some useful shortcuts, many experienced MODX users prefer to edit their documents in raw (X)HTML. You should be familiar with (X)HTML code if you are going to create web sites with or without MODX. Rich Text Editors tend to make mistakes and, unless configured correctly, can mangle your snippet tags enough to prevent them from working (for example, by changing &property into &&property after multiple saves). If you have a snippet tag that is not working or are having trouble getting a document to look right when displayed, try turning off the RTE (by unchecking the Rich Text checkbox and saving the document) and check the raw (X)HTML.

RTEs will also sometimes add unwanted <p></p> tags around some elements. TinyMCE can be configured so that it doesn't do this, but configuring it is beyond the scope of this book. See the MODX online documentation or ask in the MODX Forums.

Published On (publishedon)

The *Published On* field holds the date that the document last changed from unpublished to published (unless you edit it manually in the Page Settings tab). If you publish a document when you create it, the **publishedon** field and the **createdon** field (more on this field later) will be the same (or nearly the same since MODX records the time as well as the date). Unlike the Created On field, however, Published On can be edited later on the Page Settings tab in case you want to change it.

In a menu showing links to a series of documents or a page with summaries of a group of documents, you may want to sort the list by either the Published On date or the Created On date. Both options are available in MODX.

If you unpublish a document and later publish it again, the document will get a new Published On date.

If you want to show users when the current page was published, you can do it with the following code:

```
<p>This page was published on [[*publishedon]].</p>
```

The results of that code would look like this:

```
This page was published on 2011-08-04 12:40:00.
```

The time and date format above is the default SQL timestamp format. See the section on Filters and Modifiers toward the end of this chapter to see how to format it to meet your needs.

 Published On does not control publication. It is just a record of when the document last changed from unpublished to published (or the result of manually editing the Published On date). It's a common mistake for new users of MODX to use this field to set a future publication date. Publishing can only be controlled with the Published checkbox or the two publication dates below.

In MODX Evolution, the Published On field is not shown in the Create/Edit Resources panel.

Publish Date (pub_date)

New MODX users are often confused about this field and the following one (Unpublish Date). These are only used for resources that you wish to have published or unpublished automatically on a specific date in the future. If you will be publishing and/or unpublishing a document manually, as is often the case, leave these fields blank.

The *Publish Date* contains the date and time when a resource (document, weblink, symlink, or static resource) will be published on the web site. Until that date and time, web requests for the resource will get a "not found" response, and snippets like Wayfinder, Breadcrumbs, and getResources will ignore the resource unless instructed otherwise. There is no requirement to set this field. You can control publication manually with the Published checkbox. Obviously, you can't show users the date on the page until the page is published, but you could display upcoming pages on another (published) page by using a snippet that checks the **pub_date** field of the documents and returns a report on when they will be published.

Once the resource has been unpublished — either manually by unchecking the Published checkbox or automatically as a result of the Unpublish Date — the Publish Date is zeroed out and is no longer available, but the **publishedon** field will contain the original publication date (although that date may have been edited manually on the Page Settings tab).

Unpublish Date (unpub_date)

The *Unpublish Date* sets the date when the resource will no longer be available on the web site. After that date, requests for the page will get a "not found" response, and snippets like Wayfinder and getResources will ignore the resource unless instructed otherwise. As with Publish Date, you can leave this unset and unpublish the document by unchecking the Published checkbox and saving the document. This field is also available to you via a resource tag, and if you want to show visitors when the page will no longer be available, you can put the following code on the page:

```
<p>This page will disappear on [[*unpub_date]].</p>
```

The results of that code would look like this:

```
This page will disappear on 2011-11-04 12:50:00.
```

 Because the MODX site is idle when no users are visiting, the actual publish and unpublish actions won't occur until someone visits the site. One side effect of this is that the Published On field won't necessarily contain the date you set in the Published On field. It will contain the date when the resource was actually published, which may be later than the setting in the Published On field.

Searchable (searchable)

Sometimes, you have pages that you don't want included in a local site search. If you uncheck the *Searchable* checkbox, snippets or plugins that search the site or produce a site map can skip the document. The value of this field is available via the [[*searcheable]] resource tag, but the tag isn't very useful since it will just produce a 1 or a 0.

 The Searchable checkbox will have no effect on searches done with Google or other external search engines.

Cacheable (cacheable)

The *Cacheable* checkbox determines whether MODX will cache a resource. If it is set, MODX will put a copy of the resource in the cache, and when someone visits the page, MODX will show them the cached version rather than retrieving the content from the database. If the box is unchecked, MODX will retrieve a new version from the database every time a browser requests the page. If your site has thousands of documents, the cache can become very large, and it may be faster to store the content in a custom database table rather than creating a separate MODX resource for each page.

If there are resource tags for snippets, chunks, or template variables on a page that produce dynamic content (a snippet that shows the current time, for example), you can still cache the page, but put an exclamation point in the tag to make the output of the tag itself uncached:

```
[[!SnippetName]]
```

Unlike earlier versions of MODX, in MODX Revolution, any MODX tag can be given an exclamation point that will make it uncached.

Empty Cache (no fieldname)

The *Empty Cache* checkbox determines whether the MODX cache is cleared when you save the resource in the Manager. Unlike the other entries in this section, there is no field in the database for Empty Cache (and no resource tag to display it). Checking the Empty Cache checkbox simply sets a flag that tells MODX to clear the site cache when you save the page. MODX will remember the value of the checkbox if you uncheck it while you work on a page, but it will be set again (to the default value) when you return to the document later.

Un-checking the Empty Cache checkbox will speed up saves of the document, but the speed gain is quite small, and your changes won't show up on the site until the cache is cleared, so it's usually best just to leave it checked.

Content Type (content_type)

Most resources you create will use the default value, HTML, for this field. The *Content Type* field sets the Mime content-type set in the header of the page that tells the browser what type of content it is getting. For almost all regular web pages, that type is HTML. There are times, however, when you might want another setting for this field.

If, for example, you want to send the browser some JavaScript or CSS code but want to build the content dynamically with a snippet or plugin, you could set the Content Type to JavaScript or CSS. You might also want to send an application-specific file like an MS

Word .DOC file or a .PDF file. Setting the Content Type field appropriately will launch the appropriate application (e.g., Adobe Reader) for the user. We'll discuss this in more detail later in this chapter. Note, too, that the Content Type determines the URL suffix when using Friendly URLs (e.g., .html). In MODX Revolution, you can also create custom content types that, once created, will show up in the drop-down menu for this field.

In Revolution, it's also possible to put a CSS file in a resource, which can make it easier to edit. Just set the template to *(empty)* and the Content Type to *CSS*. Make sure to specify an alias. Put the CSS code in the Resource Content field and refer to the CSS resource in your template like this (change the 12 to the ID of the resource):

```
<link rel="stylesheet" type="text/css" href="[[~12]]">
```

Content Disposition (content_dispo)

The *Content Disposition* field tells the browser whether to display the Resource Content or offer the user a chance to download it. It does this by setting the content type in the document header that gets sent to the browser ahead of everything else. The default setting is inline, which displays the page. If you wanted the user to be able to download the page content, you would set it to *attachment*. This will tell the browser that you want users to have the chance to download the file. Depending on the browser and its settings, the user may still have the option to view the file, but they should always get the option to save it to disk. Due to the security considerations of HTML, there's no way to force a download-only option.

Class Key (class_key)

The *Class Key* field is the setting MODX uses to identify the various MODX objects (snippet, chunk, document, etc.). Only advanced developers will have any reason to change this setting. It's nice to have it there as a reminder of what the object is called internally by MODX, however, in case you need to refer to it or retrieve it in the code of a snippet or plugin.

Notice that the Resource Content field is also available at the bottom of the Page Settings tab.

The following resource fields are available either in code or via resource tags but can't be set in the MODX Manager.

Created On (createdon) and Created By (createdby)

The *Created On* resource field will give the date and time the Resource was created in the same format we saw above for Published On. The tag to display the Created On date and time looks like this:

```
[[*createdon]]
```

The **createdon** field in the database contains a permanent record of when the document was first saved. The contents of the **createdon** field can only be changed by editing the field in the database or by deleting and recreating the document.

You might think that the *Created By* field would show the name of the Resource's author. Unfortunately, it only returns the numeric ID of the author, so it is of limited use in a document's content. Later on in this chapter, we'll see a much easier method of displaying the author's name using output modifiers. Just to demonstrate MODX's flexibility, however, let's look at doing it with a very simple snippet that uses the Created By field to get the appropriate user's name and returns it:

```
<p>This page was created by [[Author]]</p>
```

The code in the Author Snippet would look like this in MODX Revolution:

```php
<?php
/* Author Snippet -
    returns the username of the current Resource's creator */
$creator = $modx->resource->getOne('CreatedBy');
return $creator->get('username');
?>
```

The user's full name (as opposed to his or her username) could also be displayed by replacing the last line of the snippet above with this code:

```php
$profile = $creator->getOne('Profile');
return $profile->get('fullname');
```

If this looks complicated, it is (a little) because user information is split into separate tables in the MODX database. A user's ID, username, and password are in one table while user attributes like full name and email address are in a second table, and user settings are in a third table.

Separating this data into different tables makes processing user security permissions more efficient, but it makes getting user information a little more complicated. Getting information about documents, system settings, chunks, and other things from inside a snippet is much more straightforward. We'll deal with the ins and outs of getting information like this inside a snippet later on in the book.

As we mentioned, later in this chapter we'll see a much easier way to get the username using an output modifier in the tag, which is how most users prefer to do it.

Edited On (editedon) and Edited By (editedby)

The *Edited On* field contains the date and time the Resource was last edited in the same format as Published On and can be displayed with the following code:

```
<p>The page was last edited on [[*editedon]].</p>
```

The *Edited By* field works just like the Created By field except that it contains the ID of the person who last edited the resource. To display the editor's name, you would need to use a snippet like the one described above or an output modifier (more on these in just a bit).

Deleted On (deletedon) and Deleted By (deletedby)

The *Deleted On* field contains the date and time that the resource was deleted. The *Deleted By* field contains the ID of the user who deleted the resource. Deleted On and Deleted By are only available directly after a document has been deleted but before the "trash" has been emptied in the Manager (by clicking on the little garbage-can icon). After the "trash" is emptied, the information may still be available in a Manager report.

Deleted (deleted)

The *Deleted* field indicates that a resource has been marked as deleted but has not been purged from the database. It can be set by right-clicking on a resource in the tree and selecting "delete resource" or by checking the "Deleted" box on the Page Settings tab of the Create/Edit Resource panel.

Freeze URI (uri_override) and URI (uri)

When you click on the Freeze URI checkbox on the Page Settings tab of the Create/Edit Resource panel, the URI input field will appear. Whatever you enter in that field will appear in the URL when the resource is displayed. The URI will be frozen with that setting and it will be unchanged even if you rename the resource, change its alias, or move it to another location in the tree.

Using Tags with Documents

Tags are a key part of MODX. They allow you to reuse content and to create dynamic content for insertion into web pages. As we learned in Chapter 2, in MODX Revolution, all tags begin with [[and end with]]. The opening brackets are followed by an optional token (such as + or $) that tells MODX what kind of tag it is. If no token is present, MODX assumes that it is a snippet tag. Table 4-1 shows the Revolution tag syntax.

Table 4-1: MODX Revolution Tags

Tag Type	Example
Resource Tag/TV	[[*ResourceField/TvName]]
Chunk Tag	[[$ChunkName]]
Snippet Tag	[[SnippetName]]
Placeholder Tag	[[+PlaceholderName]]
Link Tag	[[~ResourceID]]
Setting Tag	[[++SettingName]]
Language Tag	[[%LanguageStringKey]]

Tags can also be modified using input and output filters. The default output filter provides a number of *modifiers* for tag content. Now that we've covered the various tags, let's look at some more ways to use them in a document. Along the way, we'll see some simple modifiers in action (see the "Output Modifiers" section below for a more extensive list of the available modifiers). The modifiers described in this section can be used with any MODX tag.

Resource Tags

Resource tags take the form [[*TagName]], where TagName is the name of a resource field or template variable.

As we saw earlier, the **createdby** resource field can be used to display the user ID of the author of a particular article. Because the **createdby** field contains the ID of the author rather than his or her name, we used a snippet to get the user's name. Here's an easier way to do the same thing using an output modifier. Output modifiers, as the name suggests, modify the output of a tag. They can be used with any MODX tag, and they take the following general form:

```
[[element:modifier=`value`]]
```

Note that the value is surrounded by back-ticks (not single-quotes). Here's an example that will display the author's name:

```
[[*createdby:userinfo=`username`]]
```

This output modifier tells MODX that we want to modify the output and display the username rather than the ID. Instead of username, we could also have used *email*, *role*, or *rolename* to display the user's email, role ID (in the MODX security permissions system), or the name of the user's role. As you might guess, the :userinfo modifier can only be used with tags that return a user ID.

Suppose we want to add a copyright notice using the year that the resource was last edited. This tag will do it:

```
Copyright [[*editedon:strtotime:date=`%Y`]]
```

Note that we're using two modifiers here. Technically, this is called "chaining" modifiers. You can chain as many output modifiers as you like. If you want to format the date of any of the date resource fields (e.g., **createdon**, **editedon**, etc.), you need to insert the strtotime modifier so that the date will be converted to a Unix timestamp before the date modifier is applied.

Some modifiers alter the output in simple ways and don't require a "value" such as the ucase modifier. For example, if we wanted the Long Title of the resource in all uppercase, this tag would do that for us:

```
[[*longtitle:ucase]]
```

The cat modifier (short for concatenate) will add text to the end of the tag's output. The following tag will add "(All rights reserved)" to the end of the Long Title:

```
[[*longtitle:cat=` (All rights reserved)`]]
```

Here is another example of chained modifiers:

```
[[*longtitle:cat=` All rights reserved`:ucase]]
```

 Modifiers like ucase will act on the entire output of the tag, so everything that is output from the tag will be in uppercase.

Now suppose that we want to print a special message, but only if the page was created by the administrator (username = admin). Conditional modifiers can be constructed with if, then and else clauses. In this case, we could use the following tag:

```
[[*createdby:userinfo=`username`:is=`admin`:then=
    `Admin did this`:else=`Someone else did it`]]
```

The tag above would display "Admin did this" for any resources created by the admin Super User and "Someone else did it" for all other resources. The :is= clause will test the element against the part following the :is=. The :then clause tells MODX what to print if the condition is met. The :else clause (which is optional) specifies what to display if the condition is not met.

If we wanted no message for non-admin resources, we could leave out the :else clause. If we wanted admin resources to display no message, we could change `Admin did this` to an empty string ``. Obviously, we could use any username in our test, not just "*admin*."

In addition, the test could be for inequality (:isnot). If the value being tested is numeric, you can also test for values less than (:islt) and greater than (:isgt) the initial value.

Chunk Tags

Chunk tags simply insert the contents of the named chunk into the document. If, for example, you have a chunk called *Footer* containing the code for your footer, the following tag can go in your template where you want the footer to appear:

```
[[$Footer]]
```

If you have a chunk that contains (X)HTML tags and you would like to display it without those tags, the `notags` modifier will strip them out for you:

```
[[$ChunkName:notags]]
```

Another useful modifier for chunks is the `htmlent` modifier, which will convert the appropriate characters in the chunk to HTML entities. Any ampersands (&), for example, will be converted to & and quotation marks will be converted to ". This can be useful for (X) HTML validation:

```
[[$ChunkName:htmlent]]
```

Sometimes chunks can contain extraneous newline and tab characters, especially if you have cut and pasted them from another source. The `strip` modifier will convert them all to single spaces:

```
[[$ChunkName:strip]]
```

You might prefer that newline characters be converted to <br /> tags. In that case, you'll want the `nl2br` modifier:

```
[[$chunkName:nl2br]]
```

Snippet Tags

Snippet tags take the form [[*SnippetName*]] with no leading token. The snippet name can optionally be followed by a series of properties and their values that will be passed to the snippet as variables. We'll cover this in more detail later on in the snippet chapter (Chapter 7), but let's take a brief look at how snippet tags work in resources.

A snippet is just a bit of PHP code that performs some action or actions behind the scenes. If you are a programmer, you can think of a snippet as a function and the properties (formerly called parameters) as arguments to that function.

If the snippet returns a value (e.g., a number or some (X)HTML code), that value will replace the snippet tag in the final output that MODX sends to the browser.

If you are not a programmer, you'll be fine as long as you remember that whatever comes back from the snippet replaces the snippet tag and that snippet properties contain information we want to send to the snippet.

If the snippet tag has properties, the tag will look like this:

```
[[SnippetName? &property1=`value1` &property2=`value2`]]
```

Snippet tags (sometimes referred to as "snippet calls") always take the form above, and the various elements are important.

When there are properties in the snippet tag, the snippet name is always followed by a question mark followed by a space. This tells MODX that properties are coming. Notice that there is never a space before the question mark and always a space after it.

Each property is preceded by an ampersand (**&**). This identifies it as a property to MODX. There must be a space before the ampersand and no space after it. Each property's value must be enclosed in back-ticks (not single-quotes). Not using back-ticks is the most common error for new MODX users.

There should also be no spaces around the equals sign in snippet properties. There is no limit to the number of properties. In some versions of MODX Evolution, snippet tags must be on a single line. In MODX Revolution, however, snippet tags can be spread across multiple lines like this:

```
[[SnippetName?
    &property1=`value1`
    &property2=`value2`
]]
```

Spreading the tag across multiple lines like this makes it easier to read and edit and helps prevent syntax errors that might keep the tag from working properly.

New in MODX Revolution is another way to send properties to snippets: property sets. Snippets can also have default properties. Both of these are like properties in a snippet tag, but they can easily be created and edited in a grid in the Manager. We'll discuss them in detail in Chapter 6.

Setting Tags

Setting tags allow you to access any of the settings in the MODX System Settings grid (and some that are not in the grid). Setting tags always take the form [[++**SettingName**]]. Note the double + sign at the beginning. Be careful not to confuse these with placeholder tags, which have a single + sign.

You can see the system settings in the grid by going to **System → System Settings** on the Top Menu. A setting tag will let you display the value of a given setting. If, for example, you want to display the allowable upload file types on an Upload page, this tag will display them:

[[++upload_files]]

In addition, there are a number of settings that are set in the MODX config file but not shown in the grid. The file is:

core/config/config.inc.php

Generally, these settings should not be modified, but you can display them or use them in other tags with a standard setting tag. Table 4-2 shows a list of those settings as rendered for a localhost site at c:/xampp/htdocs/revo/.

Table 4-2: System Settings Not in Grid

Name	Tag	Example output
Site URL	[[++site_url]]	http://localhost/revo/
Base Path	[[++base_path]]	C:/xampp/htdocs/revo/
Base URL	[[++base_url]]	/revo/
Core path	[[++core_path]]	C:/xampp/htdocs/revo/core/
Manager Path	[[++manager_path]]	C:/xampp/htdocs/revo/manager/
Manager URL	[[++manager_url]]	/revo/manager/
Processors path	[[++processors_path]]	C:/xampp/htdocs/revo/core/model/modx/processors/
Assets path	[[++assets_path]]	C:/xampp/htdocs/revo/assets/
Assets URL	[[++assets_url]]	/revo/assets/
Connectors path	[[++connectors_path]]	C:/xampp/htdocs/revo/connectors/
Connectors URL	[[++connectors_url]]	/revo/connectors/
URL Scheme	[[++url_scheme]]	http://
HTTP Host	[[++http_host]]	localhost

Many system settings are Yes/No values, which are represented in the database by a zero or one. For these, a setting tag will display a 1 if the setting is true and a 0 if it is false. If you would like to display them as "Yes" and "No," you can use a conditional modifier:

```
[[++SettingName:is=`1`:then=`Yes`:else=`No`]]
```

The tag above will display Yes if the system setting is true and No if it is false. You can use any values for the yes and no clauses. You can even use a chunk tag for each to display different chunks depending on a system setting:

```
[[++SettingName:is=`1`:then=`[[$YesChunk]]`:else=`[[$NoChunk`]]
```

You can also use a snippet tag in one or both of the clauses. You could call different snippets depending on the value of the system setting:

```
[[++SettingName:is=`1`:then=`[[snippet1]]`:else=`[[Snippet2]]`]]
```

You might also want to call a snippet only if a setting were true (or false).

```
[[++SettingName:is=`1`:then=`[[MySnippet]]`]]
```

Suppose that you want to send the value of the system setting to a snippet as a property. This tag would do that:

```
[[SnippetName? &settingValue=`[[++SettingName]]`]]
```

In the tag above, the value of the system setting would be available as a variable in the snippet as $settingValue. To make this example more concrete, imagine that you are writing a file upload snippet (called FileUpload) and want to display the allowable types of files that can be uploaded. The **upload_files** system setting is a comma-delimited list of file extensions (.txt, .ZIP, .html, etc.). In order to format the display of file types, you'd like the file list to be in an array in the snippet. You could use this tag to call your snippet:

```
[[FileUpload? &fileTypes=`[[++upload_files]]`]]
```

Then, in your snippet, this code would turn the comma-delimited system setting into an array of file types:

```
$fileArray = array();
$fileArray = explode(',',$fileTypes);
```

In reality, it's unlikely that you would use the method above because the value of a system setting is available directly in a snippet using the $modx object's getOption() method (See Chapter 8).

Placeholder Tags

Placeholder tags take the form [[+*PlaceholderName*]]. Placeholder values are often set in the code of snippets and plugins. The tag displays the value of the placeholder. If you are writing a snippet, you can set a placeholder with code similar to one of the following:

```
$modx->setPlaceholder('PlaceholderName',' value`);
$modx->setPlaceholder('PlaceholderName', $variable);
```

That will set the placeholder value, which can then be displayed with a standard placeholder tag (as long as the snippet tag is above the placeholder tag):

```
[[+PlaceholderName]]
```

If you are not fluent in PHP, you will still use placeholder tags because many common MODX snippets set placeholders for you to use. We'll discuss those in detail when we cover the individual snippets later in the book. Property set values are also available using placeholder tags. We'll see how this is done in the section on property sets.

Link Tags

Link tags are used to create standard (X)HTML links in a web page to other pages on your site. They take the form [[~##]], where ## is the resource identifier of the resource being linked to. As we learned earlier, the resource identifier is shown in parentheses after the resource name in the Resource tree. It is also shown at the top of the Create/Edit Resource panel. When creating a link to a local resource on a MODX site, you should always use a link tag. If you later change the title of the resource, move the site to a new server, or turn Friendly URLs (FURLs) on or off, the link tag will still work. A hard-coded reference can be easily broken by changes in the site.

Link tags are almost always used in (X)HTML code <href> tags like the following:

```
<a href="[[~12]]">Go to Page</a>
```

If you are working in an editor in the MODX Manager and are not using raw HTML mode (i.e., you've checked the Rich Text checkbox for the resource), you can create a link to another resource by clicking on the link icon (usually an image of a little piece of chain) in the editor. In some editors (e.g., TinyMCE), the link icon won't be active until you type in and highlight the link text (the word or phrase you want the user to click on to be sent to the linked resource). After clicking on the link icon, a pop-up form will appear asking for details about the link. In the field for the link URL, simply put the appropriate link tag. If you want to link to document 12, for example, enter *[[~12]]* for the Link URL.

More advanced users may occasionally want to send a link tag as a property to a snippet with a tag like this one:

```
[[SnippetName? &url=`[[~12]]`]]
```

Using the tag above, the URL will be available to the snippet as the variable $url.

Another advanced technique involves sending parameters in the URL for use via the `$_GET` array in the resource being linked to. In MODX Revolution, you can simply include the parameters in the link tag:

```
<a href = "[[~12? &propertyName=`value`]]"> Link Text</a>
```

MODX will work out the correct form of the URL depending on whether Friendly URLs are enabled or not. With Friendly URLs off, the resulting URL would look like this:

```
index.php?id=12&propertyName=value
```

With Friendly URLs on, the resulting URL would look like this:

```
pagename.html?propertyName=value
```

The link tag also accepts a two optional properties: **&context** and **&scheme**. If a context name is specified in the **&context** property, the resulting URL will be limited to resources in that context. The **&scheme** property has several options:

-1 — Generates a relative URL based on the **site_url** system setting (default).

0 — Same as `http`.

1 — Same as `https`.

full — Generates a full absolute URL based on the **site_url** system setting.

abs — Generates a full absolute URL based on the **base_url** system setting.

http — Generates an **http://** URL.

https — Generates an **https://** URL.

To force a secure `https` URL for resource 12, for example, you would use this link tag:

```
[[~12? &scheme=`https`]]
```

Language Tags

Language tags are new in MODX Revolution. They take the form `[[%LanguageStringKey? &namespace=`NameSpaceName` &topic=`TopicName`]]`. The tag simply displays the value of the named language string.

If you leave out the properties and just use `[[%LanguageStringKey]]`, the default namespace (`core`) and the default topic (`default`) will be used.

There is a third property, (**&language**), which defaults to en. It's not recommended for use in most cases, however, since it's usually better to handle multiple language needs at the Context/System Setting level. An exception to this would be a page that uses dual language captions for form fields where every caption was displayed in two languages (e.g., French/English for a Canadian site). In that case, the **&language** property would be very useful.

The actual language strings for the MODX Manager are located in the following directory:

core/lexicon

The language strings for components are located at:

core/components/*component_name***/lexicon**

To override the language strings contained in any lexicon files, you can go to **System → Lexicon Management** on the Top Menu, select the correct Topic, and create a new entry for each string you want to override with the same key (name) but a new value. Your changes will survive any upgrades.

Nesting Tags

Nesting tags is just putting one MODX tag inside another. Within reason, tags can be nested as deeply as you want, and any tag can appear inside any other tag (although many combinations aren't likely to do anything useful). Here is an unlikely nesting that uses a snippet to return a chunk name. It produces one link if the site is online and another link if it is offline. The chunk contains a document ID number that is then used to create a link. A system setting is passed to the snippet as an argument:

```
[[~[[$[[SnippetName? &status=`[[++site_status]]`]]]]]]
```

There are obviously easier ways to accomplish what this tag does, but it demonstrates the nesting capabilities of MODX. Let's look at it from the inside out. The innermost tag calls a snippet with the **site_status** system setting as a property. In this imaginary case, the snippet checks the system setting and returns the name of the appropriate chunk. After that replacement, the tag looks like this:

`[[~[[$ChunkName]]]]`

In the next step, the chunk tag is replaced by the contents of the named chunk. Let's say the chunk contains just the number 12, which is the ID of the resource we want the link to point to. Now the tag looks like this:

`[[~12]]`

Finally, the remaining link tag is replaced by a link to document 12. If Friendly URLs are off, the result will look like this:

`index.php?id=12`

To function as a link, the whole tag would need to be embedded in an `<href>` tag like this:

`<a href="[[~[[$[[$[[SnippetName? &status=`[[++site_status]]`]]]]]]"]]">Go Here</a>`

You may be curious about how we would accomplish this task in real life (without the hard-to-decipher tag). As usual with MODX, there are many different ways to do it. Skilled PHP coders would probably just use a simple snippet tag with no properties, check the system setting in the snippet itself, and have the snippet return the link.

We could also do it with output modifiers:

`[[++site_status:is=`1`:then=`[[~12]]`:else=`[[~14]]`]]`

The tag above would create a link to resource 12 if the **site_status** is 1 and to resource 14 if it is not.

 If no resource has the ID used in a link tag, the link tag will be ignored, and the tag will be replaced with nothing.

Cache Control

Cache control is the process of determining what MODX places in its cache. In MODX, the content of resources and chunks and the code of snippets are normally kept in the database. For content that has been accessed (e.g., the content of pages in the front end that have been visited at least once), however, MODX will place the snippet and chunk content and the output of snippets in the MODX cache. Most of the time, this content will load faster than it would if it had to be retrieved from the database. MODX allows you to control whether particular content is cached or not.

The caching of resources is controlled by the Cacheable checkbox on the Page Settings tab you see when you go to the Create/Edit Resource panel. If the checkbox is checked, MODX will place the content of the resource in the cache and retrieve it from there when a browser requests the resource.

When you change the content of a resource or element, the changes won't show up until the cache is cleared, but the cache is cleared by default whenever you save a resource or element, so it's rarely necessary to clear the cache manually. If you need to do it, however, you can use **Site → Clear Cache** on the Top Menu.

The main use of uncached content is to display information that is calculated dynamically when the page is accessed. For example, any display of the current time, the number of visits of the current visitor, or the value of page-hit counters should be uncached. More specifically, anything that might have changed since the cache was last cleared should be uncached.

In earlier versions of MODX, you could identify snippets as cached or uncached by modifying the snippet tag. In MODX Revolution, any tag can be uncached by putting an exclamation point (!) after the opening brackets and before the tag's token (if any), like this:

```
[[!SnippetName]]
[[!$ChunkName]]
[[!*ResourceField/TV]]
```

The caching is also much more reliable in MODX Revolution. Reliable, universal cache control in MODX Revolution makes it possible to have very fine control of what is cached and what isn't. For example, you can now reliably have uncached snippets on cached pages. Similarly, you can have a cached page with cached chunks that contain uncached snippets.

For advanced users, there are a number of system settings that control the caching of resources and other MODX objects such as JSON data, lexicon strings, snippets, and the system settings themselves. To see a list of them, go to **System → System Settings** and put *cach* (with no "e") in the "Search by Key" box at the upper right. When you click on the grid or press the "Enter" key, you should see all the cache-related system settings in the grid. You can click on the little plus sign next to each entry for a description. It's recommended that you not change any of the default settings until you have a firm grasp of how MODX works.

Filters and Output Modifiers

We've seen examples of a number of the output modifiers available in MODX Revolution. These modifiers are part of MODX's default output filter, which is part of the tag processing sequence. In this section, we'll look at the output modifiers available in the default output filter in more detail. We'll also see how to create custom modifiers to meet specific tag-processing needs.

If you are familiar with PHX, the MODX output modifiers in Revolution now duplicate the modifiers formerly available with PHX, and a few extra ones have been added. The modifiers can be used with any MODX tag and create fewer conflicts with other add-ons than the PHX modifiers did.

Here's a complete list of the output modifiers and their aliases available at this writing. New ones may have been added by the time you read this and you can easily create new modifiers of your own. Remember that there are no uppercase letters in any modifier name. When a modifier has multiple aliases, you can use whichever one you are most comfortable with.

Conditional Operators

The conditional operators allow you to perform tests on the output of a tag and make decisions about what should be displayed based on the tests. Note that the values are marked with back-ticks, not single-quotes. It is ok to use single- or double-quotes inside the back-ticks.

Using conditional output modifiers is significantly slower than doing the same thing with a snippet. Using them is also questionable from an MVC design standpoint since they serve as controllers but are in the view level. The conditional operators are available for users who are not comfortable with PHP coding.

if (alias: **input:**) — The **if** is usually not necessary in a conditional modifier.

is (aliases: **equals, eq, equalto, isequal, isequalto**) — Tests for equality.

isnot (aliases: **isnot, isnt, ne, neq, notequals, notequalto**) — Tests for inequality.

gt (aliases: **isgt, greaterthan, isgreaterthan**) — Tests for greater than.

lt (aliases: **islt, lessthan, lowerthan, islessthan, islowerthan**) — Tests for less than.

gte (aliases: **isgte, eg, ge, equalorgreaterthan, greaterthanorequalto**) — Tests for greater than or equal to.

lte (aliases: **islte, el, le, lesthanorequalto, equaltoorlessthan**) — Tests for less than or equal to.

and — Logical and.

show — In a conditional, the **show** modifier makes the original tag value "show" if the condition is true and not show if it is false. Example (displays the contents of a chunk only if the chunk is more than 10 characters long):

```
[[$ChunkName:len:isgt=`10`:show]]
```

hide — Opposite of **show**. Hides the output of the tag if the condition is false. Example:

```
[[$ChunkName:len:islt=`10`:hide]]
```

then — Then clause of a conditional. May contain a MODX tag or plain (X)HTML.

else — Else clause of a conditional. May contain a MODX tag or plain (X)HTML.

select — Usually used to convert output to a more user-friendly form. Options are separated by an ampersand. Example:

```
[[++site_status:select=`0="OFFLINE"&1="ONLINE"`]]
```

memberof (aliases: **mo, ismember**) — Tests for membership in a user group.

More Conditional Operator Examples

Reports on the length of a chunk:

```
[[$Text:len:isgt=`10`:then=`Greater than 10`:else=`10 or less`]]
```

Only displays chunks longer than 10 characters:

```
[[$Text:len:isgt=`10`:then=`[[$Text]]`:else=`Too Short`]]
[[$Text:len:isgt=`10`:show]]
```

Displays chunks with lengths within a given range:

```
[[$Text:len:isgte=`10`:and:islte=`40`:then=`[[$Text]]`:else=`Out of Range`]]
```

Displays chunks with lengths outside a given range:

```
[[$Text:len:islt=`10`:or:isgt=`40`:then=`[[$Text]]`:else=``]]
```

Displays different chunks depending on the return value of a snippet:

```
[[IncomeLevel:isgte=`100000`:then=`[[$HighChunk]]`:else=`[[$LowChunk]]`]]
```

Display one of three chunks based on a snippet's return value:

```
[[IncomeLevel:islte=`30000`:then=`[[$LowChunk]]`]]
[[IncomeLevel:isgt=`30000`:and:islt=`100000`:then=`[[$MidChunk]]`]]
[[IncomeLevel:isgt=`100000`:then=`[[$HighChunk]]`]]
```

String Modifiers

cat — Concatenate. Adds the option value to the end of the processed tag. Example:

```
[[$Chunkname:cat=`This will be added at the end.`]]
```

lcase (aliases: **lowercase, strtolower**) — Converts all alphabetic characters to lowercase.

Example:

`[[$ChunkName:lcase]]`

ucase (aliases: **uppercase**, **strtoupper**) — Converts all alphabetic characters to uppercase. Example:

`[[$ChunkName:ucase]]`

ucwords — Converts the first letter of each word to uppercase. Example:

`[[$ChunkName:ucwords]]`

ucfirst — Converts the first letter of the first word to uppercase. Example:

`[[$ChunkName:ucfirst]]`

htmlent (alias: **htmlentities**) — Converts certain characters to their HTML entity equivalents (e.g., "&" is converted to "&"). Calls PHP's `htmlentities()` function. Example:

`[[+PlaceholderName:htmlent]]`

esc (alias: **escape**) — Escapes characters to web-safe versions. Calls PHP's `htmlspecialchars()` function. Also converts brackets and backslashes to HTML entities. Example:

`[[+PlaceholderName:esc]]`

strip — Replaces all linebreaks, tabs, and multiple spaces with a single space. Example:

`[[$ChunkName:strip]]`

notags (aliases: **striptags**, **strip_tags**) — Strips HTML tags. Calls PHP's `strip_tags()` function. Example:

`[[$ChunkName:notags]]`

length (aliases: **len**, **strlen**) — Replaces the tag with its length. Calls PHP's `strlen()` function. Example:

```
[[+ChunkName:len]]
```

reverse (alias: **strrev**) — Reverses the output of the tag character-by-character. Calls PHP's strrev() function. Example:

```
[[+ChunkName:reverse]]
```

wordwrap — Wraps text, always splitting at a space character. Inserts
\n at the end of each line. Option value is the desired width. Default is 70 characters. Calls PHP's wordwrap() function. Examples:

```
[[$ChunkName:wordwrap]]
[[$ChunkName:wordwrap=`45`]]
```

wordwrapcut — Same as **wordwrap**, but will also split words that are longer than the given width.

nl2br — Replaces newline characters with <br />. Useful to apply after the wordwrap modifier. Calls PHP's nl2br() function. Example:

```
[[$ChunkName:nl2br]]
```

limit — Truncates the output to a certain number of characters. The default is 100. Examples:

```
[[$ChunkName:limit]]
[[$ChunkName:limit=`50`]]
```

ellipsis — Like **limit**, but adds ellipsis dots ('. . .') if the string is longer than the specified length. Example:

```
[[*description:ellipsis=`50`]]
```

cdata — Surrounds the content of the tag with cdata tags: <![CDATA[and]]>; useful for making JavaScript code embedded in a chunk validate when using an XHTML Doctype. Example:

```
[[*jsChunk:cdata]]
```

Special Functions

tag — Displays the actual tag (minus the :**tag** modifier). It can be useful for displaying MODX tags in tutorials and online documentation. It is unreliable with nested tags and generally won't work unless the snippets, chunks, and resources referred to in the tag actually exist.

math — Returns the result of a math calculation. It is slow, memory-intensive, and not recommended. The question mark is replaced by the value of the tag (e.g., the return value of the snippet). Example:

```
[[SnippetName:math=`?+1+(2+3)+4/5*6`]]
```

add (aliases: **increment**, **inc**) — Returns input incremented by the option value. Default is +1. Examples:

```
[[+PlaceholderName:add]]
[[+PlaceholderName:add=`5`]]
```

subtract (aliases: **decrement**, **decr**) — Opposite of **add** modifier. Example:

```
[[SnippetName:subtract=`4`]]
```

multiply (alias: **mpy**) — Returns value multiplied by option. Default is *2. Example:

```
[[SnippetName:multiply=`1.5`]]
```

divide (alias: **div**) — Returns value divided by option. Default is /2. Example:

```
[[SnippetName:divide=`.5`]]
```

modulus (alias: **mod**) — Returns the option modulus (division remainder) on the tag value. The default is %2, which returns 0 for even numbers and 1 for odd numbers. Example (reports whether a snippet returns an odd or even value):

```
[[SnippetName:modulus:is=`1`:then=`Odd`:else=`Even`]]
```

ifempty (aliases: **default**, **isempty**, **empty**) — Returns the option value if empty. Example:

```
[[SnippetName:ifempty=`No Value Returned`]]
```

ifnotempty (aliases: **isnotempty**, **notempty**, **!empty**) — Opposite of **ifempty**. Returns the option value if tag output is not empty.

date — Displays a date formatted according to PHP's `strftime()` formatting codes. Assumes that the input is a Unix timestamp, so regular dates (including the dates in resource fields such as **createdon**, **editedon**, etc.) must be preceded by the **strtotime** modifier. Default is `%A, %d %B %Y %H:%M:%S`. Example:

```
Created on: [[*createdon:strtotime:date=`%m-%d-%Y`]]
```

strtotime — Converts a standard date (e.g., `02/23/2011`) to a unix timestamp for use with the **date** modifier. Example:

```
This page last edited on [[*editedon:strtotime:date=`%A %B %d, %Y`]]
```

md5 — Returns an MD5 hash of the input value. Calls PHP's `md5()` function. Example:

```
[[SnippetName:md5]]
```

userinfo — Returns requested user data. Input must be a valid user ID. Default is `username`. Examples:

```
[[*createdby:userinfo]]
[[*createdby:userinfo=`email`]]
[[*createdby:userinfo=`lastlogin`:date=`%m-%d-%Y`]]
```

Some available `userinfo` fields are **username**, **fullname**, **email**, **phone**, **mobilephone**, **blocked**, **blockeduntil**, **logincount**, **dob**, **gender**, **country**, **state**, **zip**, **fax**, **photo**, **comment**.

isloggedin — Returns `true` if the user is logged in, `false` if not. Examples:

```
[[$ChunkName:isloggedin:is=`1`:then=`Logged in`:else=`Not logged in`]]
[[$ChunkName:isloggedin:is=`1`:then=`[[$YesChunk]]`:else=`[[$NoChunk]]`]]
```

Note that the contents of the initial tag are not used. It can be an empty chunk, but it must exist for the tag to work. It can also be any kind of tag (e.g., a setting tag) as long as the tag is valid. This is the case for **isnotloggedin** as well.

isnotloggedin — Returns true if the user is *not* logged in. Examples:

```
[[$ChunkName:isnotloggedin:is=`1`:then=`Not logged in`:else=`Logged in`]]
[[$ChunkName:isnotloggedin:is=`1`:then=`[[$NoChunk]]`:else=`[[$YesChunk]]`]]
```

If you'd like to see the code for the output modifiers, it is in the file:

`core/model/modx/filters/modoutputfilter.class.php`

You can also check that file to see if any new modifiers or aliases have been added since this chapter was written.

 When a tag has properties, the output modifier must go between the name of the element and the question mark that precedes the properties, like this:

```
[[SnippetName:strip? &property1='value']]
[[SnippetName:ifempty=`No Value Returned`? &property1='value']]
```

Custom Output Modifiers

If none of the available output modifiers do what you want, MODX Revolution allows you to create your own custom output modifier. If MODX doesn't recognize the name of a modifier it finds in a tag, it looks for a snippet with that name and runs it. The snippet will receive the result of the tag as $input and can process that variable. If the snippet returns a value, the tag will be replaced by whatever the snippet returns. If the snippet doesn't return a value (or can't be found), the tag will be processed as if the modifier were omitted.

Let's say you want to have a chunk that mentions MODX many times. You realize that you've spelled it modX, however. You could edit the chunk, but here's how to correct it with a custom modifier. First, create a snippet called *correct_modx* containing the following line of code. This is a good time to use the Quick Create Snippet command. Go to the "Elements" tab at the left in the MODX Manager, right-click on "Snippets," and select "Quick Create Snippet." Fill in the name (*correct_modx*) and the line of code below, and click on the "Save" button.

```
return str_replace('modX','MODX',$input);
```

Then, wherever you have a tag referring to the chunk that needs correcting, add the *correct_modx* modifier to it:

```
[[$ChunkName:correct_modx]]
```

For a more practical example, let's look at a custom modifier that will highlight the output of a chunk or snippet by surrounding it with <strong></strong>. Create a snippet called *highlight* containing the following code:

```
<?php
/* highlight Snippet */
return '<strong>' . $input . '</strong>';
?>
```

Now, to highlight your output, just add the highlight custom modifier at the end of the snippet or chunk tag:

```
[[SnippetName:highlight]]
[[$ChunkName:highlight]]
```

You can also include information for the custom modifier in your modifier reference. It will be available in the modifier as the $options variable. Using the following tag, for example, the $options variable will contain 'option1,option2' as a string.

```
[[SnippetName:custom_modifier_name=`option1,option2`]]
```

The snippet code would have to parse the $options variable to separate the two options (e.g., with the PHP explode() function).

If we wanted to send the type of tag to be used as a property to the highlight snippet we created above, we could change the snippet code to:

```
$output = '<' . $options . '>';
$output .= $input;
$output .= '</' . $options . '>';
```

And use a tag like this:

```
[[$ChunkName:highlight=`strong`]]
```

In addition to the `$input` and `$options` variables, the following variables are also available in a custom modifier snippet:

- `$token` — The token at the beginning of the tag (e.g., $, ++, +, etc.); empty for snippets.
- `$name` — The element name at the beginning of the tag (e.g., the snippet or chunk name).
- `$tag` — The complete contents of the tag containing the modifier.

You can add any of the standard output modifiers after your custom modifier to further modify the output:

```
[[SnippetName:custom_modifier_name:ucase]]
```

Technically, MODX also has *Input filters* in addition to the default output filter containing the output modifiers we've discussed. The default input filter simply parses the tag in preparation for the output filter. Custom input filters that act on the element before it is processed are possible but are beyond the scope of this book.

Weblinks

A *weblink* is a MODX resource that contains a URL or MODX link tag in its Resource Content field. Note that although the link is stored in the **content** field in the database, on the Create/Edit Resource panel, the field label is Weblink.

With a weblink, the URL can be to a page at the MODX site or any other site on the Web. The main use of weblinks is to make pages from other parts of the site show up in menus created with Wayfinder or another menu snippet. If you have a **Contact** page, for example, and would like it to show up in a menu that shows a particular subpart of the tree (which doesn't contain the contact resource), you can add a weblink tied to the Contact page to that part of the tree. You can also add links to pages at any other site to your menus by creating weblinks for them.

If you're familiar with (X)HTML, you've created plenty of links already. Because a weblink is a MODX resource, however, it comes with many useful features not available with a standard (X)HTML link. It will have all the standard fields of a Resource. You can make it published or unpublished, for example, and you can give it a future publish or unpublish date.

A weblink can have a Title, a Long Title, and a Summary, although these have limited use since the user is actually forwarded to the page specified in the URL or link tag. They are available to snippets and plugins, however. The weblink's Menu Title and Menu Index fields, for example, could be used by menu and sitemap snippets.

You can also designate whether the weblink will be hidden from menus, and you can use the MODX permission system to make it unavailable to unauthorized users. If the weblink is unpublished, for example, and the document it refers to is published, a user accessing the weblink directly or via a link will not reach the page the weblink refers to. Instead, they'll be directed to your error (Page Not Found) document.

 If the weblink is to a page on the MODX site, the template used will be that of the target page rather than the template of the weblink.

Symlinks

Like a weblink, a symlink refers to another page. Unlike weblinks, however, the page must be on the MODX site. Since symlinks are also MODX Resources, they also have all the characteristics we discussed for weblinks in the previous section.

There are two important differences between weblinks and symlinks. First, while weblinks are specified by a full URL or a MODX link tag, symlinks are specified simply by the Resource ID of the document being referred to. In other words, what goes in the Symlink field on the Create/Edit Resource panel is just a number rather than a URL or link tag.

Second, while a weblink actually forwards the user to the page referred to, a symlink pulls that document into the URL of the symlink itself. In other words, when the user reaches the target page, the URL shown in the browser's address window will be that of the symlink. One use of symlinks is to allow you to serve the same page in different parts of your menu structure without duplicating the page.

Unlike weblinks, the template used will be that of the symlink rather than the template of the target page.

Static Resources

Static resources are simply resources that contain a file path in their Resource Content field. Most MODX pages have dynamic content because they contain elements, such as snippets and chunks, which may change over time. That means that the contents of the page will be created on the fly before being seen by the site visitor. When you have content that you know won't change unless you edit it yourself, however, you can save it as a file and use a *static resource* to display it. The page will display faster and will put less strain on MODX and the database.

Static Resources may also contain links to files you want to deliver to the visitor such as .PDF files or .DOC files for display or download. If you want the user to be able to download the file, simply set the Content Disposition field to *attachment*. You can even use PHP code to create dynamic .PDF files, JavaScript files, or CSS files, that the user can view or download by following a link to the static resource. This also allows you to control access to the files so some users can access them and others can't. To create the files dynamically, you'd simply create a snippet to produce the content and then create a static resource with no template and nothing but the snippet tag for its content. Set the Content Type field appropriately, and you're done.

Another use of static resources it to deliver application-specific documents such as MS Word .DOC files or .PDF files.

Let's create a static resource that will allow the user to see a .PDF file in Adobe Reader (you'll need a .PDF file somewhere on the site to do this). First, create a *static resource* (right-click anywhere in the "Resources" tree and select **Create → Create a Static Resource Here**). Set the Title to *MyStaticResource*. On the "Page Settings" tab, set the Content Type to *PDF*. Then on the Create/Edit Resource panel, set the Uses Template field to *empty* because you want nothing sent but the contents of the file. Then, click on the down arrow next to the Static Resource field, navigate to the .PDF file, and select it. Leave the Content Disposition field at its default (*inline*), and the browser will automatically launch Adobe Reader to display the content of the .PDF file when the user clicks on a link to your Static Resource. (Thanks to Jelle Jager for this example.)

Template Variables and Access Permissions

There are two tabs we haven't discussed on the Create/Edit Resource Panel. The Template Variables tab is where you set the values of any template variables you attached to the template used by the resource. Using these will be discussed in more detail in the following chapter when we cover template variables.

On the Access Permissions tab, you can assign the resource to any resource groups you have created. You assign the resource to a group by checking the checkbox next to the resource group's name on this tab. Usually, assigning resources to resource groups is done in **Security → Access Controls** by dragging the resource into a group, although you can do it here if you choose. The use of resource groups will be covered in more detail in Chapter 10 when we discuss security permissions.

Other Resource Operations

We've spent most of our time discussing the creation and editing of resources, but right-clicking on a resource in the "Resource" tree provides some other options as well. We discussed them in Chapter 3, but let's take another look at them.

View Resource

Choosing this option opens up a display with multiple tabs on the right side that lets you see (but not edit) much of the document's information. Some of the information is duplicated on the Create/Edit Resource panel, but remember that you can give users permission to view but not to edit resources. This will allow them to see all the information listed in the following section in the View panel without ever having access to the Create/Edit Resource panel.

The following sections can be opened by clicking on their tabs in the View Resource panel. Note that some of the information here is not available on the Create/Edit Resource panel.

General

The General section shows a subset of the resource fields, including the document's Title, Long Title, Description, Class Key, Alias, and Context. If any fields have not been set in the Create/Edit Resource panel, they will be blank here.

Changes

This section shows another subset of the resource fields for the resource, including the date and time the resource was created, the username of the creator, the most recent date and time that the resource was edited, and the user name of the most recent editor. If the resource is published, you can also see the date it was published and who published it.

Cache Output

This section will show the raw (X)HTML of the resource as it appears in the MODX cache. It will include the template and template variables (if any), but any uncached elements (e.g., uncached snippets, chunks, or template variables) will not be processed and will simply show as tags.

In order for anything at all to show here, the document must be set as cacheable, must be saved, and must have been either visited in the front end or previewed by a manager user. If the tab is blank, you can preview the document by right-clicking on it in the tree and selecting "Preview Resource." The tab will still be blank until you right-click on the resource and select "View Resource" again.

The information on the Cache tab can be helpful if you want to see exactly what is and isn't being cached for a particular resource since it shows you the contents of the cache directly.

Quick Update Resource

Quick Update Resource will pop up a window that allows you to make quick changes to the resource without leaving your current place in the Manager.

In the pop-up window, you can change the resource's Title, Alias, and Description. The larger window contains the Resource Content field of the resource in raw (X)HTML form. You won't have the rich text editor available, and no template variables will show, but you can make changes to the content and some basic settings in the pop-up. Maximizing the Quick Update window will give you a larger editing area. The "Save" and "Cancel" buttons are at the lower-right corner of the window.

If you expand the "Page Settings" section below the Content field, you can edit the following fields:

* Published
* Container
* Rich Text
* Searchable
* Hide From Menus
* Cacheable
* Clear Cache on Save

Quick Update is immensely useful when you are working on a chunk or snippet and want to update or review a resource. When you save the resource, the window will disappear and you'll be right where you were. Note, though, that you won't see (and can't edit) any template variables or resource group settings.

Duplicate Resource

This option lets you create a duplicate copy of a resource. When you select it, you'll be prompted for the name of the duplicate resource.

 Duplicating resources is handy for making a back-up copy of a resource before making major changes to it. It's also useful if you need to create a number of similar resources.

If the resource is a container, you'll also see a checkbox that determines if the children should also be duplicated.

Refresh Resource

Selecting this option will reload the segment of the Resource tree for that resource and any children of the resource.

Quick Create

This option is basically a duplicate of Quick Update but for resources that don't exist yet. You can create a resource in a pop-up window without leaving your current place in the Manager. As with Quick Update, you won't have access to the rich text editor or to any template variables.

Publish/Unpublish

The publish option offers a quick way to publish an unpublished resource or unpublish a published one. It's the equivalent of selecting edit, changing the Published checkbox in the Page Settings tab, and saving the resource. It is also a quick way to check to see if the document is published or unpublished. Only one of the two options will appear in the list.

Delete/Undelete

After selecting "Delete," the resource will appear in the Resource tree with a line through it. It won't be visible in the front end, won't appear in any Wayfinder menus, and can't be previewed, but it can still be edited. It can also be undeleted as long as it still appears in the tree. It will be deleted for good if you empty the trash by clicking on the little trashcan icon at the top of the tree. After emptying the trash, there is no way to recover the resource.

 Leaving deleted resources in the tree and then reusing them instead of creating new resources is a way of keeping your document IDs from growing too large.

Preview

This option will launch the resource in your browser. It will show the most recently saved version of the resource, so if you are in the process of editing it but haven't saved it, the changes will not appear.

Remember that as you preview a resource, you are still logged in as a manager. If you have things on the page that depend on the status and security permissions of a user, you may not see the page the way an actual visitor to your site will.

If you want to preview a page and see what regular visitors to your site see, the best method is to view the page in another browser where the page is in the only open window. Using another window in the same browser is not a reliable way to do this because MODX will still see you as logged in to the Manager.

Summary

Documents are the default resource type in MODX. They are stored in the MODX database. Documents are always referred to in MODX by their Resource ID numbers, shown in parentheses in the Resource tree. Documents have a number of resource fields such as `title`, `pagetitle`, `alias`, etc. They may also have one or more template variables, which are extra resource fields that you create.

The values in resource fields and template variables can be shown in a rendered page using MODX resource tags. Other content can be injected into the rendered document with chunk tags, snippet tags, setting tags, placeholder tags, link tags, and language tags. The tags can be nested within other tags, and in MODX Revolution, they can be nested as deeply as you like. Using the cache control token (!), you can prevent the content of any tag from being stored in the MODX cache, even in a cached resource.

The output of MODX tags can be formatted and controlled by the use of filters and output modifiers that duplicate the effects of the PHX plugin in MODX Evolution.

A weblink is a MODX resource that contains a URL or MODX link tag in its Resource Content field. Weblinks can be to a page on the site or to a page at another site.

Symlinks are also links to pages, but the pages must be on the MODX site. Rather than forwarding the user to the page specified in the symlink, the page is pulled into the URL of the symlink itself. When the user clicks on the link, they will see the page the symlink points to, but the URL in the browser's address window will be the URL of the symlink resource itself. Symlinks are often used to duplicate the same page in different parts of the site without having to create a whole new document.

Static resources contain a file path in their Resource Content field. The file may contain static (X)HTML or a file that you want to allow the user to download such as a .PDF or .DOC file.

Many of the operations performed on resources can be accomplished by right-clicking on the resource in the Resource tree.

MODX Evolution Notes

Most of the information in this chapter will apply to MODX Evolution. The most obvious difference is in the tag syntax, which we discussed in Chapter 1. MODX Evolution has no language tags, but it does have all the other types of tags described in this chapter, and they may be nested. Unlike Revolution tags, however, nested tags and tags within elements called through tags are not always processed correctly because of the parsing order.

Evolution has weblinks, which work as they do in Revolution, but not symlinks or static resources.

The Tree

The tree displayed at the left side of the Manager screen also looks different in MODX Evolution. In MODX Revolution, there are three trees (Resources, Elements, and Files), each on its own tab. In Evolution, only Resources are shown in the tree at the left. Elements and Files are reached through the Top Menu.

In order to create and edit elements like snippets, chunks, templates, template variables, and plugins, you need to go to **Elements → Manage Elements** on the Top Menu, and then select the appropriate tab on the right. Evolution has categories, but you create and assign them on the screen where you create and edit elements or resources. For snippets, they are on the Properties tab of the Create/Edit Snippet panel.

Quick Create and Quick Update are not available in MODX Evolution.

Templates

Templates are essentially the same in both versions except for the tag syntax for any tags they contain.

Documents

Documents (resources) and their resource fields are the same in both versions with very minor variations, except for the tag syntax. There is no Class Key field in Evolution, and there is a tab for entering Meta Tags and Keywords, although they are deprecated and seldom used (most users prefer to use template variables instead). There is also a checkbox for Log Visits, which no longer exists in Revolution.

The date resource fields will display a Unix timestamp in Evolution, and they need to be processed with either a snippet or with PHX (more on that in a bit) to show a standard date.

Snippets and Properties

Snippet tags and their properties are the same in Evolution except for the format of the tags. Evolution snippets have properties, but control of them is limited. Default properties can be specified on one line in the Default Properties field of the Properties tab of the Create/ Edit Snippet panel in Evolution. The default properties take this form:

```
&Variable1=Caption1;Type;DefaultValue&Variable2=Caption2;Type;DefaultValue2;
```

Variable1 is the name of the variable inside the snippet; *Caption* is the caption for the field on the Properties tab; *Type* is the variable type (almost always text); *DefaultValue* is the default value. Example:

```
&shoe_size=Shoe Size;text;7;
```

Once the snippet has been saved, each default property appears on a separate line on the Properties tab, is preceded by the Caption, and can be edited by the manager user. In the snippet above, the property would be available like this:

```
echo 'Shoe Size is ' . $shoe_size;
```

 If a snippet has default properties and information is also sent in with properties in the snippet tag that match the property names, the properties in the tag will override the default properties.

Setting default properties this way in Evolution is not very convenient, especially if there are many properties. Generally, all information passed to snippets in Evolution is in the form of properties in the snippet tag, and any default values are set in code within the snippet.

Revolution can parse multi-line snippet tags, but some versions of Evolution cannot. In those versions of Evolution, snippet tags must be written on a single line.

Cache Control

Cache control is more limited in Evolution. Only snippets and resources can be cached, and the caching sequence is more complicated and prone to error. Generally, the caching is reversed as you progress from outer to inner nested items such as a snippet tag used in a property inside another snippet tag. In Revolution, anything designated as uncached (with the ! token) will be uncached.

Filters and Modifiers

In Evolution, the filters and output modifiers we discussed are available only through the PHX plugin, which must be downloaded and installed.

Generally, the modifiers we discussed will work in Evolution as long as the PHX plugin is installed and enabled.

Chapter 5

Templates and Template Variables

In the previous chapter, we looked at MODX resources. In this chapter, we turn our attention to two MODX elements: templates and template variables. We've been using the MODX minimal BaseTemplate created during the install. In this chapter, we'll look more closely at the ins and outs of templates. We'll also examine template variables and how they are used with other MODX resources and elements.

Templates

In MODX, a *Template* is not classified as a resource. Technically, a template is an element. Templates don't have all of the resource fields that resources do. They don't have a published status or a publish or unpublish date. They don't have long titles, aliases, etc. They have only four editable fields: Template Name, Description, Category, and Template Code, but the only required field is the Template Name.

As we mentioned earlier in the book, a MODX *template* is something like a business letterhead. It provides a framework in which web pages are constructed.

When a browser requests a web page, the first thing MODX does is look to see what template is associated with the resource. MODX retrieves the template and proceeds to fill it in by replacing all the tags in the template before delivering the finished web page to the browser.

Creating a Template

To create a template, you can simply right-click on the "Templates" folder in the "Elements" tree in the MODX Manager and select "New Template." If you want to create a template lower down in the template hierarchy, you can right-click on an existing template (or category name if you've created categories for your templates) and select "Create a New Template Here." A third alternative is to click on an existing template and select "Duplicate Template." This last method is an excellent choice if you want to create a new version of an existing template, modify someone else's template, or just back up an existing template before messing with it.

Let's look at a relatively simple MODX template. This is an abbreviated and modified version of a template from the MODX site.

An Example Template

```html
<!-- Example Template -->
<!DOCTYPE html PUBLIC "-//W3C//DTD XHTML 1.0 Transitional//EN"
    "http://www.w3.org/TR/xhtml1/DTD/xhtml1-transitional.dtd">
<html xmlns="http://www.w3.org/1999/xhtml">
<head>
<meta http-equiv="Content-Type" content="text/html;
    charset=[[++modx_charset]]" />
<meta name="copyright" content="2011, MODX" />
<title>[[++site_name]] | [[*pagetitle]]</title>
<link href="[[++base_url]]assets/site/simple.css" rel="stylesheet"
    type="text/css" />
</head>
<body>
    <div id="header">
        <div id="logo">
            [[*longtitle]]
        </div>
    </div>
    <div id="main">
        [[*content]]
    </div>
    <div id="sidebar">
        [[$SideBar]]
    </div>
    <div id="navigation">
        [[Wayfinder? &startId=`0`]]
    </div>
    <div id="news">
        [[!getResources? &parents=`22` &tpl=`MyGrTpl`]]
    </div>
    <p><a href="[[~[[*id]]]]#" >Back to Top</a></p>
    <p><a href="[[~[[++site_start]]]]" >MODX Home Page</a></p>
    <div id="footer">
        [[$Footer]]
    </div>
</body>
</html>
```

Example Template: A Closer Look

If you are familiar with (X)HTML, you've seen a lot of this before. The standard (X)HTML tags are there (`<DOCTYPE>`, `<html>`, `<head>`, `<body>`, `<div><a href>`, etc.). Let's look at some parts of the template that show MODX at work. Along the way, we'll see some *MODX tags* in use. As you probably know, (X)HTML tags are in this format: `<TagName>`. You can spot the MODX tags because, in MODX Revolution and future versions, they are all in this format: `[[TagName]]`. First, we'll look at the `<head>` section, which contains three MODX tags.

The `<head>` Section

```
<head>
<meta http-equiv="Content-Type" content="text/html;
    charset=[[++modx_charset]]" />
<meta name="copyright" content="2011, MODX" />
<title>[[++site_name]] | [[*pagetitle]]</title>
<base href="[[!++site_url]]" />
<link href="[[!++site_url]]assets/site/simple.css" rel="stylesheet"
    type="text/css" />
</head>
```

You can see that the first two `<meta>` statements are standard (X)HTML code (but with the addition of the MODX setting tag `[[++modx_charset]]` to specify the character set). That tag will be replaced in the rendered document by the character set specified in the MODX System Settings grid.

In keeping with MODX's policy of putting as few restrictions on the user as possible, you can put any standard HTML or (X)HTML tags in a MODX template. In fact, there's no requirement to use any MODX features in any template (although it would be kind of silly to install MODX and not use its features).

Notice that what is in the `<title>` tag looks a little different. In a non-MODX site, it might contain something like `<title>My Site | Home Page</title>`. In our example, however, it uses two MODX tags to set the title of the web page. As we discussed in Chapter 1, the various MODX tags are replaced by the value they represent. Remember, too, that when this template is displayed in a browser, it will be tied to a particular MODX document, and that document will have a number of resource fields such as **pagetitle**, **longtitle**, **alias**, **id**, etc. Let's assume that this template is being used to display a document with a Resource ID of 12, a **pagetitle** of Documentation, and a **longtitle** of MODX Documentation. Let's assume, too, that in the MODX System Settings grid, the **site_name** setting value is My MODX Site.

As you probably know, the <title> (X)HTML tag sets the page title you see at the very top of your browser. The <title> tag above will set the title seen in the browser to My Modx Site | Documentation (the vertical bar is just a vertical bar, not a MODX token). The first part of the title is inserted using the setting tag [[++**site_name**]]. The second part (the title of the document) is inserted with the resource tag [[*****pagetitle**]].

If you change the title of a document or the name of your MODX site, the title will automatically change on every page that uses this template.

Notice that the **site_url** setting tag is used in the <base href> tag. This is a critical practice in all templates because it makes the paths to all links in the file relative to the site root and thus portable.

There's another MODX tag in the next line that's used as part of the path to the CSS file. The [[!++**site_url**]] tag is also a *setting tag*. MODX replaces it with the value of the **site_url** variable. The exclamation point makes it uncached. The value of **site_url** is not available in the System Settings grid. It is set automatically by MODX based on the URL the user entered the site through. The final URL will be something like **http://modx.com/ assets/site/simple.css**. This will make the site completely portable. If you move the site to another server or move it from a subdirectory to a root directory, the CSS file will still be found. Note that the line specifying the CSS file could also be done like this since the **assets_url** setting is also set automatically by MODX:

```
<link href="[[++assets_url]]site/simple.css" rel="stylesheet"
    type="text/css" />
```

The <body> Section

The Header Div

```
<div id="header">
    <div id="logo">
        [[*longtitle]]
    </div>
</div>
```

This div presents a banner heading and logo that are displayed using background images in the CSS file. It also contains a resource tag, [[*longtitle]], that displays the Long Title of the page being visited (we'll see more on resource tags in the next section).

The Main Div

```
<div id="main">
    [[*content]]
</div>
```

It's hard to find a MODX template that doesn't contain this *resource tag* referring to the resource's **content** field. This field is called the "Resource Content" field in the MODX Manager. When you create a document, you put its main content in the Resource Content field. Remember that we are dealing with document 12 in our example. When MODX sees this Tag, it replaces the [[*content]] tag with what is in the **content** field of document 12. Keep in mind that that **content** field may contain more MODX tags, which will also be replaced.

The Sidebar Div

```
<div id="sidebar">
    [[$SideBar]]
</div>
```

In the sidebar div, we see a new tag. The [[$SideBar]] tag is a *chunk tag.* The tag will be replaced by the contents of the *chunk* named SideBar. A chunk (to refresh your memory) is a chunk of (X)HTML code that you can use in multiple locations by using a chunk tag.

This tag will be replaced by the (X)HTML code/content contained in the SideBar chunk. Remember, too, that the SideBar chunk may also contain MODX tags of various kinds to be processed.

The Navigation Div

```
<div id="navigation">
    [[Wayfinder? &startId=`0`]]
</div>
```

This section contains a *snippet tag* that generates a menu using the Wayfinder snippet.

Snippets, as we discussed in Chapter 1, are sections of PHP code that execute when they are called via a snippet tag. The snippet tag is replaced by the output or return value of the snippet it calls.

Wayfinder is the name of a commonly used snippet in MODX. It contains PHP code that searches through the MODX Resource tree and creates a menu from it. The tag above allows the Wayfinder snippet to be cached. This will make your menus load faster. This is generally a good idea if all users will see the same menu. If different users will see a different menu based on their roles, however, the snippet should always be called uncached, like this:

```
[[!Wayfinder? &startId=`0`]]
```

You may recall that when a snippet is called via a snippet tag, you can send it information that it needs to do its job.

The Wayfinder snippet needs to know where in the Resource tree to start its work. In this snippet tag, we're using the **&startId** *property* to tell it to start at the very top of the tree (at 0). If we wanted a menu that showed only part of the tree, we could send it the ID of another document, and it would show all the documents below it in the tree.

Using *snippet properties*, CSS, and Tpl chunks (more on those later in the book), Wayfinder can produce just about any menu you might want — vertical, horizontal, drop-down, fly-out — you name it. The example above will produce a default Wayfinder menu — a simple list of links that are unordered, nested, and indented by level. The beauty of using Wayfinder rather than hard-coding a menu into your template is that as you add, move, rename, publish, unpublish, and delete documents at your site, all your menus will change automatically to reflect those changes.

The News Div

```
<div id="news">
    <h2>MODX News</h2>
    [[!getResources? &parents=`22` &tpl=`MyGrTpl`]]
</div>
```

The "news" div contains an aggregation (or collection) of news stories generated by another popular MODX component — the getResources snippet, which replaces the Ditto snippet used in MODX Evolution. In our example, let's say that each news story is a separate MODX document, and they are all stored under document 22 in the Resource tree. Whenever a new News item is created, getResources will automatically show it in this section. The **&tpl** property tells getResources the name of the chunk to use to format each entry.

The way we have it here, the getResources tag would show all the news stories in folder 22, no matter how many there are. Using further properties in the getResources tag, however, you could choose how many stories to show, how they are ordered, how they are formatted, and what information will be shown with each one (e.g., author, creation date, etc.).

The getResources snippet can be used to create a wide variety of aggregations. It could produce an events calendar, a selection of news stories (or summaries of news stories each with a link to the full story), a set of Blog posts, or any collection where each item is taken from a separate MODX document.

We've simplified things somewhat here. In a real site, the getResources snippet tag would be much more likely to appear in a document's Resource Content field rather than in a template, and both the getResources and Wayfinder calls would probably have many more properties. A getResources snippet tag could appear in a template, however, if it is producing an aggregation that you want to display on every page. In a blog, for example, you might want a small selection of links to recent posts on every page of the blog. In that case, you'd put the getResources tag in the desired location in your template.

You'll note that unlike the other tags in this template, this one has an exclamation point after the opening braces: [[!getResources? &parents=`22`. . .]]. This tells MODX to run the getResources snippet each time the page is visited and get a fresh result rather than getting the output from the MODX cache. The exclamation point can be used in any snippet tag, chunk tag, or resource tag, to tell MODX not to cache the results that will replace the tag.

Nested Tags

```
<p><a href="[[~[[*id]]]]#" >Back to Top</a></p>
<p><a href="[[~[[++site_start]]]]" >MODX Home
    Page</a></p>
```

This section contains *nested tags*. These are MODX tags that are inside other tags. The first line produces a *link* to the top of the current page. Let's look at the inner tag first. The [[*id]] tag is a *resource tag* that will be replaced by the Resource ID of the current document (which you'll recall is 12). After that replacement, the tag will look like this: [[~12]]. The outer tag is still there (for the moment), and the entire inner tag has been replaced by the number 12. The remaining tag (the outer tag) is a *link tag*. It will be replaced by the URL of document 12. So, if Friendly URLs are turned on (more on those later) and the **alias** resource field of the current document (document 12) is set to documentation, the result will look something like this:

```
<p><a href="http://modx.com/documentation.html#" >Back to Top</a></p>
```

The second line above also contains a nested tag. The outer tag is a link tag like the first one, but the inner tag is a *setting tag* that is replaced by the Resource ID of the site's Home page (taken from the value of the **site_start** system setting in the System Settings grid. The result will look something like this:

```
<p><a href="http://modx.com/home.html" >MODX Home Page</a></p>
```

 When you need to insert a link to a page at your site, you should always use a link tag. The name and location of the document may change, but its ID will always be the same, and the link tag will always provide a reliable link to it.

The Footer Div

```
<div id="footer">
    [[$Footer]]
</div>
```

One final tag is in the "footer" div. This is another chunk tag that will be replaced with the contents of the chunk called *Footer*. Chunks hold (X)HTML code or sometimes just straight text. You use a chunk tag when you have content that will be used on multiple pages at the site. When you want to change the footer section of pages that use this template, you simply edit the Footer chunk, and the new content will automatically appear on every page that uses a template containing the `[[$Footer]]` chunk tag.

Deciding What to Put in a Template

It's sometimes difficult to decide what to put in your template. Many things will work equally well in or out of the template. Here are some general guidelines (which you are free to ignore).

For making your sites easy to maintain, one of the most important rules is never put content in your template! Your template should always be a framework for displaying content. It should never hold that content. With very few exceptions, all content should be displayed using MODX tags. MODX is designed so that it's never necessary to put content in a template, so this rule should be easy to follow once you get used to it.

It's a good rule to have a small number of templates. Many MODX sites have just one or two templates, and the ones with two usually have a template for the Home page and a separate template for all other pages. You're free to create as many templates as you need, but having many of them will make your site more difficult to maintain. If you find yourself making the same changes to more than one template, you may have too many templates. Code that will appear in multiple templates can be moved into chunks.

Like most rules, however, there are exceptions and, for some sites, it's easier to have many templates than to try to make a single template do everything for you.

It's also a good rule to only put things that will seldom change in the template. Generally, it's more work to edit a template than to edit another MODX element. This is partly because templates tend to be bigger, so it's harder to find the part you want to change and partly because changes in a template are more likely to have side effects that affect page layout.

Finally, you might think that only things that should appear unchanged on every page can go in a template. Remember, though, that when a browser requests a particular page at your site, what visitors see will be a combination of the template and the particular MODX document associated with the URL they have accessed. The content of every document will be different, and the document may contain snippets and template variables that can make each page look different. You could, for example, have a template variable that specifies the CSS file to load for each page. The line in the template that loads the CSS file would use a tag containing that template variable to specify the file to use. That way, different pages could look very different, even though they are all based on the same template.

Using Tags in a Template

You can put any MODX tags in your template. All valid tags will be replaced before the site visitor sees the page. As we saw above, resource tags will be replaced by the values from the resource fields of the current document. Resource tags can also refer to template variables, which are extra resource fields you create that can have a different value for each document.

If that's not enough, a snippet tag in the template will be replaced by the output of that snippet. The snippet, which is written in PHP code, can actually check any number of things, such as the resource fields of the current document (including template variables), the database, a foreign database, disk files, the date and time, etc., and make intelligent decisions about what to include in the output.

A snippet, for example, could check the Resource ID and insert various chunks of content depending on which document it is. It could even check the Resource ID against the `site_start` system setting and insert particular content only if called from the site's Home page.

As you continue to use MODX, you'll get a better feel for what you want to put in your templates. There are no hard-and-fast rules, and as with so many things in MODX, it's ultimately up to you.

Template Variables

A *Template variable* (TV) is an extra resource field that you create to extend the capabilities of a MODX resource. Template variables are most often used with documents, but they can also be used with weblinks, symlinks, and static resources. For these last three, the template variables are not available via MODX tags, but they can be accessed by snippets and plugins to achieve complex results.

When to Use Template Variables

The Resource Content field is where you normally put the content of a web page. Suppose, however, that you have a page where you want to display the content in several different sections. Some of it might go in the main content section in the middle of the page, but you also want to put some of the content in the sidebar or the footer of the page. Template variables make this simple.

You always have the Resource Content field built into the Create/Edit Resource panel, but you can easily add a TV called *SidebarContent* and another TV called *FooterContent*. Once you've created these TVs, you can fill them with the appropriate content when you edit each page and display them wherever you want by placing the resource tags [[*content]], [[*SidebarContent]], and [[*FooterContent]] wherever you like in the template.

Let's look at another example involving documents. Suppose you are creating a web site for a car dealer. One section of the web site is devoted to the dealer's inventory, with each car for sale listed in its own document.

You could put all the information about each car in the Resource Content field of that car's document. Think how much better it would be, though, if you had a standard format with separate fields for the various pieces of information about each car, such as year, mileage, make, model, engine, color, price, etc.

Setting up separate fields would make the site look more professional since every car's information would be displayed in the same format. It would also simplify entering the data for each car by reminding the page editor what information was needed. Best of all, it would allow site visitors to search for the particular car they want in a variety of ways. The results could be filtered and sorted by price, age, mileage, make, etc.

Another useful feature of TVs is that they allow you to set up drop-down lists for many of the fields, so the page editor can select from the available choices rather than typing in all the values.

Template variables aren't always used to insert content directly into a web page using tags. Sometimes, they're used to control other aspects of the display. A TV, for example, could contain a background color for use on a page or part of a page. A snippet or plugin could then check the value of the TV and insert the proper CSS in the head of the document to set that background color.

A template variable can also serve as a switch that determines whether an image or a piece of content is shown on a page. If you have some boilerplate text that only needs to be shown on some pages, you can create a TV called *ShowBoilerplate* that determines whether a chunk containing the boilerplate is inserted or not.

Another handy feature of TVs is that they can be hidden from certain users. Using the MODX permission system, you can allow a user to see and edit a resource but hide one or all TVs associated with that resource. This is very useful if you want to allow users to edit a resource, but you also want to include some content on the page that the users can't edit. See the MODX Security chapter (Chapter 10) for information on how to do this.

Template variables can also control which of several CSS files are used for the whole document, what language is used for a page, or how many news articles will be summarized on the page. What you do with template variables is limited only by your imagination.

Creating Template Variables

Let's work through a simple example to create some of the TVs for the car dealer example above. We'll create a TV to hold the year, mileage, and engine type of each car (diesel or gasoline). This assumes that you've already created a template for your web site, so do that if you haven't already. If you don't have a template of your own yet, you can use the Base-Template (although you should add a DOCTYPE at the top). You can also download and install MODX templates from the repository by going to **System → Package Management** and clicking on the "Download Extras" button, but this is not recommended at this point because they are unnecessarily complicated for what we'll be doing.

We're going to want a separate template for the page that displays an individual car's information. Go to the "Templates" section of the "Elements" tab, right-click on your template, and select "Duplicate Template." Give the new template the name *Vehicle*, and click on the "Save" button.

Now that we have a template, we need a container document to hold the documents with each car's information. Click on the "Resources" tab, and right-click on the "web" folder. Select **Create → Create a Document Here**. Give the new document a Title of *Inventory*. Set the Uses Template field to *Vehicle*. This document is just a container, so we may never display it on a web page, but setting the template can make Vehicle the default template for all its children, so we won't have to set the template for each car we create under it. Check the "Published" checkbox, and click on the "Save" button.

Now, let's create a couple of cars in the inventory. We haven't created the TVs yet, but we can do that later. On the "Resources" tab, right-click on the "Vehicle" document and select **Create → Create a Document Here**.

Let's assume that we're going to put the inventory number for each car in the Title field. Make up an inventory number (e.g., 10334), and put it in the Title field. Check the "Published" checkbox, and put a brief description of the car in the Resource Content Field (e.g., "This is a great little car. It won't last long at this price"). Make sure that the Uses

Template field of the document is set to Vehicle. Click on the "Save" button. Create one or two more cars the same way (using a different inventory number for each car in the Title field). Note that the Parent Resource field is already set to the Resource ID of the Inventory container document we created.

Now, let's create our TVs. Go to the "Elements" tab, right-click on "Template Variables," and select "New Template Variable." Here's a little trick to make creating multiple TVs a little easier. Next to the Save button, you'll see three icons. If you hover the mouse over the left one, it should say "Add Another." If you click on that icon, MODX will show you a new, blank form each time you save the current one. Click on that icon. Remember to click on the center icon ("Continue Editing") after you're done creating your TVs. If you forget, the next time you save a document or TV, you'll get a new, blank form.

First, we'll create a TV for the car's model year. Put *Year* in the Variable Name and Caption fields, and set the Input Type to *Number*. Click on the "Save" button. Note that we capitalized the first letter of *Year*. TV names, like most names in MODX, are case-sensitive, so be careful when you type them.

When referring to a TV in a tag or snippet, remember that you need to use the Variable Name and not the Caption. Some people like to make them the same to avoid mistakes.

If you've set "Add Another," you should see a new blank TV form. If not, repeat the process above for creating a new TV. When you get to the blank form, create the Mileage TV by putting *Mileage* in the Variable Name and Caption fields, set the Input Type to Number, and click "Save" again.

Now, we'll create the engine-type TV. Put *Engine* in the Variable Name and Caption fields, but this time, set the Input Type to *DropDown List Menu*. In the Input Options field, put *Gas||Diesel*, and put *Gas* in the Default Value field. Click on the "Save" button. We could also have set the Input Type to *Radio Options* or *Listbox (single select)*.

In MODX Revolution, you can also right-click on "Template Variables" in the "Elements" tree and select "Quick Create TV." You have less control over the input type and no control over the output type, but it's a handy way to create a simple TV without leaving whatever you are editing.

Assigning Template Variables

We've created our TVs, but we haven't assigned them to any template yet, so they're not usable. Go to the "Elements" tab, right-click on the "Vehicle" template, and select "Edit Template." Click on the "Assigned Template Variables" tab at the right, and you should see our three TVs there. Check the checkboxes next to all three, and click on the "Save" button.

Our three TVs should now show up in the Create/Edit Resource panel for any document that uses that template. Right-click on each of the individual documents under the "Vehicle" container. For each one, select "Edit Resource," click on the "Template Variable" tab on the right, and fill in the "Year," "Mileage," and "Engine" TVs, and save each document.

There is also a green "Set to Default" icon for each TV. To see it, you have to hover the mouse over the name of the TV. When you click on the icon, MODX will ignore any current settings and return the TV to the default value (if any) set when creating or editing the TV itself.

 If you have a form customization rule that overrides the default value of the TV, that rule will be honored when you click on the "Set to Default" icon.

Displaying Template Variables

We've created and assigned each of our TVs, but they won't show up anywhere until we use MODX tags to display them. TVs are displayed with resource tags, just like the other resource fields of a document. To make them show up, we need to put resource tags in the template we created to display each car's information.

Go to the "Elements" tab, right-click on the "Vehicle" template, and select "Edit Template." Scroll down to where the [[*content]] tag is located. Change that section to include tags for our TVs:

```
<p>Inventory Number: [[*pagetitle]]</p>
<p>Year: [[*Year]]</p>
<p>Mileage: [[*Mileage]]</p>
<p>Engine: [[*Engine]]</p>
[[!*content]]
```

Save the Vehicle template. Now the TVs should be displayed any time one of the car documents is viewed. Right-click on one of the individual car documents, and select "Preview Resource." You should see the full information for each auto.

In this tutorial, we created a separate template for the page that displays each auto. We put the formatting information for that page into the template. In reality, you might not want to do it that way. Creating another template should generally be avoided if possible.

It might be better to use the main template for the site and put the TV tags and their accompanying text into a chunk instead. Then, a chunk tag with the name of the chunk could go in the Resource Content field of each car's document. We call that kind of template-like chunk a "Tpl chunk." We didn't do it that way here because we haven't covered Tpl chunks yet. We'll discuss them further in later chapters.

 If you want certain TVs available to you but hidden from any of your manager editors, or visible but not editable by certain users, you can use the Revolution permission system to create whatever scheme you need. See the Security Permissions chapter (Chapter 10) for more details.

Using a TV to Control a Snippet

Suppose you have a snippet called *NewsSummary* that displays summaries of news articles. One of the snippet's properties (**&numberToShow**) controls how many articles are shown on the page. The snippet tag might look like this:

```
[[NewsSummary? &numberToShow=`3`]]
```

You could certainly control the number of articles to show by editing the snippet tag, but suppose you have a user who is not very comfortable editing "code." If the user messes up the snippet tag, the odds are good that no articles will show at all. As an alternative, you could create a template variable called *NumberToShow* (it doesn't need to have the same name as the snippet property). Make it an integer type, put *NumberToShow* in the Caption field, and leave the output type as *default*. Now, change the snippet tag to look like this:

```
[[NewsSummary? &numberToShow=`[[*NumberToShow]]`]]
```

When your user edits the News document, the TV will show on the Create/Edit Resource panel. The user simply has to type in the number in the TV field and never has to touch the code of the snippet tag.

Template Variable Fields

Now that we've created and used a few template variables, let's look more closely at the fields available on the General Information tab of the Create/Edit Template Variable panel.

Variable Name

The Variable Name field sets the name MODX will recognize the TV by. It is the name you will use in any resource tag referring to that TV. You can also access the TV by that name and retrieve its value in a snippet or plugin. Remember that these are case-sensitive.

Caption

The Caption field is used to create the caption next to the TV in the Create/Edit Resource panel. Remember that when you create a TV tag or reference a TV in a snippet, you need to use the Variable Name and not the Caption.

Description

The optional Description field is used to describe the function of the TV. The description will appear when the user hovers the mouse over the TV's caption on the Create/Edit Resource panel. It's a good idea to put any hints about how the TV is used in this field unless it's obvious (and even then, it makes things look more professional to a client).

Category

Like any element in MODX, TVs can be assigned to a category. Assigning a category is optional and is usually only necessary when you have a lot of TVs and edit them often. It makes them easier to find in the Element tree. You might also want to do this if you'd like to hide all the TVs in a category from some users. You can see how to do this in the Security chapter (Chapter 10).

TVs can only be assigned to an existing category, so you need to create the category (by right-clicking on "Categories" in the tree and selecting "Create Category") before assigning a TV to it. If you create TVs with no category, you can always create a category later and edit the TVs to assign them to the category. TVs can also be assigned to a category by dragging and dropping them into the category folder.

Lock Variable for Editing

Checking this checkbox locks the TV so that only administrators with the appropriate credentials can edit it.

Sort Order

The value you put in this field determines the order in which the TVs will appear to editors in the Create/Edit Resource panel. TVs with lower numbers will appear first. If you leave this field empty, the TVs will generally appear in the order in which you created them. This field has no effect on where the TVs will appear in a web page. It only affects their display in the Create/Edit Resource panel.

Input Type

As of MODX 2.1, the input type is set with a drop-down menu on the Input Options tab of the Create/Edit Template Variable panel. The Input Type field determines what kind of TV you are creating. Note that it refers to how the TV will appear to a manager editing a resource in the MODX back end, not to how the TV will be rendered on a web page in the front end.

 For many types of template variables, when you select the Input Type, a form will appear that lets you set validation options for the editor's input and other options for that TV type.

We'll look more closely at the various TV input types once we've covered all the fields.

Input Option Values

As of MODX 2.1, input option values are set on the Input Options tab of the Create/Edit Template Variable panel.

Some TVs will present limited options to the manager editor of a resource in the form of radio buttons or a drop-down list or menu. For those TVs, the Input Option Values field holds the possible values separated by double pipes (||). Be sure that there is no space between the two pipes.

For a drop-down menu containing the choices red, blue, and green, for example, the Input Option Values field could contain red||blue||green.

What if the options you want to use are long and you want to show the manager editor a shorthand version (sort of like using Menu Title for documents)?

There is a more complicated version of the option string you can use with each of the choices followed by two equals (==) signs and then the longer version, like this:

```
red==Red as a rose||blue==Blue as the sky||green==Green as the grass
```

Notice that the three choices are still separated by the double pipes, but we've added ==*LongerName* after each choice. Be sure to use two equals signs if you use this method or your TV won't work.

Now, the manager editing the document will see just red, blue, and green, but the TV resource tag on the page will produce one of the three longer versions. If you set a default value for the TV, be sure to use the part after the == for the default value or it will not be set.

For input types other than radio buttons, list boxes, and drop-down menus, the Input Option Values field is ignored.

The Input Option Values field can also contain an @ binding. We'll look at those a little later in this chapter.

Default Value

The Default Value field holds the default value that will be given to the TV before it is edited by a user in the Create/Edit Resource panel. A commonly used default value is @INHERIT, which gives the TV the same value as its parent resource (the resource it is under in the Resource tree). You can also put a default value after the @INHERIT binding:

```
@INHERIT blue
```

You're not required to use a Default Value, but it's a good practice because it avoids the possibility of an empty TV appearing (actually, not appearing) on a page in the front end.

 For certain types of TVs, if you have set a default value using the form @INHERIT *value*, the TV may show no value when you create a new resource, and clicking on the "Set to Default" icon may make it appear to be empty. It still has the default value, however.

Output Type

The Output Type field determines how the TV will be rendered in the front end when displayed via a resource tag. We'll discuss these Output Types in more detail a little later in this chapter. First, we'll cover the Input Types.

TV Input Types in Detail

The following is a list of the various Input Types for TVs and how they work. Remember that these determine how the TV looks and behaves in the Create/Edit Resource panel for a manager user in the MODX back end. They have no direct effect on how the TV is rendered in the front end (or wherever the TV resource tag is used). The rendering is controlled by the Output Type field, which is described in the following section. You can also create custom TV input and output types, but the process is beyond the scope of this book. Here are the standard MODX Input Types:

Auto-Tag

The Auto-Tag TV makes it easy to place resources in one or more categories by "tagging" them for later retrieval. It can be a little confusing at first, but MODX handles most of the complexity behind the scenes. The actual content of an Auto-Tag TV is just a list of tags separated by commas.

Suppose you are posting a recipe for chicken soup on a cooking blog. You might have a TV called "ingredients" containing the following tags:

```
chicken,carrots,celery,noodles
```

A tag like the one below will show that comma-separated list on a web page, but usually Auto-Tag TVs are not displayed directly. Instead, they are used by snippets to select resources to show (e.g., showing links to all posts containing chicken).

```
[[*ingredients]]
```

When you first edit a resource with an Auto-Tag TV, the TV will simply present you with a standard text input field. The input field will be empty unless the TV has a default value. You can enter any tags for the resource, separated by commas, in the input field. The convenience comes after you have entered a few tags in various resources. Once you do that, every time you edit a resource with that TV, you'll see a list below the input field showing all the tags used for that TV in all documents that have that TV. Every time you add a new tag, it will be added to the list for all resources using the TV. Better yet, you can add existing tags to the input field just by clicking on them in the list below it. The ones actually attached to that resource will appear in the input field and will be highlighted in green in the list below it. You can also click on a tag highlighted in green to remove it from the list.

Remember that the only tags stored for the current resource are the ones in the input field. The ones below it are just there for your convenience. If you want a tag that's not on the list, you can type it in the input field. Be sure all tags in the input field are separated by commas.

Unless you are doing something unusual, all Auto-Tag TVs should have "Delimiter" as their output type and the delimiter should always be a comma.

Here is an example of a snippet that will show links to all posts containing chicken if it is listed in an Auto-Tag TV called "ingredients" (assuming that all recipes are under a container in the Resource tree called "Recipes"):

```php
<?php
$recipesContainer = $modx->getObject('modResource',
    array('pagetitle'=>'Recipes'));
$recipes = $recipesContainer->getMany('Children');
foreach ($recipes as $recipe) {
    $ingredients = explode(',',$recipe->getTVValue('ingredients'));
    if (in_array('chicken',$ingredients)) {
        $output .= '<p>Recipe: <a href="[[~' . $recipe->get('id') .
            ']]">' . $recipe->get('pagetitle') . '</a></p>';
    }
}
return $output;
```

The snippet above is very simple-minded since it only gets recipes containing chicken. More likely, you would have the tags used to select resources specified as properties in the snippet tag or in a form. By the time you read this, there may be add-on components that make use of Auto-Tag TVs to select resources and display links to them.

Checkbox

This option presents the user with a single checkbox or a group of checkboxes that can be checked or unchecked. To display a list of checkboxes, separate the values with double pipes like this:

```
red||blue||green
```

You can also used the fancier version described at the beginning of this section with both || and == delimiters to show the editor a briefer version and have the longer version set as the TV's value.

Setting a default value will determine if the checkbox is checked. Setting the default value to red will check the red checkbox in the example above. If you want more than one box checked by default, you can use this form for the default value:

```
red||green
```

Checkboxes are most often used by a snippet that checks the state of the TV and produces the appropriate output in the front end.

Date

The date option gives the user a date-picker in the form of a pop-up calendar that allows the user to select a single date.

The date selected will be shown in the front end via the TV's resource tag (which can be formatted using the output modifiers described in Chapter 4). The date TV can also be evaluated by a snippet or plugin, which can then generate the appropriate output.

DropDown List Menu

This option renders the TV as a drop-down menu of choices. The user can select any one of the choices.

The default choice (if any) is highlighted, and its value will be assigned to the TV if the user makes no selection.

Email

The email option displays a single-line text area for entering an email address. The address can be displayed with a resource tag or used in a snippet that sends email.

At this writing, the address entered is not validated in any way, but it may be in future versions.

File

This option displays a single-line text area for entering a file path along with a button that allows the user to browse to a file to select. Once the user has selected a file, it will be shown in the input field. If there is a default value, it will also be shown in the input field.

The TV will hold the path to the file selected, which can be displayed, used in an href tag, or used by a snippet or plugin.

Hidden

As you might guess, TVs with a hidden input type do not show when editing a resource. Although they won't appear on the Template Variables tab of the Create/Edit resource panel, they will still appear in the Element tree, and their values can be displayed with tags. Their values can be inherited via @ bindings (more on these later in this chapter), or set as default values (or both). Their values can also be set or retrieved in code.

The Hidden input type can be useful if you want to hide a TV without the trouble of form customization or the MODX security permissions system. You might want to have a page count TV to hold the number of times a page has been visited, for example. If you didn't want users in the Manager to be able to edit it, a Hidden TV would be a good choice.

What if you need to set the value of a hidden TV for one or more specific resources? You can change its type to Text, set its value for any resources, and (after saving the resources), set the type back to Hidden.

HTML Area

This option is deprecated. Use either Textarea or Rich Text.

Image

Like the File option, the Image option presents a single-line text box for entering the path to an image. If there is a default value, it will be shown in the box. A drop-down arrow allows the user to browse to the image file. While browsing, the user will see a preview of the image. If you expect users to browse to an image file, it's important to have a default value that will put them in the correct directory. At this writing, starting the file browser in the default directory is not implemented yet but is planned for future versions.

Once the user has selected an image, it will be shown in the box.

This input type is usually used with the Image Output Type, which has several fields that provide attributes for the image such as height, width, alt text, etc. (see the Image Output Type below).

Listbox (Multi-Select)

This option displays a listbox showing the choices in the Input Options Value field (required). The user can select more than one choice. Separate the choices with || (and optionally == as described at the beginning of this section).

The default value will be highlighted and will be assigned if the user doesn't select any choices.

Listbox (Single-Select)

This Listbox option works exactly like the Multi-Select Listbox, but the user can only select one choice. Separate the choices with || (and optionally == as described at the beginning of this section).

Number

The Number option presents a single-line text box in which the user can enter a number. At this writing, the value is not validated in any way (so the user can enter text instead of numbers), but future versions may include validation.

Radio Options

This option displays a set of standard radio buttons. The user can select only one. The default choice will be selected, and the TV will be assigned the default value if the user makes no selection. Separate the choices with || (and optionally == as described at the beginning of this section).

Resource List

When using this input type, you select the parent or parents (a comma-separated list) of the resources to display. When the TV is edited in the Manager, the user will see a drop-down list showing the page titles of all children of the specified parent(s). The actual value stored in the TV for each resource will be the resource ID of the child resource selected by the user.

Rich Text

This option displays an edit box with the Rich Text editor (e.g., TinyMCE) displayed for WYSIWYG editing.

Note that this will only work if you have a Rich Text editor installed.

 Be sure not to select "Rich Text" as the Output Type for a Rich Text TV, or the page viewer will be looking at raw (X)HTML code.

Text

The Text option presents a single line input for entering text.

The user's input can be longer than the visible area. The text will scroll as the user enters text.

Textarea

This option presents a rectangular box for entering text.

Any carriage returns will be ignored, and all text will be run together, but HTML entered by the user will be preserved. If the user's input passes the bottom of the box, a scroll bar will appear.

Textarea (mini)

This option works just like the Textarea option but with a smaller box.

TV Output Types in Detail

The following is a list of the various Output Types for TVs and how they work. Remember that these determine how the TV looks and behaves in the front end of the site (or wherever the TV resource tag is used). As of MODX 2.1, these are set on the Output Options tab of the Create/Edit Template Variable panel.

Date

Assuming that the date is a valid date (either entered by the user or selected from the date-picker widget), the date will be formatted using the conventions of the PHP `strftime()` function.

 Although the type is called "Date," it can be used for many date and time displays including day of the week, year, week number, time only, month name, etc. (see the table below).

When you select Date as the Output Type while creating or editing a TV, two more entry fields will open below the type. The first is the Date Format box where you enter the formatting code. The second field allows you to specify whether today's date will be used if there is no entry.

The default value for the Date Format is `%A %d, %B %Y`.

The first code, `%A`, specifies the full weekday name (e.g., Monday). The second, `%d`, gives you the two-digit day of the month with a leading zero for single digits. The third code, `%B`, specifies the full month name (e.g., September). The final code, `%Y`, displays the four-digit year. The comma will be rendered as a comma and the spaces as spaces. The output will look like this:

```
Monday 22, September 2011
```

Table 5-1 contains an abbreviated list of the possible formatting codes, although a given code may not always be available on the server. For a complete list and more information about how they are rendered, do a web search for *PHP strftime*.

Table 5-1: Date and Time Formatting Codes

Code	Display	Example
%a	Short weekday name	Sun
%A	Full weekday name	Sunday
%b	Short month name	Jan
%B	Full month name	January
%c	Local date and time	Wed Jan 7 00:22:10 2011
%C	Century (the year divided by 100, range 00 to 99)	20
%d	Day of the month (01 to 31)	03
%D	Same as %m/%d/%y	04/29/10
%e	Day of the month (1 to 31)	3
%H	Hour (24-hour clock)	00-23
%I	Hour (12-hour clock)	01-12
%j	Day of the year	001 to 366
%m	Month	01 to 12
%M	Minute	00 to 59
%n	Newline character	\n
%p	am or pm	amz
%P	AM or PM	AM
%r	Same as %I:%M:%S %p	08:23:11 PM
%R	Same as %H:%M	23:11
%S	Second	00 to 59
%t	Tab character	\t
%T	Same as %H:%M:%S	26:12:27
%u	Weekday (Monday=1)	01 to 07
%w	Weekday (Sunday=0)	00 to 06
%x	Date only	01/25/09
%X	Time only	02:58:12
%y	Two-digit year	09
%Y	Four-digit year	2011
%Z or %z	Time zone offset or name	-005 or EST
%%	A literal % character	%

Default

The Default option simply renders the contents of the TV as a string of text. The only exception is that if the content includes the delimiter for checkboxes, radio options, or lists (||), the delimiters are removed.

Delimiter

This option works just like the Default option except that the delimiters are replaced rather than removed. If you select this Output Type, a box will appear so that you can specify a delimiter. If you leave it blank, a comma will be used.

The best use of this option is to present a list of items with checkboxes next to them. For example, suppose you choose Checkbox for the Input Type and put *red||blue||green* in the Input Option Values field. When editing a document with this TV, three checkboxes will appear. If the manager editor of the resource checks Red and Green, the resource tag for the TV will show red,green.

This technique is of limited use for rendering output directly, but remember that a TV resource tag can be used as the value of a snippet property. The TV's value can also be accessed by a plugin.

Suppose you have a set of small bits of content that you want to show on some pages and not others. You could create a separate chunk for each bit, but it would be more efficient to just create a TV (let's call it *bits*) with checkboxes, one for each bit. Then, create a snippet that showed the appropriate ones based on which boxes were checked. The snippet would receive the comma-delimited list of bits to show when called like this:

```
[[snippet_name? &ShowBits=`[[*bits]]` ]]
```

We'll discuss this technique in more detail when we cover snippets.

HTML Tag

This option will wrap the value of the TV with the HTML tag of your choice. It is most often used with <div> (the default) and <span> tags. Using the fields that appear when you select this option, you can give the tag an id, a class, a style (e.g., {color: #090; line-height: 1.2}), and any attributes you like. Note that no quotes or equal signs are allowed in any field.

If the content of the TV is "Hello World," for example, and you set the Tag name to *div*, the ID to *MyId*, and the Class to *MyClass*, the TV resource tag will produce this (X)HTML code:

```
<div id="MyId" class="MyClass">Hello World</div>
```

Image

The Image option works like the HTML Tag option except that it surrounds the value of the TV with an image tag. The editor of the resource simply selects the image in the image browser (or types in the image path), and MODX does the rest. Clicking on the arrow at the right of the TV field will bring up the resource browser. You can navigate to the image by clicking on the tree at the left to navigate to the correct directory. Once you are in the right directory, double-click on the image you want.

When you select this Output Option while editing or creating a TV, a set of fields will drop down allowing you to set image attributes like alt text, H space, V space, align, name, class, id, etc. Attributes that are left blank will not be used in the image tag. One drawback of this option is that all images entered in the TV will have the same alt text, class, id, etc., which is usually not what you want. One alternative is to use the default output type, create separate TVs for those attributes, and make your own <img> tag containing content tags for each TV.

 When you use an Image TV, MODX creates the entire <img> tag. Be sure not to put any part of the tag in your content or the (X)HTML will be invalid, and the images won't be displayed. In other words, put nothing but the TV tag where you want the image to appear.

Rich Text

This option allows you to present the user with a rich text editor to enter content in the front end. Usually, this is used in a form that the user will submit. The submitted form will contain the rich text entered by the user. A Rich Text editor box will appear wherever the template variable resource tag is placed as long as you have a Rich Text Editor like TinyMCE installed on the site.

When you choose this Output Type, fields will appear that let you set the height and width of the text area the user sees.

String

This Output Type will display a string and provide some basic control over its formatting. The choices are:

- None (output as entered)
- Uppercase (all caps)
- Lowercase (all lowercase)
- Sentence Case (first letter capitalized)
- Capitalize (first letter of each word in caps)

 Note that Capitalize is not the same as headline case where articles and prepositions are not capitalized. Capitalize uses uppercase for the first letter of every word.

URL

This choice works like the Image and HTML Tag options. It produces a link in the rendered page. The link can be to a page at the site or anywhere on the Web.

When you select URL, new fields will drop down that allow you to set the attributes of the URL. The Display Text field is what the user will see as the text of the visible link on the rendered page. The Title field is what the user will see as a tip when hovering over the link.

The Class field will give the URL a class. Entering *MyClass* in the field will add class="MyClass" to the tag).

The Style field allows you to enter style information. Putting {color: #090; line-height: 1.2} in the field will add style="{color: #090; line-height: 1.2}" to the tag.

The Target field provides the HTML target attribute. Using *_blank* will open the link in a new window. Using *_self* will open the link in the same window. You can also use *_parent*, *_top* or the name of a frameset to open the link in.

You should never put **http://** in any of the fields (except in the rare case where you want it in the link text that appears on the page). MODX will add it for you.

If the link is to a page at your site, you should always use a MODX link tag in the default value field or as the value of the TV on the Create/Edit Resource panel. This link tag would provide a link to document 12:

```
[[~12]]
```

The default value will be used if the user doesn't enter a value. As we'll see in the section below, you can also use either @INHERIT or @INHERIT *value* as the default value.

Properties Tab

Default properties and property sets for template variables are new in MODX Revolution. Properties are basically just sets of variables, each with a name, a type, and a value. By default, your template variable has no default properties, but you can add them by clicking on "Create Property" in the grid. You'll have to unlock the grid first by clicking on "Default Properties Locked" to toggle the lock on the grid.

One use of TV properties is to set variables that will control snippets or plugins that access the template variable. If your template variable is displayed by a snippet (rather than by a resource tag), for example, you may want to set variables that will tell the snippet what to do with the TV. See the Chapter 8 for information about how to get a TV's value in a snippet.

If your TV contains placeholder tags, they will be replaced by the values from the TVs default properties or any attached property set. In other words a [[+size]] placeholder tag would be replaced by the value of the property named size. You can also set properties in the content tag used to display the TV, though this is not often done:

```
[[*TvName? &property1=`value1` &property2=`value2`]]
```

Properties and property sets are seldom used with template variables. We'll discuss them in much more detail later in the book.

Template Access Tab

On the template variable's Template Access tab, you set which templates will be able to use the TV by checking the checkbox next to each template's name. This is the equivalent of checking the TV's name on the Assigned Template Variables tab of the Create/Edit Template panel. The template variable will not show up for resources until assigned to a template using either method. If you have created TVs, and they are not showing up on the Create/Edit Resources panel, there's a good chance that you forgot this step.

Access Permissions Tab

You can determine which resource groups the TV belongs to on the Access Permissions tab. If you assign the TV to one or more resource groups, only users with rights to those groups will be able to modify it. If you don't assign the TV to any groups, all users with access to the particular resource will be able to modify it. See the Permissions chapter (Chapter 10) for more information on restricting access to template variables.

@ BINDINGS

@ bindings are a way of extending template variables. Putting an @ binding in the field of a template variable tells MODX to treat the template variable in a special way. Unlike snippet properties, @ bindings take no quotes, back-ticks, or equals signs.

 Note that @ bindings are only intended for use in the Default Value or Input Option Values fields of a template variable.

In earlier versions of MODX, some snippets were written to process the `@FILE` binding as a property in the snippet tag. This was usually used to pull in a config file in order to avoid very long snippet tags for snippets with lots of properties (e.g., getResources). It's possible that MODX Revolution snippets will do this (and you are free to create ones that do), but it's no longer necessary for two reasons. First, MODX Revolution allows multi-line snippet tags, and second, property sets are a much better solution (more on those later). So in Revolution, it's best to confine @ bindings to use in template variables.

 Unlike many MODX objects, the names of @ bindings are always in all upper-case text.

In the Default Value field of a template variable, the @ binding determines what is seen when the TV is shown (via a resource tag) in the front end. In the Input Option Values field, the @ binding determines what is shown in the Create/Edit Resource panel in the Manager. We'll give some examples of this as we go along.

Just a reminder — referring to a template variable to be rendered in the front end is done with a resource tag like this one:

`[[*template_variable_name]]`

The @INHERIT Binding

This binding gives the template variable (TV) the value contained in the TV field of its parent (the resource above it in the Resource tree). The @INHERIT binding is recursive, so if the parent also has @INHERIT in the field, the value will be retrieved from the grandparent, and so on up the chain of parents.

 With the @INHERIT binding, if no ancestor has the value set, or if all ancestors have it set to @INHERIT and there is no default value, you will see no output where the TV resource tag is placed.

Example: @INHERIT

The @INHERIT binding is extremely useful for setting both Input Option and Default Values fields for multiple documents. Let's look at an example. Suppose you want every page in a certain section of your site to output the name of a baseball team, but you want different sections of the site to have a different default value for the TV. In the Manager, perform the following steps.

1. Create the *TeamName* template variable, and assign it to a template as described above.

2. While editing the TV, set the following fields:

   - Input Type: *Radio Options*

   - Input Option Values: *Cubs||Cardinals||Twins*

   - Default Value: *@INHERIT*

   - Output Type: *Default*

3. Create two container documents that use the template with the *TeamName* TV. Set the value of the TV to *Cubs* in one and *Cardinals* in the other.

Now, all the children below the Cubs container will have the value set to Cubs, and the children below the Cardinals container will have it set to Cardinals. The appropriate team name will appear wherever you put the [[*TeamName]] tag.

Note that we could have used @INHERIT Twins for the default value of the TV, so the default would be Twins in cases where someone forgets to set the value when editing a document.

> With certain types of TVs (e.g., radio buttons), there is no way to show a value like @INHERIT Twins. In that case, the TV will appear blank or unselected for a new resource, and clicking on the "Set to Default" icon for the TV will make it appear unselected again. In both cases, the TV has the original default value; it just won't be shown.

Another use for the @INHERIT binding is to present different images in various parts of your site. Just create a TV called *DisplayImage*. Then, set the "Input Type" field to *Radio Options*, the "Input Option Values" field to the URLs of the images, separated by //, the "Default Value" to *@INHERIT* (followed optionally by the URL of a default image), and the "Output Type" to *Image*.

Where you want the image to appear in the template, place the following tag:

```
[[*DisplayImage]]
```

MODX will create the appropriate (X)HTML image tag. As we mentioned earlier, the drawback of this method is that all the images will have the same attributes (e.g., alt value). The solution to that problem is to use text as the Output Type, create separate TVs for the attributes, create your own <img> tag, and use placeholders for the various attributes:

```
<img src="[[*DisplayImage]]" alt="[[*ImageAlt]] />
```

Be careful not to change the @INHERIT value on pages that you want to inherit the value from higher up in the tree.

The @CHUNK Binding

The @CHUNK binding causes the TV resource tag to be replaced with the contents of the named chunk.

Example: @CHUNK *MyChunk*

Suppose, for example, that you have a number of products with three different Warranties (say, 1, 3, and 5 years). Each product is in its own document, but you don't want to repeat the Warranty text on every document. You can create a template variable called *Warranty* and put the three Warranties in three separate chunks (called *Warranty1*, *Warranty3*, and *Warranty5*). You can then create a set of radio buttons (using @INHERIT) as we did above for the *TeamName* TV and place three @CHUNK bindings in the "Input Options Value" field:

```
@CHUNK Warranty1||@CHUNK Waranty3||@CHUNK Warranty5
```

The Manager user who creates the product page can simply click on the appropriate Warranty, and it will replace the resource tag on the product page in the front end.

```
[[*Warranty]]
```

Another way of doing the same thing is to put all the Warranties in a single chunk (let's call it *Warranties*) using the delimiters we discussed above. The chunk's content would look like this:

```
Warranty1==Text for Warranty1 here||Warranty3==Text for Warranty3
here||Warranty5==Text for Warranty5 here
```

Now all you need to put in the Input Options Values field is this:

```
@CHUNK Warranties
```

The Manager editor will still see just the three choices (Warranty1, Warranty3, Warranty5), but the three warranties are all in the same chunk where you can edit them without jumping from chunk to chunk.

Let's look at another use for the technique we've just described. It also works to specify images to use in various parts of the site. In this case, we'd create a chunk called *Images* and use the following for its content:

```
Flowers==assets/images/flowers.jpg||Trees==assets/images/trees.jpg||
    Lake Scene==assets/images/lake.jpg
```

Now, we'd create a template variable called *Image* with the Input Type set to *Radio Options* (or one of the drop-down lists), the Input Option Values field set to *@CHUNK Images*, and the Output Type set to *Image*.

The Manager editor of each document would just see Flowers, Trees, and Lake Scene, but the following (X)HTML code would show the appropriate image:

```
<img src="[[*Image]]" />
```

The @RESOURCE Binding

Sometimes, you want to pull the **content** field of another document into the current document. In that case the @RESOURCE binding is what you want.

Example: @RESOURCE 12

The TV resource tag is replaced with the **content** field of the specified document. In MODX Evolution, this binding is called @DOCUMENT, which is deprecated in MODX Revolution.

 Remember that the document referred to in an @RESOURCE binding is specified by Resource ID, not by the document's Title.

If you create a template variable called *InsertDocument*, and give it a value of @RESOURCE 12, the following resource tag will be replaced by what is in the **content** field of document 12.

`[[*InsertDocument]]`

 You could put several @RESOURCE bindings separated by || into the Input Options field as we did above with @CHUNK to give the Manager editor several choices of documents to insert.

The @FILE Binding

With the @FILE binding, the TV resource tag will be replaced by the contents of the specified file. The part following @FILE is always a file path from the root of the MODX install and is always specified without a leading slash.

Example: @FILE assets/*my_file*

Sometimes, it is preferable to keep content in files. In some circumstances, it will speed up page loads. It also allows you to bulk-upload large amounts of content, use version control on the content, or use a specialized editor on a local machine for editing.

The @DIRECTORY binding

The @DIRECTORY binding is meant to be used in the Input Option Values field with a listbox, drop-down menu, or radio options. The Manager editor will be presented with a list of all files and folders in the directory to choose from.

One use of the @DIRECTORY binding is to provide yet another way to allow the user to select an image to display from a directory of image files. In that case, the Output Type is set to Image, and the Input Option Values field is set to @DIRECTORY name_of_image_directory/.

Example: @DIRECTORY assets/images/

As with the @FILE binding, directories are specified by absolute path from the root of the MODX install and without a leading slash. With the @DIRECTORY binding, however, a trailing slash is also necessary.

The Manager editor will see a list of just the file names, but the resource tag will contain the full path for the selected file.

The @DIRECTORY binding doesn't provide any way of filtering or sorting the list of files and directories, so its use is limited.

The @SELECT binding

The @SELECT binding produces the results of a MySQL query to the MODX database.

Example: @SELECT name, phone FROM customers

Used most often in the Input Option Values field for drop-down list TVs, this binding provides the Manager editor with a set of choices taken from the MODX database using a SELECT MySQL statement. The term following the FROM is the name of the table in the MODX database.

Example: @SELECT name, phone FROM customers

The @EVAL binding

The @EVAL binding is most often used in the Default Value field. Using @EVAL can create serious security problems if the code uses variables provided by the user or the browser (e.g., $_GET), so use it with care, or don't use it at all. The @EVAL binding replaces the TV with the results of the PHP code following @EVAL. @EVAL bindings should always have a "return" statement somewhere in the code. The value returned is what is used to replace the @EVAL binding. Because the value in an @EVAL binding is a line of PHP code, it must end with a semicolon.

Example: @EVAL return "Current time: ".time();

The @ bindings can be nested.

Example: @EVAL return "Message: @CHUNK MessageChunk";

Summary

A template is a framework for the creation of a rendered web page. MODX renders a web page by retrieving the template for the page and replacing all the MODX tags in the template. Much of the template is standard (X)HTML, but it's best not to put any actual content in the template in order to separate the content from the formatting. As a best practice, all actual content should be injected using tags.

Template variables are extra resource fields that you create. TVs have two main functions. One is to supplement the standard resource fields (**pagetitle**, **alias**, **content**, etc.) to provide extra content areas that can be filled and edited in the Create/Edit resource panel. You can limit the input options for a TV using drop-down lists, radio options, or checkboxes. The other function of TVs is to serve as variables that control the presentation or formatting of the rendered page. TVs are attached to templates, and only pages that are tied to a particular template can use its TVs. In MODX Revolution, TVs can also have property sets that can be accessed by snippets or plugins that make use of the TV.

@ bindings allow you to extend template variables. They are only used in the Default Value and Input Options Values fields of the TV. The @INHERIT binding makes the field inherit the value from the TVs of parent (or ancestor) pages. The @CHUNK binding fills the field with the content of the specified chunk. The @RESOURCE binding fills the field with the Resource Content field of the specified document. The @FILE binding fills the field with the content of the specified file. The @DIRECTORY binding uses the file names in the specified directory to fill the field. The @SELECT binding fills the field with the results of a MySQL select query. The @EVAL binding fills the field with the results of the PHP code following @EVAL. The @EVAL binding can create some serious security problems, especially if created by naïve users.

MODX Evolution Notes

Template variables are very similar in Evolution and Revolution with some minor changes in the input and output types and their names. Output Type is referred to as "Widget" in Evolution, and there are a few extra widgets not available in Revolution at this writing.

To create a template variable in Evolution, go to **Elements → Manage Elements** on the Top Menu and click on the "Template Variables" tab; then click on "New Template Variable."

Fill in the TV fields, and check the checkboxes for the Templates that will use the TV. The TV will show up on the lower part of the Create/Edit Document panel for any document that uses a template that TV has been assigned to.

When viewing a template in Evolution, the available TVs are shown on the Assigned Template Variables tab, but unlike Revolution, you can't add or remove TVs there.

Chapter 6

Chunks and Properties

A MODX *chunk* is a bit of (X)HTML content that can be plugged in anywhere in a MODX site. It can be displayed using a chunk tag, and its content can be retrieved in code in a snippet or plugin.

Properties in MODX are simply two pieces of data that are connected to each other. They exist in an element's default properties and in property sets. Properties can also be set in any element tag.

In this chapter, we'll look at chunks and how to use them. We'll also take a look at how chunks and other MODX objects interact with default properties and property sets, both of which contain individual properties.

Introducing Chunks

A *chunk*, in MODX, is just a "chunk" of content, usually text or (X)HTML code optionally containing MODX tags. When MODX finds a chunk tag, it replaces it with the contents of the chunk. A snippet (which we'll cover in detail in a later chapter) is a piece of PHP code that MODX executes whenever it encounters a snippet tag.

New users of MODX sometimes have trouble remembering the difference between snippets and chunks. It helps if you think of a snippet as a "code snippet" and a chunk as a chunk of content.

Chunks can include snippets by having a snippet tag in their content. Snippets can also make use of the content of chunks.

Chunks are often used to contain reusable content that can be placed anywhere in a MODX template or document, but they also have many other uses. In the following sections, we'll look at chunks and the various ways they can be used.

To get started with chunks, we'll create a simple chunk and display it in a document.

Creating a Simple Chunk

By now, you should have a template that displays one or more of the resource fields of a document (e.g., **longtitle** and **content**). To complete this section, you'll need a template that displays the Resource Content field of a document with a tag like this (you probably have one already):

```
[[*content]]
```

Creating the Document and Chunk

In this section, we'll create a chunk called *HelloWorld* and display it in a document called `Hello`.

Creating the Hello Document

First, create a document by right-clicking on the little "web" context icon in the "Resources" tree at the left side of the Manager and selecting **Create → Create a Document Here.**

Put *Hello* in the Title field of the new document and *My Hello Document* in the Long Title field. Make sure the document is published. In the Resource Content field of the document, enter the following line:

```
Here's my Chunk: [[$HelloWorld]]
```

Save the document, and make sure it appears in the Resource tree.

Creating the HelloWorld Chunk

Now, let's create our chunk. Go to the "Elements" tab, right-click on "Chunks," and select "New Chunk." You should see the empty form for the new chunk on the right. Put *HelloWorld* in the Name field. Be careful: chunk names, like many other things in MODX, are case-sensitive, so be sure to spell it the same way in the Name field and in the chunk tag used in your document.

In the Chunk Code (html) field of the form, enter the following line, then save the chunk.

```
Hello World. This is the content of my chunk.
```

That's all there is to it. Make sure your new chunk appears in the Element tree under Chunks.

Previewing the Hello Document

Now go to the "Resources" tab. Find the `Hello` resource you created earlier, right-click on it, and select "Preview." You should see the content of your `Hello` document in your browser window (containing the output of your chunk). If the content of the chunk isn't there, check to make sure that the chunk name is spelled the same way in the tag and in the chunk itself.

Making Changes

Try changing the content of the chunk, saving it, and previewing the `Hello` document again. You can right-click on the chunk in the "Elements" tree and select "Quick Update Chunk" to edit the chunk's content in a pop-up window. This is handy because you'll remain on the Create/Edit panel of the `Hello` document.

The content of the chunk will appear anywhere MODX sees the chunk tag referring to it. If MODX doesn't find the chunk named in the chunk tag, it will remove the tag and put nothing in its place.

You could put the chunk tag in multiple documents to show the same content on multiple pages. If you wanted the chunk's content on every page that uses a particular template, you could put the chunk tag in the template instead of in the Resource Content field of a document.

Using Chunks with Other Tags

Earlier in the book, we discussed the various tags available in MODX, such as link tags and resource tags. You can put any of the MODX tags into a chunk. When the chunk is displayed in a MODX document, all resource tags used will refer to that document. In this section, we'll modify our HelloWorld chunk so that it tells us some things about the site and about the document the chunk tag is placed in.

Modifying the HelloWorld Chunk

Here, we'll make some changes to the HelloWorld chunk. We'll rename it and then add some tags to it so that it does something useful

Renaming the HelloWorld Chunk

Right-click on the "HelloWorld" chunk in the "Elements" tree (you may have to switch to the "Elements" tab first and then expand the Chunks section within it). Select "Edit Chunk."

You should see the HelloWorld chunk in the Create/Edit Chunk panel on the right side. Change the Name field of the chunk to *Info*, and add *My Info Chunk* to the description field. Don't save it yet; we're also going to change its content.

Editing the Info Chunk

Change the text in the Info chunk to look like the following example, then save it. If you feel lazy, you can leave out some of the lines with tags in them.

```
<!--Code for the Info Chunk -->
<h2>Site Information</h2>
<ul>
    <li>Site Name: [[++site_name]]</li>
    <li>Home Page ID: [[++site_start]]</li>
    <li>Site URL: [[!++site_url]]</li>
    <li>Base Path: [[++base_path]]</li>
    <li>Base URL: [[++base_url]]</li>
    <li>Failed Login Attempts: [[++failed_login_attempts]]</li>
    <li>Manager Theme: [[++manager_theme]]</li>
    <li>Site Unavailable Message: [[++site_unavailable_message]]</li>
    <li>Allowable upload types: [[++upload_files]]</li>
    <li>Maximum upload size: [[++upload_maxsize]]</li>
    <li>Uploadable image types: [[++upload_images]]</li>
</ul>
<h2>Document Information</h2>
<ul>
    <li>Id: [[*id]]</li>
    <li>Page Title: [[*pagetitle]]</li>
    <li>Long Title: [[*longtitle]]</li>
    <li>Is Folder: [[*isfolder]]</li>
    <li>Description: [[*description]]</li>
    <li>Alias: [[*alias]]</li>
    <li>Published: [[*published]]</li>
    <li>Summary : [[*introtext]]</li>
    <li>Template ID: [[*template]]</li>
    <li>Menu Index: [[*menuindex]]</li>
    <li>Searchable: [[*searchable]]</li>
    <li>Cacheable: [[*cacheable]]</li>
    <li>Created By: [[*createdby:userinfo=`fullname`]]</li>
    <li>Created On: [[*createdon]]</li>
    <li>Edited By: [[*editedby]]</li>
    <li>Edited On: [[*editedon]]</li>
    <li>Published By: [[*publishedby]]</li>
    <li>Published On: [[*publishedon]]</li>
    <li>Menu Title: [[*menutitle]]</li>
    <li>Hide From Menus: [[*hidemenu:if=`1`:`Yes`:else=`No`]]</li>
    <li>Publish Date: [[*pub_date]]</li>
    <li>Unpublish Date: [[*unpub_date]]</li>
</ul>
```

Previewing the New Chunk

Now right-click on the "Hello" resource you created earlier, and select "Preview Resource." Our chunk is missing. It's not there because we changed its name. The tag in the Hello resource still refers to the old name. Right-click on the "Hello" resource, and select "Quick Update Resource." In the pop-up window, change *HelloWorld* to *Info* in the chunk tag, and click on the "Save" button. Now preview the Hello document again. The chunk's output should appear. It should show information about both the Hello document and your MODX site.

Improving the Info Chunk

Some of the values in the list may be blank. There are various reasons why this would be the case. In addition, some of the tags will only show a 1 or a 0. You can correct this by changing the tags to include output modifiers like this (be sure to use back-ticks rather than single-quotes around all the values):

```
[[*isfolder:is=`1`:`Yes`:else=`No`]]
[[*published:is=`1`:`Yes`:else=`No`]]
[[*searchable:is=`1`:`Yes`:else=`No`]]
[[*cacheable:is=`1`:`Yes`:else=`No`]]
[[*hidemenu:is=`1`:`Yes`:else=`No`]]
```

Make those changes, and preview the Hello resource again. Those five should now show either "Yes" or "No." If you'd like to review the conditional modifiers used to display "Yes" and "No" here, see the Output Modifiers section in Chapter 4. Note that instead of the conditional output modifiers, we could have used a very simple snippet. The snippet would be faster and more efficient. We'll see how to do this later in the book when we cover snippets.

Another reason a value is missing is that the value you are referencing in the tag is not set. If you haven't given the document an **alias**, for example, that field will be blank.

Another possibility is an error in the tag itself. All tags must start with [[and end with]]. For the setting tags in the Site Information section, all should have ++ immediately after the opening braces, and that should be followed immediately by the setting name. There should be no spaces in any of the tags. The resource tags in the Document Information section should have only one * at the beginning of the tag.

The final thing to check is the spelling of the setting or resource field in the tag. The names are case-sensitive.

It is a really good exercise in getting familiar with MODX to make sure that every line displays some value.

Notice that the Description line does not show the description of the chunk. It shows the Description field from the document it is in. Resource tags will always show the resource field value from the current resource even if they are contained in a chunk that's pulled into the current resource with a chunk tag.

Using the Chunk in Other Documents

Try creating some other documents and inserting the [[$Info]] chunk tag into their Resource Content fields.

When you preview the various documents, you'll see that each page displays different information even though they all are displaying the same chunk. The Site Information section will be the same because the information is taken from the System Settings grid using setting tags. Settings are available across the site. The Document Information section will be different for each page, however, because it uses resource tags, which always get their values from the current document.

Further Possible Improvements

If you come from a programming background or understand sound design principles, you've realized that our Info chunk is not a very good example. It mixes data with presentation logic — always to be avoided. It also uses the same repeated pattern to display each line, which is inefficient.

You could use CSS to format the lists, but if you decided that you didn't like the way the list was displayed, you'd have to edit almost every line of the chunk.

It would be much better to use a snippet to display the data and even better yet if the snippet got the format to use from one or more Tpl chunks — separate chunks with a template-like pattern for each part of the display. We'll see how to use Tpl chunks to format output later in this chapter.

Other Uses for Chunks

The most obvious use for chunks is for "boilerplate" text that you want on multiple pages, or for template sections such as a page header, footer, or sidebar. In that case, the content is simply placed in a chunk, and the chunk tag is used wherever you need that content in a document or template. The chunk can be as big or small as you like and can contain any other MODX tags, although it cannot contain any PHP code.

Plugging in reusable content isn't the only use for chunks, however. It is probably the most common use, but chunks can do much, much more. In the previous chapter, we learned how to use chunks in template variables with the @CHUNK binding. In the following sections, we'll explore how to use chunks with snippets, how to store data in chunks, how to use Tpl chunks, and how to create and use TV-based chunks.

Using Chunks with Snippets

Chunks can be used with snippets in a number of ways. Using PHP code, a snippet can grab the content of any chunk, process it and/or format it, and return it. The returned output from the snippet will replace the snippet tag.

Doing it that way would not be a very good practice since the name of the chunk would have to be hard-coded into the snippet and the snippet could only process that single chunk. It would also make it more complicated to change the name of the chunk because the snippet would have to be rewritten.

There are two better methods for having a snippet process a chunk. First, you can send the contents of the chunk in a snippet property simply by placing a chunk tag as the value of one of the properties in the snippet tag, like this:

```
[[Snippetname? &chnk=`[[$Chunkname]]` ]]
```

In the example above, the entire content of the named chunk would be available in the snippet as the variable $chnk. Notice that the entire chunk tag is placed inside the back-ticks. When MODX sees that tag, it will replace it with the content of the named chunk.

Another (usually better) way of giving a snippet access to any chunk is to send the chunk's name rather than its content in a snippet property, like this:

```
[[Snippetname? &chunkName=`ChunkName`]]
```

In the example above, the snippet can use the chunk name sent in the tag to retrieve the content of the chunk. Now the snippet can process any chunk. This method has the additional advantage of letting the snippet have a default chunk name to use if no name is sent or the named chunk can't be found.

We'll see how a snippet can retrieve the content of a chunk in the snippet chapter (Chapter 7). This is the method usually used with Tpl chunks (more about those in just a bit).

As a preview, let's create a really simple snippet to display the Info chunk we created earlier.

Displaying a Chunk with a Snippet

In the "Elements" tree, right-click on the "Snippets" item, and select "New Snippet" in the drop-down list. Put *ShowInfo* in the Snippet Name field. Now add the following code in the Snippet code (php) field:

```
return $modx->getChunk($chunkName);
```

Be careful to type the line exactly as it appears above. Be sure to notice which letters are capitalized and which are not. Click on the "Save" button.

Now, click on the "Resources" tab to see the Resource tree. Right-click on the "Hello" document, and select "Edit Resource." Change the Resource Content field by replacing the chunk tag with the following snippet tag:

```
[[ShowInfo? &chunkName=`Info`]]
```

Again, be careful to type the line exactly as it appears here (but don't use bold type — snippet properties are just shown in bold in this book to make them stand out). Be sure to use back-ticks, not single-quotes, around the name of the chunk.

Now preview the Hello document (right-click on it, and select "Preview Resource"). You should see the information display as before. If not, you've probably made a typing error. Check both the snippet code and the snippet tag.

MODX is still displaying the contents of the chunk, but the process is completely different. In the snippet tag, we've created a property called **&chunkName** that sends the name of the chunk we want to show to the snippet. In the snippet, that name is available as the variable $chunkName. The snippet simply gets the chunk with that name and returns it. MODX replaces the snippet tag with the return value of the snippet.

We could send the name of any chunk in the chunk tag and MODX would display its content where the tag appears. If you have other chunks (or create them), you can replace "Info" with any of their names, and MODX will replace the tag with their contents.

If you just want to display the content of a chunk, using a chunk tag as we did earlier is the way to go. The advantage of using a snippet is that the snippet can do more complicated processing.

You could, for example, send other properties naming other chunks and/or telling the snippet how or when you wanted the chunk or chunks to be displayed. You could display one chunk during the day and another at night. You could display one chunk for logged-in users and another for everyone else. The snippet could also combine several chunks. The possibilities are limited only by your imagination and coding skills.

Using Chunks to Store Data

MODX has a variety of ways to store data. You can put it in documents, you can store it in the MODX database or in another database, or you can put it in a file. If the data is relatively simple, however, you can put it in a chunk. With data in a chunk, the data becomes much easier to modify (you simply edit the chunk) and to retrieve.

The EZfaq snippet, for example, stores the questions and answers that appear in the FAQ in an unpublished document, but they could just as easily be in a chunk. Let's imagine, though, that they are in a chunk, in this form:

```
Q:Do I have to pay anything to use MODX?
A:Absolutely not. MODX is a free, Open-Source platform.

Q:Can a snippet tag be used inside a chunk?
A:Yes, any MODX tag can be used inside a chunk.
etc.
END-FAQ
```

The snippet that displays the FAQ would then grab the content of the chunk, parse it into questions and answers, and display them all as desired. New questions and answers can be added, and existing ones can be modified at any time simply by editing the chunk.

Any new questions and answers will be displayed automatically by the snippet. Better yet, if the name of the FAQ content chunk is sent as a property in the snippet tag, the site can have as many FAQs as you need.

Data Retrieval Example

Let's create a simple display snippet that shows a list taken from a chunk. We won't go too deeply into snippets here (that's for later), but we'll see how easy it is to display data from a chunk and get another taste of the power of snippets.

Creating the Chunk

First, create a chunk called *ListData*. In the Chunk Code (html) field of the ListData chunk, type the following list:

```
apples,peaches,cherries,carrots,lettuce,apricots,pears,turnips,cabbages
```

Be sure to type all the items as a single line with no spaces (they may wrap in the editor, but don't press the "Enter" key). Be sure that there is a comma after each item and no comma at the end of the list.

Creating the Snippet

Now, create a snippet (right-click on "Snippets" in the "Elements" tree, and select "Quick Create Snippet"). Enter *SimpleShowList* in the Name field, and enter *Display a comma-separated list* in the Description field. In the Code field, carefully type the following PHP code (be careful to match the upper- and lowercase letters). Notice the difference between curly braces and parentheses, and be sure to use the dollar signs at the beginning of the variable names. Make sure that any line with parentheses or quotes has an even number of them. Pay particular attention to which lines end in semicolons and which lines don't.

```php
<?php
/* Code for the SimpleShowList Snippet */
$list = $modx->getChunk('ListData');
$listArray = explode(',' , $list);
$output = '<ul>';
foreach($listArray as $value) {
    $value = trim($value);
    $output .= '<li>';
    $output .= $value;
    $output .= '</li>';
}
$output .= '</ul>';
return $output;
?>
```

How it Works

We'll display our list in a minute, but first, let's look at what the snippet is doing:

This line gets the content of the chunk and puts it in a variable called $list.

```
$list = $modx->getChunk('ListData');
```

The next line converts the comma-separated list into a PHP array using the comma as a delimiter:

```
$listArray = explode(',' , $list);
```

The variable called $output contains the output of the snippet. The output will be returned at the end of the code and will replace the snippet tag on the web page. The next line sets $output to the <ul> tag, which will begin our list display.

```
$output = '<ul>';
```

The foreach() statement loops through every item in the list array. The part inside the curly braces will be executed once for each item on the list. On each pass the $value variable will contain one list item (i.e., apples on the first pass, peaches on the second, etc.) until all the items have been processed.

```
foreach($listArray as $value) {
    $value = trim($value);
    $output .= '<li>';
    $output .= $value;
    $output .= '</li>';
}
```

In the foreach() loop, we first "trim" each value to remove any leading or trailing spaces. The .= operator adds the value following it to the end of the $output variable. So, on each pass through the loop, we add a <li> tag, the list item, and a </li> tag to the output.

When the foreach() loop has completed, we add a closing </ul> tag and return the output.

```
$output .= '</ul>';
return $output;
```

Displaying the List

To display our list, you simply need to place the snippet tag *[[SimpleShowList]]* in a document wherever you'd like the list to appear.

Create a new document (or use the `Hello` document you created earlier), and put the following code in the Resource Content field:

```
<p>Here's the list:</p>
[[SimpleShowList]]
```

When you preview the document, you should see your list items rendered as an unordered list with bullets.

We could improve our snippet in many ways, such as sending the name of the chunk containing the list data as a property in the snippet tag and checking in the snippet to make sure it got there. We could also define the number of items in each row and offer the option to sort the items in various ways. We could also display the data in a table. We'll see examples showing some different ways to render output later on in the snippet chapters (Chapters 7 and 8).

Introducing Tpl Chunks

Tpl Chunks are special-purpose chunks used to format the output of snippets (and sometimes Plugins). They are very much like templates, and you will sometimes see them called that, although "Tpl chunks" is the correct term for them. Calling them templates leads to confusion with the MODX template object we described earlier in the book, so it's a good idea to always refer to them by their correct name (even though they are very template-like).

You won't find the term Tpl chunk in the MODX Manager because they're just regular chunks. The only thing different about them is how and why they are used. Let's look at an example.

We won't actually create the Tpl chunks or the snippet to show them here. We'll do that in the snippet chapter (Chapter 7), but let's get a taste of how they work.

A Better Formatting Option

Our SimpleShowList snippet was a definite step up from typing all the list items and (X) HTML code together on the same page. But what if you decide to change the format of the list? You might want an ordered list with numbers, a list with three items on each line, a table, or a list where every item was a link to another page. You'd have to rewrite the PHP code of your snippet for each change.

Think how much nicer it would be to have a snippet that never changed and used one or more Tpl chunks to describe the output for the snippet. Suppose that you had three Tpl chunks: one to describe how each item should be rendered, one to describe how each row should be rendered, and one to describe how the whole list should be formatted.

The names of the three Tpl chunks would be sent to your snippet as properties. The snippet would then grab the three, fill in the data (retrieving it from the data chunk we used above or getting it from somewhere else — a database table or a file, for example), and return the finished list to be rendered by the user's browser.

We could call our three Tpl chunks *ItemTpl*, *RowTpl*, and *OuterTpl*. We'd use placeholder tags in each Tpl to mark where replacements should be made. We'd use the prefix *sl.* for all our placeholders (short for *ShowList* — the name of our snippet) so that they won't be confused with any other MODX placeholders in use at the site. Here's what the three Tpl chunks might look like (note that the tags in them are placeholder tags).

Three Example Tpl Chunks

```
<!--ItemTpl Code -->
<span class= "sl.item_class">[[+sl.item]]</span>



<!--RowTpl Code -->
<li class="sl.row_class">[[+sl.row]]</li>



<!-- OuterTpl Code -->
<div class="sl.show_list ">
   <ul class="sl.outer_class">
   [[+sl.outer]]
</ul>
</div>
```

This looks confusing at first, but think of the three chunks as being nested. The `[[+sl.outer]]` placeholder in the OuterTpl chunk will be replaced with a series of RowTpl chunks. In each of those, the `[[+sl.row]]` placeholder will be replaced with a series of ItemTpl chunks. In each of those, the `[[+sl.item]]` placeholder will be replaced with a single data item. Let's look at that process in a concrete example.

Processing the Tpl Chunks

Our snippet gets a bit more complicated. In the properties, we send it the names of the three Tpl chunks, the name of the data chunk, and how many items to put in each row. It gets the OuterTpl chunk and sees that the actual list goes where the `[[+sl.outer]]` placeholder is located.

Let's say we've told it to place three items in each row. It uses the RowTpl chunk to create each row and uses the ItemTpl chunk to format each of the three items in the row, replacing the `[[+sl.item]]` placeholder with a single item from the data chunk and replacing the `[[+sl.row]]` placeholder with the three items.

When it runs out of items, the list is done and the snippet replaces the `[[+sl.outer]]` placeholder with the complete list. The whole, formatted list `div` is returned from the snippet and replaces the snippet tag in the resource's Resource Content field.

Advantages and Refinements

Now we can change the number of items in each row simply by changing one property in the snippet tag. We can reformat the whole list by making simple edits to the three Tpl chunks. If we wanted to present the data as a table, we'd simply edit the chunks to include table tags instead of list tags.

To be well-behaved, our snippet should have three default chunks to use in case the user fails to send any in the snippet tag. It should also have a default number of items per row.

We have one problem left, however. What if we want to use the snippet for two different lists on the same page and format them differently?

We can send the names of different Tpl chunks in each snippet tag, but the CSS classes will be the same for both lists, and we might not want that.

The solution is to put the CSS class names in placeholders, too, and send three more properties with those class names. Again, a well-behaved snippet would have default values for those classes in case none are sent in the snippet tag.

The actual snippet used here is beyond the scope of this chapter, but you can see the power of Tpl chunks for separating content from format and making your site easier to maintain. We'll see what the snippet looks like in Chapter 7 and create a working version of it.

As we mentioned earlier, several standard MODX snippets, such as Wayfinder and get-Resources, use Tpl chunks in exactly the way we've described here, so it's important to understand how Tpl chunks work in order to get the most out of MODX. Wayfinder uses Tpl chunks primarily to create menus. The getResources snippet uses them to display aggregated content from various resources.

 The placeholder tags in some standard MODX snippets have dots in their names (e.g., wf.wrapper for the Wayfinder snippet). This can confuse new users who have a background in programming.

The dots are sometimes part of a prefix used to identify fields (e.g., getResources' "tv." prefix specified in the **&TvPrefix** property and the "fi." prefix that FormIt uses for fields in its forms). The primary use of this technique is to keep the names from colliding with other placeholder names and field names on the page. As far as the MODX parser is concerned, however, they have no special meaning and are just part of the placeholder name.

TV-Based Chunks

TV-based chunks are an ingenious method developed by MODX core developer Shaun McCormick (splittingred) for selecting from among various chunks to place on a page using a template variable.

The Basic Concept

As we saw in the Template Variable chapter (Chapter 5), it's not difficult to put chunk names in a drop-down list in a template variable so that the selected chunk will replace the template-variable tag. But it's annoying to have to modify the TV every time a new chunk is added or an existing one is deleted.

The beauty of Shaun's technique is that the chunks are all placed in a single category. Then, a simple snippet populates the TV with all the chunks in that category. When chunks are added or deleted, the list in the TV changes automatically.

The chunks can contain text and (X)HTML, but they could also contain links, images, paths to CSS files, or whatever else you might want to select from.

Say, for example, that you'd like to use different CSS styling for various pages that all use the same template. You could create a TV called *CssSelect* and populate it with the paths to the various CSS files. The following tag in your template would allow you, when editing each resource, to choose the CSS file that will be used when that resource is displayed as a web page:

```
<link rel="stylesheet" type="text/css" href="[[*CssSelect]]" />
```

A Simple Example

To see how TV-based chunks work, let's look at a simpler example. Since we haven't covered snippets yet, we'll use a simplified version of Shaun's method.

Remember when we created the three warranty chunks for a 1-, 3-, and 5-year warranty earlier in the book? We'll take those chunks (`Warranty1`, `Warranty3`, and `Warranty5`) and use them as TV-based chunks.

First, though, create the category by right-clicking on "Categories" on the "Elements" tab and selecting "New Category." Put *Warranty* in the Name field, and click on the "Save" button. You don't need to set the parent since you want this category at the top level of the Category tree. Note that you could also have right-clicked on "Chunks" in the tree and selected "New Category" to create the category.

As an alternative, you could have created a category called *MyCategories* and then created the Warranty category under it by selecting "MyCategories" as its parent. Our snippet is going to select the category by name, so it doesn't really matter where it is in the tree.

Now, create each of the three chunks (if they don't exist already). Call them *Warranty1*, *Warranty3*, and *Warranty5*. Put some descriptive text in each chunk (e.g., *This is the 3-year warranty*).

Next, we'll create the snippet that gets the names of the chunks and formats them for the TV input value. Create a new snippet called *GetChunks*, and enter the following code in the Snippet Code field. The comment lines (they look like this /* comment */) are not executed, and you can leave them out if you like, but be careful to delete the whole comment. If you leave the beginning or ending tag without its mate (or mistype one or the other), it will break the code. Remember that the slash character always goes on the outside.

```php
<?php
/* Code for the GetChunks Snippet */

/* Get the category object */
$category = $modx->getObject('modCategory', array('category'=>$category));

/* Get the chunk objects in the category */
$chunkArray = $category->getMany('modChunk');
$chunkNames=array();

/* Put the chunk names in an array */
foreach($chunkArray as $chunk) {
    $chunkNames[] = $chunk->get('name');
}

/* Format the chunk names for the TV and return them */
$output = implode("||",$chunkNames);
return $output;
?>
```

Finally, we'll create the template variable. Right-click on "Template Variables" on the "Elements" tab, and select "New Template Variable." Put *Warranty* in both the Variable Name and Caption fields. Set the Input Type to Radio Options. Set the Default Value to *Warranty3*. Now, carefully enter the following code (all on one line) into the Input Option Values field:

```
@EVAL return $modx->runSnippet('GetChunks', array('category'=>'Warranty'));
```

Click on the "Template Access" tab of the TV, and put a check mark next to the template (or templates) you want to use the TV with. Save your new TV.

Select a document where you'd like your warranty to appear, and edit it. Make sure it uses a template you've associated with the TV you just created. You can use your `Hello` document, create a new one, or use any existing document. Put the following tag where you'd like the Warranty to appear in the Resource Content field:

```
[[$[[*Warranty]]]]
```

This is a resource tag nested inside a chunk tag. The `[[*Warranty]]` tag will be replaced by the value of the Warranty TV for that document (which contains the name of the appropriate chunk). The chunk tag will then be replaced by the content of the chunk with the same name as the TV value.

Click on the "Template Variables" tab for the document. You should see the Warranty TV with its three radio buttons. The button next to Warranty3 should be selected (because we set it as the default value when we created the TV). Try selecting the various choices, saving the document, and previewing it. You should see the appropriate warranty chunk.

This technique is convenient for you, but it's especially useful when you have other administrative users who are not comfortable with code. All they have to do is click on a radio button to select which type of warranty will be displayed. Better yet, if you decide to create a 10-year warranty chunk, all you have to do is add it to the Warranty category and it will automatically show up in the list with its own radio button.

Shaun's original version of TV-based chunks is a little more complicated because it allows you to select multiple chunks with checkboxes and displays all of the selected ones with a second snippet. See the MODX online documentation for Shaun's version.

Introducing Properties

The two parts of a property are technically called a *key* and a *value*. The key (also referred to as the "Name") then becomes a shorthand way of referring to the value.

In the previous chapter, we used the following snippet tag:

```
[[ShowInfo? &chunkName=`Info`]]
```

In the example above, **&chunkName** is the key and "Info" is the value of the property. In the snippet, the variable named for the key ($chunkName) has the value "Info."

In MODX Evolution, properties were primarily used with snippets and were not very convenient except in snippet properties sent in the snippet tag.

In MODX Revolution, however, snippets, plugins, templates, template variables, and chunks can all have properties. These properties can be in the default properties or in property sets (more on these two in just a bit).

In addition to the key and value, properties in default properties and property sets also have a type for the value (e.g., textfield, integer, Yes/No, date, etc.) and a description (to help users understand the property).

It's somewhat like the speed-dial system on a phone. If you have your phone programmed to dial your best friend when you press the "1" key, the "1" key is the key (literally, in this case), and your friend's full number is the value.

On your MODX site, you might have a property with the key "CEO" and the value "Joe Blow." Wherever you need a reference to the CEO, you could put a tag or snippet that used the CEO property key to get its value: "Joe Blow." If someone else becomes CEO, you just have to change the value of the CEO property in one place.

Properties are a lot like system settings, which also have a key and a value but system settings are available across the whole site. In contrast, you can specify where properties will be available. In other words, properties are local in scope, and system settings are global.

Properties are also like template variables but with less overhead because they don't provide the various input and output options available with template variables. Another important difference between properties and TVs is that properties can be conveniently used as a group. A whole set of properties can be sent to a snippet very easily, for example.

Property sets can be attached to any MODX element, but they are most often used for chunks, snippets, and plugins. We'll discuss their use with snippets and plugins when we cover those objects later on in the book.

In this chapter we'll sort out the difference between default properties and property sets, and we'll see how to create, edit, and use both of them with chunks.

Sending Properties in the Chunk Tag

Before we get into default properties and property sets, let's look at the simplest way to send properties to a chunk. The properties can be sent in the chunk tag (just as snippet properties can be sent in a snippet tag). Any properties sent this way will be available as placeholders (with the same name) in the chunk. Here's a simple example:

```
[[$MyChunk? &placeholder1=`This is the value of placeholder one`]]
```

When the chunk is rendered, every instance of `[[+placeholder1]]` will be replaced with `This is the value of placeholder one`. The question mark after the chunk name is important. It tells MODX that properties are coming next. Each property name must be preceded by an ampersand and the values must be enclosed in back-ticks.

Note that values sent with this method have the highest priority. They will override any values set in the default properties or any attached property set using the methods described below. Note too that the values set in the tag will only affect the rendering of that chunk. If placeholder values have been set previously (e.g., by a snippet that uses `$modx->setPlaceholder()`), their values will be restored once the chunk has been processed.

Default Properties Versus Property Sets

Every element in MODX (chunk, snippet, plugin, template, TV, or category) has *default properties*. An element can also have one or more property sets attached to it.

At present, resources don't have default properties or attached property sets although that capability may be added in future versions of MODX.

If you edit one of the chunks you created earlier in this chapter and click on the "Properties" tab, you'll be looking at the default properties of that chunk. You'll see the word

"Default" at the upper left of the properties grid. The grid is empty because there aren't any default properties yet. If the chunk had one or more property sets attached to it, you could see them there as well.

Which is Which?

The difference between default properties and property sets can be confusing, especially since you can see both of them on the grid you just looked at, and they often appear inter-mixed. It's important to understand the differences between the two and to understand how they interact.

Where Are They Stored?

The default properties of an element (the rows in the grid) are stored in the database table where all elements of that type are stored (in the **properties** field). A snippet, for example, is a single row in the **site_snippets** table in the database. The **properties** field of that row will contain all the default properties of that snippet.

In earlier versions of MODX, the default properties are the only properties (and there is no grid to edit them in). In MODX Revolution, however, you can have independent, named property sets in addition to the default properties. Those property sets are stored in the **property_set** table in the database. Each row in that table is a property set. The properties of each property set are stored in the **properties** field of that row (just like the default properties are stored in the **properties** field of an element's row in its table).

A Source of Confusion

This is where it can get confusing. The default properties of an element are not, technically speaking, a property set even though they are a set of properties. Only the objects in the **property_set** table qualify for that term. The individual default properties are, in fact, the equivalent of a property set's properties.

The difference between default properties and property sets becomes critical when you are trying to access the properties of one or the other in a snippet, plugin, or other element. It's also important to remember that if you edit the default properties of an element that is part of a transport package, your changes will be overwritten when the package is updated. If you want your changes to survive an update, you must use a property set.

When editing and using properties in the Manager, the difference between default properties and property sets is less critical, but it's still important to remember that the default properties are treated differently than those of a property set when an element is processed for display on a web page.

Processing Differences

There are two important differences in the processing of the two groups of properties. First, the default properties are always available in an element, while property sets must be attached and specified. Second, if an individual property in the default properties has the same name (key) as a property in an attached property set, the value of the one in the property set will override the value of the default property. We'll discuss these two differences in more detail later in the chapter.

Attachment

A given property set (unlike default properties) can be attached to any element that has a tag (chunks, template variables, and snippets) or to a plugin. As of this writing, there's no way to attach a property set to a template, but there may be by the time you read this.

Remember, too, that templates, template variables, snippets, plugins, and chunks can all have default properties.

An element can have more than one attached property set, and a property set can be attached to more than one element. The property sets can also be left unattached and accessed directly by snippets and plugins, though this is less common.

Editing

In the MODX Manager, the default properties of an element (chunk, snippet, plugin, template, category, or TV) can only be created, edited, and deleted on the "Properties" tab of that element.

Property sets, on the other hand, can be created, edited, and deleted not only on the "Properties" tab of any element they are attached to, but also from the Top Menu in **Tools → Property Sets**.

Still Confused?

Although we've discussed the differences, you may still be confused about default properties and property sets. As you actually use them in the following sections, the differences
should become clearer. If you come back and read the section above after working through
the examples below, it should make more sense to you.

Working with Default Properties

In this section, we'll create some default properties for a chunk and see how they work
when the chunk is displayed. Note that they work essentially the same way with templates
and template variables. We'll see how they work with snippets and plugins later when we
cover those elements in detail.

Creating the Resource and Chunk

Before creating our default properties, we need to have a place to display them. We'll create
a document to display the default properties. Then, we'll create some properties to display.

First, create a new document called *PropertyDemo*. Give it an appropriate Long Title,
Menu Title, and Alias. Make sure it's published. Put the following chunk tag in its Resource
Content field, and then save the document:

```
[[$PropChunk]]
```

Next, create a chunk called *PropChunk*. Don't give it any content yet. We'll do that later.

Adding Default Properties

Click on the PropChunk's "Properties" tab. Click on the "Default Properties Locked" button to unlock the grid. Now click on the "Create Property" button. In the pop-up window, give the new property a name of *Prop1*, and put the following line in the "Value" field:

```
This is the default value of Prop1
```

Put the following line in the Description field:

```
This property can be displayed with the tag: [[+Prop1]]
```

Leave the "Type" set to *Textfield* (but take a look at the other options). Click on the "Done" button.

Now repeat that process to add a second property called *Prop2*.

Put the following line in the Value field:

```
This is the default value of Prop2
```

Put the following line in the Description field:

```
This property can be displayed with the tag: [[+Prop2]]
```

We're done creating our default properties. At this point, you will be tempted to click on the "Save Property Set" button. Remember, though, that the default properties are not a property set. Clicking on the button will give you an error message. The default properties will be saved automatically when you save the chunk itself.

 There is a reason why the Default Properties grid is locked. If you edit the existing default properties of an add-on component, the element could stop working. Also, your changes could be overwritten when the add-on is upgraded to a new version or reinstalled. Instead, create a new property set, and specify it in the element's tag.

It's perfectly fine to unlock the grid and add default properties to your own elements, however, since there is no risk of them being overwritten by an upgrade.

Before saving your chunk, go back to the "Create/Edit Chunk" tab and add the following code to the Chunk Code (html) field:

```
<p>This is the PropChunk</p>
<p>Here's Prop1: [[+Prop1]]</p>
<p>Here's Prop2: [[+Prop2]]</p>
```

Save your PropChunk chunk.

Seeing the Default Properties in Action

Now preview your PropertyDemo document (which contains the chunk tag for the PropChunk chunk). You should see the values of your default properties. They should appear in place of the placeholder tags in the chunk:

```
Here's Prop1: This is the default value of Prop1.
Here's Prop2: This is the default value of Prop2.
```

You can play with editing your default properties and looking at the changed values, but it's probably better not to at this point because we'll need them to see what's going on when we add property sets to the mix.

You can edit your default properties by going back to the "Properties" tab of the element, unlocking the default properties, right-clicking on a property, and selecting "Update Property" (you'll also be offered the opportunity to remove the property).

Notice that if you click on the little plus sign at the left of each property, you can see its description (if it has one). On most platforms, you can also edit a property's value by double-clicking on the "Value" field.

How Default Properties are Used

You can see from the section above that default properties are an alternative to template variables. Anywhere you have a TV shown by a resource tag, you could have a default property shown by a placeholder tag. The tag could be in the template, in a chunk, or in a document's Resource Content field.

Default properties are faster than TVs and take much less storage space. In many cases, they are also easier to edit. On the minus side, they lack some of the input and formatting options of TVs. Default properties can only be edited in the grid, and although they can show Yes/No choices and drop-down lists of options, you can't present radio options or checkboxes with them, and there is no built-in image tag formatting.

Default properties can be a good option, however, when you have a document with a number of dates or text areas that need to be edited often. A document describing the duties of a group of officers of an organization, for example, could use default properties for the names of the current officers. The names might be spread around the page, but they would all be listed together in the properties grid. They can then be updated easily after an election without any risk of messing up the formatting of the page.

Another use of default properties is to control a snippet that accesses a chunk or other element. A snippet, for example, might show the content of a chunk formatted to a certain width. The desired width could be sent as a snippet property, but it could also be a default property (an integer type) of the chunk itself. That way, different chunks could have different widths but retain those widths no matter where they are displayed. If it is a default property, it can be overridden by a property in the snippet tag. Another example is the `modx.com` download page, which is powered by a chunk that contains placeholders to show various properties.

Default Properties in Other Elements

For templates and template variables, the default properties work exactly as they do for chunks. You create the default properties in the grid on the properties tab of the element and display them with placeholder tags. If your template has small bits of text that change from time to time (e.g., a copyright date or contact email address), you can make them default properties and display them with placeholder tags.

Now that we've seen how default properties work with a chunk, let's see how property sets can be added into the mix to override the values of the default properties.

Property Sets

As we discussed earlier, ***property sets*** contain properties just like the default properties. They can be attached to multiple elements, and elements can have multiple attached property sets.

Overriding Default Properties

When a property set is used with an element, the values of any properties in the set that have the same name as default properties will override the default values.

Say, for example, that you have a chunk with a default property called "price" that is set to $2.00. You attach a property set to the chunk (we'll see how in just a bit) that also has a property called "price" set to $3.00. When you put the following tag in your chunk, $3.00 will be displayed:

```
[[+price]]
```

Two Ways to Create a Property Set

There are two different ways to create a property set. They can be created on the Properties tab of an element or from the Top Menu in **Tools → Property Sets**.

In this section, we'll create some property sets and explore how they interact with the default properties of a chunk. We'll create two property sets, one using each method. Bear in mind that if you just want to override a few default properties of an element, it's easiest to just send them as properties in the element tag.

Creating Property Sets on the Properties Tab

When you create a property set on the Properties tab of an element, that set is automatically attached to the element. All the properties in it will be available in any tag for that element that specifies the property set with @propertySetName. If you want to use a property set with a particular element, such as a chunk or snippet, the following method is the easiest and most reliable way to create the property set. Another advantage of this method is that you can see the element's default properties while creating the property set, so you won't have to enter any existing properties that you want to override.

Creating the Property Set

Load your PropChunk chunk by clicking on it in the "Elements" tree (you may have to expand the Chunks section first). Click on the "Properties" tab, and select "New Property Set" at the top right of the grid.

In the pop-up window, notice that if the property set already existed, we could edit it here by selecting it in the drop-down list. It doesn't exist yet, so check the box next to "Create New Property Set." When the box expands, fill in *MyFirstPropertySet* in the name field, and *My First Property Set* in the description field, and click the "Save" button. Note that property sets should not have spaces in their names.

You should be looking at your property set once it's saved (you'll see its name at the upper left of the grid). It looks like your set includes the two properties we set earlier. It doesn't, really, but the display takes a little getting used to. What's really happening is described at the top of the screen. For every property set, the default properties "show through" even though they are not in the set. You can tell they're not in the property set because they are rendered in gray. This will make more sense as we go along.

Adding Properties

Leave the first property alone. Right-click on the second property (Prop2), and select "Update Property." Change the Value to the following:

```
This is the overridden value of Prop2 from my first property set.
```

Don't change any of the other fields. Click on the "Done" button.

Notice that Prop2 at the left of the grid is now in green. That means that the set now contains that property, which overrides the default value. You'll also see a small red "dirty" flag next to the value. That shows that the property has been changed but not saved yet. Don't save yet; we're going to create a new property for the set.

Click on "Create Property." In the pop-up window, give the new property the Name *Prop3*. Set the Type to *Textfield*. Put the following line in the value field:

```
This is the value of Prop3 from my first property set.
```

Give Prop3 an appropriate description, and then click on the "Done" button. Notice that you could also specify a lexicon. This is useful if the element will be used in more than one language. In that case, you'd put a lexicon key in the "Description" field and the actual description in a language file. The Lexicon field would tell MODX where to look for the language string. We'll discuss that process in Chapter 13 when we cover transport packages.

Now click on the "Save Property Set" button at the top right of the grid. (Be careful: Don't click on the "Save" button at the top of the screen; we don't want to save the chunk yet).

Notice that Prop2 is in green but Prop3 is in purple. That means that Prop3 is a property that is not in the default properties. At this point, your new property set contains two properties: Prop2, which overrides the Prop2 in the default properties, and Prop3, which is not in the default properties. Prop1 is still showing, but we know it's not a member of the property set because it is in gray.

Now that we're done creating our property set, we need to go back to the "Create/Edit Chunk" tab to add a line for our third property. Add the following line at the bottom of the chunk:

```
<p>Here's Prop3: [[+Prop3]]</p>
```

Save the chunk by clicking on the "Save" button at the top right.

Seeing Our Property Set in Action

Now preview your PropertyDemo resource (right-click on it in the Resource tree, and select "Preview Resource"). Something's wrong. The first two properties look the same as they did before, and the new one is empty.

In order to use a property set, you need to attach it to the element. That happened automatically when we created the property set on the element's Properties tab, so that can't be the problem.

Specifying Our Property Set

There's another step that we left out. Because an element can have multiple property sets, we have to tell MODX which one to use. We do that in the tag that references the element. In this case that's the chunk tag in our `PropertyDemo` resource. Right-click on the "PropertyDemo" resource in the "Resources" tree, and select "Quick Update Resource." Change the chunk tag so that it looks like this:

```
[[$PropertyDemo@MyFirstPropertySet]]
```

Be sure there are no spaces in the tag. Now MODX knows it should use that property set when rendering the chunk. Specifying the property set to use always takes this form in any tag. The *@PropertySetName* is added to the end of the element name in the tag.

Previewing the Output

When you preview your `PropertyDemo` document, you should see this:

```
Here's Prop1: This is the default value of Prop1.
Here's Prop2: This is the overridden value of Prop2 from my first
    property set.
Here's Prop3: This is the value of Prop3 from my first property set.
```

You can see that the first placeholder, `[[+Prop1]]`, was replaced by the default property because there is no Prop1 in MyFirstPropertySet. Because the second placeholder, `[[+Prop2]]`, does exist in MyFirstPropertySet, the value in the property set overrides the default property's value. The third placeholder, `[[+prop3]]`, exists only in MyFirstPropertySet, so that value is used.

Our properties all used the Textfield type. Notice, though, that there are several other types available: Textarea, Yes/No, List, Date, List, and Integer. Most of these do just what you'd expect, but the List type needs a little more explanation. When users edit a List property on the Properties tab of the Create/Edit Resource panel, they will see a drop-down list showing the options for the property. This is handy if you want to limit the possible values of the property.

When you select the List type for a property, a grid will appear where you can click on the "Create Property Option" button and add a series of options, each with a Name and a Value. The Name is what the user will see in the list, the Value is the string that will replace any placeholder containing the name of the property (not the option). The values will also be available in snippets and plugins as variables named after the property. When you are done entering properties, don't forget to click on the "Save Property Set" button or else your changes will be lost when you navigate away from the element.

Editing Property Sets on the Tools Menu

As we mentioned earlier, property sets that you intend to use with a particular element should be created on the element's "Properties" tab. Occasionally, however, you want to create a property set for use with a number of elements. In that case, you might want to create the property set using the Tools Menu. Go to **Tools → Property Sets** on the Top Menu. You should see MyFirstPropertySet in the small Property Set tree in the right panel. Below it, you should see the PropChunk (you may have to click on the little arrow next to the property set to expand the tree). It appears under the property set because the two are "attached." This happened automatically when we created the property set in the PropChunk's Properties tab. Make a note, also, of the little icon next to the PropChunk. That's the chunk icon.

Click on "MyFirstPropertySet" in the tree. You should see its properties appear in the grid at the right. You could also have used the drop-down list at the top of the grid to select it.

At first, you might think that a property is missing since there are only two showing. Remember, though, that we only created two properties for MyFirstPropertySet. Prop2 was created when we edited its value. Prop3 came into existence when we created it as a new property. The value of Prop1 was "showing through" from the default properties but was never a member of MyFirstPropertySet.

You could edit the properties of MyFirstPropertySet here, just as you did on the chunk's property tab earlier, but on this grid, you don't see the default properties. They're not shown because this property set might be attached to more than one element, and MODX wouldn't know which default properties to show you.

Notice that you can right-click on a property set and Attach, Update, Duplicate, or Remove it. We'll discuss "attachment" in just a bit.

Update — Allows you to change the name and/or description of the property set. If you change the name, any existing tags that refer to it will no longer work unless you edit them to use the new name.

Duplicate — Does just what it says: you can create an exact copy of the property set (but with a different name).

Remove — Deletes the property set permanently — there is no way to recover it after you remove it.

Importing and Exporting Property Sets

Notice that in the grid you can also Export and Import property sets to and from a file. Export saves only the property set currently showing in the grid. The set is saved by default to a file called **properties.js**, but you should change the name to include the name of the property set. The file doesn't need to have the **.js** extension unless you plan to use it as JavaScript code for some other purpose.

Using Import, you can import a property set from a file. The properties in the file overwrite the current properties. All the current properties will be lost for good. Import and Export can be handy if you want to move a property set from one site to another.

Future versions of MODX may allow the option of merging the sets and selecting which values will be used when there is a collision.

 Generally, you want to create and edit properties in Tools & Property sets if you don't want to be distracted by the default properties.

If, on the other hand, you want to see the default properties (an you usually do), you should create and edit the property set on the Properties tab of the appropriate element.

If there are no default properties for the element you're concerned with, you can do it in either place, but doing it on the Properties tab of the element is usually a better choice.

Creating Property Sets from the Tools Menu

Now, let's create another property set using the alternate method. In this case, we'll create the property set from the "Tools" menu rather than from the Create/Edit Chunk panel.

Creating the Property Set

Go to **Tools → Property Sets** on the Top Menu. Rather than edit the properties of our first property set, let's create a new property set.

Click on "New Property Set" at the top of the "Property Set" tree. Call the new set *MySec-ondPropertySet*, and give it an appropriate description. Leave the Category field blank. When you've saved your new property set, click on it in the tree. You should see its name in the drop-down box in the grid. It's empty, so let's create a couple of properties for it. Create the following two properties, and save the property set:

Name: *Prop1*

Value: *This is the overridden Prop1 from my second property set.*

Name: *Prop4*

Value: *This is Prop4, a new property in my second property set.*

You've probably guessed that we have to edit our PropChunk chunk tag in order to use our new property set. If we did that now and previewed our `PropertyDemo` document, all we would see are the default properties because we haven't yet "attached" the property set to any element. If you click on the little arrow next to the new property set, nothing will appear because we haven't attached it to anything.

Right-click on the new property set in the "Property Set" tree, and select "Attach Element to Property Set." A small pop-up will appear to let you complete the attachment. First, we need to tell MODX what kind of element we're attaching. Click on the "Class Name" drop-down arrow, and select "modChunk." Notice the other element types we could attach it to. Now, we have to tell MODX which chunk we mean. Click on the "Element" drop-down arrow, and select "PropChunk."

Click on the "Save" button. You should see the PropChunk element under our new property set in the tree.

We need to edit our chunk tag, but first, edit the PropChunk chunk to add a placeholder for the new fourth property:

```
<p>Here's Prop4: [[+Prop4]]</p>
```

Now edit the chunk tag in the `PropertyDemo` resource:

```
[[$PropChunk@MySecondPropertySet]]
```

Now, we need to clear the site cache. We didn't need to do that before, because it's automatically cleared when we save an element. That doesn't happen when property sets are saved, so we need to do it manually. Go to **Site → Clear Cache** on the Top Menu. The Console will pop up to show what files were cleared from the cache. Click on the "OK" button.

Previewing the Output

Preview your `PropertyDemo` resource. You should see this:

```
Here's Prop1: This is the overridden Prop1 from my second property set.
Here's Prop2: This is the default value of Prop2.
Here's Prop3:
Here's Prop4: This is Prop4, a new property in my second property set.
```

Prop1 and Prop4 come from our second property set (they are its only properties). Prop2 comes from the default properties (which contain only Prop1 and Prop2). There is no Prop3 value because Prop3 is not in either the default properties or our second property set.

If you edit the PropChunk chunk, you should see all the property sets attached to it in the drop-down at the upper left of the grid.

 Clicking on "Revert All to Default" will make the property set that is currently showing match the default properties in every way. The values of any common properties will be reverted, and new properties in the custom set will be deleted.

The changes won't be permanent until you click on the "Save Property Set" button. You will have a chance to see what the reversion does and can click on the "Cancel" button if you don't want to save the changes.

Summary

In this chapter, we saw how chunks are displayed with chunk tags: `[[$ChunkName]]`. Chunk tags can be used in resources, in other chunks, in templates, in TVs, and as values for snippet properties. Chunks can also be accessed directly in code by snippets and plugins.

Chunks (and other elements) have default properties. Each property is a key and value pair. The value of a default property can be displayed in a chunk, template, or TV by inserting its key in a placeholder tag: `[[+propertyKey]]`. Default properties are contained in an element and don't have to be explicitly attached or specified in the element's tag.

Tpl chunks are standard MODX chunks but with a special purpose. They are used to format the output of snippets (and sometimes plugins). A Tpl chunk contains placeholders, which are set by the code of the snippet and replaced when the page is rendered. They are especially useful for snippets like getResources or Wayfinder that display the fields of multiple documents.

TV-based chunks are used to allow users editing a resource to choose specific chunks to be displayed when the page is rendered.

Property Sets are independent collections of properties that can be attached to any element. Elements can have more than one property set, and property sets can be attached to more than one element.

In order to use a property with an element, it must be attached to that element. It must also be specified in the element tag:

`[[ElementName@PropertySetName]]`

MODX Evolution Notes

Chunks

Chunks behave the same way in MODX Evolution and, as in MODX Revolution, can contain no PHP code. The tag is different, `{{ChunkName}}`, but it is still replaced by the contents of the chunk.

Chunks in Evolution, like other elements, are not shown in the tree at the left of the Manager. To create or edit a chunk in Evolution, you need to go to **Elements → Manage Elements** and click on the "Chunks" tab. Quick Update Chunk and Quick Create Chunk are not available in Evolution.

Our simple HelloWorld chunk example, above, would work fine in Evolution once we changed the chunk tag.

Our Info chunk and snippet would also work, but the setting tags and resource tags would need to be changed in addition to the chunk tag, and some system settings might be renamed or missing. In Evolution, the tags would look like this:

- Chunk tag: {{*ChunkName*}}
- Setting tag: [(*SettingName*)]
- Resource tag/TV: [**ResourceFieldName/TvName**]

The output filters and modifiers we used with tags generally work the same way in Evolution but are implemented via the PHX plugin. The plugin must be installed for them to work, and they only work with setting, placeholder, and resource field/TV tags. They do not work with chunk tags or snippet tags.

Chunks can be used with template variables (e.g., @CHUNK) in Evolution as they are in Revolution. They can also be used in snippet properties, and their content can be accessed by snippets using the $modx->getChunk() method.

Retrieving the data from a chunk as we did with the SimpleShowList snippet would be the same in Evolution, and the snippet code would be identical.

Tpl chunks work the same way in MODX Evolution, and our example would need no changes to function in Evolution.

TV-based Chunks will also work in Evolution, but the GetChunks snippet code is quite different. See TV-based Chunks in the MODX online documentation.

Properties

Elements other than snippets have no properties in MODX Evolution. Default properties and property sets are available only in MODX Revolution. In Evolution, any placeholders to be shown with placeholder tags in a chunk must be set explicitly in a snippet or plugin.

As we mentioned earlier, the section on default properties and property sets applies only to MODX Revolution because in Evolution, only snippets have properties, and there are no property sets.

Chapter 7

Snippets and Plugins

A snippet in MODX is simply a piece of PHP code that is executed when MODX encounters a snippet tag. The tag is replaced by whatever is returned from the snippet. Snippet tags can be placed in resources, chunks, and templates. Snippet tags can also be used as values for snippet properties or placed inside other MODX tags.

Snippet properties (formerly called parameters) can be sent in the snippet tag to provide information to the snippet or to control its actions. As we saw in the previous chapter, snippets also have default properties, which are overridden by any matching properties in the snippet tag. You can also specify a property set in the snippet tag as we did with chunks in the previous chapter.

For snippets with any significant number of properties or snippets that will have their properties edited often, property sets are a much better method. With property sets, there's no worrying about question marks, ampersands, or back-ticks, and you don't have to worry about misspelling the property names.

A snippet can also be used in a chunk tag to define the name of the chunk, like this:

[[$[[SnippetName]]]]

In the example above, the named snippet would return the name of a chunk. The outer tag (the chunk tag) would be replaced by the contents of that chunk. A plugin is also a piece of PHP code, but it functions behind the scenes to extend MODX itself. There is no tag for a plugin.

If you are a not familiar with PHP code, you might want to take a look at the PHP Primer in the Appendix before reading this chapter. Even if you don't plan to write any custom snippets or plugins, a little knowledge of PHP will make it much easier for you to understand the snippets and plugins written by others and will help you get the most out of MODX.

Working with Snippets

In this section, we'll review how to install an existing snippet using the MODX Package Manager. Then, we'll create some simple snippets of our own. We'll start with simple snippets and then move on to more complex ones. We'll also see how default properties and property sets can be used with snippets.

Later on in this section, we'll look at some techniques that allow snippets in MODX Revolution to interact with other MODX objects. We'll do more of that in the following chapter.

If you have trouble understanding this chapter, it will be a comfort to know that, later in the book, we'll look at how to use some standard MODX snippets without messing with their PHP code at all. We're covering the mechanics of snippets here, though, in the hope that it will help you understand how those standard MODX snippets do their work.

Installing an Existing Snippet

We've discussed this before, but just to review, you can install an existing snippet (or any other package) by going to **System → Package Management** and clicking on the "Download Extras" button. Select the desired area in the tree at the left (or use the search box). To get a snippet into the Package Manager grid, click on its "Download" button and wait for the button to change to "Downloaded." If you click on the "Details" button next to the package name, you should see a description of the package.

When you are through downloading, click on the "Finish" button. That will take you back to the Package Management grid. To install the package containing your snippet, just click on the "Install" button. Remember that you can't use anything in a package until it is installed.

A Simple Snippet

If there's no existing MODX snippet that does what you want, you can always create your own. When we covered chunks, we created a simple "Hello World" chunk. Here, we'll do something similar with snippets by creating a simple "Hello" snippet. But before we start working with snippets, let's install the CodeMirror plugin so we'll have a code editor to use when working on snippets.

Installing CodeMirror

Go to **System → Package Management** and click on the "Download Extras" button. Put *CodeMirror* in the search box and press "Enter." When CodeMirror shows up in the grid at the right, click on the "Download" button. When the package has downloaded, click on the "Finish" button to return to the Package Manager Grid. Click in the "Install" button next to CodeMirror. Follow the prompts to install the package.

At this point, CodeMirror is installed, but not yet enabled. To enable it, go to **System → System Settings** and put *which_element_editor* in the search box at the upper right. The system setting for the element editor should appear in the grid. Double-click on the value field for the system setting then use the down arrow and select CodeMirror.

CodeMirror should now be used for editing elements in the Manager. You will see line numbers and syntax highlighting when editing elements. The syntax highlighting will help you eliminate unclosed comments; mismatched parentheses, braces, and quotes; and missing semicolons. Errors are shown with a red background. It's normal for things to appear in red while you are typing since each line is incorrect until you finish typing it. When casting variables to different types, CodeMirror will sometimes flag correct code as incorrect, but this shouldn't happen with any of the examples in the book.

If you want to configure CodeMirror, you can click on it in the Element tree (under plugins) and change its default properties. Most of the default values should be fine, but you may want to change the `indent_unit` from 2 to 4 to make the indenting more obvious. For some browsers, you may also need to increase the value of the `loader_delay` property.

If you find CodeMirror annoying, you can turn it off by editing the plugin and checking the "Plugin Disabled" checkbox. I generally leave it off and enable it only when a snippet has a syntax error that I can't spot.

Creating the Snippet

Create a snippet by right-clicking on "Snippets" in the "Elements" tree and selecting "New Snippet." Enter *Hello* in the Snippet Name field.

All snippets must begin with `<?php` and end with `?>`. In the Snippet Code (php) field, you'll see that those are already filled in for you. Be careful not to remove or change them. Don't add anything before the opening `<?php` or after the closing `?>` and don't put anything else on those lines.

In the Snippet Code (php) field, between the opening and closing php tags, carefully enter the following code, then save the snippet:

```
return "<p>This is my Hello World snippet</p>";
```

Executable lines of PHP code must end in a semicolon like the one above. If you leave it out, use another symbol, or put anything after it, your snippet won't work.

Creating the Document

Now, create a new document resource called *SnippetDemo*. Put the following tag in the Resource Content field:

```
[[Hello]]
```

Save the SnippetDemo resource, and preview it. You should see the message from your snippet. If you see a PHP error message instead, it means that you didn't enter your snippet code correctly. Check it against the code above, and try again. If you see nothing at all, it usually means that you have misspelled the name of the snippet in the tag.

How it Works

When the MODX parser sees the snippet tag, it looks for a snippet with that name and executes its code. MODX replaces the entire tag with whatever the snippet returns. In this case, the snippet simply returns the message we want to display.

Properties in the Snippet Tag

A *snippet property* is just a piece of information that we want to pass to the snippet. In this section, we'll look at setting those properties in the snippet tag. Later, we'll see how to set them using default properties and property sets.

A snippet with properties must have a question mark (followed by a space) after the snippet name. The question mark tells the MODX parser that properties are coming. Each property must begin with an ampersand, and the value being sent must be surrounded with back-ticks (not single-quotes):

`[[SnippetName? &property1=`value1` &property2=`value2`]]`

Here's a more concrete example:

`[[GetCars? &year=`2009` &make=`Ford` &model=`Mustang` &color=`red`]]`

The properties are available as variables in the snippet. In the example above, the PHP variable $year would be set to 2009, $make would be set to Ford, $model would be set to Mustang, and $color would be set to Red.

In this real-world example, the snippet could simply display the information for the car, or it could search a database for cars that meet the criteria and return a list of them. The form of the return value would depend on what you wished to do with it. One common form would be the (X)HTML for an unordered list.

A snippet can also have another snippet as a value for one of its properties. Here's an example:

`[[SnippetName? &varName=`[[OtherSnippetName]]`]]`

In the example above, the value returned by the "other" snippet would be sent as a property to the snippet called by the tag.

Actually, any MODX tag can be used for the value of a snippet property. Nested tags can be used there as well:

`[[SnippetName? &varName=`[[~[[12]]]]`]]`

The example above would send a link to document 12 to the snippet.

A Slightly Less Simple Snippet

Now that we've created a really simple snippet, let's modify it to use some snippet properties. We'll also use a variable to return the output.

Although snippet properties begin with an ampersand, they appear in the snippet as PHP variables. MODX sets the value of those variables when it processes the snippet tag.

PHP Variables

Variable names in PHP always begin with the $ symbol and must begin with a letter. Good practice dictates that they contain only alphanumeric characters and underscores. Variable names are case-sensitive, so $count and $Count are two different variables. Before writing any significant code of your own for MODX, especially if you plan to share that code with the MODX community, you should check out the MODX Code Standards page, currently at:

```
http://rtfm.modx.com/display/revolution20/Code Standards
```

Snippet Output

If you use one of the standard PHP output statements such as echo or print, the output will be displayed as the snippet executes, but it is considered a bad practice in MODX. Well-behaved snippets in MODX don't use echo or print. Instead, the return value is placed in a variable. Returning the value in a variable makes the snippet easier to understand and maintain, and when you use echo or print, you have less control over where the output will appear on the rendered page.

We could use any name for the variable, but in MODX it's almost always called $output to make your snippet easier for others to understand. Occasionally, in a long and complex snippet, the coder will use $o instead to save typing.

Let's modify our Hello snippet to include some properties and return its value in the $output variable. First, however, let's look at a couple more basic PHP concepts.

The PHP . and .= Operators

The dot operator (.) in PHP concatenates (puts together) the things on either side of it. Example:

```
$first = "John";
$last = "Doe";
$output = $first . " " . $last;
return $output;
```

After the code above executes, the value of the $output variable is set to John Doe (the middle part of the next-to-last line just puts the space between the two).

The .= operator tacks the value at the right onto the end of the current value of the variable at the left. It's used often in MODX snippets. So here's another way of doing the same thing:

```
$output = "John";
$output .= " Doe";
return $output;
```

After the lines above have executed, $output is again set to John Doe.

Modifying the Resource

Now it's time to modify our resource and snippet. Edit the Hello document. Make sure that the Rich Text box is not checked to make sure that the rich text editor doesn't mess up your snippet tag. If the Rich Text box is checked, uncheck it, and save the resource before proceeding. Change the snippet tag in the Resource Content field of the SnippetDemo resource to look like this (use your own name if you like):

```
[[Hello? &firstName=`John` &lastName=`Doe`]]
```

Modifying the Snippet

Now, let's modify our snippet. Change the code of the Hello snippet to look like this:

```
$output = "<p>";
$output .= "Hello, my name is ";
$output .= $firstName . " " . $lastName;
$output .= ".</p>";
return $output;
```

Notice that we've used = in the first line, but in the other lines, we've used the .= operator to tack the new string onto the end of the $output variable.

Viewing the Output

Save the snippet, and preview the SnippetDemo resource. You should see the following:

```
Hello, my name is John Doe.
```

In the snippet tag, we passed the first and last name as properties in the snippet tag. The snippet simply puts them together as a string in the $output variable and returns it. MODX then replaces the snippet tag with the contents of the $output variable returned from the snippet.

Using Placeholders with Snippets

In the previous section, we generated output in our Hello snippet by returning a long string of (X)HTML code from the snippet in the $output variable. This is fine if your snippet's output is short and simple. If the snippet's output is more complicated, however, and is longer than a single line, it's much better to display the results with placeholder tags.

In this section, we'll redo our SnippetDemo document and use placeholder tags to display the output. Then we'll alter our snippet to set those placeholders.

Adding the Placeholder Tags

Edit your SnippetDemo document, and replace everything in the Resource Content field with this:

```
[[Hello? &firstName=`John` &lastName=`Doe`]]
<p>My name is: [[+first_name]] [[+last_name]].</p>
```

 Property values in snippet tags are always enclosed in back-ticks. Quoted strings in snippet code are always enclosed in single- or double-quotes. Back-ticks are never used in snippet code. Note that quotes can be used in snippet property values inside the back-ticks (e.g., &lastName=`O'Connor`).

Snippet properties always begin with an ampersand (&). Variable names in snippet code always begin with a dollar sign ($).

Modifying the Snippet

Now, edit your Hello snippet. Replace all the code with the following:

```php
<?php
$modx->setPlaceholder('first_name', $firstName);
$modx->setPlaceholder('last_name', $lastName);
return "";
?>
```

Be careful — those are single-quotes, not back-ticks. Back-ticks are only used in snippet properties. Save the snippet.

Viewing the Output

Preview the `Hello` document. You should see this:

```
My name is: John Doe.
```

Notice that there is no output from the snippet tag itself (and no `return` statement). To verify this, you can put an "X" on each side of the snippet tag in the `SnippetDemo` document:

```
X[[Hello? &firstName=`John` &lastName=`Doe`]]X
```

You'll see "XX" when you preview the document. That's because our snippet doesn't return anything. Instead, it sets the two placeholders.

How it Works

Let's look at what's happening in more detail. The first line of the snippet sets the `first_name` placeholder.

```php
$modx->setPlaceholder('first_name', $firstName);
```

The snippet property **&firstName** is available in the snippet as the variable $firstName. Its value is set to John. The line of code simply sets the value of the placeholder first_name to John. The second line sets the last_name placeholder the same way.

When MODX is processing the SnippetDemo document, it sees the two placeholder tags. It looks to see if those placeholders have values, and since they do, it replaces the placeholder tags with those values (which were set in the snippet). If the values were empty, MODX would remove the placeholder tags from the output.

One advantage of this method is that we can now change the way the output is displayed without rewriting the snippet code. If we wanted the name displayed as Doe, John, for example, we'd just change the code in the document to look like this:

```
<p>Name: [[+last_name]], [[+first_name]].</p>
```

It's both a curse and a blessing that there are almost always a number of ways to do the same thing in MODX. In Chapter 6, we saw how to set placeholder values by using properties with chunks. In this section, we've seen how to do it directly in a snippet.

In the following sections, we'll explore how to do the same thing with default properties, property sets, and Tpl chunks.

Snippet Default Properties and Property Sets

Earlier, we saw how default properties and property sets could be used with placeholders in a chunk. The properties in a property set override any default properties with the same names.

Snippets also have default properties, and can be used with property sets, but the properties are not displayed with placeholder tags. Instead, the properties set the values of variables in the snippet.

 For snippets with any significant number of properties, property sets and default properties are much better than typing in lists of properties in the snippet tag because there's no worrying about question marks, ampersands, or back-ticks, and you don't have to worry about misspelling the property names.

Snippet properties set in snippet tags have the highest priority. They override both default properties and properties in property sets. Here's a list of the three kinds of properties, with the highest-priority ones on top:

- Properties in tags
- Properties in property sets
- Properties in the default properties

In a simple snippet, there may be no default properties and no attached property set. In that case, only the properties in the tag are processed.

Let's look at the processing sequence for properties in a snippet.

When MODX starts processing a snippet, it first gets the default properties of the snippet (if any) and sets variables with their values. In other words, if there is a default property called name and its value is set to John, MODX will create the variable $name with the value John.

In the next step, MODX checks all the properties in an attached property set (if any). If any properties in the property set have the same names as variables created from the default properties, those variables will be reset using the values from the property set.

For new properties in the property set (ones not contained in the default properties), MODX creates new variables and sets their values from the values in the property set.

Finally, MODX processes any properties sent in the snippet tag. If any of the names match existing variables (from either the default properties or those from the property set), the existing variables are reset to the values from the properties in the tag. If there are new variables in the properties in the tag, new variables are created based on the values sent.

In other words, values in a property set override default properties (as they did in chunks), and properties sent in the snippet tag override everything else. Every property in the default properties, an attached property set, or in the snippet tag, will have a variable named after it in the snippet.

Using Default Properties with Snippets

Default properties for snippets are created and edited exactly as they were for chunks. Default properties can only be created and edited on the Properties tab of the snippet.

Edit the Hello snippet, and click on the "Properties" tab. Unlock the Default Properties by clicking on the "Default Properties Locked" button, and create two new properties. Create one named *firstName* (with the value *Joe*) and one named *LastName* with the value *BLow*. Notice that we're using the property names here, not the placeholder names we used with chunks. Save the snippet (don't click on the "Save Property Set" button).

We've said this before, but it bears repeating. The Default Properties are locked for a reason. It's perfectly fine to edit them for a snippet of your own.

For snippets downloaded and installed with the Package Manager, however, your changes may be undone if you reinstall or upgrade the package.

For those snippets, you should always create your own property set, which will override the default properties or use properties in the snippet tag.

Preview the `SnippetDemo` document. It still says "John Doe." Why? Because the snippet properties we sent in the snippet tag override the default properties. Edit the `SnippetDemo` document, and remove the two properties from the snippet tag. In other words, change the snippet tag back to this:

```
[[Hello]]
```

Now clear the Site Cache and preview the `SnippetDemo` document again. You should see "Joe Blow" in the output.

When we used default properties with chunks, we used the placeholder names as the property names, and MODX automatically set the placeholder values. This technique doesn't work with snippets. The snippet must explicitly set the placeholder values using the values of the properties.

 When using placeholders with a snippet, it's easy to confuse placeholder names and property names. To help you remember which is which, it's a good idea to put the property names in mixed case with no space between the words (e.g., *propertyName*) and the placeholder names in all lowercase with underscores between the words (e.g., *placeholder_name*).

Using Property Sets with Snippets

As we learned in Chapter 6, property sets can be created on the Properties tab or from the Top Menu in **Tools → Property Sets.** Let's create a property set to use with our snippet.

Creating the Property Set

Go to **Tools → Property Sets**, and create a new property set called *DemoProperties*. Click on the "Save" button. Now, use the down arrow in the grid at the right to select the "DemoProperties" property set. In the grid, add one property named *LastName*, and give it the value *Blowkowski*.

If we were to preview our `SnippetDemo` document now, it would still say Joe Blow even though properties in property sets are supposed to override the default properties. To make the new property set take effect, we need to attach our property set to our snippet.

Attaching the Property Set

Still in **Tools → Property Sets**, right-click on "DemoProperties" in the tree, and select "Attach Element to Property Set." Click on the down arrow next to "Class Name," and select "ModSnippet." Now click on the down arrow next to "Element," and select the Hello snippet. Click on the "Save Property Set" button. Note that if we had created our property set on the Properties tab of the Hello snippet, this step would be unnecessary.

Is it time to preview our `SnippetDemo` document? If we did, it would still say Joe Blow (try it). What did we forget? We need to specify our property set in the snippet tag.

Specifying the Property Set

Edit the `SnippetDemo` document, and change the snippet tag:

```
[[Hello@DemoProperties]]
```

Viewing the Output

Now, preview the `SnippetDemo` document. It should say `Joe Blowkowski`. It's getting `Joe` from the default properties of the snippet and `Blowkowski` from the DemoProperties property set (which overrides any values in the default properties).

A Final Modification

Edit the Hello snippet, and go to the "Properties" tab. You should see our two default properties with the values `Joe` and `Blow`. Now click on the down arrow in the grid, and take a look at the DemoProperties property set. You should see `Joe` in gray. It's not in the

DemoProperties property set, but it's showing through from the default properties. You should also see the one property in the DemoProperties (with the value `Blowkowski`) displayed in green to show that it's overriding the default property.

Let's try one more thing. Edit your `SnippetDemo` document, and change the snippet tag so it looks like this:

```
[[Hello@DemoProperties? &firstName=`Sylvester`]]
```

Save the document. Can you guess what the preview will show? The snippet property in the tag will take precedence over everything else, so it should show `Sylvester Blowkowski`.

Further Operations

Continue changing values in the default properties, the property set, and the properties in the snippet tag. Try to guess what effect each change will have on the output. It will help you understand the precedence of the properties and will give you practice in finding and editing them.

Replacing Conditional Modifiers with a Snippet

We mentioned earlier that the conditional modifiers available with the default output filter are slow and inefficient and should be replaced with snippets. In this section, we'll create a snippet that plays the same role as a conditional modifier like this one:

```
[[++SettingName:is=`1`:then=`Yes`:else=`No`]]
```

The tag above will be replaced by "Yes" if the named setting is `1` or by "No" if the setting is `0`.

Let's replace this with a simple snippet called *YesNo* that will do the same thing. The snippet tag will look like this:

```
[[YesNo? &value=`[[*ResourceField]]`]]
```

To test your snippet, you'll have to replace *ResourceField* with the name of an actual resource field. Of course, the tag that sets the **&value** property could be anything that returns a `0` or `1`, such as a setting like **hidemenu**, **searchable**, or **published**.

Creating the Resource

Create a new document called *YesNoDemo*, and put the following line in its Resource Content Field:

```
Searchable: [[YesNo? &value=`[[*searchable]]`]]
```

Creating the Snippet

Now, create a snippet called *YesNo* with the following code:

```php
<?php
/* Code for YesNo Snippet */

If ($value) {
    $output = 'Yes';
} else {
    $output = 'No';
}
return $output;
?>
```

Viewing the Output

Try checking and unchecking the "Searchable" checkbox on the "Page Settings" tab for your YesNoDemo document and preview it to see the results of the snippet. You may need to clear your browser cache between tests.

Using the Ternary Operator

If you are a PHP programmer, you'll have recognized that our YesNo snippet could be done more efficiently in a single line:

```php
<?php
return $value == true ? 'Yes': 'No';
?>
```

This is an example of the PHP ternary operator, which is seen often in MODX snippet and plugin code. The code above returns whatever comes after the return statement.

Using the ternary operator (the part after `return`), the code to the left of the question mark is evaluated. If it's `true`, the part just after the question mark becomes the value. If not, the part after the colon (not including the semicolon that ends the line) becomes the value. In PHP the double equals sign is a test for equality and a value of `1` is always equal to the logical value `true`. The `$value` variable will contain whatever we sent in the **&value** property. So this code returns `Yes` if `$value==true` and `No` if not. Note that the following code, also using the ternary operator, would be even more efficient:

```
return $value ? 'Yes': 'No';
```

The code above works because we only need to test the logical value (`true` or `false`) of `$value`. As before, if `$value` is true, `Yes` will be returned, and if not, `No` will be returned. If our test were more complicated, we'd have to use the longer form above.

Making the Snippet More Useful

Our snippet is very limited. It accepts only `0` and `1` for a value and returns only `Yes` and `No`. Let's make it a little more generic. Change the snippet tag in the `YesNoDemo` document to look like this:

```
[[YesNo?
    &value=`[[*searchable]]`
    &yesValue=`1`
    &yes=`Yes`
    &no=`No`
]]
```

Change the code in your YesNo snippet to look like this:

```
<?php
$yes = empty($yes)? 'Yes' : $yes;
$no = empty($no)? 'No' : $no;
return $value == $yesValue ? $yes : $no;
?>
```

How It Works

The first two lines of our snippet set default values for the `$yes` and `$no` variables (to `Yes` and `No`) in case none are sent in the snippet tag. In other words, if the value of `$yes` is empty, its value is set to `'Yes'`, and if not, its value is set to `'No'`. The same thing is done with the `$no` variable.

The third line compares the value sent in the **&value** property against the value sent in the **&yesValue** property. If they match, it returns the $yes variable. If they don't match, it returns the $no variable.

Notice that if you want a Yes or No return, you can leave out the **&yes** and **&no** properties since we set Yes and No as defaults in the snippet (try it).

Now our snippet can return an appropriate message for any value sent to it as long as there are only two choices. For example, you can display a message telling whether the site is online or not with this tag:

```
[[YesNo?
    &value=`[[++site_status]]`
    &yesValue=`1`
    &yes=`Site is online.`
    &no=`Site is offline.`
]]
```

If the site is online, the value of the **site_status** setting will be 1. That will match the **&yesValue** and the **&yes** message will be returned. If not, the **&no** message will be returned.

A Final Improvement

There is one more improvement we could make to our snippet: Create three default properties on the Properties tab of the snippet. They would be called *yesValue* (with a value of 1), *yes* (with a value of Yes), and *no* (with a value of No). That way, only the **&value** property needs to be sent in the snippet tag for simple "Yes" and "No" cases. The snippet will get the values of the other variables from the default properties. Now, the two lines in our snippet that set the default values can be removed since they are set in the snippet's default properties.

If you want to use the snippet for other purposes (e.g., "You have new messages" or "You have no new messages"), you can either create a property set for each use (don't forget to attach it to the snippet and specify it in the snippet tag) or send the other properties in the snippet tag, in which case they will override the default properties.

Tpl Chunks

In Chapter 6, we discussed Tpl Chunks. You might want to refresh your memory by reviewing that section before continuing.

In this section, we're going to create a new version of the SimpleShowList snippet we discussed in that chapter. Our new version will display a formatted list with class names for the list, each row, and each item.

The snippet will display any kind of list using a specified delimiter (defaults to a comma). It will, optionally, sort the list in ascending or descending order, or randomize it. It also allows us to specify the number of items in each row and to specify a separator between items in the list (defaults to a comma and a space).

Creating the Chunks

Before continuing, create the three chunks (*ItemTpl*, *RowTpl*, and *OuterTpl*) from the code in the Chunks chapter (Chapter 6). If you didn't create the *ListData* chunk earlier, do that also. You might want to create a category called *ShowList* and drag all the chunks in it to make them easier to find.

Creating the Resource

Now create a new document called *TplChunkDemo*, and put the following tag in the Resource Content field:

```
[[!Showlist?
    &listChunk=`ListData`
    &itemTpl=`ItemTpl`
    &rowTpl=`RowTpl`
    &outerTpl=`OuterTpl`
    &itemsInRow=`3`
    &delimiter=`,`
    &separator=`, `
    &sortType=`RANDOM`
]]
```

Creating the Snippet

Create a snippet called *ShowList* (or reuse the one you created earlier, but be sure to change its name to *ShowList*), and use the following code for it:

```php
<?php
/* Code for ShowList Snippet */

/* Get our three chunks */
$outerChunk = $modx->getChunk($outerTpl);
$rowChunk = $modx->getChunk($rowTpl);
$itemChunk = $modx->getChunk($itemTpl);
/* Make sure we have all of them */
if (empty($outerChunk))
    return "Didn't get " . $outerTpl;
if (empty($rowChunk))
    return "Didn't get " . $rowTpl;
if (empty($itemChunk))
    return "Didn't get " . $itemTpl;
/* Set default items in a row to 3 */
$itemsInRow = empty($itemsInRow)? '3' : $itemsInRow;
/* Set default separator within rows */
$separator = empty($separator)? ', ' : $separator;
/* Keep HTML code from being all on one line */
$crlf = "\n";
$output = "";
/* Set default sort type */
$sortType = empty($sortType)? 'NONE' : $sortType;
/* Set default list delimiter to comma */
$delimiter = empty($delimiter) ? ',' : $delimiter;
/* Create array of list items */
$list = $modx->getChunk($listChunk);
$listArray = explode($delimiter , $list);
/* Sort the list if directed to */
switch ($sortType) {
    case 'RANDOM':
        shuffle($listArray);
        break;
    case 'ASC':
        sort($listArray);
        break;
    case 'DESC':
        rsort($listArray);
        break;
}
```

```
/* Create array for formatted rows */
$rowArray = array();
$count = 0; /* Items in current row */
$itemCount = count($listArray); /*total items */
$currentRow = ""; /* Contents of current row */
/* Walk though the list items and add them to the current row */
foreach($listArray as $key=>$value) {
    $itemCount--; /* Decrement itemCount */
    $count++;      /* Increment count */
    /* Remove extra white space */
    $value = trim($value);
    /* Add separator if we're not at end of row or end of list */
    if ($count != $itemsInRow && $itemCount > 0) {
        $value .= $separator;
    }
    /* Plug value into our item tpl and add to current row */
    $value = str_replace('[[+sl.item]]', $value, $itemChunk);
    $currentRow .= $value;
    /* If we're at the end of row or end of list, format the current row
     * with our row Tpl and add it to the row array */
    if ($count == $itemsInRow || $itemCount == 0) {
        $rowArray[] = str_replace('[[+sl.row]]',$currentRow,$rowChunk);
        $count = 0;
        $currentRow = "";
    }
}
/* Collapse row array in to one string, separating rows with $crlf
   then plug the string into the outer tpl and return the result */
$output = implode ($crlf,$rowArray);
$output = str_replace('[[+sl.outer]]',$output,$outerChunk);
return $output;
```

```
?>
```

Our snippet is not up to the quality of Wayfinder or getResources, but it's not bad. The comments in the code explain what each part is doing.

The snippet is capable of showing many kinds of lists in a variety of formats. You can use a variety of separators and delimiters. You can set the number of items in each row. You can even sort the items or randomize them.

If you want an ordered list with numbers, you simply need to change the `<ul>` and `</ul>` tags to `<ol>` and `</ol>` in the OuterTpl chunk.

If you'd rather show your list as a table, you can insert table tags in the Tpl chunks. Because all the elements have classes, you can use CSS to format the output in any way you want. All this is possible without touching the data in the chunk. Note that we've called the snippet uncached by using the ! token at the beginning of the snippet tag.

Possible Improvements

We've used standard PHP functions for all the operations of our snippet to make it easier to follow. It would be more efficient (and shorter) if we used MODX's `getChunk()` method in a different way.

By adding a second argument to `getChunk()`, we could have MODX replace the placeholders for us as it gets the chunk. Instead of getting the three chunks at the beginning of the snippet, we'd just name them in all the `getChunk()` calls and add them to the output at the same time.

Instead of this:

```
$itemChunk = $modx->getChunk($itemTpl);
$value = str_replace('[[+sl.item]]', $value, $itemChunk);
$currentRow .= $value;
```

We'd have this:

```
$currentRow .= $modx->getChunk($itemTpl, array('sl.item'=>$value));
```

MODX will then replace every occurrence of the sl.item placeholder with $value as it gets the chunk. Note that the second argument to the getChunk() method will take any associative array (an array of key/value pairs) and replace every key it finds in the chunk with the associated value.

There are several other improvements we could make to our snippet. It should really have default chunks to use in case any of the three Tpl chunks are not sent. These could either be three default chunk names, or you could put the (X)HTML code of the three default chunks directly into the snippet. This would replace the test to see if the chunks were retrieved.

The class names for the various parts of the list could be sent in the snippet tag (with default values in the snippet). There should also be an option to send the path to a CSS file as a property (again with a default path in the snippet). The CSS file could then be injected into the head of the document with this line of code:

```
$modx->regClientCSS($cssPath);
```

Having the option of providing the class names and CSS file path would allow us to show more than one list with different formatting on the same page.

Finally, the default values for all the properties should be assigned to default properties on the snippet's Properties tab.

The implementation of these improvements is left as an exercise for the reader.

Working with Plugins

A *plugin* is a piece of PHP code like a snippet. Unlike a snippet, however, there is no tag to get the output of a plugin. Instead, a plugin listens for particular MODX system events, and the plugin's code executes when a system event it is listening for "fires." Plugins are a great way to extend the MODX platform without hacking the core code.

Earlier in the book, we created a snippet that highlights the output of snippets and chunks. What if, however, you wanted to highlight any of a set of key words on a whole web page? A snippet wouldn't have access to the whole page because some of the key words might be in the template, in the template variable, in chunks, or produced by other snippets.

The answer is a plugin that intercepts the rendered output of a web page just before it goes out to the user's browser and inserts the highlighting. In this section, we'll create a simple plugin that removes offensive words on a web page.

In our first version, the words and the replacement for them will be in the plugin itself. Then we'll move them into the plugin's default properties. In the process, you should get a feel for how plugins operate.

When you work through the following tutorial, it's important to use the exact code, resource names, and elements names we've used in the tutorial. You can try changing things later, but plugins are tricky and hard to debug. It's best if you stick with what's here until you get it working.

MODX System Events

As MODX goes about its business, it periodically "fires" (the technical term is "invokes") any one of a number of system events (see the Appendix for a list of the system events and when they are invoked). This allows you to step in with a plugin and perform operations before MODX continues.

In other programming environments, things like MODX system events are often called "hooks." System event names in MODX are easy to recognize because they all begin with the word "On."

A plugin "listens" for one or more system events. When they fire, the plugin takes control. It performs its operations and then returns control to the MODX core. System events fire when MODX executes the following code:

```
$modx->invokeEvent('OnEventName');
```

Let's look at system events again from MODX's perspective. When MODX executes the invokeEvent() method, it looks to see if any plugins are attached to the named event. If so, it executes their code before continuing.

The system event we'll use here is **OnWebPagePrerender**, which fires just before a page is sent off to the browser. At that point, the entire page is stored in the $modx->resource->_output variable. Our first plugin will modify that variable by highlighting our key words before returning control.

In case you're curious, the event is triggered in this file:

```
core/model/modx/modresponse.class.php
```

It is triggered by the following code:

```
$this->modx->invokeEvent('OnWebPagePrerender');
```

Creating a Simple Filter Plugin

In this section, we'll create a plugin called BadWords that operates in the MODX front end to filter out a list of bad words and replace them with [expletive deleted]. This plugin could be used on a blog, for example, to prevent offensive language in comments.

Creating a Demo Resource and Chunk

We need a resource to demonstrate our plugin. The plugin will be triggered for every page at the site, but we need a page that actually contains our key words. Create a new document called *PluginDemo*, make sure it is published, and put the following in its Resource Content field:

```
This is the content of our damned plugin demonstration resource.
Will it modify scrap and seashells? It should also modify the hell
out of the content of the following damn chunk: [[$PluginDemoChunk]].
```

Now, create a chunk called *PluginDemoChunk* containing the following text:

```
This damned text is inside our chunk.
Our damned plugin should modify the crap out of it.
```

Creating the Plugin

Create a plugin called *BadWords* using the following code:

```php
<?php
/* Code for BadWords Plugin */
$output =& $modx->resource->_output;
$replacement = '[Expletive Deleted]';
$words = array('damned', 'damn', 'hell', 'crap');
$output = str_replace($words, $replacement, $output);
unset($words);
?>
```

How It Works

Our plugin is simple enough. The first thing it does is set $output to the content of the page. Notice the ampersand in front of the dollar sign in that statement. That makes $output a reference variable. In other words, it tells PHP that we want a reference to the actual object rather than a copy of it. That means any changes we make will change the original page content, which is what we want.

Next, we set the replacement, then the array of words. Then we do the replacement using the PHP str_replace() function.

Notice that we don't have a return value. Plugins do sometimes return a value, but in this case, we've altered the page content directly in the snippet, so there's no need. In fact, the `OnWebPagePrerender` event ignores any value returned to it.

If you preview your `PluginDemo` resource now, you won't see any replacements in the text from our plugin. That's because our plugin isn't listening to any system events. Let's fix that.

Attaching the Plugin to a System Event

Edit your BadWords plugin. Click on the "System Events" tab. On the tab, you'll see a long list of system events.

Notice that each plugin has a priority and a property set (though most of these will be blank since they have not been set). The priority determines when the plugin executes compared with other plugins listening to the same event. Plugins with a lower number execute first. The Property Set is the ID of a property set that will be available to the plugin. We don't care about either of these for our plugin, so leave them alone.

Check the box next to `OnWebPagePrerender`. That's the system event we want our plugin to listen for. You'll need to save your plugin to make that take effect, but before you leave, you might want to browse through the list of system events. You can attach a plugin to any system events on the list. Some plugins listen for several events and perform different actions depending on which event has fired.

Viewing the Output

If you preview your `PluginDemo` resource now, you should see the bad words replaced by our replacement string (along with some problems). This will be true for the words in the chunk also, even if you create a snippet that uses `getChunk()` to return the chunk's content.

It will all work because `OnWebPagePrerender` intercepts the process just before the page is sent to the browser, after MODX is finished processing it and replacing all the tags.

Note, too, that the plugin doesn't change anything in the database. It just alters the output to the browser. If you look at the resource and chunk, you can see that they are unchanged.

Improving Our Plugin

As it is now, our plugin is a little clunky and dangerous. For one thing, it doesn't look for whole words, so it will replace words that are embedded in other words (like "shell" and "scrap"). The search is also case-sensitive, which we probably don't want.

A more serious problem, however, is that if a word on the list appears in a file path (say, a path to a CSS file), a page title, or a link to another page title, things can get very messed up. If you are operating within the MODX demo content site, try adding "modx" as a bad word to see the problem.

Let's improve our search by using `preg_replace()` to look for whole words regardless of case. Replace the `str_replace()` statement in the plugin with this code:

```
foreach($words as $k => $word) {
    $pattern[$k] = "/\b($word)\b/is";
    $replace[$k] = $replacement;
}
unset($word);
$output = preg_replace($pattern, $replacement, $output);
```

We haven't solved all our plugin's problems, but it's a lot better. It looks for whole words now and isn't case-sensitive.

Let's improve it some more by using the plugin's default properties to set the replacement and bad-word list.

Using Properties with Plugins

When we want to send information that might change from time to time to a snippet, we can use propertiess in the snippet tag. Since there is no plugin tag, however, that method won't work with plugins. Like all other elements, though, MODX plugins have a set of default properties. These appear on the Properties tab of the Create/Edit Plugin panel. Putting information in the plugin's default properties allows you to edit it easily without altering the plugin's code. Let's change our plugin so that it uses default properties for the list of bad words and the phrase used to replace them.

First, edit the plugin, and replace the two lines that set the replacement and the word list with the following code. In other words, remove these two lines:

```
$replacement = '[Expletive Deleted]';
$words = array('damned', 'damn', 'hell', 'crap');
```

Replace them with this line:

```
$words = explode(',' , $useWords);
```

Now, edit the plugin, and click on its "Properties" tab. With an installed third-party component, you don't want to mess with the default properties because they'll be overwritten if the component is updated or reinstalled. For them, then, you'll want to create a separate property set instead. This is our own plugin, however, and it can't possibly be overwritten by any upgrades. In this case, using the default properties is fine.

Click on the "Default Properties Locked" button to unlock the default properties. Click on "Create Property," and create a new property called *replacement* with a value of *[<i>expletive deleted</i>]*. Now create a second new property called *useWords* with a value of *damn,damned,hell,crap*.

Now you can change the replacement or the word list easily by simply editing the plugin's default properties on its Properties tab.

We could also have created a new property set (or used an existing one) and made the properties in it available to our plugin. There's seldom a need to do this with a plugin of your own, since the default properties are easier to use, and in a custom plugin, there's no chance of them being overwritten by an update or reinstall, but let's look at how it's done anyway.

The process of using property sets with plugins is a little different because plugins have no tag. Edit your plugin. On the "Properties" tab, click on "Add Property Set" and then on the "Create New Property Set" checkbox. Give your property set a name and description and click on the Save button. This will create the property set and attach it to the plugin. Creating and attaching the property set can also be done in **System → Property Sets** as we demonstrated earlier.

If the property set existed already, you could have gone to the Properties tab of the plugin, clicked on "Add Property Set" and selected the property set from the drop-down list.

We still need to specify the property set (or sets) that the plugin will use, however, because more than one property set can be attached to a given plugin. To specify the property set, click on the "System Events" tab when editing the plugin. Find a system event that the plugin is listening to and double click in the "Property Set" column. Select the desired property set from the drop-down list. Don't forget to save the plugin when you're finished. Note that if your plugin listens to more than one system event, each one can use a different property set, though this is seldom done. When each system event fires, the appropriate property set will be loaded before the plugin code executes.

As a further improvement to our plugin, changing the preg_replace() statement so that the search is confined to the <body> section (or a particular div) and ignores text in (X) HTML tags is left as an exercise for the reader.

Tuning the Plugin

Our plugin now operates on every page at the web site, but we might not want that. How can we make our plugin act only with selected pages? As often happens in MODX, there are a number of different ways to do this. One of the simplest methods is to create a template variable that controls the plugin. Call the template variable *runPlugin*, and give it a default value of 0. Set it to 1 on the pages where you want the plugin to execute, and add this code to the top of the plugin:

```
$tv = $modx->getObject('modTemplateVar', array('name'=>'runPlugin'));
if (! $tv->getValue($modx->resource->id)) {
    return;
}
```

Now the plugin will return without executing whenever the template variable doesn't exist in a template or is set to 0. If you want the plugin to execute on almost all pages, you can set the default value of the runPlugin TV to 1.

If you have a large site and want the plugin to execute on only a very few pages, you can skip the TV and just test for the IDs of the pages at the top of the plugin.

Our BadWords plugin still has two disadvantages. First, it slows down the site because it executes every time a page is requested. Second, either it acts on the whole web page (not just the content), or it has to take the time to parse the web page so that it can act only on part of it. A better approach might be to replace the bad words in the Resource Content field when the document is saved. In the following section, we'll modify the plugin to work on a resource's content when it is saved.

BadWords Manager Plugin

This new version of our BadWords plugin will make its replacements in the Resource Content field of a resource after the user has edited it in the Manager and just before the resource is saved to the database.

Disabling the BadWords Plugin

Before creating the new version, it's important to disable the old version. Otherwise, you won't know which version is doing the replacing. Edit your BadWords plugin. Click on the "System Events" tab, and uncheck **OnWebPagePrerender**. Save the plugin. Clear the cache, and preview your PluginDemo resource to make sure the plugin is no longer working. You may have to clear your browser cache as well.

Creating the New Plugin

Create a new plugin called *BadWordsMgr*. Create both the *useWords* and *replacement* default properties. Give them the same values they had in our BadWords plugin. Next, switch to the "System Events" tab. Find and check the **OnBeforeDocFormSave** event. Be careful: several events have similar names.

Use the following code for the new plugin:

```php
<?php
/* Code for BadWordsMgr Plugin */
$words = explode(',',$useWords);
foreach($words as $k => $word) {
    $pattern[$k] = "/\b($word)\b/is";
    $replace[$k] = $replacement;
}
unset($word);
$content = $resource->getContent();
$newContent = preg_replace($pattern, $replacement, $content);
$resource->setContent($newContent);
?>
```

How It Works

Because this plugin operates in the back end (the MODX Manager), it has to use a different method for modifying the resource's content. In the back end, the resource object is available as $resource. Fields are available with $resource->get('*fieldName*'), but there is a special method for getting the content field: $resource->getContent(). In the last line, we update the content field with $resource->setContent() using $newContent, which contains our replacements. Actually, we could replace the last three lines with this single line of code:

```
$resource->setContent(preg_replace($pattern,
    $replacement,
    $resource->getContent() ));
```

We've modified the content field, but we could use a similar method to modify any of the resource fields (e.g., **alias**, **pagetitle**, **longtitle**, etc.) in a plugin. We'd have to use the set() and get() methods, however, instead of setContent() and getContent(). The following code would add a prefix to the resource's **alias** field:

```
$resource->set('alias', $newPrefix . $resource->get('alias'));
```

The line of code above should be modified to make sure the prefix is not already there. Otherwise, the alias will keep getting longer and longer:

```
if ( ! strstr($resource->get('alias'), $newPrefix )) {
    $resource->set('alias', $newPrefix . $resource->get('alias'));
}
```

Viewing the Results

Now load your PluginDemo resource. It should look the same as before until you save it. After saving it, you should see the bad words replaced by your replacement text. When you preview the PluginDemo resource, you'll notice that some of the words have been replaced, but the bad words in the included chunk have not been altered.

Listening to Another System Event

You may already have guessed how to fix the problem. Edit your BadWordsMgr plugin, and switch to the "System Events" tab. Check **OnBeforeChunkFormSave**. Don't uncheck **OnBeforeDocFormSave**.

Now our plugin will listen for both events. It will fire whenever either a chunk or a resource is saved. Before saving the plugin, we have to make some changes in the code so it will handle chunks properly.

Modifying the Code

Change the BadWordsMgr plugin code to look like this:

```php
<?php
/* New Code for BadWords Plugin */
$words = explode(',',$useWords);
foreach($words as $k => $word) {
    $pattern[$k] = "/\b($word)\b/is";
    $replace[$k] = $replacement;
}
unset($word);
switch ($modx->event->name) {
    case 'OnBeforeDocFormSave':
        $resource->setContent(preg_replace(
            $pattern,
            $replacement,
            $resource->getContent() ));
        break;
    case 'OnBeforeChunkFormSave':
        $chunk->setContent(preg_replace(
            $pattern,
            $replacement,
            $chunk->getContent() ));
        break;
}
?>
```

How It Works

Because our plugin is listening to more than one system event, we needed to add the switch statement to know which event has fired so the plugin can respond appropriately. The name of the event that is currently active will always be contained in the $modx->event->name variable. Once we've identified the event, we call the appropriate object's getContent() and setContent() methods.

Save the plugin. Now edit your PluginDemoChunk, and save it. When you preview your PluginDemo resource, you should see all the bad words replaced, even the ones in the chunk.

Using techniques similar to the ones we used in our BadWordsMgr plugin, we could intercept a reader's comments in a front-end blog just before they were saved to the database or perform other operations on user content.

We could warn the user about using forbidden words (rather than replacing them), perform a spelling or grammar check, highlight key words, or perform any other transformation that could be done in PHP code — all without touching the MODX core code.

Another useful job for this technique is to make typographical changes such as changing ' -- ' to '—' in (X)HTML code.

Our plugin executes each time a chunk or plugin is saved. That's probably a good idea since both can be edited at any time. There are some situations, however, where you might want a plugin to execute only when an object (e.g, a user, resource, or element) is created. You might, for example, want to add a user to one or more user groups when the user is created. In other situations, you might want a plugin that executes only when an object is updated (say, to email a user when the user's activation status changes). You could also have a plugin that does one thing when an object is created and something else when it is updated. Events that fire in relation to the creation and updating of objects receive a variable, $mode, that indicates whether the object is new or being updated. The two possible values for the $mode variable are:

```
modSystemEvent::MODE_NEW
modSystemEvent::MODE_UPD
```

In your plugin, you can check the value of the $mode variable to find out if the object is new or being updated:

```
if ($mode === modSystemEvent::MODE_NEW) {
    /* Object is being created - do something */
} else {
    /* Object is being updated - do something else */
}
```

Note that there are three equal signs in the test of the $mode variable. This makes sure that the $mode variable's value is not only equal to, but of the same PHP type as the modSystemEvent::MODE_NEW constant.

The Captcha Plugin

The Captcha plugin shows another way of using plugins. In this section, we'll work our way through it to see how it uses events.

As you probably know, a CAPTCHA system presents the user with an image. The user has to enter the characters displayed in the image in order to prove he or she is human and proceed. The most common use of a CAPTCHA system is to prevent automated bots from entering spam in a web form.

Like our final BadWordsMgr plugin, the Captcha plugin listens to more than one event. You can set a plugin to listen to any and all system events (though I've never seen a plugin that listens to more than two or three).

The Captcha plugin "listens" for both the **OnBeforeManagerLogin** and **OnManagerLogin-FormRender** events. If you install the Captcha plugin in the Package Manager and look at its code, you'll see something like this (the code that performs the actions has been left out to save space):

```
switch ($modx->event->name) {
    case 'OnBeforeManagerLogin':
        /* Verify the Captcha code */
        break;
    case 'OnManagerLoginFormRender':
        /* Display the Captcha code */
}
```

The Captcha plugin runs when either event "fires." As usual, it checks to see which event is currently active by looking at the event name in $modx->event->name.

The MODX Event Model

The Captcha plugin is also different from some other plugins in how it functions. Plugins like our BadWords plugin directly alter the output that was just about to be rendered by changing the resource's **$_output** variable. Our BadWordsMgr plugin modified the field of the object to be saved before the database was updated..

The Captcha plugin, however, stores information in the **$_output** variable of the event itself ($modx->event->_output).

To understand how the `$_output` value is used, we have to look at the *MODX Event Model*. As we discussed earlier, an event is triggered whenever MODX executes the `$modx->invokeEvent()` method. The name of the event is given as an argument to `invokeEvent()`.

When a plugin places a value in the event's `$_output` variable, MODX adds it to an array attached to that event. All plugins listening to an event can contribute return values to that array. The full array is returned from `$modx->invokeEvent()` wherever it appears. After MODX is through executing all the plugins attached to the event, it goes on with the code following the call to `invokeEvent()`. That code can then examine the array to see if any of the plugins returned information.

Rendering the Login Form

In the case of the **OnManagerLoginFormRender** event, the Captcha plugin prepares the (X)HTML code that will display the Captcha image and its prompts as a single string and returns that string. In the MODX login code that renders the login form, just after the event is invoked, MODX adds the string (along with any others coming from other plugins listening for that event) to the page output.

During this phase, the Captcha plugin also stores the correct answer to the Captcha challenge in a `$_SESSION` variable for later use in verifying the user's input.

Validating the User's Input

In the case of the **OnBeforeManagerLogin** event, the Captcha plugin verifies that the user answered the challenge correctly. It checks the user's input (obtained from the `$_POST` array) against the value stored in the `$_SESSION` variable. If the two match, the plugin stores `true` in the `$_output` variable. If not, it stores an error message there.

The code in MODX's **login.php** is in the following directory:

core/model/modx/processors

It verifies the user's username and password, but before it does that, it invokes the **OnBeforeManagerLogin** event and checks the return value. All plugins listening to that event return `true` if the user passes the test and an error string if not. The code in the login file loops through all members of the array returned by the event. The order of processing in the loop is determined by the plugins' relative priority settings.

If all the return values are true, the user passes and processing moves on to finding the user in the database. On the first non-true return, however, the error message returned from the first plugin that returned false is presented to the user, and the login sequence is restarted.

Additional Login Tests

In theory, you can add as many login tests as you like as long as they return appropriate values in the event's $_ouput variable. Each will be evaluated in turn (based on the plugin priority settings), and if all return true, the user will be passed on.

The additional login tests can be based on the user's IP; answering a common-sense question; a third-party service such as reCAPTCHA, Mollom, or BotScout; or any other method — all without touching the MODX core.

Page-Not-Found Plugin

Here's another example of the power of plugins. When a user requests a non-existent page at a MODX site, MODX normally redirects the user to the Error (page not found) page designated in the System Setting grid (**error_page**). Suppose, however, that a client wants some custom behavior when a page isn't found. The client wants users to be sent to one page during business hours and to another page during off hours.

We could do this in a number of different ways (e.g., a snippet on the Error page), but using a plugin will be slightly faster.

Our plugin will listen for the **OnPageNotFound** event, check the time, and use $modx->sendForward() to redirect the user to the appropriate page.

 When creating a plugin, it's often a good idea to create it as a snippet first. It's much easier to debug code in a snippet. Snippets display echo and print statements and will often show a helpful error message if there are any errors in the PHP code. Plugins do neither. If a plugin contains syntax errors, it will do nothing at all and produce no output, though it may place an error in the MODX Error log.

By creating a snippet first, you can make sure that the snippet's logic is correct and that it returns the correct values before converting it to a plugin.

Let's create that plugin. We'll do it first as a snippet, and then we'll convert it to a plugin. This is often a good practice since snippets are much easier to debug than plugins.

Creating the Resources

We'll assume that the business hours of your web site are from 9 to 5 (9 to 17 on a 24-hour system). Create two documents, one called *DayErrorPage* and another called *NightErrorPage*.

Add appropriate content to each one so you can tell them apart. Make sure both are published, and save them. Preview both pages to see how they look. Before going on, make a note of their Resource ID numbers in the tree.

Creating the Snippet

Create a *PageNotFound* snippet using the following code. Use the Resource IDs of the DayErrorPage and the NightErrorPage for lines 3 and 4 of the following code.

```php
<?php
/* Code for PageNotFound Snippet */
$busStart = 9;
$busEnd = 17;
$dayPageId = 37;
$nightPageId = 38;

$busStartSecs = $busStart * 3600;
$busEndSecs = $busEnd * 3600;

$secsSinceMidnight = (date("G") * 3600) + (date("i") * 60) + date("s");

if ($secsSinceMidnight >= $busStartSecs
    &&
$secsSinceMidnight <= $busEndSecs) {
    $modx->sendForward($dayPageId);
} else {
    $modx->sendForward($nightPageId);
}
?>
```

Viewing the Results

Once you've created your PageNotFound snippet, create a resource called *PageNotFound-Demo* to display it. Put the following code in the Resource Content field of that resource:

```
[[!PageNotFound]]
```

If you preview your PageNotFoundDemo resource, you should be forwarded to the appropriate Error page depending on the time of day. If you'd rather not wait until the business day starts or ends, you can reverse the ID numbers in the snippet.

Remember that the redirection will depend on the time where your server is. If the server time is off, you can add a call to PHP's date_default_timezone_set() function.

If you have trouble getting the snippet to work, you can always comment out the lines that redirect the user and return messages instead.

Creating the Plugin

Once the snippet is working as it should, converting it to a plugin couldn't be much simpler. Just create a plugin called *PageNotFound*, remove any debugging code, and paste the snippet's code into the plugin (minus the PHP start and end tags). Set the plugin to listen to the **OnPageNotFound** event on the "System Event" tab of the Create/Edit Plugin panel.

 Never include PHP begin and end code (<?php, ?>) in a plugin. Because the plugin is inserted into the middle of other code, the tags are unnecessary, and they will break the code.

If you want to improve things a little, you can leave out the first four lines and make them default properties of the plugin (remember to leave off the dollar sign in the property names). You could also add a runPlugin default property with a value of 1 and add the following line to your plugin:

```
if (! $runPlugin) return;
```

That way, the plugin will only act when the value of the runPlugin property is set to 1.

Note that to test your plugin, you need to request a non-existent page in your browser. If you are not using Friendly URLs, you will need to request the page with **http://yoursite.com/index.php?id=99**, where 99 is the ID of a nonexistent document.

Rather than putting the Resource IDs in the default properties of the plugin, you could also make `dayPageId` and `nightPageId` system settings and retrieve them with these lines:

```
$dayPageId = $modx->getOption('dayPageId');
$nightPageId = $modx->getOption('nightPageId');
```

Summary

A snippet in MODX is a piece of PHP code that is executed when MODX sees a snippet tag. The tag is replaced by the output returned from the snippet. Snippet properties are bits of information sent in the snippet tag. They can provide information to the snippet or control its actions.

Default properties and property sets serve the same purpose as properties sent in snippet tags, but properties in tags will take precedence over them and override their values. If you modify default properties, your changes will be removed if you update the snippet. You should create your own property sets to avoid this. Property sets must be attached to the snippet, and they must be specified in the snippet tag like this:

```
[[Hello@DemoProperties]]
```

Snippets in third-party components can be installed using Package Manager. You can also create snippets yourself in the MODX Manager. Snippets often set placeholders that will be used to replace placeholder tags in rendered content. This is especially common when snippets use Tpl chunks to format their output.

Plugins, like snippets, are pieces of PHP code but with no tag to display them. They work to extend the MODX engine by listening for particular system events and executing when the system event "fires." As with snippets, plugins have default properties, and they can also have property sets. Using property sets will avoid having the properties overwritten when a third-party plugin is updated.

MODX Evolution Notes

Snippets and plugins are very similar in Evolution and Revolution, although the methods they use to interact with the database are very different, and in Revolution, default properties and property sets play a much bigger role.

Snippets

In this section, we'll look at the similarities and differences between snippets in MODX Evolution and MODX Revolution. There is no element tree in Evolution. Instead, snippets are accessed through the Top Menu: **Elements → Manage Elements → Snippets tab**.

Installation

One of the biggest differences in snippets between the two versions is that MODX Revolution supports transport packages, so snippets can be downloaded and installed through the Package Manager. In Evolution, a few snippets have auto-installation tools, but most require you to create a snippet manually in the Manager and paste the snippet code into it. You may also need to physically install support files and create chunks as well.

Tags, Properties, and Placeholders

The tag for a cached snippet is the same for both versions: `[[SnippetName]]`. For an uncached snippet, MODX Evolution uses this tag: `[!SnippetName!]`. MODX Revolution uses this tag for an uncached snippet: `[[!SnippetName]]`.

In both, snippets with properties must have a question mark after the snippet name. Properties are exactly the same for both versions. They begin with an ampersand, and their values are enclosed in back-ticks:

&property=`value`

MODX Revolution uses both property sets and default properties. MODX Evolution has default properties, but they are awkward and seldom used. Evolution has no property sets.

Placeholders work the same way in both versions but with slightly different tag styles:

Revolution: `[[+PlaceholderName]]`

Evolution: `[+PlaceholderName+]`

Except for the changes in the tag syntax and the use of default properties and property sets, our Hello, YesNo and ShowList snippets will work in Evolution. Tpl chunks also work the same way in both versions.

The Current Resource

Information about the current resource is available in Evolution via the `$modx->documentObject` array. The field names are the same as they are in MODX Revolution. Here are some examples:

```
$alias = $modx->documentObject['alias'];
$pagetitle = $modx->documentObject['pagetitle'];
$isFolder = $modx->documentObject['isfolder'];
$parent = $modx->documentObject['parent'];
```

The `getTemplateVar()` and `getTemplateVarOutput()` methods will get the raw and processed values of a template variable in Evolution.

User Information

In Evolution, the `$modx->userLoggedIn()` method will tell you if the current user is logged in. You can use the `$modx->getLoginUserID()` and `$modx->getLoginUserName()` methods to get information about a logged-in user.

Plugins

Plugins are very similar in the two versions. They both respond to the same system events, and in both, the event name is available in the `$modx->event->name` variable. Since Evolution has no Package Management area, third-party plugins must be downloaded and their code pasted into a newly created plugin. As in Revolution, Evolution plugins should not have the php tags `<?php` and `?>` in them.

There is no Element tree in Evolution. Instead, plugins are accessed through the Top Menu: **Elements → Manage Elements → Plugins tab.**

In Evolution, plugins have default properties, but there is no way to create or edit them in the MODX Manager, so they are seldom used.

Chapter 8

Advanced Snippet Operations

This section is for advanced developers who want to create sophisticated custom snippets. It documents various operations that snippets can use to interact with documents, system settings, chunks, users, etc.

You might be tempted to experiment with some of the code in the following sections, but you might want to wait until the second part of the chapter where we'll have some step-by-step tutorials. The first part of the chapter is mainly for reference and to introduce the various methods. The methods below are organized by type. In the second part of the chapter, we'll use a more practical organization and see how to use the various methods with resources, elements, and users.

MODX get*() Methods

The following methods are members of the $xpdo object, an instantiation of the xPDO class, which is the base class for all objects in MODX. All of these methods start with the word get, and almost all of them are used to get a specific object or an array of MODX objects (users, snippets, resources, chunks, template variables, etc.). Because the $modx object extends the $xpdo object, all of them can (and should) be called like this in any snippet or plugin:

```
$modx->methodName()
```

Some of the methods are generic. They can be used with any MODX object. Others can only be used with the specific object for which they were designed.

Generic Methods

The methods below can be used to retrieve any MODX object or an array of MODX objects. Note that except for getOption(), which returns a string of text, the methods return the objects themselves not their names or IDs.

Using getObject()

In order to get information from MODX objects, you need to first get a reference to the object you want, then you can access its fields using its get() method. (The get() method is discussed in the Object Methods section below.) Often, the first step is accomplished with $modx->getObject()$. The getObject() method searches for and returns a single MODX object, such as a resource, snippet, chunk, template, template variable, or user. The getObject() method takes two forms:

```
$resource = $modx->getObject($classKey, $id);
$resource = $modx->getObject($classKey, $criteria);
```

The $classKey argument is the name of the class key of the object you are looking for. Here are the most commonly used class keys:

- modResource
- modChunk
- modSnippet
- modPlugin
- modCategory
- modTemplate
- modTemplateVar
- modUser
- modUserProfile

The second argument is either the ID of the object you want (i.e., an integer) or an associative array describing the criteria for finding the object. If you know the ID of the object you're looking for, using that method is faster. This code will get the resource with the ID of 12:

```
$resource = $modx->getObject('modResource', 12);
```

Sometimes, however, you need to create a $criteria array to tell MODX how to search for the object. The possible criteria are too extensive to list here, but you can see them in the MODX Objects Reference in the Appendix. Here are some simple examples:

```
$resource = $modx->getObject('modResource', array('pagetitle'=>'Home'));
$chunk = $modx->getObject('modChunk', array('name'=>'ListData'));
$user = $modx->getObject('modUser', array('username'=>'admin'));
```

The first part of each array object is the name of a field in the MODX database table containing the object.

Notice that you have to use the appropriate field name in the criteria argument. All three of the examples above are searching for an object by name, but the name of the "name" field is different for each one. For resources, the name of the resource is in the `pagetitle` field; for chunks, it is in the `name` field; for users, it is in the `username` field.

Our examples above used only a single criterion, but you can specify as many as you like, and you can assign the criteria array to a variable and use that variable as the second argument to getObject():

```
$criteria = array(
    'pagetitle'=>'Home',
    'alias'=>'home',
    'longtitle'=>'Home Page',
);


$resource = $modx->getObject('modResource', $criteria);
```

It might seem that the more characteristics you specify in your criteria, the faster the object will be found. Actually, the reverse is true since the more criteria there are, the longer it takes to compare them all before returning the result.

When getObject() fails to find an object that fits the criteria, it returns null. You can test the return value of getObject() for failure with this code:

```
if ($modx->getObject($classKey, $criteria) === null)
```

If you want to work with the current resource being shown in the front end, there is no need to use getObject() because MODX provides it as $modx->resource. Instead of any of the lines above, you'd use:

```
$resource =& $modx->resource;
```

Note that when assigning a variable to the current resource, you should always use =& instead of the = operator. Using =& here instead of = tells PHP to connect the $resource variable with the actual $modx->resource object rather than making a copy of the object. Getting a direct reference to the object saves both time and memory. Technically, it's called an *assignment by reference*.

It's not necessary to use =& when calling a method that returns an object (e.g., any of the get*() methods), but you should always do so when assigning a variable to the current object ($modx->resource or $modx->user), especially if you plan to modify the object and save it. You could just use $modx->resource everywhere, but assigning it to the $resource variable will save you some typing.

Using getCollection() and getIterator()

If your criteria fit more than one object, getObject() will return the first one it finds. If you want an array of objects, you can use getCollection(), which takes the same arguments as getObject() but returns an array of objects. If only one object fitting the criteria is found, the array will contain only one member. The following code will retrieve an array of modResource objects. The array will contain all the published immediate children of the resource with the ID of 12 (i.e., the published resources directly below resource 12 in the Resource tree):

```
$resources = array();
$criteria = array (
    'published'=>'1',
    'parent'=>'12',
);
$resources = $modx->getCollection('modResource', $criteria);
```

When getCollection() fails to find any objects, it returns an empty array. To test getCollection() for failure, you can use this code:

```
if (empty($resources))
```

The criteria sent in the second argument to getCollection() can also be in the form of an xPDO query, created with $modx->newQuery(). We'll discuss queries in further detail later in the chapter when we work with getting resource information. An xPDO query can also be used as a second argument to getObject(), getOne(), getMany(), and the graph methods.

The getIterator() method is used exactly like getCollection() and takes the same arguments. The difference is that while getCollection() gets all the items into memory, getIterator() gets references to them but they are not pulled from the database until they are used. With getCollection() the initial query will be slower and will use more memory, but a loop processing the items retrieved will be faster. With getIterator() the reverse is true, so it is the preferred method when the number of objects to be retrieved is very large. With small data sets getCollection() is usually the preferred method.

Using getOption()

All settings values (system settings, context settings, and user settings) are available with `$modx->getOption()`. Rather than retrieving MODX objects, `getOption()` retrieves the actual setting, which is always a string (though the string may contain an integer value). It takes this form:

```
$modx->getOption('OptionName')
```

As we discussed earlier in the book, context settings override system settings, and user settings (for the current logged-in user) override the other two. When you use `getOption()`, you will get the value of the setting with the highest precedence. In the common case where you haven't created any context or user settings, you'll get the system setting.

There is no way from inside the snippet to see where a setting is coming from since they all end up in the same array. This is as it should be because the precedence of the various values is part of MODX's architecture, and it would violate the logic of MODX for the snippet to be able to override the precedence rules.

The `getOption()` method has other uses as well. It can be used to search any array or to get a property of a snippet. We'll see how to use it for those purposes a little later in the chapter.

Other Generic Methods

There are two more generic methods: `getObjectGraph()` and `getCollectionGraph()`. They are used to get objects and their related objects in a single step by retrieving objects from multiple tables in the MODX database. We'll cover them later in the chapter after we've discussed related objects.

Specific Methods

The methods discussed in this section only work with specific objects. The last one (`getChunk()`) is used only with chunks. The others are used only with resources. The `getChildIds()` method returns an array containing any children of the specified resource. Similarly, the `getParentIds()` method returns an array containing the IDs of all ancestors up the tree. The `getPlaceholder()` method returns the value of the named placeholder.

Note that, with the exception of `getPlaceholder()`, none of these methods return MODX objects. The `getPlaceholder()` method will retrieve a MODX object if one has been stored with setPlaceholder(), although it is seldom used this way. Most of the time, getPlaceholder() is used to retrieve a string previously saved with setPlaceholder(), setPlaceholders(), toPlaceholder(), or toPlaceholders().

Using getChildIds()

You can get the ID numbers of the children of any resource (as an array) with getChildIds($id, $depth). The first argument, $id, is the Resource ID of the resource you want the children of. The second argument, $depth, is the number of levels you want to traverse. The second argument is optional and defaults to 10. Remember that the return value is an array of numbers, not resource objects. If you want the resource objects themselves, you need to use one of the generic methods from the previous section.

If you want to retrieve the IDs of children of the current resource with getChildIds(), you need to get its ID first:

```
$id = $modx->resource->get('id');
$children = $modx->getChildIds($id);
```

The return value is always an array of ID numbers or an empty array if the specified resource has no children. If you set $id to 0, you'll get all the resources in the current context provided that the depth argument is sufficiently large. You can't count on the order of the resources in the array. Note that unlike some other methods, this one doesn't default to the current resource if one is not specified (though this could change in future versions). At this writing, you must always specify a resource ID in the first argument of getChildIds().

Using getParentIds()

Sometimes, you might want all ancestors of the current resource. You could work your way up the tree, getting each object, using its get() method to find the contents of the **parent** field, and moving on to the next one, but there is a much easier way. The getParentIds($id, $height) method will get them all. It walks up the Resource tree getting each parent in turn and putting it into an array.

Note that as we did with `getChildIds()`, we have to get the ID of the current resource first. The `getParentIds()` method takes a second argument, `$height`, which determines the number of levels traversed. The `$height` argument defaults to 10, so you can omit it in most cases.

```
$parents = $modx->getParentIds($id);
if (! empty($parents)) {
    foreach($parents as $parent) {
        if ($parent) { /* make sure it's not 0 */
            $obj = $modx->getObject( 'modResource' , $parent);
            /* do something with the $obj resource here */
        }
    }
}
```

The `getParentIds()` method will give you the IDs in order. The first one will be ID of the parent of the specified resource, then its grandparent, and so on up the tree. Unless stopped by the `$height` limit, the final ID in the list will be 0 because the top resource has no parent resource. If we wanted the ancestor objects instead of just their IDs, we would need to get each of them with `getObject()`.

Like the `getChildIds()` method, at this writing `getParentIds()` doesn't default to the current resource if one is not specified. You must always specify a resource ID in the first argument of `getParentIds()`.

Using getPlaceholder()

You can display the value of a placeholder by inserting a placeholder tag in a document or template, but what if you want that value in a snippet? The `getPlaceholder()` method will retrieve it for you:

```
$ph = $modx->getPlaceholder('MyPlaceholder');
```

The returned value will depend on what was stored in the placeholder with `setPlaceholder()`, which will accept any MODX or PHP object. Most MODX users, however, employ it only for strings.

Using getChunk()

In its simplest form, getChunk() retrieves the processed output of a chunk. Obviously, this method only makes sense when used with chunks. It takes this form:

```
$text = $modx->getChunk('ChunkName');
```

The line above will set the variable $text to the content of the named chunk. All tags in the chunk will be processed before the variable is set. Note that the argument must be a chunk name. At this writing, the getChunk() method will not accept a chunk ID instead.

The getChunk() method can also be used to set the values of placeholder tags in the chunk during the call by sending an associative array as a second argument. We'll see how to do that later in this chapter.

Getting Related Objects with getOne() and getMany()

We learned earlier that getObject() gets a MODX object and that getCollection() gets an array of MODX objects. Now, we need to discuss getOne() and getMany(), which also get MODX objects. The difference between getObject() and getOne() seems confusing at first, but it's an important distinction and not all that complicated once you understand it. The same goes for the difference between getCollection() and getMany(). The key is to understand the concept of *related objects*.

Many MODX users have trouble sorting out the various get*() methods, so please be patient if we seem to be repeating things in this section.

Related Objects

A *related object* is simply a MODX object that is related to some other MODX object. The relationships are defined in an XML file that defines the *schema* for the MODX database. If you'd like to look at it, the file is:

core/model/schema/modx/modx.mysql.schema.php

You can also look at the MODX Objects Reference in the Appendix. That section also shows the relationships and is a bit more readable. The XML file, however, actually defines the relationships that MODX uses when processing the various get*() methods and, unlike the section in the Appendix, it is more likely to be accurate and up-to-date. We'll discuss the schema file further at the end of this section.

Many MODX objects have one or more related objects. A resource, for example, has one Parent related object and (potentially) many Children related objects. A user has a Profile related object and a template has Resources related objects. Note that all related object names start with a capital letter. The fields of an object always start with a lowercase letter.

Remember that in order to retrieve its related objects, you must have a variable pointing to the object itself. In the case of the current resource or the current user, MODX furnishes the variables for you: $modx->resource and $modx->user. In almost all other cases, you must get the object yourself using one of the methods described above (e.g., $modx->getObject()).

While getObject() and getCollection() get objects specified in their criteria argument, getOne() and getMany() methods get related objects of the object they are methods of:

```
$resource->getOne('Parent');
$resource->getMany('Children');
```

Note that these methods are not methods of the $modx object. Instead, they are methods of specific objects like snippets, resources, chunks, etc. Code that calls these methods always starts with the variable referring to the object, never $modx->.

Notice, also, that with these methods you don't need to specify any criteria at all. MODX knows that you just want the related objects of the object whose method you are calling. You can specify criteria in a second argument, however, if you don't want all of the objects. The following code, for example, would retrieve only published children of a resource called MyResource:

```
$resource = $modx->getObject('modResource',
    array('pagetitle'=>'MyResource'));
$children = $resource->getMany('Children', array('published'=>'1'));
```

The schema file we mentioned earlier in this section is confusing at first, but it is a valuable reference for understanding the relationships between the various MODX objects. Here is the section that defines the user group object (modUserGroup):

```
<object class="modUserGroup" table="membergroup_names"
    extends="modPrincipal">
        <field key="name" dbtype="varchar" precision="255" phptype="string"
            null="false" default="" index="unique" />
        <field key="parent" dbtype="int" precision="10"
            attributes="unsigned" phptype="integer" null="false"
            default="0" index="index" />
```

```
<aggregate alias="Parent" class="modUserGroup" local="parent"
    foreign="id" cardinality="one" owner="foreign" />
<aggregate alias="Children" class="modUserGroup" local="id"
    foreign="parent" cardinality="many" owner="local" />
<composite alias="UserGroupMembers" class="modUserGroupMember"
    local="id" foreign="user_group" cardinality="many"
    owner="local" />
</object->
```

The first line defines the class name and the name of the table in the MODX database that holds this object. Each modUserGroup object is a row in that table. Next, the two fields, **name** and **parent**, are defined along with their field attributes in the database. Finally, the class that the modUserGroup class extends is specified. The modUserGroup class will inherit all methods of the modPrincipal.

The two aggregate alias lines define the two related objects of a user group (note the initial capital letters in the aliases). The Parent and Children objects are also objects of the class modUserGroup. Every aggregate alias line in the file describes the relationship between the class being defined and one of its related objects.

Notice the cardinality settings. The cardinality of a Parent is one because a user group can have only one parent. The cardinality of Children is many because a user group can have many children. This tells us that if you wanted to get a user group's Parent, you would use its getOne() method. If you wanted its Children, on the other hand, you would use its getMany() method.

The last line describes a composite alias. There is a many-to-many relationship between users and user groups. A user can be in more than one group, and a group may have multiple members. As a result, there is a table for users and a table for user groups, but there is also an intersect table (containing modUserGroupMember objects) that ties users to groups (and vice versa). The rows in that table each have three important fields: **user_group** (the ID of the group), **member** (the ID of the user), and **role** (the ID of the user's role in the group). The composite alias line describes the relationship between the user group object and the intersect object. There is a similar line in the sections of the file that define the modUser and modUserGroupMember objects. The modUserGroupMember section defines all three fields.

Using getOne()

Suppose you retrieve a resource with getObject() and want to get the user object for the person who created the document. You could use get() and getObject() to get the user object via the **createdby** field:

```
$userId = $resource->get('createdby');
$user = $modx->getObject('modUser',array('id'=>$userId));
```

Because of MODX's xPDO roots, however, there is an easier (and faster) way using related objects. In this case, there is a related object called CreatedBy. It is the user object we ended up with in the code above. Using getOne(), we can get it in a single step:

```
$user = $resource->getOne('CreatedBy');
```

Note that after the code above executes, the $user variable contains a reference to the user object (technically, a modUser object), which we've retrieved without messing with user IDs or usernames.

The arguments used in many of the get*() methods (e.g., getObject() and getCollection()) are field names, so they are in all lowercase type (e.g., **pagetitle, createdby**).

In contrast, the related object names used in a call to getOne() or getMany() are all in camel case (e.g., Parent, CreatedBy). They always start with an uppercase letter.

Related objects retrieved with getMany() have plural names (e.g., Children, TemplateVars, CreatedResources). Related objects retrieved with getOne() have singular names (e.g., Parent, Profile, Category).

Using getMany()

The key to knowing whether to use getOne() or getMany() is to ask whether there could ever be more than one of what you're looking for. If so, you want getMany(). A resource can only have one parent, so the appropriate code to get that parent (a modResource object) is:

```
$resource->getOne('Parent');
```

On the other hand, a resource can have more than child. To get the array of child objects for a resource, you'd use this code:

```
$resource->getMany('Children');
```

If the object could have many related objects of the type you are retrieving, you must use getMany() even if there is only one object to find. A resource might have only one child, but if you wanted to retrieve that child object directly, you'd still have to use getMany('Children'). If you look at the MODX Objects Reference in the Appendix, you can see which objects are available with getOne() and which are available with getMany(). Always use the appropriate method to get related objects or your search will fail.

The Graph Methods

If you are concerned about efficiency, there are two very elegant xPDO methods that allow you to get data from multiple tables in a single query. They are called getObjectGraph() and getCollectionGraph().

Both methods can get an object (or an array of objects) along with any related objects in a single line of code.

Using getObjectGraph()

When you want information on an object and its related objects, you can get the object and then get the related object or objects with getOne() or getMany(). This takes several steps (and several queries to the database). You can often do it more efficiently with getObjectGraph(). Suppose you want information about the current user, including both **username** and **fullname**. The first is in the $modx->user object. The second is in the user's profile. You can get both at once with this code:

```
$user = $modx->getObjectGraph('modUser', array('Profile' => array()));
```

Since the code above gets the current user, you should make sure a user is logged in before executing it (see hasSessionContext()). The second argument to getObjectGraph() must always be an array, even if you only want one related object. If you want more than one, you can just add the other related object names to the array.

The function can take four arguments, but we've left the last two blank (they are optional). The third argument contains the criteria for the search. Leaving it blank gets the current user (or the current resource if the first argument is 'modResource'). The fourth argument (true/false) tells xPDO whether to cache the result (see the xPDO reference section of the Appendix).

After executing the getObjectGraph() call above, the current user's data is available with $user->get('**fieldName**').

```
$name = $user->get('username');
```

If that's all we needed, we could have just used:

```
$name = $modx->user->get('username');
```

But since we used getObjectGraph(), we also have all of the user's profile information, available with $user->Profile->get('**fieldName**'). Notice the capital 'P' in Profile. Related object names always start with a capital letter.

```
$fullName= $user->Profile->get('fullname');
```

What if we wanted the information on another user? All we need to do is fill in the third argument in the call to getObjectGraph():

```
$user = $modx->getObjectGraph('modUser',
    array('Profile' => array()),
    array('username' => 'JoeBlow'));
```

We've used getObjectGraph() here to get user data, but it can be used to get any MODX object and its related objects. You could get a resource and its related creator, last editor, publisher, and/or parent object, for example:

```
$resource = $modx->getObjectGraph('modDocument',
    array('CreatedBy' => array(),'EditedBy' => array()),
    array('pagetitle' => 'SomeDocument'));

$output = '<p>Creator: ' . $resource->CreatdBy->get('username') . '</p>';
$output .= '<p>Editor: ' . $resource->EditedBy->get('username') . '</p>';
return $output;
```

See the MODX Objects Reference section of the Appendix for a list of MODX objects and their related objects.

You need to be careful when using getObjectGraph(), however, because each related object returned may or may not be an object. Instead, it may be an array of objects.

If you get a user Profile, for example, you'll get a single object, but if you get any of the other related objects, such as CreatedResources or PublishedResources, you'll get an array of objects.

Similarly for resources, if you ask for the CreatedBy or EditedBy related field, you'll get a single user object back. If, on the other hand, you ask for TemplateVars or Children, you'll get an array of template variable objects or child resource objects.

To know what you'll get, look at the MODX Objects Reference in the Appendix. If the related object is available with getOne(), you'll get a single object. If it's available with getMany(), you'll get an array of objects.

If the related object returns an array, you may also get an empty array back (e.g., for a user who has created no resources or a resource with no children), so you should always test the return value before trying to extract anything from it:

```
if (!empty($user->CreatedResources)){
    // extract info here
}
```

This test is important because calling any of the get*() methods on a non-existent object will lead to a PHP error complaining that you've tried to call a method of a non-object.

Using getCollectionGraph()

If you want more than a single object, you can use getCollectionGraph(), which is just like getObjectGraph() but for getting multiple objects at once with their related objects.

If we wanted an array containing all the active users and their profiles, we could use this code:

```
$users = $modx->getCollectionGraph('modUser',
    array('Profile' => array()),
    array('active' => '1'));
```

We could then display the user names and full names with this code:

```
foreach($users as $user) {
  $output .= '<p>USER: ' . $user->get('username') . '/p>';
  $output .= '<p>FULLNAME: ' . $user->Profile->get('fullname') .
      '</p><br />';
}
return $output;
```

As with getObjectGraph(), always be aware that some related objects will be objects, and some will be arrays of objects. If the related object is available with getOne(), it will be an object. If it is available with getMany(), it will be an array of objects.

The return value can also be empty, so you should always test it before trying to extract any information.

 The various "get" methods (get(), getObject(), getOne(), getMany(), getCollection(), etc.) discussed here are not really methods of the modX class. They are inherited from the xPDO class. Since the modX class extends the xPDO class, however, you can call them with $modx->*methodName*() in any snippet or plugin.

The only exception to this is in scripts contained in transport packages. The $modx object is not available there, but you can create a temporary $modx variable that points to the $xpdo object with the following code at the top of the file:

$modx =& $object->xpdo;

Once you have done that, the usual $modx->methodName() calls will work.

The methods of both classes are documented in the MODX API section in the Appendix.

Object Methods

Earlier in this chapter, we saw the `getOne()` and `getMany()` object methods. In this section, we'll look at some more. Many of the methods discussed above retrieve MODX objects. Once you have an object, you usually want some information from it. The methods below are designed to retrieve that information. These are methods of the objects themselves, not the `$modx` object. Some are generic and some are used only with specific objects. Obviously, you must first have an object before you can call one of its methods (see Sanity Checking later in this chapter). All object methods are called this way:

```
$object->methodName();
```

Generic Object Methods

The methods in this section will work with any MODX object. They allow you to get the object's fields, either individually or in an array.

Using get()

Once you have a reference to an object, you can get any of its fields with this code:

```
$object->get('fieldName');
```

Here are some examples. In each case you would have to get a reference to the object and perform sanity checks before attempting to get the field:

```
$resouce>get('pagetitle');
$chunk>get('name');
$user->get('username');
```

Remember that MODX always provides a reference to the current resource as `$modx->resource` and the current user as `$modx->user`. For the current values, then, you could use this code:

```
$modx->resource->get('id');
$modx->user->get('username');
```

The examples above return a single string. The `get()` method also has another form, however, that lets you get multiple fields at once. It returns an associative array.

```
$fields = $modx->resource->get(array('id','username'));
```

With the code above, `$fields` would contain an array like this after the call:

```
array(
    'id' => 1,
    'username' => 'JoeBlow',
);
```

If you wanted the username, it would then be available with `$fields['username']`. If you want all the fields of the object, you should use the object's `toArray()` method, which we'll discuss in just a bit.

The `get()` method is used a lot in MODX, and we'll see many examples of it later in the chapter. There is also a `set()` object method, which sets the value of a specific field. We'll discuss that later in the chapter when we cover creating and changing objects.

Using getContent()

The `getContent()` method gets the raw, unprocessed content of an element or resource's main content field as a string. For snippets, plugins, chunks, and templates, it is the code of the element. For resources, it is the unprocessed resource content field (with any MODX tags intact). This method is seldom used in snippets, because users usually want the processed content of the element or resource. Occasionally, however, you might want the raw content. You might, for example, want to get the raw content of a snippet and save it somewhere so that you could later roll back the snippet to its previous version.

There is also a `setContent()` object method. We'll discuss that later in the chapter when we cover creating and saving objects.

Using toArray()

All MODX objects are actually rows in a particular table in the database. While `get()` gets the content of a single field from that row, `toArray()` gets the entire row as an associative array. In other words, it gets all the fields of the object into an associative array where each key is a field name and each value is the content of that field. This code would put all the fields of the current resource into an associative array:

```
$fields = $modx->resource->toArray();
```

Using process()

The `process()` method is seldom used except in MODX's internal code. It retrieves the processed output of a MODX object. It is unreliable with resources and templates, however, because some tags will not be processed due to their cache status. In most cases, there is another way to get the processed output of an object. For template variables, you can use `$tv->renderOutput()`. For snippets, there is `runSnippet()`. For chunks, there is `getChunk()`. These methods meet the needs of most users. If you need `process()` for something, it takes this form:

```
$processedOutput = $object->process();
```

Specific Object Methods

The following methods relate to specific types of MODX objects. They are sometimes called "convenience" functions because they perform functions that could be done with the methods above but in a single step. Like the generic object methods above, they are called with this form:

```
$object->MethodName();
```

Using hasChildren()

The `hasChildren()` method provides a quick way to find out if a resource has children and how many children it has. It takes no arguments and simply returns the number of children. To get the number of children of the current document, for example, you'd use this code:

```
$numChildren = $modx->resource->hasChildren();
```

Note that the **isfolder** resource field indicates whether the resource is designated as a container. In MODX Revolution, `hasChildren()` and **isfolder** are independent. A resource marked as a container with **isfolder** doesn't necessarily have any children, and a resource with children doesn't necessarily have its **isfolder** field set. This is not the case in MODX Evolution where all resources with children automatically have their **isfolder** field set.

Using getValue() and renderOutput()

This pair of methods is specifically for use with template variables (TVs). The `getValue()` method gets the raw, unprocessed value of the TV. Remember that you have to get the TV first (usually with `$modx->getObject()`) before calling its `getValue()` method. Here is the form:

```
$tv->getValue($id);
```

The `$id` variable represents the ID of the resource you want the TV's value from. In other words, the `$id` used here is always the resource ID of the document whose TV value you want, not the ID of the TV itself. If you want the TV's value for a specific resource, you need to include the resource's ID in the call. If you leave it out, you will get the default value of the TV.

The following example would get the raw value of a TV called MyTv for the current document:

```
$tv = $modx->getObject('modTemplateVar', array('name'=>'MyTv'));
$val = $tv->getValue($modx->resource->get('id'));
```

It's hard to test this method because if the TV contains one or more tags and you return the value from a snippet for display on a page, any tags will be processed when MODX renders the page. Suppose that the MyTv template variable contains the tag `[[*pagetitle]]`. Returning the results of the code above would display the current resource's Title rather than the tag even though the tag is the raw content of the TV. If you needed to debug the code above to see what's actually being returned from `getValue()`, you could add the following two lines at the end of the code:

```
$val = str_replace('[[', '[ [', $val);
return $val;
```

The added code will put a space between the opening braces of all MODX tags. That will keep MODX from processing them, and you will be able to see them in the output. Don't forget to remove that line when you're finished debugging.

The renderOutput() method gets the processed value of the TV. Any tags or @ bindings in the TV will be processed. In all other ways, it is the same as the getValue() method:

```
$tv = $modx->getObject('modTemplateVar', array('name'=>'MyTv'));
$val = $tv->renderOutput($modx->resource->get('id'));
```

If you want the value of a TV from the current resource or you already have a variable pointing to the resource, an easier method is to call the resource's getTVValue() method, which takes two forms:

```
$val = $resource->getTVValue('TvName');
$val = $resource->getTVValue($id);
```

In the second version, $id is the ID of the TV, not the resource. It's easy to confuse getValue() and getTVValue(). While getValue() is a method of the TV itself and returns the raw value, getTVValue() is a method of the resource and returns the processed output of the TV. In fact, if you look at the code for getTVValue(), you'll see that it calls the TV's renderOutput() method. Another thing to watch out for is the spelling of getTVValue(). It's easy to misspell it as getTvValue(), which doesn't exist.

MODX Evolution uses the getTemplateVarOutput() method, which is deprecated in MODX Revolution.

Using hasTemplate() and hasTemplateVar()

The hasTemplate() method is used to find out if a particular template variable is attached to a given template. You must first get a reference to the TV object with one of the get*() methods. The method is called like this:

```
$tv->hasTemplate($template);
```

The $template variable can be the name or ID of the template. The method returns true if the TV is attached to that template and false if not.

The hasTemplateVar() method tests the opposite relationship. It reports whether a particular template has a given template variable. In this case, you need a reference to the template object and you call the method like this:

```
$template->hasTemplateVar($tv);
```

The $tv variable can be the name or ID of the template variable.

Using joinGroup() and leaveGroup()

The `joinGroup()` method can be used with both resources and users.

It is used with resources to add the resource to a resource group. You must first obtain a reference to the resource object using one of the `get*()` methods (or use `$modx->resource` for the current resource). It takes this form:

```
$resource->joinGroup($group);
```

The `$group` variable can be a resource group object, the name of the resource group, or the ID of the resource group. Using the ID is slightly faster.

When used with a user object, `joinGroup()` adds the user to the user group:

```
$user->joinGroup($group);
```

In this case, the `$group` variable must be either the name or the ID of the user group. As with resources, you must first get a reference to the user object, and using the ID is slightly faster.

Note that these are both methods of the user and resource objects, not the `$modx` object, so they should never be called with `$modx->joinGroup()`.

At this writing, the `leaveGroup()` method is only available for the user object.

It removes the user from the specified user group. It is called like this:

```
$user->leaveGroup($group);
```

The `$group` variable can be the name or the ID of the user group.

Sanity Checking

In order to keep our code simple and brief and to avoid redundancy, we've often left out tests that make sure what we get back from MODX methods is what we want. Testing the return values is often called a "sanity check," and how you do it depends on what you are expecting to get back from a method.

Although we've often left it out of much of the code in the book, code going into production environments should always contain sanity checks.

Sanity checks are especially important with the get*() methods because if they fail, and you call any of the object's methods (e.g., the object's get() method), your site visitor may be left looking at a white screen with a PHP error message at the top complaining about calling get() on a non-object.

In this section we'll look at sanity checking with isset(), is_array(), empty(), ===, is_object(), and instanceof. All of these can be handy for sanity checking in snippets. Note that these are part of PHP, not MODX.

Using isset()

The isset() function tells you whether a variable exists and has some value other than null. A variable set to 0 or false will still be considered "set" if it exists.

```
if (isset($v)) {
    $output .= 'isset() returned true';
}
```

The code above will do nothing unless the variable $v exists and is set to something. If you add this line before the test, the snippet will report that isset() returned true:

```
$v = false;
```

Even though $v is set to false, it still exists and has a value, so it is considered "set." The next line would make $v fail the test.

```
unset($v);
```

The isset() function is often used in snippets to see if the user sent along a particular property in the snippet tag (or if it is set in the default properties or a property set). If the variable is set, the snippet uses it. If not, the snippet uses a default value.

```
if (isset($width)) {
    $pageWidth = $width;
} else {
    $pageWidth = 65;
}
```

More often, you'll see the same thing done in a single line with the PHP ternary operator. The following line is the equivalent of the code above:

```
$pageWidth = isset($width)? $width : 65;
```

If you're not familiar with the PHP ternary operator, there is a section on it in the PHP Primer in the Appendix.

In MODX Evolution, isset() is a reliable way of checking whether the user has sent a property to a snippet. In MODX Revolution, however, many snippets have default properties. If the snippet has a default property (or a property in an attached property set), isset() will always return true for that property, regardless of the value of the default property, or whether the user has included it as a property in the snippet tag. The return from isset() will be true even if the property has no value at all.

Using is_array()

The is_array() function simply tells us if a variable is an array.

```
if (is_array($v)) {
    $output .= "it's an Array";
}
```

If you are expecting an array, you can use is_array() to make sure you have one before trying to use it.

Some MODX methods (functions) can take either an array or a non-array as an argument. Often, they do different things depending on the type of the argument. If they receive a single string, for example, they might process the string. If they receive an array of strings, they'll loop through the array and process each string. Those methods use is_array() to check the incoming argument.

Using empty()

If a MODX method normally returns an array, it will usually return an empty array on any error. If you call getMany('Children') with a resource that has no children, for example, you'll get an empty array back. If getCollection() doesn't find any of the objects you are looking for, it will also return an empty array. You can check the return value for "emptiness" with the PHP empty() function.

The empty() function has many uses because it will test a variety of objects for emptiness. The following are all considered to be empty:

- "" (empty string)
- 0 (0 as an integer)
- "0" (0 as a string)
- null
- false
- array() (an empty array)
- var $var; (a variable declared in a class, but not set)

The empty() function can test to see if an array is empty, whether a snippet property has been set to true or some other non-false value, or whether a given string variable has any content.

Remember that a property, variable, $_POST, or $_GET member that is explicitly set to "", " ", '', ' ', 0, or '0' is still empty.

Using ===

Sometimes, you want to check to see if a value is really equal to PHP true or false. Suppose something returns false on an error but sets a number value on success (and the number might be 0). The empty() function won't tell you whether the return value is false or 0 since both are considered empty. You're in a similar situation with a function that returns false on error and a string (that might be an empty string) on success.

In those cases, you can test the return value by using the PHP === operator which tests for exact equality:

```
if ($return === false)
```

The test above will fail if $return contains an empty string or an integer with a value of 0. Note that there are three = signs in the operator. If you used == in the above example, empty strings and 0 integers would pass the test.

Using is_object()

What about MODX methods that normally return an object, such as `getOne()` and `getObject()`? These methods return an object on success but `null` on failure. Using `empty()` won't always work here. A better test is to see if the thing returned is an object or not using the PHP `is_object()` function:

```
if (is_object($modx->getOne('Parent')))
```

Using instanceof

Sometimes, it's not enough to know that you have an object. You need to know if it is the right kind of object. In those cases you can use PHP's `instanceof` operator (only available in PHP5):

```
if ($result instanceof modUser)
```

The code above tests to see if `$result` contains an instance of a MODX `modUser` object. Note that there are no quotes around `modUser`, and there is no equals sign in the test.

You can also test to see if the object is not an instance of a class using the PHP `Not` operator (`!`), but you need an extra set of parentheses to make it work:

```
if (! ($result instanceof modUser) )
```

You have to be careful with `instanceof` because it is designed for use with objects. If `$result` is a string or an integer, for example, the code above will throw an error. To prevent your code from crashing, you should always make sure that the thing you're testing is an object before using `instanceof`. The easiest way to do that is with a double test:

```
if (is_object($result) && ($result instanceof modUser) )
```

Because PHP evaluates the line above from left to right, the `instanceof` part won't execute if `$result` is not an object.

Since all the objects we would want to use in MODX are descended from the xPDOObject class, we could just use this test in all cases:

```
if (is_object($result) && ($result instanceof xPDOObject) ) {
    /* Object is OK, go ahead and process it */
} else {
    /* Error */
}
```

All MODX user, resource, and element objects and their related objects will pass that test if they are successfully retrieved. The reverse version using the PHP Not (!) and Or (||) operators will also work:

```
if (!is_object($result) || !($result instanceof xPDOObject)) {
    /* Error */
} else {
    /* Object is OK, go ahead and process it */
}
```

Creating and Changing Objects

There are many cases where you want to either create new MODX objects or modify existing ones in the code of a snippet or plugin. The following methods will allow you to do either task simply and reliably.

Using newObject()

If you would like to create a MODX object, you should always use the newObject() method. The code is simple, and MODX will handle the details for you. Here is the form:

```
$modx->newObject('ObjectType', $fields);
```

The first argument will be a MODX object class name (e.g., modSnippet, modResource, modChunk, etc.). The second argument is optional. The $fields argument provides an array of field names and values to populate the fields of the new object. The following code will create a new resource and populate some of its fields:

```
$fields = array(
    'pagetitle' => 'Test Page',
    'alias' => 'test-page',
    'menutitle' => 'Testing',

);
$resource = $modx->newObject('modResource', $fields);
$resource->save(); /* save it to the database */
return '<p>Resource created</p>';
```

Remember that once created with newObject(), the object exists in memory, but it is not in the MODX database until you call its save() method.

Using set()

The set() method can be used to change any field of an object. Of course you have to know the field names in order to set them. See the MODX Objects Reference in the Appendix for a list of object fields. You have to get the object first if it already exists or create it with newObject() before setting any fields. The code below is equivalent to the code we used with newObject() above:

```
$resource = $modx->newObject('modResource');
$resource->set('pagetitle', 'Test Page');
$resource->set('alias', 'test-page');
$resource->set('menutitle', 'Testing');
$resource->save(); /* save it to the database */
return '<p>Resource created</p>';
```

 Most MODX objects have an **id** field, which is created and filled automatically when the object is saved to the database for the first time. Never change or set the **id** field in your code.

Using setContent()

When you create an object, you usually want to set its main content field, but it can be hard to remember what that field is called. For resources it is called **content**, but for chunks and snippets it is called **snippet**. The object's setContent() method will always set the main content field of an object. If we wanted to set the **content** field of the resource we just created, the best method would be to use this code:

```
$resource->setContent('<p>I created this page in code</p>');
```

It's best to use this method to set the main content field of MODX objects because it will always work, even if the name of that field changes in future versions of MODX.

Using fromArray()

The fromArray() method allows you to set multiple fields of an object from an associative array of keys and values. The keys in the array will be the names of the fields of the object and the values will be the values you want in the fields. This method is essentially the reverse of the `toArray()` method we saw earlier in this chapter. The `fromArray()` method is most often called with a single argument, which is the array of keys and values. Here is an example using a simple snippet:

```
$fields = array(
    'name'=>'SimpleSnippet',
    'description'=>'Prints "Hello World" ',
    'snippet' => 'return "Hello World";',
);
$snippet = $modx->newObject('modSnippet');
$snippet->fromArray($fields);
$snippet->save();
```

Note that **snippet** is the name of the field that holds a snippet's code. The `fromArray()` method takes an optional second argument specifying a prefix to remove from the beginning of each field name. It also has several other optional arguments that are seldom used outside of MODX's internal code or transport packages.

Although we used the **snippet** field in our `fromArray()` example, we really should have left out that array member and used this instead:

```
$snippet->setContent('return "Hello World";');
```

Using addOne()

Sometimes, you want to create and save an object and one or more of its related objects at the same time. For example, what if you create a new user with `$modx->newObject()` and would like to add the user's full name and email address before saving the user? The full name and zip code are stored in the user's profile, not in the user object, and our user doesn't even have a profile yet. The answer is to create a new profile object, set its fields, and add it to the user object with the user object's `addOne()` method. We need to use `addOne()` because the profile is a related object of the user. Here's how to do it:

```
$user = $modx->newObject('modUser', array ('username'=>'MyUser'));
$user->set('password', 'desired_password');
$userProfile = $modx->newObject('modUserProfile');
$userProfile->set('fullname','My User');
$userProfile->set('email','myuser@gmail.com');
$success = $user->addOne($userProfile);
if ($success) {
```

```
        $user->save();
        return '<p>User object and profile created</p>';
    } else {
        return '<p>failed to add profile. User not saved.</p>';
    }
```

Notice that we didn't have to explicitly save the user profile. In fact, we can't at first. MODX wouldn't know which user it belonged to. Once we have connected it to the user object with addOne(), we could save it, but there's no need because it will be saved automatically when the user is saved. Note that you always call the save() method of the object whose addOne() method you called (in the case above, the $user object). MODX will automatically create and store the password hash for the specified password using the default hashing algorithm (MD5 or PBKDF2).

The addOne() method is a member of the user object itself, not the $modx object, so you should never call it with $modx->addOne().

You might expect that you'd use addOne() whenever you only have a single object to add, but this is not the case. Like getOne(), addOne() is only used when there can never be more than one related object to be added. Before using addOne(), be sure to review the section below on addMany().

Using addMany()

The relationship between addOne() and addMany() is like the relationship between getOne() and getMany(). Which method you use depends on the relationship between the two objects. We chose to add a user profile to a user in the example above because each user can have only one profile. If we were adding a snippet to a category instead, we would have to use addMany() because a category can have many snippets.

The key is to ask, "If I were getting this object (the one being added in the first argument of the method), would I use getOne() or getMany()?" If the answer is getOne(), use addOne(). If the answer is getMany(), use addMany(). You may need to review the section above on getOne() and getMany().

If you wanted to add a snippet called MySnippet to a category called MySnippets, you'd first create the category, then add the snippet to it using the following code:

```
$category = $modx->newObject('modCategory',array('category'=>'MySnippets'));
$snippet = $modx->getObject('modSnippet',array('name'=>'MySnippet'));
$category->addMany($snippet);
$category->save();
return '<p>Snippet categorized</p>';
```

Note that **category** is the "name" field for categories. We didn't have to save the snippet because it is automatically saved when we save the category.

Because snippets and categories are related objects, we could also have made the connection the other way around by using these two lines of code to replace the third and fourth lines above:

```
$snippet->addOne($category);
$snippet->save();
```

Why are we using addOne() here instead of addMany()? We have to use addOne() because a snippet has only one category. We used addMany() before because a category can have many snippets. Notice, too, that we had to save the snippet instead of the category. Otherwise, the category would have been created, but the snippet would not have been placed in that category. Always save the object whose add*() method you have called.

Using save()

We've seen a number of examples of the save() method in the sections above. Once you have a reference to an object (either by finding it with one of the get*() methods or by creating it), you can save it to the database by calling its save() method. Remember that the object is transient and doesn't exist in the database until its save() method has been called:

```
$object->save();
```

The save() method takes an optional argument that determines whether the object will be saved in the cache as well as in the database. If the argument is a positive number, the object will be cached for that many seconds. If the argument is `true`, the object will be cached indefinitely. The argument defaults to `null`, in which case the object will not be cached. With the following code, the object will be cached for 45 seconds:

```
$object->save(45);
```

Using remove()

At some point, you might want to remove a MODX object from the database in the code of a snippet or plugin. The process is very easy. You simply get the object and then call its `remove()` method:

```
$user = $modx->getObject('modUser', array('username'=>'MyUser'));
$user->remove();
```

Once `remove()` has been successfully executed, the removal process is not reversible.

Modifying Existing Objects

All of the methods we detailed above can be used with existing objects. Instead of creating a new object with `$modx->newObject()`, however, you simply get the object with one of the `get*()` methods, modify it, and then call its `save()` method. The following code, for example, will change the alias field of the current resource:

```
$resource =& $modx->resource;
$resource->set('alias', 'NewAlias');
$resource->save();
```

Setting Placeholders

A placeholder is also a MODX object, but it is a relatively simple one when compared to resource and element objects. Like all MODX tags, its class extends the `modTag` class. The simplest way to set placeholders in a snippet or plugin is with the `setPlaceholder()` method:

```
$modx->setPlaceholder($key, $value);
```

The code above sets a placeholder with the name held in `$key` to the value held in `$value`.

In other words, the $key/$value pair is added to the associative array holding all place-holders that are currently set. The following code sets a placeholder named *Hello* to the string *Welcome to the web site!*:

```
$modx->setPlaceholder('Hello', 'Welcome to the web site!');
```

Once set, the placeholder can be retrieved with this code:

```
$msg = getPlaceholder('Hello');
```

The placeholder can also be displayed on a web page by using the appropriate placeholder tag:

```
[[+Hello]]
```

Here is an example that includes a personal greeting for the user:

```
$user = $modx->user->get('username');
$modx->setPlaceholder('Hello', 'Hello ' . $user . ', welcome back!');
```

The [[+Hello]] placeholder could then be used to display the greeting in a template, a chunk, a template variable, or in the Resource Content field of a resource.

Placeholders can also contain other MODX tags, which will be processed before the place-holder tag is rendered:

```
$modx->setPlaceholder ('DisplaySiteStart',
    'The Site Start is [[++site_start]]');
```

With the code above, the placeholder tag [[+DisplaySiteStart]] would show this message (assuming that your Home Page has a resource ID of 1):

```
The Site Start is 1
```

The first argument to setPlaceholder() must be a string. The second can be a string, but it can also contain any PHP variable type as well as any MODX object. Placeholders that will be displayed with a placeholder tag, however, should always contain strings.

If you would like to add a prefix to your placeholders without adding it manually, you can add it by using `toPlaceholder()` instead of `setPlaceholder()`. When using `toPlaceholder()` the first two arguments are the same as those of `setPlaceholder()`. The third argument is the prefix to use, and the fourth is the separator (which defaults to a dot):

```
$modx->toPlaceholder('name', 'John Doe', 'userdata');
```

The code above adds the prefix `userdata.` to the `name` placeholder when setting it. To display the value (John Doe), you would use the following tag:

```
[[+userdata.name]]
```

The `toPlaceholder()` method can be handy if you are writing a snippet that will be part of a transport package. The prefix helps keep your placeholders from colliding with place-holders set by other snippets.

The `setPlaceholders()` method (notice the "s" on the end of the name) will allow you to set multiple placeholders at one time. In its simplest form, you send an associative array as the only argument, and it sets the placeholders.

```
$ph = array(
    'first_name'=>'John',
    'last_name'=>'Doe',
);
$modx->setPlaceholders($ph);
```

In a web page, you could then display the user's full name like this:

```
Name: [[+last_name]], [[+first_name]]
```

You can add a second argument to `setPlaceholders()` containing a prefix to prepend to all placeholder names. The `setPlaceholders()` method does not allow you to specify a separator character, so you need to include it in the second argument:

```
$modx->setPlaceholders($ph, 'userdata.');
```

Another method, `toPlaceholders()`, does allow you to specify the separator character in a third argument, and like `toPlaceholder()`, it defaults to a dot:

```
$modx->toPlaceholders($ph, 'userdata' , '.');
```

If you would like to delete your placeholder entries after using them, you can use `unsetPlaceholder($key)` or `unsetPlaceholders($keys)`. Using these methods in a snippet will keep the placeholder tags from working, so they should only be used if the placeholder values will never be displayed with tags. Much of the information in the section above will be repeated later in this chapter when we work though practical examples involving resources, elements, and users.

Using the Lexicon

If you are writing a snippet that may be used in different languages, every message the snippet displays should be in the form of a MODX language string. SPForm, for example, displays a number of prompts and messages on the contact form. All the messages are language strings. That way, the snippet can be translated for use in another language without touching the code itself. This is all possible using the MODX lexicon.

So what exactly is a lexicon? Technically, a *lexicon* is a MODX service (which can be treated as an object) into which you can load a set of language strings divided into various namespaces and topics. Once loaded, the language strings can be retrieved by their keys and displayed in the Manager or on pages in the front end. Generally, only one language is loaded into the lexicon at a time. That sounds complicated, but the process is fairly simple. You create a properly formatted lexicon file, put it in the right place, load the lexicon in your snippet, and refer to the lexicon entries with the appropriate code.

Lexicon Files

The language strings are stored in files. The lexicon files for the MODX core are below the **core/lexicon** directory (each in a specific language directory, e.g., **core/lexicon/en**). The standard location for the English lexicon files of add-on components is:

core/components/component_name/lexicon/en/

The English language file for the SPForm component, for example, is:

core/components/spform/lexicon/en/default.inc.php

The name of every language file must be in this form:

topicName.**inc.php**

In code, you never have to refer to the file name of a language file. You simply load the topic by its name into the Lexicon (more on this in a bit).

Each line in the lexicon file is a lexicon entry. Each lexicon entry has a key (used to retrieve it), a value (the string that's displayed in place of the language tag), a namespace, a topic, and a language. Only the keys and values are used in the lexicon file. The field containing the key is called **name**. The lines in a language file must be in this form:

```
$_lang['send-to'] = "Send To";
$_lang['your-name'] = "Your name";
$_lang['email-address'] = "Email address";
$_lang['subject'] = "Subject";
```

The part in the square brackets is the key, and the part to the right of the equals sign is the value. All lexicon entries in all languages begin with $_lang[].

Users can override the values for individual lexicon entries in the grid in **System → Lexicon Management**. If you edit lexicon entries in the grid, however, always be sure you select the correct namespace, topic, and language before editing any entries.

Changes made in the grid are shown in green and are saved in the **lexicon_entries** table of the MODX database. They will survive any upgrades of MODX or components. This means that you can freely change the language strings for the MODX core or any add-on component in the grid without worrying about them being overwritten when you upgrade MODX or the add-on component.

Component Namespaces

A *namespace* is like a category tag for third-party components. It lets the component load a particular set of language strings into the lexicon. It also contains a path to the component's support files (if any) and tells MODX where to look for the component's lexicon files. In future versions of MODX, the namespace may also play a role in MODX security by allowing or denying access to specific components.

Any MODX third-party component can (and should) have its own namespace and the namespace may have multiple topics. Every namespace should have a "default" topic with lexicon entries in a `default.inc.php` file. Generally, MODX add-on components have a single namespace, which is simply an all-lowercase version of the component's name. Many components also get by with only a "default" topic.

Namespaces for add-on components re created by transport packages during the installation process. You can also create them manually by going to **System → Namespaces**. The *namespace path* always takes this form:

`{core_path}components/componentName/`

Note that `{core_path}` is a literal string that should be typed as it appears here. MODX will translate it to the actual path of the MODX core directory. The namespace path should always end with a slash and there should be no slash between `{core_path}` and `components`.

Languages

Language strings can be grouped by their *language,* although the term "language" is somewhat misleading. The language strings in a language can represent anything you like. You could have a verbose language and a terse language. British English and American English are considered different languages. You could even have a technical language and a layperson's language and let users switch between them by creating a user setting.

Displaying a Lexicon String

When you want to display a language string in MODX, you refer to it by its key, and MODX gets the string from whatever language is currently loaded in the lexicon.

This code will make sure the lexicon service is available (though it is usually unnecessary when running code inside MODX):

```
$modx->getService('lexicon','modLexicon');
```

Language strings are loaded into the lexicon using the lexicon's `load()` method. They must be loaded before accessing them by key. The `load()` method takes a variable number of arguments.

Each argument must specify a topic and, optionally, precede the topic with a namespace and/or language. They must be specified in this order and format: `language:namespace:topic`. Here are all the possible versions:

```
$modx->lexicon->load('Language:namespace:topic');
$modx->lexicon->load('namespace:topic');
$modx->lexicon->load('topic');
```

Note that the argument in the examples above is a single string and specifies a single topic. To load multiple topics, you can add more arguments separated by commas:

```
$modx->lexicon->load('default', 'user', 'chunk');
```

 Unlike the language strings in the files or the Lexicon Management grid, language strings loaded in the lexicon have only a key and a value. They do not have a language or a namespace. Loading a language string with the same name (key) as an existing entry will overwrite that entry even if they are in different languages or namespaces. If you are writing an add-on component, you should always specify the namespace when you load a topic into the lexicon. You should also use a prefix on the lexicon keys to avoid collisions. For SPForm, for example, you might see `$modx->lexicon('spf.bad_email')`.

When you want to display a language string in a snippet, you use code like this:

```
$output .= $modx->lexicon('keyName');
```

This code will get the language string with the key `keyName`. You can only get one language string at a time, and at present, there is no way to specify a namespace or language.

It is the developer's responsibility to make sure that the proper namespace and topics are loaded into the lexicon before retrieving them when using lexicon strings in code. This is not the case with language tags used to display language strings since they can (and should) include the language, namespace, and topic as well as the key:

```
[[%LanguageStringKey?
    &language=`en`
    &namespace=`NameSpaceName`
    &topic=`TopicName`
]]

[[%file-not-found?
    &language=`en`
    &namespace=`spform`
    &topic=`default`
]]
```

When a third-party component is first distributed as part of a transport package, all of its language strings will usually be in a single, default language. Later, other language packs will become available for the component. Each language pack will contain all the same strings (with the same keys) but with their values translated into the alternate language. Each language pack will, typically, be added as part of the transport package, though they can be distributed in a separate package as well. Once the alternate language files are created, a set of strings in a specific language can be loaded into the lexicon with `$modx->lexicon->load()` and used anywhere in the MODX front or back end.

The information above can be somewhat confusing, but for most snippets or other components, the method for using language strings is fairly simple. We'll see how to do it later in this chapter.

Working with Resources, Elements, and Users

In the following sections, we'll explore some practical uses for the methods we discussed earlier in this chapter. We'll see how to work with the current resource and other resources. We'll take a look at getting information about the snippet itself, and we'll see how to work with other elements. We'll also try out some operations with users. Along the way, we'll work with default properties, property sets, and the $scriptProperties array. We'll also take a look at getChunk() and runSnippet(). We'll tackle using the MODX lexicon in snippets, and we'll close with a practical example showing how to create a page-count snippet and display its results on every page of our site.

Some of the demonstration code in this section assumes that you still have the resources, chunks, and snippets created earlier in the book. If not, you'll need to create them (or at least shortened versions of them).

Setting Things Up

We'll need a place to show the work we do in this chapter, so let's create a snippet to try things out in and a display area to show the results. As we go along, we'll add and remove sections to try out different advanced snippet techniques.

Before going any further, we'll create a resource called *ObjectDemo* and a snippet with the same name so we can experiment with some of the techniques used in this chapter.

Creating the Resource

Create a new resource called *ObjectDemo* and put the following snippet tag in its Resource Content field:

```
[[!ObjectDemo]]
```

Make sure you fill in the various optional fields such as Alias, Long Title, Description, etc. Set the template to your main template. Make sure the resource is published, and save it.

Creating the Snippet

Create a new snippet, also called *ObjectDemo*, and put this code in its Snippet code (php) field:

```php
<?php
/* Code for ObjectDemo Snippet */
$output = '<h2>Object Demo Snippet Output</h2>';
/* ------ Add lines here ------ */


/* -------------------------- */
return $output;
?>
```

As you go through the sections below, add the suggested lines to the middle of this snippet. Be sure to use `.=` rather than `=` so that all the lines will be added to the output. You can preview the ObjectDemo resource after each addition to see the code at work. Once you've explored any of the methods below, you may get tired of looking at their output. You can always add the new code at the top of the snippet and put a return statement below the new code:

```php
return $output
```

The rest of the code will be ignored when the snippet executes. It's best not to delete code because some sections will involve adding to or modifying the code you just created.

In snippets, a lot of time is spent working with resources because they are at the heart of the web site's front end. Much of the time, you want to work with the current resource. There are times, however, when you want to deal with other resources on the site. In the following section, we'll explore some ways to deal with both the current resource and any other resources on the site.

Working with Resources

As we learned earlier, a reference to the current resource (the one currently being viewed or previewed in the front end) is always available as the $modx->resource object. This is true even if the snippet tag is in a template, chunk, or template variable. As long as the tag is part of the current resource in some way, $modx->resource will resolve to the current resource the web site visitor is looking at.

You can use the various methods of the resource object to get information about the current resource and, if necessary, to change and save it. Working with other resources is exactly the same, except that we need to get a reference to the object first by using one of the `$modx->get*()` methods.

In the sections that follow, we'll use a variable called `$resource` to point to the resource we're working with. The name of the variable is arbitrary, but using `$resource` is a MODX convention. We'll also leave out most sanity checks for the sake of brevity, but you should definitely add them before putting any of this code on a live site. In all the examples below, assume that we've set the `$resource` variable with something similar to one of the following lines of code. The first is for the current resource, and the others are for any other resource.

```
$resource =& $modx->resource;
$resource = $modx->getObject('modResource', $id);
$resource = $modx->getObject('modResource',
    array('pagetitle'=>'resourceName'));
$resource = $modx->getObject('modResource', $criteria);
```

In the second line, `$id` is the resource ID of the resource you're looking for. Using this method is faster, and it will still retrieve the resource object if its Title field changes. Note the field name **pagetitle** in the third line. That's the name of the field in the database that holds a resource's Title field. It's a very common mistake to use "name" or "title" here. If you do that, the resource will never be found and it may take you a while to figure out why.

Note that we used `=&` instead of `=` for the assignment in the first line above as described in the first part of this chapter. You should always use `=&` when assigning the current resource (or the current user) to a variable.

Working with get()

Once you have a reference to the `$resource` object, you can get any field with the object's `get()` method:

```
$resource->get('fieldName');
```

If you would like to put multiple fields into an array in the snippet code, you can call **get()** like this:

```
$fields = $resource->get(array('id','pagetitle','alias'));
```

All fields are available with `get()`. Add some lines like the following ones to your Object-Demo snippet to display various fields from the current resource and preview your *Object-Demo* resource to see what they produce:

```
$output .= '<h3>Current Resource Info</h3>';
$resource =& $modx->resource;
$output .= '<p>Title: ' . $resource->get('pagetitle') . '</p>';
$output .= '<p>Alias: ' . $resource->get('alias') . '</p>';
```

Working with toArray()

If you want all the fields of a resource, its `toArray()` method will retrieve them in the form of an associative array. Instead of the code above, try this code in your ObjectDemo snippet:

```
$output .= '<h3>Current Resource Info</h3>';
$resource =& $modx->resource;
$fields = $resource->toArray();
$output .= '<pre>' . print_r($fields, true) . '</pre>';
```

Don't be surprised if this produces a long list — resources have a lot of fields. This will give you some idea how much overhead there is in using resources to store data. If you are working with a blog that will have many posts, for example, creating a new document for each blog post is fairly wasteful because most of the fields will contain information that you don't really need to display the post. The same goes for an e-commerce site with many products where each product has its own resource. In those cases, it's better to create a custom database table containing just the information you need for each item and use a snippet and a Tpl chunk to display them all, though the details of doing that are beyond the scope of this book.

Remember that the `toArray()` method can be used with any MODX object.

Working with hasChildren() and isfolder

The hasChildren() method tells us whether a resource has any children under it in the Resource tree. The **isfolder** resource field indicates whether the resource is designated as a container. In MODX Revolution, hasChildren() and **isfolder** are independent.

In MODX Evolution, the **isfolder** field is set automatically when a resource has children and the hasChildren() method doesn't exist. In Evolution, the **isfolder** field can't be changed. This is not the case in Revolution where a resource can be marked as a container but have no children and a resource with children can be designated as a non-container. This can be handy in styling menus or the output from Wayfinder or getResources tags.

Notice that hasChildren() is a method of the resource, and **isfolder** is a resource field. To find out if a resource has any children, you can use the following method. It returns the number of children:

```
$numberOfChildren = $resource->hasChildren();
```

To see if a document is marked as a container, use this code, which returns true or false:

```
$folderStatus=$resource->get('isfolder');
```

The resource object's hasChildren() method returns the number of children. The **isfolder** resource field shows the value of the Container checkbox (1 or 0). Neither of these will give you any information about the children themselves, though. For that we need to use other methods.

You can display the number of children and the **isfolder** status for any resource with this code. Try it out in your ObjectDemo snippet:

```
$resource = $modx->getObject('modResource',
    array('pagetitle'=>'DocName'));
$output .= '<p>The ' . $resource->get('pagetitle') . ' resource has ';
$output .= $resource->hasChildren() . ' children.';
if ($resource->get('isfolder')) {
    $output .= ' and it is a folder.';
} else {
    $output .= ' and it is not a folder';
}
$output .= '</p>';
```

Be sure to replace *DocName* with the name of an actual resource. Try it with various resources with varying numbers of children. Note that this method is a member of the resource object, so it must always be called with $resource->hasChildren(), where $resource is the name of the variable pointing to the resource. Be careful, because if you use it's a folder or it's not a folder in your output, you'll need to use double-quotes. If you don't, the extra single-quotes will cause a PHP syntax error.

Working with getChildIds()

You can get the ID numbers of the children of any resource (as an array) with getChildIds($id, $depth). The first argument, $id, is the Resource ID of the resource you want the children of. The second argument, $depth, is the number of levels you want to traverse. The second argument is optional and defaults to 10. Unlike hasChildren(), getChildIds() is a method of the $modx object, so it must always be called with:

```
$modx->getChildIds($id);
```

If you want to get the IDs of children of a document with getChildIds(), you need to get the document's resource ID first:

```
$id = $resource->get('id');
$children = $modx->getChildIds($id);
```

As we learned earlier, the return value is always an array of ID numbers or an empty array if the specified resource has no children.

Try adding the following code just below the section we used with hasChildren() in your ObjectDemo snippet:

```
if ($resource->hasChildren()) {
    $id = $resource->get('id');
    $children = $modx->getChildIds($id);
    $output = '<p>Children: ';
    $output .= implode(',', $children) . '</p>';
}
```

In the page output, you should see a comma-delimited list of the children's IDs (if any).

If you want the child objects themselves, you can use their IDs to get them with $modx->getObject(), but you can also retrieve them with $resource->getMany('Children').

Working with getParentIds() and the parent field

If you want the ID of a resource's immediate parent, it is available in the resource's **parent** field. You can retrieve it with the resource's `get()` method:

```
$resource->get('parent');
```

Sometimes, however, you want all the ancestors going up the tree. You could walk up the tree using `getObject()` with the contents of each resource's **parent** field, but the ancestor's IDs are available with `$modx->getParentIds()`. Because `getParentIds()` is a method of the `$modx` object, you must always include the ID of the resource you want the ancestors of as an argument and call the method like this:

```
$modx->getParentIds($id);
```

Put the following code in your ObjectDemo snippet just below the code we used above to get the child IDs. Try previewing the `ObjectDemo` resource several times with different resources selected. Try to use resources that have a few ancestors (i.e., are deeper in the tree):

```
$resourceArray = $modx->getParentIds($id);
$output .= '<p>Parents: ' . implode(', ', resourceArray) . '</p>';
```

As with the children, you can get the parent objects themselves by using their IDs with `$modx->getObject($id)`, but you can also get them with the resource's `getMany()` method.

Working with getOne() and getMany()

As we learned earlier in the chapter, `getOne()` and `getMany()` retrieve related objects. If there can only be one object (e.g., `Parent`, `Template`, or `Category`), you use `getOne()`. If there can be more than one object (e.g., `Children`, or `TemplateVars`), you use `getMany()`. Remember that these methods retrieve whole MODX objects. If you just want the content of a resource field, you need to use the object's `get()` method.

Here's a brief list of some of the related objects for resources. Their class types are in parentheses. For a more comprehensive list, see the MODX Objects Reference in the Appendix.

Related Objects available with getOne():

- Parent (modResource)
- Template (modTemplate)
- CreatedBy (modUser)
- EditedBy (modUser)
- DeletedBy (modUser)
- PublishedBy (modUser)
- Category (modCategory)
- ContentType (modContentType)
- Context (modContext)

Related Objects available with getMany():

- Children (modResource)
- TemplateVars (modTemplateVar)

Remember that the aliases used in getOne() and getMany() are in CamelCase. They always start with an uppercase letter. The aliases for getOne() are always singular (e.g., Parent), and the aliases for getMany() are always plural (e.g. Children), even if there is only one object to retrieve.

Let's get the parent object of the current resource. Because a resource can have only one parent, we'll use getOne(). Put the following code in your ObjectDemo snippet:

```
$resource =& $modx->resource;
$parentObject = $resource->getOne('Parent');
$parentTitle = $parentObject->get('pagetitle');
$output .= '<h4>My Parent</h4>';
$output .= '<p>Parent Title: ' . $parentTitle . '</p>';
```

Note that the code above will fail with an error message if the current resource has no parent (i.e., it's at the top level of the Resource tree). That's because we forgot to put in any sanity checks. To make it work, you can drag the resource under another resource in the tree so it will have a parent. To avoid the error message, we could replace the third line above with this:

```
if ($parentObject) {
    $parentTitle = $parentObject->get('pagetitle');
} else {
    $parentTitle = 'No Parent';
}
```

If we wanted the parent of another resource, we could get it the same way by replacing the first line of the code above with something like this (after setting $id to the resource ID of the page we want):

```
$resource = $modx->getObject('modResource', $id);
```

There are a number of other objects available with a resource's getOne() method. Several of them are user objects. The creator, publisher, and most recent editor, for example, are available as related objects. To display the username of the original creator of the resource, you could add this code to your ObjectDemo snippet:

```
$output .= '<h4>My Creator</h4>';
$creator = $resource->getOne('CreatedBy');
$username = $creator->get('username');
$output .= '<p>I was created by: ' . $username . '</p>';
```

Now that we've retrieved the parent object and the creator of the current resource, let's try getting the children's names. We have to use getMany() here because a resource can have more than one child. Because getMany() returns an array, we have to process that array after retrieving it. If your ObjectDemo resource doesn't have any children, you'll have to add some. Add this code to your ObjectDemo snippet:

```
$resource =& $modx->resource;
$children = $resource->getMany('Children');
$output .= '<h4>My Children</h4>';
foreach ($children as $child) {
    $childTitle = $child->get('pagetitle');
    $output .= '<p>Child Title: ' . $childTitle . '</p>';
}
```

Note that the first line is unnecessary if you have it earlier in the code. When you preview your ObjectDemo resource, you should see a list of the children's page titles. Earlier, we got the resource's parent object with getOne(). In some cases, though, you might want all the ancestors of the current resource going up the tree (or another resource). In that case we have to use $modx->getParentIds() because there is no related object for a resource's ancestors. The following code will get the ancestors of a document and display their titles:

```
$resource = $modx->getObject('modResource',
    array('pagetitle'=>'DocName'));
$ancestorIds = $modx->getParentIds($resource->get('id'));
$output .= '<h4>Ancestors</h4>';
foreach ($ancestorsIds as $resourceId) {
    $ancestor = $modx->getObject('modResource', $resourceId);
    $ancestorTitle = $ancestor->get('pagetitle');
    $output .= '<p>Ancestor Title: ' . $ancestorTitle . '</p>';
}
```

Obviously, this won't show anything for resources at the top level of the Resource tree because they don't have any ancestors. Put the code above in your ObjectDemo snippet, replacing DocName with the title of a resource with several ancestors.

We'll see some more examples of getOne() and getMany() when we talk about template variables and users later in the chapter.

Working with getCollection()

The getCollection() method is essentially a plural version of getObject(). Both methods get objects of the type specified in the first argument that meet the criteria specified in the second argument. While getObject() returns a single object (or null), getCollection() returns an array of objects (or an empty array).

Say, for example, that you want to retrieve all published resources on the site. This code would do it:

```
$resources = $modx->getCollection('modResource', array('published'=>'1'));
```

That's a fairly simple request. What if we wanted just the IDs and page titles of all published documents created by the admin (whose user ID is 1) and we wanted them sorted by Resource ID number? For that we would need to use an xPDO query:

```
$output .= '<h2>Published Resources</h2>';
$c = $modx->newQuery('modResource');
$c->select(array('id','pagetitle'));
$c->where(array('published'=>'1',
    'createdby'=>'1',));
$c->sortby('id', 'ASC');
$docs = $modx->getCollection('modResource', $c);
foreach ($docs as $doc) {
    $output .= '<p>Title:' . $doc->get('pagetitle') .
        ' ID:' . $doc->get('id') .'</p>';
}
return $output;
```

Queries like the one above can be quite complicated and can involve any SQL operations such as joins, GROUPBY, ORs, INs, etc. For example, add this line to the $c->where array above and you'll only get resources with the letter "r" in their page titles:

```
'pagetitle:LIKE' => '%r%'
```

Using this line instead will show all the resources without an "r" in their page titles:

```
'pagetitle:NOT LIKE' => '%r%'
```

Here's an example that will get all resources, sorted by creation date, where the resource is published and the pagetitle contains "hello" or "welcome":

```
$c = newQuery('modResource');
$c->sortBy('createdon');
$c->where(array(
    'published'=> 1,
    array('pagetitle:LIKE'=> 'hello',
    'OR: pagetitle:LIKE'=> 'welcome')));
$resources = $modx->getCollection('modResource', $c);
```

Explaining all the possible query operations is beyond the scope of this book. See the xPDO online documentation for details.

The getOne() method can also accept an xPDO query as a second argument, though it is seldom necessary. An xPDO query can also be used as a second argument with getOne() and getMany() and with either of the graph methods if you don't want all of the objects that they might retrieve or if you want to sort them using one of the resource fields.

Working with getObjectGraph()

Both getObjectGraph() and getCollectionGraph() can be used to retrieve resources and their related objects in one step. For example, the following code will get a resource and its parent object with a single query and will display their page titles:

```
$output .= '<h2>Me and My Parent</h2>';
$id = $modx->resource->get('id');
$resource = $modx->getObjectGraph('modResource',
    array('Parent' => array()),
    $id);
$output .= '<p>Me: ' . $resource->get('pagetitle') . '</p>';
$output .= 'My Parent: ' . $resource->Parent->get('pagetitle') . '</p>';
```

Add the code above to your ObjectDemo snippet and then move your ObjectDemo resource under some other page by dragging it in the tree or by setting its parent when editing it.

When you preview your `ObjectDemo` resource, you should see its title and the title of the parent page in your output. Be careful because if the `ObjectDemo` resource doesn't have a parent, the code will fail. For a live site, we would have tested the return value of both the resource and the parent before calling their `get()` methods.

Working with getCollectionGraph()

What if we wanted to retrieve a group of resources and their parents or children? We would have to use `getCollectionGraph()`. The following code will display the names of all the published resources on the site and their children (if any):

```
$output .= '<h2>Resources and their Children</h2>';
$criteria = array('published'=>'1');
$resources = $modx->getCollectionGraph('modResource',
    array('Children' => array()),
    $criteria);
foreach($resources as $resource) {
    $output .= '<p>Resource: ' . $resource->get('pagetitle');
    if ($resource->hasChildren($resource->get('id')) ) {
        foreach ($resource->Children as $child) {
            $output .= ' >> ' . $child->get('pagetitle');
        }
    } else {
        $output .= ' >> No Children';
    }
    $output .= '</p>';
}
```

Notice that because we asked for `Children`, the related object is an array. If we had asked for the `Parent` instead, we wouldn't need the inner `foreach` loop. You should always be aware of what you're asking for when using `getCollectionGraph()`.

Sometimes, you just want to get the **id** of an object, but don't need the object itself. You can use $modx->getObject() to retrieve it and $object->get('**id**') to get the ID, but here is a more efficient method for retrieving any single field of an object:

```
$pagetitle = 'MyDocument';
/* build a new xPDOQuery object, similar to getObject() *
$query = $modx->newQuery('modResource', array('pagetitle' => $pagetitle));
/* indicate you only want to select the id column */
$query->select('id');
/* prepare the PDOStatement and execute it directly */
if ($query->prepare() && $query->stmt->execute()) {
    $id = $query->stmt->fetchColumn();
} else {
    /* error */
}
```

Working with Properties

The current element when working in a snippet is, of course, the snippet itself. Snippets often need to access the values sent as snippet properties in the tag as well as their default properties and properties in an attached property set.

As you know, any properties of a snippet sent in the snippet tag are available as variables in the snippet. So the property **&firstName** is available in the snippet as the variable $firstName. But all the properties are available in an array called $scriptProperties. You can get them out of that array by asking for them by name using the $scriptProperties array or by using the $modx->getOption() method.

Working with the $scriptProperties Array

On occasion, you might need to process or use all the properties of the snippet. They are available as the associative array $scriptProperties. Each member of the array contains the name of the property and its value. The properties are also available individually as:

```
$scriptProperties['propertyName'].
```

If you have a lot of properties, you can save a little typing by assigning them to an array with a shorter name:

```
$opts =& $scriptProperties;
$prop = $opts['propertyName'];
```

Add the following lines to your ObjectDemo snippet to display all its properties:

```
$output .= '<h3>Properties</h3>';
foreach($scriptProperties as $key=>$value) {
    $output .= '<p>KEY: ' . $key . '=>' . ' VALUE: ' . $value . '</p>';
}
```

Note that the code won't display much unless your snippet has some properties. You can start by adding some properties in the snippet tag in your ObjectDemo resource:

```
[[!ObjectDemo? &firstName=`John` &lastName=`Doe` &age=`21`]]
```

After viewing those, add some default properties on the "Properties" tab of the ObjectDemo snippet. Finally, create some more properties in an independent property set, attach them to the snippet, and specify them in the snippet tag. If necessary, you can review how to do that in the section on property sets in Chapter 6. In fact, you may already have a property set you can use that is left over from the exercise in Chapter 6.

The code above that prints out the $scriptProperties array is handy for debugging when there are a lot of properties and you want to see the ones that are reaching the snippet (and what their values are). The array will include all snippet properties sent in the snippet tag, all default properties, and any properties in an attached property set. In each case, you'll see both the key and value of the property. As usual, the values set in a property set will override the values in the snippet's default properties, and properties sent in the snippet tag will override both of those.

There is also a shorthand method in PHP to print out all the keys and values in an array. This can be handy for quick debugging:

```
print_r($arrayName);
```

If you want to return the value of `print_r()` as the output of a snippet, you need to use this form in the snippet:

```
return print_r($arrayName, true);
```

If you want a much longer but nicely formatted version, you can add `<pre>` and `</pre>` tags to the output like this:

```
return '<pre>' . print_r($arrayName,true) . '</pre>';
```

Using getOption()

In the section above, we saw how to get a property of a snippet with this code:

```
$props = $scriptProperties['propertyName'];
```

Let's look at another way to get the values of snippet properties: `$modx->getOption()`. When used with a single argument, `getOption()` will search the settings for the value in the first argument (more on this in the next section). However, `getOption()` can also take an optional second argument, which allows it to search other arrays. The second argument specifies the array to search.

The following code will search through all properties sent in the snippet tag, all default properties, and any attached property set (in other words, the `$scriptProperties` array), looking for the value in the first argument.

```
$modx->getOption('propertyName', $scriptProperties, 'default value');
```

The third argument (`'default'`) is also optional. It provides a default value to use if the search comes up empty. Note that `getOption()` also searches for any setting (system setting, user setting, or context setting) if the value is not found in the specified array (e.g., `$scriptProperties`). If it then finds a system setting with that name, it will use the system setting, and the `'default'` argument will be ignored. It's a good idea, then, to choose names for your snippet properties that aren't likely to collide with any setting names. The best way to do that is to add a prefix to all the property names.

You can use `$modx->getOption()` to search any PHP associative array. It's handy because, in a single line of code, you can search the array and specify a default value to use if the value is not found. Be careful, however, if the snippet has default properties or an attached property set. If you use `getOption()` to retrieve a property that exists in the default properties or an attached property set, the default value you set as the third argument will never be used, regardless of the property setting, because the `getOption()` call will always be successful even if the property has no value.

Where Are the Properties Coming From?

From inside the snippet, there is no way to see where any particular property is coming from since properties sent in the snippet tag, default properties, and properties from property sets all end up in the same array.

In creating the array, MODX starts with the default properties, then overwrites any properties set in an attached property set, then overwrites any properties sent in the snippet tag. If you put some properties with the same names in the snippet tag, the default properties, and the attached property set, you can confirm that the properties in the snippet tag have the highest priority, the attached property set is second, and the default properties have the lowest priority.

Working with Other Elements

To accomplish all the tasks you might want to do in a snippet, you need to understand how to work with chunks, other snippets, template variables, and settings. We'll explore how to work with those objects in the following sections.

Working with getChunk()

One of the most common operations in a snippet is getting, processing, and returning the content of chunks (including Tpl chunks). Quite often in a snippet, you want to grab the content of a chunk and insert it into the output. This is easily done with the following code:

```
$output .= $modx->getChunk('ChunkName');
```

MODX will retrieve the named chunk for you. It will also process the chunk to resolve any tags contained in the chunk such as chunk, snippet, or setting tags. If the chunk contains placeholder tags that refer to the chunk's default properties or properties in an attached property set, those will be processed as well.

If there are other placeholder tags in the chunk that are not related to the default properties, they can be set with $modx->setPlaceholder() before getChunk() is called. They can also be replaced by the snippet itself using str_replace(), or something similar, after getChunk() has been called, but before adding the chunk's content to the output. You may remember doing that with Tpl chunks earlier in the book.

If you put your placeholder names and the values you want to replace them with in an associative array, you can pass them as a second argument to getChunk(). MODX will replace the placeholders in the chunk before returning it. In that case, the code looks like this:

```
$placeholderArray = array('name'=>'John Doe' ,'age'=>'27');
$output .= $modx->getChunk('ChunkName', $placeholderArray,
    $prefix, $suffix);
```

The last two variables define the prefix and suffix (if any) of the tags that will be replaced. They default to '[[+' and ']]' so they are unnecessary for replacing standard placeholder tags. They are optional and usually omitted, but they can be used in cases where you want to create your own custom MODX tags.

When a chunk's content is retrieved with getChunk(), any default properties will be processed. The situation is different with an attached property set, however. In a chunk tag, we can specify a property set with @PropertySetName. In a snippet using getChunk(), however, we need to include the property set ourselves.

In the section above, we sent an associative array along as a second argument to getChunk(). Since the properties in a property set are already an associative array of keys and values, we can send them the same way:

```
$modx->getChunk('ChunkName', $properties);
```

Of course we need to obtain those properties before we send them. For the next section, you'll need the MyFirstPropertySet and PropChunk objects you created in Chapter 6. The first is a property set, and the second is a chunk. In the exercise in Chapter 6, we specified the property set in the chunk tag using @MyFirstPropertySet. We can't do that from inside a snippet, though, so we'll have to use another method.

To use a property set (rather than the default properties) in a call to getChunk() (or runSnippet()), we must first get the property set using getObject(), extract its properties, and then send those properties in the second argument to getChunk() or runSnippet(). The following code uses the properties from MyFirstPropertySet with the PropChunk chunk:

```
$set = $modx->getObject('modPropertySet',
    array('name'=>'MyFirstPropertySet'));
$props = $set->getProperties();
$output .= $modx->getChunk('PropChunk', $props);
```

Note that it's not the property set you want to send in the call to getChunk(). It's the property set's properties, which we get in the second line of the code above. The process is exactly the same for runSnippet(), which allows you to run another snippet from inside the current snippet. The output of the other snippet will be returned by runSnippet(). Sending the properties along so they will be available in the other snippet works just like it does in getChunk(). The steps are identical:

- Get the property set with getObject().

- Extract its properties with getProperties().

- Send the properties as the second argument in the function call.

If you add the code above to your ObjectDemo snippet, you should see the same output you got with the chunk tag in Chapter 6. We'll work through an example using runSnippet() a little later in this chapter.

It's worth noting that using a property set's properties this way with getChunk() or runSnippet() is something you would seldom, if ever, do. Typically, you'd just specify the property set in a snippet or chunk tag with @PropertySetName. The property set's properties would then be in the $scriptProperties array for a snippet and placeholders would automatically be set for a chunk. Getting the property set and its properties directly could be handy, though, in some rare cases, and the example above may help give you a better understanding of properties and property sets.

Working with Tpl Chunks

Another common process in snippets is displaying the content of another resource using a Tpl chunk to format the output. You can do this easily with the getResources() snippet, but let's look at how it's done. It will help you understand getResources(), and someday you may need to use the information here for a situation where getResources() won't quite do what you want. In this section, we'll display a brief summary of a document with a link for people who want to see the whole document. We'll get the document with getObject(), turn its fields into an array with toArray(), then call getChunk() with the fields as a second argument. Any placeholders in the chunk will be replaced by the values in the fields.

First, create a Tpl chunk called *ShowTeaserTpl* containing the following code:

```
<h3>Title: [[+pagetitle]]</h3>
<p>[[+introtext]]<br /> . . . <a href=[[~[[+link_id]]]]>read more</a></p>
```

Next, create a snippet called *ShowTeaser* with the following code:

```
$resource = $modx->getObject('modResource',
    array('pagetitle'=>'Election Results'));
$modx->setPlaceholder('link_id',$resource->get('id'));
$output .= $modx->getChunk('ShowTeaserTpl',
    $resource->toArray());
return $output;
```

Now, put the following lines in your ObjectDemo resource:

```
<h2>Resource Summary</h2>
[[!ShowTeaser]]
```

We'll need a resource to show, so create one called *Election Results* and put the following text (or lines of your own) in its Resource Content field. If you are using a Rich Text editor, leave out the tags. If you care about it being valid (X)HTML, replace the double-quotes with " entities.

```
<p>Arthur Dracula, an admitted Vampire was elected Mayor of Roseville in
last Friday's closely fought election.</p>

<p>Dracula was something of a dark-horse candidate who rarely appeared
during the campaign except at occasional late-night events. "I don't
really like being out in the sun," Dracula said during an interview at
his home late Friday night, "it makes my skin itch and burn. I guess you
could call it kind of an allergy."</p>
```

```
<p>Dracula ran on a platform of lower taxes and more late-night activities
for teenagers. It is thought that his surprise win in the election was
largely do to the last-minute revelation that his opponent was a ruthless
serial killer who is wanted in 14 states.</p>
```

Put a quick summary of the story in the Summary (**introtext**) field, and save the resource.

If you preview your ObjectDemo resource, you should see the summary along with a link to the full story.

Our snippet isn't very well-behaved or flexible. It could be improved by sending the ID of the page we want as a property in the snippet tag (call it **&doc_id**), and it would be nice if the summary showed the first part of the story if the resource's **introtext** field was empty. An error return if the resource wasn't found would also be in order. In that case, it would look something like this:

```
$resource = $modx->getObject('modResource', $doc_id);
if (! $resource) {
    return 'Could not find resource';
}
$fields = $resource->toArray();
if ( empty($fields['introtext'])) {
    $fields['introtext'] = substr($fields['content'], 0, 100)
}
$modx->setPlaceholder('link_id', $doc_id);
$output .= $modx->getChunk('ShowTeaserTpl', $fields);
return $output;
```

Notice that we had to move the toArray() call up. Otherwise, it would have overwritten the value of **introtext**. Add the **&doc_id** property to your snippet tag:

```
[[!ShowTeaser? &doc_id=`##`]]
```

Replace ## with the ID of your news story, and delete the content from the news story's Summary (**introtext**) field. If you preview the ObjectDemo resource again, you should see the first 100 characters of the story in the teaser.

Making the summary break at a word boundary and using a snippet property for the length of the summary would be nice improvements. We could also use getCollection() and retrieve a selection of resources. Say the resources were all in a folder with an ID of 12. We could do something like this:

```
$resources = $modx->getCollection('modResource', array('parent'=>'12'));
```

Then put our original version of the code inside a loop:

```
foreach($resources as $resource) {
    /* original code here */
}
```

As an alternative, we could replace that first line with these two:

```
$resourceObj = $modx->getObject('modResource', '12');
$resources = $resourceObj->getMany('Children');
```

Since we only need two of the fields of each resource, we're wasting some memory here (but only temporarily). We could create an xPDO query to use as the second argument to getCollection() and use its select() member to limit the fields returned.

If you've worked through the exercises above, you should have a new understanding of how snippets like getResources() work. The getResources() code is more complex because of the error reporting, debugging, access control, and template variable processing. Toward the end of the code, however, you'll see a getCollection() call just like the one we used here.

Working with runSnippet()

Another, less common, operation inside a snippet is adding the results of another snippet to the output. You can't use MODX tags in a snippet. Instead, you need to call the runSnippet() method of the $modx object. In some cases, it's as simple as this:

```
$output .= $modx->runSnippet('SnippetName');
```

In the code above, the return value of the snippet is simply appended to the output.

It becomes a little more complicated, though, when we want to use properties with the snippet we're running. If the snippet has default properties, they will be available to the snippet automatically. Any properties of the outer snippet (the one with the code that called runSnippet(), are in the $scriptProperties array and can just be sent on to the other snippet like this:

```
$modx->runSnippet('SnippetName', $scriptProperties);
```

Any other properties, however, must be sent as an array in the second argument to runSnippet(), like this:

```
$props = array(
    'color' => 'red',
    'size' => 'large',
    'weight' => 'heavy',
);
$output .= $modx->runSnippet('ProcessOrder', $props);
```

Using the code above, the properties will be available in the ProcessOrder snippet as the variables $color, $size, and $weight. They will also be available as members of the $scriptProperties array, which will also include any default properties of the other snippet that are not in the $props array. If there are collisions (e.g., there is a default property called 'color' in the ProcessOrder snippet), the ones sent in the runSnippet() call will take precedence, because they have the status of properties sent in a snippet tag.

What if we have created a property set and would like to use its properties for the snippet? As we described with chunks, in order to send a property set's properties along in the call to runSnippet(), we can get the property set and then get its properties. We get the properties in exactly the same way we got them in the section above on working with getChunk():

```
$set = $modx->getObject('modPropertySet',array('name'=>'PropertySetName'));
$propSet = $set->getProperties();
$output .= $modx->runSnippet('SnippetName', $propSet);
```

Of course, if all you want to do is send on the properties of the outer snippet, you'd just send the $scriptProperties array as the second argument.

What if you want to send your own properties (from the properties in your own snippet tag and/or its default properties) and the ones from the property set? Simply merge the two arrays, and send the merged array:

```
$allProps = array_merge($scriptProperties, $propSet);
$output .= $modx->runSnippet('SnippetName', $allProps);
```

Note that in the array_merge() call, for any properties common to both arrays, the values in the second argument will overwrite those in the first argument. You can reverse the arguments if you want your own properties to take precedence.

For the next section, you'll need the ShowList snippet we created in Chapter 7 and its Tpl chunks. Add the following code to your ObjectDemo snippet to display the results of the ShowList snippet. If you have created the appropriate default properties for the ShowList snippet, you can leave out the property array at the top of the code and the $props argument in the runSnippet() call.

```
$propSet = array(
    'listChunk' => 'ListData',
    'itemTpl' => 'ItemTpl',
    'rowTpl' => 'RowTpl',
    'outerTpl' => 'OuterTpl',
);
$output .= '<h2>runSnippet</h2>';
$output .= $modx->runSnippet('ShowList', $propSet);
```

You should see the same output you got with the snippet tag in Chapter 7.

Getting Template Variables

Getting the values of template variables (TVs) in a snippet is a very common operation. Often, a snippet will use the value of a TV to fill in part of its output. The TV might contain plain text, HTML, a path to an image, a path to a CSS file, or the name of a resource or chunk to be used in the snippet. In other cases, the snippet uses the content of the TV to control what it does. The snippet uses the value of the TV in an if() or switch() statement that determines whether certain parts of the code execute or not.

If you get a TV with getObject(), you are getting the TV object that's associated with one or more templates. If you get its value, you will be getting the default value (if any) you set when you created the TV. That's usually not what you want.

Getting template variable values can be tricky since a single TV can have different values in different resources. You also have to decide if you want the raw value of the TV (@INHERIT, for example) or the processed output of the TV (the value that will appear on a page when MODX renders the TV tag).

If you want the processed output of a TV in the current resource, the resource's getTVValue() method is the fastest and easiest way. Either of these will work (in the second, ## is the ID of the TV not the resource):

```
$modx->resource->getTVValue('TvName');
$modx->resource->getTVValue(##);
```

For the raw content of a TV in the current resource or either kind of content from a TV in another resource, you need to tell MODX the Resource ID of the resource (not the TV). The following code will get the raw content or the processed content of a TV in any resource:

```
/* First, get the resource */
/* For the current resource */
$resource =& $modx->resource;
/* For another Resource */
$resource = $modx->getObject('modResource',
    array('pagetitle'=>'ResourceName'));
$id = $resource->get('id');
/* Get the TV object */
$tv = $modx->getObject('modTemplateVar',
    array('name'=>'MyTV'));

/* get the raw content of the TV */
$rawValue = $tv->getValue($id);

/* get the processed content of the TV */
$processedValue = $tv->renderOutput($id);
```

Although we retrieved the resource and TV by name in the code above, it's usually better (and faster) to retrieve them by ID since the name may change:

```
$resource = $modx->getObject('modResource',12);
$tv = $modx->getObject('modTemplateVar',2);
$processedValue = $tv->renderOutput($resource->get('id'));
```

Note that in the second line above, you need to use the ID of the TV, not the resource it is attached to.

Working with Template Variables

Let's create a template variable that will control the text color of a page. We'll use the `Election Results` news story we created earlier in this chapter. We'll create four separate CSS files that set the text inside any `<p>` tag to four different colors. Then we'll create a template variable to hold the path to the desired CSS file. Finally, we'll create a snippet that uses the TV to select the right CSS file and then injects the CSS into the `<head>` section of the document before it is rendered. This process demonstrates some very useful TV techniques as well as how to use a snippet to control the CSS of a page.

First, we'll create the four CSS files. Create a file called **black.css** in the **assets/css/** directory of your MODX site (create the **assets** and **css** folders if necessary). Use the following CSS code for the content of the file:

```
p {
    color:black;
}
```

Now, create three more CSS files: **red.css**, **green.css**, and **blue.css**. Change the color name for each to the appropriate color.

Next, create a template variable called *TextColor*. Use the following values:

Name: *TextColor*

Caption: *Text Color*

Default Value: *assets/css/black.css*

On the "Template Access" tab of the TV, check the box for the template used by your `Election Results` resource, and click on the "Save" button.

Put the following snippet tag at the top of the Resource Content field of the `Election Results` resource:

```
[[!TextColor]]
```

Now, create a snippet called *TextColor* using the following code:

```
$tvValue = $modx->resource->getTVValue('TextColor');
$modx->regClientCSS($tvValue);
return "";
```

Notice that there's no content in the `return` statement in our snippet. We don't want any output from it to put on the page. We just want it to inject the correct CSS file into the `<head>` section of the document with the MODX `regClientCSS()` method. If you click on the "Template Variables" tab, you should see the new TV there with its default value.

If you preview the `Election Results` resource, you should see the text there, still in black. Now edit the `Election Results` resource and change the TV (on the Template Variables tab) to the path to one of the other files, and save the resource. If you preview it again, the color should have changed.

Our TV isn't very convenient. To use it, you have to know the path to each CSS file and enter it correctly each time you want to make a change. In the Element tree, right-click on the "TextColor" TV (not the snippet), and select "Edit TV." Change the Input Type to Radio Options, and put the following line in the Input Option Values field:

```
Red==assets/css/red.css||Blue==assets/css/blue.css||
    Green==assets/css/green.css
```

Save the TV. Now you should just see three radio buttons with "Red," "Blue," and "Green" on the Template Variable tab when editing your resource, but the TV will still be set correctly because MODX will return the path to the snippet. Clear the site cache, and try previewing the resource with various settings of the TV. The TV's setting should control the text color.

As with so many things in MODX, there are many different ways to accomplish what we just did. To list just ten of them, we could have:

- Made the path or the color name a user setting and had the snippet use that setting to select the correct CSS file to inject. This would be useful if you wanted to let users pick the color and remember their choices.

- Sent the path or the color name as a content tag in a snippet property and used a switch() statement in the snippet based on that property.

- Put the paths or the color names into the snippet's default properties or an attached property set.

- Had the snippet output a <style> tag at the top of the content section of the document.

- Sent the <style> tag as a snippet property.

- Put the <style> tag in chunks named for the colors and retrieved the correct file with content tag nested inside a chunk tag: [[$[[*TextColor]]]].

- Put three comma-separated paths in a chunk and had the snippet parse them and select the proper one based on a property or TV.

- Put the CSS in three separate chunks and used different chunk tags on different pages.

- Put the CSS in three separate chunks and used a property or TV to select among them.

- Used the TV as class name for the <p> tag and altered the CSS file to use the class names: <p class="[[*TextColor]]">

The method you use should be based on the ease of creation, the ease of maintenance (figuring in how often they will change), the ease of use (figuring in how skilled the intended user is), and how well they separate the view from the data. In the list above, the last example might be the best choice because it involves no chunks or snippets, requires only one CSS file, and won't affect other <p> tags on the page.

Our example above is trivial, but if you use your imagination, you can see that we could change the whole look of the site with it by having a more extensive CSS file. Every new page you create that uses a template attached to the TV will already have the TV, and you could put the snippet tag in the template.

Working with Settings

As we saw earlier, getOption() can be used to get any property of a snippet or to search an array specified as a second argument. It can also be used to get settings (system settings, context settings, and user settings). In fact, it is the only convenient way to do so. It takes this form:

```
$modx->getOption('setting_name');
```

User settings have the highest priority, context settings come second, and system settings have the lowest priority. In many cases, you won't have any user settings or context settings. In that case getOption() will get the named system setting.

Add the following code to your ObjectDemo snippet to display some settings:

```
$output .= '<h2>Settings</h2>';
$output .= '<p>Site Start ID: ' . $modx->getOption('site_start') . '</p>';
$output .= '<p>Character Encoding: ' .
    $modx->getOption('modx_charset') . '</p>';
```

If you go to **System → System Settings**, you can see the grid containing all the system settings. You can display any of them with the code above, and you should see the same value that appears in the System Settings grid unless you have context or user settings with the same name. Remember that user settings will not be retrieved unless the user is currently logged on in the front end.

Working with Users

Working with users is very much like working with resources. Almost all the same methods apply and are used in the same way. Of course users have no template variables, properties, templates, parents, or children, but all the generic get*() methods and getOne() and getMany() work as they do for resources.

For resources, much of the information we want is stored directly in the resource fields of the resource object or in template variables. For the user object, however, the **username** and **id** are the only commonly used fields in the object. Much of the information we might want about a user is stored in the user profile, a related object that must be retrieved with the user's getOne() method.

There is also user information stored in a resource object. The resource fields of the resource contain the IDs of the creator, publisher, most recent editor, and deleter (if any). The related user objects for those users are also available with the resource's getOne() method.

So, there are really three kinds of user information you might want in a snippet. First, you might want information on the current user (the one who requested the current page on the web site). Second, you might want to know about the user or users who created, published, or edited the current resource. Finally, you might want information about another registered user on the site (say, to make a list of all the registered users who live in a certain zip code) or the user who created, published, or edited some other document on the web site.

In the following sections, we'll see practical examples of how to use the methods discussed in the first part of this chapter to get information about the site's users.

Working with the Current User

Getting the current user is very easy because on every page request, MODX gets the current user for you. The code below is a reference to the current user (in the form of a moduser object):

```
$modx->user
```

The moduser object we get in the code above contains only the **id**, **username**, and encrypted **password** of the user (if the user is logged in). They are available with the user object's get() method:

```
$userID = $modx->user->get('id');
$userName = $modx->user->get('username');
$userPwd = $modx->user->get('password');
```

If the user is not a logged-in registered user, the **id** will be 0, the **username** will be (anonymous), and the **password** will be empty.

 As we mentioned earlier in the book, in the front end of the site, the current user's ID and username are always available using these placeholders:

```
[[+modx.user.id]]
[[+modx.user.username]]
```

If the user is registered and logged in, the user attributes (e.g., **fullname**, **phone**, **city**, **state**, **zip**, etc.) can be found through another related object: the *user profile*, also known as the **Profile** related object. The following code will get the user profile and some of its information if the user is registered and logged in — add it to your ObjectDemo snippet:

```
$output .= '<h2>User info</h2>';
$output .= '<h3>Current User</h3>';
$username = $modx->user->get('username');
$output .= '<p>Username: ' . $username . '</p>';

if ($username != '(anonymous)') {
    $profile = $modx->user->getOne('Profile');
    $fullname = $profile->get('fullname');
    $email = $profile->get('email');

    $output .= '<p>User Full Name: '. $fullname . '</p>';
    $output .= '<p>User email: '. $email . '</p>';
}
```

Note that the parentheses in "(anonymous)" are actually part of the username and that no other user has them in his or her username. The code above should print the username, full name, and email address of the admin Super User if you preview the ObjectDemo document from the Manager. If, however, you paste the URL into another browser and visit the page (make sure the page is published), you will only see the username (anonymous).

 At this writing, a user previewing a resource from the MODX Manager is logged in when visiting the front end, but this could change in future versions of MODX.

The test in the code above that checks the $username against (anonymous) is important. If you leave it out, the page will crash with a PHP error when visited from another browser (although it will work fine if the user logs in first).

It crashes because the "(anonymous)" user has no user profile. That means getOne('Profile') will return null instead of a profile object. When we try to use $profile->get(), we'll get an error message telling us that we tried to use the get() method of a non-object.

As we discussed earlier in this chapter, it's always a good idea to test the return value of any MODX get*() method that retrieves an object before calling the object's get() method.

Note that we could also have used the sanity checking code we described earlier in this chapter:

```
if (! (is_object($profile) && $profile instanceof xPDOObject) ) {
    return 'User has no Profile';
}
```

This would be significantly slower, however, because it would try (and fail) to get the profile for all anonymous users.

Setting Placeholders

Sometimes, you'll want to set placeholders with the user information rather than using it immediately in a snippet or plugin. The advantages of this method are that the formatting can be moved out of the snippet and the various pieces of user information don't all have to appear in the same place. You can set the individual placeholders yourself in the code (assuming that you have successfully retrieved the user profile first):

```
$email = $profile->get('email');
$modx->setPlaceholder('email',$email);
```

Once you've done that, you can put an [[+email]] placeholder anywhere on the page (or in a Tpl chunk) to display the value of that field.

If you are using a number of fields, however, it's often easier to convert the object fields to an associative array with the user object's toArray() method and then use the MODX object's toPlaceholders() method to set multiple placeholders at once. The following code will set a placeholder for every field in the user profile of the current user (e.g. [[+**fullname**]], [[+**username**]], etc.):

```
if ($modx->user->getOne('Profile')) {
    $modx->toPlaceholders($modx->user->Profile->toArray());
}
```

If you want to set only a few placeholders, you can send their names in an array in the call to the profile object's get() method:

```
if ($modx->user->getOne('Profile')) {
    $modx->toPlaceholders($modx->user->Profile->get(array(
        'email',
        'fullname',
        )));
}
```

As we did earlier in the chapter with resources, you can get the user object information and the user profile for the current user in a single step with getObjectGraph(). We can then set placeholders for the profile data as well as the user's name and ID at the same time. This code will do that for the current user:

```
$user = $modx->getObjectGraph('modUser', array('Profile' => array()));
$userData = array_merge($user->toArray(), $user->Profile->toArray());
$modx->toPlaceholders($userData);
```

Once the code above has executed, all the possible placeholders have been set with information contained in both the user object and the user profile.

Is the User Logged In?

We could check the user's ID or username with one of the methods above, but there is a more efficient way — calling the user object's hasSessionContext() method. As we mentioned, for any page request, MODX creates a $user object.

The user object's hasSessionContext() method will return true if the user is logged in (authenticated) and false if the user is not logged in.

If you are only using the default web context (and if you don't know, then you are), the following code will tell you if the current user is logged in to the front end:

```
$isAuthenticated = $modx->user->hasSessionContext('web');
```

If you are using multiple contexts and want to know if the user is logged in to the current context, you can do this:

```
$isAuthenticated = $modx->user->hasSessionContext(
    $modx->context->get('key'));
```

If you are using multiple contexts and want to know if the user is logged in to any of them, this code will do it:

```
$isAuthenticated = $modx->user->hasSessionContext(array(
    'context1',
    'context2',
    'context3',
    ));
```

If you are previewing the site from the MODX Manager, the methods above will still work as described. You will not be authenticated unless you log in using a login form in the front end. Remember, though, that you are still logged in to the Manager, so you may still see unpublished documents and can have manager permissions that a normal front-end user doesn't have. To see the site as regular users see it, it's best to preview the site in another browser where you are not logged in to the Manager.

 The Login package provides a snippet called isLoggedIn that will check the user's login status for you. If the user is not logged in to the current context, it will automatically redirect the user to the unauthorized page or to a page you specify in the snippet properties.

Is the User a Member of a User Group?

You can check to see if a user is a member of a group with the user object's `isMember()` method. It will accept a user group name or an array of user group names. The method will return `true` if the user is in the group or list of groups and `false` if not. At this writing, `isMember()` will not accept a user group ID as the argument.

```
/* Is user a member of the Editors user group? */
$isEditor = $modx->user->isMember('Editors');

/* Is user a member of one of these groups */
$groups = array(
    'Editors',
    'CopyEditors',
    'Proofers',
);
$isEmployee = $modx->user->isMember($groups);
```

It's seldom necessary to deal with user groups directly in MODX Revolution code because it's usually easier and more reliable to do it with the Access Control system, but `isMember()` can be useful if you want to put different content on the same page for different user groups, as we'll see in the following section.

Using isMember() to Select Content

There are occasions when you might want to show different content on a page to members of different user groups. This is easy to do with chunks and `isMember()`. Say, for example, that you have a school site and want to show one chunk to teachers and another to students. Just create two user groups — Teachers and Students — and add some users to them. Then create a snippet called *StudentTeacher* with the following code:

```
/* StudentTeacher snippet */
$output = "";
if ($modx->user->isMember('Students')) {
    $output = $modx->getChunk('StudentChunk');
} else if ($modx->user->isMember('Teachers')) {
    $output = $modx->getChunk('TeacherChunk');
}
return $output;
```

Create a chunk called *StudentChunk* and another chunk called *TeacherChunk* containing different content.

In your ObjectDemo resource, put the tag [[!StudentTeacher]] where you want the content to appear. Teachers will see the content of one chunk, students will see the content of the other chunk, and anonymous users will see nothing. Of course the users will have to be logged on in the front end in order to see the content of the chunks.

It would be easy to extend this method to include the names of the user groups and the names of the chunks to be shown to each group as or properties for the snippet.

Users Related to the Current Resource

Instead of getting information about the current user, suppose you want information about the user or users who created, edited, or published the current resource. You could get the user's ID using get() to retrieve the contents of the appropriate field and then use getObject() to get the user, but there's a simpler way. The current resource object is always available as $modx->resource, so the user objects are MODX related objects and can be obtained by using the resource's getOne() method. Try out the following code in your ObjectDemo snippet:

```
$resource =& $modx->resource;
$creator = $resource->getOne('CreatedBy');
$editor = $resource->getOne('EditedBy');
$publisher = $resource->getOne('PublishedBy');
$output .= "<h3>current doc's related users.</h3>";
$output .= '<p>Most Recent Editor: ' . $editor->get('username') . '</p>';
$output .= '<p>Published by: ' . $publisher->get('username') . '</p>';
$output .= '<p>Created by: ' . $creator->get('username') . '</p>';
```

As we mentioned earlier, using =& instead of just = when getting the resource tells PHP to assign $resource variable to the $modx->resource object rather than making a copy of it. This makes the code more efficient.

If you wanted to use the code above on a real web site, you'd probably put the (X)HTML in a Tpl chunk with placeholders for the user names. The snippet would then set the placeholders and call getChunk() or pass a placeholder array as a second argument to getChunk().

If you need a lot of the fields for each user, the following code would set all of them for the three related users with an appropriate prefix:

```
$creator = $modx->getObjectGraph('modUser',
    array('Profile' => array()),
    $modx->user->get('createdby'));
$creatorFields = array_merge($creator->toArray(),
    $creator->Profile->toArray());
$modx->toPlaceholders($creatorFields, 'creator');
$editor = $modx->getObjectGraph('modUser',
    array('Profile' => array()),
    $modx->user->get('editedby'));
$editorFields = array_merge($editor->toArray(),
    $editor->Profile->toArray());
$modx->toPlaceholders($editorFields, 'editor');
$publisher = $modx->getObjectGraph('modUser',
    array('Profile' => array()),
    $modx->user->get('publishedby'));
$publisherFields = array_merge($publisher->toArray(),
    $publisher->Profile->toArray());
$modx->toPlaceholders($publisherFields, 'publisher');
```

Note that we used all lowercase letters in the last argument to getObjectGraph() because we are using the resource field rather than the related object — we want the ID of the related user, not the user object here. Also, notice that we specified a prefix in the second argument to each toPlaceholders() call so that the placeholders for creators, editors, and users would have different names. If we hadn't done that, each successive toPlaceholders() call would overwrite the previous values and all placeholder tags would contain the values from the Publisher. Because we left out the separator argument, the default dot separator will be used. Be sure to use toPlaceholders() rather than setPlaceholders() because the latter won't set any prefixes.

After the code above has executed, all the following placeholders (and many others) will have the appropriate values:

```
[[+creator.username]]
[[+creator.fullname]]
[[+editor.id]]
[[+editor.zip]]
[[+publisher.username]]
[[+publisher.state]]
```

Try using the getObjectGraph() code in your ObjectDemo snippet instead of the code we used earlier. Put the following line at the end of the code:

```
$output .= $modx->GetChunk('RelatedUserTpl');
```

Put tags like the ones just above in a Tpl chunk called *RelatedUserTpl*. Note that we didn't have to send any placeholders in the getChunk() call because we set them all with toPlaceholders(). If we had sent the fields in the getChunk() call, the prefixes would not have been set unless we added them to each array with separate code.

Users Related to Another Resource

Getting the related objects of another resource is simply a matter of getting a reference to the desired resource and then using the methods we saw above for the current resource.

What if you wanted to get the creator, editor, or publisher of some resource other than the current one? All you need to do is to get a reference to the other resource using getObject() and then use that object's getOne() method to retrieve the related users. Try the following code in your ObjectDemo snippet. It gets the creator of the YesNoDemo resource we created earlier in the book.

```
$output .= "<h3>YesNoDemo doc's related users.</h3>";
$resource = $modx->getObject('modResource',
    array('pagetitle'=>'YesNoDemo'));
$creator = $resource->getOne('CreatedBy');
$output .= '<p>YesNoDemo was Created by: '.
    $creator->get('username') . '</p>';
```

Notice that we used double-quotes for the <h3> line because the string we want to use contains a single-quote (doc's). If we used single-quotes to enclose this, PHP would throw an error.

There is another resource related object that only applies to deleted resources: the user who deleted the resource. The following code will only work with resources that have been deleted but not purged from the tree. The first version gets the deleter's ID. The second one gets the user object for the deleter:

```
$deleterId = $resource->get('deletedby');
$deleterObject = $resource->getOne('DeletedBy');
```

Suppose you want a list of all the published documents at your site and the username of the user who published them. This code will produce the list:

```
$output .= '<h3>Publishers</h3>';
$docs = $modx->getCollection('modResource', array('published'=>'1'));

$output .= '<p>Name : Publisher' . '</p>';
foreach ($docs as $doc) {
    $name = $doc->get('pagetitle');
    $publisher = $doc->getOne('PublishedBy');
    if ($publisher) {
        $uName = $publisher->get('username');
    } else {
        $uName = 'Unknown';
    }
$output .= '<p>' . $name . ': ' . $uName . '</p>';
}
```

The 'if ($publisher)' line in the code above is an important sanity check. Some documents created during the install or by an add-on component may not have anything in the **publishedby** field. In those cases, the call to $publisher->get() will generate a PHP error.

If you need information from the user profile of the publisher, you could use code like this once the $publisher variable is set:

```
$profile = $publisher->getOne('Profile');
$userFullname = $profile->get('fullname');
```

You could also use getObjectGraph() to get the user object's information and the user profile in one step:

```
$publisher = $modx->getObjectGraph('modUser',
    array('Profile' => array()),
    $doc->get('publishedby'));
```

Using getObjectGraph(), the following code would get the user name and full name of the publisher:

```
$uName = $publisher->get('username');
$fullName = $publisher->Profile->get('fullname');
```

Note that "Profile" begins with a capital letter because it's a related field, while "publishedby" in the code above is in all lowercase letters because it is a field name.

Users in General

Sometimes, you want to find a particular user or a group of users independent of any documents. Maybe you want a list of all users in a particular zip code, for example. The answer is a simple getObject() or getCollection() call with the criteria for the user specified. The following code will get the user with the username JohnDoe:

```
$user = $modx->getObject('modUser', array('username'=>'JohnDoe'));
```

Getting users in a zip code is more complicated because the zip code is in the user profile, not the user object. This code will put all users in the 55127 zip code into an array called $zipUsers using getCollection() to get all users first:

```
$zip = '55147';
$zipUsers = array();
/* get all active users */
$users = $modx->getCollection('modUser',array('active' => '1'));
foreach ($users as $user) {
```

```
    /* get the user's profile */
    $profile = $user->getOne('Profile');
    /* get the user's zip code */
    $userZip = $profile->get('zip');
    /* if the user has the zip code, add them to the array */
    if ($userZip == $zip) {
        $zipUsers[] = $user->get('username');
    }
}
```

Note that our $zipUsers array contains just the usernames. We could just as easily have made it an array of user objects by doing this instead:

```
$zipUsers[] = $user;
```

With the array of user objects, a foreach() loop could process all the users (getting each user profile, if necessary) and extract any information about each user.

 Shaun McCormick's Peoples package, available in Package Manager provides simple snippets for listing users, user attributes, user groups, and user group members.

It's also possible to get all the active users in that zip code with a single query by using an xPDO query object as the second argument to getCollection(). The code would look like this:

```
$zip = '55433';
$c = $modx->newQuery('modUser');
$c->select($modx->getSelectColumns('modUser','modUser',"",
    array('id','username')));
$c->innerJoin('modUserProfile','Profile');
$c->where(array(
    'Profile.zip' => $zip,
    'modUser.active' => true));
$users = $modx->getCollection('modUser',$c);

$output = '<h3>Users in 55433</h3>';
$output .= '<ul>';
foreach ($users as $user) {
```

```
    $output .= '    <li>' .
    $user->get('username') . '</li>';
}
$output .= '</ul>';
```

Sanity Checks

To keep the code brief, we've left out some sanity checks in many of our examples. For a live web site, you'd definitely want to test the return values of the various methods to make sure that they were successful before calling any of the get*() methods of the specific objects. This is especially important with the current user because there may not be a logged in user, in which case the current user has no profile.

Working with Extended User Fields

Extended user fields are new in MODX Revolution. They provide a convenient place to put other information about the user (e.g., political affiliation, height, weight, astrological sign, etc.). The benefit of using the extended user fields is that they can be created and edited on the Extended Fields tab when updating the user's profile. The downside is that they are a little trickier to get and set in code because they are all in a single field of the user's profile.

 If all you need to do is display user extended fields on a web page, you can use the Profile snippet included in the Login package. Putting [[!Profile]] at the top of the page will set placeholders for all fields in the user profile, including any extended fields. The optional (but recommended) &prefix property will let you define a prefix for the placeholders. If you don't need any extended fields, use [[!Profile? &useExtended=`0`]].

The examples above will get the information for the current user. If you want another user's information, you can include the &user property with the user's username or ID: [[!Profile? &user=`12`]], [[!Profile? &user=`JoeBlow`]].

Creating and using extended user fields can be very simple thanks to several snippets included in the Login package: Register, Profile, and UpdateProfile. If the form you present with the Register snippet contains fields that are not standard user fields, when the registration form is submitted, the Register snippet will create extended fields based on the field names and store their values in those extended fields. Once the extended fields exist, the Profile snippet will set placeholders for them so they can be displayed. The UpdateProfile snippet will then allow you or your users to update those extended fields in the front end of the site.

In the Register snippet, you can use validators, such as `:required` or `:email`, to validate the extended fields as you would any other field.

What if you are using extra fields in your registration form that you don't want stored permanently in extended user fields (e.g., a hidden no-spam field)? You can prevent the snippet from creating the fields by putting the names of those fields as a comma-separated list in the **&excludeExtended** property:

```
&excludeExtended=`no-spam,extra-field1`
```

The method described above will work fine if you just want to create, update, and display extended user fields. There may be situations, however, where you need to work with the extended fields in code. You might, for example, want to add and/or set one or more new extended user fields after a large number of users have already registered. In the following section, we'll look at how to deal with extended user fields in code.

The extended fields are stored in JSON format in the database in the **extended** field of the user's profile. Luckily, MODX converts them to a PHP associative array when you retrieve them with the user profile's `get()` method:

```
$extendedFields = $user->Profile->get('extended');
```

Remember that `$extendedFields` will be an array here. A standard PHP associative array of user fields will also be converted to JSON format automatically when you call the profile's `set()` method:

```
$fields = array(
    'sign'=>'Leo',
    'FavoriteColor'=>'Red',
);
$profile->set('extended', $fields);
```

Let's create a couple of user extended fields for our user Jane Doe and then retrieve them in a snippet. Create a user with the user name JaneDoe if you haven't done so already.

Go to **Security → Manage Users**. Right-click on "JaneDoe," and select "Update User." Click on the "Extended Fields" tab, then on the "Add Attribute" button. Use the following values, and click on the "Save" button:

Name: *sign*

Value: *Leo*

You should see the new extended field in the grid. Add another one with the following settings:

Name: *party*

Value: *Independent*

You can edit either one by clicking on it in the grid, changing the Name or Value at the right, and clicking on the "Set" button. The field isn't changed until you click on the "Set" button. Note, too, that no changes (including the creation of the fields) will be permanent until you click on the "Save" button at the upper right to save the user. Do that now.

 At this writing, saving a new or existing extended user field with an empty Value field can cause serious problems. Always give every field some value. If you'd like to leave the field empty, use *0, (blank)*, or something similar.

Let's get the values from Jane Doe's extended fields in our ObjectDemo snippet. Add the following code:

```
$user = $modx->getObjectGraph('modUser',
    array('Profile' => array()),
    array('username'=>'JaneDoe'));
$modx->toPlaceholders($user->toArray(),'user');
$modx->toPlaceholders($user->Profile->get('extended'),'extended');
```

Now, add the following code to your ObjectDemo resource:

```
<h3>Jane Doe's Info</h3>
<p>User name: [[+user.username]] . '</p>';
<p>Sign: [[+extended.sign]] . '</p>'
<p>Party: [[+extended.party]] . '</p>'
```

You should see the values when you preview the resource. Notice that we added the prefixes *user* and *extended* when we set the placeholders and used them in the placeholder tags. This isn't necessary, but it's a good idea. It helps keep the placeholders from conflicting with other placeholders on the page.

What if we wanted to change the value of one of Jane Doe's extended fields in a snippet? We'd have to get the user object and the extended fields, make the change, and save the user. If we want to change Jane Doe's astrological sign to Virgo, for example, this code would do it:

```
$user = $modx->getObjectGraph('modUser',
    array('Profile' => array()),
    array('username'=>'JaneDoe'));
$extFields = $user->Profile->get('extended');
$extFields['sign'] = 'Virgo';
$user->Profile->set('extended',$extFields);
$user->save();
```

We could have just used $user->Profile->save() in the code above, but saving the user object will save any other changes we might have made for the user.

 The Login package includes an UpdateProfile snippet that will allow users to update their profiles (including any extended fields) in the front end of the site.

You can also create new user extended fields in a snippet, but you should always get the current ones first. Otherwise you will wipe out any existing extended fields. At present, adding an extended field for one user in the Manager won't create that field for other users (although that may be added as an option in future versions of MODX). If you'd like to create a new user field called *new-field* for all active users, this code would do it:

```
$users = $modx->getCollectionGraph('modUser',
    array('Profile' => array()),
    array('active'=>'1'));

foreach($users as $user) {
    $extFields = $user->Profile->get('extended');
    $extFields['new-field'] = '(blank)';
    $user->Profile->set('extended',$extFields);
    $user->Profile->save();
}
return '<p>Fields Created</p>';
```

Getting the extended fields with $user->Profile->get('extended') is critical here. If we didn't do that, any other extended fields would be lost when we saved the user profile. Because we didn't change any fields of the user object, we used $user->Profile->save() instead of $user->save(). Either one would work because the related user profile would be saved automatically when the user was saved, but saving just the profile is faster and more efficient.

Creating and Modifying MODX Objects

After working through the examples above, you probably have some sense of how to modify existing objects. Most of the time, it's simply a matter of getting the object with one of the get*() methods, modifying its fields with the object's set() method (or setContent()), and calling the object's save() method. Creating new objects is very similar except that you need to create the object itself first by using $modx->newObject(). There are also more fields to set, because in a new object, they are all empty unless MODX sets their default values.

It is possible to create new MODX objects by direct manipulation of the database, but it is generally a very bad idea. You would also have to create the relationships to other MODX objects in all the appropriate tables, and if you make a mistake, your MODX database could be corrupted. When you create objects with newObject(), MODX will take care of updating all the related tables automatically when you save the object.

Creating a Resource

This code will create a new resource called *Test Page*:

```
$fields = array(
    'pagetitle' => 'Test Page',
    'alias' => 'test-page',
    'menutitle' => 'Testing',
);
$resource = $modx->newObject('modResource', $fields);
$resource->save(); /* save it to the database */
$output .= '<p>Resource created</p>';
```

Try out the code above in your ObjectDemo snippet. After previewing the `ObjectDemo` page, you should see the new document in the tree, although you will have to refresh the tree first. You can set any of the object's fields in the `newObject()` call, or you can set them using the object's `set()` method.

Working with set()

The code below is equivalent to the code we used with newObject() above:

```
$resource = $modx->newObject('modResource');
$resource->set('pagetitle', 'Test Page');
$resource->set('alias', 'test-page');
$resource->set('menutitle', 'Testing');
$resource->save(); /* save it to the database */
$output .= '<p>Resource created</p>';
```

Working with setContent()

The page we created above doesn't have any content. Let's give it some. First, in your ObjectDemo snippet, delete (or comment out) the code that created the page because we don't want two test pages. Then add the following code:

```
$resource = $modx->getObject('modResource',
    array('pagetitle'=>'Test Page'));
$resource->setContent('<p>I created this page in code</p>');
$resource->save();
```

Be sure the pagetitle is the same as the one you used when creating the resource. After previewing your ObjectDemo resource, you should be able to edit your Test Page and see the new content in the Resource Content field. If we wanted to set the content when creating the element, we'd just need to add the setContent() line above just below the line with newObject(). You should always use setContent() to set the main content field of any resource or element because MODX will know the correct name of the field, even if that field name changes in future versions of MODX.

Creating Elements

Creating any of the various elements is just like creating a resource. There are fewer fields involved because you usually only need to give the name of the element and call its setContent() method. The following code will create a snippet, a chunk, and a template:

```
$snippet = $modx->newObject('modSnippet', array('name'=>'MySnippet'));
$snippet->setContent("/* My Snippet */ \n return('In My Snippet'); ?>");
$snippet->save();
$chunk = $modx->newObject('modChunk', array('name'=>'MyChunk'));
$chunk>setContent(

    "<p>This is My Chunk</p>\n<p>Here is it's second paragraph</p>");
$chunk>save();
$template = $modx->newObject('modTemplate',
    array('templatename'=>'MyTemplate'));
$template->setContent(
    "<html>\n
        <head>
            <title>Not Much of a Template</title>\n
        </head>)\n
        <body>\n
            [*content]]\n
        </body>\n
    </html>\n"
);
$template->save();
return "<p>Elements Created</p>";
```

Notice that the "name" field for a template is *templatename*. We've added a newline character (\n) at the end of each line so that the content won't all run together on a single line. In order for the newline character to be translated (and to make it possible to use single-quotes in the line), we need to use double-quotes around the string.

Try out the code above in your ObjectDemo snippet. After previewing your ObjectDemo resource and refreshing the Element tree, you should see all three of your newly created elements in the tree.

Working with Categories

If you want to place new elements in a category, you simply need to find out the category's ID and use it to set the element's **category** field. If necessary, you can create the category first (if the category exists, just leave out the first two lines below). This code assumes that you have already created or retrieved the snippet object and have a reference to it in the `$snippet` variable:

```
$category = $modx->newObject('modCategory',
    array('category'=>'MyCategory'));
$category->save();
$category = $modx->getObject('modCategory',
    array('category'=>'MyCategory'));
$snippet->addOne($category);
$snippet->save();
```

Note that the "name" field for categories is "category." The `addOne()` call must appear after the snippet is created but before it is saved.

Here's another way to do it that is handy if you will be creating a lot of objects and want to add them all to the same existing category. The code below assumes that you have obtained a reference to the category object `$category` with `getObject()` and that you have references to the snippet, chunk, and template:

```
$elements = array();
$elements[] = $snippet;
$elements[] = $chunk;
$elements[] = $template;
$category->addMany($elements);
$category->save();
```

This code could go at the end of the code above to assign all the elements to the category rather than assigning them as we went along. If you'd like to try it out, change the names of the elements (e.g., by putting the number 2 at the end of their names) and add this code at the end. Notice that we had to use `addMany()` because a category can have many elements. We also had to save the category because we retrieved it with `getObject()` rather than as a related field of any element, so it would not be saved automatically when saving an element. If we only had one element to assign to the category, we would still need to use addMany(), but the array would be unnecessary.

```
$category->addMany($snippet);
$category->save();
```

Creating Template Variables

Template variables are elements, but they are more complicated because they're connected to both templates and resources and they can have a different value for each resource. The situation with TVs is further complicated by that fact that there is a many-to-many relationship between templates and TVs. One template can have many TVs, and one TV can be attached to many templates. Template variables also require the setting of a number of fields. Here is the code to create a template variable called *NewTV*:

```
$fields = array(
    'name'=>'NewTV',
    'type'=>'option',
    'caption'=>'New TV',
    'description'=>'My New TV',
    'elements'=> 'red||blue||green',
    'default_text'=>'red',
    'display'=>'default',
);

$tv = $modx->newObject('modTemplateVar', $fields);
$tv->save();
```

The type of this TV is "option," which creates a radio option TV. The fields correspond to the fields on the Create/Edit Template Variable panel, and they must all be strings. The **elements** field corresponds to the Input Option Values field.

The possible values for the **type** (Input Type) field are: checkbox, date, dropdown, email, file, image, listbox, listbox-multiple, number, option, resourcelist, richtext, tag, text, textarea, textareamini, textbox, and url.

The possible values for the display (Output Type) field are: date, default, delim, htmltag, image, richtext, string, text, and url. Note that some output types only make sense with certain input types and that some of the output types require extra information in the **input_properties** or **output_properties** fields. The easiest way to determine what you need is to create a TV that meets your needs, make sure it works properly, and then examine its record in the `modx_site_templvars` table using PhpMyAdmin. The **input_properties**, **output_properties**, and **properties** fields hold JSON strings but MODX automatically converts them to and from regular PHP associative arrays when you call the TV's `get()` or `set()` method for those fields.

See the sections on template variable input and output types in Chapter 5 for details on how each option works.

The TV we created with the code above is not attached to any templates, so it won't be available in any resources until we edit both the template and the TV itself to attach it. We can attach it in the code, but it's not as simple as adding it to the template because of the many-to-many relationship between templates and TVs. Instead, we need to create the intersect object (a `modTemplateVarTemplate` object) for the intersect table. We already have the TV, but we need to get a reference to the template. Here's the code to add to the bottom of the code above:

```
$template = $modx->getObject('modTemplate',array('templatename'=>'main'));
$intersect = $modx->newObject('modTemplateVarTemplate');
$intersect->addOne($tv);
$intersect->addOne($template);
$intersect->save();
```

Make sure the template name matches the main template of your site, and try this code in your ObjectDemo snippet. After previewing your `ObjectDemo` resource, you should be able to edit your TV and see the main template checked. You should also be able to edit the main template and see the TV checked. If you edit a resource that uses the main template, you should see the new TV on the Template Variables tab.

If you would like to add the TV to all templates on the site, you would use this code instead:

```
$templates = $modx->getCollection('modTemplate');
foreach($templates as $template) {
    $intersect = $modx->newObject('modTemplateVarTemplate');
    $intersect->addOne($tv);
    $intersect->addOne($template);
    $intersect->save();
}
```

If you test the code above, use a new template variable name so you don't try to create the same template variable twice.

Now, our TV exists and is attached to one or more templates. It still doesn't have a value for any particular resource, however. If you want to set the value of your template variable for specific resources, you must do the attachment above and save the intersect object before setting any values. Once the TV is attached to the template, you can set the value for a specific resource by using the TV's `setValue()` method with the ID of the resource you want to set it for:

```
$tv->setValue($id,'value');
$tv->save();
```

You can't use the TV's `setContent()` method to set the value for a specific resource because `setContent()` sets the default value of the TV itself.

Creating Users

Creating users is much like creating any other object except that much of the user's information is in the `UserProfile` related object. To add a user and set some of the profile information at the same time, we need to create two objects with `newObject()`: a user and a user profile. Then, we need to connect the two. We do that by adding the profile to the user object with `addOne()`. We use `addOne()` because a user can have only one profile.

Let's create a user called Sally Rand (username: SallyRand). Add the following code to your ObjectDemo snippet:

```
$user = $modx->newObject('modUser', array ('username'=>'SallyRand'));
$userProfile = $modx->newObject('modUserProfile');
$userProfile->set('fullname','Sally Rand');
$userProfile->set('email','sally@gmail.com');
$success = $user->addOne($userProfile);
if ($success) {
    $user->save();
    return '<p>User object and profile created</p>';
} else {
    return '<p>failed to add profile. User not saved.</p>';
}
```

If you add the code above to your ObjectDemo snippet and preview your ObjectDemo resource, once you see the success message you should be able to go to **Security → Manage Users** and see your new user there. If you update the user, you should see the full name and email address in the profile.

 The Login package provides a snippet called UpdateProfile that will allow users to update their profiles in the front end of the site.

Using xPDO Transactions

Sanity checking is especially important whenever you save an object and its related objects in one step as we did above. If something goes wrong, it's possible that one of the objects will be saved but not the other. Sanity checks that test all the objects returned from the get*() functions will help here, but another useful approach is to use transaction processing with the three xPDO transaction methods. Because the $modx object extends the $xpdo object, you can call them like this:

```
$modx->beginTransaction();
$modx->rollback();
$modx->commit();
```

Unfortunately, transaction processing is not available with most MySQL databases because they use the MyISAM storage engine, which does not support transaction processing (though it may in the future). At present, in order to use transactions, you need a database that uses the InnoDB storage engine.

If you have an InnoDB database, you can call beginTransaction() before any modifications are made to the database (i.e., before any save() call). At any future point, you can call rollBack() to undo all changes to the database that occurred after the beginTransaction() call or call commit() and permanently commit all the changes to the database.

An object's save() method will return null if an error occurs, so we could replace the save() call in the code above with this transaction processing code:

```
$modx->beginTransaction();
if (! $user->save()) {
    $modx->rollBack();
    return '<p>Error. Transaction rolled back.</p>';

} else {
    $modx->commit();
    return '<p>User object and profile created</p>';
}
```

Working with User Groups

User groups are like template variables in that they have a many-to-many relationship with users. One user can be in many groups, and most groups will have multiple users. To add a user to a group, we need to create an intersect object as we did earlier with template variables. For TVs, we used this line:

```
$intersect = $modx->newObject('modTemplateVarTemplate');
```

For user groups, the appropriate line is:

```
$intersect = $modx->newObject('modUserGroupMember');
```

Let's create a user, a user group, and a role all at once. We'll put the user in the new group with the new role. Add the following code to your ObjectDemo snippet.

```
$group = $modx->newObject('modUserGroup',array('name'=>'PhotoEditors'));
$user = $modx->newObject('modUser', array('username'=>'BillSmith'));
$profile = $modx->newObject('modUserProfile');
$profile->set('fullname','Bill Smith');
$profile->set('email','bill@gmail.com');
$user->addOne($profile);
$role = $modx->newObject('modUserGroupRole',
    array('name'=>'PhotoEditor',
    'authority'=>'7'));
$intersect = $modx->newObject('modUserGroupMember');
$intersect->addOne($user);
$intersect->addOne($group);
$intersect->addOne($role);
if (! $intersect->save()) {
    $output .= '<p>An error occurred — user, role, and group not saved</p>';
} else {
    $modx->commit();
    $output .= '<p>User, role, and Group Created</p>';
}
```

We didn't have to save the user, the user group, or the role because we added them to the $intersect object with getOne(). They will be saved automatically when the $intersect object is saved.

Notice that we use addOne() with the intersect object even though we're dealing with a many-to-many relationship. This makes sense because the modUserGroupMember intersect object itself holds a single user ID, a single user group ID, and a single role ID.

Note that we could also have used the following convenience function to add the user to the group rather than creating the intersect object, but then we would have to save the user and the user group as separate operations and would need a more complicated test to know if the operation succeeded.

```
$user->joinGroup($group, $role)
```

After previewing your ObjectDemo resource, you should see the new user group, the new role, and the new user in the Manager. If you update the user group, you should see your new user in it with a role of PhotoEditor.

Suppose we wanted to add all active users to a new user group called Readers with a role of PhotoEditor (and the role already existed). This code would do it:

```
$role = $modx->getObject('modUserGroupRole', array('name'=>'PhotoEditor'));
$role->set('description','Photo Editors');
$users = $modxGetCollection('modUser',array('active'=>'1'));
$group = $modx->newObject('modUserGroup',array('name'=>'Readers'));
foreach($users as $user) {
    $intersect = $modx->newObject('modUserGroupMember');
    $intersect->addOne($user);
    $intersect->addOne($group);
    $intersect->addOne($role);
    $intersect->save();
}
```

Because the role and the users already exist, we don't need to create them. We simply get references to them with getObject() and getCollection().

There is also a convenience function for adding a user to a user group, although the code above would be slightly faster if you already have the user and group objects:

```
$user->joinGroup($group);
```

The $group variable can be the name or the ID of the user group. As usual, using the ID is slightly faster. When used with the $user object, joinGroup() takes an optional second argument that assigns a role for the user in the group:

```
$user->joinGroup($group, $role);
```

The $role variable can be either the name or the ID of the role you want to assign to the user. If $role is omitted, the user is added to the group with no assigned role.

Other Intersect Objects

Whenever there is a many-to-many relationship between objects, there must be an intersect table to manage the relationship. Each row in the intersect table can be considered an intersect object in xPDO. We've already seen this with templates/TVs and with users/user groups, but it also applies to a number of other MODX object relationships such as resources/resource groups, plugins/events, and elements/property sets. There are also a number of intersect objects involved in security permissions. The following code shows how to use an intersect object with resources/resource groups, plugins/events, and elements/property sets. It's assumed that you already have a reference to the objects to be added using either `$modx->getObject()` for existing objects or `$modx->newObject()` for objects you create.

```
/* Add a resource to a resource group */
$intersect = $modx->newObject('modResourceGroupResource');
$intersect->addOne($resource);
$intersect->addOne($group);
$intersect->save();
/* Alternate method using a convenience function. $group can
 * be a resource group object, the ID of the resource group,
 * or the name of the resource group.
 */
$resource->joinGroup($group);

/* Connect an event to a plugin */
$intersect = $modx->newObject('modPluginEvent');
$intersect->addOne($plugin);
$intersect->addOne($event);
$intersect->save();
/* Connect an element and a property set */
$intersect = $modx->newObject('modElementPropertySet');
$intersect->addOne($element);
$intersect->addOne($propertySet);
$intersect->save();
```

Calling the Processors

MODX objects can also be created and updated by calling the appropriate processors directly, but this method is not fully implemented or documented at this writing. It will be a good way to create and modify objects because MODX will set many of the default fields for you and will perform some important sanity checks. The resource processor is currently available and serves as an example of what the method will look like. Here's an example that will create a new resource using the `resource/create` processor:

```
$response = $modx->runProcessor('resource/create',
    array(
        'pagetitle' => 'My Page',
        'published' => true,
        'content' => 'stuff here',
        /* any other fields can be set here */
    )
);
```

The resource created with this code will have the default template and the default settings for fields such as **hidemenu**, **richtext**, **cachable**, and **searchable**. If the **automatic_alias** system setting is set to Yes, an alias will be generated automatically for the new resource.

Custom Database Tables

If you have data that doesn't fit in the existing tables of the MODX database, you'll want to create custom database tables to hold it. You should never modify the existing tables by creating new fields in them. With a little effort, you can also create xPDO objects for the rows of your tables so that you can use all the xPDO methods listed above with them.

Even if you can put your data in the existing tables, it's still, in many cases, worthwhile to create custom tables to improve the efficiency of the site. It's very convenient to use MODX resources to store everything. You can create a blog where each post and comment is a separate MODX resource or an e-Commerce site where every product is stored in its own resource. This is fine as long as the site doesn't grow too large. Resources, however, carry a lot of overhead. They have many fields that you probably aren't using, and if you have thousands of resources on the site, using resources as your storage object may slow things down. The Resource tree will also get very large and rendering it will slow down the Manager. In that case, you may want to create a custom table with just the fields you need in each row.

Adding New Tables

You can add new tables to the MODX database using PhpMyAdmin or any other data-base tool. MODX will ignore those tables, and you can access them using standard PDO techniques. There is nothing wrong with using PDO, but you won't be able to use the incredibly convenient and efficient xPDO methods described in this chapter for those tables without some extra work. You also won't be able to use another database platform without rewriting all your code.

Making Your Tables xPDO-friendly

Setting things up so that your custom database tables will work with xPDO takes a little effort, but it's generally well worth it. You only have to do it once, and when you're done, you'll be able to create, retrieve, update, and delete any object in your database using the xPDO methods detailed earlier in this chapter. For example, you can query the database with getCollection() and add new rows to it with newObject(). You can also get related objects with getOne() and getMany() and add new ones with addOne() and addMany(). Better yet, you can move your database tables to any platform that xPDO supports by simply migrating the data and changing the **config.inc.php** file to specify the new platform. None of your code will have to change.

The details of setting things up for xPDO are beyond the scope of this book, but there are several tutorials showing how to do it on the Web, including one at **http://bobsguides.com**. The process involves several fairly straightforward steps. There are various methods for doing this, but here is how I generally do it:

- Design the database tables. Make sure they include all the fields that you need and de-termine the type of each field.

- Create the tables, and add them to the MODX database. They can have the same prefix as the MODX tables, but I generally prefer to use a different prefix.

- Using two methods of xPDO's xpdogenerator class (writeSchema() and parseSchema()), write a snippet that generates an xPDO schema and creates xPDO class and map files. The class and map files will be created under the **core/components** directory in a directory named for your new component.

- Modify the schema file after running writeSchema() and before running parseSchema(). Generally, this step is only necessary if you want to use related objects with your tables.

Once you've completed the steps above, all you need to do to use xPDO with the objects in your custom tables is to add code like this at the top of any snippets or plugins that use xPDO methods:

```
$path = MODX_CORE_PATH . 'components/mycomponent/';
$result = $modx->addPackage('mycomponent', $path . 'model/','prefix_');
```

It may take you a bit of effort to create the files properly and get up to speed with xPDO, but I can promise that you'll never regret it. Once you get used to working with xPDO, you'll wonder how you ever lived without it.

Working with the Lexicon

As we learned earlier in this chapter, lexicon strings are used to internationalize a component. Let's look at an example for a simple snippet that does nothing but display a couple of language tags. We'll create a snippet called *MySnippet* with its own namespace and lexicon file. Then we'll display the lexicon strings in the snippet.

Creating the Namespace

First, we'll need to create a namespace for the snippet. Go to **System → Namespaces** and click on the "Create New" button. Fill in the following fields exactly as they appear here:

Name: *mysnippet*

Path: *{core_path}components/mysnippet/*

MODX will replace the {core_path} part with the actual path to your **core** directory. If we later move the core directory (which is easy to do in MODX Revolution), MODX will still be able to find our snippet's files. Notice that the path is in all lowercase letters, following the MODX guideline that all filenames and directory names should be in lowercase.

Creating the Lexicon File

Next, we'll need to create the lexicon file containing the language strings and put it in the correct location. Create the directories for the following path (the **core** and **components** directories should already exist, but you will have to create the others). Be sure to use all lowercase letters:

core/components/mysnippet/lexicon/en/

Now create a file called **default.inc.php** in the **en** directory, and put this code in it:

```
$_lang['ms.file-not-found'] = "File Not Found";
$_lang['ms.bad-email'] = "Improper Email Address";
```

We used the `ms.` prefix on our language strings (`ms` for MySnippet) to prevent collisions with other language strings that might be in the lexicon.

Creating the Snippet

To use the language strings in our snippet, all we need to do is load them into the lexicon and specify them. Create a snippet called *MySnippet* with the following code:

```
$modx->getService('lexicon','modLexicon');
$modx->lexicon->load('mysnippet:default');
/* file not found error */
$output .= '<p>File not found message: ' .
    $modx->lexicon('ms.file-not-found') . '</p>';
/* bad email address error */
$output .= '<p>Bad email message: ' .
    $modx->lexicon('ms.bad-email') . '</p>';
return $output;
```

Because we specified the path to our component when we created the namespace, MODX knows where to look when we call `$modx->lexicon->load()` with the namespace and the topic. Note that although the topic is `default`, MODX will look for a file called **default.inc.php**.

Displaying the Language Strings

Create a resource called *LanguageDemo* with the following content:

```
<h2>Language Demo</h2>
[[MySnippet]]
```

When you preview the resource, you should see your language strings on the page. Normally, of course, we'd be using a more complicated snippet and those error messages would only be inserted into the page output if an error were discovered in a form field. Typically, we'd set the error messages with $modx->toPlaceholder() and display them with placeholder tags.

Sometimes, however, you might want to display the language strings in a chunk, template, or template variable, or in the content of a resource without using a snippet. In that case, we'd use language tags. Because there is no snippet to load the lexicon file, we'd need to include the namespace and topic in the language tag:

```
[[%ms.file-not-found? &namespace=`MySnippet` &topic=`default`]]
[[%ms.bad-email? &namespace=`MySnippet` &topic=`default`]]
```

The namespace and topic are required because if they are omitted, MODX will look for the strings in the default topic of the core namespace and won't find them.

Creating a Page Count Snippet

Let's end this chapter with something truly useful. We'll put together some of the things we've learned about MODX objects to create a simple page counter for our site. Every page will show the number of visits, and every visit will update the page count for that page.

Creating the Elements

We'll need one template variable and one very simple snippet for our page counter. We could create the template variable in code with $modx->newObject() and attach it to all templates with addMany(), but since we only need one template variable, it's much easier to create it manually in the MODX Manager.

Create a template variable called *PageCount*, and (on its Template Access tab) attach it to all the templates used in the front end of your site. Put *PageCount* in the Name field, and leave the other fields at their default values. Save the TV.

Next, create a snippet called *PageCount* with the following code:

```php
<?php
/* Code for the PageCount Snippet */
$id = $modx->resource->get('id');
$tv = $modx->getObject('modTemplateVar', array('name'=>'PageCount'));
$count = $tv->getValue($id);
$count++;
$tv->setValue($id,$count);
$tv->save();
return $count;
?>
```

Our snippet first gets the ID of the current page. We'll need that when calling the TV's setValue() method. Next, the snippet gets the template variable itself with getObject(). Then the snippet gets the current value of the TV in the $count variable, increments it by 1, and uses it to update the TV's value with setValue() and save(). Finally, the snippet returns the new value of $count so it can be displayed on the page with a snippet tag.

Displaying the Page Count

In your templates, put the following code where you want the page count to appear:

```
<p>Page Count: [[!PageCount]]</p>
```

The page count should increase every time the page is visited. Notice that we've used the ! token to make the snippet uncached. That way, even if the page is cached, we'll get an up-to-date page count when the page is visited. Because we're storing the page count in a regular TV, you can also cheat by simply editing that TV on the Template Variable tab for any page to make that page appear more popular than it really is (not that you'd ever do that). To avoid the temptation, you could hide the TV using the form customization rules discussed in Chapter 11.

Summary

In this chapter, we learned how to use the built-in MODX objects and their methods to get information inside a snippet or plugin. Information about an object is available using the object's get() method. Information about related objects can be retrieved from the database using the object's getOne() and getMany() methods.

You can also retrieve objects themselves from the database by using the $modx->getObject() and $modx->getCollection() methods. Objects and their related objects can be retrieved in a single step with the $modx->getObjectGraph() and $modx->getCollectionGraph() methods.

In a snippet, any properties sent in the snippet tag, default properties, and properties from property sets (if any) are available in the $scriptProperties array.

The $modx->getOption() method will retrieve a value from any properties in the snippet tag, default properties, and property sets. It will also search for MODX settings and, optionally, a specified array.

The $modx->getChunk() method will retrieve the processed content of the specified chunk and will allow you to send a property set that will be used to replace placeholder tags in the chunk.

The $modx->runSnippet() method will let you run another snippet from inside a snippet and, optionally, send properties to be used by the snippet.

When retrieving the value of a template variable inside a snippet, it is necessary to specify the ID of the resource you want the TV value for.

Using the MODX lexicon allows you to internationalize your site by presenting the snippet's output in a particular language.

Advanced developers can create and change objects in the MODX database from inside a snippet by retrieving an object or creating a new one with $modx->newObject(), creating or changing its content, and using the object's save() method.

MODX Evolution Notes

This area is where we see the biggest differences between the two versions. The convenient $modx object, getObject(), get(), getOne(), getMany(), getCollection(), and hasChildren() methods don't exist in MODX Evolution, nor do the graph methods, and there are no related objects. The getChildIds(), getParentIds(), getChunk(), parseChunk(), and runSnippet() methods do exist in Evolution.

Context settings and user settings don't exist in Evolution, but system settings do. The method for getting system settings in Evolution looks like this:

```
$setting = $modx->config['SettingName'];
```

There is no MODX lexicon object in Evolution, and language strings are generally loaded as a single array and accessed with $_lang['keyName'].

Modifying MODX objects is generally performed by direct queries to the MODX database. See the DBAPI section of the MODX online documentation for more information. Note that the DBAPI is deprecated in MODX Revolution. In Revolution, the information in the database can always be retrieved and changed with the xPDO get*() and set*() methods instead.

Chapter 9

Site Organization and Contexts

In earlier versions of MODX, there are fixed locations and names for the directories containing the MODX core files. There is no way to modify this without major hacking of the MODX core.

In MODX Revolution, however, you can easily move and rename the major directories. Sites can be made much more secure, and several MODX sites can now share the same MODX core files and add-on components.

Another change is the introduction of contexts, which allow users to divide sites into separate areas by context or to use contexts to maintain separate sites within a single MODX install. Different users can be allowed access to different contexts in both the front and back end of the site, and each context can have its own independent context settings, which will override any system settings with the same name.

In this chapter, we'll look at how to move and/or rename the **core** and **manager** directories. We'll also look at contexts and various ways they can be used to solve common problems

Site Organization

MODX Evolution has a potential security problem in the placement of raw PHP code for some snippets in the **assets/snippets** directory. Since the snippet code is Open Source, any vulnerability that is discovered by examining the snippet code can be exploited on almost any MODX site. A well-written snippet would not contain any vulnerabilities, but since snippets can be submitted by anyone, it's hard for naïve users to be sure that a particular snippet is sufficiently hardened.

In MODX Revolution, the **core** directory (with all its subdirectories) can be moved outside of the web root so that any snippet code placed under the **core** directory will not be available via the Web.

A second vulnerability exists in the fixed placement and name of the **manager** directory. In MODX Evolution, hackers can assume that the MODX Manager can be accessed via http://*yoursite.com*/**manager**. This opens up the site to brute-force attempts to capture the Manager login (especially when naïve users leave the admin Super User name at the default: admin). Bots can be programmed to go to the Manager URL, enter "admin," and guess a password. On most sites, they would be blocked for an hour after several unsuccessful attempts to log in, but by using multiple servers and a lot of patience, hackers could eventually get the Super User's password. Imagine how much more secure the site would be if the name of the **manager** directory were unknown.

Reorganizing the Site

In the following sections, we'll look at how to move and rename the **core** and **manager** directories. The moving and renaming can be done during the install when using the Advanced distribution of MODX, but the Advanced distribution will not install on all platforms. If you have installed the Traditional distribution, the method below will let you do the job later on. Even if you use the Advanced distribution to move and/or rename the directories, the following sections will help you understand how MODX handles the changes and where to look if things aren't working properly.

How MODX Knows Where Things Are

While MODX Evolution has a single configuration file, MODX Revolution has several. The master config file is here:

core/config/config.inc.php

You edit the **config.inc.php** file to rename and/or move the manager.

There are also four **config.core.php** files that identify the location of the MODX core. There is a **config.core.php** file in each of the following directories:

- *MODX root directory*
- **/manager/**
- **/connectors/**
- **/setup/includes/**

Note that when using the Advanced distribution of MODX, the initial settings will be taken from the **setup/includes/config.core.php** file. They will be displayed during the installation process, and you can modify them to move and rename the directories. The settings in the **core/config/config.inc.php** file and the other **config.core.php** files will be set automatically from your input, and the directories will be renamed and moved for you.

Moving/Renaming the MODX Core
(Advanced distribution)

If you have not already installed MODX and would like to move and/or rename the core, you can try downloading and installing the Advanced distribution of MODX. It will install on most (but not all) platforms and provides tools to move and/or rename both the **core** and the **manager** directories. It's not much more difficult to do the same thing with the Traditional distribution, however, using the techniques outlined below.

 Important: Before making any modifications to the site structure of a new site using the Traditional distribution, do a standard install with everything in the default locations, but do not delete the **setup/** directory. Then log in to the Manager, and try the Top Menu items and the file browser to make sure things are working correctly.

You may also want to create a resource and an element and save them. It's important to have a fully working MODX site before making alterations.

If the site is on a public server, be sure to delete the **setup/** directory once you know everything is working. Don't leave the **setup/** directory in place any longer than you absolutely have to because it presents a serious security vulnerability.

Moving/Renaming the MODX Core
(Traditional distribution)

You can move and/or rename the **core** directory with the Traditional distribution by editing the config files. Note that you can't rename any of the files or directories in the **core** directory, just the directory itself. First, change the name and/or move the directory and all its files to a location anywhere on the same server. Then enter the new path to the **core** directory in the four **config.core.php** files listed above. Rather than calculate the new path, it's usually easier to hard-code the full path in each file (see below). At this writing, you also have to modify the MODX_PROCESSORS_PATH setting in

path_to_your_new_core/**config/config.inc.php**

if it's not correct. Then, run Setup in upgrade mode.

If you're going to the trouble of moving the **core** directory, you might as well move it out of the MODX site into a directory with a boring name for extra security and give the **core** directory another boring name.

Suppose, for example, that your MODX site is in the following directory:

*username***/usr/public_html/modx**

The **config.core.php** file would contain this line to start with:

```
define('MODX_CORE_PATH', 'username/usr/public_html/modx/core/');
```

If you rename the **core** directory to **old** and move it to *username***/usr/css/**, you would edit the lines in the four **config.core.php** files to look like this:

```
define('MODX_CORE_PATH', 'username/usr/css/old/');
```

Be sure to leave the trailing slash in the path. It is a general rule in MODX that all path specifications end in a slash.

Run Setup in upgrade mode, and you should have a working site with your new core directory. If the Manager doesn't look right or you get an error message when logging in, check the **config.inc.php** file in the **user/usr/css/old/** directory. Find the line that sets the $modx_processor_path and change it to:

```
$modx_processors_path = 'username/usr/css/old/model/modx/processors/';
```

Not only do the core and its directory have boring names now, the **core** directory and all files below it are no longer accessible via URL. Be sure to delete the old **core** directory after the move/rename. Before deleting the old directory, it's good idea to rename it and clear the site cache first to make sure that MODX is actually using the new core. Remember that you'll have to edit these files again and perform an upgrade Setup if you move the site.

When you upgrade MODX, you'll have to extract the files somewhere else and copy the files in the **core** directory to the **old** directory of your site. Be sure to upgrade all the files in your MODX site at the same time, so the version of the core will match the version of all the other files. It's not recommended that you move/rename the core when using the Development version of MODX because you will want to upgrade it regularly and it's just too much trouble.

Renaming the Manager Directory

Renaming the **manager** directory in MODX Revolution is remarkably simple. There are just three steps:

* Rename the **manager** directory
* Edit the **core/config/config.inc.php** file to include the new name
* Run Setup in upgrade mode

Say, for example, that you want to rename the **manager** directory to **mymanager** in a local-host site where the MODX installation is in the `htdocs/modx/` directory.

First, rename the **manager** directory to **mymanager**.

Next, change this part of the **config.inc.php** file in your **core/config/** directory (if you've renamed and/or moved the core, you'll have to look for it in your new core directory):

```
$modx_manager_path = 'C:/xampp/htdocs/modx/manager/';
$modx_manager_url = '/modx/manager/';
```

to this:

```
$modx_manager_path = 'C:/xampp/htdocs/modx/mymanager/';
$modx_manager_url = '/modx/mymanager/';
```

Be careful to leave any leading and trailing slashes in place.

Then run Setup. Make sure that upgrade is checked, and make sure that the manager path looks as it should on the Setup screen.

You can now log in to the MODX Manager by entering **http://yoursite.com/mymanager** in your browser's address window. You could also move the **manager** directory to another location using the same technique, though (unlike the **core** directory) it can't be moved outside the site because it needs to be accessible via URL. Once you have changed the name, there's not much point in moving it.

As we mentioned earlier, when you upgrade MODX, you'll have to extract the files somewhere and then copy (or FTP) the files to the appropriate locations. Copy the files in the **manager** directory to the **mymanager** directory at your site. As with the **core** directory, it's not recommended to rename or move the **manager** directory when using the Development version of MODX.

MODX should read the location and name of the **manager** directory from the config file during the upgrade install, but watch during Setup to make sure it has been read correctly.

Contexts

Contexts are new in MODX Revolution. A *context* is essentially a group of resources with their own system settings (called context settings) that override the settings in the Manager's System Settings grid. The resources in each context will be displayed in a separate section of the Resource tree. By creating context-specific ACL entries, a context can also have its own users.

Why Use Contexts?

Contexts can be used to isolate the parts of a multi-language site or two separate web sites sharing the same MODX core and Manager. Contexts can also be used to isolate the separate parts of a large, complex site (e.g., a corporate or educational web site).

In an enterprise corporate site, for example, management, labor, and customers might each access different contexts (each with its own login page). In an educational site, faculty, administrators, staff, and students could be similarly isolated.

You could do the same thing with resource groups and ACLs, but there is an added level of security when the users are in separate contexts. It saves you from having to worry about getting all the settings right or forgetting to add a new resource to the proper resource groups. When users are logged in to a particular context, they can only see that context's resources. Links to resources in another context will lead to the File Not Found page.

When thinking about using contexts, it's a good idea to remember that a front-end user in MODX can only be in one context at a time. If front-end users will be jumping back and forth between contexts frequently, you probably don't want to be using contexts in the first place. In addition, contexts do complicate things, so they should not be used unless you've put a fair amount of thought into whether you really need them.

The mgr and web Contexts

Many sites will only use the two default contexts (mgr and web). The mgr context is a special context that includes everything in the MODX Manager.

When a user is logged in and working in the Manager, that user is always in the mgr context. We should mention that it is theoretically possible to create multiple Manager interfaces with MODX using additional mgr-style contexts, but doing so is well beyond the scope of this book.

The web context and any other contexts you create are essentially the front end of the site. All resources in those contexts can be viewed in the Manager (by logged-in users with the appropriate permissions) and by users in the front end. Normally, front-end users can only see the resources of the context they are in at the moment.

Sharing the Database

One resource-saving measure when you have two MODX sites on the same server is to have the two sites share the same database. To share the database, just create one database and specify it in both installs but with a different table prefix. Each site will only use the tables with the table prefix specified in this file:

`core/config/config.inc.php`

If you were to examine the **core/config.inc.php** files of the two sites after the install, you'd find the only difference would be in this line:

`$table_prefix = 'modx_';`

This method doesn't do a very good job of conserving resources, however. We've reduced the number of databases by one, but we've still duplicated all MODX tables and all MODX files. A much better method is to have both sites share everything but the actual resources of the two sites.

Multiple Sites – One Core

If you have two relatively small MODX sites on the same server, it's wasteful to create two separate installations of MODX. There are literally thousands of files in a MODX install, and duplicating all of them is a waste of resources.

By using separate contexts, the two sites can share all the files of the MODX install, not just the database. When it's time to upgrade MODX to a new version, you only need to copy one set of files for both sites.

Unlike the other exercises in this book, it's not recommended that you actually do this one (though you can if you want to) unless you really have a need for multiple contexts. In the following sections, we'll discuss two different methods for handling multiple sites with contexts.

In the first, we'll have a separate site in a different subdirectory and put its resources in a separate context. Users will be going to two separate URLs, and we'll determine the context they will access in each site's **index.php** file.

In the second, we'll have two sites both pointed to the same directory. We'll direct the users to the correct context with a plugin.

Two Contexts, Two Directories

In MODX Revolution, users are placed in a particular context with a single line of code:

```
$modx->initialize('contextName');
```

If you look in the **index.php** file in the root of your MODX site, you'll see this line near the end of the file:

```
$modx->initialize('web');
```

This places every user who visits the front end of your site in the web context. In this section, we'll have another MODX site in a subdirectory (accessed by a separate URL). Before going any further, if you have Friendly URLs on, turn them off for now, and rename the **.htaccess** file in the MODX root to **ht.access**, so we won't have to worry about the rewrite rules.

Let's assume that you're doing this all on a localhost install where the MODX root directory is called **modx**, and you access it by going to **localhost/modx**.

Now, we'll create a subdirectory under that called **alt** which will be accessed via **localhost/modx/alt**. We could just have a complete second install of MODX in the subdirectory, but that's what we're trying to avoid. Instead, we'll use contexts to let the two sites share the MODX core and database.

Create the **modx/alt/** subdirectory, and put an **index.php** file in it with just this code:

```
<?
return 'Alt Site Home Page';
?>
```

Go to **localhost/modx/alt**, and make sure that the message appears, so we know we have things set up correctly before going any further. We're going to replace that **index. php** file in just a bit.

Keep in mind that, for both sites, you will be going to the Manager at **localhost/modx/manager**.

Creating the Second index.php File and config.core.php

Copy the **index.php** file in the **localhost/modx** directory to **localhost/modx/alt** (overwriting the one we created just above). Now do the same with **config.core.php** file in the MODX root.

Because both sites will be using the same core, we don't need to change the **config.core.php** file. We do need to edit the new **index.php** file, however.

We're going to call our second context **alt**, so edit the **index.php** file in the **alt** subdirectory, and find the following line near the bottom of the file:

```
$modx->initialize('web');
```

Change it to this:

```
$modx->initialize('alt');
```

Save the **index.php** file. That's really all there is to the file part of creating our second context. Of course you'd want to put any images or context-specific CSS files for the **alt** context in place in the subdirectory, but as far as MODX is concerned, we're all set. Now it's time to actually create our second context.

Creating the Second Context

In the MODX manager at **localhost/modx/manager**, go to **System → Contexts**. You should see the two default contexts, mgr and web. Click on the "Create New" button. Put *alt* in the first field, add an appropriate description, and click on the "Save" button. In the Resource tree at the left, click on the double-arrow refresh icon. You should see the new context in the tree.

The name of the other context doesn't have to match the name of the subdirectory we created earlier, but making them the same keeps you from having to figure out which one to use where. It can also eliminate some really frustrating errors.

In the Resource tree, under the web context, duplicate the Home page (and the Error and Unauthorized pages if you have them). Drag those duplicate pages, one at a time, into the `alt` context. Once they appear under the new context, edit their names and content appropriately. It's still too soon to preview our `alt` site. First, we need to adjust some settings to tell MODX where things are.

Context Settings

All contexts inherit the settings in the System Settings grid. There is a **`site_start`** system setting that tells MODX where the Home page is. Can you guess what would happen if we previewed the `alt` site now? The **`index.php`** would execute and place the user in the `alt` context. Then, it would try to send the user to the **`site_start`** page specified in the System Settings. Since that is set to the Home page of the web context (which we're not in), we'd get redirected to the Error (File not Found) page of the web context. That, in turn, would not be found, and we'd be redirected to it over and over. Eventually, we'd most likely get a "Too many forward attempts" error message.

We could change the **`site_start`** system setting, but then the original site wouldn't work. Remember that context settings will override system settings. We need to create a new context setting to send the user to the right place.

Go to **System → Contexts**. Right-click on the `alt` entry in the grid, select "Update Context," and click on the "Context Settings" tab.

You'll see an empty (or nearly empty) grid that looks just like the System Settings grid. We'll add some new settings to straighten things out. Click on the "Create New" button. Enter the following information:

Key: **`site_start`**
Name: *Home*
Value: *##*

Replace ## with the Resource ID of the alt context's Home page.

You can enter a description if you like, but don't change any of the other fields. Click on the "Save" button. If you have an Error page and an Unauthorized page for your `alt` site, create two more settings with *error_page* and *unauthorized_page* in the "Key" fields and the IDs of the two pages in the "Value" fields.

You'll also need a few more context settings to make links work properly.

Key: **`base_url`**
Name: *Base URL*
Value: */*

Key: `site_url`
Name: *Site URL*
Value: *http://localhost/modx/alt/*

Key: `http_host`
Name *HTTP Host*
Value: *localhost/modx/alt*

Don't forget the trailing slash on the `site_url` setting.

You should now be able to enter `localhost/modx/alt` in the browser window and see the Home page of your `alt` site. Create a few more pages in the `alt` context, and put links to them on the Home page of the `alt` site (using MODX link tags: `[[~##]]`). Check to make sure that they work properly.

You're probably going to want a different template for your `alt` site. The easiest way to do this is to duplicate the template in the Element tree, rename the duplicate to *Alt Template*, and create a new *default_template* context setting (as we did above) for the `alt` context, setting the Value field to the ID of the new template. Since you'll be putting images and CSS files under the `alt` directory, be sure to change the `<base href>` tag in the `<head>` section of the template and copy or create any necessary files.

Since we now have more than one context, you'll also want to update the `web` context settings. Go to **System → Contexts**. Right-click on the `web` context, and select "Update Context." Create the same context settings we created above but use the appropriate values for the `web` context.

Creating a Virtual Host

Suppose that you'd like visitors to go to **http://alt.modx** instead of **http://localhost/modx/alt**. You need to create `alt.modx` as a *virtual host*.

Most hosts have a utility for creating add-on domains. This allows you to point a domain name at any directory (assuming that you own the domain name). The technique varies from host to host. In cPanel, you can usually select Add-on Domains in the Domains section.

Once you've created the virtual host, users can go to the host name you've given it and see the `alt` site.

Since we're doing this on a localhost install, we'll give a quick example of how to create a virtual host on Windows and XAMPP. We'll call our virtual host *alt.modx*, but you can call it anything you want.

On Windows, you first need to tell Windows to accept the new domain name. If you are on a newer version of Windows, you'll need to right-click on notepad, and select "Run as Administrator" in order to edit the **hosts** file. Navigate to this directory:

/windows/system32/drivers/etc/

Change the file mask to show all files. Open the **hosts** file, and add this line to the bottom:

```
127.0.0.1        alt.modx
```

Save the file. Now, navigate to this directory:

xampp/apache/conf/extra

Make a back-up copy of the **httpd-vhosts.conf** file. Load the **httpd-vhosts.conf** file. Add the following code to the bottom of the file, and save it. Do this very carefully because if there is a syntax error in this file, the Apache server won't start. Adjust the paths to match your configuration, and notice that some lines use backslashes. The backslashes are not necessary on some versions of Windows, and they should not be used on a *nix install.

```
NameVirtualHost *:80
<VirtualHost *:80>
  DocumentRoot "C:\xampp\htdocs"
  ServerName localhost
</VirtualHost>
<VirtualHost *:80>
  DocumentRoot "C:\xampp\htdocs\modx\alt"
  ServerAdmin webmaster@alt.modx
  ServerName alt.modx
  ErrorLog "C:\xampp\apache\logs\alt.error.log"
 <Directory "C:\xampp\htdocs\modx\alt">
    Options Indexes FollowSymLinks Includes ExecCGI
    AllowOverride All
    Order allow,deny
    Allow from all
  </Directory>
</VirtualHost>
```

At this point, it's a good idea to go to the DOS command line, navigate to the **apache/bin** directory, and enter:

```
apache -S
```

Be sure to use a capital letter S. Apache will then tell you if there are any problems with the file you just edited.

Once you have the syntax correct, you need to restart Apache in order for the new rules to take effect. Once Apache has restarted, you should be able to enter `alt.modx` in your browser's address bar and see your `alt` site Home page. Note that you no longer enter **localhost** in front of the URL.

Now, you need to alter the context settings you created for your `alt` context to reflect the new URL. The **site_url** setting should be *http://alt.modx*, and the **http_host** should be *alt.modx*.

Once those changes have been made, you should be able to hover over the links you created earlier and see the virtual host name instead of the subdirectory.

Two Contexts, One Directory

Suppose that your two sites will share many of the same files. Rather than creating second copies of all the files in the **alt** directory, there's a way to put both sites in the same directory.

The answer is to edit the **httpd-vhosts.conf** file again and change the DocumentRoot of the virtual domain to point to the MODX root directory. This is the line you'll be changing:

```
DocumentRoot "C:\xampp\htdocs\modx\alt"
```

The new version will be:

```
DocumentRoot "C:\xampp\htdocs\modx"
```

We no longer need the `<directory></directory>` section, but it won't hurt to leave it there. Before going any further, make sure you can restart Apache. If there's an error in the **httpd-vhosts.conf** file, Apache won't start.

Now, both URLs (**modx** and **alt.modx**) point to the same directory. How will MODX know which context to serve up? The answer is a plugin that initializes the correct context based on the URL.

Since we won't be using the /alt/ subdirectory we created earlier, rename it to make sure it's not being used.

Important: If you created an **http_host** context setting for the web context, delete it before doing anything else. Otherwise, that setting will override the URL the user comes in on, and your alt context will never be initialized by the plugin.

Create a plugin called *Gateway* with the following code:

```php
<?php
/* Code for the Gateway Plugin */

if ($modx->context->get('key') == 'mgr') {
    return;
}

switch ($modx->getOption('http_host')) {
    case 'alt.modx':
    case 'alt.modx:80':
        $modx->switchContext('alt');
        break;

    default:
        /* by default, don't do anything -- index.php */
        /* will already have initialized the web context */
        break;
}
?>
```

After entering the plugin code, switch to the "System Events" tab, and check the box next to the **OnHandleRequest** event. Save the plugin, and clear the MODX cache (you may also need to clear your browser cache).

The two contexts should now be sharing the same directory. If you point your browser to **http://localhost/modx**, you should see the web context. If you point it at **http://alt.modx**, you should see the alt context. The links we created between the two contexts should also work.

You can (and should) still have the separate context settings we created earlier. Your separate templates should still work, and if you create a new document in one of the contexts, it should use the default template specified in the context settings with the **default_template** setting. You can create context settings to override any system setting for each context with context-specific values. The two contexts can have different context settings that determine whether pages are published by default, whether the rich-text editor is used, the allowable upload file types, whether Friendly URLs are enabled, etc.

Remember that any settings that should be common to both sites should be set as system settings. Settings that will differ between contexts should be set as context settings for both contexts. Settings that are only shared by specific resources or elements should generally be put in property sets.

Context Security Permissions

Because there are no ACL entries linking our new context or its resources to a user group, all the resources in the new context are unprotected and visible to all users.

You can protect all the resources in a context by creating a Context Access ACL entry for the Administrator user group with an Authority level of 0 and a Context of alt. This will hide the entire context in the Manager from everyone but the admin Super User. You can use this technique to give different users access to different contexts (see the following chapter for details on using ACLs).

You can create Context Access ACL entries by going to **Security** → **Access Controls** and updating a user group. Using that method, you can create a Context Access ACL entry for any context. You can also create them by going to **System** → **Contexts**, right-clicking on a context, and selecting "Update Context." An easier method is to just right-click on the context in the Resource Tree and select "Edit Context." Both methods take you to the same place. If you then select the "Access Permissions" tab, you can add a new Context Access ACL entry by clicking on the "Add Access Control" button (but only for the context you are editing).

As we'll see in the next chapter, if you would like to protect specific resources within a context, you can put the resources in a resource group and create a Resource Group Access ACL linking them to a specific user group.

Any contexts you create are just like the web context in the sense that protecting resources in them will hide them in the front end.

Other Uses for Contexts

Contexts can be used any time you want to have different sites or different versions of a site that share the same MODX core. Two common uses are serving multiple sites and creating multi-language sites.

Many Sites, One Core

In the section above, we saw how two sites can share the same core with contexts. We could just as well have created two or three more sites, each with its own context. At some point, especially if the sites have many visitors, the sites will start to slow down as the core tries to serve all of them. For small sites with little traffic, however, there's no reason a number of sites can't share the same core.

Multi-language Sites

Multiple contexts are often used to create a multi-language site. Each context contains resources in a particular language. This technique works best when all the language-specific contexts will display their pages in a similar format.

Remember, too, that the sites will be sharing all the elements on the site, including all snippets, chunks, and plugins. Most MODX add-on components are well-behaved and use placeholders for all output, but some are not. You may have to rewrite (or duplicate) certain snippets and have them check a context setting to determine what language to use. In MODX Revolution, placeholder tags can include language tags, and language tags can contain setting tags, so you can do something like this:

```
[[+[[%file_not_found?
    &namespace=`NameSpaceName`
    &topic=`default`
    &language=`[[++language]]`
]]
```

Do You Need Another Context?

Contexts complicate the administration of the web site, so before implementing them, you should be sure that there's no way to achieve what you want without them. To hide subsets of resources from certain users, for example, it's generally better to use resource groups and ACL entries rather than contexts. Similarly, letting users choose the "look" of the site should be done with different CSS files, not different contexts.

Summary

MODX sites can be made more secure by moving key directories outside the web root and by renaming them. The process can be done by editing the config files or during Setup when using the Advanced distribution of MODX.

Contexts are new in MODX Revolution, and they can be used to isolate and control user access to various parts of the site. Users can only access protected contexts when given explicit access to them in the MODX security permissions system. Contexts can also be used to allow a single MODX core to serve several different front-end sites or to configure multi-language sites. When MODX is upgraded, only the core is changed, so in multi-context sites, only one upgrade is required no matter how many sites are using the same core.

MODX Evolution Notes

Most of this chapter simply doesn't apply to MODX Evolution. In Evolution, you can't rename or move the **manager** directory without hacking the core code, and there is no **core** directory.

Since there are no contexts in Evolution, there's nothing you can do with them.

There are several multi-language solutions for MODX Evolution. The most popular one is called YAMS (Yet Another Multilingual Solution). See the MODX Forums for more information.

Chapter 10

MODX Security

In this chapter, we'll look at how you can use the MODX Revolution security system to control what users can do and see in both the front end and back end of MODX. Before implementing any security controls in a real site, be sure to read Chapter 11 where we discuss customizing the MODX Manager. Many security goals can be accomplished with less work simply by customizing the Manager so that users can't see the things they shouldn't have access to (e.g., the Elements and Files tabs).

Before we discuss the tasks necessary to set up a security strategy, we'll look at the security system as a whole and at the building blocks used to control user access to parts of a MODX site.

Security System Overview

In MODX Revolution, you can control access not only to resources, but also to parts of the MODX Manager. Controlling access to specific resources is done, as it was in MODX Evolution, by creating user groups and resource groups and linking the two. Control of access to elements in Revolution is accomplished by putting the elements in a category and linking the category to a user group — something that cannot be done at all in MODX Evolution. In the following sections, we'll look at the building blocks of the MODX security system. These sections can be confusing at first, and it may be some comfort to know that later in the chapter, we'll work through some practical applications that should help you understand how the system works.

Protecting Resources, Elements, and Contexts

One of the basic concepts of the security system is something we'll call "protection." By default, the objects in a resource group, a category, or a context, are unprotected and can be accessed by all users in both the front end and the MODX Manager. When any users are given specific access to one of these three objects, the object or objects they have been given access to become protected. Other users will then have no access to them unless a rule is created to grant that access.

We've already seen user groups, resource groups, categories, and contexts earlier in the book. User groups contain users, resource groups contain resources, and categories contain elements like snippets, chunks, and plugins. Contexts also contain resources. The key to the MODX security system is protecting specific resources, elements, and contexts by associating them with a user group.

Protected Resources

Resources become protected when a user group is associated with a resource group. The users in the user group will have access to the resources in the resource group. Other users will be denied that access unless a rule is created that gives them access as well. In MODX Revolution, the link between a user group and a resource group is created by adding an Access Control List (ACL) entry — more on these in just a bit.

Once a group of resources is protected by being associated with a user group, no one outside the user group (including the admin Super User) can edit the resources or elements unless explicitly given permission to do so. Unauthorized users won't even see the protected resources in the Manager. Don't be alarmed if resources disappear from the Resource tree while you are playing with access controls. They're not gone, just hidden.

Protected Elements

Elements (plugins, templates, template variables, snippets, and chunks) are protected by linking a user group with a category. The elements in the category are then off-limits to all other users unless they too are granted access. As with a resource, the link between a user group and a category is in a particular ACL entry.

Protected Contexts

Contexts are also protected when they are associated with any user group. While resources and elements are all unprotected by default, this is not true of contexts. The two default contexts in a new install are mgr and web. Both are protected by default because they are already associated with the Administrator user group (which has only the admin Super User as a member). This means that when you create a new user group, the users in that group will not be able to log in to the Manager unless you explicitly give them access to the protected mgr context. Even if they have mgr access, they still won't see any resources in the Resource tree until you also give them access to the protected web context (or other contexts you create). Creating a **tree_root_id** setting for the user (more on that in a bit) will also affect which resources the user can see in the Resource tree.

 One stumbling block for people learning the MODX security system is the **udperms_allowroot** system setting. By default, users other than the Super User cannot create resources at the root level of the site. You can spend hours messing with security permissions and security settings and wondering why your users can't create resources. If you want your users to be able to create resources at the top level of the tree, set the **udperms_allowroot** system setting to *Yes* before you do anything else.

Important: As of MODX 2.1, this capability is controlled by the **new_document_in_root** permission and the **udperms_allowroot** system setting is ignored. The system setting will likely be removed in future versions.

Security Permissions and Roles

If you are used to security in MODX Evolution, it's easy to be confused by the Revolution security system. First, Revolution does away with the distinction between web users and manager users. Second, security permissions in Revolution can be inherited within a user group. Finally, roles have a very different function in Revolution, users can have different permissions in different groups, and one user can have multiple roles.

Inheriting Security Permissions

When a user is assigned to a user group, he or she is assigned a specific role in that group. In MODX Evolution, roles are defined with specific permissions that control the user's capabilities. In MODX Revolution, on the other hand, when a user is added to a user group, an access policy is associated with the user's role. In Revolution, it is the individual permissions in the access policy that determine what the user can and can't do or see. In MODX Revolution, users can have different roles in different groups.

Every role has an authority number associated with it. You assign the numbers when you create the role. In a particular user group, users inherit the security permissions of roles with an authority number greater or equal to the one associated with their role in the group.

In other words, a user with a role that has an authority number of 5, will also have the security permissions of the other roles in that group with authority numbers greater than or equal to 5. This is only true within the user group. The user won't inherit security permissions of roles with higher numbers that exist in other user groups.

Multiple Security Permissions

Users can be in more than one group, so rules controlling their ability to perform a particular action might conflict with one another. A user might be in one group where they can see but not edit a particular resource. The same user might be in another group, however, with security permissions that let them both see and edit the same resource. In cases like this, the most permissive condition applies.

If a user belongs to a group and has permission to see and edit a particular resource, no permission setting in any other group can take that capability away.

Access in the Front End

In earlier versions of MODX, users were divided into manager users and web users. In MODX Revolution, however, this distinction is gone. There are just users. Access to resources in the front end is now controlled using contexts (e.g., the mgr context and the web context) — more on these in a bit.

When you create a rule (technically, an ACL entry) that protects resources or elements, you specify the context where the rule applies. The web context is the default front-end context. The mgr context is the default back-end (Manager) context. Resources that are protected with a rule that specifies the web context can only be seen by front-end users who are logged in and authorized to see them.

Access Control Lists (ACLs)

When you read about MODX Revolution security settings, you'll see a lot of discussion about Access Control Lists (ACLs) and setting context access and resource group access for users by creating ACL entries. It's not immediately obvious where this happens. It's easy enough to figure out how to create and populate user groups and resource groups. It's also easy to understand the creation of roles and policies.

The real work of managing security settings, however, is done in ACLs. To find the ACL area, go to **Security → Access Controls** and click on the "User Group" tab. Then, right-click on a user group and select "Update User Group." This will show you the User Group Editing panel where you can select one of the three ACL grids visible on the three right-hand tabs.

The Context Access tab contains the ACL grid where you set which contexts the user group can access (generally in the Manager). The Resource Group Access tab contains the ACL grid where you set which Resource Groups the user group can access. The Element Category Access tab contains the ACL grid where you control user access to elements in specific categories.

Once you have created the appropriate groups, roles, and policies, these ACL grids are where you actually implement the security system. We'll walk through creating a security system once we have covered the various elements in the following section.

 At this writing, all security controls must be applied to user groups. Setting security controls for individual users is on the roadmap, however, and may be possible by the time you read this.

Security Elements

The following elements all work together to control access to resources and parts of the Manager. It's important to have a basic understanding of them before you begin working with the security system.

A good first step, before you mess with any permissions, is to go to **Security → Access Controls** and click on the "User Group" tab. Right-click on the Administrator user group and select "Update User Group" on the drop-down list. Click on the "Context Access" tab. You should see the two default ACL entries there. Write down the values in each field. They should look like this:

Context: mgr
Minimum role: Super User - 0
Policy: Administrator

Context: web
Minimum role: Super User - 0
Policy: Resource

Now, look at the "Users" tab. You should see the admin Super User as the only user with a role of Super User. If you look at the "Resource Group Access" tab and the "Element Category Access" tabs, you'll see that the grids in both are empty. Click on the "Cancel" button at the upper right to go back to the main "Access Controls" panel. On the "User Groups" tab, click on the little triangle next to the Administrator user group to expand it. You'll see that the admin Super User is the only member. On the "Roles" tab, you'll see that the Super User role has an authority level of 0.

These are the default permission settings. If you completely mess up the permissions for your site, you can come back here, delete any extra entries, and edit the default entries to return things to normal. Be sure to select **Security → Flush Permissions** and **Security → Flush All Sessions** after making your changes.

To help keep you from shooting yourself in the foot, never edit any of these default entries. Always duplicate entries or create new ones and edit those.

Permissions

Permissions are the lowest level of the security system. They control access to basic actions and parts of the manager. The `save_element` permission, for example, allows users to save elements in the MODX Manager. The `file_tree` permission allows users to see the File tree in the manager.

Not having a particular permission, such as the `save_element` permission, may cause the user to see an "Access Denied" error message when attempting to perform an action. In other cases, like the `file_tree` permission, it will simply hide parts of the Manager.

In earlier versions of MODX, security permissions were assigned directly to roles. In MODX Revolution, however, security permissions can only be assigned as part of an access policy.

Access Policies and Policy Templates

An *access policy* is simply a list of security permissions. If a particular permission is enabled (by checking the checkbox next to its name), users can perform the action specified by the permission. If the permission is not enabled, the user can't perform that action. Access policies are assigned in an Access Control List (ACL).

An *access policy template*, is just a list of the permissions that will be available to be enabled in a policy. The policy template has no direct effect on what users can do and see — it simply determines the permissions that will appear in any policies based on it. There is no way to add new permissions (built-in or custom) directly to a policy. Instead, you add them to the appropriate policy template. Once you have done that, the new permissions will show up to be enabled or disabled in every policy based on that policy template.

Access policies are created by going to **Security → Access Controls** and selecting the "Access Policies" tab. Usually, you will create a new policy by duplicating an existing one rather than creating a new one from scratch. On the "Policy Templates" tab, you can create, modify, delete, and duplicate policy templates. As with policies, you will generally modify existing policy templates rather than creating new ones.

Creating and Altering Policies

By default, your install will contain a standard *Administrator policy*, a standard *Resource policy*, and a standard *Element policy*. These policies contain all the possible security permissions and give the user full rights. Important: You should never alter these three policies because that will take permissions away from the admin Super User. There is a *Load Only policy* that is typically used to allow viewers in the front end to see resources but do nothing with them.

There is also a *Load, List, and View policy* that is usually used to give users in the Manager the right to see resources and view their attributes but not to edit them. A ContentEditor policy is also included that may meet your needs for users who can edit resources but have limited rights in the MODX Manager. The Element policy is used in Element Category Access ACL entries and is used to specify what users can do with the elements in a particular category. The Object policy is a more limited version of the element policy.

When creating your own access policies, you have two choices. The easiest method is to duplicate one of the standard policies (by right-clicking on the policy and selecting "Duplicate"). After duplicating the policy, you simply right-click on it, select "Edit," rename it, and disable the permissions that you don't want the users to have by unchecking the checkboxes next to them in the grid.

The second method for creating your own access policies is to duplicate one of the built-in policy templates and then create a new policy based on the duplicate template. This second method is a little more trouble, but it allows you to completely remove permissions from the policy template that you never want to use. The standard templates (especially the Administrator template) have many permissions, and that can make it hard to find the specific ones you want to enable or disable. If you duplicate the standard Administrator template, you can easily disable specific permissions, but there is no safe way to remove permissions you don't need. Removing permissions from the Administrator template will take those permissions away from the admin Super User.

You can also add your own custom security permissions (or restore ones you accidentally removed) by editing a policy's policy template. This is best done by creating a new policy template containing just the custom permissions and creating a new policy based on it so that you are altering your own template rather than one of the built-in templates.

Types of Policies

There are two general types of policies. There are manager action policies (e.g., the standard Administrator policy) and Object policies (e.g., the standard Resource and Element policies and the Object policy). Understanding the difference between the two is critical. Table 10-1 shows the types of policies and the tabs they should be used on.

Access Controls Tab	Default Policy	Type
Context Access	Administrator	Manager Action
Resource Group Access	Resource	Object
Element Category Access	Element	Object

Manager Action policies (e.g., the Administrator policy) control what the user can do in general in the MODX Manager. Object policies (e.g., the Resource and Element policies) control what the user can do with individual resources and elements (i.e., resource, snippets, chunks, etc.). Earlier, we mentioned the three Access Control List (ACL) grids available in the User Group Editing panel. The following critical principles govern the assigning of policies on those grids:

- Policies assigned on the Context Access tab should be based on the standard Administrator policy.

- Policies assigned on the Resource Group Access tab should be based on the standard Resource policy.

- Policies assigned on the Element Category Access tab should be based on the standard Element policy.

If you create a policy of your own by duplicating an existing policy, be sure to duplicate the appropriate policy for the kind of ACL entries you will create for it. Consult the list above to see which policy is the right one for you. If you duplicate a policy and it doesn't show up as an option when you create an ACL entry, it means that you duplicated the wrong policy. Generally, only the appropriate types of policies will show up as options.

In all cases the policies you create will have fewer permissions enabled than the standard policies if you want to restrict the users' actions. In some cases, only a few permissions will be enabled.

As we said earlier, if you find that there are many permissions in a policy that you don't need, you may want to duplicate the appropriate policy template, remove permissions you are sure you will never need, and create a new policy based on that template. That way, the unnecessary permissions won't clutter up the list. This is hard to do after-the-fact, because at this writing, there is no way to change the policy template a policy is based on. As a rule, then, we recommend one of two approaches. The safest is to simply duplicate an existing policy and just uncheck (and ignore) permissions you don't the users to have. The other method is to duplicate a policy template, rather than a policy, and create a new policy based on that template. In the second case, you can delete permissions from the template so they will no longer show in the policy without altering any of the default templates or policies.

If you will be removing permissions, it's best to duplicate a policy template rather than a specific policy. If you will be adding permissions, it's best to create a new policy template and a new policy. We'll work through both methods later in this chapter.

Roles

As we mentioned earlier, *Roles* play a very different part in MODX Revolution than they did in previous versions of MODX. In MODX Evolution, when you create a role, you define exactly which manager actions a user with that role can perform. In other words, permissions in Evolution are tied directly to specific roles.

In MODX Revolution, however, the only things you set when you create a role are the name of the role, the authority number associated with that role, and an optional description of the role. In Revolution, permissions are tied to specific access policies.

When you add a user to a user group, you give the user a role in the group. The user might have different roles in different groups. The role doesn't directly determine the user's rights in the group, however. Instead, it is the access policy that determines what the user can and can't do.

The only function of the role in MODX Revolution is to assign that user an authority number in the group so that the user will inherit the security permissions of other users in the group with greater or equal authority numbers. The authority numbers are completely arbitrary. The only guideline for them is leave some room between the numbers you create in case you want to add users with an intermediate authority level later.

Roles are created by going to **Security → Access Controls** and selecting the "Roles" tab. Clicking on the "Create New" button will open the Create Role dialog. Roles can be removed by right-clicking on them and selecting "Remove Role."

Users

Earlier versions of MODX distinguished between web users and manager users. The separation of the two kinds of users meant that users often had to belong to two separate groups (a web user group and a manager user group) and use a separate login for the front end and the Manager. In MODX Revolution, there are just users. A user who can log in on a Login page in the front end of the site can log in to the Manager with the same credentials (assuming that they have permission to do so). If you want to restrict users to the front end, you can easily add them to a user group and deny that user group access to the Manager (in fact, that is the default behavior for users granted access to only the web context).

New users can be created in the MODX Manager by going to **Security → Manage Users** and clicking on the "New User" button. This will take you to the Create/Edit User panel, which allows you to enter the user's profile data including a username and password on the General Information tab. No user security permissions are set in the profile other than those affecting whether the user is totally blocked from logging in.

You can also right-click on a user and select "Update User" to update the user's profile data, settings, or user group membership. Another right-click option is "Remove User," which removes the user from the database. Removing the user can't be undone except by creating a new user.

When you select either "New User" or "Update User," you'll also see a Settings tab where you can set *user settings* for that user that will override both regular system settings and context settings. You can, for example, set the `manager_language` setting for just that user. You can also create a `tree_root_id` user setting, which sets the top of the Resource tree for that user to the resource with the specified ID. This will prevent the user from seeing resources above the specified resource in the tree but will show any resources below it. This can be very handy if you have a site with many users who each have access to a single page or just one section of the site. The `tree_root_id` setting also accepts a comma-delimited list of IDs, so the user can see only the resources specified and any resources below them in the tree. See Chapter 12 for details on using these two settings.

On the Access Permissions tab, you can add the user to a user group and specify the user's role in that group. This can also be done in the User Groups section.

User Groups

A user group is a just group of users who have been assigned group membership. User groups are created and filled by going to **Security → Access Controls** and selecting the "User Groups" tab.

To create a new user group, you can either click on the "New User Group" button or right-click on one of the existing groups in the User-Group tree and select "Create User Group." Either method will open the Create User Group dialog. Once the user group has been created, you can right-click on it and select "Update User Group." This will take you to the User Group Edit panel where you will see five tabs.

 Whenever you create a new user group, always add yourself to it with a role of admin Super User. That will prevent you from losing privileges and access to resources and elements when you create ACL entries for that group.

The General Information tab lets you set the name and, optionally, the parent of the group. The parent is just used for organizing the tree at present, but in future versions, it may be possible to have children inherit security settings from their parents. You will need to give the group a name and save it before you can add any users.

The Users tab allows you to add and remove users. You can add a user by clicking on the "Add User to Group" button, which will open the Add User to Group dialog. In the dialog, you can select the user from the drop-down list.

When you add a user, you specify a role for the user in that group from a drop-down list of existing roles. Obviously, you can only do this if the role you want has already been created. If you're not sure what the user's role will be, you can select "None" for the role and add a role later.

Remember that the role assigned to the user only operates in that group and has no effect on the user's status in other groups to which he or she belongs.

In MODX Revolution, users can have very different roles and capabilities in different user groups. If the specifications overlap, the most permissive rule takes precedence.

By right-clicking on an existing user, you can either remove the user or update the user's role on the Update User Role dialog. Remember that when you update the user's role you are only changing the user's role in the user group you are updating. The user's role in other user groups will be unchanged.

The Context Access, Resource Group Access, and Element Category Access tabs, as you might guess, control access to contexts, resource groups, and elements in specific categories. These will be covered below when we discuss Access Control Lists (ACLs).

Resource Groups

A *resource group* is simply a set of resources. Resource groups are created by going to **Security → Resource Groups** and clicking on the "Create Resource Group" button or by right-clicking in the Resource Group tree and selecting "Create Resource Group." Either action will open the Create Resource Group dialog.

Once you have created a resource group, you can add resources to it by dragging and dropping them from the Resource tree at the right. You may have to expand the tree first. Note that, at this writing, you can't drag and drop resources from the main Resource tree on the left side of the Manager.

You can remove resources from a group either by dragging them to another group or by dragging them back to the Resource tree at the right.

The Resource Group panel only allows you to create and remove resource groups and to add and remove resources from them. No security limitations are set here. Security limitations are created by applying the roles, policies, and permissions you have created to user groups and resource groups using an Access Control List (ACL).

Access Control Lists (ACLs)

Access Control Lists (ACLs) are the heart of the MODX Revolution security system and, unfortunately, one of its most confusing parts. Because the Revolution security system is so powerful and flexible, it can be a challenge to understand. Once you understand the basic principles, however, it's not that difficult to use.

One stumbling block is that the term ACL does not appear in the Manager (although it may by the time you read this). Every user group has, potentially, three types of ACLs associated with it. The ACLs are found by going to **Security → Access Controls**, clicking on the "User Groups" tab, right-clicking on a user group, and selecting "Update User Group." This will take you to the User Group Edit panel where the three right-hand tabs will display the three ACLs: the Context Access ACL, Resource Group Access ACL, and the Element Category Access ACL. Each ACL is a list containing a set of *ACL entries*. Each ACL entry connects user group members to a specific context, resource group or element category. Let's look at the three tabs.

Context Access Tab

The rules you set on the *Context Access tab* can be thought of as *Manager action rules*. They determine what Manager actions (e.g., load, save, save_chunk, publish_document, new_user, etc.) the user can perform while working in a particular context. New entries are created by clicking on the "Add Context" button to open the User Group Context Access dialog. In the dialog, you can enter a Context, a Minimum Role, and an Access Policy specified. Let's look at those entries:

Context — The context where the rule applies. The rule won't affect any other context.

Minimum Role — The Minimum Role necessary for the specified Access Policy to apply. Users in the group that meet the minimum role criterion (as determined by the role's authority number) will have the security permissions contained in the specified Access Policy and any policies attached to roles with an equal or greater authority number in the group. The access policy will not apply to users with higher authority numbers (i.e., less authority) than the minimum role specified in the ACL entry. Remember that higher authority numbers always mean less authority. The admin Super User always has an authority of 0 — the highest possible authority level. The admin Super User will inherit all the permissions granted to all other users of the group. This can only happen, however, if the admin Super User is a *member* of the group, so you should always add yourself, with a role of admin Super User, to any user group you create unless members of the group should have permissions that you don't have.

Access Policy — Specifies a policy containing a set of security permissions that users with the Minimum Role will have in that context.

Remember that you are working with a particular user group here, so the settings you enter will only apply to the users in that group. Note, also, that what you do on this tab will have no effect on what pages users can visit in the front end. Protecting contexts here only protects them in the Manager, and resources in the context will all be visible (if published) in the front end unless you protect them on the Resource Group Access tab.

As we discussed earlier, a context is unprotected by default, but if there is a single context ACL entry (in any user group at the site) specifying that context, it becomes protected in the Manager and can only be accessed by users who have been given explicit access to it. That access can only be granted in an ACL.

The default MODX Revolution install contains an Administrator user group with context ACL entries for the mgr and web contexts. That means that those two contexts are protected in the Manager unless you remove those entries. If all of your users will have full access to all resources, elements, and manager actions, you won't need any more ACL entries — you can simply add the users to the Administrator group with a role of Super User (authority level 0).

Unless they have been added to the Administrator user group or given access in some other way, new users won't be able to log in to the MODX Manager because the mgr context (essentially, the MODX back end) is protected. If you grant them access to the mgr context, they will be able to log in, but still won't be able to see any resources in the Resource tree (because the web context is also protected) until you also give them access to the web context (or other contexts you create).

There are two ways to give users access to those contexts:

- Add them to the Administrator user group with a role and policy that will allow them to perform actions in the mgr context and access the web context.
- Add them to some other user group and add ACL entries there for both the web and mgr contexts with the appropriate roles and policies.

Which route you take depends on your overall security strategy. Both techniques work, but the second method provides more flexibility for customizing the Manager, so it is usually a better choice.

Note that when you give users access to the web context in a Context Access ACL entry, it lets them see the resource in the web context in the Manager. Don't forget, though, that it also determines what Manager actions they can perform in the front end.

If a plugin or snippet in the front end performs Manager actions such as changing security permissions, modifying the database, etc., the code won't execute unless the user belongs to a group with proper permissions in the policy you assign in the web Context Access ACL entry. The policy won't affect what they can do in the Manager, however. That can only be affected by a mgr Context Access ACL entry. Most plugins and snippets don't perform any Manager actions, so this is seldom an issue. For a plugin that allows front-end editing and saving of resources or elements, however, users would need to be granted the appropriate rights.

Often, it's enough to use a policy that just contains the load permission when creating a web Context Access ACL entry. That will allow users to see resources in the front end, and that's often all you want them to be able to do.

Resource Group Access Tab

The *Resource Group Access tab* is where you create Resource Group Access ACL entries. These rules protect resource groups in a specified context and, depending on the policy assigned, determine what resource actions users can perform on the resources in the resource group using tools in that context. In the previous section, we called the Context Access rules "Manager action" rules because they determine what manager actions a user can perform. The rules on the Resource Group Access tab, on the other hand, should be thought of as "object" rules. They determine what users can do with resource objects in a particular resource group.

The most common use of Resource Group Access ACL entries is to hide groups of resources from users in the front or back end. They can also be used to control what actions users can perform on the resources in a resource group.

Note that the Manager action rules take precedence here, so users with `save` permission in a resource policy won't be able to save any protected resources unless they also have the `save_document` permission in a Context Access policy with a context of `mgr`. Users with the `save_document` permission in the administrator Context Access ACL, for example, still won't be able to save the protected resources unless they also have the `save` permission in the Resource Group Access ACL.

The fact that users need both permissions in some situations might seem to contradict the principle we mentioned earlier that when permissions conflict, the most permissive takes precedence. There is no contradiction, however. That earlier principle only applies when the two permissions are the same. Here, they're different permissions altogether.

The `save` permission gives users the right to save objects in the Manager. Without the `save permission`, a user can't save any documents. The `save_document` permission, on the other hand, gives users the right to save documents in a specific resource group. Without the `save_document` permission, users can't save documents in that group.

You create new entries by clicking on the "Add Resource Group" button to open the Add Resource Group dialog. Each ACL entry on this tab has a Resource Group, a Minimum Role, an Access Policy, and a Context where the rule applies:

Resource Group — The resource group affected by the ACL entry.

Minimum Role — The minimum role necessary for the specified access policy to apply to resources in the resource group. Users who don't have the necessary role won't have the permissions specified in the access policy for the resources in the resource group.

Access Policy — The set of specific resource permissions users in the user group with the minimum role will have when dealing with the resource objects of the resource group in the specified context.

Context — The context where the rule applies.

Policies in Resource Group Access ACL entries should always be based on the standard Resource policy. If you don't want users to have all the permissions in the standard Resource policy, don't edit that policy. Instead, duplicate it, and disable the unwanted permissions in the duplicate by unchecking the checkboxes for them. Then use that duplicate as the policy in your Resource Group Access ACL entries.

Of course you can have multiple policies here and assign different policies to different user groups. You can also create multiple ACL entries for one user group but specify different minimum roles so that different rules will apply to different users in the group. As always, users will inherit policies with equal or higher authority numbers in the Resource Context Access ACL.

Element Category Access tab

The *Element Category Access tab*, like the Resource Group Access tab, contains "object" rules that determine what a user can do with particular objects. The rules on this tab, however, apply to elements (templates, snippets, chunks, etc.) rather than resources. Since elements (except for TVs) don't go in resource groups, they are grouped by being placed in a category.

Create entries here by clicking on the Add Category button to open the Add Category dialog.

The ACL entries you create on this tab control access to elements in a specific category in the MODX Manager and determine what actions (e.g., create, view, save, edit, etc.) users can perform in the Manager.

As we saw with resource policies, these are overridden by administrator policies in any Context Access ACL, so users with save permission for a chunk in a category won't be able to save the chunk unless they also have the save_chunk permission in the appropriate administrator Context Access ACL. Users with the save_chunk permission in the administrator Context Access ACL still won't be able to save the chunk unless they also have the save permission in the Element Category Access ACL.

Each ACL entry on this tab has a Category, a Minimum Role, an Access Policy, and a Context where the rule applies:

Category — The category affected by the ACL entry. Access to the category itself and the elements in it will be controlled by the ACL entry.

Minimum Role — The minimum role necessary for the specified policy to grant permissions for the elements in the category. Users who don't have the necessary role won't have the permissions in the specified policy for the category or any elements under it in the Element tree.

Access Policy — The set of element permissions users in the user group with the minimum role will have when dealing with the elements in the category in the specified context.

Context — The context where the rule applies. This should match the context where the users will be working with the elements you want to apply the rule to (usually the mgr context).

Policies in Element Category Access ACL entries should always be based on the standard Element policy. If you don't want users to have all the security permissions in the standard policy, don't edit that policy. Instead, duplicate it, rename it, and disable the unwanted permissions in the duplicate by unchecking their checkboxes. Then use that duplicate in your Element Category Access ACL entries.

Of course you can have multiple policies for a given user group here, and you can assign different policies to different user groups. As always, users will inherit policies with equal or higher authority numbers in the Element Category Access ACL.

Working with MODX Security

Confused? Let's work through a relatively simple example. Remember the news stories we displayed with getResources? Let's create an Editors user group that can see and edit only those resources in the MODX Manager. A little later in this chapter, we'll see how to hide the Element tree and the File tree from those users and limit what they can do in the Manager.

Before diving into the creation of a complex security system for your site and adding ACL entries, you may want to take a look at the following chapter on customizing the MODX Manager.

In many cases, it is easier to accomplish security goals by simply hiding parts of the Manager. Almost any menu item, tab, template variable, or individual resource form field can be hidden from specific groups of users.

Limiting the Editors' Access to Resources in the Manager

We'll start by determining what resources our Editor users can and can't see in the MODX Manager (the back end).

Creating the Documents

If you haven't done so already, create a *Home* page and a *News* page. Make sure that both are published and use the main template, and that the News page is a container. Make sure that the **site_start** System Setting is set to the Home page's Resource ID.

Now create three news stories (*News1*, *News2*, and *News3*) under the News folder (by right-clicking on the "News" folder and selecting "Create Document Here"). Again, make sure all are published and use the main template.

Creating the Resource Groups

Go to **Security → Resource Groups**. We'll create two resource groups here. First, we'll create an "AllDocs" group that contains all the documents on the site. This will protect all the documents so that the Editors can only see the documents we give them access to. Click on "Create Resource Group." Put *AllDocs* in the Name field of the Create Resource Group dialog, and save the group. Now expand the web context in the tree at the right, and drag all the documents there into the AllDocs group on the left. Make sure you drag the News page and all three news story pages.

Now create a new resource group called *News*, and drag just the three news story pages into it (but not the News container).

Note that we haven't actually protected any pages yet. Any new user will still see all the pages (as long as they have access to the web and mgr contexts) because we haven't protected them by creating an ACL entry. Putting resources in a resource group, by itself, does not protect them in any way unless the there is a Resource Group Access ACL entry linking that resource group with a user group.

 When working on security, you often want to go back to the previous panel after saving your work. Usually, the "Cancel" button at the upper right will act as a "Back" button. Be sure you've saved your work before clicking on it.

Creating the User and User Group

Create a user named *JoeBlow* (if you haven't already). Make a note of Joe's username and password because you'll need to be logging in as Joe.

Create a user group called *Editors*.

Go to **Security → Access Controls → Roles tab**. Create a new role called *Editor* with an authority of *10*. Click on the "Save" button to save the role.

Add Joe to the Editors user group with a role of Editor by clicking on the "User Groups" tab, then right-clicking on the "Editors" group and selecting "Add User to Group" on the drop-down menu.

Creating the Policies

Go to the "Access Policies" tab in **Security → Access Controls**. Right-click on the "Administrator" policy, and select "Duplicate."

Right-click on the "Duplicate of Administrator" policy, and select "Update Policy."

Change the name of the duplicate policy to *EditorAdmin*, enter an appropriate description and save the policy. Don't change any of the permissions at this point.

Now do the same for the Resource policy. Duplicate it, then update the duplicate, and change the name to *EditorResource*.

If you try to log in as JoeBlow at this point, you'll get an "Access Denied" error message because we haven't given Joe access to the mgr context. We'll do this by updating the Editors User group, which Joe is a member of.

Creating the Context Access ACL Entry

Go to **Security → Access Controls → User Groups tab**. On the Access Controls panel, right-click on the Editors user group, and select "Update User Group." Go to the "Context Access" tab. Click on "Add Context." That will take you to the User Group Context Access dialog. Use the following settings:

Context: *mgr*

Minimum Role: *Editor*

Access Policy: *EditorAdmin*

Click on the "Save" button in the dialog.

When working on security permissions, changes won't take effect until you select Security → Flush Permissions. If the changes affect a user's access in the Manager, you also have to select Security → Flush All Sessions (which will log you off).

If you make a change and it doesn't take effect, try both before assuming that you've made a mistake.

The ACL entry above gives Joe access to the `mgr` context. The rule affects him because he meets the minimum role requirements. In the Manager, he will have all the rights granted in the EditorAdmin policy. Since that's essentially a duplicate of the Administrator policy, he will have all the rights of the admin Super User. If we quit now, however, our Editor (JoeBlow) could log in to the Manager, but the Resource tree would be empty because we haven't given him access to the `web` context.

Right-click (again) on the Editors user group, and select "Update User Group." Go to the "Context Access" tab. Click on "Add Context." Use the following settings in the User Group Context Access dialog:

Context: *web*

Minimum Role: *Editor*

Access Policy: *EditorAdmin*

Click on the "Save" button in the dialog.

Flush the permissions and the sessions (on the Security menu). Now Joe can log in and can see the resources in the `web` context. Log in as JoeBlow. You (as Joe) should see the Resource tree with all the resources (including the `Home` page). You should also be able to edit any of the resources. Why are all the resources visible? They're visible because we haven't protected any resources with a Resource Group Access ACL entry.

New MODX Revolution users often forget this second step of creating a `web` context ACL entry because they think of the `web` context as the front end. Normally, it is, but because the `web` context is protected by the Context Access ACL entry for the Administrator group, users who are not in the Administrator group have no access to it until we provide it. Without access to the `web` context, the users won't see any of its resources in the Manager.

Creating the Resource Group Access ACLs

Now it's time to protect (hide) the pages we don't want Joe to see. Log out, and log back in as the admin Super User.

Go to **Security → Access Controls → User Groups tab**. Right-click on the Editors group, and select "Update User Group." Click on the "Resource Group Access" tab. Click on "Add Resource Group." In the Add Resource Group dialog, use the following settings:

Resource Group: *AllDocs*

Minimum Role: *Super User*

Access Policy: *Resource*

Context: *mgr*

Click on the "Save" button.

On the Security menu, select "Flush Permissions," and then "Flush All Sessions." Log in as JoeBlow.

Notice that all the resources are gone from the tree. See if you can guess why.

By creating the Resource Access ACL entry for the AllDocs resource group, we've protected all the resources in that resource group (which contains all the resources of the site). The ACL entry we created sets a Minimum Role of Super User (authority number: 0) for those resources, and Joe doesn't meet that criteria because his role in the group is Editor (with an authority number of 10).

Log out, and log back in as the admin Super User. The resources are still missing. We protected them from everyone by creating the Resource Access ACL. We've made it so Editors group members with a role of Super User have access to the AllDocs resources, but the admin Super User is not a member of the Editors user group. To get the resources back in the tree for the admin, you can do one of two things:

1. Add the admin Super User to the Editors user group with a role of *Super User*.

2. Update the Administrators user group, and add a Resource Access ACL for the AllDocs resource group with a Minimum Role of *Super User*, an Access Policy of *Resource*, and a Context of *mgr*.

Number 1 is easier and usually a better choice, so do that. After you flush the permissions and the tree reloads, the resources should be visible again.

Now, we need to give our editors access to the news pages.

Go to **Security → Access Controls → User Groups tab**. Right-click on the Editors group, and select "Update User Group." Click on the "Resource Group Access" tab. Click on "Add Resource Group." In the Add Resource Group dialog, use the following settings:

Resource Group: *News*

Minimum Role: *Editor*

Access Policy: *EditorResource*

Context: *mgr*

Click on the "Save" button.

Flush Permissions and Sessions, and log in as JoeBlow. Why aren't the three news pages visible? We gave the members of the Editors group permission to see those pages, but we forgot something: they don't have access to the News container document. Without that being visible, its three children won't show up in the tree. So we have a little more work to do.

Creating a ViewOnly Resource Group and Policy

We could just add the News container document to the News Resource Group, but let's assume that we don't want the editors to be able to mess with that page. We need to use a policy that allows them to see the page and its children in the tree but not to edit it, delete it, unpublish it, or do anything else with it. Log out, and log back in as the admin Super User.

Go to **Security → Access Controls → Access Policies tab**. Right-click on the Resource policy and select "Duplicate Policy". Once the policy has been duplicated, right-click the Duplicate of Resource policy and select "Update Policy." Change the name to *ResourceViewOnly*. Uncheck the checkboxes to disable all permissions except load, list, view, and add_children. Enter an appropriate description and click on the "Save" button.

You may be wondering why we didn't use the built-in Load, List, and View policy. That policy is based on the Object template, which does not include the add_children permission. We want our Editors to be able to create new resources under the News resource. We could have altered the Object policy template to add that permission, but it's best not to alter any of the built-in templates. We could have duplicated the Object template and added the add_children permission to the duplicate, but what we did is slightly easier, and there may be other resource permissions you would like to include for the Editors group.

Now go to **Security → Resource Groups**, and create a new Resource Group called *ViewOnly*. Drag the News container document into the group. We'll give our Editor users "view-only" rights to that resource group.

Go to **Security** → **Access Controls** →**User Groups tab**. Right-click on the Editors user group, and select "Update User Group." Click on the "Resource Group Access" tab and then on the "Add Resource Group" button. On the Add Resource Group dialog, use the following settings:

Resource Group: *ViewOnly*

Minimum Role: *Editor*

Access Policy: *ResourceViewOnly*

Context: *mgr*

Click on the "Save" button.

Flush the Permissions and Sessions, and log in as JoeBlow. You should see all the news pages (including the container document). The Home page is not visible because we haven't given the Editors access to it. It's protected because it's in the AllDocs resource group, but it's not in the News or ViewOnly groups, which are the only groups the Editors have resource access to. Attempts to edit the News page should fail, because Joe has ViewOnly access to it, but Joe should be able to edit any of the three News resources.

 If we had just wanted to limit the users' capabilities in the Manager without hiding any resources in the tree, the process would have been much simpler. The Editors user group and the News resource group would be unnecessary. We'd have simply added the Editor users to the Administrator user group with a policy of EditorAdmin and edited that policy to disable permissions we didn't want them to have.

None of what we've done affects access in the front end because all the Resource Group Access ACL entries we created refer to the mgr context. Anonymous visitors in the front end are in the web context. They can still see all the documents because none are protected in that context.

Limiting the Editors' Access to Elements in the Manager

Unless you limit their access, users can see and edit everything in the Element tree (chunks, snippets, plugins, templates, and template variables). For some users, you may want to hide the entire Element tree. We'll see how to do that in the next section of this chapter. In other cases, though, you'll want to hide or control access to specific elements. In this section, we'll see how that's done using Element Category Access ACL entries.

Resources are protected when we put them in resource groups. Elements, on the other hand, can't go in a resource group because they're not resources. Instead, we put them in categories. The methods here are essentially the same as the ones we used above to hide and control access to resources. The only difference is that they involve categories rather than resource groups.

Creating the Category

Select the Elements tab on the left side of the Manager. Right-click on the "Categories" folder at the bottom, and select "New Category." Put *AdminOnly* in the "Name" field of the New Category dialog. Leave the "Parent" field blank, and click on the "Save" button. You should see the new *AdminOnly* category in the tree.

Creating the Elements

Create a new chunk called *Chunk1* by right-clicking on the "Chunks" item in the Element tree and selecting "New Chunk" or "Quick Create Chunk" from the drop-down menu. Enter *Chunk1* in the "Name" field. You could set the category here, but let's do it another way. Click on the "Save" button. Expand both the "Chunks" section and the "Category" section of the tree. Now click on "Chunk1," and drag it to the "AdminOnly" category. Notice that a yellow AdminOnly folder has appeared in the Chunks section. If you expand it, you should see Chunk1 under it. Create several more chunks (*Chunk2*, *Chunk3*, etc.), and drag them to the AdminOnly folder. You can drag them to either of the AdminOnly category folders (there's now one under Chunks and one under Categories). If you make a mistake, just drag the chunk again and put it in the right place.

Create some other types of elements (e.g., *Snippet1*, *Plugin1*, etc.), and drag them to the AdminOnly category. When you do this, you'll see a new category folder appear in the appropriate section of the tree with your new element under it.

Creating the User and User Group

If you've completed the section above, you can skip this step. Be sure you are logged in as the admin Super User. Create a user named *JoeBlow* (if you haven't already). Make a note of Joe's username and password because you'll need to be logging in as Joe.

Create a user group called *Editors*.

Go to **Security → Access Controls → Roles tab**. Create a new role called *Editor* with an authority of *10*.

Add Joe to the Editors user group with a role of Editor. Create the `mgr` Context Access ACL entry for the Editors users group as described earlier, (or add Joe to the Administrator user group with a role of Editor).

Creating the Policy

Go to the "Access Policies" tab in **Security → Access Controls**. Right-click on the "Element" policy, and select "Duplicate Policy." After duplicating the policy, right-click on the "Duplicate of Element" policy and select "Update Policy." Change the name to *EditorElement*, enter an appropriate description, and click on the "Save" button.

Creating the Context Access ACL Entry

Go to **Security → Access Controls → User Groups tab**. On the Access Controls panel, right-click on the Administrator user group (not the Editor user group), and select "Update User Group." Now, go to the "Element Category Access" tab. Click on "Add Category." Use the following settings in the Add Category dialog:

Category: *AdminOnly*

Minimum Role: *Super User*

Access Policy: *Element*

Click on the "Save" button in the dialog.

Why did we edit the Administrator group rather than the Editors group? By connecting the AdminOnly category to users with a role of Super User, we've protected that category. Only users in the Administrator group with a role of Super User can see that category. If you flush the permissions and sessions (**Security → Flush Permissions, Security → Flush all Sessions**) and log back in as JoeBlow, you'll see that the AdminOnly category and all elements in it are now completely hidden. At this point, when logged in as the Super User, you can drag any element to the AdminOnly category, and it will be hidden from all members of the Editors user group.

Finer Control

What if, instead of hiding the entire AdminOnly category, we wanted to have it visible in the tree but limit what the Editors can do with the elements? We could edit the Element policy, but that would limit the Super User's access to the elements. Instead, we need to create another ACL entry for the Editors group.

On the "User Groups" tab, right-click on the Editors user group, and select "Update User Group." Go to the "Element Category Access" tab, and click on the "Add Category" button. Use the following settings in the Add Category dialog:

Category: *AdminOnly*

Minimum Role: *Editor*

Access Policy: *EditorElement*

Click on the "Save" button in the dialog.

Now the Editors have full rights to that category. That's because we based the EditorElement policy on a duplicate of the standard Element policy, which contains all possible element permissions. Flush permissions and sessions, and log back in as JoeBlow. The elements in the AdminOnly category should be back in view.

To limit what the Editors can do with the elements in the AdminOnly category, we simply need to edit the EditorElement policy. Go to **Security → Access Controls**, and click on the "Access Policies" tab. Right-click on the "EditorElement" policy, and select "Edit." Disable any permissions you don't want the Editors to have by unchecking the checkbox next to them in the grid. Disabling the permissions won't affect the admin Super User's rights because the Administrator user group has a different Access Policy (Element) for those elements.

Limiting the Editors' Options in the Manager

Remember that we based the EditorAdmin policy on the standard Administrator policy, which contains all possible Manager action permissions. We then assigned that policy to the Editors in the mgr Context Access ACL entry we created earlier. This means that unless we edit that EditorAdmin policy, our Editor users are, in many ways, Super Users. Although they can't see all the resources, they have full access to all the functions of the Manager.

 As we've said before, never edit the standard policies or policy templates.

Always create a duplicate, and edit the duplicate. That way, you'll always have the standard policies and policy templates as a reference and they won't be overwritten when you upgrade MODX.

It's also a good idea to use the terms "Admin," "Resource," and "Element" in the duplicate names so that you can tell which policy or template they are based on.

The Editors can change system settings, create new users, install Transport Packages, create and edit snippets and plugins, or do anything else the admin Super User can do. They can even change the security settings to give themselves access to all the resources and contexts on the site and alter their own roles and permissions.

The solution is to update the EditorAdmin policy to limit their capabilities. Remember that this policy is used to control which Manager actions the user can perform in a particular context (as opposed to the "object" policies that determine what the user can do with particular objects such as resources and elements).

Editing the EditorAdmin policy

Go to **Security → Access Controls →Access Policies tab**. Right-click on the "EditorAdmin" policy, and select "Update Policy." The list on the screen shows all the security permissions associated with the EditorAdmin policy.

Limiting the user's capabilities in the Manager is simply a matter of disabling the permissions you don't want them to have by unchecking their checkboxes. Each permission has a description that indicates what it does.

One important permission to disable is `access_permissions`. This will prevent the user from changing the security rules for the site. A user with that permission could lock the admin Super User out of the manager and make himself or herself a Super User. Disabling this permission will actually hide the menu choices related to changing the security settings.

You might also want to hide the Element tree and the File tree at the left of the screen by disabling the `element_tree` and `file_tree` permissions. Disabling the `resource_tree` permission will hide the Resource tree in the left panel, though hiding it is seldom done. Note that if the Element tree is hidden, the changes we made earlier to the EditorElement policy are less critical since the user can't see any elements at all, although the users could still access elements if they guess the appropriate URL to get to them in the Manager.

As we have set things up, the security permissions you disable will only affect the members of user groups who have a role of Editor in the user group. They will be denied those permissions as long as those permissions aren't enabled in policies assigned to roles with higher authority numbers for the Editors user group.

Let's look at an example. If you limit the Editor group's permissions in the `mgr` context and then create another Context Access ACL entry for your Editors group (also in the `mgr` context) that has an authority number of 20 and a policy of Administrator, your Editors will go back to being Super Users because with a role of Editor, they have an authority level of 10, so they will inherit all the permissions of that higher-numbered role.

In general, it's a good idea to avoid having the user get an "Access Denied" message. It's frustrating for users to spend time editing a document only to get an error message when they try to save it. If you don't want users to edit a specific document, it's better to disable the `edit_document` permission than the `save_document` permission. It's often even better to hide it from view altogether (using Resource Group Access ACLs) for users who don't have the right to edit it.

Editing Object Policies

As with the EditorAdmin policy, you disable any security permissions that you don't want the user to have from a resource or element policy, such as our EditorResource and EditorElement policies. Remember that these are object policies. They determine the user's access to particular objects (resources and elements). The warning above about users inheriting policies/permissions via higher-numbered roles applies here as well.

Object policies are less often edited because you can keep the user from performing certain actions by customizing the MODX Manager, by hiding particular resource groups or categories using ACL entries, or by disabling permissions from their version of the Administrator policy.

There are cases, however, where you might want to reserve certain security permissions for the admin Super User but only for certain groups of resources or elements. You could, for example, disable specific permissions such as publish, unpublish, undelete, and remove for a set of News items. You might also want to let users in a particular user group see the code of a snippet, but not change it. If you want to restrict a user in general, rather than restricting actions the user can perform with specific resources and elements, it's usually much easier just to edit the administrator policy that applies to that user in the mgr Context Access ACL.

Using the tree_root_id User Setting

In previous versions of MODX, if you wanted to restrict a user's access to a single page or specific sections of the site, it was necessary to create a user group for every user and a resource group for every group of resources. In the current version of MODX Revolution, you can do this very easily with a user setting.

The **tree_root_id** setting sets the top of the Resource tree just for that user. Once you have set **tree_root_id** to the Resource ID of a page, the user can see only that resource and the resources below it in the tree. The setting also accepts a comma-delimited list of IDs, so you can let the user see multiple parts of the tree. This works across contexts if the user has access to more than one front-end context, so the IDs specified don't have to be in the same context.

If you use this technique, you should remember that the **tree_root_id** user setting is not a permission and does not reliably protect any resources. It determines what resources show in the Resource tree, but clever users who know or can guess a resource's ID can manually alter the URL and edit any document on the site. This technique, then, should only be used where the Manager users can be trusted not to do that. If you need real security inside the Manager, resources should be protected with resource groups and ACL entries. Another way of truly protecting the resource would be to create a plugin that protects resources in the Manager based on the **tree_root_id** user setting. Later in the book, we'll see how to use the **tree_root_id** user setting to protect resources in the front end and the plugin we use there could be adapted to protect resources in the Manager.

To set the **tree_root_id** for a user, go to **Security → Manage Users**, and right-click on the user's name. Select "Update User," and then click on the "Settings" tab. Click on the "Create New" button to open the Create New Setting dialog. Enter *tree_root_id* in the "Key" field and the ID or IDs of the resources you want the user to see in the "Value" field. If you use a comma-delimited list, be sure there are no spaces in the line. The other fields are optional, but it's not a bad idea to give the setting a name and a description. If you enter the ID of a container, the user will automatically see any descendants of that container, so you don't need to include their IDs. Click on the "Save" button.

 To hide parts of the Resource tree from all users except the admin Super User, create a **tree_root_id** user setting for the admin Super User with a value of 0. Then, change the **tree_root_id** system setting to the ID (or IDs, separated by commas) of the parts of the Resource tree the other users should be allowed to see. The admin Super User will see the whole Resource tree and all other users will see just the part of the tree specified in the system setting. You can override this behavior for any specific user by creating a **tree_root_id** user setting for that user.

Although the **tree_root_id** setting can be used to control what users can see in the MODX Manager, remember that you may still need to put users into a user group and create ACL entries to restrict the actions they can perform in the Manager and to implement form customization rules and customize the Manager for them. Remember, too, that the **tree_root_id** setting has no effect on which resources the user can see in the front end. Later on, we'll see a method for making the **tree_root_id** setting apply in the front end as well as the Manager.

Using the filemanager_path Setting

The **filemanager_path** setting works just like the **tree_root_id** setting except that it takes a file path rather than an integer, and (at this writing) only one path is accepted. If this is set as a user setting, the user will only see files in the specified path in the File tree tab in the MODX Manager.

 To restrict all users except the admin Super User to a particular part of the File tree, create a **filemanager_path** user setting for the admin Super User and leave the value blank. Then, change the **filemanager_path** system setting to the restricted tree (e.g., **assets/**). The admin Super User will see the whole file tree and all other users will see just the folders below the assets directory. You can override this behavior for any specific user by creating a **filemanager_path** user setting for that user.

Remember that the **tree_root_id** and **filemanager_path** settings have no effect on what users will see in the front end of the site. They only affect the rendering of the Resource tree and the File tree in the MODX Manager.

Controlling Access in the Front End

One simple way of hiding documents in the front end is to unpublish them. They will no longer show in any Wayfinder menus. Protecting documents using Resource Group Access ACLs (with a context of web), however, will allow you to make them available to users who are logged on in the front end.

We'll discuss how to control access to pages in the front end in the following sections — first, though, a word about previewing from the Manager. We discussed this earlier, but it bears repeating.

When you are logged in to the Manager as the admin Super User and preview a document in the front end, you are in the web context (or other context you create), but you are not logged in (authenticated) in that context unless you fill in a login form in the front end. Because you are also logged in to the mgr context, however, you may see unpublished documents and have manager security permissions that regular users don't have (though this may change in future versions of MODX).

It's always a good idea to preview the site in another browser where you are not logged in to the Manager to see the site as regular users see it, especially when what you're doing doesn't seem to be working. You may also need to flush permissions and/or clear the site cache before seeing changes in the front end.

Hiding Pages with a Snippet

It's easy enough to hide a page with a simple snippet, though it is seldom a good idea (we'll see why in just a bit). This section is more educational than practical, and although it's not a good security solution, you may need the functions explained here for other purposes at some point.

The following code will tell you if the current user is logged in to the current context in either the front or back end:

```
$ctx = $modx->context->get('key');
$isAuthenticated = $modx->user->hasSessionContext($ctx);
```

In the code above, $ctx is set to the name of the current context. If you know that you are in the default web context, you can use this single line of code:

```
$isAuthenticated = $modx->user->hasSessionContext('web');
```

If you have only one set of pages you want to protect and want all logged-in users to be able to see them, you can protect them with a simple snippet. You can insert the snippet at the top of the page or, more likely, the page's template. The snippet simply checks for an authenticated user and forwards anonymous users to the Error (page not found) page or the Unauthorized page using one of the following:

```
$modx->sendErrorPage();
$modx->sendUnauthorizedPage();
```

If you need to check whether the current user is authenticated (logged in) in any of several contexts, you can do this:

```
$isAuthenticated = $modx->user->hasSessionContext(array(
    'web',
    'mgr',
    'otherContext'));
```

The snippet (let's call it *HidePages*) would look something like this:

```
<?php
/* HidePages Snippet */
$ctx = $modx->context->get('key');
$isAuthenticated = $modx->user->hasSessionContext($ctx);
if (! isAuthenticated) {
    $modx->sendUnauthorizedPage();
}
```

Note that this method will not distinguish between users who have different roles or belong to different user groups. It will show the page to any user who is logged in to the front end and deny it to any user who is not. Worse yet, it will run afoul of standard MODX snippets like Wayfinder and getResources, which need to decide which links and pages to show before the pages are accessed. Those snippets will show everyone (logged in or not) links and/or content from the pages you are trying to hide.

For more discriminating access control, you should use ACLs.

Working with Access Control Lists (ACLs)

If you have several sets of users and want to restrict them to various subsets of the site's pages, you'll most likely want to use Access Control Lists (ACLs) to control access to them.

Let's create a page that can only be viewed by members of a particular user group. We'll do it with ACLs, user groups, and resource groups. The basic process involves putting the users in a user group, putting the document in a resource group, and connecting the two with a Resource Group Access ACL entry for the user group. Notice that this is just like protecting resources in the Manager as we did earlier in the chapter except that the context will be web rather than mgr.

Creating the Document

First, we need a page to hide. Right-click on the "web" icon in the Resource tree, and select **Create → Create a Document Here**. Call the document *Private Document*. Check the "Published" box, and put the following in the Resource Content field:

Only members of the PrivateViewers group can see this page.

Creating the Resource Group

Next, we need a Resource Group to put our *Private Document* in. Go to **Security → Resource Groups**, and click on the "Create Resource Group" button to open the Create Resource Group dialog. Call the group *Private*, and click on the "Save" button. Expand the tree on the right, and drag the "*Private Document*" resource into the "Private" resource group at the left.

Creating the User Group

Go to **Security → Access Controls**. Select the "User Groups" tab, and click on the "New User Group" button to open the Create User Group dialog. Call the group *PrivateViewers*, and click on the "Save" button. We'll want to add users to the group, but first we need to create a Role and an Access Policy for them. We'll also need to create the users themselves.

 When working on one of the Access Controls tabs, after saving your work, you can get back to the main Access Controls screen by clicking on the "Cancel" button.

Creating a Role and an Access Policy

Click on the "Roles" tab and then on the "Create New" button to open the Create Role dialog. Call the new role *FeViewer* (Fe for "front end"), set the Authority number to *15*, enter an appropriate description, and click on the "Save" button. You should see your new Role in the list.

Click on the "Policy Template" tab. Right-click on the "Object" template and select "Duplicate Template." After creating the template, right click on the "Duplicate of Object" template and change the name to *FeViewTemplate*. Save the template.

Now, click on the "Access Policies" tab. Click on the "Create Access Policy" button. On the Create Access Policy dialog, create a new policy called *FeView* based on the *FeViewTemplate*. Enter an appropriate description, uncheck all permissions except load and view, then click on the "Save" button.

Note that we could have just duplicated the Resource policy and changed the name of the duplicate, but later in this chapter, we're going to add a custom permission to the template and it's best not to edit the built-in templates. We've chosen the Object template because it has fewer permissions. We don't need the extra permissions in the Resource template.

Creating the Users

Now let's create a couple of users — one who can see the pages and one who can't. Go to **Security → User Management**, and click on the "New User" button. Create a user called *Registered* and a user called *Unregistered*. Select the "Let me specify the password" radio option. You can give them the same password, but be sure to make a note of it. Use your own email address in the Email field. The only required fields are Username, Password, and Email.

Adding the Registered User to the User Group

The next step is to put our Registered user into the PrivateViewers user group. Go to **Security → Access Controls**, and select the "User Groups" tab. On the Add User to Group dialog, right-click on the "PrivateViewers" group, and select "Add User to Group." Use the drop-downs to select the Registered user and a role of "FeViewer." Click on the "Save" button.

Creating the ACL Entry

Now, it's time to connect the user group to the resource group with an ACL entry. Right-click on the "PrivateViewers" user group, and select "Update User Group." Click on the "Resource Group Access" tab and then on the "Add Resource Group" button. Use the following settings in the Add Resource Group dialog:

Resource Group: *Private*

Minimum Role: *FeViewer*

Access Policy: *FeView*

Context: *web*

Click on the "Save" button in the dialog.

What we just did "protects" the resources in the Private resource group in the front end (because we specified the web context). The resources can only be viewed by users in the PrivateViewers user group and they will only see them if they are logged on in the front end of the site. As we learned earlier, resources are unprotected in a context until a Resource Group Access ACL entry ties them to a user group.

Creating the Login Page

We're almost there. We've created our users and their roles and access policies. We've protected the Private Document by putting it in a resource group and connecting that group to the PrivateViewers user group with an ACL entry in the web context. Note that nothing we've done will restrict access to the Private Document in the MODX Manager. Because our ACL entry specifies the web context, it will only apply in the front end. The final step is to give our PrivateViewers a way to log in to the front end of the site.

Go to **System → Package Management**. Click on the "Download Extras" button and download the latest version of the Login package. Install the Login package.

If you look in the Element tree under the Login category, you'll see that, in addition to the Login snippet, you've also installed several other snippets that will let you register users, send them a password if they've forgotten it, and let them reset their passwords or update their user profiles. You'll also see several login and registration Tpl chunks in the Element tree.

Right-click on the "web" icon in the Resource tree, and select **Create → Create a Document Here.** Call the document *Login*, make sure the document is published, and put this snippet tag in the Resource Content field:

```
[[!Login? &loginResourceId=`12`]]
```

Important: Change the *12* to the ID of your Private Document page. Be sure to save the document. When the Login page is visited, the user will see a login form. If the user successfully logs in, he or she will be forwarded to the Private Document page. If the login is unsuccessful, the user will remain on the login page and should see a message explaining that he or she has failed to log in.

When logged-in users visit the Login page, they will see a link that allows them to log out. This is handy because you can put the Login snippet in your template. New visitors will see the login form, and logged-in users will see the logout link. You can style the login and logout sections by using Tpl chunks specified in the following properties:

```
&loginTpl=`LoginChunkName`
&logoutTpl=`LogoutChunkName`
&errTpl=`LogoutChunkName`
```

At this writing, the Login snippet is one of the few snippets that allow you to store the Tpls in various forms. Two additional properties, **&tplType** and **&errTplType**, tell the snippet where to find the Tpls named in the properties above. The first property specifies the type of the login and logout Tpls. The second property does the same for the error Tpl. Here are the options for those properties and what they tell the snippet:

modChunk — Use the chunk named in the property as the Tpl.

file — Use the property value as the absolute path to a Tpl file.

inline — Use the literal content of the property value as the Tpl.

embedded — The Tpl is already in the page; just set the placeholders.

You can also add **&redirectToPrior=`1`** as a property in the Login snippet tag to send the user back to the page they were on before going to the Login page, but don't add that now because we want the user sent to the Private Document.

Testing the Security Settings

Go to **Security → Flush Permissions** to make sure that the permissions you set will be applied. Edit the Login page, and make sure that the **&loginResourceId** property is set to the Resource ID of the Private Document. If the Resource ID of the Private Document has a Resource ID of 5, for example, the Login snippet tag would look like this:

```
[[!Login? &loginResourceId=`5`]]
```

Make sure that the ID in the property is surrounded by back-ticks, not single-quotes. Make sure, too, that your Private Document is published. Go to **Site → Clear Cache**. After logging in on the Login page, the Registered user should be redirected to the Private Document. The Unregistered user should be redirected to the site's error (page not found) page. By default, this is the site's Home page, so don't be surprised if you end up there unless you've changed the **error_page** system setting to the Resource ID of another page (it's not a bad idea to create a custom Page Not Found page if you haven't already — be sure to change the **error_page** system setting to point to the page).

Note the ID of your Login page. Now, either log out of the Manager or use a fresh session in another browser. Put this in the browser's address line:

```
yoursite.com/index.php?id=##
```

Replace *yoursite.com* with the URL of your site and ## with the ID of the Login page. You should see the login form. Log in as the Registered user. If all has gone well, you'll see the Private Document after logging in. Click the "back" button in your browser to go back to the Login page. You should see the "logout" link. Click on it, and then log in as the Unregistered user. If you don't see the Private Document after logging in, you've successfully protected that page.

Obviously, you can add as many users as you want to the PrivateViewers user group. All of them will be able to access the Private Document or any other documents you add to the Private resource group, and no one else will have that access.

You can have as many user groups and resource groups as you like. If you connect each user group to a resource group with an ACL entry as we did above, users will only have access to the documents that you have assigned them to. Remember that anonymous (not-logged-in) visitors to the front end will not be able to see any of the pages you have protected with ACL entries in this way.

Avoiding the Error Page

MODX Revolution handles unauthorized access in a different way than MODX Evolution. In Evolution, users who try to access a page they're not authorized to see are redirected to the Unauthorized page — the page specified by the **unauthorized_page** system setting. In Revolution, however, pages you are not authorized to see don't officially "exist," so you are redirected to the Error (page not found) page — the page specified in the **error_page** system setting.

There is a way around this if you would like users redirected to the Unauthorized page instead. The secret is to give the "(anonymous)" user group load permission in the front end. Here are the steps you would follow:

* Create an Unauthorized page (make sure it is published), and set the **unauthorized_page** system setting to its resource ID.

* Update the *(anonymous)* user group.

* Create a new Resource Group Access ACL entry with the following settings in the Add Resource Group dialog:

  * Resource Group: *Private*

  * Context: *web*

  * Minimum Role: *Member - 9999*

  * Access Policy: *Load Only*

Repeat the second step for each protected resource group. Users in the front end who have not logged in are all honorary members of the (anonymous) user group. Now, they will all have the load permission in the web context (front end). They still won't see protected resources, but the resources officially "exist" for them because they have permission to load them. As a result, they'll be redirected to the Unauthorized page. Be sure to flush permissions, clear the cache, and flush all sessions after making the changes.

Note that this won't solve the problem for users who are logged on in the front end but are trying to access pages they are not authorized to see. To make it work for them, you'll have to add them to the user groups who are authorized to see the pages but with a role of "Member." Then update those user groups to add a new Resource Group Access ACL entry with the Resource Group set to the group of the protected resources, the Role set to "Member," and a policy of "Load Only."

At this writing, some snippets, such as Wayfinder and getResources have trouble with this method because they assume that users with the load permission have rights to the resources. Wayfinder will show the private resources in menus (though the user can't access them), and getResources will show their content.

By the time you read this, those problems may have been corrected by having those snippets check for the list and/or view permissions before showing a resource.

Registering Users

In the section above, we saw how to let users log in and out. But if you will have a lot of users, it's a pain to create all of them yourself, so let's set up a way for them to register themselves. You probably don't want spammers to be able to register and log in immediately, so we'll send the new users an activation email message on registration. The email message will contain a link to activate the account. Since spammers won't usually enter their own email address, their registrations will never be activated.

There are several components necessary for the registration process, and luckily, most of them are included in the Login package (install it now if you haven't done so already).

 It is fairly likely that you will want to alter some of the chunks used in the registration process. Rather than alter the ones provided, duplicate them, and refer to the duplicates in the tags and forms you use. That way, they won't be overwritten when you update the package.

It's recommended that you use the forms as provided until you have everything working.

We need three resources (documents) for the registration process. Here are their names and functions:

Register — A registration resource containing a call to the register snippet and a form for the user to fill out.

Thanks for Registering — A page to redirect the users to after they successfully fill in the Register form.

Confirm Registration — A page that the registration email link points to containing the ConfirmRegister snippet and a welcome for the new user.

We also need at least two chunks:

lgnRegisterForm — The actual registration form.

lgnActivateEmailTpl — The Tpl chunk for the registration email.

Creating the Thank You Page

Create this resource first because we'll need to use its Resource ID later. Call the resource *Thank You*, and make sure it is published and hidden from menus.

Put an appropriate message in the Resource Content field:

```
<p>Thank You for registering. You will receive an email message soon
that will allow you to activate your registration.</p>
```

Creating the Confirm Registration Page

This also needs to be done before we create the `Register` page because we'll need its Resource ID for that page. Call it *Confirm Registration* and make sure that it is published but hidden from menus. Put the following code in the Resource Content field:

```
[[!ConfirmRegister]]
<p>Welcome. You have successfully completed the registration process.
Please go here to log in <a href="[[~##]]"> Log in</a></p>
```

Replace ## with the Resource ID of the `Login` page, and make a note of the `Confirm Registration` page's Resource ID.

Creating the Register Page

Create a resource called *Register*. Make sure it is published. You probably want to hide it from menus as well since there will be a link to it on the Login page. Put the following code in the Resource Content Field:

```
[[Register?
    &submitVar=`registerbtn`
    &activationResourceId=`##`
    &activationEmailTpl=`MylgnActivationEmailTpl`
    &activationEmailSubject=`Please activate your account`
    &submittedResourceId=`##`
    &usergroups=`Editors`
]]
[[$MylgnRegisterForm]]
```

Set the **&activationResourceId** property to the Resource ID of the Confirm Registra-tion page (replace the ## with it in the code above).

Set the **&submittedResourceId** property to the Resource ID of the Thank You page (replace the ## with it in the code above).

We've told the snippet that we'd like the new user to be a member of the Editors user group (be sure that group exists). You can specify several user groups in the **&usergroups** property by separating them with commas:

```
&usergroups=`Editors,Supervisors,Auditors`
```

Notice that we've changed the name of the Tpl chunk and the login form chunk. Those are not the names of the chunks in the Login package (look in the chunks section of the Element tree under the Login category). Be careful with the spelling in the following two steps because the names are case-sensitive.

Duplicate the lgnActivationEmailTpl chunk, and name the new chunk *MylgnActivationEmailTpl*.

Duplicate the lgnRegisterForm chunk, and call the new chunk *MylgnRegisterForm*. Be sure the spelling exactly matches the spelling in the Register resource.

You will almost certainly want to modify these at some point, and using your own chunks will prevent them from being overwritten if you update the Login package down the road.

There is one last thing we need to do to make everything work. We need to make sure that the **&submitVar** is set properly to help foil spammers. The **&submitVar** property in the Register snippet tag (on the `Register` page) will be checked in the Login snippet. It must match the `name` attribute in the registration form's submit button. We've set it to *registerbtn* in the snippet tag, so the line near the end of the MyIgnRegisterForm chunk must look like this:

```
<input type="submit" name="registerbtn" value="Register" />
```

This makes it a little harder for spam-bots to submit the form successfully. You can (and probably should) change the name and the property value, but be sure they match, or else the user will end up back at a blank registration form after submitting it.

Modifying the Login Page

To finish setting up the registration process, we need a link to the `Register` page on the `Login` page. Edit the `Login` resource, and add the following line below the Login snippet tag:

```
<a href="[[~##]]">Register</a>
```

Replace ## with the Resource ID of the `Register` page.

How It All Works

When a user clicks on the `Register` link on the `Login` page, he or she will be sent to the `Register` page. The `Register` snippet will execute but will simply return an empty string because the form has not been filled out yet.

Once the form has been filled out and submitted, if the **&submitVar** property is set correctly, the validation will be performed. If the form passes validation, the Register snippet will fill in the MyIgnEmailTpl chunk, send off the email message to the user, and forward the user to the `Thank You` page. Be sure to enter your own email address when testing the form. If the email message is not sent, you can install and test the QuickEmail package. You may need to use SMTP to send the email (especially if this is a localhost install on your own computer). If so, see the SMTP section in Chapter 12.

At this point, the user will be entered in the MODX database (in the **users** table) but with the **active** field set to 0. The user will also be registered in the database as a member of the Editors user group but won't be able to log in because of the inactive status.

The link in the registration email message will take the user to the `Confirm Register` page. If the credentials submitted in the URL are legitimate, the user's status will be changed to active (the active field in the **users** table will change from 0 to 1). The user will then see the welcome message on the Confirm Register page and the link to the Login page. If something is wrong with the credentials, the user will be sent to the MODX error (page not found) page without seeing the rest of the Confirm Register page.

At this writing, the login form is not particularly attractive, and you will probably want to improve it by adding some CSS and/or altering the Tpl chunk.

Further Enhancements

The Login package includes some other useful snippets related to user information and credentials. The UpdateProfile snippet allows users to update their profiles using a form in the front end of the site. The Profile snippet sets placeholders for all user fields, including extended fields in the user profile. It can be used on any page where you need to display user information. The ForgotPassword snippet, in conjunction with the ResetPassword snippet, can be used on the Login page to help registered users who have forgotten their passwords. See the online documentation for more information on how to use these snippets.

The Login, UpdateProfile, and Register snippets each have two additional properties, **&preHooks** and **&postHooks**, that allow you to run custom snippets of your own before or after the main code of each snippet executes. A preHook, for example, might be used to pre-populate form fields. A postHook might add the user to one or more user groups based on selections made in the registration form. See the online documentation for more details. We'll see an example of a preHook in action when we discuss the FormIt snippet later on in the book.

Checking the User's Status

Suppose that you want to keep anonymous users from viewing certain pages on the site. Earlier in this chapter, we saw how to send anonymous users to the Unauthorized page or the Error page with a snippet. A simple modification of that snippet will send them to the Login page instead:

```
/* CheckStatus snippet */
$ctx = $modx->context->get('key');
$isAuthenticated = $modx->user->hasSessionContext($ctx);
if (! isAuthenticated) {
    $modx->sendRedirect($modx->makeUrl(##));
}
```

Replace ## with the Resource ID of the Login page. Once you create the snippet, adding the following snippet tag to the template used by the pages you want to protect will forward all users who are not logged in to the Login page, where they can either log in or register.

```
[[!CheckStatus]]
```

Remember that this won't work when you are previewing pages from the Manager. You'll need to view the pages from another browser where you are not logged on in the Manager.

In addition to the Login, Profile, Register, and ConfirmRegister snippets, the Login package now comes with a number of other useful snippets that you may wish to include on your login page: a ChangePassword snippet, a ForgotPassword snippet, and a ResetPassword snippet.

Hiding Template Variables in the Manager

This section really belongs above in the section on controlling access in the Manager, but we wanted to keep it together with the following section on hiding template variables (TVs) in the front end of the site, since they use some of the same resources and elements.

There are a number of cases where you might want to hide a template variable (or its output) in either the Manager or the front end. In this section, we'll see how to do that by putting TVs in resource groups. Note that you can also hide them from members of specific user groups with form customization rules as we'll see in the following chapter.

Suppose, for example, that you want a user to be able to access a resource in the MODX Manager, but you want to hide one or more (but not all) of the template variables available for that resource so that the user can't see or edit them when editing the resource. In the following chapter, we'll learn how to hide individual TVs or the entire Template Variables tab with a form customization rule. In this section, we'll see how to hide specific TVs by putting them in protected resource groups.

Like resources, template variables can also belong to resource groups. Unlike resources, however, they don't appear in the tree in **Security → Resource Groups**. Instead, you have to assign them to groups using the Access Permissions tab of the Create/Edit Template Variable panel.

Assigning the TV to a Resource Group

To assign a TV to a resource group, right-click on the TV in the "Elements" tree, and select "Edit TV." Then click on the "Access Permissions" tab to see a list of all the resource groups. Check the checkbox next to each group that you want to assign the TV to. Obviously, the resource groups need to exist before you can assign TVs to them.

If a TV is assigned to a resource group, and that resource group is connected with a user group by an ACL entry, only users in that group will be able to see the TV when editing resources.

 At this writing, you can hide or show TVs by putting them in resource groups, but there is no way to control specific actions (such as view, edit, and save) for TVs.

At present, what the user can do with any TV when editing a resource in the MODX Manager is not affected by the user's Manager access permissions. Those only affect the editing of the TV itself in the Element tree.

For example, let's say we want to hide a template variable called *TV1* from everyone but members of the Administrators user group.

Go to **Security → Resource Groups**, and click on the "Create Resource Group" button. In the Create Resource Group dialog, call the resource group *HiddenTVs*, and click on the "Save" button.

Now, go to the Element tree, right-click on "TV1" (create it if you haven't already), and select "Edit TV." Go to the "Access Permissions" tab, and check the box next to the "HiddenTVs" group. Check the "Template Access" tab, and make sure the TV is attached to your main template. Save the TV.

Create the Editors user group if you haven't already, and add a user called *JoeBlow* to it. Log out, and log back in as JoeBlow. Edit a document that uses the main template, and click on the "Template Variables" tab to make sure that TV1 is visible. It should be, because we haven't protected it yet.

Connecting the User Group to the Resource Group

Log out, and log back in as the admin Super User. Go to **Security → Access Controls**, and select the "User Groups" tab. Right-click on the "Administrators" group, and select "Update User group." Select the "Resource Group Access" tab, and click on the "Add Resource Group" button. Use the following settings in the Add Resource Group dialog:

Resource Group: *HiddenTVs*

Minimum role: *Super User*

Access Policy: *Resource*

Context: *mgr*

Click on the "Save" button.

Testing the Security Settings

Log out, and log back in as JoeBlow. Edit a document that uses the main template, and click on the "Template Variables" tab. The TV1 template variable should be hidden because it is now only available to the admin Super User.

Further Options

If you would like to allow some other users to see TV1, you can do it in several different ways. One option is to add the users to the Administrators group (presumably with a role other than Super User). You'll have to use a Minimum Role in the Resource Access ACL entry that matches whatever role they hold in the group. This is usually not the best choice because it can interfere with form customization rules you might want to create.

A second option is to add a Resource Group Access ACL entry to any other group the users belong to, and give them access to the HiddenTVs group there.

A final way of granting the users access to the TV is to create a new user group and add them to it, and then create a Resource Group Access ACL entry for that group giving access to the HiddenTVs group.

As always, if you protect a TV by creating a Resource Group Access ACL entry for a specific user group, add yourself to that user group with a role of admin Super User so you won't be hiding it from yourself.

Hiding TVs in the Front End

There are many situations where you might want to hide specific TVs from a subset of your users in the front end of the site. Say, for example, that you want a link to a private part of the site to be shown only to users in the Editors user group who are logged on in the front end of your site.

The process is very similar to what we did in the section above. We'll assume that you have created a TV called *TV1* and put it in the HiddenTVs group and that you've created the Editors user group and added members to it. You'll also need the Login snippet, a login page, and a landing page that users will be sent to after logging in. The landing page should display the TV. You should have the login and landing page and the login snippet from the earlier exercises in this chapter. If you don't, you'll have to create them.

Connecting the User Group to the Resource Group

Go to **Security → Access Controls**, and select the "User Groups" tab. Right-click on the "Editors" group, and select "Update User group." Select the "Resource Group Access" tab, and click on the "Add Resource Group" button. Use the following settings in the Add Resource Group dialog:

Resource Group: *HiddenTVs*

Minimum role: *Editor*

Access Policy: *Resource*

Context: *web*

Notice that this is essentially the same process that we used to hide the TV in the Manager. We've created a link (this time in the web context) between the user group and the resource group by adding a Resource Group Access ACL entry. Now, only logged in members of the Editors user group will see the TV in the front end.

Testing the Security Settings

To test your work, put a tag for TV1 on the landing page specified in your Login snippet (make sure TV1 has some content and that the landing page is published and not a member of any resource groups):

```
<p>This is the TV that we hid: [[*TV1]].</p>
```

Go to **Security → Flush Permissions** and then **Site → Clear Cache**. Now visit the page as an anonymous user. You should not see the content of the TV. Now, visit the page by Logging in (on the Login page) as a member of the Editors user group. The TV's content should be visible.

Hiding Resources with Custom Permissions

There is another way to hide resources in the front end that bypasses some of the steps we used above. The secret is to create a custom permission, assign it to members of a user group by adding it to an access policy, and use a snippet to deny access to users who don't have that permission.

Before we go any further, we should mention a significant drawback to this method. Because this method doesn't involve resource groups, the access restrictions won't be honored by standard snippets like getResources and Wayfinder. Wayfinder will show the restricted documents in menus, and getResources will show their content.

So, like the method we discussed earlier for hiding pages with a simple snippet that checks for an authenticated user, this method is usually a bad idea.

There may still be times when this method will work for you (and it can be used to hide parts of a page as we'll see later), but you should be aware of its limitations. Explaining how it works, though, may help you understand how MODX processes security permissions and we'll see some techniques that are useful for other situations along the way. Using custom permissions is also a good technique for customizing the Manager's Top Menu, as we'll see in the following chapter.

The $modx object has a method called hasPermission() that checks to see if the current user has a particular permission.

In the following section, we'll hide a resource from certain users without using resource groups.

Creating the Document

Create a new resource called *Private Document 2*. Make sure it is published, and put the following in the Resource Content field:

```
This is the NEW Private Document.
```

Check the Access Permissions tab of the Create/Edit Resource panel while editing the document, and make sure that the new document is not assigned to any resource groups (all checkboxes should be unchecked). This means that our new document is not protected in any way. You could delete the resource group you created earlier because we don't need any resource groups for this method.

In fact, this technique won't work with documents that are in a resource group that is protected by a Resource Group Access ACL entry unless you create a Resource Group Access ACL entry giving the (anonymous) user group access to that resource group. This means that it's not very practical to use both the ACL method and this method on the same site.

Editing the Login Page

Now edit the Login page, and change the Login snippet tag to redirect the user to our new document by changing the **&loginResourceId** property to the Resource ID of *Private Document 2*.

Verify that both the Registered and Unregistered user can see the new page in the front end by visiting the Login page and logging in as each of them in turn. This will also make sure that you have the **&loginResourceId** property set correctly.

Creating the Custom Permission

Now, we'll add our new custom permission to the FeView access policy.

Note: If you skipped the section above using ACLs, you'll have to create the user group, role, and *FeViewTemplate* access policy template described there.

Go to **Security → Access Controls → Policy Templates tab**. Right-click on the "FeView-Template" and select "Update Policy Template." Click on the "Add Permission to Template" button. Use the following settings in the Add Permission to Template dialog (be careful not to click on the down arrow, which will make the drop-down list appear):

Name: *my_allow_private*

Description: *Allow front-end viewing of private documents*

Click on the "Add" button. Now (this is important), click on the "Save" button at the upper right. You should see your new permission in the list.

Remember that the FeView access policy is connected to the PrivateViewers user group and that our Registered user is a member of that group (and the Unregistered viewer is not). This means that the Registered user now has that permission (and the Unregistered user doesn't).

Important: In order for the Registered user to have the permission in the front end, permission must be granted to the front-end context in a Context Access ACL. We did this earlier in the ACL section, but if you deleted it or skipped that section, you'll have to "Update" the PrivateViewers user group and make sure that there is a Context Access ACL with a context of *web*, a Minimum Role of *FeViewer*, and an Access Policy of *FeView*.

Creating the Unauthorized Page

In a bit, we'll create a snippet that redirects users who don't have the custom permission (my_allow_private) we just created. We could easily redirect unauthorized users to the Error (page not found) page or to the MODX Unauthorized page, but let's create a new page to send them to. It will be a good example of MODX's flexibility. We can send them anywhere (even to a page that isn't on the site).

Create a new document called *Unauthorized*. Make sure it's published, and put this in the Resource Content Field:

```
<p>Oops, you aren't allowed to see that document.</p>
```

Save the document.

Edit the Private Document resource we created earlier, and insert the following snippet tag at the top of the Resource Content field:

```
[[CheckPermission? &redirectURL=`##`]]
```

Replace the ## with the Resource ID of the Unauthorized (Oops) document we just created, and save the document.

Creating the CheckPermission Snippet

Now, create a new snippet called *CheckPermission* (be sure to spell it exactly as it's spelled in the snippet tag, and be sure to spell the function and variable names carefully — they're case-sensitive), and put the following code in it:

CheckPermission Snippet

```php
<?php
if ($modx->hasPermission('my_allow_private')) {
    return "";
} else {
    $newURL = $modx->makeURL($redirectURL);
    $modx->sendRedirect($newURL);
}
?>
```

The snippet simply checks to see if the user has the my_allow_private permission. If so, the snippet returns an empty string. If not, it redirects the user to the resource specified in the $redirectURL snippet property.

Testing the Security Settings

Now, visit the Login page in your browser, and log in as the Registered and Unregistered user. After logging in, the Registered user should see the new Private Document. The unregistered user should see the Unauthorized (Oops) page.

Further Options

With some modifications, this method can be very flexible. You could redirect the user to the Login page. Different pages could have a different $redirectURL property in the snippet tag. You could also place the snippet tag in the template (above any resource tags) rather than in the document itself, and different templates could have different versions of the snippet tag.

Because we're using a snippet to control access, we could also add other features to the snippet, such as logging authorized and/or unauthorized visits.

We could also use this technique to hide just part of a page by adding a call to $modx->getChunk() in the snippet. That way we could show the chunk (containing restricted content or a special menu) only to users who have the custom permission.

Member Pages

One common need for web sites is to restrict users to their own individual page or section of the site. It's possible to do this with ACL entries, but it's tedious and time-consuming. You need to create a resource group for every page or group of pages and a separate user group for each user. Then you need to create ACL entries to link each user to his or her resource group. If you have hundreds of users, this could be quite unpleasant.

Earlier in this chapter, we saw how to restrict users to a single page or group of pages in the MODX Manager by using the **tree_root_id** user setting. In this section, we'll see how to use a snippet to apply that restriction in the front end. Along the way, we'll also see how to modify a form in the Manager to make it easier to create the user setting.

General Strategy

To restrict users to a specific page, we'll place a snippet in the template used by all the individual member pages. The snippet will forward the user to another page if their **tree_root_id** user setting doesn't match the current page ID. For each user, we'll create a **tree_root_id** user setting and set to the ID of his or her personal page. Later, we'll create a plugin to modify the Create/Edit User form and add a Tree Root field. The user setting will be created or updated automatically when that form is saved. We'll also modify the snippet so that users can access any children of their personal pages and add a method to send each user to his or her personal page after the login.

Setting Things Up

In order to develop and test your snippet you'll need to install the login snippet and create a login page (if you haven't already). You'll also need several users and individual member pages for each of them. If you've been creating the users and snippets described earlier in the book, you should have most of that already. If not, create the users and the login page.

Create a resource called Members and designate it as a container by checking the Container checkbox. Make sure that it uses your main template. Put the following code in the Resource Content field of the Members resource:

```
<h2>Members Page</h2>
[[!Wayfinder? &startId=`[[*id]]` ]]
```

The tag above will create a menu containing links to the children of the current page.

Duplicate your main template and change the name to *Member*.

Place a page under the Members page for each user and make sure it uses the *Member* template. Use the member's name for the **pagetitle**, **alias**, and **menutitle** fields. Make sure all the user pages are published and place a message in each one that indicates whose page it is:

```
<p>This is Jane Doe's Page</p>
```

Change the tag on your login page so it looks like this (replace ## with the ID of your Members page).

```
[[!Login? &loginResourceId=`##`]]
```

Preview your Members page and make sure that all the links work and all the pages show the appropriate message. All the pages are now available for all users because we haven't protected them yet. To do that, we need to create our MemberPages snippet and call it in our Member template.

Creating the Snippet

Create a snippet called *MemberPages* using the following code (replace ## with the ID of your Members page):

```php
<?php
/* MemberPages Snippet */
/* First, reject any users who are not logged in */
if (!$isAuthenticated =
    $modx->user->hasSessionContext($modx->context->get('key')) ) {
    $modx->sendUnauthorizedPage();
    /* could also redirect to the Register page here */
}
/* if it's not the user's page, send them to the Members page */
$tr = $modx->getOption('tree_root_id');
if ($tr != $modx->resource->get('id') ) {
    /* return "Wrong Page Tree Root:" . $tr . " Page ID: " .
        $modx->resource->get('id');
    */


    /* replace ## with the ID of the Members page */
    $modx->sendRedirect($modx->makeUrl(##));
}
return "";
```

Our snippet first kicks out any users who are not logged in. Then it gets the **tree_root_id** setting with $modx->getOption() and checks it against the current page ID. Because user settings have override system settings, we should get the user setting here for any logged-in user who has one. If they don't match, it sends the user back to the Members page. If they do match, it does nothing, and the rest of the page is rendered. The commented out section is for debugging. It displays the **tree_root_id** setting and the current page ID. This will help you figure out what's happening if things aren't working correctly.

The snippet doesn't do anything yet because we're not calling it anywhere. Edit your Member template and put the following snippet tag just below the <body> tag:

```
[[!MemberPages]]
```

If you log in, you should see the Members page, but clicking on any link should leave you there. That's because no user has a **tree_root_id** setting, so every user is rejected from every member page and sent back to the Members page.

Go to **Security → Manage Users**. Right-click on one of your users and select "Update User." Go to the "Settings" tab and click on the "Create New" button. In the Create New Setting dialog, enter the following values:

Key: *tree_root_id*

Name: *Tree Root ID*

Value: *(enter the ID of the user's page)*

Leave the other settings at their default values, and click on the "Save" button. You should see your new setting in the grid. Double-check the spelling of **tree_root_id** and make sure that the Value is set to the ID of the user's personal page. Now, in another browser, type or paste the URL of the Login page into the address bar. Log in as the user you just edited. You should see the Members page. If you click on that user's page, you should see it, but if you click on the link for another user's page, you should stay on the Members page.

 If you try out your code here by previewing from the Manager, you can get very strange results. That's because the user settings may not be cleared when you log out in the front end (because you're still logged on in the Manager). The current **tree_root_id** setting may not be for the current user.

Be sure to visit the site from another browser where you're not logged in to the Manager.

We could create a **tree_root_id** setting for each user, but it's a pain to have to create the setting for each user. Let's create a plugin that modifies the User form so that we can enter the setting value on the main page and the setting will be created automatically when the user is saved.

Creating the Plugin

Normally, we'd create our plugin as a snippet first, because snippets are easier to debug. We can't do that here, though, because this plugin only operates in the Manager, and it modifies a Manager form. Create a plugin called *MemberPages* using the following code. Type carefully because if there are any syntax errors in the plugin, it won't do anything and it will be very difficult to debug. Pay particular attention to the single- and double-quotes.

```php
<?php
/* MemberPages Plugin */
switch ($modx->event->name) {
    case 'OnUserFormRender':
        /* set field to the current value (if any) */
        /* The user ID is always available as $id */
        $v = "";
        $treeRoot = $modx->getObject('modUserSetting',
            array('user'=>$id,'key'=>'tree_root_id'));
        if ($treeRoot) { /* the user already has the setting */
            $v = $treeRoot->get('value');
        }
        /* now do the HTML */
        $fields = '<div class="x-form-item x-tab-item">
            <label class="x-form-item-label" style="width:152px;">
                <b>Tree Root</b></label>
            <div class="x-form-element">
                <input type="text" name="TreeRoot" value="'. $v .
                    '" class="x-form-text x-form-field" />
            </div>
        </div>';
        $modx->event->output($fields);
        break;
    case 'OnUserFormSave':
        if (isset($_POST['TreeRoot'])){  /* field is filled in */
            $setting = $modx->getObject('modUserSetting',
                array('user'=>$id,'key'=>'tree_root_id'));
```

```
        if ($setting) { /* user setting already exists - update it */
            if ($setting->get('value') != $_POST['TreeRoot']){
                /* user changed it */
                $setting->set('value',$_POST['TreeRoot']);
                $setting->save();
            }
        } else { /* create a new one  */
            $setting =& $modx->newObject('modUserSetting');
            $setting->set('user',$id);
            $setting->set('key','tree_root_id');
            $setting->set('value',$_POST['TreeRoot']);
            $setting->set('namespace','core');
            $setting->save();
        }
    }
    break;
}
return;
?>
```

Before saving the plugin, click on the "System Settings" tab. We need to specify which system settings the plugin will listen for. Check the box next to the two system settings names in the plugin (**OnUserFormRender** and **OnUserFormSave**). Be careful because some other system events have similar names.

How It Works

Our plugin first checks to see what system setting has triggered it. If it's **OnUserFormRender**, it checks to see if the current user already has the user setting. If so, it sets the value of $v for use in the form field. Then it adds the HTML code for the field to appear in the form and returns it.

The MODX code that renders the Create/Edit User form fires the **OnUserFormRender** event and adds any output returned from it to the form. We've put the field label in bold type so it will be easy to spot. You can remove the bold tags later if you wish. The various classes and styles in the HTML aren't necessary, but they will make the field look like the other fields in the form.

If the **OnUserFormSave** event has triggered our plugin, the second part of the code executes. That event fires just after the user is saved to the database. If we attached our plugin to the

OnBeforeUserFormSave event, it wouldn't work because at that point, the user has no ID to use in creating the user setting. The user's ID doesn't exist until he or she is saved to the database.

If our plugin has been triggered by the **OnUserFormSave** event, the plugin checks to see if there is anything in our form field. If the field is empty, it does nothing. If the field is filled in, the plugin attempts to get the existing setting with $modx->getObject(). The $setting variable will be equal to the user's **tree_root_id** setting if it exists and null if it does not. If $setting and $_POST['TreeRoot'] are the same, no action is necessary. If they are different, either the user setting has been changed, or it doesn't exist. The plugin then checks to see if the setting exists and either updates the setting or creates it, whichever is appropriate, using the value of $_POST['TreeRoot'] for the value of the setting.

Now, if you've entered the code correctly, you can set the value for each of your users. Go to **Security → Manage Users**, right-click on a user, and select "Update User." Fill in the Tree Root field with the ID of the user's personal page, and click on the "Save" button. Once you've done that for each user, they should all be limited to their personal pages. For new users, you can fill in the field when you create each user, and the setting will be created and set to the value you enter.

Improvements

You might also want to allow users to access any children under their **tree_root_id** resource. You can accomplish that with a simple change to the snippet (not the plugin). Leave the section that rejects users who are not logged in alone, but change the test below it so it looks like this:

```
$tr = $modx->getOption('tree_root_id');
$children = $modx->getChildIds($tr);
$children[] = $tr;
if (! in_array($modx->resource->get('id'),$children)) {
    /* return "Wrong Page Tree Root:".$tr . " Page ID: " .
        $modx->resource->get('id');
    */
    $modx->sendRedirect($modx->makeUrl(##));
}
```

Be sure to change ## to the ID of your Members resource and make sure that any child pages you create are published and use the Members template.

Another change you might want to make involves the use of the **tree_root_id** setting in the Manager. The **tree_root_id** setting accepts a comma-delimited list of resource IDs.

In the Manager, users will be allowed to see any resources on the list (and their children). If you are using **tree_root_id** this way (or might in the future), you'll want to modify the code above to create an array containing the listed resources and all of their children before calling in_array(). The test code would then look like this:

```
$tr = $modx->getOption('tree_root_id');
/* create an array out of the roots */
$roots = explode(',' , $tr);
/* add the roots to the full list */
$fullList = $roots;

foreach ($roots as $root) {
    $children = $modx->getChildIds($root);
    if (! empty($children)) { /* add the children (if any) */
        $fullList = array_merge($fullList, $children);
    }
}

/* return print_r($fullList,true); */
if (! in_array($modx->resource->get('id'),$fullList)) {
    $modx->sendRedirect($modx->makeUrl(##));
}
```

The code above will work fine even if the user has a single **tree_root_id**, so it's a good generic version of the snippet. You could add a property called **&includeChildren** to the snippet. The property would determine whether the user is allowed to access the child pages. You could also create a new plugin that would add a Personal User field to the Create/Edit Resource panel and create the **tree_root_id** setting when the user's page is saved. The plugin would be very similar to the one above, but it would be connected to the **OnDocFormRender** and **OnDocFormSave** events. It would have access to the resource ID of the document in the $id variable, and it would get the user's ID from the form field. With a few more fields, you could create the user there as well. You could actually create both plugins so that the setting could be created or updated from either form. The two plugins would not interfere with one another because they would be triggered by separate events. You could also alter our original plugin so that it would create the user's personal page, set its template, and use a Tpl chunk for the content.

If you feel really ambitious, you can skip the plugins and create your own resource containing a custom form that would create the user, the user's page, and the user setting on submission. It could be done using a single snippet. As we've seen before, there are usually many ways to accomplish a given goal in MODX. What you can do with MODX is limited only by your imagination and your coding skills.

A whole other way of approaching this problem would be to use an extended user field instead of `tree_root_id`. Once the new extended field has been created for the user, the field would automatically show up on the Extended Fields tab of the Create/Edit user panel. It would be trickier to get and set the field in code, since it's in the user profile rather than the user object, but it could be done. See Chapter 8 for information on working with extended user fields.

Summary

The MODX Revolution security permissions system has changed significantly from MODX Evolution. It allows much finer control of what users can see and do.

In MODX Revolution, users are no longer divided into web users and manager users — they are simply users. Similarly, there is only one set of resource groups. In Revolution, what users can see and do is no longer completely controlled by their roles. Instead, it is controlled by Access Control Lists (ACLs). Roles in Revolution simply assign authority levels that allow users to inherit permissions tied to roles with higher authority numbers within a given user group.

In Revolution, it's possible to have users who have different levels of access to resources and Manager actions in the same user group. Lists of specific permissions called "access policies" control what users can do with resources and which actions they can perform in the Manager. A standard Resource policy, a standard Administrator policy, and a standard Element policy with full permissions are provided to serve as models. These three policies should never be edited. If you want to modify them, duplicate them, and modify the duplicates. Policies used in Context Access ACLs should be based on the standard Administrator policy. Policies used in Resource Group Access ACLs should be based on the standard Resource policy. Policies in Element Category Access ACLs should be based on the standard Element policy.

Policy templates determine which permissions appear in a policy. The permissions can be checked or unchecked in the policy to enable or disable them.

Both contexts and resource groups become protected when they are associated with a user group by an ACL entry. Once they are protected, only users who are given explicit access in an ACL entry can see them. ACLs controlling access to the `mgr` context protect them in the back end. ACLs controlling access to the `web` context (or other contexts you create) protect them in the front end.

You can also control access to resources in the front end with a snippet.

MODX Evolution Notes

In MODX Evolution, the security system is similar to the Revolution system, but is much less flexible and powerful.

General Security Principles

There are still user groups and resource groups, and as in Revolution, resources in Evolution are protected by connecting a user group to a resource group.

In Evolution, however, there are separate user groups and resource groups for the front and back ends. Users are divided into Manager Users and Web Users, and resource groups are divided into Manager Resource Groups and Web Resource Groups.

When a Manager Resource Group is connected to a Manager User Group, only members of that group can see the resources in the Manager. This has no effect on documents in the front end. When a Web Resource Group is connected to a Web User group, only members of the user group can see the resources in the front end. This has no effect on what is visible in the Manager.

The connections for the Manager are made in the
Security → Manager Permissions → User/Resource Group Links tab.
The connections for the front end are made in the
Security → Web Permissions → User/Resource Group Links tab.

Here are the basic rules of Evolution permissions:

- Any document that is not assigned to a document group is open to everyone.

- Documents in a document group not connected to a user group are open to everyone.

- As soon as a document is assigned to a document group that is connected to a user group, it can only be accessed by users belonging to that user group.

- The above rules apply to both Manager User and Web User permissions, BUT:

- Manager User permissions (which apply in the Manager), and Web User permissions (which apply in the front-end), are entirely separate.

- Setting Manager User permissions has no effect on Web Users and vice versa.

- The same document group can be connected to either or both, however.

There are no ACLs or contexts in MODX Evolution and no inheritance of permissions with a group. Users in a user group can have different permissions if they have different roles.

User Capabilities

What users can do in Evolution is controlled by each user's Role. When you create a Role, you specify what the user can and can't do.

Unlike Revolution, where users can have a different role in each user group they belong to, in Evolution, users can have only one role. If the user is a Web User, the role applies to the front end. If the user is a Manager user, the role applies to the Manager.

Users can have more than one identity, of course, but they have to log out and log back in as a different user to change the role they currently operate under. Manager Users have no rights in the front end, and Web Users have no rights in the Manager.

Other Differences

There are no authority numbers or policies in Evolution, there are simply roles, and there are no custom security permissions.

The Login snippet works much the same way in Evolution as it does in Revolution except that in Evolution it only affects the rights of Web users.

Our Member Pages system could be created in Evolution, but it would require substantial changes because of the differences in database access, the difficulty of customizing Manager pages, and the fact that there are no user settings in Evolution.

Chapter 11

Customizing the MODX Manager

In MODX Revolution, it's now possible to have very fine control over how the MODX Manager looks to various users. You might want to hide certain parts of the Manager from some users for security reasons. In other cases, you might just want to alter the Manager for naïve users so that they're not intimidated the Manager's complexity. You might also want to add your own custom menu items to perform tasks necessary for your site or change the order of the existing items.

MODX Revolution makes it relatively easy to rearrange or add items on the Top Menu. It's also fairly simple to hide parts of the menu, tabs in the tree, or even parts of the individual forms used to create and edit resources and elements. All this can be done without touching the MODX core and, often, without creating any ACL entries.

In this chapter, we'll look at altering the Manager's Top Menu, modifying the Create/Edit Resource panel with form customization, and creating Custom Manager pages (CMPs).

Altering the Top Menu

You can change the MODX Manager's Top Menu either by rearranging its items or by hiding some of them from selected users. You can also add new entries that point to existing actions or to custom actions you create. In the following sections, we'll look first at the methods used to modify the Top Menu, then in the following section we'll work through some practical examples.

 Be careful here. Any changes that you make to the menu will be permanent unless you undo them yourself. Your changes will survive clearing the cache, re-running Setup, and in most cases, updating to a new version of MODX. There is no "return to default menus" option (unless one has been added by the time you read this).

It's advised that you not make any permanent changes to the MODX menus until you are fairly familiar with MODX and have a good reason for making the changes. It's also not a bad idea to write down the default menu structure before making any changes.

Top Menu Concepts

The Revolution menu system has a completely new architecture. It has almost nothing in common with the Evolution menu system except for the names of many of the menu choices. It isn't necessary to understand the new menu system to customize it, but it helps to have some grasp of how things are done, especially if you are going to create Custom Manager Pages that will be accessed through the Menu.

The Top Menu Tree

Go to **System → Actions**, and you'll see the underpinnings of the menu system. The tree at the right (Top Menu) contains the actual menu items and subitems. If you expand the various sections, you'll see that it is an exact duplicate of the Manager's Top menu. The top-level items are what you see across the top of the screen in the Manager. They are almost always containers for the subitems, which drop down under each main item.

Each of the subitems in the tree corresponds to a Manager action. When you click on a subitem, the Manager action occurs (e.g., clearing the site cache or going to the Access Controls panel). Actually, the top-level items can be actions, but none of the default top-level items are configured that way.

What happens when you click on an item in the menu is actually defined here, on the Top Menu section of the page you're viewing. As we'll see, you can easily redefine what happens when you click on a menu item, and you can rename, hide, or remove items from the list. You can also add items to the Menu and define what will happen when they are clicked on. In fact, you could create a whole new menu system for the Manager that would replace the existing one, and different users could see a completely different menu. This can all be done without touching the MODX core.

The physical display of the Top Menu is also determined here. It's not a coincidence that all the items are in the same order as they are in the Top Menu. If you move them in the tree, the Top Menu will change when the page is reloaded.

We're going to look at some of the Manager actions here, but be careful not to change them — Click on the "Cancel" button after viewing them.

In the right-hand (Top Menu) tree, right-click on the "Site" item and select "Update Menu." The Update Menu dialog will pop up with the fields that define that menu action:

Lexicon Key — A lexicon key for the menu item (or the menu item itself)

Description — A lexicon key for the description (or the description itself)

Action — A specification of a PHP file that will be executed

Icon — An optional icon for the menu option

Parameters — Optional $_GET parameters for the URL

Handler — JS code that will be executed

Permissions — A comma-separated list of necessary permissions

Notice that most of the fields of the Site item are blank. There is no Action, no Handler, and the Permissions field is blank. That's because it is a container for the subitems under it. If you click on the "Site" menu choice in the Top Menu, nothing happens.

Let's look at a menu option that does something. Click on "Cancel" to close the dialog, expand the "Site" section of the tree in the right panel, right-click on the "Clear Cache" option under "Site," and select "Update Menu."

Notice that the Clear Cache option has a Handler and a Permissions entry. The Permissions field tells us that a user can't execute this option unless he or she has the clear_cache permission. The Handler is the actual JS code that will execute when you select this option. All options that actually do something have either an Action or a Handler. If there is a Handler, its code simply runs and the action field is ignored. If there is no Handler, on the other hand, the action specified in the Action field occurs. The Action is actually a pointer to either a controller file, or one of the actions in the Actions tree at the left side of the panel (which points to a controller file). Close the dialog by clicking on the "Cancel" button.

Let's look at a menu option with an action. Download and install the Batcher extra in Package Manager, reload the Manager page in your browser, then come back to **System → Actions**. In the Components section of the right-hand tree (expand it, if necessary by clicking on it), right-click on "Batcher" and select "Update Menu." Now we have an Action rather than a Handler: batcher - index. Now that the Components menu has a subitem, it shows up in the Top Menu. Close the Update Menu dialog for the right panel by clicking on the "Cancel" button.

In the left panel, all the top-level entries are namespaces. In the Actions tree at the left, expand the "batcher" namespace. You should see the index Action. That's the action that the Batcher menu choice we just looked at in the right panel is pointing to. We'll look at a little more closely in just a bit.

We'll discuss the Actions tree in more detail in the section below, but first, let's look at what you can do with the Top Menu tree. Later, we'll make some actual changes to it.

The items in the Top Menu tree can be rearranged by dragging them around in the tree. If you move an item in the tree, the actual Top Menu of the Manager will change to match, although you'll have to reload the Manager page to see the changes.

To add an item to the Top Menu, you can right-click somewhere in the tree and select "Place Action Here." To add an item at the top level of the tree, you can also click on the "Create Menu" button.

Menu items can be removed by right-clicking on them and selecting "Remove Menu Item." If you remove an item, the content of its fields will be lost and any children of the item will be deleted as well. This action is not reversible.

If you want to remove a menu option without actually deleting it (almost always the best practice), you can hide it simply by putting something in the Permissions field. If there is already something there, add a comma and some new permission name at the end. As long as it is a permission that no one has, the menu choice will be invisible. You can make it reappear by deleting the permission name. If you'd like to show the menu option to some (but not all) users, just create a new policy template containing just the custom permission, create a new policy based on that template, and create a mgr Context Access ACL entry that applies to those users and assigns that policy (more on this in a bit).

To change the caption of a Top Menu item, make a note of its Lexicon Key. Then, go to **System → Lexicon Management**. Select the "core" Namespace and the "topmenu" Topic.

The Topic drop-down list can have more than one page, so you may have to go to the second page to find the "topmenu" topic. Find the lexicon key for the menu item, double-click on the value and change it. Any changes you make here will survive upgrades of MODX or any add-on components.

The method just described will only work for built-in core menu choices. For an add-on component's menu choice, you'd have to look in the add-on's namespace rather than the core namespace. If you wanted to change the Basher menu choice, for example, you'd change the Lexicon Key's value in the basher namespace in Lexicon Management.

The Actions Tree

Return to **System → Actions** if you're not still there. In the left panel, click on the "index" action under the "batcher" namespace and select "Update Action" in the drop-down list. Remember that this is the action that the Batcher menu item in the right panel points to. You'll see that the Controller for that action is index and the Namespace is batcher. If we went to **System → Namespaces** at this point, we'd see that the batcher namespace path is:

```
{core_path}components/batcher/
```

In looking for a controller to execute when the "Batcher" Top Menu item is clicked on, MODX will create a full path like this:

```
namespace_path + controller_name + .php
```

In other words, assuming that the core is at its default location, MODX will look for and execute the controller file at:

```
core/components/batcher/index.php
```

If you look at that file, you'll see that it just "includes" the **index.php** file in the **core/components/batcher/controllers** directory, which loads the Batcher class and initializes it — launching Batcher in the Manager. We'll create a new menu choice in the Components menu a little later in this chapter when we create our custom manager pages.

Here is a description of the fields in the Update Action dialog:

Controller — The name of the file that will be executed (`.php` is appended to it).

Namespace — The namespace of the action (determines the path to the file and any lexicon topic files).

Load Headers — If checked, the file's output will be displayed surrounded by the Manager UI.

Language Topics — Lexicon topics to load for the action.

Assets — Currently not used by MODX.

Many of the menu items in the right panel do not have actions shown for them in the left panel. That's because the paths to their controllers are stored in the MODX database and shouldn't be edited (at least not easily). They're stored in the `modx_actions` table. Each action has an ID number and a path to its controller. It also has a help URL for context-sensitive help when that controller is active and several other fields. For the actions that show in the Action panel at the left, you can see the ID in parentheses next to the action name.

Adding a menu choice to the tree for any Manager action is simply a matter of creating the menu choice in the right panel and specifying the correct Action (controller) or adding a Handler. If the controller already exists, you can just select it in the Action drop-down. If not, you have to create an Action in the left panel that points to the controller. There is no menu choice for creating a new user, for example, but since there is a controller file for it, it could be easily added as a Top Menu choice. It would simply be a matter of creating a menu item on the right and setting its Action to `core - security/user/create`. As you would expect, a menu choice on the Top Menu that has a handler but no action (like the Clear Cache menu item) has no corresponding action in the Action tree. It doesn't need one because the handler contains the code for it. Rather than launching the controller, MODX simply executes the code in the handler field.

Handling Menu Clicks

Take a look at the index action for the Batcher namespace in the left panel. Make a note of its ID. When you click on an item in the Top Menu, MODX gets its ID. It then generates a Manager URL for that page and forwards the user to it. In my localhost install of MODX, the ID of the batcher index action is 70. When I click on Batcher in the Top Menu, the URL in the browser address bar is:

```
http://localhost/modx/manager/?a=70
```

If you click on the Batcher menu option, you should see a similar URL showing the ID of your Batcher index action. When the request handler gets that URL, it looks up that menu object in the database, makes sure the user has permission to execute it, sets the help URL, and executes the controller pointed to by the action (unless there is a handler, in which case it executes the JS code of the handler). If the Load Headers checkbox is checked for that action, the output from the controller is displayed surrounded by the Manager UI.

Working with the Top Menu

Now that we have seen how MODX handles menu items and their associated actions, let's modify the actual Top Menu in the Manager. The methods are fairly simple, and you don't have to understand the inner workings of the MODX menu/action system to use them.

Be careful here because your changes will survive an upgrade of the site and there's no simple way to revert to the default menu. Most of the things we're doing here are easily reversible, but you might want to write down the original menu structure before changing anything. It's best to make these changes in a MODX installation that you won't be using for a live site.

Rearranging the Top Menu

You can rearrange any of the Top Menu items on the Manager screen or any of the individual subitems under them. Go to **System → Actions**, and expand the Menu tree on the right-hand side (under the Top Menu heading).

As we learned earlier, this tree is the basis for the Manager's Top Menu. You can reorganize the Top Menu by dragging and dropping menu items. Just click on the menu item you want to move, and, holding the mouse button down, drag it to where you want it, then release the button. You can change the order of the items on the Top Menu, or the order of the subitems on any submenu. You can move subitems to another menu. You can also make subitems into main items by dragging them and dropping them on the Top Menu folder. You'll have to reload the Manager page to see your changes. Try reversing the order of the Flush Permissions and Flush All Sessions options on the Security menu.

Adding and Removing Menu Items

Adding a new menu item is quite simple. Just go to **System → Actions**, and expand the Menu tree on the right-hand side (under the Top Menu heading). Select the part of the menu you want to add to, and click on the "Create Menu" button (or right-click and select "Place Action Here"). Put the name of your menu item in the Lexicon Key field, and click on the "Save" button. Usually, MODX users put new menu items in the Components menu, but you can put them anywhere. To remove a menu item, you can right-click on it, and select "Remove Menu Item."

 We've put the caption to be used for the menu item in the Lexicon Key field for this exercise. That's fine if a single language will be used in the Manager.

If users might see the Manager in more than one language, however, you'll want to create a core lexicon entry in each language and use the actual lexicon key rather than a language-specific caption for that field of the menu item.

If you create a third-party add-on that adds any items or subitems to the MODX Top Menu, you should definitely create new lexicon entries and use lexicon keys here so that speakers of other languages can easily modify the menu selections without having to customize their own Manager menus.

If you add a new menu item, and then click on the "Reload" button in your browser, you may not see your new menu item in the Top Menu. Menu items with no children and no specified Action or Handler do not show up on the menu. That's why the Component menu choice you see in the tree doesn't show up in the Top Menu when you first install MODX Revolution — no components are installed yet. If your new menu choice is under the Components item, however, both the Components item and your new one should show up in the Top Menu when you reload the page.

As a simple exercise, let's create a new custom Top Menu item that takes you to your favorite sections of the Manager. Let's assume that you are doing work that requires frequent visits to the System Settings panel, the Create/Edit document panel, and the Access Controls panel. We'll create a new Top Menu item called *MyMenu* that takes you to them. Note that all our work will be in the right-hand (Top Menu) panel.

Go to **System → Actions**, and (in the Top Menu tree) click on the "Create Menu" button. Put *MyMenu* in the Lexicon Key field, and click on the "Save" button.

Next, we'll create our subitems under it. Right-click on the "MyMenu" item, and select "Place Action Here." Fill in the following fields:

Lexicon Key: *Create a Document*

Action: *core - resource/create*

Click on the "Save" button. Now create two more items in the same way with the following field settings:

Lexicon Key: *System Settings*

Action: *core - system/settings*

Lexicon Key: *Access Controls*

Action: *core - security/permission*

Check to make sure that your three new menu items are subitems under MyMenu. If they're not, drag them there with the mouse. Depending on where you drag them, you can create a three- or four-level menu, but it's not very practical. It's easy to do this by accident when dragging them around. Correct it by dragging them to the menu item you want them under. You can also change the order of the items and subitems by dragging them around, though it may take you more than one try.

Once you have the items where you want them, reload the Manager page in your browser. You should see the new MyMenu item in the Top Menu with the three subitems below it and the subitems should take you to the appropriate panels in the Manager.

Suppose that you're constantly going to the "Access Controls" menu and don't want to bother with dropping down the MyMenu item to get there. Just go to **System → Actions**, and drag the "Access Controls" item you created earlier to the Top Menu entry and drop it. It should appear at the bottom of the menu list.

Now, when you reload the page, you should see a new Top Menu item at the right called "Access Controls." Clicking on it will take you directly to the Access Controls panel. Note that we haven't done anything with the original "Access Controls" menu, so it should still be there and will work as it did before.

As of this writing, MODX sometimes gets confused when you do a lot of dragging and dropping, and menu items you've created can disappear from the tree. If this happens, just navigate away from the Actions panel and come back. They should be there again.

If you'd like to remove any of the menu items you've created, just go to **System → Actions**, right-click on them, and select "Remove Menu item." It's a good idea to remove all the subitems before removing a Top Menu item to make sure they don't remain in the database.

Hiding Menu Items

In addition to rearranging menu items, you can also hide them by using security permissions attached to the menu item. Go to **System → Actions**, and expand the Menu tree on the right-hand side (under the Top Menu heading).

Right-click on any menu item or subitem, and select "Update Menu." A dialog will pop up with an input field at the bottom labeled "Permissions." Be careful not to change any of the other fields.

If you try this with some of the existing menu items, you will see that some of them have permissions listed in the Permissions box, and some do not. How you hide the items will depend on whether the box is empty or not.

If the Permissions box contains a permission listing, you can create a new access policy (or edit an existing one) to disable that permission, and the menu item will be hidden. This could have unwanted side effects, though, because other Manager actions might depend on that same permission. A better method is to add an additional custom permission specification to the box.

The Permissions box will accept a comma-separated list of permissions. Only users with all the listed permissions can see the menu item.

Let's look at an example. Imagine that you would like to hide the Manage Users subitem on the Security menu from everyone but the admin Super User.

Go to **System → Actions** and expand the Menu tree, then right-click on the "Manage Users" item, and select "Update Menu." The permissions box should contain `view_user`. We're going to add another permission called *my_view_user_menu*. Edit the permissions box so that it contains *view_user,my_view_user_menu*. Be sure there are no spaces in the entry. Now users need both those permissions, and since no one has the second one (because we just made it up), no one can see the menu. It's a good idea to put "my" in front of permissions you create so you can tell them from the original permissions. Using the my_ prefix will help keep you from deleting critical default permissions if you decide to change things later on.

For menu items that have no permission, the procedure is essentially the same. You just add your new custom permission to the empty Permissions box.

Now that we've added our custom permission, the admin Super User can no longer see the Manage Users menu subitem. To correct that, we need to give the admin Super User that permission. If you plan to do this on a real site, you should always give the admin Super User the permission first, before creating the custom permission.

Because the standard Administrator group is protected in the Manager, you need to create a new policy template containing just the custom permission and a new policy based on it. You can put all your custom permissions in that policy template. Click on the "Create Policy Template" tab. Use the following values for the dialog:

Name: *CustomPermissionsTemplate*

Template Group: *Admin*

Description: *My custom permissions*

Click on the "Save" button. Next, click on the

Now, right-click on the "CustomPermissions" template and select "Update Policy Template." Then click on the "Add Permission to Template button." Use the following values in the dialog:

Name: *my_view_user_menu*

Description: *Permission to see the User menu*

Click on the "Add" button, then on the "Save" button.

Next, click on the "Access Policies" tab, then on the "Create Access Policy" button. Use the following values in the dialog:

Name: *CustomPermissions*

Policy Template: *CustomPermissionsTemplate*

Description: *My custom permissions*

Click on the "Save" button"

Right-click on the "CustomPermissions" policy and select "Update Policy." Scroll down to the my_view_user_menu permission and check the box next to it. Click on the "Save" button at the upper right.

Now, we need to give the admin Super User that permission by creating a new Context Access ACL entry. Go to **Security → Access Controls → User Groups tab**. Right-click on the "Administrator" user group and select "Update User Group." Click on the "Context Access" tab and then on the "Add Context" button. Use the following values in the dialog:

Context: *mgr*

Minimum role: *Super User - 0*

Policy: *CustomPermissions*

In the Top Menu, select **Security → Access Controls**. Now no one can see the menu item except the admin Super User (and anyone else with that policy). If you log in as one of your Editor users, the Manage Users subitem on the Access Controls menu should be missing.

You can (and often should) hide the Access Controls menu itself from low-level users with the technique described above, but be sure to read the warning first about giving the admin Super User the permission before adding that permission to in the Action panel.

When you hide a main Top Menu option, the menu items under it will be hidden automatically. If you hide the Access Controls menu option, for example, there's no need to hide the subitems under it.

 Hiding menu items by adding custom permissions means that the action associated with the menu choice can no longer be performed by anyone until they have that custom permission. It's possible to paint yourself into a corner with this method. If you hide the "Actions" subitem or the "System" Top Menu item, for example, you will have no way to unhide them and no way to perform any actions on them.

The solution is to give the admin Super User the custom permission before hiding the menu item. This is a good practice in general because, otherwise, the only way out is to edit the database directly to grant the admin Super User the necessary permission.

Custom Menus for Selected Users

You can combine the techniques from the previous two sections to create a custom menu for a particular user group (which could have just one user in it), or you can simply hide menu items that a user should not see by using the steps described above to give the admin Super User alone permission to see selected menu items.

You could create a new Top Menu item with all the actions the user group members need as subitems under it by creating new menu items in **System** → **Actions** and duplicating the values from the existing ones. By the time you read this, it may be possible to simply duplicate the menu items and subitems, which would make this task easier.

Then, you can hide all the original Top Menu items from those users with custom security permissions that everyone else has except that user group. Members of the user group will see only the new menu items you created. A possible next step would be to hide the new custom menu from the admin Super User (who would still see the original menu) using the same technique.

If you only need two levels of menu (e.g., one for the admin Super User and one for everyone else), you can use a single custom permission (say, `my_view_admin_menu`) in your custom policy template. If you need different menus for multiple user groups, you can use more specific permissions (e.g., `my_view_user_menu`, `my_view_access_menu`, etc.) in the custom policy template and then create multiple policies based on that template, each with different permissions checked. Then create a new Context Access ACL entry for each group assigning the appropriate policy.

The only catch with this technique is that the Top Menu is not always the only way to get to a Manager panel. Some panels have links to other panels (although this is fairly rare), and some actions can be performed on multiple panels. This is seldom a problem because the cases where this is true tend to be on panels that will be hidden from low-level users.

Form Customization

In the section above, we learned how to modify the menus of the MODX Manager. In this section, we'll see how to customize the Manager's Create/Edit Resource panel.

In earlier versions of MODX Revolution, *Form customization* allowed you to alter the Create/Edit panels for resources, templates, chunks, snippets, and plugins. At this writing, however, it is limited to the Create/Edit Resource panel. The other capabilities may be added back in future versions. See the online documentation for details.

In a way, there are really two separate Create/Edit Resource forms in the Manager: one for creating new resources and the other for updating existing resources. Although the two forms look the same, they don't have to because you can alter each one with separate form customization rules. When you're finished, the two forms can look very different. Technically, those Create/Edit forms are called "Actions," and that is how they are referred to in the form customization dialog. There is a resource/create action and a resource/update action.

The most common alteration is simply hiding fields that the user doesn't need to see, but you can also set field default values, hide tabs, move TVs to another tab, create new tabs, and change captions. You can even customize the Create/Edit Resource panel for particular user groups or resources attached to a particular template. This accomplishes much of what was done in MODX Evolution with the ManagerManager plugin.

In the previous chapter, we learned how to hide TVs with ACL entries. Here, we'll see how to do it with form customization. Many users find form customization easier to understand than the access permission rules, and using ACL entries won't let you hide TVs when editing specific documents or documents with specific field values. Form customization can give you finer control and let you do things like hiding a form field or setting a default field value only for certain users, certain documents, or documents that use a certain template.

Let's assume that you don't want the Editors user group we created earlier to be able to edit any template variables. You might think the way to accomplish this would be to change the EditorResource policy to disable the `view_tv`, `edit_tv`, or `save_tv` permissions. This only affects their ability to use the Template Variable Create/Edit panel, however. In other words, it controls the user's ability to work on the template variable itself in the Template Variable section of the Element tree. It won't affect the ability to set TV values when editing a resource.

Instead, what we need to do is to hide the Template Variables tab on the Create/Edit Resource panel for the Editors user group using form customization. We could also hide particular TVs from all users or a particular user group. We'll see how to do that in a bit. First, let's look at the form customization process.

Form Customization Overview

In this section, we'll look at the process of customizing forms in the MODX Manager. We'll take a brief tour of the form customization process and then, in the following sections, we'll create some practical form customization rules.

At this writing, the Form Customization section of the Manager has just been redesigned, and it may undergo further alteration before you read this. Currently, there are three main components to the form customization process: profiles, sets, and rules. There are also constraints, which determine when a rule should be applied. The organization can be confusing at first, but it's very simple and easy to work with once you get used to it. Let's look at it from the bottom up.

Rules

A *form customization rule* is specification for one modification of the Create/Edit Resource form. In other words, a form customization rule just determines which tab or field is being altered and the nature of the alteration. A rule may hide a field or template variable, set a default value, create a new tab, or move a field or template variable to a different tab.

The rules fall into three groups: Field rules, Tab rules, and TV rules.

Field Rules alter a specific field of the Create/Edit Resource form and provide the following options:

- Setting the default value of the field
- Setting the field's label
- Showing or hiding the field

Tab Rules let you control the following options:

- Setting a tab's title
- Showing or hiding the tab
- Creating a new tab

TV Rules allow you to alter a specific template variable in the following ways:

- Setting the default value of the TV
- Setting the label of the TV
- Showing or hiding the TV
- Moving the TV to another tab
- Controlling the placement of the tab containing the TV

Rules can also have *constraints*. Constraints are optional, and they allow finer-grained control of when the rule applies. A constraint, for example, could make the rule apply only when editing a specific resource, the children of a specific resource, resources that use a specific template, or even just resources created by a specific user.

Sets

Rules are grouped into form customization sets. Each set of rules is tied to a specific action, so the rules in the set will only apply when creating or updating a resource, but not both. Sets can be tied to specific templates, or they can apply to all templates. Sets can also be tied to specific user groups or they can apply to all user groups. Rule sets are almost always tied to specific user groups because you generally don't want the rules to apply to the admin Super User. Like rules, sets can also have constraints, in which case the rules in the set will only apply if the constraint condition is met. A set can be designated as active or inactive. When a set is inactive, none of the rules in the set will apply.

Profiles

Sets are grouped into *form customization profiles*. Like sets, profiles can also be designated as active or inactive. When a profile is inactive, none of the rules in any of its sets will apply. Unlike sets and rules, profiles do not have constraints.

Review

Although we've covered things from the bottom up, you'll need to create them from the top down. You need a profile to create any sets, and you need a set to create any rules. It's not a bad idea to plan out your form customization strategy on paper. Remember that applying rules to specific user groups or specific templates is done at the set level. Most constraints are created at the rule level, though occasionally, you might want a constraint to apply to all the rules in a set. For example, you might want to apply a whole set of rules to the children of a specific folder. Remember, too, that most of the time you'll need both a resource/create rule set and a resource/update rule set. Often the two will contain many of the same rules.

 When working with the three levels of form customization (profiles, sets, and rules), you can go down to the next lowest level by right-clicking on a profile or set and selecting edit. You can move back up to the level just above the one you're on by clicking on the "Cancel" button at the upper right. Be sure to save any changes you've made, though, before clicking on the "Cancel" button.

Both profiles and sets can be duplicated from the right-click menu, and sets can be exported to an XML file and imported into a different profile.

Working with Form Customization Rules

This section describes the current state of the form customization system. By the time you read this, there may be other rules or capabilities, and some of the identifiers used here may have changed. See the MODX online documentation for details.

Setting a Template Variable's Default Value

You know that the default value of a template variable can be set when editing the TV itself. With form customization, however, you can override that setting for members of a specific user group or for resources that use a specific template. You can also override the TV's default value for everyone, but there isn't much point in doing that since it's easier just to set the default value in the TV itself.

Create at least three template variables if you haven't done so already, and assign them to the template that is used by the site's Home page. Call them *tv one*, *tv two*, and *tv three*. Create a default value for each TV and make sure the default value is appropriate for the type of TV. For a radio options TV with input option values of *red||blue||green*, for example, an appropriate default value would be *blue*.

When you create your form customization rules, make any default value different from the TV's default value so you can see that it overrides the original default value. Edit the Home page, and click on the "Template Variables" tab. Make sure your TVs show up there. Edit the Resource Content field, and add tags for your three TVs:

```
<p>TV 1: [[*tv one]]</p>
<p>TV 2: [[*tv two]]</p>
<p>TV 3: [[*tv three]]</p>
```

Create an *Editors* user group if you haven't already and add at least one user (who is not the admin Super User) to it so you can log in as that user to test the rules.

To set the default value of *tv one* for the *Editors* user group, we first need to create a profile for that group. Go to **Security → Form Customization**, and click on the "Create New Profile" button.

Set the following fields:

Name: *EditorProfile*

Description: *Form customization rules for Editors*

Check the "Active" checkbox, and click on the "Save" button. Now, right-click on the Editors profile in the grid and select "Edit" from the drop-down list. This will take you to the Sets grid.

Click on the "Create New Set" button, and set the following fields:

Action: *Create Resource*

Description: *Rules for new resources*

Constraint Field: *Leave Blank*

Constraint: *Leave Blank*

Make sure the "Active" checkbox is checked, and click on the "Save" button. Click again on the "Create New Set" button, and set the following fields:

Action: *Update Resource*

Description: *Rules for existing resources*

Constraint Field: *Leave Blank*

Constraint: *Leave Blank*

Make sure the "Active" checkbox is checked, and click on the "Save" button.

Note that we left the template field blank so that our rules would apply to all templates. In many cases, however, you might want to tie the rule set to a particular template. Doing so will speed up the Manager for pages using other templates since MODX won't have to check the form customization rules for those pages.

To attach the rule sets to our Editors user group, click on the "User Groups" tab at the top of the grid and then click on the "Add User Group" button. Select the Editors user group in the drop-down list, and click on the "Save" button in the pop-up dialog. Next, click on the "Save" button at the upper right. If you forget this second save, MODX will not attach the rule set to the Editors user group. Notice that we could have attached our rule sets to more than one user group here. Click on the "Save" button to save the set.

> To test your form customization rules, you'll have to log out and log back in as an Editor user. You can avoid this by temporarily adding the Administrator group on the User Group tab. Remember to remove the Administrator user group later when you're done testing your rules. To do so, go to the Sets grid, click on the "User Groups" tab, right-click on the "Administrator" group, and select "Remove User Group From Profile." Don't forget to save the set.

Now it's time to create our rule. Click on the Profile tab to return to the rule set grid. Right-click on the "resource/create" rule set and select "Edit" from the drop-down list. This will take you to the rules grid. You'll see fields at the top that allow you to set a template and constraints for the rule set, but don't change those now.

Notice that there are three tabs at the top: Set Information and Fields, Tabs, and Template Variables.

On the Set Information and Fields tab, you can see a list of all the page settings fields in one part of the grid and the resource fields in another part. The Resource Content field has its own section of the grid. Using the grid, we could change the Label, visibility, and default value for any field.

On the Tabs tab, you can create a new tab for the Create/Edit Resource panel or set the title and/or visibility of any tab.

We want the "Template Variables" tab, so click on that. You should see your template variables in the grid. The grid shows the name of each, whether it is active, whether it is visible or not, its Label, its Default Value, its Original Value, the name of the tab it appears on, and the rank of that tab. The Original Value is the default value of the TV itself (if any), and the rank determines where the TV tab appears among the tabs of the Create/Edit resource panel.

Double-click on the "Default Value" column for TV One. Set a different value than the Original Value. If there are Input Option Values settings for the TV, be sure to use one of them for the Default Value. Click on the "Save" button. We could create the same rule for the resource/update set, but there's no point because TV default values only apply when a new resource is created.

When a member of your Editors group creates a new document, the default value of *tv1* should be set by the form customization rule. The rule will only apply to Editors because we specified that user group earlier when we edited the set. If we had left the User Group field blank, the rule would apply to everyone (including the admin Super User).

 Default values of TVs may not be shown for a resource that has ever been saved because the saved value will show. When testing to make sure any default value rules are working, always create a new document. Once you see that the defaults are set correctly, you can click on the "Cancel" button.

Hiding or Moving a Specific Template Variable

Let's create a form customization rule that will hide a particular TV.

Go to **Security → Form Customization** in the Top Menu, and drill down to the rule sets page. You'll know you're in the right place when you see the Template Variables tab. Click on the "Template Variables" tab. Right-click on the "resource/create" set and select "Edit" from the drop-down list. Uncheck the "Visible" checkbox for TV Two. Click on the "Save" button. Now click on the "Cancel" button to return to the Sets panel. Create the same rule for editing existing resources by right-clicking on the "resource/update" set and selecting "Edit," then uncheck the "Visible" checkbox, and click on the "Save" button.

At this point, when an Editor creates or edits a resource and looks at the Template Variables tab, the TV you have specified should be hidden.

You can also move a TV to a different tab on the Create/Edit Resource panel. Edit the resource/create set as we did above, and click on the "Template Variables" tab. Double-click on the "Tab" column for TV Three. Change the value to *modx-resource-settings* and then click on the "Save" button. Now that TV will appear on the main tab along with the Title, Long Title, and Alias rather than on the TV tab. To see the names of other tabs you could use, click on the "Tabs" tab at the top of the grid. If you want to move the TV to the second tab (Page Settings), use *modx-page-settings* instead of *modx-resource-settings*.

Normally, you'd want a rule like this to apply when creating new documents and editing existing ones. In that case you'd need to repeat the process above with the resource/update rule set.

 Be careful when entering form customization rules for tabs. If you misspell the name of a tab, the rule won't work. You may also have to flush permissions and/or clear the cache to see some form customization changes.

Hiding the Template Variables Tab

Suppose that we'd like to hide the entire Template Variables tab from the Editors user group. Go to **Security → Form Customization** in the Top Menu, drill down to the Rules page, and click on the "Tabs" tab. Uncheck the "Visible" checkbox for the *modx-panel-resource-tv* tab. Click on the "Save" button.

Now the entire Template Variables tab should be hidden from the Editors user group. Again, we could apply this rule to all users by leaving the User Group field blank, but then the rule would apply to the admin Super User too. We could also hide the Access Permissions tab with a similar rule by unchecking the "Visible" checkbox for the *modx-resource-access-permissions* tab.

 Remember, if you want a form customization rule to apply for both creating and updating resources, you'll need to create a rule for both the resource/create and resource/update rule sets.

Setting a Constraint

Constraints limit the application of a rule to a specific situation. Suppose that we'd like our rule that hides the Template Variables tab to affect just the Home page. We'll assume that the Home page ID is 1 (use the actual ID if it's different).

Go to **Security → Form Customization** in the Top Menu. Right-click on the "Editors" profile and select "Edit" from the drop-down list. Because we don't want the other rules in the sets we created before to apply just to the Home page, we need to create a new rule set. Click on the "Create New Set" button, and set the following fields:

Action: *Create Resource*

Description: *Home Page Rules*

Template: *Leave blank or select the Home page's template*

Constraint field: *id*

Constraint: *1*

Click on the "Save" button. Now repeat that process, but use Update Resource for the action. Click on the "Save" button at the upper right to save the two new rule sets.

Edit the new resource/create set, select the "Tabs" tab, and uncheck the "Visible" checkbox for the *modx-panel-resource-tv* tab. Click on the "Save" button. Now repeat that process for the new resource/update set.

The Template Variables tab should now be hidden for any Editor users editing the Home page. Note that we could also go to the "Template Variables" tab if we wanted to hide specific TVs rather than the entire TV tab.

You can set a constraint on any resource field. You could limit a rule to the immediate children of a particular document, for example, by using **parent** as the Constraint Field and putting the ID of the parent document as the Constraint. Similarly, you could limit the rule to resources that use a particular template by using **template** as the Constraint

Field and the ID of the template as the Constraint. At this writing, you can't set a constraint based on the content of a template variable, but it's likely that this will be possible in future versions of MODX.

Creating a New Tab

It's very easy to create a new tab for the Create/Edit Resource panel with a few form customization rules. For example, you might want to hide the existing Template Variables tab but move a few TVs to a new tab with a custom name. To create a new tab called My New Tab for the Create/Edit Resource panel, right-click on the original "resource/create" rule set (the one we created earlier), select "Edit," and then click on the "Tabs" tab. Click on the "Create New Tab" button, and use the following field values:

ID: *my-new-tab*

Title: *My New Tab*

Now, we'll move TV One to the new tab. Click on the "Template Variables" tab. Double-click on the "Tab" column for TV One, and change the value to *my-new-tab*. Click on the "Save" button. Repeat the two steps above for the original resource/update set. Now, when an Editor user creates or edits a resource, a new tab with the label "My New Tab" should be visible and will show just TV One.

Hiding a Field

You can hide any individual field on the Create/Edit Resource panel in the MODX Manager with a form customization rule. The field names are the same ones you use to get the fields with an object's `get()` method. Let's hide the Summary (`introtext`) field on the Create/Edit Resource panel. Right-click on the original "resource/create" rule set, select "edit," then click on the "Set Information and Fields" tab. Uncheck the "Visible" checkbox for the "introtext" field, and click on the "Save" button. Now repeat that process for the resource/update rule set.

You can hide the field for specific users or resources that use a particular template as we discussed earlier. You can also set a constraint that determines when the rule will apply. Be careful, though, because setting a constraint will apply to all rules in a set. If you need to have a constraint apply only to a single rule, you need to create a new rule set just for that rule. Actually, you usually need to create two new rule sets, one for resource/create and one for resource/update.

Setting Field Default Values and Labels

Setting field default values and labels works just like hiding the field except that you set the Default Value column rather than the Visible checkbox.

You can also set the label (caption) for a template variable by using the method we saw above for changing a TV's default field but changing the Label column instead of the Default Value column.

Bulk Actions

There is a **Bulk Actions** drop-down menu above the top of the grid on both the Profile panel and the Sets panel. This allows you to make changes to groups of profiles or rule sets. You can check the checkbox at the left side of the grid to select every profile or rule set you want to modify. Once you've made your selections, you can activate, deactivate, or remove the selected items by choosing an option on the Bulk Actions menu. Don't forget to click on the "Save" button after making any changes.

Custom Manager Pages

The creation of Custom Manager Pages (CMPs) is an advanced topic for those who want to add their own pages to the MODX Manager. It requires some knowledge of PHP coding and, optionally, ExtJS and Smarty templating.

The development of a full add-on component using ExtJS and Smarty is beyond the scope of this book. To see how it is done, you can look at the MODX documentation or examine the code of an existing component such as Quip or Gallery. Here, we'll create a very simple CMP using HTML to present a MODX cheat sheet.

Cheat Sheet Custom Manager Page

Since we're learning about Custom Manager Pages (CMPs), we might as well produce something useful. In this section, we'll create a very simple CMP that displays a MODX cheat sheet showing the format of MODX Revolution tags and some common system settings. We'll make it a menu choice on the "Components" menu in the Manager, and we'll display the cheat sheet in the right-hand panel. Our cheat sheet will have two separate pages with links to each other.

Creating the Namespace

All add-on components should have a namespace. It provides an identification string that MODX uses for the component's pieces and a path where they can be found. It also specifies the location of the component's lexicon strings. Namespace names are generally in all lowercase.

Go to **System → Namespaces**, and click on the "Create New" button. Use the following values for the namespace (exactly as they appear here), and click on the "Save" button:

Name: *cheatsheet*

Path: *{core_path}components/cheatsheet/*

Be sure to include the trailing slash in the path.

Creating the Action

Go to **System → Actions**. The right-hand panel will show two trees. The left one (Actions) shows actions, which are abstractions of MODX controllers. They are basically events that can occur in the Manager. The right-hand tree (Top Menu) shows all the items in the Manager's Top Menu. We'll start by telling MODX what action is associated with our cheat sheet. Then we'll connect it to a Top Menu item.

In the Actions tree (at the left), right-click on "cheatsheet," and select "Create Action Here." Enter the following values, and then click on the "Save" button.

Controller: *index*

Namespace: *cheatsheet*

Parent Controller: *No Action*

Load Headers: *checked*

Language Topics: *cheatsheet:default*

Assets: *leave blank*

Let's look at these values and what they mean. Remember that we specified a path when we created our cheatsheet namespace. The top two entries above tell MODX that when the `cheatsheet` action is triggered, MODX should execute the **index.php** file found in the `cheatsheet` namespace path. Notice that the **.php** extension is left off the file name. MODX adds it automatically. Here is the file that will be executed:

core/components/cheatsheet/index.php

We'll create that file in a bit. First, though, we need to associate our CheatSheet action with a Top Menu item.

At present, the Parent Controller entry has no effect in MODX Revolution, so it can be set to "No Action" or left blank.

The Load Headers checkbox tells MODX that you want the standard Manager headers and footers. You would turn this off only if you wanted a page that did not look like a Manager page.

The Language Topics entry is a comma-separated list of topics used in your component. We'll only have a default topic, so we've entered that.

The Assets entry is not used by MODX Revolution, so we've left it blank.

Creating the Menu Subitem

Now, we need a menu item to execute the action we created above. In the right-hand (Top Menu) tree of the **System → Actions** panel, right-click on the "Components" menu item, and select "Place Action Here." The Action is selected from the drop-down list, which should show the cheatsheet - index action we created earlier. (At this writing, it doesn't show in the drop-down until you clear the cache and reload the Manager page in your browser.) Enter the following values, and then click on the "Save" button.

Lexicon Key (Name): *cheatsheet_name*

Description: *cheatsheet_desc*

Action: *cheatsheet - index*

Icon: *leave blank*

Parameters: *leave blank*

Handlers: *leave blank*

Let's look at those entries in more detail. The Lexicon Key is the name of the component as it will appear in the menu under Components. We use a lexicon key here because the menu title should be translated for other languages. We'll discuss creating the lexicon file at the end of this section.

The Icon field specifies an icon image to show next to the menu item. It is not implemented in the MODX Revolution Manager at this writing, but it is there for developers who want to create their own Manager or custom pages within MODX.

The Parameters field allows you to enter parameters that will be available in the $_GET array when the action file executes.

The Handlers field allows you to specify a JavaScript handler that will execute instead of the action file we specified earlier. If this field is filled in, the JS will execute, and the action file will be ignored.

You can either put all the JavaScript in the field itself or enter a call to an existing JS function. Use this method if you want your component to execute a JS action instead of loading a page.

For example, the Preview Top Menu subitem (under Site) has this Handler:

```
window.open("../");
```

The Logout menu subitem has this Handler:

```
MODX.logout();
```

Creating the Lexicon Entries

If you preview the menu item we just created on the "Components" menu (after reloading the page), you'll see the lexicon keys rather than the values we want them to have. That's because we haven't created the lexicon entries yet.

We could just add our lexicon entries manually in the Lexicon Management section of the MODX Manager. Instead, let's do it properly with a lexicon file, which will makes it easier to maintain and translate the entries and provides a source if we want to make a transport package out of our component.

For simple components that you're sure will never be translated or packaged, you can just use the names rather than lexicon keys in the fields. If MODX doesn't find a lexicon entry, it always displays the lexicon key instead.

The English language lexicon file should be:

core/components/cheatsheet/lexicon/en/default.inc.php

Remember that **core/components/cheatsheet/** is the path of the cheatsheet namespace. It should be visible in **System → Namespaces** as **{core_path}components/cheatsheet/**. The file should look like this:

```
<?php
/*
 * @topic default
 * @namespace cheatsheet
 * @language en
 */
$_lang['cheatsheet_name']='Cheat Sheet';
$_lang['cheatsheet_desc']='MODX Cheat Sheet';
```

Remember that the lexicon file must be in the proper place in order for MODX to use the lexicon entries.

Creating the index.php File

Clear the Site Cache and reload the Manager page in your browser. Select "CheatSheet" on the Components menu. MODX will try to execute the action we specified earlier for that menu item. Since we haven't created any code yet, you should see a message something like this:

```
Could not find action file at: C:/yoursite/core/components/cheatsheet/index.
php
```

The line you see when you try to execute the Cheat Sheet menu item tells you where to put the **index.php** file that will produce the cheat sheet. Create an **index.php** file in that location, and add the following code to it:

```
<?php
/* Code for index.php File */
$path = $modx->getOption('assets_url');
$modx->regClientCSS($path . 'components/cheatsheet/cheatsheet.css');
$output = '<div class="cheatsheet">';
$output .= '<h2>MODX Cheat Sheet</h2>';
```

```
/* get page to show from URL */
switch($_GET['page']) {
    case '2':
        $output .= $modx->getChunk( 'CheatSheet2');
        break;
    default: /* default to page 1 */
        $output .= $modx->getChunk( 'CheatSheet');
}
$output .= '</div>';
return $output;
?>
```

The first line of the code above will inject a reference to a CSS file (which we'll create in just a bit) into the <head> section of the Manager page.

In order to tell the **index.php** file which page to show, we'll put *page=1* or *page=2* in our URL as a parameter. The switch statement in the code uses $_GET to determine which chunk to retrieve.

Now, we'll create the two chunks that contain the content we want to display on the two pages of our Custom Manager Page. Create a chunk called *CheatSheet*, and put the following code in the chunk:

```
<!-- Code for the CheatSheet Chunk ->
<h3>MODX Tags</h3>
<table>
    <tr>
        <th>Name</th>
        <th>Form</th>
        <th>Example</th>
    </tr>
    <tr>
        <td>Resource Tag</td>
        <td>[<!-- ->[*ResourceField/TV]]</td>
        <td>[<!-- ->[*pagetitle]]</td>
    </tr>
    <tr>
        <td>Link Tag</td>
        <td>[<!-- ->[~id]]</td>
        <td>[<!-- ->[~12]]</td>
    </tr>
```

```
    <tr>
        <td>Snippet Tag</td>
        <td>[<!-- ->[SnippetName]]</td>
        <td>[<!-- ->[MySnippet]]</td>
    </tr>
    <tr>
        <td>Chunk Tag</td>
        <td>[<!-- ->[$ChunkName]]</td>
        <td><!-- ->[[$MyChunk]]</td>
    </tr>
    <tr>
        <td>Placeholder</td>
        <td>[[+PlaceholderName]]</td>
        <td>[<!-- ->[+MyPlaceholder]]</td>
    </tr>
    <tr>
        <td>System Setting</td>
        <td>[[++SettingName]]</td>
        <td>[<!-- ->[++site_url]]</td>
    </tr>
    <tr>
        <td>Language Tag</td>
        <td>[<!-- ->[%LanguageKey]]</td>
        <td>[<!-- ->[%file_not_found]]</td>
    </tr>
</table>
<br /><br />
<h3>Common System Settings</h3>
<table>
    <tr>
        <th>Function</th>
        <th>System Setting
        </th>
    </tr>
    <tr>
        <td>Home page</td>
        <td>site_start</td>
    </tr>
    <tr>
        <td>Site Name</td>
```

```
        <td>site_name</td>
    </tr>
    <tr>
        <td>Error Page</td>
        <td>error_page</td>
    </tr>
    <tr>
        <td>Unauthorized Page</td>
        <td>unauthorized_page</td>
    </tr>
    <tr>
        <td>New Docs Published by Default</td>
        <td>publish_default</td>
    </tr>
    <tr>
        <td>Use Friendly URLs</td>
        <td>friendly_urls</td>
    </tr>
    <tr>
        <td>Enable Rich Text Editor</td>
        <td>use_editor</td>
    </tr>
        <tr>
        <td>Editor to use</td>
        <td>which_editor</td>
    </tr>
    <tr>
        <td>New Docs Rich Text by Default</td>
        <td>rich_text_default</td>
    </tr>
    <tr>
        <td>New Docs Cacheable by Default</td>
        <td>cache_default</td>
    </tr>
    <tr>
        <td>Show Preview in Manager</td>
        <td>show_preview</td>
    </tr>
</table>
<br />
<a href="[[++manager_url]]?a=12&page=2">Page 2 >></a><br />
```

Notice the empty HTML comments <!-- -> between the two opening brackets of the MODX tags in the chunk. These keep MODX from trying to process them as tags. This is one technique to use if you need to display examples of MODX tags on your site (you can also do it with a plugin).

Feel free to abbreviate the code by leaving out most of the rows of our table.

Notice the link at the bottom of the file:

```
<a href="[[++manager_url]]?a=12&page=2">Page 2 >></a><br />
```

Using a regular link tag won't work because we want to stay on that Manager panel. Instead we use the URL of the Manager followed by the ?a=12 parameter, which tells MODX which action (page of the Manager) to load. Important: To make this link work, you'll have to replace the *12* with the ID of your CheatSheet action (visible in the left tree of **System → Actions**). Because we're creating a link to Page 2, we send along **&page**=2 as a second parameter to be read with $_GET['page'] in the **index.php** file we created earlier.

Now create another chunk called *CheatSheet2* and add the following code to it:

```
<!-- Code for the CheatSheet2 Chunk ->
<h3>Page 2</h3>
<p>This is page 2</p>
<br />
<a href="[[++manager_url]]?a=12&page=1"><< Page 1</a><br />
```

This chunk doesn't have any real content yet. We just created it to show how to have multiple pages in a CMP. Notice the link back to Page 1 at the bottom. Be sure to change the *12* to the same ID you used in the other chunk, or the link won't work.

Now, let's add the CSS file to beautify our cheat sheet. Remember that we already created code to inject the CSS into the <head> section of the document in our **index.php** file. Create a file called **cheatsheet.css** in this directory:

assets/components/cheatsheet/

Add the following CSS code to it:

```
/* Code for the cheatsheet.css File */
div.cheatsheet table {
    border: 3px solid #5E5E5E;
    margin: 0;
    padding: 20;
    text-align: left;
    width: 50%;
}
```

```
div.cheatsheet th {
    background-color:#ccc;
    padding: 10px;
    border: 1px solid #ccc;
    font-weight: bold;
}

div.cheatsheet td {
    background-color:#FFFFFF;
    padding: 10px;
    border: 1px solid #CCCCCC;
}
```

If you reload the Manager page, you should see the Components item in the Top Menu and our Cheat Sheet as a subitem under it. If you select the subitem, you should see our attractively styled cheat sheet in the right-hand panel of the Manager.

Feel free to play with the design and styling. Anti-table CSS purists may object to using tables here, but we're displaying tabular data after all. Formatting it with table-free CSS inside a Manager panel can be quite a challenge. If we wanted to be able to edit the table and, optionally, update the database, we could use Smarty and MODExt.

Why is our CSS file under `assets/components/cheatsheet` and not `core/components/cheatsheet` with the `index.php` file? CSS files must be available via URL. If the CSS file is under the core directory and the core directory is moved outside of the web root to make the site more secure, the **cheatsheet.css** file will no longer be available.

More Sophisticated Custom Manager Pages

Our Cheat Sheet CMP is quite simple, but what you can do with custom manager pages is limited only by your imagination and coding skills. You could, for example, create a backup system for backing up and restoring your site or a database editor for direct editing of the MODX database. In fact, those components may exist by the time you read this.

More complex CMPs will normally involve Smarty templating and MODExt, the ExtJS extension that is part of MODX. You can learn more about Smarty at the Smarty web site: **http://smarty.net**. There is information about MODExt in the MODX online documentation. You can see some full-featured CMPs by looking at the code in the Doodles, Quip, Batcher, or Gallery transport packages. Shaun McCormick has also created a tutorial on creating MODX third-party components that uses Doodles as an example. The Doodles package shows how to query a custom table, create a CMP, and build a transport package.

See the MODX online documentation for more information.

Note that MODX tags (e.g., snippet and chunk tags) in CMP HTML code will not be processed, although links in chunks will be processed if you retrieve them with `$modx->getChunk()`.

Links to other pages at the site will take you out of the Manager, and they will display those pages full-screen unless you include **/manager** in the path as we did above and preserve the `?a=` parameter to tell the Manager what action is being performed. That's generally the preferred method, but you can also create a separate action for each page and link to them by using each action's ID in the `?a=` parameter.

Summary

You can customize the MODX Top Menu (and hide parts of it from specific users) by going to **System → Actions**.

Individual forms and tabs can be hidden and altered using form customization by going to **Security → Form Customization**. Form customization can be used to hide fields, tabs, and specific template variables. It can also be used to set the default values of TVs and move them to other tabs. By using constraints, these modifications can be limited to specific documents, groups of documents, and/or specific users or groups of users.

You can also create custom Manager pages to let users perform specific tasks such as modifying the database or configuring a plugin. Custom Manager pages can use Smarty templating and MODExt to create pages like those already in the MODX Manager.

MODX Evolution Notes

There are no form customization rules in Evolution and the visibility of parts of the Manager is not controlled via security permissions. Instead, the ManagerManager plugin (which is similar to Revolution's form customization system) allows customization of the Manager. See the documentation for ManagerManager for more details.

The Evolution equivalent of a custom manager page is called a *module*. For more information on creating a module, see Susan Ottwell's excellent tutorial at: `http://www.sottwell.com/create-module.html`.

Chapter 12

Using Common MODX Components

In this chapter, we'll look at how to install and configure some commonly used snippets in MODX. We'll start with the easy ones. EZfaq creates an FAQ page with sliding windows that expose the answers to common questions. SPForm provides a simple "Contact Us" form with various spam-proofing options. The Breadcrumbs snippet shows the path to the current document.

Then we'll move on to the more complicated and flexible snippets. Wayfinder creates simple or complex dynamic menus for your site. The getResources snippet (the recommended replacement for the Ditto snippet) is a lightweight snippet that aggregates content in a variety of ways. FormIt (the recommended replacement for the eForm snippet) is a powerful user form and email snippet.

Installing Components and Creating Property Sets for Them

To use a MODX third-party add-on component, you need to do two things. First, you need to download and install the component. Second, if the component has default properties, you need to either create a new property set so that any properties you change won't be overwritten if you upgrade the component, or set all properties in the snippet tag.

Installing Components

The components in this chapter are all installed with some variation of the following method.

 In order to see packages in the grid, you'll need cURL or sockets enabled (MODX recommends cURL). This is usually no problem on a public server, but if you are using XAMPP on your local machine, you may need to modify this file:

xampp\php\php.ini

Uncomment this line (remove the semicolon) to enable cURL:

;extension=php_curl.dll

Go to **System → Package Management**, and click on the "Download Extras" button. Find the latest version of the add-on you want. You'll have to expand the tree at the left to see the versions. Clicking on the "Details" button in the grid will give you more information about the package. If you know the name of the component you are looking for, it's usually faster to type the name in the search box. The component should then come up on the right side of the screen.

Clicking on the "Download" button will download the package to the Package Management grid. Wait until the button changes to "Downloaded" before proceeding. When you are done downloading packages, click on the "Finish" button at the bottom of the grid.

In a moment, you should see any add-ons you've selected in the Package Management grid at your site. The packages have been downloaded to the **core/packages** directory but have not been installed. To install one, click on the "Install" button in the grid. Most add-ons will have a License and Readme screens, and some will have questions for you to answer during the installation. We'll discuss those in the sections below when appropriate.

Once you've made your way past the screens, the Console will pop up, and you'll see progress messages as the package is installed. Depending on the state of the installer and the package, you may see error messages in the console. As long as you see the blue message telling you that the package was installed successfully, you should be fine. Click on the "OK" button to close the console.

When you go to the appropriate part of the tree (e.g., the snippets section of the Element tree), you should see your newly installed add-on component there.

Alternate Installation Methods

This section deals with add-on components that are not available through Package Manager but can still be installed in MODX Revolution.

Packages Not Downloadable Through Package Management

If the add-on component has a transport package but doesn't show up when you click on the "Download Extras" button, it is still installable through Package Manager, but you need to use a different method to get it into the grid. To find out if there is a transport package for a component, look for the word "package" in the description. The name of the file will also end in .transport.zip. Transport packages that aren't in the repository are usually found at the developer's web site or as an attachment to a message in the MODX Forums. In rare cases, problems in the configuration of your platform can prevent the packages in the repository from being downloaded in Package Manager.

These packages can still be installed through Package Management, but you have to put them in place manually. To install them, just download the .ZIP file from **http://modx.com/extras** and FTP it to the **core/packages/** directory at your site.

Then go to **System → Package Management**. Click on "Add New Package," and then select "Search Locally for Packages." Click on "Next," and then click on the "Yes" button. You should now see the package in the grid. Right-click on it, and install it as you would any other package.

Add-ons With No Transport Package

Add-ons with no transport package have to be installed the old-fashioned way. Download them, and extract everything in the .ZIP file. Look for a **readme.txt** file describing how to install the add-on. If you don't find one, look for comments in the main **.php** file for the add-on describing how to install and use it. Usually, it involves creating new elements and pasting the code from the downloaded files into them.

If the add-on isn't listed as supporting MODX Revolution, it may still work as long as you use the correct Revolution tags. If not, you can install it and try to rewrite it to work with Revolution, but it's a good idea to back up your site first or install it in a test site in case the add-on causes any trouble with the site.

Creating Property Sets

We covered this earlier in the book, so this is a quick review. Many MODX Revolution add-ons have default properties that control how the add-on works. These can be modified in the Properties tab of the Create/Edit panel when editing the element.

The problem with editing the default properties is that they may be overwritten and set back to their defaults when you upgrade or reinstall the add-on. The solution is to create a new property set of your own and use that for the element. This is most common with snippets, so we'll use that for our example. You might want to stick a bookmark in this page and the installation page above because you'll be using these techniques for many of the snippets covered in this chapter.

After you've downloaded and installed a snippet, right-click on it in the Element tree, and select "Edit Snippet." Click on the "Properties" tab. You should see the default properties. If there aren't any, you don't need to do anything more, and you can skip this section.

Click on "Add Property Set." You need to name the property set, and, if you always use a name like the following, it will save you some time (put the actual name of the snippet in place of *Snippetname*):

My*Snippetname*Props

Click on the "Save Property Set" button. Now you're free to edit any of the properties without worrying about them being overwritten. When you come back to edit them later, be sure to switch to your property set by selecting it in the drop-down list at the upper left of the Properties grid rather than editing the default properties. The default properties are locked to remind you to do this. Unless you are developing a new add-on, you should never need to unlock the default properties except to examine their descriptions.

There is one last critical point to make here. In order for MODX to use your property set, you need to put a reference to it in any tag referring to the element:

```
[[SnippetName@MySnippenameProps]]
```

If you forget, MODX will use the default properties, any changes you made to properties in your set will be ignored, and you'll wonder why your changes have no effect. Remember that for any properties in your set that you don't change from their default values, the default properties' values will still be available in the snippet.

Creating an FAQ Page with EZfaq

Installing EZfaq

Go to **System → Package Management**, and click on the "Download Extras" button. Find the latest version of EZfaq (it should be under "Content"). Expand the tree to show the current version of EZfaq, and select it. Click on the "Download" button and wait for it to change to "Downloaded." You can get back to the Package Management grid by clicking on the "Finish" button at the lower left.

 If you prefer, you can download all the snippets used in this chapter before clicking on the "Finish" button: EZfaq, SPForm, Breadcrumbs, Wayfinder, get-Resources, and FormIt.

The Package Management grid should now show EZfaq.

Click on the "Install" button to install EZfaq. Click past the License and Readme sections. Be sure to check the checkbox to install the sample FAQ page.

You should see the installation console, which will show progress messages as it installs the EZfaq package. Click on the "OK" button when the install finishes.

When you go to the "Elements" tab of the tree, you should see EZfaq in the snippet section. At this time, it has no default properties (though it may by the time you read this). If they've been added, you can either create a new property set as described above or just use the properties described below in the snippet tag to override the default values.

On the Resources tab, you should see two new resources. FAQ and (as a child under it) FAQ Content.

If you look at the FAQ resource, you should see the snippet tag that calls the EZfaq snippet. The **&docID** property should be set to the Resource ID of the FAQ Content page. Check to make sure it is, and modify the property value if it isn't.

If you right-click on the *FAQ* resource and select "Preview," you'll see a bare-bones FAQ page with a couple of questions and answers along with buttons to show and hide all the answers.

 If you haven't created a template yet, your FAQ page will be unstyled and quite ugly and the buttons won't work. EZfaq uses the default template, and MODX inserts the CSS and JavaScript for the FAQ page into the template. It can't do that unless you have a default template for the site.

You can change the fields at the top of the FAQ resource (e.g., Title, Longtitle, etc.), but the Resource Content field should generally be left alone except to add properties to the snippet tag. The exception would be if you want to create multiple FAQ pages. In that case, you'd want to duplicate the FAQ and FAQ Content pages and change the **&docID** property on the new ones to the appropriate value (pointing to the FAQ Content resource for that FAQ). Content should always be added in the FAQ Content resource, not the FAQ resource. The FAQ Content resource should remain unpublished and hidden from menus because it's simply a place to store the data and its content is always shown through the FAQ resource. When viewed directly, the FAQ Content resource would be quite ugly.

Adding Your Own Content

Using your own content on the FAQ Content page is very simple. You just edit the FAQ Content resource. All questions must start with Q: and all answers with A:. Don't put a space after the tokens. The snippet will insert one for you. You can have as many questions and answers as you like, but make sure that every question is followed by exactly one answer.

 Only the **content** field of the FAQ Content resource is used. Changing any of the other fields will have no effect. If you want to schedule publication, for example, set the Publish Date on the FAQ resource instead.

White space between the questions is ignored, so you can format them any way you like, but don't use any carriage returns within a question or answer. If you want to separate paragraphs, you can insert <p> or <br> tags. You can also use <b>, <strong>, <i>, <em>, and <pre> tags for formatting. Most other (X)HTML tags will work as well (e.g., links and image tags).

In some cases, you may want to place content in between the question and answer pairs. For example, you might want to put a set of links to sections of the FAQ at the top and anchors and/or section headings at the top of each section. Any content above the first Q: will be rendered at the top. For the section headings/anchors, use Extra: at the beginning of those lines. They will be inserted outside of the question and answer pairs.

 Be careful to use Extra: and not EXTRA:. EXTRA: ends with A: and that will confuse the snippet when it parses the content.

At the end of the FAQ content, you can add Q:FAQ-END. That line and any content below that point will be ignored. It's a good place to put notes to yourself or work in progress that you plan to add to the FAQ later.

Styling the FAQ Page

What the FAQ page looks like is controlled in two ways: adding properties to the EZfaq snippet tag and editing the CSS file.

The optional properties shown below can be added to the snippet tag to control the look of the FAQ page.

&showHideAllOption — Display the show/hide all buttons. Default: true.

&statusOpenHTML — Symbol to put next to open topics (can be an image URL). Default: [-].

&statusClosedHTML — Symbol to put next to closed topics (can be an image URL). Default: [+]

&openColor — Color for open questions (name or hex value #ffffff). Default: red

&closedColor — Color for closed questions (name or hex value #ffffff). Default: black

&setPersist — Does open state persist across visits/reloads. Default: true

&collapsePrevious — If set, only one answer can be open at a time. Default: true.

&defaultExpanded — Expand answers n1 through n2 (`0,1` expands items 1 through 2) when page is opened. Default: no.

&cssPath — Path to CSS file. Set to `` for no CSS file. Default: **assets/components/ezfaq/ezfaq.css**.

&faqPath — Path to the EZfaq directory. Default: **/assets/components/ezfaq**.

The default CSS file can be found here:

assets/components/ezfaq/ezfaq.css

You can edit it to control the fonts, colors, and background colors of the various parts of the FAQ page. The file is relatively short, and it contains comments explaining what each section controls.

Creating a Contact Page with SPForm

SPForm provides a simple, spam-proof contact form for your site. It's easy to install and user and the contact form should work as soon as you finish installing SPForm (assuming that your mail service works). SPForm is not a good choice, however, if you need to customize the fields of the form. SPForm provides standard contact-form fields and will allow you to have a drop-down list of recipients to sent message to, but if you need a custom contact form, FormIt is a much better choice, though FormIt is more difficult to install and configure. We'll discuss FormIt later in this chapter.

Installing SPForm

Go to **System → Package Management**, and click on the "Download Extras" button. Download and install SPForm using the method described at the beginning of this chapter. During the install, enter the email address you would like SPForm to send mail to (you'll be able to edit it later, if necessary).

Create a new property set for both the SPForm and SPFResponse snippets as described at the beginning of this chapter.

Working with SPForm

In this section, we'll discuss how to test, customize, and style the contact form. Before going into detail, let's look first at an overview of SPForm.

How SPForm Works

When a site visitor requests the Contact page, the following steps occur:

- MODX gets the template and begins replacing the tags on the page.

- When the SPForm snippet tag is encountered, the snippet is executed.

- The snippet checks the properties of the snippet to set various options.

- If CAPTCHA is turned on, the snippet adds the spfcaptchaTpl chunk to the output and sets the placeholders used by the chunk. The CAPTCHA plugin must be installed for this to work.

- The snippet then adds the spformTpl chunk to the output and sets the placeholders for it based on the options previously set for the snippet.

- After the snippet returns its output, the finished page is rendered and sent to the browser where the user sees the complete form.

- The user fills in the form and clicks on submit.

- Some JavaScript code validates certain fields while the form is still on the screen. Once the form passes the JS validation, the form is reposted, and the snippet executes again.

- The snippet sees that this is a repost and does some further validation. If something is still wrong, it inserts the spformprocTpl chunk (used as the error page) and sets the placeholders used on that page. It may also log some information if certain logging options are set. The error page is then sent to the browser.

- If the snippet doesn't see any problems on the repost, it sends the email, and forwards the user to the Thank You page where another snippet inserts the spfresponseTpl chunk and sets any placeholders it uses.

 SPForm is designed to be a really simple, single-purpose contact form. It has many spam-proofing options and will send email to multiple recipients, but it is not designed to accept extra fields. You can rename existing fields and/or change their prompts, but you would have to modify the snippet's code to add extra fields in the form. Use the FormIt snippet if you need a more complex form.

Testing SPForm

Once the form is installed, you should have a working contact form on the site. In the resource tree, find the resource called "Contact." Right-click on it, and select preview. You should see the contact form, and it should work to send email to the address you entered during the install. You should end up on the Thank You page.

If everything looks good but no email is sent (and you know the email address you entered is correct), the most likely problem is that your host has the mail() function turned off or your localhost install has no mail server. See the section below on using SMTP with SPForm.

Editing the Contact Resource

There are a limited number of things you can do to change the Contact resource. One thing you should not do here is change the Resource Content field except to edit the SPForm tag. All the content for the contact form comes from other places that we'll discuss below.

What you can do here is edit the other fields such as Title, Long Title, Alias, Menu Title, and Publish Date to control the appearance of menus, URLs, headings, etc. The effect of these changes will depend, to some extent, on the site's default template. If there's no [[*longtitle]] tag in the template, for example, changing the Long Title field won't have any effect.

Editing the Tpl Chunks and CSS File

Most of the content of the contact form is contained in the SPFormTpl chunks described above. If you go to the "Elements" tab, expand the Chunks section and then the SPForm folder, you'll see the four Tpl chunks involved:

spformTpl — Contains most of the content of the form itself.

spfcaptchaTpl — Contains the content of the CAPTCHA image and prompts.

spformprocTpl — Contains the content of the error/validation screen.

spfresponseTpl — Contains the content of the Thank You page.

Here is the code contained in the SPFormTpl chunk:

```
<!-- Code for the spformTpl Chunk ->
<div id="spf_form">

    <form action="[[~[[*id]]]]" method="post"
        onsubmit="return checkform(this);">
      [[+spf-use-mouse-or-keyboard1]]
      [[+spf-use-mouse-or-keyboard2]]
      [[+spf-use-hidden-field]]
      [[+spf-use-timer]]
      [[+spf-cookie-message]]
      <div class="spf_recipient">[[+spf-recipient]]</div>
```

```
    <div class="spf_input_pair">
       <span class="spf_block_prompt"> [[+spf-name-prompt]]: </span>
       <span class= "spf_normal_input">
          <input type="text" id="name" name="name" size="30" />
       </span>
    </div>
    <div class="spf_input_pair">
       <span class="spf_block_prompt"> [[+spf-email-prompt]]: </span>
       <span class="spf_normal_input">
          <input type= "text" id="email" name="email" size="30" />
       </span>
    </div>
    <div class="spf_input_pair">
       <span class="spf_block_prompt"> [[+spf-subject-prompt]]: </span>
       <span class="spf_normal_input">
          <input type="text" id="subject" name="subject" size="30" />
       </span><br />
    </div>
    [[+spf-captcha-stuff]]
    <div class="spf_block_prompt">[[+spf-comments-prompt]]:</div>
    <div class="spf_textarea">
       <textarea name="comments" rows="[[+spf-text-rows]]"
          cols="[[+spf-text-cols]]">
       </textarea>
    </div>
    <div class="spf_buttons">
       <input type="submit" name="s" value="[[+spf-submit]]" /> 
       [[+spf-reset]]
    </div>
  </form>
</div>
```

If you look closely at the code above, you'll see that it contains no actual content at all. There is nothing there but placeholders and (X)HTML code. This is a "best practices" example for MODX in which content and display code are completely separated.

Altering the chunk changes the format for displaying the content but not the content itself. In fact, it's unlikely that you would need to alter the chunk. Editing the CSS file or changing the SPForm options will accomplish most changes you would want to make.

Let's look at some of the code in the chunk.

The [[~[[*id]]]] tag at the beginning of the form simply sets the link for the form to post back to itself. This is a MODX resource tag inside a MODX link tag. The inner tag is replaced by the Resource ID of the Contact page, and then the outer link is replaced by the URL of the Contact page.

```
<span class="spf_block_prompt">
```

The span tag above surrounds the prompts and input fields for each line of the form. The CSS file displays the prompt and the input field on different lines. To display each pair on a single line, you could edit the CSS file, but the CSS file already contains a class called spf_inline_prompt. Changing spf_block_prompt to spf_inline_prompt throughout the chunk will display each prompt and input field on the same line.

All the other MODX tags in the chunk are placeholder tags. They are replaced by the values for them set in the snippet. Many of them may be empty, depending on the current setting of the snippet's options. The tags for unused options could be removed, but there is no harm in leaving them there since they will produce no output.

The default CSS file is called spform.css and can be found here:

```
/assets/components/spform/css
```

You can use a different CSS form by adding the following property to the snippet tag:

```
&spfCssPath=`path_to_css_file`
```

You can also add the SPForm CSS code to your main CSS file and tell SPForm not to load any CSS by using this property instead:

```
&spfCssPath=`""`
```

If you look at the other SPForm Tpl chunks, you will see that they are similar to the one above.

Where is the content?

There is definitely content when you look at the Contact form. Where does it come from?

You might think that it is in the SPForm snippet, but that would violate the separation of code and content. In fact, it is in the SPForm lexicon file:

```
core/components/spform/lexicon/en/default.inc.php
```

If you want to change some of the specific language strings, you could edit the file, but a better way is to edit the entries in the grid at **System → Lexicon Management**. Select the "spform" namespace in the drop-down list at the top left, then select the "default" topic in the Topic drop-down list (you may need to do this even if it already says "default"). You can edit any of the lexicon entries here by double-clicking on the "Value" field. The ones you've altered will show up in green. Values entered here will override those in the language file. They will be saved in the MODX database, and they will survive any upgrades of MODX or SPForm.

If you want to translate SPForm to another language, you could create all the alternate entries in the grid, but you shouldn't. A better method is to duplicate the file itself, and then translate the values in the duplicate file. To create a French language version, for example, copy the file

```
core/components/spform/lexicon/en/default.inc.php
```

to

```
core/components/spform/lexicon/fr/default.inc.php
```

Then, translate all the language strings in the new file. When French is specified as the Manager language, MODX will automatically use the French language file. Doing it this way makes the French language file easy to move to other sites. It also lets you share the French language file with other users of MODX who might need it.

Setting SPForm's Options

The options for SPForm can be set using properties in the snippet tag, but in MODX Revolution, it's much easier and more reliable to set them in the properties section of the two snippets (SPForm and SPFResponse).

Before changing any of the properties, be sure that you've created new property sets for each snippet (*MySPFormProps* and *MySPFResponseProps*) as described at the beginning of this chapter. Edit the Contact form resource, and change the snippet tag so it looks like this:

```
[[!SPForm@MySPFormProps]]
```

This tells MODX that you want it to use a property set called *MySPFormProps* with the snippet.

Now edit the "Thank You" resource (it's a child of the Contact resource) so that the snippet tag looks like this:

```
[[!SPFResponse@MySPFResponseProps]]
```

To see the SPForm options, edit the SPForm snippet, and click on the "Properties" tab. The grid will show all of the snippet's default properties. The default properties are locked, and we're going to leave them that way.

Use the drop-down box at the upper left of the grid to select the "MySPFormProps" property set. Now you're looking at your own property set. It appears to contain all the default properties, but it really doesn't. MODX will use the default properties for any properties you don't alter in your property set. In the grid, the default properties "show through" for convenience even though they're not really part of your property set. If that's confusing, you might want to review the section on property sets earlier in the book.

You can click on the plus sign next to each property to see a description of what it is for and/or how it is used.

Many of the properties control spam-proofing options that can be turned off or on. Try re-setting a few of them by double clicking on the "Value" field or by right-clicking on the property and selecting "Update Property." Notice that as you change them, the color of the property changes to green (this may not happen until after you save the property set). The green color indicates properties that are actually in your property set.

You can always set them back to their default values by clicking on "Revert All to Default" at the top of the grid.

We're not going to cover all the properties here because most of them are well documented in the grid, but let's look at some that are often changed.

The recipientArray property at the top of the grid controls what is shown in the TO: section of the contact form and what addresses the form will send email to. By default, the form has only a single recipient called Webmaster with whatever address you entered during the install. Nothing is shown in the form because the *showSingleRecipientTo* property further down in the form is set to No. This tells SPForm not to show anything if there is only one recipient.

To have multiple recipients, change the *recipientArray* property to list the recipients, separated by commas. Each recipient should be in this form:

```
recipient:email
```

So you might have this for your *recipientArray* value:

```
Webmaster:you@yourdoman.com,Support:support@yourdomain.com
```

With this setting, the form will show a drop-down list with Webmaster and Support. The email addresses will never show in the form or in the source code of the page, so spam-bots can't harvest them. You can have as many addresses as you like as long as the property is formatted correctly.

Check the *formProcALLowedReferers* property. It should have been set to your domain (and your domain preceded by www.) during the install.

Because hosts often have the mail() function disabled, it is often necessary to use SMTP to send mail successfully with SPForm. Although SPForm has properties that allow you to use SMTP to send the mail, they are usually unnecessary in MODX Revolution because you can now set SMTP system settings that force MODX to use SMTP by default to send mail.

The only reason to use SPForm's SMTP properties is if you want SPForm to use a different SMTP server than the one set in the MODX SMTP system settings.

Note that if SMTP is enabled in the system settings, you should not use the SPForm SMTP options. You want to let MODX handle all the SMTP operations.

Some of the properties control which events are logged in the MODX error log. Use these with caution because spam-bots may be hitting your form quite often, and your error log can get very large very quickly.

There are also some settable properties attached to the SPFResponse snippet. The only one you're likely to change is the *takeMeBack* property. By default, the Thank You page shows a link that takes the user back to the page they were on before jumping to the Contact page. The link depends on the $_SERVER['HTTP_REFERER'] variable which some servers delete.

If the "Take Me Back" links don't work on your site, you'll want to set the *takeMeBack* property to *No*, which will prevent the links from showing. If you change this, you may want to create a property set for the SPFResponse snippet as we did above for the SPForm snippet or use a snippet property in the tag to turn off the option so that your change won't be overwritten when upgrading the SPForm package:

```
&takeMeBack=`0`
```

One last configuration option for SPForm involves banning people from using the form by email address, domain name, or IP number. This is not done with the snippet properties but by editing the spfBanlist chunk. Comments in the chunk describe the format used.

Using Breadcrumbs to Show the Current Path

Many web sites offer breadcrumbs as a convenience to the user. Some simple sites use breadcrumbs instead of a menu. The breadcrumbs appear on a single line, usually near the top of the screen, and they show each page in the hierarchy of pages leading to the current page as a link to that page.

The trail of breadcrumbs is based on the Resource tree, and it's important to remember that it shows the path to the current page but not necessarily the path that the user took to get there.

For example, the Resource tree for an auto dealership might look like this:

```
Home
      Inventory
              New
              Used
      Service
      Directions
```

A user visiting the Used Vehicles page might see breadcrumbs like this:

```
Home >> Inventory >> Used
```

On the Service page, the breadcrumbs might look like this:

```
Home >> Service
```

In both cases, the user could click on any page in the breadcrumbs to jump to that page.

Installing Breadcrumbs

Download and install the Breadcrumbs snippet. At this writing, it has no default properties, so there's no need to create a property set. If default properties have been added, you can either create a new property set as described at the beginning of this chapter or just use the properties listed here in the snippet tag. If you create new properties, be sure to refer to them in the snippet tag.

The Breadcrumbs snippet is very simple, and once you've downloaded and installed it using the method described at the beginning of this chapter, all you need to do is put the following snippet tag in your template where you want the breadcrumbs to appear:

```
[[!Breadcrumbs]]
```

If you create a property set, use this tag:

```
[[!Breadcrumbs@MyBreadcrumbsProps]]]
```

By default, the snippet does not show breadcrumbs on the Home page, but you can change that.

Breadcrumbs Properties

Here are the options that can be set using properties in the snippet tag (or on the Properties tab of the snippet if they have been added there):

&homePageId — Sets the Home page's ID. Defaults to the **site_start** system setting. Useful for having different breadcrumbs in different sections of the site.

&maxCrumbs — Maximum number of crumbs shown. Default is 100.

&maxDelimiter — The string that will show if **&maxCrumbs** is exceeded. Default is . . ..

&pathThruUnPub — Default is 1. Set to 0 to hide unpublished documents.

&respectHidemenu — Default is 1. Set to 0 to show resources with "Hide From Menus" checked.

&showHomeCrumb — Default is 1. Set to 0 to hide the home crumb.

&showCrumbsAtHome — Default is 0. Set to 1 to show crumbs on the Home page.

&showCurrentCrumb — Default is 1. Set to 0 to hide crumb for the current page.

&currentAsLink — Default is 1, which shows the crumb for the current page as a link. Set to 0 to show it as plain text.

&crumbSeparator — String shown between crumbs. Default is >>.

&homeCrumbTitle — Sets name of home crumb. Default is Home.

&homeCrumbDescription — Text shown when the user hovers over the home crumb. Default is $homeCrumbTitle (property just above).

&titleField — Field used for crumbs other than the home crumb. Default is **pagetitle**.

&descField — Field shown when hovering over non-home crumbs. Default is **description**. If **description** is empty, **&titleField** (property above) is shown. If **&titleField** is empty, **&pagetitle** is shown.

Breadcrumbs CSS

There is no CSS file included with the Breadcrumbs snippet. You can create one and put a reference to it in your template, or you can add styling using the following class names in your main CSS file:

.B_crumbBox — Class of span surrounding the entire breadcrumb snippet output.

.B_hideCrumb — Class of span that surrounds the ellipsis (. . .) if there are more crumbs than the **&maxCrumbs** limit.

.B_currentCrumb — Class for <a> tag or span surrounding the current crumb.

.B_firstCrumb — Class of span surrounding the first crumb (whether it is the home crumb or not).

.B_lastCrumb — Class of span surrounding last crumb (whether it is the current page or not).

.B_crumb — Class given to each <a> tag around all crumbs other than home crumb or hidden crumb.

.B_homeCrumb — Class of the home crumb.

Here's a sample of Breadcrumbs output (» is rendered as >>, which is the default separator character):

```
<span class="B_crumbBox">
    <span class="B_firstCrumb">
        <a class="B_homeCrumb" href="/site.com" title="Home">Home</a>
    </span>
    &raquo;
    <span class= "B_crumb">
        <a class="B_crumb" href="/site.com/inventory.html"
            title="Inventory">Inventory</a> &raquo;
    </span>
    <span class=" B_lastCrumb">
        <a class="B_crumb" href="site.com/inventory/used.html"
            title="Used Vehicles">Used Vehicles</a>
    </span>
</span>
```

The following CSS example shows the breadcrumbs with a white background, the separators in black, visited links in purple, and other links in blue. The last crumb is underlined, and hover turns the background of any crumb to gray:

```
.B_crumbBox {
    font-family:Arial, Verdana, Helvetica, sans-serif;
    color:#000;
    background-color:#FFF;
}
.B_crumbBox a:link {
    color:navy;
    background-color:#FFF;
}
```

```
.B_crumbBox a:visited {
    color:purple;
    background-color:#FFF;
}
.B_crumbBox a:hover {
    background-color:#DDD;
}
.B_lastCrumb a, .B_lastCrumb a:visited {
  text-decoration: underline;
}
```

Using Wayfinder to Create a Menu

Wayfinder is a MODX snippet that is designed to produce site menus based on the Resource tree (or parts of it). Wayfinder can produce anything from simple list menus to complex drop-down fly-out menus or JavaScript sliding accordion menus. The odds are that if you have seen a menu on a web site, it can be done with Wayfinder.

The beauty of Wayfinder is that when you create, delete, publish, and unpublish pages on the site, Wayfinder automatically adjusts the menu to reflect the changes. Once you have Wayfinder producing the menu you want, you never have to touch it again. Better yet, you can completely restyle any Wayfinder menu just by editing the Wayfinder CSS file and/or one or two Tpl chunks.

Wayfinder can also be used to produce tables, event listings, and all kinds of other things. Those are beyond the scope of this book, however. We'll just be looking at menus here.

As we discuss Wayfinder menus, we'll only be scratching the surface of Wayfinder, which is a very powerful snippet. There is, in fact, a whole book on Wayfinder by MODX community member Kongondo: *The (almost) complete guide to creating menus in MODX using Wayfinder*. By the time you read this, it may be published and available at **http://modx.com**. If not, you should be able to find the .PDF version of it on the Web.

In the following sections, we'll look at how to construct and style a Wayfinder menu. We'll see how to customize the menu using Wayfinder properties, placeholders, Tpl chunks, and CSS. At the end of this chapter, there is a quick reference guide to Wayfinder properties and placeholders.

Before we can use Wayfinder, however, we need documents to show in our menu.

Preparing to Use Wayfinder

Download and install the current version of Wayfinder using the method described at the beginning of this chapter.

By now, you should have a template that uses the **pagetitle**, **longtitle**, and **content** fields that you can attach as the template for the pages we're going to create here. If not, go back to the Templates chapter (Chapter 5) and create one.

Before we can create a menu, we need some resources to show in it. We're going to want all our documents published at first. Before creating any documents, go to **System → System Settings**, and change the setting for "Published default" to Yes (type *Published* in the "Filter" box to find it). While you're there, make sure that the template you want to use for these pages is set as the default template (type "default" in the filter box to find it). Look at the Templates section of the Element tree to see the ID of the template, and set the Default Template setting to that number.

Right-click in the Resource tree, and create a set of documents with the structure shown in the tree below. Create the top one first by right-clicking on the "web" icon in the tree. Then you can create each new document by right-clicking on its parent and selecting "Create" and then "Create a Document Here."

 After creating the first document (*MODX Motors*), click and drag it to the top of the Resource tree. That will make it easier to find as you make the rest. You can always drag it somewhere else later if you need to.

There's an alternate method that might be somewhat faster, although it can be a little more confusing. This alternate method is handy when you're creating a number of resources or elements at the same time. When you create the first page (or any other page), select the icon in the upper-right corner with the little plus sign (the left one of the three; it shows "Add another if you hover the mouse over it). Once the "Add another" button is selected, after you save each document, you'll see a new form for creating another one. Be sure to set the correct parent for each document by clicking on the drop-down arrow next to "Parent Resource" then on the parent before saving it (when you use the other method, this is set for you).

You only need to click on the icon once to set it. When you do the last page, be sure to click on the middle icon (Continue Editing) before saving it. Otherwise, every time you save a document, you'll see a new empty form. If that happens, click on "Cancel," edit any document, click on the middle icon, and save the document (you'll have to make some minor change to the document in order to be able to save it).

 At this writing, Add Another carries over to other resources and elements once it is set. If you use it, there's a good chance that you'll forget to change it when you're done. Later, you'll save a resource or element and wonder why you're looking at a blank form after the save.

Use the terms below for the Title field. In the Long Title field, put the title followed by the word "Page" for now. If you were creating a real site, you might also fill in the Menu Title and Alias fields, but leave them blank for now. If you like, you can put a little content in the Resource Content field for each page.

Create these pages:

```
MODX Motors

        Hours and Directions

        Sales

                Sales Team

                        Joe Blow

                        Jane Doe

                        Richard Roe

                Inventory

                        New

                        Used

        Service and Parts

                Parts

                Service

                Specials
```

When you've created all the pages, take a look at the Resource tree to make sure that they are all in the right places. If not, just click and drag them to the proper location (you could also edit them and set the correct parent).

Make a note of the Resource ID of the MODX Motors page (in parentheses next to the name). Now, go to the "Elements" tab, expand the "Templates" section if necessary, and edit your default template. Add the following tag just above the [[*longtitle]] tag (replace *12* with the actual Resource ID of the MODX Motors page):

```
[[!Wayfinder? &startId=`12`]]
```

Now preview your MODX Motors page. You should see the menu for all the pages you created at the top of the page, rendered as an unordered list of links. The submenus should be indented. If you click on any link, it should take you to that page. All the pages will show the menu at the top because the Wayfinder tag is in your template.

Congratulations. You've just created your first Wayfinder menu. You can add or delete pages anywhere under the MODX Motors page, and the menu will always be accurate. The menu will only show published pages (though you can change this using Wayfinder properties). If you'd like to see the (X)HTML code that Wayfinder creates by default, do a "View Source" in your browser while viewing one of the pages. You can see that, in addition to the list of links, Wayfinder has created a number of classes you can use to style the menu with CSS.

Note that if all users will see the same menu, you can make the Wayfinder call cached by removing the exclamation point and calling it like this:

```
[[Wayfinder? &startId=`12`]]
```

Calling Wayfinder cached will make your menus load faster because they will come from the site cache rather than the database. If different users will see a different menu depending on their roles, however, Wayfinder must be called uncached (with the exclamation point). If you hide certain resources from some user groups by placing them in protected resource groups, Wayfinder needs to calculate which items to show every time it is called rather than just pulling the content from the site cache.

Styling the Wayfinder Menu

By default, Wayfinder only assigns classes to the <li> items. At each level of the menu, the first item gets the class "first," and the last item gets the class "last." The current page also gets the class "active." Any middle items get no class at all unless they refer to the current page, in which case they get the "active" class.

If you use a Tpl chunk to wrap the whole menu in a `<div>` with a specified class, you can then use CSS to style just the `<li>` items in the menu. You can also tell Wayfinder which classes to use for the various parts of the menu by using specific properties. Here are the properties that assign classes to menu parts. The first two default to `first` and `last`. The rest are not inserted into the output unless set:

&firstClass — Class applied to the first item at each level.

&lastClass — Class applied to the last item at each level.

&hereClass — Class applied to the current page and all its ancestors up the tree.

&selfClass — Class applied just to the current page.

&parentClass — Class applied to each item that has children.

&rowClass — Class applied to every item in the menu.

&levelClass — Class applied to every item, but with the level number of that item appended.

&outerClass — Class applied to the outerTpl container.

&innerClass — Class applied to the innerTpl container.

&webLinkClass — Class applied to any item that is a link.

Injecting CSS and JS

There are two Wayfinder properties that let you specify a chunk containing CSS or JavaScript:

&cssTpl — The CSS code in the named chunk will be injected into the `<head>` section of the page.

&jsTpl — The JS code in the named chunk will be injected into the `<head>` section of the page.

Modifying the Wayfinder Menu

Wayfinder Menus can be modified in a variety of ways. You can use the "Hide From Menus" checkbox, you can create and edit Tpl chunks for the various parts of the menu (using Wayfinder placeholders), and you can set Wayfinder properties. In the following sections, we'll look at how to use those various methods.

Using the "Hide From Menus" Checkbox

When you unpublish a document, it will disappear from any Wayfinder menus. What if we want the page published but not shown in a menu? Simply edit the page, check the "Hide From Menus" checkbox, and save it.

Let's imagine that Joe Blow's personal page will be shown only when people click on his picture on a page showing a gallery of salespeople. The page has to be published so people can see it, but we don't want it in any menus. Edit his page. Check the "Hide From Menus" checkbox, and save the page.

Now preview any of the pages under MODX Motors. His link should be missing from the menu. You can put it back by unchecking the "Hide From Menus" checkbox on his page and saving it. Note that his page is still there, and any external links or bookmarks that link to it will still work. To make it unavailable, you'd need to uncheck the "Published" checkbox. That will take it out of the menu and make it unavailable to site visitors. You could also protect it with MODX security permissions.

Using Wayfinder Tpl Chunks

We've seen Tpl chunks at several points earlier in the book. In Wayfinder, you specify the Tpl chunks to use for the menu. They are optional, and if you don't specify any, you'll get the default unordered list format we saw for the MODX Motors page above.

Some of the Wayfinder options may seem like overkill, and not all are needed for every menu. Remember, though, that you might want to have more than one Wayfinder menu on a page. By assigning specific Tpl chunks and classes in the Wayfinder tag, each menu can have a completely different style.

All Wayfinder Tpl chunks should contain a [+wf.wrapper+] tag. That tag tells Wayfinder where to put all the processed items that go inside the current Tpl. Let's create a standard drop-down fly-out menu for our MODX Motors site. Note that this menu will not work with IE6. If you need IE6 compatibility, you need a separate IE6 CSS file and IE conditional comments in some of the Tpl chunks. See the Wayfinder documentation for details.

First, create the following five Tpl chunks. Use the names and code below for the five chunks:

```
<!-- WayfinderOuter Chunk ->
<div[[+wf.classes]]>
    <ul>
        [[+wf.wrapper]]
    </ul>
</div>
```

```
<!-- WayfinderInner Chunk ->
<ul>
    [[+wf.wrapper]]
</ul>


<!-- WayfinderRow Chunk ->
<li[[+wf.classes]]><a href="[[+wf.link]]" title="[[+wf.title]]">[[+wf.
linktext]]</a>[[+wf.wrapper]]</li>


<!-- WayfinderParentRow Chunk ->
<li><a [[+wf.classes]] href="[[+wf.link]]" title="[[+wf.title]]">[[+wf.
linktext]]</a>[[+wf.wrapper]]</li>


<!-- WayfinderCss Chunk ->
<link rel="stylesheet" media="all" type="text/css" href="assets/components/
wayfinder/examples/cssplay/dropdown.css" />
```

Now change the Wayfinder tag in your template to look like this:

```
[[!Wayfinder?
    &startId=`0`
    &outerTpl=`WayfinderOuter`
    &innerTpl=`WayfinderInner`
    &parentRowTpl=`WayfinderParentRow`
    &rowTpl=`WayfinderRow`
    &cssTpl=`WayfinderCss`
    &outerClass=`menu`
    &parentClass=`hide`
]]
```

If you preview your MODX Motors page, you should see a nicely styled drop-down menu.

 If you are used to working with an earlier version of MODX, be careful when entering the tags above. They must be MODX Revolution tags, which all start with [[and end with]].

Let's look at some of the placeholders used in the Tpl chunks above:

[[+wf.wrapper]] — Stands for all items that will be inserted inside the current Tpl chunk.

[[+wf.classes]] — Will be replaced by the classes specified in the Wayfinder class properties.

[[+wf.title]] — The contents of each resource's **pagetitle** field will go here.

[[+wf.link]] — The URL of each resource will go here.

[[+wf.linktext]] — The text the user clicks on to reach the resource will go here.

The following placeholders are available for use in the inner Tpl chunks (rowTpl, parentRowTpl, parentRowHereTpl, hereTpl, innerRowTpl, innerHereTpl, activeParentRowTpl, categoryFoldersTpl, and startItemTpl):

[[+wf.classes]] — Inserts class names with `class=" "`.

[[+wf.classnames]] — Inserts the class names without `class=" ")`.

[[+wf.link]] — The link URL.

[[+wf.title]] — The resource's Title field.

[[+wf.linktext]] — Text for the user to click on.

[[+wf.wrapper]] — Placeholder for all items placed inside the current Tpl chunk.

[[+wf.id]] — Inserts the unique ID specified in the **&id** property.

[[+wf.attributes]] — Inserts link attributes.

[[+wf.docid]] — Inserts the Resource ID for the current item.

[[+wf.subitemcount]] — Inserts the number of items in a folder. **&showSubDocCount** must be set to `true`.

[[+wf.description]] — Inserts the resource's **description** field.

[[+wf.introtext]] — Inserts the resource's **introtext** field.

Wayfinder can create just about any kind of menu given the appropriate Tpl chunks and CSS or JS code. There are a number of sites on the Web containing Wayfinder menu examples. You can also adapt almost any kind of menu to work in Wayfinder. Fisheye menus, expanding and animated menus, and even circular menus can all be done with Wayfinder.

Using Wayfinder Properties

In the example above, we controlled Wayfinder with properties in the snippet tag. We could also use one or more property sets to do the same thing.

As we've seen with some other snippets in this chapter, Wayfinder has a set of default properties that we don't want to be overwritten when we upgrade Wayfinder. To avoid that, we need to create our own property set. Create a new property set on the Properties tab of the Wayfinder snippet (call it *MyWayfinderProps*) using the method described at the beginning of this chapter. Change the beginning of the Wayfinder tag in your template to look like this:

```
[[!Wayfinder@MyWayfinderProps? . . .]]
```

This won't have any effect until we change some of the properties because Wayfinder was already using the default properties. As always, leave the default properties locked, and always edit your MyWayfinderProps property set.

Take a look at the properties (be sure you're looking at your property set rather than the default properties). The properties we described above can be set here. Remember that any property set you specify in the snippet tag will override the default properties. Remember, too, that properties sent in the snippet tag will take precedence over all the others, so if you want to use a property set, you need to remove the properties from the snippet tag. Select your property set in the drop-down list at the top of the grid on the Wayfinder snippet's Properties tab. This won't have any effect until we change some of the properties because Wayfinder was already using the default properties. As always, leave the default properties locked, and always edit your MyWayfinderProps property set. Select your property set in the drop-down list at the top of the grid on the Wayfinder snippet's Properties tab.

Here are some additional properties that control the Wayfinder snippet:

&level — Controls the number of levels shown in the menu. If you set it to 1, for example, you'll only see the three main sections in the menu. Default is 0, which shows all levels.

&includeDocs — Lets you specify a comma-separated list of resources to include in the menu. Only those resources will be shown, and they must be below the **&startId** document. Resources that are below a non-shown resource in the tree won't be shown.

&excludeDocs — Lets you specify a comma-separated list of resources to hide from the list. Resources below the hidden resources in the tree also won't be shown.

&ph — Forces Wayfinder to store the complete menu in the placeholder named in the property rather than placing it where the Wayfinder tag is. This lets you have multiple copies of a Wayfinder menu on the same page with a single Wayfinder tag. Example:

&ph=`MyMenu`

Using the property above in the Wayfinder tag will put the menu wherever the [[+MyMenu]] placeholder tag appears. By putting the placeholder tag in the Resource Content field of a document (and the Wayfinder tag with the **&ph** property in the template), for example, you can put the menu in different places on different pages.

&debug — Turns on Wayfinder debugging. If this is set to Yes, Wayfinder will output an incredible amount of information about how it processed the menu. The display will show below the menu.

&ignoreHidden — Tells Wayfinder to ignore the "Hide From Menus" checkbox. Normally, menu items with the "Hide From Menus" box checked will not be shown. If this is set to Yes, Wayfinder will ignore the checkbox and show them anyway. This is useful for sitemaps or any time you want to show all pages regardless of their "Hide From Menus" checkbox settings.

&hideSubMenus — Hides all but the top-level menu items except for the current page. This is a very handy property. When set to Yes, the top-level items will always show, but the sub-menus under them will only show for items below the current page.

&fullLink — Tells Wayfinder to create full links to all resources rather than relative links.

&sortOrder — Tells Wayfinder the order to use in sorting the resources in the menu. Default is ASC (ascending). The only other accepted value is DESC (descending). It is generally used with $sortBy.

&sortBy — Tells Wayfinder the resource field to sort on. Default is **menuindex**, but you can use any field. The most commonly used fields are **pagetitle**, **id**, **alias**, **createdon**, **publishedon**, and **createdby**.

&limit — Sets the total number of menu items to be processed per level. The default is 0, which shows all items. If Menu Index values are set, the items displayed will be the ones with the highest priority. If no Menu Index values are set, the count will start from the top of the menu for each level and work down.

&displayStart — Determines whether the **&startId** resource is shown. Default is false. This property has no effect if **&startId=`0`**.

Using getResources to Aggregate Content

There are a number of situations where you want to aggregate content from a number of pages and display it on a single page. Say, for example, that you have a news section where each page is a complete news story. On your Home page, you'd like to show a summary for each news story and display a link to the full story. In the following section, we'll create a news summary using the getResources snippet. The getResources snippet is designed to be a replacement for the Ditto snippet, which is deprecated in MODX Revolution. Most of the properties for getResources are the same as the Ditto properties.

The getResources snippet is one of the few standard MODX snippets that starts with a lowercase letter. It's easy to forget and call it GetResources, in which case nothing will appear where the tag is placed.

If you leave out the &tpl property, getResources will print out a long code dump showing all the available resource fields for each document.

If your &parents property contains a comma-delimited list, make sure there are no spaces in the list.

News Summary

First, make sure that the current version of the getResources snippet is installed. Before creating any pages, make sure that you have told MODX to make new pages published by default.

Go to **System → System Settings**, and type *published* in the filter box at the upper right of the grid. Set the *Published Default* setting to *Yes*.

Now create a document called *News* that uses your main template. Check the "Container" checkbox, and make sure it's published. Save it.

Now, right-click on the News folder, and select "Create," and then "Create a Document Here." Do this four times to create four news stories using the following values for the fields (change the number for each news story — *1*, *2*, *3*, or*4* — and change the title and text to match the number):

Title: *News Story 1*

Long Title: *News Story One*

Alias: *news-1*

Menu Title: *News One*

Summary (introtext): *This is the summary for News Story One.*

Resource Content: *This is the content of News Story One. The actual news story will go here.*

Before we can display our aggregation, we need to create a Tpl chunk to format each entry. Create a chunk called *GetResourcesTpl* with the following code:

```
<!-- GetResourcesTpl Chunk ->
<div class="grItem">Item [[+idx]]: [[+pagetitle]]
<br />
Author: [[+createdby:userinfo=`fullname`]]
Date: [[+createdon:strtotime:date=`%A %B %d, %Y`]]
<br />
[[+introtext]] . . . <a href="[[~[[+id]]]]">Read More</a>
</div><br />
```

Notice that we've used placeholder tags ([[+*placeholder*]]) rather than resource tags ([[*fieldname]]) for all the fields. The getResources snippet will set all these placeholders for us (and many more). We can't use resource tags here because they would retrieve the values for the current document (the one containing the getResources tag) rather than the values for the document being pulled for each item.

Now we need a getResources tag to gather the content and display it. You can put this tag in the News container document, in your template, or on your Home page. For now, put it in the Resource Content field of the News container document. The tag should look like this:

```
[[!getResources?
    &tpl=`GetResourcesTpl`
    &idx=`1`
]]
```

When you preview your News container document, you should see an abbreviated version of all the news stories with links that will take you to the full story. Try modifying the GetResourcesTpl chunk to create different formats for the news item teasers.

You can add classes to the Tpl chunk and modify your CSS file to style the news items and add background color, text color, different fonts, etc. to make the items look the way you want them to.

In the example above, we display the **introtext** (summary) field as the teaser. A better method is to show the first part of the **content** field if the **introtext** field is blank. To use this method, change the snippet tag to:

```
[[!getResources?
    &tpl=`GetResourcesTpl`
    &idx=`1`
    &includeContent=`1`
]]
```

Next, change the placeholder that shows the content in the GetResourcesTpl chunk to look like this:

```
[[+introtext:default=`[[+content:ellipsis=`100`]]`]] <a href="[[~[[+id]]]]">
Read More</a>
```

Now the tag will show the introtext field if it is not empty. If the **introtext** field is empty, the tag will display the first 100 characters of the **content** field followed by an ellipsis (three dots). We needed to add the **&includeContent** property because, by default, getResources saves time by not retrieving the **content** field.

Additional Properties

There are a number of additional properties for the getResources snippet that will help you control and style its output:

&limit — Specifies the number of items that will be displayed. The default value is 5.

&tplOdd — Specifies the name of a Tpl chunk that will be used for the odd-numbered items. The chunk specified in **&tpl** will be used for the even-numbered items. Use this if you want to have a different style for alternate items.

 If your items are displayed as a long array showing all the resource fields of each object, it means getResources can't find a Tpl chunk to use for the display. Either you haven't specified or created a Tpl chunk, or you've spelled its name incorrectly.

This display (unlike Ditto's) is getResources' default Tpl. It can be useful if you want to know the names of all the available resource fields. Simply leave out any **&tpl** property, and you'll see the list of available fields.

&tplFirst, **&tplLast** — Specify the names of different Tpl chunks for the first and last items in the list. You can use either one alone, or you can use both of them together.

&tpl_n — Specifies the name of the Tpl chunk that will be used for the *n*th item in the list. The chunk named in the **&tpl_3** property, for example, will be used for the third item. You can use as many of these properties as you like, so it's possible to have a separate Tpl chunk for every item on the list. The underscore is required.

&hideContainers — Skips documents designated as containers even if they have children. In Revolution (unlike Evolution), the **isfolder** page setting does not indicate whether the resource has children or not.

&parents — Takes a comma-delimited list of IDs specifying the parents to look under when retrieving documents for the list. The default value is the current document's ID. If your getResources snippet tag is not in the content section of the container document holding the items to be selected, you must specify at least one parent.

&includeContent — By default, getResources assumes that you don't want the **content** field and are using the **description** or summary (**introtext**) field (or some other field) for your teaser. If you *do* want to use the **content** field, you need to set this property to `1` so it will be available.

&depth — Contains an integer value that specifies how deeply getResources will look for items under each parent. Note that this property specifies the number of levels in the tree to be traversed, not the number of items to be retrieved. In our example, setting **&depth=`1`** will still get all four news stories since they are all one level below the parent. The default value is **10**.

&sortby — Specifies the field to sort the list by. It will accept any resource field, although the date fields are the most commonly used. The default value is **publishedon**.

&sortdir — Specifies the direction of the sort. Acceptable values are ASC (ascending) and DESC (descending). Default is DESC. If you are sorting by a date field, the default (DESC) will show the newest items first. If you are sorting by a text field, such as **pagetitle**, you probably want to change the direction to ASC.

&sortbyAlias — Allows you to specify a query alias for the sort. The default is modResource.

&offset — Specifies the number of items to skip at the beginning of the list. Those items will not be displayed. The default value is **0**.

&idx — Allows you to set the starting value for the [[+idx]] placeholder used to number your items. This is only necessary if you want a starting value other than the default: 1.

&first, &last — These specify the idx numbers of the items that will use the **&tplFirst** and **&tplLast** Tpl chunks. You can use either one alone or both together.

&showHidden — By default, getResources ignores resources if they have the "Hide From Menus" checkbox checked. Set this property to `1` to show them.

&includeTVs — To increase the speed of getResources, template variables are not included in the retrieved items unless you set this property to `1`.

&processTVs — By default, the raw values of TVs are retrieved. For example, a TV set to @INHERIT will be displayed as @INHERIT rather than the inherited value. If you set this property to `1`, the processed values of the TVs will be displayed.

&tvPrefix — By default, getResources prepends "tv." to all TVs when they are retrieved. If you don't set this property, all TV names must be in the form [[*tv.*TvName*]]. Use this property to set a different prefix or no prefix.

 If getResources is not showing your TVs, it's almost always because you forgot to use **&includeTVs** and/or **&tvPrefix**. If the TVs are being shown but don't look right, it's probably because you forgot to use **&processTVs**. If you don't want to mess with TV prefixes, just put **&tvPrefix** =`` in every getResources tag that shows TVs.

&tvFilters — Allows you to show only items that have TVs set to a certain value or values.

This property allows you to set a filter to specify the criteria to be used to select items. For a TV called `Show` that is set to `IncludeMe` in some resources, you could show only those resources with `Show` set to `IncludeMe` with this filter:

`&tvFilters=`IncludeMe==1``

Here is a more complex example with two filters set (separated by a comma):

`&tvFilters=`IncludeMe==1,Filter==Dog%||Filter==Cat``

The example above will show only items with `Show` set to `Yes` and another TV, called `Filter`, set to `Dog%` or `Cat`. The `%` symbol is a wildcard, so items with `Filter` set to `Dog`, `Dogs`, or `Cat` will be selected for display.

You can also leave out the TV name:

`&tvFilters=`IncludeMe``

The example above will select items where any TV associated with the resource is set to `IncludeMe`.

Where's Ditto?

Those of you coming from MODX Evolution may be wondering why there is no coverage of the Ditto snippet in the book. Ditto is a very old and well-known snippet with a lot of options and some cobbled-together capabilities. In MODX Revolution, Ditto is available (and Evolution users already know how to use it), but it is deprecated and no longer being developed or supported. The getResources snippet is newer and faster, and it uses less memory, so MODX strongly recommends that you use getResources for content aggregation. Most of the properties are the same, and it is usually fairly easy to convert a Ditto tag to use getResources. If you need pagination, the getPage snippet will add that capability to getResources.

Blogging with getResources

If you think about the News Summary we just created, you can see that each news item could be a blog post. A related snippet called Quip can be used to allow comments for your blog with various options such as moderation, trusted users, CAPTCHA, spam protection, etc. A Revolution version of Jot is in beta development at this writing.

Another related snippet called Reflect creates date-based archives of MODX blog posts. There is no MODX Revolution version of Reflect at this writing, but Reflect or a replacement for it may be available by the time you read this.

Blogging has always been something of a weak point for MODX, though many MODX-based blogs do exist. Many MODX users have opted to install WordPress, a much more mature blog platform, on their MODX sites and have integrated it with MODX in various ways. Several MODX blogging tools for Revolution are under development, however, and there may be a full-featured blog transport package available by the time you read this.

Using FormIt to Create and Process Forms

FormIt is a flexible form-processing snippet that can create a wide variety of forms for use on web pages.

FormIt can validate form fields, email the form results, and redirect the user to another page. It can also do custom validation and custom processing of the form (e.g., to store form data in the MODX database) using snippets written by the user. You can also extend FormIt with both built-in and custom snippets called hooks and preHooks.

 Note that the "I" in FormIt is capitalized. If you use "Formit" in your tags, MODX will simply remove them from the output and put nothing in their place because it won't find the snippet.

How FormIt Works

With FormIt, you create a standard (X)HTML form and place the FormIt snippet above it on the page. The **&validate** property in the snippet tag tells FormIt how to validate the form. There are a number of built-in validators, but you can add your own using custom snippets. You can have as many custom validators as you like, although the built-in validators can probably handle most of your needs. Here's a brief example:

```
[[!FormIt? &validate=
    `name:required,
     age:required:isNumber,
     department:required:ValidateDepartment`
     &customValidators=`ValidateDepartment=`accounting,sales` `
]]
<h2>Profile</h2>
<form action="[[~[[*id]]]]" method="post" class="MyForm">
Name: <input type= "text" name="name " id="name" value="[[+fi.name]]" />
<br />
Age: <input type= "text" name="age " id="age" value="[[+fi.age]]" />
<br />
Department: <input type= "text" name="department" id="department"
    value="[[+fi.department]]" /><br />
</form>
```

The form above presents three input fields: Name, Age, and Department. The **&validate** property tells FormIt that all are required and that the value entered in the Age field must be a number. The Department field will also be validated by a custom validator snippet called ValidateDepartment that we would have to write.

FormIt Properties

FormIt is constantly evolving and may have more properties by the time you read this. These are the available FormIt properties at this writing:

&clearFieldsOnSuccess — If set to 1, the fields will be cleared on any successful submission that does not redirect. Default: 1.

&customValidators — A comma-separated list of custom snippets to use for validating form fields. The custom validators must be specified here *and* in the **&validate** property.

&errTpl — A bit of (X)HTML code used to format error messages. Note that this is not a chunk name — it is the actual code. Default:

```
<span class="error">[[+error]]</span>
```

&hooks — A comma-separated list of built-in or custom hooks to execute once the form has been validated; if a hook returns `false`, processing will stop.

&language — The language to use in FormIt responses.

&placeholderPrefix — The prefix used with FormIt fields. The fi. prefix is used by default.

&preHooks — A comma-separated list of custom hooks to execute when a form is loaded. The preHooks execute before any hooks specified in the **&hooks** property and before any validators have been applied. If a preHook returns `false`, processing will stop.

&store — If set to 1, form field values will remain in the cache for use by the FormItRetriever snippet. Default: 0.

&storeTime — Time to store the values in the cache (in seconds). Default: 300 (5 minutes).

&submitVar — The name of an optional required variable specified in the form. If this property is set and the variable is not present in the $_POST array, processing will not continue.

&validate — A comma-separated list of fields to validate and the validators to use with them in the form: fieldName:validatorName (e.g., email:required). Multiple validators can be chained (e.g., email:email:required). This property can be specified on multiple lines.

&placeholderPrefix — Placeholder to be set by FormIt for all fields.

&successMessage — Message to display on successful submission if not using the redirect hook.

&successMessagePlaceholder — Name of the placeholder for the success message. Default: fi.successMessage.

&recaptchaTheme — Theme to use for the reCAPTCHA image. Options are red, white, blackglass, clean, and custom.

The properties above are used by the FormIt snippet. If you send more properties, however, they will be available to any hooks or validators that are processed. In the code of a hook or validator, the properties will be available as:

```
$prop = $scriptProperties['propertyName'];
```

A separate snippet, FormItRetriever, is also included in the FormIt package. If you want the data from the form to be available on another page (e.g., a "Thank You" page), use **&store=`1`** in the FormIt tag. Then, place this code at the top of the "Thank You" page:

```
[[!FormItRetriever]]
```

The form's placeholders will then be available on the "Thank You" page if you want to personalize the message there:

```
<p>Thanks [[+fi.name]] for your submission.</p>
<p>You will receive an email at [[+fi.email]].</p>
```

FormIt Validators

FormIt Validators, do just what you would expect. They make sure that the information the user has entered in the form is valid. The built-in validators will handle most cases, but you can also create your own custom validators if none of the built-in ones do what you want. All validators return `true` if the form field is valid and `false` if not.

Built-in FormIt Validators

Using the built-in FormIt validators, you can require that a form field be filled out or that it be blank. FormIt can test fields for legal email addresses, minimum and maximum lengths, and minimum and maximum values. It can also check to see if a field matches another field (e.g., duplicate password or email fields).

All FormIt validators are specified in the **&validate** property. The form fields to be validated are separated by commas. Multiple validators can be chained together for use on a single form field by separating them with commas. Validator parameters (if any) are sent to the validator by adding them after the validator name with an equals sign and back-ticks like this:

```
&validate=`password:minLength=`8`:maxLength=`12` `
```

Note the space between the final two back-ticks. This is required if your **&validate** property ends with two consecutive back-ticks. In theory, FormIt validators can be used together without limit, and they will be executed in the order you specify them. It is recommended that you put separate validators on separate lines. Here is a more complex example (the form field names are in bold):

```
&validate=`password:minLength=`8`:maxLength=`12`,
    url:minLength=`6`:contains=`.com`,
    username:required:isLower:minLengeh=`6`,
    user_email:email:required`
```

Here is the full list of built-in validators (as of this writing). Note that all of these must be specified in the **&validate** property of the FormIt tag, not in the form field:

allowTags — Allow HTML tags in the field; tags are stripped from fields by default (see stripTags below).

blank — Require that the field be blank. Example:

```
last_name:blank
```

Validation will fail if the field is filled in.

contains — Require that the field contain the string in the parameter. Example:

```
subject:contains=`Contact`
```

email — Require a valid email address. Example:

```
emailaddr:email
```

isDate — Require the field to be resolvable to a date. An optional parameter sets the format of the date. Examples:

```
eventDate:isDate
eventDate:isDate=`%Y-%m-%d`
```

islowercase — Require that the field be all lowercase letters. Example:

```
subject:islowercase
```

isNumber — Require that the field be a numeric value. Example:

```
age:isNumber
```

isuppercase — Require that the field contain all uppercase letters. Example:

```
subject:isuppercase
```

maxLength — Require the field to be no more than *x* characters long. Can be stacked with minLength. Examples:

```
password:maxLength=`10`
password:minLength=`6`:maxLength=`9`
```

maxValue — Require the field to be less than or equal to the parameter. Examples:

```
price:maxValue=`300`
price:isNumber:maxValue=`300`
```

minLength — Require the field to be at least *x* characters long. Example:

```
password:minLength=`8`
```

minValue — Require the field to be greater than or equal to the parameter. Examples:

```
hours_worked:minValue=`1`
hours_worked:isNumber:minValue=`1`
```

password_confirm — Require that the field match another specified field; takes the name of the other field as a parameter. Example:

```
password2:password_confirm=`password`
```

required — Require that the field be filled. Example:

```
username:required
```

strip — Remove the string sent in the parameter from the field. Example:

```
text:strip=`badword`
```

stripTags — Strip all tags from the field; takes an optional parameter containing a list of allowed tags. Examples:

```
text:stripTags
text:stripTags=`<p><b><i>`
```

Note that if the HTML is not valid, stripTags can end up removing more or less than you want.

FormIt Custom Validators

For custom validation, you simply create a MODX snippet with the name of the custom validator. The validator can be as simple or as complex as you like as long as it returns true on success and false on failure to validate. Custom validators must be specified in the **&customValidators** property of the FormIt tag.

Suppose that you want your form to reject submitters who don't live in one of several local zip codes. You could use this custom validator for the zip form field:

```
&customValidators =`zip:allowedZips=`55433,55126,55113` `
```

To enforce validation of that field, you'd create the following snippet named *allowedZips*:

```php
<?php
/* Code for allowedZip Snippet */
$zips = explode(',',$param);
if (in_array($value, $zips)) {
    return true;
} else {
    $validator->addError($key,'Invalid Zip Code.');
    return false;
}
?>
```

Note that we sent the allowed zip codes as a parameter in the validator. We could also have placed the allowed zip codes in the default properties of the snippet as a property called `legalZips`. The first line of the snippet would then be:

```
$zips = explode(',', $scriptProperties['legalZips'],
```

The content of the field being validated will always be available in the snippet as `$value`. As we mentioned earlier, all properties in the FormIt tag are available in any validator as `$scriptProperties['propertyName']`. These additional variables are also available in the `$scriptProperties` array for every validator:

`$value` — The current value of the field being validated.

`$key` — The numeric key (index) of the field being validated.

`$type` — The name of the validator (or snippet).

`$param` — The value of the parameter sent with the validator (if any).

`$validator` — A reference to the fiValidator object (the validator class instance).

Processing with PreHooks and Hooks

FormIt *preHooks* and *hooks* are custom snippets that you write to help with form processing. The preHooks, specified in the **&preHooks** property, execute when the page loads — before the form is processed. The hooks, specified in the **&hooks** property, execute after the form is validated. Each property takes a comma-delimited list of preHooks or hooks to execute. The terms specified in the comma-separated list are the names of MODX snippets. The snippets can be existing snippets installed by a transport package or custom snippets that you write yourself. This allows you to add a lot of form-processing power and flexibility without touching the code of the FormIt snippet.

At this writing, FormIt has several built-in hooks: email, redirect, spam, recaptcha, math, and FormItAutoResponder. The email hook emails the submitted form data using a Tpl chunk to format it, the redirect hook redirects the user to another page after the form has been processed, the spam hook filters spam emails, and the recaptcha hook uses the reCAPTCHA web utility to make sure the email is being submitted by a human rather than a spam-bot. The spam hook requires that cURL or sockets be enabled. The FormItAutoResponder hook sends an automatic email response to the user after the form is successfully submitted.

You can have as many hooks or preHooks as you like. They will execute in the order that you specify them in the **&hooks** or **&preHooks** properties. If any hook returns `false` (indicating an error), the remaining ones will not be processed.

When processing the **&hooks** property, if FormIt comes to a hook that is not built-in, it will look for a snippet with that name and execute it as a hook.

Let's take a closer look at the built-in validators and hooks.

FormIt Built-in Hooks

FormIt hooks execute after the form has been validated. At this writing, there are only six built-in hooks: email, redirect, spam, recaptcha, math, and FormItAutoResponder. The FormIt *email hook* emails the form. The FormIt *redirect hook* simply redirects the user to a specified page on the site. The *spam hook* checks to see if the email is from a known spammer by consulting **StopForumSpam.com**. The recaptcha hook displays an image containing text from **http://recaptcha.net** that the user must match. The *math hook* places a simple math question in your form to foil spammers. The *FormItAutoResponder hook* sends an email to the user who submitted the form.

At this writing, FormIt itself has only the properties listed above, though more may be added later. The FormIt tag often contains other properties, however, since those properties are passed to and used by the hooks and preHooks themselves.

Let's work through a very simple example that uses the FormIt email hook to display and mail a contact form and the redirect hook to forward the user to another page after the form has been emailed.

FormIt Email and Redirect Hooks

The email hook emails the form on the page. Here is a typical example of the tag you would use. Notice that it also includes the *redirect* hook to forward the user to another page after the form is emailed.

```
[[!FormIt?
    &hooks=`email,redirect`
    &emailUseFieldForSubject=`1`
    &emailTpl=`MyEmailTpl`
    &emailTo=`your@yourdomain.com`
    &redirectTo=`12`
]]
```

The tag above sets the minimum properties for the email and redirect actions. The first property (**&hooks**) tells FormIt to execute the email hook and then, if the email hook is successful, to execute the redirect hook.

The **&emailTpl** property specifies the chunk that will be used for the email. Note that this is not the contact form — it is the Tpl chunk that will be used to format the email message being sent.

The **&emailTo** property tells FormIt's email hook where to send the email message.

The **&redirectTo** property specifies the ID of the page the user will be redirected to after the email is sent. It usually refers to a Thank You page.

The FormIt snippet tag should be placed at the top of the page, usually just above the form itself.

FormIt Spam, Recaptcha, and Math Hooks

To implement the spam hook, you just need to add spam to the list of hooks. You can also add the **&spamEmailFields** property, which specifies which fields the spam service should check (the default is email):

```
&spamEmailFields=`email,subject`
```

The service will also check the sender's IP address, so the default (email) is usually fine. Unless you are a spammer, this hook is difficult to test. Even if you use the email address of a known spammer, the IP address will not match, and the email will still be sent. The service used by the spam hook (Stop Forum Spam) currently limits queries to 5,000 per day. Stop Forum Spam also requires that you not sell software that includes their service, although my understanding is that you can protect a commercial site with it when the Stop Forum Spam service is contained in an Open Source product like MODX. See **http:// stopforumspam.com** for current information and details.

To use the recaptcha hook, you need to add `recaptcha` to the list of hooks and add the following placeholders in your email form:

```
[[+formit.recaptcha_html]]
[[+fi.error.recaptcha]]
```

The reCAPTCHA image will replace the first placeholder. If the user fails the reCAPTCHA challenge, an error message will appear where the second placeholder is located when the form is submitted.

You also need to add the first two of the following properties to the snippet tag (the third is optional):

&formit.recaptcha_public_key — Your reCAPTCHA public key.

&formit.recaptcha_private_key — Your reCAPTCHA private key.

&formit.recaptcha_use_ssl — whether to use SSL (default: false).

To obtain the two keys, you need to register at **http://recaptcha.net/**.

The FormIt math hook requires the user to solve a simple math equation in order to submit the form. To use it, add *math* to the beginning of your **&hooks** property and add this code somewhere inside the form:

```
<label>[[!+fi.op1]] [[!+fi.operator]] [[!+fi.op2]]?</label>
[[!+fi.error.math]]
<input type="text" name="math:required" value="[[!+fi.math]]" />
<input type="hidden" name="op1" value="[[!+fi.op1]]" />
<input type="hidden" name="op2" value="[[!+fi.op2]]" />
<input type="hidden" name="operator" value="[[!+fi.operator]]" />
```

At this writing, the math hook does not work unless your **&validate** property is all on one line.

The Contact Form

Of course, none of the above will work without an actual contact form. Here's an example of what that form might look like:

```
<!--FormIt Contact Form Example ->
<h3>Contact Us</h3>
[[!+fi.error_message:notempty=`<p>[[!+fi.error_message]]</p>`]]
[[!+fi.validation_error_message:`<p>[[!+fi.validation_error_message]]</p>`]]
<form action="[[~[[*id]]]]" method="post" class="form">
<input type="hidden" name="last_name" value="" />
Name:
<span class= "error">[[+fi.error.name]]</span><br />
<input type="text" name="name" id="name" value="[[+fi.name]]" /><br />
Email:
<span class="error">[[+fi.error.email]]</span><br >
<input type="text" name="email" id="email" value="[[+fi.email]]" /><br />
Subject:
<span class="error">[[+fi.error.subject]]</span><br />
<input type="text" name="subject" id="subject" value="[[+fi.subject]]" />
<br />
Message:
<span class="error">[[+fi.error.text]]</span><br />
<textarea name="text" id="text" cols="55" rows="7" value="[[+fi.text]]">
    [[+fi.text]]
</textarea><br />
<br class="clear" />
<div class="form-buttons">
<input type="submit" value= "Send Contact Inquiry" />
</div>
</form>
```

Let's look at some parts of the form in more detail.

```
<form action="[[~[[*id]]]]" method="post" class="form">
```

The line above simply posts the form to itself. MODX will replace the tag with the URL of the current page.

```
[[!+fi.error_message:notempty=`<p>[[!+fi.error_message]]</p>`]]
[[!+fi.validation_error_message:`<p>[[!+fi.validation_error_message]]</p>`]]
```

The first line above provides a placeholder for general error messages from the form (e.g., "mail not sent"). The second line will tell the user if there are any validation errors in the form. Because of the :notempty output modifier, the messages will not be displayed unless there is an error.

The other fi.error placeholders in the form are for error messages from the validators for those fields. All these placeholders will be empty when the form is first displayed. If there are errors in the form when it is submitted, the fi.error placeholders will be set for any errors detected by the validators. The "error" class span allows you to style the error messages (e.g., bold and/or colored text) with CSS.

All of the fi. placeholders will be available for use (without the prefix) in the Tpl chunk used to format the email message.

```
<input type="hidden" name= "last_name" value="" />
```

The line above is used to foil spam-bots. It hides the last_name input field from users, but spam-bots will see it. If they fill it in (as they often will), the form will be rejected (assuming that you have included last_name:blank in your **&validate** property).

The <br /> tags will make the form look acceptable as written, but in a real form, you would normally remove them and style the form with CSS.

The emailTpl Chunk

Here is the content of the `MyEmailTpl` chunk we specified in the **&emailTpl** property. It is used to format the email message:

```
<p>Sent from FormIt Email Snippet:</p>
<br />[[+name]] <[[+email]]> Wrote: <br />
[[+text]]
```

The placeholders in the chunk above will be replaced by the values submitted by the user in the contact form. It is a good practice to put the user's email address in the body of the message because there are some situations where the return address is modified by the host. When sending via Gmail with SMTP, for example, Gmail will replace the `From` address with your own email address, making it impossible to reply to the sender.

Testing the FormIt Contact Form

Install the FormIt snippet package if you haven't done so already.

Create a chunk called *MyEmailTpl*, and put the Tpl code (shown in the previous section) into the code field. Click on the "Save" button.

Create a contact page resource called *Contact Us*. Give it an appropriate Long Title, Alias, and Menu Title. Put the following FormIt snippet tag at the top of the Resource Content field, followed by the contact form listed above. Make sure the resource is published.

```
[[!FormIt?
    &hooks=`email,redirect`
    &emailUseFieldForSubject=`1`
    &emailTpl=`MyEmailTpl`
    &emailTo=`you@yourdomain.com`
    &redirectTo=`## `
    &validate=`last_name:blank,
        name:required,
        email:email:required,
        subject:required,
        text:required:stripTags`
]]
```

Just below the FormIt snippet tag, add the example contact form code from earlier in this section. Change the value of the **&emailTo** property to the address to which you want email sent. Click on the "Save" button.

Create a *Thank You* page as a child of the Contact page. Check the "Hide From Menus" box and the "Published" box. Put *Thank you! Your message has been submitted* in the Resource Content field, and click on the "Save" button. Now, go back to the Contact page and put the ID of the Thank You page in the **&redirectTo** property of the FormIt tag. Save the page.

Right-click on the Contact Us resource in the tree, and select "Preview Resource." You should see your contact form. Try submitting it with empty fields and with an invalid email address (leave out the @ sign) to see if the validators are working. If you fill in all the fields correctly, you should receive an email from the form.

 If you are testing your form on a localhost install, you probably don't have a mail server to send the mail. You could install one, but it is often difficult to do. Usually, it is easier to use SMTP. Any email account that you have with an SMTP server will work (including Gmail).

MODX Revolution can be configured to send via SMTP by default. Go to System → System Settings, and put *smtp* in the "Search by Key" box. You'll see the SMTP system settings in the grid.

At this writing, the following settings will work with Gmail:

SMTP Authentication: Yes
SMTP Connection Prefix: tls
SMTP Hosts: smtp.gmail.com
SMTP Password: *yourGmailPassword*
SMTP Port: 465
SMTP User: *yourGmailUsername*
Use SMTP: Yes

Here is a list of the properties for the email hook. The first two are required:

&emailTpl — The Tpl chunk for the email message.

&emailTo — A comma-separated list of email addresses to send to.

The following settings are optional:

&emailSubject — The subject of the email. Use this if you don't want the user to supply the subject or if the subject field is not required.

&emailUseFieldForSubject —If `true` (default), FormIt will use the `'fi.subject'` field as the message subject.

&emailToName — A comma-separated list of names to pair with the **&emailTo** values.

&emailFrom — If set, this will specify the `From:` address for the email. If not set, FormIt will first look for an `'fi.email'` form field. If none is found, it will use the **emailsender** System Setting.

&emailFromName — If set, this will specify the `From:` name for the email.

&emailHtml — Determines whether or not the email should be in (X)HTML format. Default is `true`.

The redirect hook has only one property, and it is required:

&redirectTo — The resource ID of the page to redirect to.

The Spam Hook

To use the built-in spam hook, just add *spam,* at the beginning of your **&hooks** property. The spam hook will check to see if the email address is that of a known spammer and will also check the sender's IP against those of known spammers. Be sure to put the spam hook ahead of the email hook:

```
&hooks=`spam,email,redirect`
```

The spam hook has only one property, and it is optional:

&spamEmailFields — An optional, comma-delimited list of email fields to check. The default value is `'email'`.

The FormItAutoResponder Hook

The FormItAutoResponder Hook will send an automated email response to the user when the form is successfully submitted. It takes the following properties (which must be added to the FormIt tag). The first property is required — the rest are optional:

&fiarTpl — The name of a Tpl chunk to use for the auto-response message.

&fiarSubject — The subject of the email.

&fiarToField — The form field to use as the submitter's email. Defaults to `email`.

&fiarFrom — The From: address to use for the email. Defaults to **emailsender** system setting.

&fiarFromName — The FromName: for the email.

&fiarHtml — Whether or not the email should be in HTML format. Defaults to `true`.

&fiarReplyTo — The ReplyTo: field for the email.

&fiarReplyToName — The name for the ReplyTo: field.

&fiarCC — A comma-separated list of email addresses to send to via CC.

&fiarCCName — A comma-separated list of names to pair with the **&fiarCC** values.

&fiarBCC — A comma-separated list of email addresses to send to via BCC.

&fiarBCCName —A comma-separated list of names to pair with the **&fiarBCC** values.

FormIt Custom Hooks

If the FormIt built-in hooks don't do what you want, you can create *FormIt custom hooks* very easily.

Creating Custom Hooks

To use a custom hook, you just create a snippet and add the name of it to the **&hooks** property in the FormIt tag.

```
[[FormIt? &hooks=`SnippetName`]]
```

Multiple hooks can be entered in a comma-separated list, and custom hooks can be mixed with the built-in hooks. The hooks will execute in the order they are specified in the property.

Say, for example, that you wanted to update a log file or database table with data from an emailed form before redirecting the user to another page. You'd write a snippet to do the update. Let's call it *UpdateData*.

If you wanted the update to occur only after the form had been successfully emailed, the **&hooks** property in your FormIt tag would look like this:

```
&hooks=`email,UpdateData,redirect`
```

Custom hooks (like the built-in hooks) should return `true` on success. On failure, they should set an error field and return `false`. If any hook returns `false`, the hooks after it in the property list won't execute. If a hook is not found, however, hooks after it in the list will execute.

Information Passed to a Custom Hook

A snippet used as a custom hook has access to the $modx object (as all snippets do) and several pieces of information sent to it by FormIt. The properties in the FormIt tag are available in the $scriptProperties array:

```
$scriptProperties['propertyName']
```

If you used **&userGroup**=`Editors` in the FormIt tag, for example, the following code would set the $userGroup variable to Editors:

```
$userGroup=$scriptProperties['userGroup'];
```

The $hook object itself is available as the $scriptProperties['hook'] member. This is an instance of the fiHooks class defined in **fihooks.class.php**. This gives you access to the member variables of the $hook object:

```
$hook = $scriptProperties['hook'];
$hook->errors   /* The array of errors for this hook /*
$hook->hooks    /* The array of previously processed hook names */
$hook->formit   /* A reference to the instance of the $formit object */
$hook->modx     /* A reference to the $modx object */
```

In addition, the fields of the submitted form (with any fi. prefixes removed) are available using $hook->getValue('fieldName'):

```
$email = $hook->getValue('email');
```

Hooks and preHooks can also set field values with code like this:

```
$hook->setValue('fieldName', 'value');
$hook->setValue('fieldName', $value);
```

Returning Errors from a Custom Hook

As we saw above, hooks have access to the hook object, which holds the array of generic errors. If the snippet detects an error, you can load errors into that array in a custom hook snippet using the following method:

```
$errorMsg = 'User not found';
$hook->addError('user', $errorMsg);
return false;
```

If you were creating an add-on component to work with FormIt, you might want to put the error message in the FormIt lexicon instead of hard-coding it into the snippet. Then, you'd replace the first line with this code:

```
$errorMsg = $modx->lexicon('formit.user_not_found');
```

If you are returning `false` from a failed hook, you can also set any placeholders on the page (before the return, of course) with the usual:

```
$modx->setPlaceholder('placeholderName','value');
```

Those placeholder values will be displayed when the form is reloaded after the failed return from the custom hook snippet.

Example Custom Hook

Let's create a simple hook that will let a user update his or her email address in the front end.

The first step is to create a new resource, called *ChangeEmail*, with the following code in its Resource Content field:

```
[[!FormIt?
    &preHooks=`PreFormIt`
    &hooks=`ChangeEmail,redirect`
    &store=`1`
    &redirectTo=`##`
    &validate=`email:email:required`


 ]]


<h3>New Email Address</h3>
<p>[[+fi.error.error_message]]</p>
<form class="form" action="[[~[[*id]]]]" method="post">
Name: [[+fi.name]]<br /><br />
Email:
<span class="error"><strong> [[+fi.error.email]]</strong></span>
<input id="email" name="email" type="text" value="[[+fi.email]]" /><br />
<br class="clear" />
<div class="form-buttons">
<input name="Submit" type="submit" value="Submit" />
</div>
</form>
```

The form above is mostly an abbreviated version of the email form with our custom hook name replacing the email hook. Notice that we've added a custom preHook called *Pre-FormIt*. It doesn't exist yet, but we'll create it and see what it does in just a bit.

Create a resource called *Confirmation* containing the code below:

```
[[!FormItRetriever]]

<p>Congratulations [[+modx.user.username]].</p>
<p>Your username has been changed to [[+fi.email]].</p>
```

Save the Confirmation resource, and check its resource ID in the tree. Replace the ## in the **&redirectTo** property of the ChangeEmail resource with the ID of the Confirmation resource. Notice that in the code above, we had to use [[+modx.user.username]] in the resource to display the user's username. That field is not actually a form field in the ChangeEmail resource form, so it's not available as an fi. placeholder on the confirmation page. Luckily, [[+modx.user.username]] is set automatically as a placeholder in every MODX page.

Our user will have to log on in the front end in order to use our ChangeEmail page, so we'll also need a Login page. You can use the one you created in the MODX Security chapter (Chapter 10) or follow the directions there to create a new one. Set the **&loginResourceId** property in the Login snippet tag to the Resource ID of the ChangeEmail document we just created.

You'll also want to create a user or two (other than the admin Super User) to test the page and our custom hook.

We could show the user a blank form, but since the user will need to be logged in, we'll fill it in based on the user's profile. We'll also chase away any visitors who are not logged in. We'll do this in a preHook called PreFormIt. Note that we could use the Profile snippet included in the Login package here, which sets placeholders for all the fields in the user profile. Doing it this way will be more efficient, however, since we only need two of the fields.

Remember that we specified a preHook called PreFormIt in our FormIt snippet tag. Now it's time to create that custom preHook. Create a new snippet called *PreFormIt* with the following code:

```php
<?php
/* Code for PreFormIt Snippet */
$isAuthenticated = $modx->user->hasSessionContext(
    $modx->context->get('key'));
if (!$isAuthenticated) {
    $modx->sendUnauthorizedPage();
}
$profile = $modx->user->getOne('Profile');
$name = $modx->user->get('username');
$email = $profile->get('email');
$hook->setValue('name', $name);
$hook->setValue('email', $email);
return true;
```

In the first few lines, the snippet checks to see if the user is logged in. If not, the user is sent to the page designated in the System Settings grid by the **unauthorized_page** setting.

Next, we get the username and email of the user. Notice that we have to use a different method for each one. The username (and the user's ID) is in the $modx->user object, which is always available. That means that we can get it with the user object's get() method:

```php
$name = $modx->user->get('username');
```

Other information about the user, such as the user's full name, email address, etc., is in the *user profile*. The profile is a related object of the user object, so we retrieve it with the user object's getOne() method:

```php
$profile = $modx->user->getOne('Profile');
```

Finally, we set the placeholders for the two form fields using the hook's setValue() method so that they will be filled in when the form is displayed. We return true from the snippet to indicate success.

At this point, you should be able to preview the Login page, log in as another user, and see the filled-in form. You can test the validators by submitting an empty email field or one without the @ sign. You'll also be forwarded to the confirmation page with a successful submission.

Let's build our custom hook snippet. Create a new snippet called *ChangeEmail*, and put the following code in it:

```php
<?php
/* Code for ChangeEmail Snippet */

$profile = $modx->user->getOne('Profile');
if ($profile == null) {
    $hook->setError('user', "Sorry, cannot find you in the Database");
    return false;
}
$modx->setPlaceholder( 'new_email',$scriptProperties['fields']['email']);

$profile->set('email', $hook->getValue('email'));
$profile->save();
return true;
```

The first few lines of the code above get the current user's profile. If the user can't be found, we return an error message. Then, we set the profile's email field from the user's input and save it.

Finally, we return true to indicate success, although it wouldn't be a bad idea to set an error message if $profile->save() returns false.

Now, you should be able to change the user's email address in the MODX database using the form. Remember that the form will only be visible if you are logged on in the front end. After changing the email address, you should be able to re-visit the form and see the new address.

We used our form to change just the user's email address, but by adding more fields to the form and the two snippets, we could have let the user edit the entire user profile. We should mention that the Login transport package contains an UpdateProfile snippet that will do the same thing. In fact, several recent additions to the Login package provide easier ways to perform a number of tasks related to the login process. The Profile snippet, for example, will set placeholders for all the user fields. There is also a ChangePassword snippet, a ResetPassword snippet, and a ForgotPassword snippet.

Summary

In this chapter, we learned how to install common MODX components such as EZfaq, SPForm, Breadcrumbs, Wayfinder, getResources, and FormIt. EZfaq creates easily edited FAQ pages. SPForm creates a simple contact form for the site. Breadcrumbs displays a trail of links to the current page. Wayfinder is the standard MODX component for creating dynamic menus. The getResources snippet aggregates content (and replaces the MODX Evolution Ditto snippet). FormIt is used to create custom forms and to process those forms on submission (replacing the Evolution eForm snippet).

We also looked at the snippet properties used by these add-on components and discussed how to work with default properties and property sets for them.

MODX Evolution Notes

Since Evolution has no transport packages, installing components is more complex. In addition, some of the components we discussed above don't exist for Evolution.

Installing Components

In Evolution, installing a component involves physically copying the components files and manually creating any necessary resources and elements by cutting and pasting code. The files have to be copied to the correct locations (though you can usually expand the .ZIP file in **assets/snippets** to install them). The snippets, chunks, plugins, resources, templates, and template variables have to be created manually in the MODX Manager. Most components come with a **readme.txt** file explaining how to install them, but for some, you have to guess.

If you are new to MODX, EZfaq and SPForm are good snippets to start with because they have detailed installation instructions that will help you understand how snippets are installed and used, and both have online tutorials at:

http://bobsguides.com.

Snippets in Evolution have default properties, but they are not in the handy grid form found in Revolution, so using them is not very practical. They have to be entered in a single line on the snippet's Properties tab like this:

```
&Variable1=Caption1;Type;DefaultValue&Variable2=Caption2;Type;DefaultValue2;
```

Snippet properties are almost always specified in the snippet tag in Evolution. In earlier versions of Evolution, snippet tags had to be written as a single line. With recent versions, this is no longer the case, so you can do this:

```
[[SnippetName?
    &property1=`some_value`
    &property2=`some_other_value`
]]
```

Common Snippets

EZfaq, SPForm, Wayfinder, and Breadcrumbs, once they are installed, work pretty much the same way in Evolution and have the same properties, although SPForm has a config file for setting the properties.

The getResources snippet doesn't exist in Evolution, nor does FormIt. The eForm snippet is the form-creation and email snippet in Evolution, though it is nothing like FormIt. It will do validation, and it can have custom "hooks," although you'll need to read the documentation to use those features.

MODX Evolution can't be configured to send email with SMTP by default (unless you hack the core code). SPForm can be configured to use SMTP, but to get eForm to do so, you'll need to edit its code.

Chapter 13

Creating Transport Packages

This chapter is for MODX Revolution users who want to share their work with other members of the MODX community. You don't need to know anything in this chapter to use MODX. The information here is necessary, though, if you'd like to create a transport package so other MODX users can download and install your add-on component.

Third-party components for MODX Revolution can be installed the old-fashioned way by pasting code into new snippets, chunks, plugins, etc. In MODX Revolution, however, you also have the option of using transport packages. A *transport package* is a .ZIP file that auto-installs MODX third-party components and other things via the Package Management section of the MODX Manager.

Transport packages can be very simple (e.g., a package that just installs a single snippet or chunk), or they can be quite complex. A complex transport package might create new system settings and install several snippets, chunks, and plugins, each with default properties. It can also show a license agreement, `readme.txt` file, and a changelog during the install and interact with the user to ask, for example, which parts of the component should be installed.

Transport packages can also include validation tests that make sure it's ok to install the component and even auxiliary PHP scripts that perform any action that can be done using PHP. They can also behave differently when installing, upgrading, or uninstalling a component.

Since transport packages can include any MODX object and can modify existing objects, a transport package could actually install a complete web site containing many resources and elements along with system settings, custom manager pages, property sets, templates, CSS files, etc. In fact, the MODX Sample Site does just that. In theory, upgrades of MODX itself could be installed as transport packages and it is likely that this capability will be available in future versions.

Down the road, there will almost certainly be MODX transport packages containing full-featured blogs, forums, user-management systems, web sites for custom markets such as real estate and auto sales, etc. Maybe you will create one of them.

In this chapter, we'll look first at a minimal transport package that installs a very simple snippet. Then we'll add some bells and whistles to the package.

Transport Package Overview

For our first package, we're going to create a simple "Hello World" snippet and package it. The script to create the transport package will be the code of a snippet called *MakeHello*. We'll put a snippet tag to call that snippet in a resource (document) also called *MakeHello*. When we preview the MakeHello document, the script will run and will create the transport package.

 There is a MODX Manager add-on called PackMan that is a tool for creating transport packages. It will do some of what we describe in this chapter, but at this writing, it is limited to relatively simple cases. By the time you read this, there may be a full-featured package-building tool available for download. There will probably always be cases, however, where users need to create packages that are beyond the capabilities of any existing tool. If you need to create a more complex transport package, you will need the information presented in this chapter.

In the code of the script that builds our package, we'll first initialize the package-builder object and assign it to a variable called $builder. We'll then use the various methods of that object to create and save the transport package.

I like to create transport packages with a script that runs in my editor (JetBrains' PhpStorm) outside of MODX. By convention, the script is called **build.transport.php**. You may not have an editor that will do this, however, so the examples in this chapter will assume that you're creating the transport package with a snippet running in a MODX install as described above. If you do have an editor that can run a PHP script, or if you would like to create the transport package by running the **build.transport.php** script from the command line, you need to add the following lines to the top of the script so that it will run outside of MODX:

```
define('MODX_CORE_PATH', 'full/path/to/your/modx/core/');
define('MODX_CONFIG_KEY', 'config');
require_once MODX_CORE_PATH . 'model/modx/modx.class.php';
$modx= new modX();
$modx->initialize('mgr');
```

File Locations

Most non-trivial components will have a number of files associated with them. A component may need image files, CSS files, documentation files, example files, data files, etc. There may also be files used to build the transport package, which may or may not be placed in the final install. In fact, a proper transport package for even a minimal snippet will have at least 20 associated files.

As we've seen earlier in this book, MODX is remarkably unrestrictive when it comes to file locations. Files associated with an add-on component can be placed just about anywhere in a MODX install. In this section, we'll discuss some guidelines for file placement. You're free to violate them, but following them will make your files easier to find (both for others and for you) and in some cases, will make your component more secure.

We'll look first at where to put the files used to create the component's transport package. Then we'll discuss where to place any files transferred during the install. We'll use the terms *source* and *target* for these two locations (and the variables $source and $target in our transport-package build script). The source is the location where the file exists in your build environment — before being placed in the transport package. The target is the location where the file will exist in any site where the package is installed — after the transport package has been installed. Not all of the files involved in building the package will be "transported." Some of them will be used only during the build process.

We should also mention an important convention in MODX: All file and directory names should be entirely in lowercase. Using lowercase file and directory names will prevent many headaches on Unix installs where file and directory names are all case-sensitive. On Windows, for example, using the name **file1** to access a file called **File1** will work fine. If the site is moved to a remote server, however, it will usually fail.

Files Used to Build the Transport Package

The files used to build a transport package can be anywhere, but they are usually placed under this directory:

assets/components/component_name**/**

Files used in only the build phase but not transferred to the final install usually go in or under the **_build/** directory:

assets/components/component_name**/_build/**

It's up to you to determine which files will be transferred during the installation of a component. Obviously, support files such as CSS and image files will have to be transferred, and it makes sense to transfer documentation and example files. Any lexicon files must also be transferred.

Some people like to provide the user with PHP class files, **readme.txt** files, lexicon files, changelogs that describe changes in each new version, etc., even though it's not necessary to do so. Transferring those files can make the component easier to understand and to modify. It also makes it possible for the end user to print the files for reference.

It's best to place files that will be transferred during the install in a directory structure that mimics their locations after the transport package is installed because files are transferred by directory rather than individually. We'll say more about this in the following sections.

File Placement during the Install

As part of the build process, you'll tell MODX where you want the files placed during the install. You're free to place support files for a component, such as image and CSS files, anywhere you like as long as they are available to your component. The standard place to put these files, however, is under one of two directories:

/core/components/component_name**/**
/assets/components/component_name**/**

Many components use both locations. The **/core** directory is more secure (especially in MODX Revolution where it can be placed outside of the **public_html** directory), so the rule of thumb is to put all files that don't need to be web-accessible under the **/core** directory. PHP source files, examples, lexicon files, and documentation should all go there. CSS and image files, on the other hand, need to be available via the Web because they are referenced in (X)HTML code, so they go under the **/assets** directory. If they are placed under the **/core** directory, they won't be available if the user moves that directory outside the web root — something that is often done to make the site more secure.

 Unlike other support files for a component, the lexicon files have a standard location where MODX will look for them. The standard location for the English (en) language lexicon files, for example, would be in the following directory (assuming that MODX_CORE_PATH is set to **core/**):

core/components/*component_name***/lexicon/en/**

It's technically possible to put them somewhere else by adjusting the namespace path of the component, but this is almost never done and is discouraged.

Because users can rename and move both the **/core** and **/assets** directories in MODX Revolution, it's important to always refer to them using the MODX constants: MODX_CORE_PATH, MODX_ASSETS_PATH, and MODX_ASSETS_URL.

 When writing PHP code that refers to a web resource, such as a CSS, JS, or image file, always remember to use MODX_ASSETS_URL rather than MODX_ASSETS_PATH. Forgetting this can lead to extended periods of extreme frustration.

Here are some example directories for final placement of files:

```
MODX_CORE_PATH . components/component_name/examples/
MODX_CORE_PATH . components/component_name/elements/snippets/
MODX_CORE_PATH . components/component_name/elements/chunks/
MODX_CORE_PATH . components/component_name/lexicon/
MODX_ASSETS_URL . components/component_name/images/
MODX_ASSETS_URL . components/component_name/css/
```

File Location Guidelines

In the transport-package build script, you must specify a source and a target for any files to be transferred. The files are transferred with something called a file resolver (more on this in a bit).

Since some files will go under the **/core** directory and some under the **/assets** directory, organizing your source files into the following three directories makes sense, though it looks a bit odd at first:

/assets/*component_name***/_build/**
/assets/*component_name*/core/*component_name*/
/assets/*component_name*/assets/*component_name*/

Files used only in the build go in the **_build** directory. Files intended to be placed under the **/core** and **/assets** directories during the install go in the other two locations. Notice that the files you work on when developing the component are all placed under the assets directory, but in a location where they won't conflict with the copies of those same files that will be created when you install the package on the same site.

With the above structure, the specification in the transport package might look like this for the files to be installed below the **/core** directory:

```
$source = MODX_ASSETS_PATH . 'component_name' . '/core/component_name/';
$target "return MODX_CORE_PATH . 'components/';";
```

For the files to be installed below the **/assets** directory, the specification would look like this:

```
$source = MODX_ASSETS_PATH . 'component_name' . '/assets/component_name/';
$target = "return MODX_ASSETS_PATH . 'components/';";
```

Note that the specification never lists specific files, only directories, and that in the $target lines, it's not necessary to specify the *component_name* directory name. The directory specified in the $source line and all files below it will be included in the transport package and will automatically be placed below the directory specified as the $target.

Version Control Considerations

Many component developers, especially those with complex components, like to use a version-control system such as SVN or Git to manage the files used by their components. MODX currently uses Git. A full explanation of version control is beyond the scope of this book, but here is a brief overview. Version-control systems store all files in a "repository." The repository not only stores the current versions of the files, but also contains previous versions. This allows you to "revert" to a previous version when changes you make break your component. You can also examine all the changes you've made to any file in the component to see what might be causing the problem.

Using SVN, you "check out" files before working on them and "commit" them back to the repository after making and testing changes. You can also "update" to include changes made by others to the repository. The process is similar with Git, except that you "clone" the repository to start and "fetch" and "merge" any changes made by others. With each commit, you record a comment specifying what you changed. The repository's "log" contains all the comments from every commit, and you can revert to any previous version. You can see how handy version control would be when working on a complex component over a long period of time.

A Simple Transport Package

For our first transport package, we're simply going to package up our Hello World snippet. Since you may already have a `Hello` snippet, we'll call this one *Hello2*. No files at all are involved in this example, so there's no need to specify any source or target directories. We'll add some files later when we enhance our simple package.

Our First Version

The first version of our transport package will simply include the Hello2 snippet and nothing more.

Creating the Build Script

Here is the full code of the transport script to create the package. Put this code in your *MakeHello* snippet (MakeHello is the snippet that builds the package containing our Hello2 snippet):

```php
<?php
/* MakeHello Package Building Script */
echo 'Creating Package';

/* package variables */
define('PKG_NAME', 'Hello2');
```

```
define('PKG_NAME_LOWER', strtolower(PKG_NAME));
define('PKG_VERSION', '1.0.0');
define('PKG_RELEASE', 'beta1');

/* now load the package builder and create the package */
$modx->loadClass('transport.modPackageBuilder',"",false, true);
$builder = new modPackageBuilder($modx);
$builder->createPackage(PKG_NAME_LOWER, PKG_VERSION, PKG_RELEASE);
$builder->registerNamespace(PKG_NAME_LOWER, false,true,
    '{core_path}components/' . PKG_NAME_LOWER.'/');

/* create or get the object to be packaged */
$obj= $modx->newObject('modSnippet');

/* alternative method gets the object from the DB:
 * $obj = $modx->getObject('modSnippet', array('name'=>'Hello2'));
 * if the object is retrieved from the
 * DB, the following three lines
 * are not necessary
 */
$obj->set('name', 'Hello2');
$obj->set('description', 'Hello2 1.0 beta1 - prints: Hello World.');
$obj->setContent("return 'Hello World';");

/* alternate method gets the content from a file:
 * $obj->setContent(file_get_contents('path_to file'));
 */

/* create a vehicle to carry the object we've just created */
$attributes = array(
    xPDOTransport::UNIQUE_KEY => 'name',
    xPDOTransport::UPDATE_OBJECT => true,
    xPDOTransport::PRESERVE_KEYS => false,
);
$vehicle = $builder->createVehicle($obj, $attributes);

/* insert the vehicle into the transport package */
$builder->putVehicle($vehicle);
```

```
/* zip up the package (will go to /core/packages) */
$builder->pack();

echo '<br />Package complete.';
?>
```

A Closer Look

Let's look at our build script one section at a time to see what it's doing.

In the first section, we print a message indicating that we're creating the package, and we set the package variables. The name of the package as it appears in the **/core/packages** directory and in the Transport Packages grid will be a combination of the first three of these variables. The last two variables are for the package's namespace. The {core_path} specification is a placeholder that MODX will replace with the actual core path.

```
echo 'Creating Package';

/* package variables */
define('PKG_NAME', 'Hello2');
define('PKG_NAME_LOWER', strtolower(PKG_NAME));
define('PKG_VERSION', '1.0.0');
define('PKG_RELEASE', 'beta1');
```

Notice that we've created a lowercase version of the package name and that all the values except the first are in all lowercase. This is important so that the package will install on servers where file names are case-sensitive. Next, we load the package-builder class and assign a new instance of it to the $builder variable. This code will be the same for all packages:

```
/* now load the package builder and create the package */
$modx->loadClass('transport.modPackageBuilder', "", false, true);
$builder = new modPackageBuilder($modx);
```

The following code creates the new package (using the variables we set above) and sets its namespace. This code will also be the same for all packages:

```
$builder->createPackage(PKG_NAME_LOWER,PKG_VERSION,PKG_RELEASE);
$builder->registerNamespace(PKG_NAME_LOWER, false, true,
    '{core_path}components/' . PKG_NAME_LOWER . '/');
```

Now, we need to create the snippet object we are packaging. Notice that there's an alternative method here. If the object already exists in the MODX install, we can simply get it from the database with $modx->getObject(). We didn't use that method here because we want to test the package and see if it actually installs the component, so we want the component to be missing until after the package is installed.

```
/* create or get the object to be packaged */
$obj = $modx->newObject('modSnippet');

/* alternative method gets the object from the DB:
 * $obj = $modx->getObject('modSnippet', array('name'=>'Hello2'));
 * if the object is retrieved from the
 * DB, the following three lines
 * are not necessary
 */
```

Now that the snippet object exists, we can set its resource fields using the set() method and its content using the setContent() method.

```
$obj->set('name', 'Hello2');
$obj->set('description', 'Hello2 1.0 beta1 - prints: Hello World.');
$obj->setContent("return 'Hello World';");
```

 We could have set the snippet's "content" field using
$obj->set('snippet', "return 'Hello World';") because **snippet** is the
actual field name. It is much wiser to use setContent(), however, since the
actual field name involved may change in future versions of MODX.

The following alternative method sets the snippet's content to the contents of a file. Some users prefer this method because the contents of the file can be put under version control:

```
/* alternate method gets the content from a file: */
 * $obj->setContent(file_get_contents('path_to_file'));
 */
```

Note that if you use the method above, the file must not contain either <?php at the top or ?> at the bottom — just the code. As an alternative, you can include those lines but get the file's content and strip them out with str_replace() before calling setContent() using code like this:

```
$o = file_get_contents('path_to_file');
$o = str_replace('<?php',"",$o);
$o = str_replace('?>',"",$o);
$o = trim($o);
$obj->setContent($o);
```

There is no need to do that with elements that don't contain PHP code. It's only necessary with snippets and plugins.

Now that we have the snippet object, we need a vehicle to put it in. Any object to be transported in a transport package must be contained in a vehicle. Vehicles not only carry objects, but can also have validators and resolvers that carry files to be copied and scripts to be run. We don't need a validator or a resolver for this simple example, so we'll skip adding one. We'll see how to add validators and resolvers later in this chapter.

When we create a vehicle, we need to create an attributes array to tell MODX how to handle the object. The UNIQUE_KEY attribute specifies the unique key of the object (in this case 'name') used in the database. This is the "name" field of the object. For resources it would be **pagetitle**, for categories it would be **category**, and for templates it would be **templatename**. It would be **name** for most other elements.

The UPDATE_OBJECT attribute tells MODX whether to modify the object if it already exists. The PRESERVE_KEYS attribute tells MODX whether to update the primary key(s) of the object if it already exists. The last two will only come into play if the snippet is upgraded or reinstalled. Usually, the following settings for the last two attributes are fine:

```
/* create a vehicle to carry the object we've just created */
$attributes= array(
    xPDOTransport::UNIQUE_KEY => 'name',
    xPDOTransport::UPDATE_OBJECT => true,
    xPDOTransport::PRESERVE_KEYS => false,
);
$vehicle = $builder->createVehicle($obj, $attributes);

/* insert the vehicle into the transport package */
$builder->putVehicle($vehicle);
```

Now that our package is complete and contains the vehicle that carries our snippet object, it's time to create the .ZIP file and tell the user that we're finished:

```
/* zip up the package (will go to /core/packages) */
$builder->pack();
echo '<br />Package complete.';
```

The transport package object automatically creates the final .ZIP file of a transport package in the site's **/core/packages** directory.

When you preview your MakeHello document, the package should be created. You should see a file called **hello2-1.0.0-beta1.transport.zip** in your **core/packages** directory.

To install the new package you've created (for testing), simply go to **System → Package Management** on the Top Menu. Select "Add New Package" and "Search Locally for Packages." The new package should show up in the grid. Once it's there, simply click on its "Install" button.

You should see a new snippet called Hello2 with the code we created for it. If you go to **System → Namespaces**, you should also see the hello2 namespace.

Enhancing Our Simple Package

There are several ways of enhancing our simple transport package. We could give it lexicon strings to prepare it for internationalization. We could transfer some support files (e.g., image files, CSS files, etc.). We could also show the user a **readme.txt** file and ask the user to agree to a license before installing the component. In addition, we could create a script (called a PHP resolver) that would interact with the user, so the user could set options during the install or create a PHP script (called a validator) that checks conditions to make sure the install should proceed. In the following sections, we'll discuss how to accomplish these tasks.

Internationalization

A well-behaved add-on component is ready for internationalization. All strings used in a component that can be viewed by a user (e.g., prompts, instructions, error messages, property descriptions, etc.) are contained in a set of lexicon entries. To internationalize our snippet, all we need (at a minimum) is an English language file containing the lexicon entries that will end up being installed as:

core/components/*component_name*/lexicon/en/default.inc.php

In our case, that would be:

core/components/hello2/lexicon/en/default.inc.php

That's where the file will end up, but where do we create it for the build process? Since it will go under the core directory, we want it at:

assets/hello2/core/hello2/lexicon/en/default.inc.php

In the **en** directory, we then create a file called **default.inc.php** containing the following line:

```
$_lang['hello'] = "Hello World";
```

During the install, the contents of our **/assets/hello2/core/** directory will be transferred to the **core/** directory. The lexicon directory will be automatically installed in its proper location during this process.

Next, we need to change the content of the Hello2 snippet to this:

```
$modx->lexicon->load('hello2:default');
return $modx->lexicon('hello');
```

The first line above tells MODX to load the language strings from the `default` topic of the `hello2` namespace (in the current language specified in the **manager_language** system setting) into the MODX lexicon object. MODX knows where to find them because it knows the namespace path. The second line tells MODX to return the language string from the lexicon that is associated with the key: `hello`.

The final step is the addition of the lexicon to our package. As long as the language files are in the proper place, they will be transported to the correct location when the package is installed. Remember, the default topic for the English language lexicon will be placed here for the build phase:

/assets/hello2/core/hello2/lexicon/en/default.inc.php

To make the add-on work with other languages, we'd simply add a new **default.inc.php** file for each language in a directory under the **lexicon** directory. For a French version, for example, we'd create a **lexicon/fr/** directory and a **default.inc.php** file in that directory with the following line:

```
$_lang['hello'] = "Bonjour Tout le Monde";
```

The French language file will be packaged along with the English one when the transport package file is created. We'll see how to add the file to our package in the following section.

File Resolvers

As we mentioned earlier, components often have files that need to be transferred in the package. There might be images used in the component or CSS files. We might also want to transfer documentation files or files containing examples of how to use the component, and we certainly want to transport our lexicon file. Transporting those files is the job of a file resolver.

In every transport package there is at least one vehicle. As we said earlier, every object to be transported in a package must be inside a vehicle. Vehicles can also have resolvers, however. A *resolver* is kind of an extra passenger in a transport package vehicle that carries something other than a MODX object.

Resolvers come in two flavors: a *file resolver* is a part of a vehicle that transfers files; a *PHP resolver* is a script that will be executed at the end of the install (more on those later). Resolvers act after the main part of a transport package has been installed, so any elements and resources installed in the package will be in place before any resolvers do their work.

 Resolvers must be attached to a vehicle. You can have a vehicle without a resolver, but you can't have a resolver without a vehicle. A *file resolver* simply copies one or more files and is very simple. You just specify the path to the directory containing the files you want to transfer and the path to where you want those files placed. To use a file resolver, you specify the two paths (source and target) after you've created a vehicle and before you put the vehicle in the package:

```
$vehicle = $builder->createVehicle($obj, $attributes);
$vehicle->resolve('file', array(
    'source' => $resolver_source,
    'target' => $resolver_target,
));
$builder->putVehicle($vehicle);
```

For example, we have all the files we want to place under the core directory stored in this directory:

assets/hello2/core/hello2/

You want them to end up here after the transfer:

/core/components/hello2/

You'd use this code:

```
$source = MODX_ASSETS_PATH . 'hello2/core/hello2';
$target = "return MODX_CORE_PATH . 'components/';";
$vehicle->resolve('file', array(
    'source' => $source,
    'target' => $target,
));
```

The transport package will grab the **hello2/** directory that is in **assets/hello2/core/** and all the files under it and install that **hello2/** directory in the **core/components/** directory. Because the lexicon file we created is also under the **assets/hello2/core/** directory, it will come along for the ride automatically.

Both the source and the target must be directory names, and the source directory name (**hello2** in this case) should not be in the specification of the target. It will automatically be created under the target directory. The $source specification is always the path to a directory to be packaged. The $target specification must be a line of PHP code that specifies the directory where the source file or directory should go. Note that the target path must end with a slash, but the source path should not.

If you need to transfer files to more than one location, you can add several file resolvers to a vehicle. If we had files we wanted to place under the assets directory, we'd have them stored in the **assets/hello2/assets/hello2/** directory and we'd use this code:

```
$source = MODX_ASSETS_PATH . 'hello2/assets/hello2';
$target = "return MODX_ASSETS_PATH . 'components/';";
$vehicle->resolve('file', array(
    'source' => $source,
    'target' => $target,
));
```

File Vehicles

Although it's not common, you might want to create a package that just transfers files and has no resources or elements. In that case, there's no object to attach a file resolver to. Instead of a file resolver, then, you need to use a *file vehicle*, an xPDO object that contains only files. The file vehicle object's class name is xPDOFileVehicle.

This code for a transport package will transfer the **hello2/** directory (located at **_build/ hello2/** on the local machine) to **/assets/components/hello2/** on the site where the package is installed:

```
$sourcePath = '_build/hello2';
$targetPath = "return MODX_ASSETS_PATH . 'components/ ';";
$obj = array ('source' => $sourcePath,'target' =>$targetPath);
$attributes = array('vehicle_class' => 'xPDOFileVehicle');
$package->put($obj, $attributes);
```

Adding the 'Special' Files

There are four files that have special status and are not transferred with a file resolver: a **readme.txt** file, a **license.txt** file, a **changelog.txt** file, and an (X)HTML file to be presented to the user during the install. All four are optional, but it is good form to include them. To use any of these, we need to create the files: **readme.txt**, **license.txt**, **changelog.txt**, and **user.input.html**. The names are arbitrary, and you can change them if you like, although the first three are very standard. The keys to the array — readme, license, changelog, and setup-options — must have those names.

To package our four files, we simply need to add this code just above the $builder->pack() line:

```
$builder->setPackageAttributes(array(
    'readme' => file_get_contents('path_to_readme_file'),
    'license' => file_get_contents('path_to_license_file'),
    'changelog' => file_get_contents('path_to_changelog_file'),
    'setup-options' => array(
        'source' => 'path_to_user_input_file',
    )
));
```

As we mentioned above, all four files are optional, and you can leave out any member of the array above. A **readme.txt** file should be included for every component, however. It will be shown to the user during the install. The file usually explains what the component does and how to use it along with one or more examples. It should also contain the version number, the author of the component, and the URL of the support page for the component (if any). The URL of the MODX Forums support topic for the component (if any) should be included as well.

The first three files are just plain text files containing the **readme.txt** info, a license (e.g., the GPL license) that the user needs to agree to before installing the add-on component, and a changelog showing changes to the various versions of the component. You don't need to create any code to handle these files. If there is a **readme.txt** file in the package, the installer will show it to the user during the install. The **changelog.txt** file, if any, will be shown below the readme information. If there is a license file in a package, the installer will automatically display the license and ask the user to agree to the license. The install will abort if the user does not agree to the license.

The fourth file, which we'll call **user.input.html**, allows you to interact with the user during the install. It requires further explanation (and a PHP resolver to process the user's input). We'll see how it works in the next section.

Interacting with the User

If you would like to interact with the user during the install, you need two extra files, which are normally placed in this directory:

assets/component_name**/_build/**

The first is an (X)HTML file that presents the user with a form. The second is a PHP script file that processes the user's input. We'll call these two files **user.input.html** and **install.script.php**, although the file names are arbitrary.

To demonstrate how the two files work together, we'll extend our package to ask the user during the install if we should create a document to display the results of our Hello2 snippet. We'll call that document *Hello2Demo*. Our package will automatically install the Hello2 snippet during the install, but it won't install the Hello2Demo document unless the user selects that option.

The user is automatically presented with the form contained in the **user.input.php** file specified in the optional setup-options member of the setPackageAttributes array shown above.

Be careful when constructing your **user.input.php** file. If it is not valid PHP code, or if you get the variable names wrong, the package installation could hang.

Here is the code of the **user.input.php** file:

```php
<?php
/* user.input.php code */
$output = '<input type="checkbox" name="install_sample"
    id="install_sample" value = "Yes" align="left" >  ';
$output .= '<label for = "install_sample">Install Demo Document
    (recommended).</label>';
$output .= '<p> </p>';
$output .= '<p><b>Check the box to install a sample page that calls
    your Hello2 snippet.</b></p>';
return $output;
```

The code above presents an HTML form with a checkbox the user can check to install a sample page containing a snippet tag to call the Hello2 snippet. If the user checks the box, the install_sample variable will be set to Yes. Notice that this is actually a PHP script, much like a snippet, and we could perform many other operations in addition to creating the form's output.

The installation will show the form to the user, and any variables in the form will be available in the **install.script.php** script as $options['*variable_name*'].

In our **install.script.php** code, we'll check to see whether the user selected the option. If the option has been selected, we'll create the Hello2Demo page and give it the default template.

Here is the code of the **install.script.php** file. Be careful to enter the code exactly as it appears here. The install will hang if there are any PHP syntax errors:

```php
<?php
/* Code for install.script.php File */
/* Make the $modx object available */
$modx =& $object->xpdo;
/* get the default template */
$default_template = $modx->config['default_template'];

$success = false;
switch($options[xPDOTransport::PACKAGE_ACTION]) {

    case xPDOTransport::ACTION_INSTALL:
        if (isset($options['install_sample'])
            && $options['install_sample'] == 'Yes' ) {
            $modx->log(xPDO::LOG_LEVEL_INFO, "Creating Hello2Demo");
            $r = $modx->newObject('modResource');
            $r->set('class_key','modDocument');
            $r->set('context_key','web');
            $r->set('type','document');
            $r->set('contentType','text/html');
            $r->set('pagetitle','Hello2Demo');
            $r->set('longtitle','Hello2Demo Page');
            $r->set('description','Show output of Hello2 Snippet');
            $r->set('alias','hello2-demo');
            $r->set('published','1');
            $r->set('parent','0');
            $r->setContent('[[Hello2]]');
            $r->set('richtext','0');
            $r->set('menuindex','99');
            $r->set('searchable','1');
            $r->set('cacheable','1');
            $r->set('menutitle','Hello');
```

```
                $r->set('hidemenu','0');
                $r->set('template', $default_template);
                $r->save();
            }
            $success = true;
            break;

        case xPDOTransport::ACTION_UPGRADE:
            $success = true;
            break;

        case xPDOTransport::ACTION_UNINSTALL:
            if (false === $modx->removeObject('modResource',
                array('name'=>'Hello2Demo'))) {
                    $modx->log(xPDO::LOG_LEVEL_INFO,
                    "<br /><b> NOTE: You may have to remove the
                    Hello2Demo Page manually</b><br />");
            }
            $success = true;
            break;
    }
return $success;
?>
```

This script will execute when the package is installed, but it will also execute when the package is upgraded or uninstalled. That's why we need the three case statements to respond appropriately to the three conditions. The value of $options[xPDOTransport::PACKAGE_ACTION] is set automatically by MODX to one of these three constants:

```
xPDOTransport::ACTION_INSTALL
xPDOTransport::ACTION_UPGRADE
xPDOTransport::ACTION_UNINSTALL
```

All three cases should return true to let MODX know that the code executed successfully unless an error condition is detected during the execution of a particular case. We haven't included any error-checking code in our example, but it would be a good idea to add some error checks and set $success to false if an error is detected. In the case of an upgrade, we don't want to create the resource because it should already exist.

Notice that in the uninstall case, we try to remove the Hello2Demo page, and if we're not successful (probably because the user has renamed the document), we warn the user that he or she will have to manually remove the page.

Elements and resources created in the main part of a transport package (e.g., our Hello2 snippet) will be removed automatically on uninstall. This is not the case, however, for elements or resources created with a PHP resolver script. Those have to be removed in the uninstall case of the script.

We have one last task to perform to make these two scripts work together. We've already told the transport package the name of the **user.input.html** file (when we set the package attributes above). Now, we need to add the **install.script.php** file to the package so that it will be executed on install. To do that, we need to create a PHP resolver and attach it to the vehicle we created earlier:

```
$vehicle->resolve('php', array(
    'type' => 'php',
    'source' => 'install.script.php',
));
```

The code above is placed just above the `$builder->pack()` line, usually after any file resolvers. The code of any PHP resolvers will execute at the end of the installation process.

Validators

Validators, like resolvers, are extra passengers that are attached to vehicles. Unlike resolvers, however, validators execute before any other parts of the transport package.

A *file validator* works exactly like a file resolver except that it runs at the beginning of the install rather than at the end. It simply stores directories from the source (and the files under them) into the transport package to be installed at the target location. File validators must be attached to a vehicle like this:

```
$vehicle->validate('file', array(
    'type' => 'file',
    'source' => $file_source,
    'target' => $file_target,
));
```

A *PHP validator* works exactly like a PHP resolver except that it operates at the beginning of the install instead of at the end. PHP validators must return `true` or `false`. If the return value is `false`, the install halts before performing any other actions. In order for the validator to abort the install, you must include this line in the attributes array for the vehicle containing the validator:

```
$attr[xPDOTransport::ABORT_INSTALL_ON_VEHICLE_FAIL] = true;
```

PHP validators must be attached to a vehicle like this:

```
$vehicle->validate('php', array(
    'type' => 'php',
    'source' => '_build/preinstall.script.php',
));
```

A component that should only be installed by the admin Super User, for example, could check to make sure that the admin Super User is logged in before proceeding. A component that requires CAPTCHA might have a PHP validator that checks to see that the CAPTCHA plugin is installed before proceeding, as in this example:

```
$obj = $transport->xpdo->getObject('modPlugin', array('name'=>'Captcha'));
$success = ($obj != null);
unset($obj); /* free up memory */
return $success;
```

PHP validators are added to a vehicle in the same way that PHP resolvers are:

```
$vehicle->validate('php', array(
    'type'=>'php',
    'source'=> $path_to_validator_source_file,
));
```

 All validators run in the order they were created in the build script at the beginning of an install, before any objects are installed. All resolvers run in the order they were created in the build script at the end of an install, after all objects are installed.

Further Enhancements

It is good form to put all the elements in a transport package into a category (named after the package), especially if there are many of them. This is relatively easy to do using some xPDO methods in the build script. The code below shows how to do that with the snippet object we packaged earlier. Once we have the snippet, we can create the category and add the snippet (and any other elements) to it using the category's addMany() method. We also have to modify the attributes array we used above to tell the package builder that we're including some related objects. We'll use the PKG_NAME we defined earlier for the category name. The code for that section would look like this:

```
/* create category */
$category= $modx->newObject('modCategory');
$category->set('id', 1);
$category->set('category', PKG_NAME);


/* add snippet (remember $obj is our snippet) */
$snippets = array();
$snippets[] = $obj;
$category->addMany($snippets);
/* If we had chunks or other elements, we'd add them
 * separately:
 * $category->addMany($chunks);
 */
$attributes = array(
    xPDOTransport::UNIQUE_KEY => 'category',
    xPDOTransport::PRESERVE_KEYS => false,
    xPDOTransport::UPDATE_OBJECT => true,
    xPDOTransport::RELATED_OBJECTS => true,
    xPDOTransport::RELATED_OBJECT_ATTRIBUTES => array (
        'Snippets' => array(
            xPDOTransport::PRESERVE_KEYS => false,
            xPDOTransport::UPDATE_OBJECT => true,
            xPDOTransport::UNIQUE_KEY => 'name',
        ),
        /* If we had some chunks or other elements to add
         * They would go here in separate arrays
         * 'Chunks' => array (
         *    xPDOTransport::PRESERVE_KEYS => false,
         *    xPDOTransport::UPDATE_OBJECT => true,
         *    xPDOTransport::UNIQUE_KEY => 'name',
         * ),
         */
    ),
);
```

```
$vehicle = $builder->createVehicle($category, $attributes);
/* Any validators or resolvers would go here */
$builder->putVehicle($vehicle);
```

The rest of the build script would be the same as the one we saw earlier in this chapter. Notice that we had to put our snippet in an array because the argument to addMany() must be an array of objects rather than a single object. Using this method, there's no need to create vehicles for any of the other objects. When the category is placed in the vehicle by the last line in the code above, all the other objects will come along for the ride because we have added them to the category as related objects.

The method above is extremely common in build scripts, especially those with multiple elements. The element objects are created first and placed in an array. Then the category is created. Finally, each element array is added to the category with the category's addMany() method. The elements in each array must all be of the same class type (e.g., all snippets in one array, all chunks in another, etc.), and each must be named in a separate member of the $attributes array as in the code above. All elements can be added this way.

The method of adding objects to a category doesn't work for resources, however, because they don't have a category. Each resource must have its own vehicle in a transport package. In the example above, we added a resource in the script resolver. Resources can also be added in the **build.transport.php** file. First, the $resource object is created:

```
$resource = $modx->newObject('modResource');
```

Its fields are set as we saw earlier in this chapter. Then, the resource is added to the package like this:

```
$attributes= array(
    xPDOTransport::PRESERVE_KEYS => false,
    xPDOTransport::UPDATE_OBJECT => true,
    xPDOTransport::UNIQUE_KEY => 'pagetitle',
    xPDOTransport::RELATED_OBJECTS => true,
    xPDOTransport::RELATED_OBJECT_ATTRIBUTES => array (
        'ContentType' => array(
            xPDOTransport::PRESERVE_KEYS => false,
            xPDOTransport::UPDATE_OBJECT => true,
            xPDOTransport::UNIQUE_KEY => 'name',
        ),
    ),
);
$vehicle = $builder->createVehicle($resource, $attributes);
$builder->putVehicle($vehicle);
```

As we mentioned earlier, each resource must have its own vehicle, so the last two lines are repeated for each resource you want to add to the package. The `$attributes` array only needs to be created once since it can be reused for each resource.

Creating an Array of File Paths

This enhancement isn't necessary, but it's very common to create an array called `$sources[]` containing all the paths used in the build script. It simplifies the code and makes it easier to reuse the code when you want to build another transport package. Here's an example:

```
$root = dirname(dirname(__FILE__)) . '/';
$sources= array (
    'root' => $root,
    'build' => $root . '_build/',
    /* note that unlike all the other paths,
       the next two must *not* have a trailing slash */
    'source_core' => $root . 'core/components/'.PKG_NAME_LOWER,
    'source_assets' => $root . 'assets/components/'.PKG_NAME_LOWER,
    'resolvers' => $root . '_build/resolvers/',
    'validators'=> $root . '_build/validators/',
    'data' => $root . '_build/data/',
    'docs' => $root . 'core/components/' . PKG_NAME_LOWER . '/docs/',
    'install_options' => $root . '_build/install.options/',
    'packages'=> $root . 'core/packages',
);
unset($root);
```

The example above is fairly comprehensive and, as you might guess, many simple transport packages might only need a few of those paths. The `source_core` and `source_assets` members are particularly useful. If they are set correctly, every package can transfer its files with the following code:

```
$vehicle->resolve('file', array(
    'source' => $sources['source_core'],
    'target' => "return MODX_CORE_PATH . 'components/';",
));
$vehicle->resolve('file', array(
    'source' => $sources['source_assets'],
    'target' => "return MODX_ASSETS_PATH . 'components/';",
));
```

Running the Script Outside of MODX

Most people who create MODX build scripts write the code in a code editor rather than in the MODX Manager. The build-script code could be copied and pasted into a snippet, but it's much easier to just run the code directly from the editor. This means that the build script is no longer a snippet and the $modx object is not automatically available. Some minor changes are required in the build script to allow it to run outside of MODX. First, the $modx object has to be initialized at the top of the build file with code like this:

```
require_once $sources['build'] . 'build.config.php';
$sources['build'] = MODX_ASSETS_PATH . 'mycomponent/_build';
require_once MODX_CORE_PATH . 'model/modx/modx.class.php';
$modx= new modX();
$modx->initialize('mgr');
```

The code above simply loads the MODX class file and creates a new $modx object for use in the build script. The constants necessary for the build script, such as MODX_ASSETS_PATH and MODX_CORE_PATH, are defined in the build.config.php file, which might look like this:

```
<?php
define('MODX_CORE_PATH',
    dirname(dirname(dirname(dirname(dirname(__FILE__))))) . '/core/');
define('MODX_BASE_PATH',
    dirname(dirname(dirname(dirname(dirname(__FILE__))))) . '/');
define('MODX_MANAGER_PATH',
    MODX_BASE_PATH . 'manager/');
define('MODX_CONNECTORS_PATH',
    MODX_BASE_PATH . 'connectors/');
define('MODX_ASSETS_PATH',
    MODX_BASE_PATH . 'assets/');
```

A second change involves using the $modx object's log() method rather than echo to provided feedback while the build script is running:

```
$modx->setLogLevel(xPDO::LOG_LEVEL_INFO);
$modx->setLogTarget(XPDO_CLI_MODE ? 'ECHO' : 'HTML');
$modx->log(modX::LOG_LEVEL_INFO, 'Creating Package.');
/* . . . */
$modx->log(modX::LOG_LEVEL_INFO, 'Adding in snippets.');
```

With the exception of the two changes above, a build script to be run outside of MODX will look exactly the same as the one in our snippet.

More Information

There is now a very complete build-script template called MyComponent that contains examples of almost everything you might want to do in a build script. It's designed so that you can modify it to create your own build script. To install it on your site, go to Package Manager, click on the "Download Extras" button, and look for the GetMyComponent package. There is a tutorial for MyComponent at `http://bobsguides.com`.

Summary

A transport package contains an installable third-party component. Transport packages are installed using Package Manager, and they can also be updated and uninstalled there. The packages can be very simple, such as a simple snippet, or much more complicated with many MODX files, resources, and elements. Transport packages can interact with the user during the install process to allow the user to control the installation and set options and properties.

Transport packages are created using PHP code, and in the chapter, we looked at how files can be transported and how MODX resources and elements can be created and installed by the package.

We built a simple transport package and then enhanced it to include internationalization. Every object to be transported in a package must be inside a vehicle. Vehicles can also have resolvers, however. A *resolver* is kind of an extra passenger in a transport package vehicle that carries something other than a MODX object. File resolvers carry files, and PHP resolvers contain scripts that will be executed at the end of the install. Packages can also use file vehicles to carry files when there is no MODX object along for the ride. A readme file, a license file, a changelog, and a setup-options file can be included in the package. The setup-options file is used to interact with the user during the install.

Validators are also attached to vehicles. They execute before the package is installed. A file validator installs files that might be needed during the install. A PHP validator is a PHP script that will run before the install begins. If a PHP validator returns `true`, the installation will continue. If it returns `false`, the installation will halt.

MODX Evolution Notes

There are no transport packages in Evolution. Most Evolution add-on components do not have an installation package and must be installed manually. It is possible to create an installation script for an Evolution component, but it involves direct manipulation of the database, usually using the MODX DBAPI.

MODX API

The MODX API is a set of PHP variables and methods (functions) that you can use to interact with MODX in snippets and plugins. The classes containing the variables and methods documented here are the xPDO class, the xPDOObject class, the modX class, and the modUser class. Some seldom-used methods have been omitted, as have some methods that are only for internal use by MODX.

Because the modX class is a direct descendant of the xPDO class, the preferred method of calling all the methods listed below for the modX class and the xPDO class is:

```
$modx->methodName();
```

There are some situations, however, where the $modx object is not available, such as in some plugins (depending on the event that triggers them) and scripts attached to a transport package. In those cases, the methods need to be called like this:

```
$xpdo->methodName();
```

You can also create a $modx reference variable so that you can call those methods with $modx->methodName() with this line at the top of your code:

```
$modx =& $xpdo;
```

The xPDOObject methods are available for all resources and elements. Once you have a reference to an object, you can call the xPDOObject method as a method of that object. The general form is:

```
$object->methodName();
```

Here is an example:

```
$resource = $modx->getObject('modDocument', array('pagetitle'=>'Home'));
$id = $resource->get('id');
```

In the code above, the resource ID of the resource object is retrieved by calling the resource object's get() method.

The following lists contain the most commonly used public methods of the four classes. The classes also have member variables, but their values should almost always be retrieved using one of the following methods. A full reference to all MODX Revolution methods and variables is available at **http://api.modx.com/**. Arguments in square brackets are optional.

xPDO Class

These are the most commonly used methods of the xPDO class. Some of them are discussed in detail in Chapter 8. Note that individual object classes may override these methods, and those overridden methods may take different arguments. In the case of users, resources, and elements, the arguments are usually the same as those documented here.

addPackage([string $pkg = ''], [string $path = ''], [string|null $prefix = null])

— Adds a package (an xPDO package, not a transport package) to xPDO. This function doesn't actually load any classes. Instead, it tells xPDO where to look for the class files in the named package. **$pkg** is the name of the directory containing the package. **$path** is the path to that directory. The third argument specifies a package-specific table prefix and is seldom used. This method returns true on success and false on failure. In the following example, MODX will register this package:

```
MODX_CORE_PATH/components/captcha
```

It will load this file:

```
MODX_CORE_PATH/components/captcha/model/captcha/veriword.class.php:
```

Here is the code:

```
$captcha_core_path = MODX_CORE_PATH.'components/captcha/';
$modx->addPackage('captcha', $captcha_core_path .'model/');
$modx->loadClass('captcha.veriword',
    $captcha_core_path . 'model/',true,true);
$vword = new VeriWord($modx,$width,$height);
```

beginTransaction() — Begin an xPDO DB transaction (PHP5, InnoDB engine only). Returns true on success.

commit() — End an xPDO DB transaction (PHP5, InnoDB engine only). Returns true on success.

connect([array $driverOptions = array()]) — Creates an xPDO connection. This is generally not needed to connect to the MODX database, which will be connected automatically. Returns `true` on success.

errorCode() — Returns an `SQLSTATE` string. See the PHP PDO docs for details.

errorInfo() — Returns a three-member array containing `SQLSTATE`, driver-specific error code, and driver-specific error message. Here are the three members of the returned array:

> **0** — `SQLSTATE` error code (a five-character alphanumeric identifier defined in the `ANSI SQL` standard).
> **1** — Driver-specific error code.
> **2** — Driver-specific error message.

exec(string $query) — Executes the SQL `$query` string (PHP5 only). Returns the number of rows affected. Does not return the results of a SELECT query (see `query()`).

getAggregates(string $className) — Returns a string containing the foreign key relationship definitions for the named class (available with `$obj->getOne()` or `$obj->GetMany()`). Example:

```
$aggs = $xpdo->getAggregates('modResource');
return print_r($aggs));
```

getAncestry(string $className, [boolean $includeSelf = true]) — On success, returns an array containing the names of all classes from which the named class is a descendant. Returns an empty array on failure.

getAttribute($attribute) — Returns the value of the named database connection attribute (PHP5 only). See the PHP PDO docs for possible attributes.

getCacheManager([string $class = 'cache.xPDOCacheManager'], [$options = array('path' => XPDO_CORE_PATH, 'ignorePkg' => true)], string $path, boolean $ignorePkg) — Returns a handle to the MODX cache manager object. Usually called with no arguments.

getCachePath() — Returns the absolute path to the MODX **cache** directory as a string.

getCollection(string $className, [object|array|string $criteria = null], [mixed $cacheFlag = true]) — Returns the array of MODX objects specified by the `$criteria` argument. Returns `null` on failure. Examples:

```
/* get all chunks in category 7 */
$chunks = $modx->getCollection('modChunk', array('category'=>'7'));
foreach ($chunks as $chunk) {
    echo $chunk->get('name') . '<br />';
}
```

```
/* get all docs fitting a set of criteria, sorted by ID */
$c = $modx->newQuery('modResource');
$c->where(array(
    'published'=>'1',
    'createdby'=>'1',
    'richtext'=>'1',
));
$c->sortby('id','ASC');
$docs = $modx->getCollection('modResource', $c);
foreach ($docs as $doc) {
    echo $doc->get('pagetitle') . ' (' . $doc->get('id') . ')' . '<br />';
}
```

getCollectionGraph(string $className, mixed $graph, [mixed $criteria = null],[mixed $cacheFlag = true]) — Like getCollection(), but $graph specifies related objects to retrieve along with the named object (in JSON or PHP array format) in a single query. Returns an array of objects or an empty array on failure. Sending an empty array for $criteria will get all objects. Set $cacheFlag to false if you don't want the results cached. Example:

```
/* get all active users and their profiles */
$users = $modx->getCollectionGraph('modUser',
    array('Profile' =>array()),
    array('active'=> '1'));
/* JSON form equivalent to above . . .
$users = $modx->getCollectionGraph('modUser',
    '{"Profile":{}}', array('active' => '1'));
*/
/* get all users except JoeBlow . . .
$users = $modx->getCollectionGraph('modUser',
    array('Profile' =>array()),
    array('username:!='=> 'JoeBlow'))';
*/
/* display user data with Tpl chunk */
foreach ($users as $user) {
    $output[] = $modx->getChunk('userTpl',
        array_merge($user->toArray(),
        $user->Profile->toArray()));
}
return implode('<br />', $output);
```

getComposites(string $className) — Returns an array of strings with composite foreign key relationship definitions for the named class.

getCount(string $className, [mixed $criteria = null]) — Like getCollection(), but returns only the number of objects found as an integer.

getDebug() — Reports on the debug state. Returns true if debug is on.

getDebugBacktrace() — Returns an array containing abbreviated backtrace information.

getFields(string $className) — Returns an array containing the field name => default value pairs for the named class. Returns an empty array on failure.

getIterator(string $className, [object|array|string $criteria = null], [mixed $cacheFlag = true]) — Exactly like getCollection() except that the actual objects are not pulled from the database until they are used. With getCollection(), the initial query is slower and uses more memory, but a loop that processed the items will be faster. The opposite is true with getIterator(), which will use less memory and allow elements to be processed as they are referred to.

getManager() — Returns an instance of the manager class for the current connection (or null on failure). The manager object has methods for operations such as creating or altering table structures and other advanced operations that are seldom used.

getMicroTime() — Returns a float containing the current microtime() value in seconds.

getObject(string $className, [mixed $criteria = null], [mixed $cacheFlag = true]) — Like getCollection(), but returns a single object or null on failure. If the second argument is an integer, it will get the object with that ID. Example:

```
$modx->getObject('modResource', array('pagetitle'=>'Home'));
$modx->getObject('modResource', 12);
```

getObjectGraph(string $className, mixed $graph, [mixed $criteria = null],[mixed $cacheFlag = true]) — Like getObject(), but $graph specifies related objects to retrieve along with the named object (in JSON or PHP array format) in a single query. Returns a single object or null on failure. Logs an error if more than one object is found. Set $cacheFlag to false if you don't need to cache the results. Example:

```
$user = $modx->getObjectGraph('modUser',
    array('Profile' =>array()),
    array('username'=> 'JoeBlow', false));
/* JSON form equivalent to above . . .
$user = $modx->getObjectGraph('modUser',
    '{"Profile":{}}',
    array('username' => 'JoeBlow'));
*/
```

```
/* display user data with Tpl chunk */
$output[] = $modx->getChunk('userTpl',
    array_merge($user->toArray(),
    $user->Profile->toArray()));
return implode('<br />', $output);
```

getOption(string $key, [array $options = null], [mixed $default = null])
— Gets an xPDO option value (or a value from the $options array). The third argument
is a default value to use if the option is not found. Also searches system settings if the key
is not found. Examples:

```
$tablePrefix = $modx->getOption(xPDO::OPT_TABLE_PREFIX);
$siteStatus = $modx->getOption('site_status');
$opt = $modx->getOption('use_captcha', $scriptProperties, false);
```

getPackage(string $className) — Returns a string containing the package name of
the named class.

getPK(string $className) — Returns the primary key for the named class as a string
or an array of strings for compound primary keys. Returns null if the class has no defined
primary key.

getPKType(string $className, [$pk = false]) — Returns a string with the type
of the primary key of the named class or null if no primary key is defined.

getTableName(string $className, [boolean $includeDb = false]) — Returns a
string containing the full table name for the named class or null on failure. The second argument, which allows the specification of the database name, is generally not used. Example:

```
$table = getTableName('modResource');
```

lastInsertId() — Returns the ID of the last row inserted into the database. Can be used
to get the resource ID of a newly created resource.

**loadClass(string $fqn, [$path = ''], [$ignorePkg = false],
[$transient = false])** — Loads a PHP class file. $fqn is in the form
$dir_1 . $dir_2 . classname. $path is the path to dir_1. Returns the class name on
success, null on failure. In the following example, MODX will look for this file:

MODX_CORE_ PATH/components/wayfinder/wayfinder.class.php

(See also the example for addPackage() above.)

For add-on packages, the third and fourth arguments are usually set to true. Their default is false, and for built-in classes, they are usually omitted:

```
$wayfinder_base = $modx->getOption('core_path') . 'components/wayfinder/';
if (!$modx->loadClass('Wayfinder', $wayfinder_base, true, true)) {
    return 'error: Wayfinder class not found';
}
$wf = new Wayfinder($modx, $scriptProperties);
```

log(integer $level, string $msg, [mixed $target = ''], [string $def = ''], [string $file = ''], [string $line = '']) — Logs a message to the current logTarget unless the $target argument is set. If you are logging to your own file, $target will be an array (see setLogTarget() and setLogLevel().

Arguments:

> **$level** — Choices are:
>
> > **xPDO::LOG_LEVEL_FATAL**
> > **xPDO::LOG_LEVEL_INFO**
> > **xPDO::LOG_LEVEL_WARN**
> > **xPDO::LOG_LEVEL_ERROR**
> > **xPDO::LOG_LEVEL_DEBUG**
>
> **$msg** — Message to record.
>
> **$target** — Choices are:
>
> > **ECHO** — Send to STDOUT.
> > **HTML** — Same as ECHO but with HTML formatting.
> > **FILE** — Send to a file.
>
> **$def** — Defining structure (e.g., name of class where error occurred).
> **$file** — Name of file in which the error occurred.
> **$line** — Line number where the error occurred.

newObject(string $className, [array $fields = array()]) — Creates a new xPDO object of the named class, loads it, and passes the current xPDO instance to it. $fields allows you to set fields of the object. Returns the new object or null on failure. Objects are transient until $object->save() is called. Example:

```
$chunk = $modx->newObject('modChunk', array('name'=>'MyChunk'));
$chunk->set('description', 'My new chunk');
$chunk->setContent('This is my new chunk');
$chunk->save();
```

newQuery(string $class, [mixed $criteria = null], [boolean|integer $cacheFlag = true]) — Returns an xPDO query on the named class for use in getCollection() and other get methods. $cacheFlag caches the query if true. If $cacheFlag is an integer, the query will be cached for that many seconds. If $cacheFlag is 0, the query will be cached indefinitely. Criteria are the same as those for getObject() and getCollection().

prepare($statement, [$driver_options = array()]) — Prepares an SQL statement for execution. See exec() and query() (PHP5 only). Used for optimization of statements that will be executed more than once with different parameters. Returns a PDOStatement or a PDOException on failure.

query($statement) — Executes a PDOStatement (PHP5 only). Returns a PDOStatement or PDOException on failure.

removeCollection(string $className, mixed $criteria) — Removes the specified collection from the database without instantiating it. Returns true on success, false on failure.

removeObject(string $className, mixed $criteria) — Removes the specified object from the database without instantiating it. Returns true on success, false on failure.

rollBack() — Rolls back a transaction to the point where beginTransaction() was called (PHP5, InnoDB engine only). Returns true on success, false on failure.

setAttribute($attribute, $value) — Sets a PDO attribute value (PHP5 only).

setDebug([boolean $v = true]) — Sets the xPDO debug state.

setLogLevel([integer $level = xPDO::LOG_LEVEL_FATAL]) — Sets the level of XPDO log messages.

setLogTarget([string $target = 'ECHO'], mixed 1) — Sets the current log target. Returns the current target so you can set it back after logging a message. The choices for target are ECHO, HTML, and FILE. HTML echoes the message with HTML formatting. FILE defaults to the MODX error log. To set a particular file as a target, use this form:

```
$modx->setLogTarget('FILE');
$target = array(
    'target' => 'FILE',
    'options' => array(
        'filename' => 'path_to_file'),
);
$modx->log(xPDO::LOG_LEVEL_ERROR, 'Error Message', $target);
```

setOption(string $key, mixed $value) — Sets an xPDO option (MODX system setting) value. Does not alter the database. The change persists only for the duration of the current request. Example:

```
$modx->setOption('site_start', $id);
```

xPDOObject Class

All MODX Revolution objects are descended from the xPDOObject class, so the methods of the class are available for all resources and elements. Once you have a reference to an object, you can call the xPDOObject method as a method of that object:

```
$resource = $modx->getObject('modDocument', array('name'=>'Home Page'));
$id = $resource->get('id');
```

These are the most commonly used methods of the xPDOObject class. Many of them are discussed in detail in Chapter 8. Note that individual object classes may override these methods and those overridden methods may take different arguments. In the case of users, resources, and elements, the arguments are usually the same as those documented here.

addMany(mixed &$obj, [string $alias = '']) — Adds a related object or an array of related objects to the object. Only valid when there can be many related object of the type. The related object(s) will be saved when the object is saved. The $alias argument is only necessary if there are multiple relations for the class. Returns true on success, false on failure. Example:

```
$category = $modx->newObject('modCategory',
    array('category'=>'MySnippets'));
$snippet = $modx->getObject('modSnippet', array('name'=>'MySnippet'));
$category->addMany($snippet);
$category->save();
```

addOne(mixed &$obj, [string $alias = '']) — Like addMany(), but adds a single related object. Only valid when there can be only one related object with the type. Returns true on success, false on failure. Example:

```
$user = $modx->newObject('modUser', array('username'=>'MyUser'));
$userProfile = $modx->newObject('modUserProfile');
$userProfile->set('fullname', 'My User');
$userProfile->set('email', 'myuser@gmail.com');
$user->addOne($userProfile);
$user->save();
```

fromArray(array $fldarray, [string $keyPrefix = ''], [boolean $setPrimaryKeys = false], [boolean $rawValues = false], [boolean $adhocValues = false]) — Sets object fields from an associative array. $keyPrefix is an optional prefix that will be stripped from all fields. The other fields are seldom used except in MODX internal code and transport packages. Example:

```
$resource = $modx->newObject('modResource');
$fields = array(
    'pagetitle'=>'Home',
    'alias'=>'home',
    'published'=>'1',
    'menutitle'=>'Home Page',
);
$resource->fromArray($fields);
$resource->save();
```

fromJSON(string $jsonSource, [string $keyPrefix = ''], [boolean $setPrimaryKeys = false], [boolean $rawValues = false], [boolean $adhocValues = false]) — Like fromArray(), but with a JSON formatted string as the first argument.

get(string|array $key, [string|array $format = null], [mixed $formatTemplate = null]) — Gets a field or fields from the object. The last two arguments are seldom used. Returns the value of the named field or an associative array of field names and values. Examples:

```
$modx->resource->get('pagetitle');
$modx->resource->get(array('pagetitle','alias','longtitle'));
```

getMany(string $alias, [object $criteria = null], [boolean|integer $cacheFlag = true]) — Gets a group of related objects for the current object. Only valid when there can be more than one related object with the alias. The $criteria argument specifies criteria for the search. The $cacheFlag argument specifies whether the results will be cached. If $cacheFlag is an integer, it will specify how many seconds to cache the result. Returns the array of objects or an empty array on failure. Examples:

```
$kids = $modx->resource->getMany('Children');
$publishedKids = $modx->resource->getMany('Children',
    array('published'=>'1'));
/* get published children of the current resource sorted by pagetitle */
$criteria = $modx->newQuery('modResource');
$criteria->where(array(
    'published' => '1',
));
$criteria->sortby('pagetitle', 'ASC');
$children = $modx->resource->getMany('Children', $criteria);
```

getOne(string $alias, [object $criteria = null], [boolean|integer $cacheFlag = true]) — like getMany(), but gets a single related object. Only valid if there can be only one object with the alias. Returns the object or null if no instance exists. Example:

```
$modx->resource->getOne('Parent');
```

isNew() — Indicates whether the object is new and has not been permanently saved. Returns true if the object has not been saved or false if it has been saved.

remove([$ancestors = array()]) — Permanently removes the object and any objects that are dependent on it from the database. The $ancestors array is used internally to prevent circular references and should not be set. Returns true on success, false on failure. Example:

```
$obj->remove();
```

save([boolean|integer $cacheFlag = null]) — Saves an object to the database along with any changed related objects. $cacheflag specifies whether the object should be saved in the cache and, if it is an integer, for how many seconds. Example:

```
$obj->save();
```

set(string $key, [[mixed $value = null], [string|callable $vType = '']) — Sets a field of the object. $key is the name of the field to set. $value is the value to set it to. $vType is an optional string indicating the format of the value sent or a callable function that will set the value. Format options are 'integer' and 'utc'. If $vType is a function, it will execute to set the value, overriding the default behavior. Returns true if the value is set and the value is different from the previous value (i.e., object is now "dirty"). Returns false in all other cases. Automatically sets the dirty flag for the field. Example:

```
if ($resource->set('alias', 'newAlias')) {
    $resource->save();
}
```

toArray([string $keyPrefix = ''], [boolean $rawValues = false], [boolean $excludeLazy = false]) — Copies fieldnames and their values to an associative array. $keyPrefix is an optional prefix to prepend to all keys. If $rawValues is true, will get the raw values of the fields instead of the processed values returned by the object's get() method. Often called with no arguments for resources and elements. Returns the array on success and null on failure.

```
$fields = $modx->resource->toArray();
return print_r($fields, true);
```

toJSON([string $keyPrefix = ''], [boolean $rawValues = false]) — The same as toArray(), but returns a JSON-format string containing the keys and values. Returns an empty string on failure.

modX Class

These methods can all be called with $modx->*methodName*(). Because the modX class is a direct descendant of the xPDO class, all of the methods in the previous section can also be called with $modx->*methodName*(). The reverse is not true, however. The methods below cannot be called with $xpdo->*methodName*().

In some situations, the $modx object is not available (e.g., transport package scripts and some plugin events). In those cases, you'll either need to use xPDO class methods or load the modX class and instantiate an instance of the $modx object like this:

```
$corePath = 'path_to_modx_core';
require_once $corePath . 'model/modx/modx.class.php';
$modx = new modX();
$modx->initialize('mgr');
```

In all other cases, $modx->*MethodName*() is the preferred method.

These are the most commonly used methods of the modX class. The ones described as deprecated will be removed in future versions of MODX (most have been removed as of MODX 2.1), but at present, they are often used in MODX Evolution.

addEventListener(event $event, int $id) — Adds a plugin to the event map for the duration of the current request.

changePassword(string $oldPwd, string $newPwd) — Changes the current user's password. Returns true on success, an error message on failure.

changeWebUserPassword($oldPwd, $newPwd) — Deprecated. Use changePassword().

checkPreview() — Deprecated.

checkSession([string $sessionContext = 'web']) — Checks to see if the user has a session set in the named context ('mgr' for the back end, 'web' for the front end, or a user-created context name). Returns true if the user session is set.

cleanDocumentIdentifier(string|integer $qOrig) — Deprecated.

getActiveChildren([$id = 0], [$sort = 'menuindex'], [$dir = 'ASC'], [$fields = 'id, pagetitle, description, parent, alias, menutitle, class_key, context_key']) — Deprecated. Use getChildIds().

getAllChildren([$id = 0], [$sort = 'menuindex'], [$dir = 'ASC'], [$fields = 'id, pagetitle, description, parent, alias, menutitle, class_key, context_key']) — Deprecated. Use getChildIds().

getAuthenticatedUser([string $contextKey = '']) — Returns the user object for the currently logged-in user (if any) in the named context or null on failure. The current context is used by default if no argument is sent. This function is for internal use by MODX and shouldn't be called directly. Instead, use `$modx->user->hasSessionContext()` or `$modx->user->isAuthenticated()`. Examples:

```
$isAuthenticated = $modx->user->hasSessionContext(
    $modx->context->get('key'));
$isAuthenticated = $modx->user->isAuthenticated('web');
```

getCacheManager() — Gets a reference to the MODX cache manager object. Example:

```
$cacheManager= $modx->getCacheManager();
$cacheManager->clearCache();
```

getChildIds([integer $id = null], [integer $depth = 10]) — Returns an array containing the Resource IDs of all children of the resource with the named ID. The current resource's ID is used by default. $depth determines how many levels (not resources) are searched. Returns an empty array if no children are found. Examples:

```
/* get and display all TVs of the children of doc 12 */
$ids = $modx->getChildIds(12);
foreach ($ids as $id) {
    $obj = $modx->getObject('modDocument', array('id'=>$id));
    $tvs = $obj->getMany('TemplateVars');
    $output .= 'Pagetitle:' . $obj->get('pagetitle') .
        ' (' . $id . ')' . '<br />';
    foreach($tvs as $tv) {
        $output .= '   TvName: ' . $tv->get('name') .
            ' ----- Raw Value: ' . $tv->getValue($id) .
            ' ----- Processed Value: ' . $tv->renderOutput($id) . '<br />';
    }
}
return $output;
/* Get and display a single TV for all children of doc 12 */
$ids = $modx->getChildIds(12);
$tv = $modx->getObject('modTemplateVar', array('name'=>'MyTv'));
foreach($ids as $id) {
    $output .= 'Page Id: ' . $id . ' ----- Raw Value: ' .
        $tv->getValue($id) . ' ----- Processed Value: ' .
        $tv->renderOutput($id) . '<br />';
}
return $output;
```

getChunk(string $chunkName, [array $properties = array()]) — Returns the content of the named chunk as a string. $properties is an array of key/value pairs. For placeholder tags in the chunk, key placeholders will be replaced with the associated value. Other tags in the chunk (e.g., chunk and snippet tags) will also be processed.

getConfig() — Returns an associative array of key/value pairs containing the MODX configuration settings (e.g., modx_base_url, modx_base_path, modx_core_path, etc. See **core/model/modx/modx.class.php** for the full list) and all MODX system settings (see the System Settings grid in the Manager for others). Returns null on failure.

getContext(string $contextKey) — Returns the named context object (without initializing it).

getDocGroups() — Deprecated. Use getCollection().

getDocument([$id = 0], [$fields = "*"], [$published = 1], [$deleted = 0]) — Deprecated. Use getObject().

getDocumentChildren([$id = 1], [$published = 1], [$deleted = 0], [$fields = "*"], [$where = ''], [$sort = "menuindex"], [$dir = "ASC"], [$limit = ""]) — Deprecated. Use getChildIds() or getMany('Children').

getDocumentChildrenTVars([$parentid = 0], [$tvidnames = array()], [$published = 1], [$docsort = "menuindex"], [$docsortdir = "ASC"], [$tvfields = "*"], [$tvsort = "rank"], [$tvsortdir = "ASC"]) — Deprecated. Use getChildIds() and getMany('TemplateVars') in a foreach() loop.

getDocumentIdentifier(string $method) — Deprecated. Use $resource->get('id') or, for the current resource, $modx->resource->get('id').

getDocumentMethod() — Deprecated.

getDocumentObject(string $method, string|int $identifier) — Deprecated. Use $modx->getObject().

getDocuments([$ids = array()], [$published = 1], [$deleted = 0], [$fields = "*"], [$where = ''], [$sort = "menuindex"], [$dir = "ASC"], [$limit = ""]) — Deprecated. Use getCollection().

getEventMap(string $contextKey) — Returns an array containing all events and their associated plugins for the named context. $contextKey is required. There is no error return.

getFullTableName($tbl) — Deprecated. Use getTableName().

getKeywords([integer $id = 0]) — Deprecated. Use template variables for key words.

getLoginUserID([string $context = '']) — Returns the user ID of the currently logged-in user in the named context. Uses the current context by default.

getLoginUserName([string $context = '']) — Returns the username of the currently logged-in user in the named context. Uses the current context by default.

getLoginUserType() — Deprecated. Revolution makes no distinction between manager users and web users. Use $modx->user.

getManagerPath() — Deprecated. Use MODX_MANAGER_PATH or $modx->getOption('manager_path').

getMETATags([integer $id = 0]) — Deprecated. Use template variables for meta tags.

getPageInfo([integer $pageid = -1], [integer $active = 1], [string $fields = 'id, pagetitle, description, alias, class_key, context_key']) — Deprecated. Use $modx->getObject() and $object->get('fieldName').

getParent([integer $pid = -1], [integer $active = 1], [string $fields = 'id, pagetitle, description, alias, parent, class_key, context_key']) — Deprecated. Use $resource->get('parent') for the ID or $resource->getOne('Parent') for the object.

getParentIds([integer $id = null], [integer $height = 10]) — Returns an array containing the ancestor Resource IDs up the tree. $height is the number of levels (not resources) to search. The immediate parent will be the first member, the grandparent will be the second, and so on.

getParser() — Returns the modParser object for the current modx instance.

getPlaceholder(string $key) — Returns the value of the named placeholder.

getRegisteredClientScripts() — Returns a string containing the parsed HTML output of all registered JavaScript blocks. See the reg* methods below.

getRegisteredClientStartupScripts() — Returns a string containing the parsed HTML output of all registered CSS, JS, and/or HTML blocks. See the reg* methods below.

getRequest([$string $class = 'modRequest'], [$path $path = '']) — Attempts to load the named request handler class. Loads the modRequest class by default. $path is the absolute path to the class. $path defaults to the current model path. Returns true on success, false on failure.

getResponse([$string $class = 'modResponse'], [$path $path = '']) — Attempts to load the named response handler class. Loads the modResponse class by default. $path is the absolute path to the class. $path defaults to the current model path. Returns true on success, false on failure.

getService(string $name, [string $class = ''], [string $path = ''], [array $params = array()]) — Loads and returns an instance of the named service class or null on failure. $name is the variable name of the returned instance. If $class is empty, $name is used for the class. $path defaults to XPDO_CORE_PATH. $params contains an optional array of parameters to pass to the class constructor.

getSessionState() — Returns an integer describing the state of the current settings. Possible values are:

> **modX::SESSION_STATE_UNINITIALIZED**
> **modX::SESSION_STATE_UNAVAILABLE**
> **modX::SESSION_STATE_EXTERNAL**
> **modX::SESSION_STATE_INITIALIZED**

getSettings() — An alias for getConfig().

getTemplateVar([string $idname = ""], [string $fields = "*"], [$resourceId = ""], [integer $published = 1], integer $docid) — Deprecated. Use getObject(). Examples:

```
$tv = $modx->getObject('modTemplateVar', array('name'=>'MyTv'));
$tv = $modx->getObject('modTemplateVar', 12);
```

getTemplateVarOutput([array $idnames = array()], [integer $resourceId = ""], [integer $published = 1]) — Deprecated. Use: $modx->getObject() and $tv->renderOutput($id). Example:

```
/* get the value of the 'MyTv' in document 12 */
$tv = $modx->getObject('modTemplateVar', array('name'=>'MyTv'));
$rawValue = $tv->getValue(12);
$processedValue = $tv->renderOuput(12);
```

getTemplateVars([array $idnames = array()], [$fields = "*"], [$resourceId = ""], [$published = 1], [$sort = "tv.rank, tvtpl.rank"], [$dir = "ASC,ASC"]) — Deprecated. Use $modx->getObject() and $obj->getMany('TemplateVars'). Example:

```
$obj = $modx->getObject('modResource', array('name'=>'MyDoc'));
$id = $obj->get('id');
$tvs = $obj->getMany('TemplateVars');
foreach ($tvs as $tv) {
    $rawValue = $tv->getValue($id);
    $processedValue = $tv->renderOutput($id);
}
```

getTree([int|array $id = null], [int $depth = 10]) — Returns a site tree as an array of Resource IDs. $id can be a single Resource ID or an array of Resource IDs to use as the head(s) of the tree. Uses the current resource by default. $depth is the number of levels to search.

getUser([string $contextKey = '']) — Returns a modUser object. By default, gets the current user from the current context. Used internally by MODX. Use $modx->user.

getUserDocGroups([boolean $resolveIds = false]) — Deprecated. Use getCollection('modResourceGroup').

getUserInfo(integer $uid) — Deprecated. Use $modx->user and/or $user->getOne('Profile').

getVersionData() — Returns an array containing the version information for the current MODX install. Array members:

> **version** — Current version (e.g., 2).
> **major_version** — Current major version (e.g., 0).
> **minor_version** — Current minor version (e.g., 1).
> **patch_level** — Current patch level (e.g., beta-3).
> **code_name** — Current codename (e.g., Revolution).
> **full_version** — All of the above.
> **full_appname** — 'MODX' . code_name | full_version (if code_name is empty).

getWebUserInfo(integer $uid) — Deprecated. Use getUser().

handleRequest() — Initialize, cleanse, and handle a request from a browser. Returns the result of the process.

hasPermission(string $pm) — Returns true if the current user has the specified policy permission or false if not. Example:

```
$ok = $modx->hasPermission('edit_resource');
```

initialize([string $contextKey = 'web']) — Initializes the MODX engine for the named context (or the current context by default). Loads common classes and objects and all system/configuration settings. Example:

```
$modx->initialize('mgr');
```

insideManager() — Deprecated. Use $modx->context->get('key'). Example:

```
if ($modx->context->get('key') == 'mgr') {
    return ('Inside Manager');
}
```

invokeEvent(string $eventName, [array $params = array()]) — Fires the named event with optional parameters. Example:

```
$modx->invokeEvent('OnUserFormPrerender', array(
    'id' => 0,
    'mode' => modSystemEvent::MODE_NEW,
));
```

isBackend() — Deprecated. Use $modx->context->get('key').

isFrontend() — Deprecated. Use $modx->context->get('key').

isMemberOfWebGroup([array $groupNames = array()]) — Deprecated. Revolution has no web groups, only user groups.

lexicon(string $key, [array $params = array()]) — Returns a lexicon string. Use $modx->lexicon->load(namespace:topic) first for non-core messages. Example:

```
$modx->lexicon->load('spform:default');
return $modx->lexicon('unauthorized');
```

logEvent(integer $evtid, integer $type, string $msg, [string $source = 'Parser']) — Deprecated. See xPDO->log().

logManagerAction(string $action, string $class_key, mixed $item) — Log an event to the Manager Action log. $action is the lexicon key of the event (e.g., 'chunk_create', 'resource_update'). $class_key is the class key of the object the action is performed on (e.g., 'modChunk', 'modResource'). $item is the ID or array of IDs for the object(s) being acted on (e.g., $resource->get('id')).

makeUrl(integer $id, [string $context = ''], [string $args = ''], [mixed $scheme = -1]) — Returns the URL to the resource with the named ID (optionally in the specified context). $args is an optional query string to append to the URL. $scheme has the following possible values:

-1 — Relative URL from the site root.
0 — Alias of http below.
1 — Alias of https below.
full — Full absolute URL from **site_url**.
abs — Full absolute URL from **base_url**.
http — Absolute URL forced to http scheme.
https — Absolute URL forced to https scheme.

If you need to send parameters in the URL for use with $_GET, you can use this form:

```
$modx->makeUrl($id, '', 'paramName=value');
```

mergeChunkContent($content) — Deprecated.
Use modParser::processElementTags().

mergeDocumentContent($content) — Deprecated.
Use modParser::processElementTags().

mergePlaceholderContent($content) — Deprecated.
Use modParser::processElementTags().

mergeSettingsContent($content) — Deprecated.
Use modParser::processElementTags().

messageQuit([$msg = 'unspecified error'], [$query = ''], [$is_error = true], [$nr = ''], [$file = ''], [$source = ''], [$text = ''], [$line = '']) — Deprecated. Legacy fatal error message.

parseChunk(string $chunkName, array $chunkArr, [string $prefix = '[[+'], [string $suffix = ']]']) — Replaces placeholder tags in the named chunk using the associative array in $chunkArr. $prefix and $suffix default to standard placeholder tag tokens but can be changed to process custom tags. Seldom used (see $modx->getChunk()). Returns the processed chunk as a string. Example:

```
$modx->parseChunk('MyChunk',
    array('name'=>$username ,
    'email'=>$userEmail));
```

putChunk($chunkName) — Deprecated. Alias of getChunk().

reg* — The following five methods insert CSS, JS, or HTML at various points of a document. In all cases, the script is registered with MODX so that it won't be injected more than once. Multiple scripts are injected in the order in which they are registered.

regClientCSS(string $src) — Places the string just above the closing </head> tag of the document. If $src contains '<link' or '<style', it will be inserted as written. Otherwise, it will be wrapped as follows:

```
'<link rel="stylesheet" href="' . $src . '" type="text/css" />'
```

regClientHTMLBlock(string $html) — Places the string, as written, just above the closing </body> tag of the document.

regClientScript(string $src, [boolean $plaintext = false]) — Inserts the string (assumed to be JavaScript) just above the closing </body> tag of the document. If $src contains '<script' or $plaintext is set to true, $src will be injected as written. Otherwise, it will be wrapped as follows:

```
'<script type="text/javascript" src="' . $src . '"></script>'
```

regClientStartupHTMLBlock(string $html) — Like regClientHTMLBlock() except that the string is injected just before the closing </head> tag.

regClientStartupScript(string $src, [boolean $plaintext = false]) — Like regClientScript() except that the string is injected just before the closing </head> tag.

reloadConfig() — Repeats loadConfig().

removeAllEventListener() — Removes all events from the event map (for the duration of the current request) so they cannot be invoked.

removeEventListener(string $eventName) — Removes the named event from the event map (for the duration of the current request) so it cannot be invoked.

runSnippet(string $snippetName, [array $params = array()]) — Executes the named snippet and returns its output. $params is an associative array of snippet properties that will override the default properties (if any) of the snippet.

sendError([string $type = ''], [array $options = array()]) — Sends the user to a type-specific error page generated by the function. Basically "includes" the file found at **MODX_CORE_PATH/error/$type/include.php**, makes a page out of it (using the optional $options array), and sends it to the browser. By default, delivers a page containing a fatal "error 500". Generally used only internally by MODX.

sendErrorPage([array $options = null]) — Invokes the OnPageNotFound event with the options specified and forwards the user to the "page not found" error page defined by the error_page system setting.

sendForward(integer $id, [string $options = null]) — Forwards the user to the page specified by $id (without changing the current URL). $options specifies options for the forward: response_code, error_type, error_header, error_pagetitle, and error_message.

sendRedirect(string $url, [integer $count_attempts = 0], [string $type = '']) — Redirects the user to the specified URL (URL is changed) optionally trying $count_attempts times. Options for $type are:

> **REDIRECT_REFRESH** — Uses the header refresh method.
> **REDIRECT_META** — Sends a META HTTP-EQUIV="Refresh" tag to the output.
> **REDIRECT_HEADER** — (default) Uses the header location method.

sendUnauthorizedPage([array $options = null]) — Invokes the OnPageUnauthorized event with the options specified and redirects the user to the page specified in the unauthorized_page system setting. $options are the same as for sendErrorPage().

setDebug([boolean|int $debug = true], [boolean $stopOnNotice = false]) — Sets the debug state of the MODX instance, optionally using $debug as a bitwise integer to specify the state. If $stopOnNotice is true, execution will stop on E_NOTICE PHP errors. Returns the previous debug state, so it can be reverted.

setPlaceholder(string $key, mixed $value) — Sets the placeholder identified by $key to $value. Example:

```
setPlaceholder('day', 'Friday');
```

setPlaceholders(array|object $placeholders, [string $namespace = ''])
— Sets multiple placeholders. If $placeholders is an array of key/value pairs, place-holders named with the key will be created or updated based on their respective values. If $placeholders is an object, placeholders will be created or updated using the name of all properties (member variables) of the object and set to the values of those properties. Unlike toPlaceholders(), no prefixes are set and no separators are used. Example:

```
$placeholders = array('name'=>'Joe Blow', 'age'=>'33'));
$modx->setPlaceholders($placeholders);
```

stripTags($html, [$allowed = ''], [$patterns = array()]) — Strips HTML tags, PHP code, and, optionally, other patterns from a string. Calls the PHP strip_tags($html, $allowed) function. Optional $patterns is an array of regular expressions that will be removed from the string with PHP preg_replace().

switchContext(string $contextKey) — Switches the context for the current MODX instance. The new context still uses the current session. Example:

```
$modx->switchContext('web');
```

toPlaceholder(string $key, mixed $value, [string $prefix = ''], [string $separator = '.']) — Recursively sets placeholders. $key is the placeholder name; $value is the value to set. If $prefix is sent, it is prepended to the placeholder name separated by $separator (defaults to a period).

toPlaceholders(array|object $subject, [string $prefix = ''], [string $separator = '.']) — If $subject is an array of key/value pairs, key placeholders are set to their respective values. If $subject is an object, placeholders are created or updated using the name of each property (member variable) of the object and set to the value of that property. The $prefix and $separator variables operate as they do for toPlaceholder().

unsetPlaceholder(string $key) — Unsets the named placeholder.

unsetPlaceholders(string|array $keys) — Unsets multiple placeholders. $keys can be a prefix, in which case all placeholders with that prefix will be unset.

userLoggedIn() — Deprecated. Use hasSessionContext() or getAuthenticatedUser().

modUser Class

The following methods are available for all user objects. For the current user, you can use:

```
$modx->user->methodName();
```

For other users, you can get the user object first with one of the get*() methods and then call the method:

```
$user = $modx->getObject('modUser', array('username'=>'JoeBlow'));
$user->methodName();
```

changePassword(string $newPassword, string $oldPassword) — Changes the users password from $oldPassword to $newPassword.

getSettings() — Returns an associative array containing the user's user settings as key/value pairs.

getUserGroups() — Returns an array containing the IDs of the user groups the user is a member of.

getUserGroupNames() — Returns an array of strings containing the names of the user groups the user is a member of.

hasSessionContext(mixed $context) — Returns true if the user is logged on in the specified context, false if not. $context can be the name of a context (e.g., 'web') or an array of context names.

isAuthenticated([string $sessionContext]) — Returns true if the user is logged on in the named context, false if not. $sessionContext defaults to 'web'.

isMember(mixed $groups, [boolean $matchAll]) — $groups can be the name of a user group or an array of user group names. Returns true if the user is a member of any of the specified groups, false if not. If the optional $matchAll argument is true, the user must be a member of *all* specified groups (defaults to false).

joinGroup(mixed $group, [integer $role]) — Adds the user as a member of the specified user group. $group can be the ID of a user group or the name of a user group. The optional $role argument can be set to the ID of a particular role or the name of a role and that role will be set for the user in the group (defaults to null). Using the IDs is faster. Returns true on success, false on failure.

leaveGroup(mixed $group) — Removes the member from the specified user group. $group can be the ID of a user group or the name of a user group. Using the group ID is faster. Returns true on success, false on failure.

remove() — Permanently removes the user object from the database.

save([mixed $cacheFlag = true]) — Saves the user object to the database.

sendEmail(string $message, [array $options]) — Sends the user an email with $message as the body. The user's full name from his or her profile is used for the "to" value. The $options variable can hold an associative array of values as follows:

> **from** — Used to set MAIL_FROM. Defaults to the **emailsender** system setting.
> **fromName** — Used to set MAIL_FROM_NAME. Defaults to the **site_name** system setting.
> **sender** — Used to set MAIL_SENDER and reply-to. Defaults to the **emailsender** system setting.
> **subject** — Used to set MAIL_SUBJECT. Defaults to the **emailsubject** system setting.
> **html** — Used to set whether the email will be in HTML. Defaults to true.

Additional Methods

These are not methods of the above classes but are useful for getting and setting object fields.

getContent([array $options]) — Available for all resources and elements. Gets the raw, unprocessed value of the main content field of the object. For resources, this is the **content** field. For plugins, snippets, templates, and chunks, it is the code of the object. For template variables, it gets the default value of the TV. The $options array contains an associative array with options that can modify the default behavior of the method. For resources and elements, the $options argument is ignored. Example:

```
$resource = $modx->getObject('modDocument', array('pagetitle'=>'Home'));
$content = $resource->getContent();
```

setContent(string $content, [array $options]) — Available for all resources and elements. Sets the raw, unprocessed value of the main content field of the object. For resources, this is the **content** field. For plugins, snippets, templates, and chunks, it is the code of the object. For template variables, it sets the default value of the TV. The $options array contains an associative array with options that can modify the default behavior of the method. For resources and elements, the $options argument is ignored. Example:

```
$resource = $modx->getObject('modDocument', array('pagetitle'=>'Home'));
$resource->setContent('<p>This is the Home page.</p>');
$resource->save();
```

getValue ([int $id]) — Gets the raw, unprocessed value of a template variable (e.g., @INHERIT). $id is the resource ID of the resource you want the TV from. If $id is not sent, the current resource is used. Example:

```
$id = 12;
$tv = $modx->getObject('modTemplateVar', array('name'=>'MyTV'));
$rawValue = $tv->getValue($id);
```

renderOutput([int $id]) — Gets the processed value of a template variable. $id is the resource ID of the resource you want the TV from. If $id is not sent, the current resource is used. Example:

```
$id = 12;
$tv = $modx->getObject('modTemplateVar',array('name'=>'MyTV'));
$processedValue = $tv->renderOutput($id);
```

PHP Primer

If you are absolutely determined not to learn anything about PHP coding, MODX might not be the CMS for you. You can certainly create a simple "brochure" web site with MODX without doing any coding, but to get the most out of MODX, it really helps to learn a little PHP.

PHP is a programming language designed specifically for use in creating dynamic web pages. The purpose of this section is not to make you an ace PHP programmer. Rather, it's to give you a basic working knowledge of PHP at a level that will let you handle 90 percent of the PHP needs for a MODX site. It will also prepare you to read the code of existing snippets and plugins to understand how they work and to modify them to meet your needs.

We will be skipping the quirks and advanced features of PHP. We'll also neglect some of the finer points involved in making your code fast and efficient, and we'll be leaving out some of the more complex ways to use certain PHP functions.

If you want to know more, there are some excellent PHP tutorials on the Web. Just do a web search for *php tutorial*. If you need information about built-in PHP functions, **http://php.net** is an excellent resource, and it provides valuable comments from users about the quirks and capabilities of the various functions and excellent examples of how to use the functions to solve common problems.

We'll start with a simple PHP program (placed in a MODX snippet). Then we'll discuss various PHP principles and methods.

Hello World

In keeping with long-standing tradition, our first PHP program will simply print "Hello World" on the screen. All **PHP code** begins with `<?php` and ends with `?>`. MODX will generally add these for you at the beginning and end of snippets or plugins. Let's create the simplest possible snippet, called *PhpDemo*. Use the following line for the snippet:

```
return 'Hello World';
```

Each executable line of PHP code must end with a semicolon. Leaving it out is a very common mistake for beginners. Another common mistake is having an odd number of quotes, brackets, or curly braces. Any opening quote, bracket, or curly brace must have a matching closing partner.

Now create a resource to display the results of our snippet. Call it *PhpDemo* also. Add the following to the Resource Content Field:

```
[[PhpDemo]]
```

When you preview your `PhpDemo` resource, you should see `Hello World` on the resulting web page (as long as you've copied the example exactly). MODX replaces the snippet tag with whatever the snippet code returns. Congratulations, you're a PHP programmer.

Comments

Comments are an important and often neglected part of PHP programming. **PHP comments** have no effect on the execution of the PHP code. They are there to help humans reading the code understand what it's doing and why. Over 90% of the PHP code I look at has what I consider to be inadequate comments.

As you are writing PHP code, you'll find yourself thinking, "I don't have to comment this; I'll remember what it's doing and why I did it this way." Later, when you return to work on the code, you'll wish you could go back in time and say to yourself, "no, you won't."

The key to writing good comments is simple. Imagine that someday a not-very-bright person will have to work on the code. The person will have an angry boss and a very short deadline. Write comments to help this person out. You'll never regret it.

There are two kinds of comments in PHP: single-line and block comments. The single line comments look like this:

```
// This is a comment.
# This is another comment.
```

When PHP sees # or // at the very beginning of a line, it will ignore everything else on that line. In MODX, single-line comments are frowned on, and you should generally avoid them.

Block comments begin with /* and end with */. Everything between the comment markers will be ignored no matter where they appear or how far apart they are:

```
/* This is a block comment
    PHP will ignore all
    of it */
```

Of course the block comments can still be on a single line:

```
/* This comment is all on one line */
```

Always use this comment style for comments in MODX. Be very careful not to reverse either of the comment markers. The asterisks must go inside the slashes at both ends. Make sure, also, that there is no space between the asterisk and the slash. Note, too, that nested comments (comments within comments) will confuse the parser.

Some people prefer to do block comments like this to make it clear that the whole block is a comment:

```
/* This is a comment
 * that is on more than
 * one line */
```

For especially important comments, you may also see this style:

```
/* * * * * * * * * * * *
 *   This is a really   *
 *   important comment   *
 * * * * * * * * * * * */
```

As long as there is a /* at the beginning and a */ at the end, you can use any style you want for your comments, but never put a comment inside another comment.

Be very careful when typing comment tags. Getting them wrong will make your code fail every time. There are four ways to place the stars and slashes in a comment, and only one of them is correct: /* comment */. The stars always go on the inside. If you forget the closing */ or get it wrong, the parser will consider all the rest of the code to be a comment.

By convention, all comments in MODX core code take the form above. Single line comment tags (// and #) are not used.

Variables

PHP variables are simply holders of information. They always start with a dollar sign followed by a letter. Variable names can have numbers in them but shouldn't start with a number, and in MODX, they generally contain nothing but letters and occasionally underscore characters. In MODX (and elsewhere) variables usually start with a lowercase letter, and any additional words have their first letter in uppercase:

```
$firstName = 'Bob';
```

Variables are case-sensitive in PHP, so $number is not the same as $Number. Failing to match the case or misspelling variable names is another common beginner mistake.

There are a number of types of variables in PHP. The most commonly used are: Boolean (true/false), integer (usually called int), float (floating point numbers), string (a series of alphanumeric characters), array (an indexed group of variables), and object (more on these later).

There are two special variable types. Resource variables are variables that point to external resources like files and databases. A variable that points to a file resource is usually called a "file handle," and the conventional variable name used for them is $fp (for "file pointer"). A handle to a database is also a resource variable. The other special type is the null value, which represents a variable with no value:

```
$content = null;
```

The null value is often returned by functions to indicate failure. Unlike most things in PHP, null can be in either upper or lowercase. By convention, it is written as null in MODX.

In PHP, variables get their values in various ways. The most common is with the equals sign (technically, the "assignment operator"):

```
$number = 5;
return $number;
```

The code above assigns the value 5 to the variable $number. If you put that code in a snippet, the snippet tag would be replaced by the number 5.

Variables can hold a number of different kinds of things, but almost all of them hold a number, a string, an array, or an object (more on arrays and objects later). A string is just a sequence of alphanumeric characters. Here is a version of our Hello snippet that uses a string variable:

```
$output = 'Hello World';
return $output;
```

In the code above, we assign the string 'Hello World' to the variable $output. It is a MODX convention to use a variable called $output to hold the value that will be returned from a snippet.

PHP is very forgiving about converting back and forth between strings and numbers. For example, this works fine:

```
$number1 = '5';
$number2 = '2';
$sum = $number1 + $number2;
return $sum;
```

A snippet with the above code will return 7, even though the two variables being added are strings.

Variables can also hold two special values: true and false. These are logical values often used in conditional statements in PHP. The rules for what counts as true and false are actually quite complicated, but in most cases, anything that evaluates to 0 is false, and anything else is true:

```
0       /* (false) */
1       /* (true) */
7       /* (true) */
0 + 0   /* (false) */
'0'     /* (false) */
'1'     /* (true) */
'7'     /* (true) */
```

Unlike almost everything else in PHP (except the null value), the keywords true and false are case-insensitive, so true, True, and TRUE are equivalent as are false, False, and FALSE. It is a MODX convention, however, to always type them in lowercase (true, false).

Reserved Words

PHP Reserved Words are words that should never be used as variable names or function names because PHP is already using them for something else. The list is too long to provide here, but it includes all of the PHP terms used in this primer (e.g., true, false, null, else, if, for, foreach, while, do, etc.). For a more complete list, do a web search for *PHP Reserved Words*. In MODX, it's a good idea to avoid using the names of MODX object fields like **name**, **pagetitle**, **alias**, **content**, **id**, etc. as variable names.

Quoted Strings

String variables in PHP are specified using either single or double- quotes. The following two lines are equivalent.

```
$name = 'John Doe';
$name = "John Doe";
```

This does not mean that single and double-quotes are always interchangeable, however. The correct use of single- and double-quotes is a stumbling block for many new PHP users.

Before we discuss the differences between single- and double-quotes, we should mention that, above all, quotes must match. A string with a single-quote at the beginning must have a single-quote at the end. The same goes for double-quotes. For every opening quote, there must be exactly one closing quote of the same type:

```
$s = 'Hello';   /* ok */
$s = "Hello";   /* ok */
$s = 'Hello";   /* error */
$s = "Hello';   /* error */
$s = "Hello;    /* error */
$s = Hello";    /* error */
$s = 'Hello;    /* error */
$s = Hello';    /* error */
```

Single-quotes are taken literally by PHP. That is, the material inside the quotes is quoted as written without any processing. Consider the following example:

```
$string = 'XXX';
$string2 = 'Hello $string Goodbye';
```

You might think that that `$string2` would be output as `Hello XXX Goodbye`, but it's not. It is output as `Hello $string Goodbye`.

When using double-quotes, however, the segment inside the quotes will be processed. So if we redid our example above with double-quotes, the result would be `Hello XXX Goodbye`.

Another feature of double-quotes is that the backslash character inside double-quotes will "escape" the character that follows it. That next character will be taken literally as a character:

```
$s = "Hello \"Bob\" Goodbye";
```

In the example above, `$s` will have the value: `Hello "Bob" Goodbye`. Without the backslashes, it would generate an error because the second `"` (the one before `Bob`) would be interpreted as a closing quote.

Often, you want to render a string with quotes in it. For example, you might want to return an (X)HTML `<href>` tag in a snippet. Suppose you want to return the following tag:

```
<a href="assets/dog.jpg">My Dog</a>
```

Just putting double-quotes around the whole line would generate an error. There are two ways to solve this:

```
$output = "<a href=\"assets/dog.jpg\">My Dog</a>";
$output = '<a href="assets/dog.jpg">My Dog</a>';
```

In the first line above, we've used double-quotes and "escaped" the inside quotes by putting a backslash character in front of them. In the second, we've use single-quotes around the whole string, so the double- quotes will be taken literally.

Single-quotes inside double-quotes will be taken literally, and double-quotes inside single-quotes will be taken literally. The following two lines will both work fine:

```
$s = "O'reilly, O'Connor, O'Brien";
$s = 'I said "No" to him';
```

When mixing variables and literal strings in the return from a snippet, the code often becomes convoluted, and you have to be very careful with the quotes. Here we use the dot (`.`) operator to concatenate separate strings into one. These are equivalent:

```
$s = "<a href=\"" . $url . "\">My Dog</a>";
$s = '<a href="' . $url . '">My Dog</a>';
```

658 MODX: The Official Guide

Notice that when part of the string we're building is a variable name, it gets no quotes.

So, which should you use, single or double-quotes? It's largely a matter of personal preference. The convention in MODX is to use single-quotes whenever possible because they are slightly faster (since the text inside the quotes is not processed). In the MODX code, single-quotes are used almost everywhere except in cases like this:

```
$s = "Can't find that file.\n";
```

In the example above, the double-quotes are necessary because the quoted string contains a single-quote and because the \n at the end needs to be interpreted as a newline character. Any output that follows the code above will appear on a new line.

The speed difference is very small, but if you use single-quotes whenever possible, you'll find the MODX code easier to read, and your code will be clearer to most MODX users.

 Many word processing programs (and some web pages) use "smart" or 'smart' quotes (like the ones around the word smart). They're also called "curly" quotes. If you paste code with these quotes into MODX, your code will fail because those quotes are not recognized as single- or double- quotes by PHP. If the opening and closing quotes look different, PHP will have trouble with the code, and you'll usually get a very non-helpful error message.

If you have a simple text editor, such as an older version of Notepad, you can paste the code there first before pasting it to MODX. Sadly, this doesn't work in most modern editors, and you have to edit all the quotes manually in the MODX Manager.

Operators

We won't be covering all the PHP operators here, just the most common ones. They're called operators because they operate on values.

Arithmetic Operators

These are the most obvious operators. They operate on numeric values and generally do what you would expect. Assume that $x = 3. The resulting values of $x are in parentheses:

```
Addition: $x = $x + 4;        /* (7) */
Subtraction: $x = $x - 1;     /* (2) */
Multiplication: $x = $x * 2;  /* (6) */
Division: $x = $x / 3;        /* (1) */
Modulus: $x % 2 ;             /* (division remainder) (1) */
Increment: $x++;              /* (4) */
Decrement: $x--;              /* (3) */
```

Assignment Operators

Assignment operators assign what is on the right to what is on the left. Assume that $x = 3. The resulting values of $x are in parentheses:

```
$x = 7;        /* (7) */
$x = 'Hello'; /* (Hello) */
$x += 2;       /* (5) */
$x -= 2;       /* (1) */
$x *= 4;       /* (12) */
$x /= 3;       /* (1) */
$x %= 2;       /* (1) */
```

Another assignment operator, the concatenation operator (.), is used quite often with strings in MODX. Here's an example:

```
$x = 'Hello' . ' World'; /* (Hello World) */
```

The method shown above is very useful when you want to mix literal strings (strings defined directly with quotes) and variables in an assignment:

```
$firstName = 'Joe';
$lastName = 'Blow';
$output = 'First Name: ' . $firstName . '<br />' .
    'Last Name: ' . $lastName;
return $output;
```

With the code above in a snippet, the web page containing the snippet tag would show the following:

```
First Name: Joe
Last Name: Blow
```

Notice that there are five parts being concatenated above, each separated by the dot operator. Notice too, that literal strings are completely enclosed in quotes while variables ($firstName and $lastName) have no quotes around them.

In combination with the = character, the dot operator appends the part after the equals sign to the part before it Example:

```
$x = 'Hello';
$x .= ' World'; /* output: Hello World */
```

The .= operator is used a lot in MODX. Sometimes a large section of (X)HTML code is assigned to a single variable by using the .= operator:

```
$output = '<h3>This is my web page</h3>';
$output .= '<p>This is my first paragraph.</p>';
$output .= '<p>This is my second paragraph.</p>';
return $output;
```

Comparison Operators

In conditional statements (discussed below), you often want to compare things. The *PHP comparison operators* are used for this. PHP compares the things on each side of the comparison operators and converts the whole statement to true or false depending on the comparison. In the following examples, the result of the comparison is in parentheses:

Equality

```
5 == 5    /* (true) */
5 == 7    /* (false) */
```

Inequality

```
5 != 7    /* (true) */
5 != 5    /* (false) */
5 <> 7    /* (true) */
5 <> 5    /* (false) */
(The <> version of the inequality operator is seldom used.)
```

Greater than

```
5 > 3    /* (true) */
5 > 7    /* (false) */
5 > 5    /* (false) */
```

Less than

```
5 < 7    /* (true) */
5 < 3    /* (false) */
5 < 5    /* (false) */
```

Greater or equal

```
5 >= 4    /* (true) */
5 >= 6    /* (false) */
5 >= 5    /* (true) */
```

Less than or equal

```
5 <= 7    /* (true) */
5 <= 4    /* (false) */
5 <= 5    /* (true) */
```

Note that although we used numbers in the above examples, you can also compare variables and, in some cases, strings:

```
if ($x == 'Yes')
    /* do something */
if ($x == $y)
    /* do something */
if ($userName == 'admin')
    /* do something */
```

A common beginner mistake in PHP is confusing the assignment operator (=) with the equality operator (==). The assignment operator actually assigns the value on the right to whatever is on the left. The equality operator simply tests to see if the two are equal.

The most common form of this mistake is to write the conditional statement above like this:

```
if ($x = 'Yes')
```

Doing that assigns 'Yes' to $x rather than testing $x to see if it equals 'Yes'.

Logical Operators

There are three **PHP logical operators**, usually used in conditional expressions (more on those in a bit). The three logical operators are `&&` (and), `||` (or), and `!` (not). As we saw above, expressions evaluate to `true` or `false`. For example: `5 > 3` evaluates to `true`. The logical operators allow for more complex expressions like this:

```
5 > 3 && 3 < 2
```

The expression above uses the **logical and operator** (`&&`). It would only be `true` if both parts were `true`. That is, it would be `true` if `5 > 3` were `true` and `3 < 2` were `true`. The expression above is `false` because 3 is not less than 2. Parentheses can be used to group parts of an expression. The bits inside a pair of parentheses will be evaluated before being compared to the rest of the expression:

```
(5 > 3) && (3 < 2)
```

If you understand the order of precedence of all PHP operators, some parentheses (like the ones just above) are unnecessary, but there is little harm in including them anyway. It slows the processing down by a few milliseconds, but it makes the code easier to understand, and it prevents some difficult-to-find bugs. We'll use some extra parentheses here to make things a little easier for you.

Think about the following expression:

```
(5 > 3) || (3 < 2)
```

Because we've used the **logical or operator**, the expression is `true` if either side is `true`. Since `5 > 3` evaluates to `true`, the expression is `true`.

The **logical not operator** (`!`) just reverses the value of what follows it. All of the following evaluate to `true`:

```
! false
! (3 < 2)
(5 > 3) && ! ( 3 < 2)
```

The logical operators are evaluated from left to right, so if PHP can draw a conclusion after evaluating one expression, the expressions to the right of it won't be evaluated. You can use this to speed up your code by putting tests that are more likely to determine the outcome on the left. We also saw this technique when we covered sanity checks earlier in the book. In a sanity check, we put expressions that might generate an error to the right of expressions that determine whether it's safe to evaluate them:

```
if (is_object($result) && ($result instanceof xPDOObject) ) {
    /* Object is OK, go ahead and process it */
}
```

The `instanceof` operator will generate an error if the variable is not an object, but that part of the test won't execute if the `is_object()` test is `false`.

In the following examples, the right-hand test will not be performed:

```
if (5 < 3 && 4 < 7)
if (5 > 3 || 4 < 8)
```

In the first example, PHP knows that the expression is `false` after evaluating the left-hand part. In the second, PHP knows that the expression is `true` after evaluating the left-hand part. Note that in the following expressions, both parts will be evaluated:

```
if (5 > 3 && 4 < 7)
if (5 < 3 || 4 < 8)
```

Conditionals

In PHP code, we often want to perform some action only if certain conditions are `true` (or `false`). To do this, you can use an `if` statement (with optional `else` and `elseif` clauses), a `switch` statement, or the ternary operator. Note that conditionals do not end with a semicolon because there will be code following them that may execute.

The if Statement

The simplest way of doing this is with the *PHP `if` statement*. It looks like this:

```
if (condition) {
    /* do something */
}
```

An `if` statement must always be followed by a set of parentheses. The curly braces mark the section of code that will be executed if the expression inside the parentheses evaluates to `true`. If there is only one line of code to be executed, the curly braces are optional, but it is a very good practice to include them anyway. Here's a practical example of an `if` statement:

```
if ($username == 'admin') {
    /* allow something */
}
```

If you want the code to execute only if the condition is `false`, you can use the logical not operator (`!`):

```
if (! condition) {
    /* do something */
}
```

Often, you want to do something if the condition is `true` and something else if it is `false`. In that case you need a *PHP else statement*:

```
if ($username == 'admin') {
    /* allow something */
} else {
    /* tell the user they can't do it */
}
```

The curly braces (`{` and `}`) delimit sections of code that will execute based on the condition. If there is only one line to execute, they are unnecessary, but you should always include them because they make the code more readable and help prevent logic errors.

What if you have more conditions to test? You can use the *PHP elseif statement*:

```
if ($username == 'admin') {
    /* allow something */
} elseif ($username == 'JoeBlow') {
    /* allow something else */
} else {
    /* tell the user they can't do it */
}
```

You can use as many `elseif` statements as you need but only one `else` statement, which must come at the end.

If you want either the admin Super User or Joe Blow to be allowed to do something, you can use the logical or operator (`||`):

```
if ( ($username == 'admin') || ($username == 'JoeBlow') ){
    /* allow something */
} else {
    /* tell the user they can't do it */
}
```

The if statement (and its elses and elseifs) only apply to the code in the curly braces:

```
if ($username == 'admin') {
    /* this will happen for the admin */
} else {
    /* this will happen for non-admins */
}
/* this will happen no matter what */
```

All conditionals can be written on a single line, and the curly braces can be omitted if there is only one line of code to execute, but this is considered a bad practice in MODX because it makes the code harder to read and to maintain:

```
if ($username == 'admin') $admin = true;
```

The switch Statement

When you have a bunch of possibilities to check, you can use the *PHP switch statement*:

```
switch($username) {
    case 'admin':
        /* do something */
        break;
    case 'JoeBlow':
        /* do something else */
        break;
    case 'JaneDoe':
        /* do something else */
        break;
    default:
        /* handle all other cases */
        /* or maybe return an error message */
}
```

The value in the parentheses after the word `switch` will be compared to each case, and the first one that matches will have its code executed. The `break;` statement at the end of each case is very important (and easily forgotten). It stops the processing of the `switch` statement, and the program continues after the final closing curly brace of the `switch`. If you forget the `break;` statement, the program will "fall through" to the next `case`, and its code will be executed too. This will create a confusing and hard-to-debug error, so generally, you should be careful to always end every `case` with a `break;` statement. Sometimes, however, you want the code to "fall through" (as in the case where the admin Super User and Joe Blow get the same treatment):

```
switch($username) {
    case 'admin':
    case 'JoeBlow':
        /* do something */
        break;
    case 'JaneDoe':
        /* do something else */
        break;
    default:
        /* handle all other cases */
        /* or maybe return an error message */
}
```

In the above code, having no `break;` after the 'admin' `case` lets the code below execute for both 'admin' and 'JoeBlow'.

It's also a good practice to have a `default` case at the end of your `switch` statement so that something sensible will happen if there are no matches.

The Ternary Operator

One more way of conditionally executing code is a common sight in MODX snippets. It's called the *PHP ternary operator*, and it's easier than it looks. Here is its basic form:

```
condition ? value1 : value2;
```

If `condition` evaluates to `true`, the whole expressions gets `value1`; if condition is `false`, the whole expression gets `value2`. Here's an example:

```
$isAdmin = ($userName == 'admin') ? 'Yes' : 'No';
```

If $userName is admin, $isAdmin will be Yes; otherwise, it will be No. You will see this operator very often at the beginning of snippets. It is used to set a default value for a snippet property in case the property is not set (in the snippet tag, the snippet's default properties, or in an attached property set). In the following example, the empty() function is used to test whether the **&rowTpl** property is set:

```
$rowTpl = empty($rowTpl) ? 'defaultRowTpl' : $rowTpl;
```

If $rowTpl is empty, $rowTpl is set to 'defaultRowTpl'. Otherwise, it gets the value set in the tag, default properties, or attached property set ($rowTpl). The single line of code above is equivalent to this longer version:

```
if (empty($rowTpl)) {
    $rowTpl = 'defaultRowTpl';
} else {
    $rowTpl = $rowTpl;
}
```

Arrays

A *PHP array* is just a variable that contains a collection of other variables. PHP has simple arrays and associative arrays.

Simple Arrays

Here is a simple array called $colors:

```
$colors = array ('red', 'blue', 'green');
```

Arrays have an index (which always starts at 0). In the above array, $colors[0] is red, $colors[1] is blue, and $colors[2] is green. Array indexes in PHP always start at 0. Each member of an array can be retrieved by putting its index number in braces after the array name:

```
$myColor = $colors[1];
```

The code above sets the variable $myColor to blue.

In the example above, we created the array all at once. We could also have created an empty array and added the color names to it. This code is the exact equivalent to the code above:

```
$colors = array();
$colors[] = 'red';
$colors[] = 'blue';
$colors[] = 'green';
```

The empty square brackets tell PHP to add the value to the right as a new member of the array. Notice that we didn't have to give the index numbers when adding the color names to the array (although we could have). PHP automatically figures out what the index numbers should be.

Associative Arrays

The example above is a very simple array. Much more common, though, is something called a *PHP associative array*. In an associative array, the variables contained in the array get names rather than index numbers, and the values can be retrieved by those names. Technically, the names are called *keys*, and the values are called *values*. Here is a simple associative array:

```
$animals = array('cat'=>'feline', 'dog'=>'canine', 'frog'=>'amphibian');
```

Because PHP arrays don't need to be all on the same line, this is exactly equivalent to the code above:

```
$animals = array(
    'cat'=>'feline',
    'dog'=>'canine',
    'frog'=>'amphibian',
);
```

Arrays in MODX are often written like the code above to make them easier to read and to help prevent typos. The comma after the next-to-last line is optional, but it's a good practice, because it will prevent an error if you decide to add more items to the end of the array and forget to insert it.

As we did with our simple array above, we could also create an empty array and add the animals to it:

```
$animals = array();
$animals['cat'] = 'feline';
$animals['dog'] = 'canine';
$animals['frog'] = 'amphibian';
```

Once the associative array exists, we can retrieve the value for any member by using its key:

```
$catSpecies = $animals['cat'];
```

The code above sets the variable $catSpecies to 'feline'. Associative arrays are very common in MODX. Default properties, for example, are associative arrays. In MODX Evolution, the system settings are available as the $modx->config[] array. You can get the value of the **site_start** system setting in Evolution using its key:

```
$home = $modx->config['site_start'];
```

Program Flow

We've already seen how you can control the flow of a PHP program with the `if` statement. Sometimes, however, you want to repeat certain parts of a program. You might want to read a file one line at a time until there are no more lines to read. Or, you might want to print out each member of an array. To accomplish this, PHP has several looping mechanisms: the foreach loop, the while loop, and the for loop. We'll start with the `foreach` loop because it's the most commonly used in MODX. The Revolution code has over 800 `foreach` loops.

The foreach Loop

The *PHP foreach loop* is specifically designed for use with arrays. In fact, it only works with arrays. Whatever code is inside the loop will be performed for each member of the array. This code will loop through our `$colors` array and print the key and value of each member:

```
$colors = array('red', 'blue', 'green');
$output = "";
foreach ($colors as $key => $value) {
    $output .= 'Key:' . $key;
    $output .= ' Value:' . $value;
    $output .= '<br />';
}
return $output;
```

The code above will produce this output:

```
Key:0 Value:red
Key:1 Value:blue
Key:2 Value:green
```

The variable names `$key` and `$value` are arbitrary. We could use any variable names, but `$key` and `$value` are traditional (sometimes `$k` and `$v` are used instead). The lines inside the curly braces will be executed once for each member of the `$colors` array. On each pass, the `$key` and `$value` will be set to the key and value for the current member.

If we use the exact same `foreach` loop for our `$animals` associative array (changing `$colors` to `$animals` in the `foreach` statement), the output would look like this:

```
Key:cat Value:feline
Key:dog Value:canine
Key:frog Value:amphibian
```

Any time you want to process or display the members of an array, the `foreach` loop is almost always the way to go.

The while Loop

The *PHP while loop* performs operations as long as the condition specified in the while statement is true. There are about 50 while loops in the MODX code. The following code will print Hello ten times:

```
$count = 10;
$output = "";
while ($count) {
    $output .= 'Hello<br />';
    $count--;
}
return $output;
```

Each time through the loop, we decrement the value of $count (with $count--). When it reaches 0, it evaluates to false, the loop ends, and processing continues with the next line after the closing curly brace of the loop. It is critical to make sure that the condition changes inside the while loop; otherwise, the loop will go on forever.

Here is an example of code that reads a file line by line and puts the lines into an array:

```
$lines = array();
$filename = 'somefile.txt';
$fp = fopen($filename,'r');
while(!feof($fp)) {
    $lines[] = fgets($fp,4096);
}
fclose($fp);
```

The *PHP fgets() function* reads one line of code from the file and moves the file pointer to the next line, and the *PHP feof() function* in the code above tests for the end of file marker (eof). The code simply reads the lines, one at a time, from the file and adds them to the $lines array.

The for Loop

The third looping form is the *PHP for loop*. In the for loop, a variable is used as a counter. There are also about 50 for loops in the MODX code. This for loop uses the variable $i as a counter (a common convention). It will print Hello 10 times:

```
$output = "";
for ($i=1; $i <=10; $i++) {
    $output .= 'Hello<br />';
}
return $output;
```

The three terms of the `for` loop are always separated by semicolons. The first one sets the initial value of the index. The second is the test that determines whether the loop will continue. The third changes the counter. If we changed the third term of the `for` loop above from `$i++` to `$i += 2`, `Hello` would be printed five times. The values of the index would be 1, 3, 5, 7, 9, and 11. When the index reached 11, the loop would end, the code inside it would not execute, and the program would continue after the closing curly brace.

Coding Style

No discussion of PHP would be complete without saying a little bit about ***PHP coding style***. PHP doesn't care about white space (spaces, tabs, and carriage returns) unless it is inside of quotation marks. In fact, each example program above could be written as a single line of code. That would take up less space, but it would make life very hard for anyone who had to read the code.

The term "coding style" refers to the conventions for formatting code. There are a number of coding styles commonly used by programmers. The style used in this book, and in most of the MODX code, is called K&R style. It's named after Brian Kernighan and Dennis Ritchie, the authors of The C Programming Language, considered by many to be the finest computer-programming book ever written.

The main features of K&R style can be illustrated with an `if` statement:

```
if (condition) {
    do something;
    then do something else;
}
```

Notice that the first curly brace is at the end of the first line, everything inside the curly braces is indented by the same amount, and the final curly brace lines up with the beginning of the first line. Here are a couple of alternate styles:

```
if (condition)
    {
    do something;
    then do something else;
    }

if (condition)
{
    do something;
    then do something else;
}
```

You're free to use any coding style you like, but if you use K&R style, you'll find it easier to read MODX code, and if you share any of your code with the MODX community, others will have an easier time reading your code. It is also a convention in the MODX community that you use spaces rather than tabs for indenting. The depth of the indenting is up to you, but four spaces is fairly common.

Here's a more complex example of K&R style showing the indenting of nested blocks of code:

```php
<?php
if (condition1) {
    do something;
    if (condition2) {
        do something;
    } else {
        do something else;
    }
    do something;
}
do this no matter what;
?>
```

The code inside any `if`, `for`, `while`, `foreach`, or `switch` statement and the code inside any loop, class, or function should always be indented.

User-defined Functions

PHP functions are just blocks of code that return a value. They take this form:

```php
function function-name(arguments) {
    code;
    return something;
}
```

The arguments are pieces of information (numbers, strings, variables, etc.) that are passed to the function. *PHP arguments* are always separated by commas. A curly brace marks the beginning and end of the function. There are many built-in functions in PHP, and you can create your own user-defined functions.

PHP user-defined functions are ones that you create and place in your code. Here's a simple user-defined function called `add` that adds two numbers and returns the result:

```php
function add ($num1, $num2) {
    return $num1 + $num2;
}
```

The code above is called a function declaration (also, a function prototype and sometimes a function definition). Usually, function declarations are placed at the end of a snippet or plugin.

Here's some code that uses our add function:

```
$x = 5;
$y = 10;
$output = "";
$output .= add($x,$y);
$output .= '<br />';
$output .= add(1,3);
return $output;
function add($num1, $num2) {
    return $num1 + $num2;
}
```

Here is the output of the code above:

```
15
4
```

The variable names used in the function declaration are arbitrary, so we could use any other variable names in place of $num1 and $num2 as long as we used those same names inside the function.

Functions can also have default arguments. These are values that the arguments get if the user doesn't send an argument:

```
function add($num1 = 6, $num2 = 9) {
    return $num1 + $num2;
}
```

Using the version of our function above, our example would give the same results, but add(), called with no arguments, would return 15 (6 + 9), and add(3) would return 12 (3 + 9). It's possible to have default values for some of the argument but not for others, but the ones with default values must come at the end of the argument list:

```
function add($num1, $num2 = 9) {
    return $num1 + $num2;
}
```

With the code above, we can still send two arguments, but only the first is required. So add(1) would return 10 (1 + 9). The following function definition is wrong because the argument with a default value is on the left:

```
function add($num1 = 3, $num2) {
    return $num1 + $num2;
}
```

When using default values for arguments, no argument without a default value can appear to the right of an argument that has a default value in the function definition.

Functions can return strings or arrays as well as numbers. This example would splice (concatenate) two strings together and return the resulting string:

```
function stringSplice($s1, $s2) {
    return $s1 . $s2;
}
```

The following example will add its arguments to an array and return the array:

```
function addToArray($s1, $s2, $s3) {
    $ary = array();
    $ary[] = $s1;
    $ary[] = $s2;
    $ary[] = $s3;
    return $ary;
}
```

Functions can also receive arrays as arguments. The following example creates an output string from all the members of the array sent to it:

```
function aryFormat($stringArray) {
    $output = "";
    foreach($stringArray as $key=>$value) {
        $output .= $value . '<br />';
    }
    return $output;
}
```

Built-in Functions

There are over 700 **PHP built-in functions**. The complete list can be found at **http://www.php.net/quickref.php** with each entry as a link to the function's manual page.

The following section covers the basics of some of the most commonly used built-in functions.

echo and print

The `echo` statement echoes a message to the screen. No parentheses are necessary, and arguments can be separated with commas. It returns nothing. Example:

```
$s = 'on the screen';
echo 'This is ', $s;
```

The `print` statement also echoes a message to the screen — no parentheses needed. It can only have one argument (no commas). Example:

```
$s = 'on the screen';
print 'This is ' . $s;
```

echo versus print

These are fairly interchangeable. Echo is more common and slightly faster. Actually, both are almost never used in MODX except for debugging. Instead, a variable (usually `$output`) is used to return output.

String Functions

trim($string) — Removes white space from both sides of a string. Takes an optional second argument specifying which characters to trim. Returns the trimmed string.

rtrim($string) — Like `trim()` but only trims the right side.

ltrim($string) — Like `trim()` but only trims the left side.

strtolower($string) — Converts the string to all lowercase. Returns the lowercase string.

strtoupper($string) — Converts the string to all uppercase. Returns the uppercase string.

strlen($string) — Returns the length of the string as an `int`.

strstr($haystack, $needle, [true/false]) — Finds the first occurrence of `$needle` in `$haystack`. Returns `$needle` and the rest (right end) of `$haystack`. If the optional third argument (only available since PHP 5.3.0) is `true`, `strstr()` returns the left side of `$haystack`, up to and including `$needle`. Examples:

```
$haystack = 'This is our example sentence.';
$needle = 'example';
$s = strstr($haystack, $needle);
/* $s = 'example sentence.' */
$s = strstr($haystack, $needle, true);
/* $s = 'This is our example' */
```

stristr($haystack, $needle, [true/false]) — Case-insensitive version of srtstr().

strpos($haystack, $needle) — Returns the position of $needle in $haystack (starting from position 0). Example:

```
$haystack = 'This is our example sentence.';
$needle = 'example';
$pos = strpos($haystack, $needle);
/* $pos = 12 */
```

stripos($haystack, $needle) — Case-insensitive version of strpos().

substr($string, $start, [$length]) — Returns the portion of $string from the position defined by $start to the end (starting with position 0). Returns $length characters from $start if the third argument (a number) is included. Example:

```
$string = 'This is our example sentence.';
$start = 12;
$s = substr($string, $start, 7);
/* $s = 'example' */
```

str_replace($search, $replace, $subject) — Replaces all instances of $search with $replace in $subject. Returns the altered $subject. If $search and $replace are arrays, then str_replace() takes a value from each array and uses them to do search and replace on $subject. If $replace has fewer values than $search, an empty string is used for the rest of the replacements. If $search is an array and $replace is a string, then $replace is used for every replacement. If $replace is an array and $search is a string, the results are undefined. Example:

```
$subject = 'This is our example sentence.';
$search = 'example';
$replace = 'new';
$s = str_replace($subject, $search, $replace);
/* $s = 'This is our new sentence' */
```

str_ireplace($search, $replace, $subject) — Case-insensitive version of str_replace(). It does *not* preserve the original case pattern of the things replaced.

Array Functions

count($arrayName) — Returns the number of entries in $arrayName as an integer.

explode($delimiter, $string) — Converts a delimited string into an array and returns that array. For example, $myArray = explode(',' 'red,blue,green') will set $myArray to an array with three members: red, blue, and green. The delimiters are removed and are not part of the array. This is often used in MODX code to convert a comma-delimited string into an array.

implode($glue, $pieces), implode($pieces) — The reverse of explode(). Converts the $pieces array to a string delimited by $glue. For the array in the explode() example, this will turn it back into its original form: implode(',' , $myArray). If used with a single argument ($pieces), the pieces will be glued together with no delimiter.

File Functions

file_exists($filename) — Returns true if the file or directory exists, false if not.

file_get_contents($filename) — Returns the entire contents of the file as a string.

file_put_contents($filename, $string, [$flags]) — Writes the $string to the named file, which will be created if it doesn't exist. This will overwrite an existing file unless the optional $flags argument is set to FILE_APPEND (no quotes), in which case $string will be appended to the file's contents. Returns the number of bytes written or false on failure.

fopen($filename, $mode) — Opens a file for reading and/or writing (depending on the $mode argument) and returns a handle to the file. The most commonly used modes are 'r' (read), 'w' (write), 'r+', 'w+' (read and write), 'a' (append write), and 'a+' (append read and write). Example:

```
$fp = fopen('c:/myfile','r');
```

fclose($handle) — Closes a file opened with fopen(). Example:

```
fclose($fp);
```

fread($handle, $length) — Reads $length bytes from the file pointed to by $handle. Returns a string containing the bytes read. Returns false on failure.

fwrite($handle, $string) — Writes $string to the file pointed to by $handle. Returns the number of bytes written as an integer or false on failure.

fgets($handle) — Returns a string containing a single line from the file ending with a newline (which is included in the string) or false on failure. After each call to fgets() the file pointer is advanced to the next line.

fputs() — An alias of `fwrite()`.

unlink($filename) — Deletes a file. Returns `true` on success, `false` on failure.

Date and Time Functions

time() — Returns a Unix timestamp, which is the number of seconds since January 1, 1970, 00:00:00 GMT (Greenwich Mean Time).

date($format, [$time]) — Returns a string with the formatted time and/or date based on the pattern in `$format` (see **http://php.net/manual** for the format string options). The optional second argument is a Unix timestamp. If `$time` is omitted, the current time/date is used.

strftime($format, [$time]) — Like date except that it uses the current locale setting.

strtotime($datestring) — Converts a date/time string to a Unix timestamp. It will accept almost any format for `$datestring` (e.g., `'02/04/09 7:21 pm'`). Returns the Unix timestamp or `false` on failure. Examples:

```
strtotime("now")
strtotime("10 September 2000")
strtotime("+1 day")
strtotime("+1 week")
strtotime("+1 week 2 days 4 hours 2 seconds")
strtotime("next Thursday")
strtotime("last Monday")
```

Objects

PHP and MODX are both moving in the direction of *Object-oriented Programming* (OOP). A full discussion of OOP is beyond the scope of this book, but we'll discuss the concept and some of its advantages. OOP techniques make code much more reliable and easier to maintain. Many MODX snippets use OOP techniques, so it's helpful to know a little bit about it in order to understand their code.

OOP Concepts

Pre-OOP code is procedural, and processing moves through the code jumping from place to place as necessary. It's hard to find the code you need to modify, and modifying it can have unpleasant side-effects. Consider the document, for example. In pre-OOP code, information about documents would be in the database. You might have code for editing, updating, and displaying the document. That code might be scattered in several files, and each piece would interact with the database. Altering the editing code might break the update and display code.

In OOP, everything is built around objects. Objects each contain their own data and their own methods (functions). Now, the document is an object. The document object contains all the data about the document (**pagetitle**, **longtitle**, **published**, **alias**, etc.). It also contains the methods (functions) used for displaying, updating, and editing the document.

In an OOP approach, rather than running code to edit the document and more code to update the database, you might get a reference to the document object and pass it to the editor object. The editor object would let the user edit the document, and when the user clicked on the "Save" button, it would tell the document object to save itself (by invoking the document's `save()` method).

If this is done properly, the document object doesn't need to know anything about how the editor works, and the editor doesn't need to know anything about how to save a document to the database. Similarly, when you want to display a document on a web page, you might tell the document object to display itself (by invoking the document's `display()` method).

Objects in MODX Revolution

To use an object, you get a reference to it. In MODX, MODX itself is an object that contains many of the MODX utility functions as methods. It is referenced by the `$modx` variable, which is automatically available in all snippets. To execute a method (function) of an object, you use:

```
$object->methodName().
```

So, to get a reference to a document object in MODX, you execute the `$modx` object's `getObject()` method. To get a reference to the document with the Resource ID of 12, for example, you do this:

```
$doc = $modx->getObject('modDocument',12)
```

Now that you have a reference to the document object, you can get any of its resource fields by calling its `get()` method:

```
$doc->get('pagetitle');
```

If you want to change the **pagetitle**, you can use the document's `set()` method:

```
$doc->set('pagetitle', 'New Title');
```

Now you can update the database with the changed version of the document by invoking the document's `save()` method:

```
$doc->save();
```

Objects in PHP can be descended from other objects (in PHP, they are said to "extend" the classes they are descended from), in which case they inherit the variables and methods of the classes they extend.

Resources (including documents) in MODX belong to the `modResource` class. The code below is a very simplified version of the MODX code that defines the `modResource` class. We've left out some variables and methods and omitted the actual code inside the methods.

The `modResource` class extends the `modAccessibleSimpleObject` class, which extends the `modAccessibleObject` class, which extends the `xPDOObject` class. Some of the methods and variables listed here are not in the `modResource` class but are inherited from the classes it extends.

```
class modResource extends modAccessibleSimpleObject {
var $_content;
var $_output;
var $_fields;
/* constructor (creates the object) */
function modResource(& $xpdo) {
}
/* process the resource for display */
function process() {
}
function get($fieldname) {
}
function set($fieldname,$value) {
}
function save() {
}
function hasChildren() {
}
function getContent($options = array()) {
}
function setContent($content, $options = array()) {
}}
```

Notice that, in keeping with good OOP design, we never manipulate or retrieve the member variables of the object directly. Instead, we call methods of the object (like get(), set(), and setContent()) that do it for us. That way, if the MODX installation switches to a different kind of database, we don't care because the methods will still do what we want. No code outside the object has to change.

If you want to see the actual code for the modResource class, it is here:

/core/model/modx/modresource.class.php

Creating a Simple Object Class

Here is a really simple example of a PHP class that contains information for a dog object. The dog object has three member variables representing the dog's name, age, and gender. It also has a constructor (which creates the object) and public methods to get and set the three variables. The constructor is used by PHP to create the object whenever code calls for a new object of the dog class. Here is the class code for our dog object:

```php
class dog {
    var $_name;
    var $_age;
    var $_gender;
/* PHP5 Constructor */
    function __construct($name, $age, $gender) {
        $this->_name = $name;
        $this->_age = $age;
        $this->_gender = $gender;
    }
    function get($field) {
        switch ($field) {
            case 'name':
                return $this->_name;
                break;
            case 'age':
                return $this->_age;
                break;
            case 'gender':
                return $this->_gender;
                break;
        }
        return $this->_name;
    }
```

```
function set($field, $value) {
    switch ($field) {
        case 'name':
            $this->_name = $value;
            break;
        case 'age':
            $this->_age = $value;
            break;
        case 'gender':
            $this->_gender = $value;
            break;
    }
}
}
```

Member Variables

This code declares our three member variables:

```
var $_name;
var $_age;
var $_gender;
```

We've used an underscore character to begin each of the member variable names. This is a long-standing programming convention used to indicate that these variables should never be accessed directly from outside the class. It is also used for function (method) names that should only be used internally by the class itself and should never be called from outside the class.

Inside the class, each of the member variables is accessible with:

```
$this->$_variable_name;
```

Outside the class, the variables are accessed by calling the object's get() method. Inside a class, the $this variable always points to the object itself.

One of the principles of OOP is to only deal with classes through their *public methods*. That way, major changes to the internal workings of the class won't have any effect on existing code outside the class. That code will always work fine as long as the public methods of the class still provide the same interface. We'll discuss this further in a bit, but first, a word about constructors.

Constructors

Every PHP object must have a constructor. A ***PHP constructor*** is simply a function (method) that creates the object. In this example, we've use the PHP5 from of the constructor. Revolution requires PHP5 so we can be sure it will work. Our constructor has three jobs:

- Allocate memory for the object
- Set the three member variables
- Return a handle to the object

The first and third jobs are handled by PHP behind the scenes. The second one is done in the code of the constructor.

get() and set() Methods

The `get()` method in the code above just returns the value of the internal variable named in the argument to the method. The `set()` method sets the value of the variable named in the first argument to the value set in the second one. By providing these two methods, there's no need to know how the class works internally. The data for each dog could be stored in a database or in a file, and we could add a `save()` method that saved the dog's information.

Using Our Dog Class

Imagine that you want to use the dog class in a snippet. Creating a new dog object would be as simple as this:

```php
$obj = new dog('Rex', '8', 'M');
```

The code above calls the dog class constructor and passes it the values for the three variables. The constructor creates the dog object, sets the three variables, and returns the new object. Once the constructor has executed, we can get any of the three variables like this:

```php
$name = $obj->get('name');
```

If Rex has a birthday, we can do this to update his age:

```php
$age = $obj->get('age');
$age = $age + 1;
$obj->set('age', $age);
```

Note that in the code above, we created our new dog object with the PHP new operator. In MODX, however, you are almost always creating new MODX objects such as snippets, users, resources, etc. Rather than new, you should always create MODX objects with $modx->newObject(). MODX will use the constructor to create a new object and will handle any other necessary housekeeping tasks.

By itself, our dog class isn't very useful. But you can see how well it would work if you think about another class called dogs. The dogs class would contain an array of dog objects. Its constructor could get all the dogs in the database and put them into that internal array. It could have a getDog() method that would return a single dog by name and a getDogs() method that would either return the whole array or a subset of dogs selected by age or gender.

To update a particular dog's information (e.g., on Rex's birthday), you could do something like this (assuming that the dogs object already existed as $dogs):

```
$dog = $dogs->getDog('Rex');
$age = $dog->get('age');
$dog->set('age', $age + 1);
$dog->save();
```

Notice that to do this, you don't need to know anything about how the information for the dogs is stored. You just need to know the names of the public methods and what arguments they take.

This method is used extensively in MODX. The various MODX objects (templates, documents, template variables, chunks, snippets, etc.) are stored in the database. You can get a handle to any of them by calling the $modx->getObject() method of the $modx object like this:

```
$resource = $modx->getObject( 'modResource', array('name'=>'MyPage'));
```

Once you have that handle, you can get member variables of the object by calling the object's get() method, like this:

```
$title = $resource->get('pagetitle');
```

You can change the value of any of the member variables by using the object's set() method, like this:

```
$resource->set('pagetitle', 'New Title');
```

And you can save the altered object to the database by using the object's save() method:

```
$resource->save();
```

All MODX objects also have a `remove()` method, which removes them permanently from the database. Resources also have a `delete()` method, which marks them for deletion but does not remove them from the database.

Just like our dog object, there's no need to know anything about how MODX stores or retrieves the object. You just need to know the public methods of the object and how to call them (referred to collectively as the API). You could, in theory, tell MODX to use a different kind of database other than MySQL to store its objects, and none of your object-related code outside the class would have to change.

Debugging

Debugging is the process of removing the errors from your PHP code. There are PHP debuggers that will run MODX snippets and plugins, but using them is beyond the scope of this book. This section describes debugging snippets and plugins the old-fashioned way. We'll look at snippets first, then at plugins.

Is the Snippet Executing?

Put the following line at the beginning of the snippet:

```
return 'In Snippet';
```

Next, put something around your snippet tag in a document, like this:

```
XXX[[SnippetName]]XXX.
```

When you preview a document containing your snippet tag, if you see nothing at all where the snippet tag is (in other words, you see XXXXXX on the page), check the spelling of your snippet name in the tag and the snippet to make sure they match. Make sure there is no space between the opening and closing brackets in the snippet tag, and look at the raw (X)HTML (turn off the Rich Text Editor) to make sure it hasn't mangled the snippet tag. Once you see the "In Snippet" message, remove that line from the code. If you get a syntax error before seeing the "In Snippet" message, see the next section.

Syntax Errors

If your snippet contains a PHP syntax error, you'll see an error message on the screen when you preview your document (even if the error comes after the return statement). Sometimes, the error message is useful. If it refers to parentheses or tokens, or if it contains the word "expecting," the odds are fair that you have one of the following problems:

* missing semicolon
* missing quotation mark
* mismatched quotes
* missing parenthesis
* missing closing curly brace
* improperly formatted comment

You need a semicolon at the end of each executable line (but not after a control statement ending in a curly brace). If a line of code wraps across more than one line, there should be only one semicolon, and it should be at the very end of the line.

Count your single-quotes, double-quotes, left parentheses, right parentheses, left brackets, right brackets, left curly braces, and right curly braces. There should be an even number of single-quotes and an even number of double-quotes. For parentheses, braces, and brackets, the number of lefts should equal the number of rights of the same type. Using K&R style as described above and indenting properly should help you find mismatches.

If you're still at a loss, try commenting out lines and sections of code until the message goes away. Start with the most complex lines of code, especially ones with lots of quotes and/or parentheses in them.

PHP doesn't like it when you put comments inside of other comments, so be careful not to create nested comments. Also, be careful that you don't create another syntax error with your comments by having one member of a pair of curly braces inside the comment and another outside it.

Once the comments make the error go away, you can start uncommenting the code, one line at a time, until it comes back. This should enable you to find and fix the error. If you find the line but can't see what's wrong with it, post the line on the MODX Forums. You're likely to get help almost immediately.

If you see a message that refers to a "non-object," the odds are that you have either called an object's method (usually get()) after failing to retrieve the object or referred to the $modx object variable inside a function. To make the latter work, you need to put the following line at the top of the function (inside the curly braces):

```
global $modx;
```

If you have code inside functions calling other functions and you still see the "non-object" error, you may need to send the $modx variable as an argument to the later functions.

Dead Variables

Once the syntax errors are gone, the most likely cause of a snippet that doesn't do what it should is variables that don't have the correct value. Most often, they have no value at all, either because their names are misspelled or their values aren't available where they should be. Start at the top of your snippet, and find the first string or integer variable (don't do this with the $modx variable). Put the following line just after the variable:

```
return '<br />VariableName: ' . $variableName;
```

Then, preview the document with the snippet tag, and see if the variable has the proper value. Move the return line down from variable to variable, and make sure they all are set as they should be. You may prefer to check all of them at once using the following code for all of them instead of a return statement:

```
$output .= '<br />VariableName: ' . $variableName;
```

Note that if a variable's value is set outside any function and you later try to access it inside a function, you need to put the following line at the top of the function (inside the curly braces):

```
global $variableName;
```

Otherwise, PHP will create a new variable with that name inside the function, and it will have no value.

If you need to see if an array has the proper values, use this code:

```
$output .= '<pre>' . print_r($arrayName, true) . '</pre>';
return $output;
```

That will print out the key and value of each member of the array.

Logic Errors

What if you're not getting any syntax errors and all the variables are set properly, but the code doesn't do what you want? Now you're looking for a logic error in your code. Sometimes, it helps to write down the logic flow of your code on paper.

When trying to solve a logic problem, look first for an if, else, or elseif statement that uses = instead of ==. Next, look closely at all the conditional statements to make sure that they are doing what they should. Often, it helps to insert return statements with diagnostic messages at various points to see if certain parts of the code are executing at all (e.g., inside an if statement).

Sometimes, you want to eliminate sections of your code to help you see what's happening. If you have a section of code containing comments, you can't comment out the whole section because that would create nested comments. Here's a trick for taking a section of code out of play. Surround the code with a conditional that contains just `true` or `false` as the condition:

```
if (false) {
    /* your code section here */
}
```

You can then turn that section of code on and off simply by changing the condition between `false` and `true`. Make sure, though, that any curly braces, quotes, or parentheses have their matching closer inside the block.

If you're using a built-in PHP function and are not sure you have it right, go to **http://www.php.net/manual** and check. Read the comments below the function's manual section to see if any of the comments are relevant to your situation.

If you're completely stumped, post your code in a message at the MODX Forums (**http://modx.com/forums**), and ask for help. The MODX community is quite generous about helping out in situations like this. Do try to solve the problem yourself first, though. It's considered bad form to ask other people to write your code for you.

Debugging Plugins

Many of the suggestions for debugging snippets will work with plugins. If your plugin returns some output that goes on the screen, you can place debugging information in that output. Unfortunately, plugins designed to work in the Manager (like our BadWordsMgr plugin) produce no output, and worse yet, any syntax error in the plugin can hang the Manager. Reloading the page in your browser will usually get the Manager working again, but you don't get any information on what went wrong. One solution is to write your plugin as a snippet first and then convert it to a plugin after it's working properly.

In some plugins, you can insert debugging information by adding code like this at an appropriate point in the plugin:

```
/* example one */
echo 'Variable: ', $variableName;
die();
/* example two */
die('Variable: ', $variableName);
/* example three (for arrays) */
die('<pre>' . print_r($arrayName, true));
```

If the return value of the plugin is not used (and it often isn't), you can have the plugin return a string. The string can be built dynamically in the plugin code to contain any information you want. The string will not appear on the screen, but it will be written to the MODX error log. In other cases, you just need to try to fix the plugin using trial and error. As we mentioned earlier, it's always a good idea to implement your plugin as a snippet first because snippets are easier to debug.

Here is a neat trick for debugging plugins. Create a chunk called *debug*. Put code like this in your plugin:

```
$chunk = $modx->getObject('modChunk', array('name'=>'debug'));
/* Put any debugging information in the string, $s */
$ids = $modx->getParentIds(58); /* example function */
$s = 'Debug output' . "\n\n";
$s .= print_r($ids,true); /* example debug output */
$chunk->setContent($s);
$chunk->save();
```

You can examine the debug chunk to see the debugging information using Quick Update Chunk after the plugin has executed. The chunk's content will be reset each time the plugin executes.

There is some discussion of adding a debugging console to MODX that will display error messages and debugging information. It may exist by the time you read this.

MODX Objects Reference

The following table lists some of the more commonly used MODX objects in MODX Revolution and some of their properties. "Deprecated" means that the object should not be used and will likely be removed in future versions of MODX. Some of the deprecated items below may have been removed by the time you read this.

Document/Resource (class key = 'modResource')

id (int - Resource ID)
pagetitle (text)
isfolder (int 0/1)
longtitle (text)
description (text)
alias (text)
published (int 0/1)
introtext (text - aka summary)
content (text)
template (int - template ID number)
menuindex (int)
searchable (int 0/1)
cacheable (int 0/1)
createdby (int user ID number)
editedby (int user ID number)
deleted (int 0/1)
deletedby (int user ID number)
publishedby (int user ID number)
createdon (date - date of first save)
publishedon (date - date of most recent change to published)
editedon (date - date it was last edited)
menutitle (text)
donthit (int 0/1) (deprecated)
haskeywords (int 0/1) (deprecated)
hasmetatags (int 0/1) (deprecated)
hidemenu (int 0/1)

Resource-related Objects Available with getOne()

Parent (class='modResource')
Template (class='modTemplate')
CreatedBy (class='modUser')
EditedBy (class='modUser')
DeletedBy (class='modUser')
PublishedBy (class='modUser')
ContentType (class='modContentType')
Context (class='modContext')

Resource-related Objects Available with getMany()

Children (class='modResource')
TemplateVars (class='modTemplateVar')
TemplateVarTemplates (class='modTemplateVarTemplate')

Chunk (class key = 'modChunk')

name (text)
description (text)
category (int - category ID number)
snippet (text - chunk's contents)
locked (int 0/1 - AKA locked for editing)

Chunk-related Objects Available with getOne()

Category (class='modCategory')

Chunk-related Objects Available with getMany()

PropertySets (class='modElementPropertySet')

Snippet (class key = 'modSnippet')

name (text)
description (text)
category (int - category ID number)
snippet (text - snippet's code)
locked (int 0/1 - AKA locked for editing)
properties (text)

Snippet-related Objects Available with getOne()

Category (class='modCategory')

Snippet-related Objects Available with getMany()

PropertySets (class='modElementPropertySet')

Plugin (class key = 'modPlugin')

name (text)
description (text)
category (int - category ID number)
plugincode (text - plugin's code)
locked (int 0/1 - AKA locked for editing)
properties (text)
disabled (int 0/1)

Plugin-related Objects Available with getOne()

Category (class='modCategory')

Plugin-related Objects Available with getMany()

PropertySets (class='modElementPropertySet')
PluginEvents (class='modPluginEvent')

Template (class key = 'modTemplate')

templatename (text)
description (text)
category (int - category ID number)
content (text)
icon (text)
locked (int 0/1)

Template-related Objects Available with getOne()

Category (class='modCategory')

Template-related Objects Available with getMany()

PropertySets (class='modElementPropertySet')
TemplateVarTemplates (class='modTemplateVarTemplate')

Template Variable (class key = 'modTemplateVar')

type (text)
name (text)
caption (text)
description (text)
category (int - category ID)
locked (int 0/1)
elements (text)
rank (int)
display (text)
display_params (text)
default_text (text)

Template-variable-related Objects Available with getOne()

Category (class='modCategory')

Template-variable-related Objects
Available with getMany()

PropertySets (class='modElementPropertySet')
TemplateVarTemplates (class='modTemplateVarTemplate')
TemplateVarResources (class='modTemplateVarResource')
TemplateVarResourceGroups (class='modTemplateVarResourceGroup')

User (class key = 'modUser')

username (text)
password (text)
cachepwd (text)

User-related Objects Available with getOne()

Profile (class='modUserProfile')

User-related Objects Available with getMany()

CreatedResources (class='modResource')
EditedResources (class='modResource')
DeletedResources (class='modResource')
PublishedResources (class='modResource')
SentMessages (class='modUserMessage')
ReceivedMessages (class='modUserMessage')
UserSettings (class='modUserSetting')
UserGroupMembers (class='modUserGroupMember')

User Profile (class key = 'modUserProfile')

fullname (text)
role (int)
email (text)
phone (text)
mobilephone (text)
blocked (int 0/1)
blockeduntil (int - date)
blockedafter (int - date)
logincount (int)
lastlogin (int - date)
thislogin (int - date)
failedlogincount (int)
sessionid (text)
dob (int - date)
gender (int 0/1)
country (text)
state (text)
zip (text)
fax (text)
photo (text)
comment (text)

User-profile-related Objects Available with getOne()

User (class='modUser')
UserRole (class='modUserRole')

Using SMTP to Send Mail in MODX

Many MODX third-party components send email messages, and MODX itself can send an email to new users created in the MODX Manager. When a hosting service has the PHP `mail()` function turned off (as many do), it may be necessary to use SMTP to send the mail.

Some (though not all) MODX third-party components can be configured to use SMTP, and it is possible (though often difficult) to set up a localhost XAMPP install with mail service. Fortunately, with MODX Revolution, these steps are no longer necessary. MODX now has system settings that will make it use SMTP for all mail transactions.

If you have an SMTP account on any server, you can set the following MODX system settings, and MODX will use that account to send mail from the core or from any component that uses the MODX mail service.

The following example shows how to use a free Google Gmail account to send mail with SMTP from inside MODX. Go to **Create → Create a Document Here**, type "smtp" in the search box, and press Enter. Set the following values in the SMTP system settings:

SMTP System Settings

Setting	Value
Use SMTP (`mail_use_smtp`)	Yes
SMTP Authentication (`mail_smtp_auth`)	Yes
SMTP Connection Prefix (`mail_smtp_prefix`)	tls
SMTP Hosts (`mail_smtp_hosts`)	mail.gmail.com
SMTP User (`mail_smtp_user`)	*Your Gmail username*
SMTP Password (`mail_smtp_pass`)	*Your Gmail password*
SMTP Port (`mail_smtp_port`)	465

 Gmail will change the "From" email address of the message to your Gmail address. If you are creating a contact form, you'll want to include the user's email address somewhere in the Tpl chunk you use for the message. Otherwise, you won't be able to reply to the user. As an alternative, Gmail now has an option to set your preferred email sender account to an external account.

For SMTP hosts other than Gmail, you may not need SMTP authentication or a prefix. Check with your hosting service or search their forum for SMTP.

MODX System Events

The following sections provide a reference to all the *system events* available in MODX Revolution. System events are essentially triggers for plugins, which listen for specific system events and execute when they fire.

In the new Quick Create and Quick Update methods for resources and elements, saving the object will invoke the **OnBeforeObjectFormSave** and **OnObjectFormSave** events. As of this writing, however, the other events (e.g., **Render** and **Prerender** family) will not be invoked. That may have changed by the time you read this.

As MODX evolves, system events may be added or removed from the core code. The true list of system events can be found by looking at the System Events tab when editing or creating any plugin. Note that if you click on the "Name" header at the top of the System Events grid, the events will be sorted alphabetically by name. If you click on the "Group" header, they will be grouped according to the objects to which they apply.

You will notice that for MODX objects that can be manipulated in the MODX Manager (e.g., resources, snippets, TVs, etc.), there are four system events that will be triggered when the form's object is saved. The first two fire before the object is saved to the database, and the last two fire after it has been saved. Here are the current names (in order of when they fire):

* **OnBeforeObjectFormSave**
* **OnBeforeObjectSave**
* (Object is saved to the DB at this point)
* **OnObjectSave**
* **OnObjectFormSave**

Notice the word "form" in the first and last events. It may seem redundant to have two "before" events and two "after" events, but they take place in different "layers" of MODX. The first and last events in the list above occur in the "form" layer. That is, they "fire" when a user saves the object in the Manager by clicking on the "Save" button in one of the Manager panels. The inner two events occur in the object class itself (technically, the "model" layer). These inner events fire regardless of whether the save was caused by a user saving a form or by a line of code calling the object's save() method. When PHP code calls an object's save() method, the outer two events don't occur because there is no form involved.

Most of the time, you'll want to connect your plugins to one or both of the outer two (the "form" events) so that they're tied to user actions. The BadWords plugin we created earlier in the book, for example, shouldn't execute when a utility snippet changes the alias of all resources. Similarly, a plugin that logs user actions should only execute when a user performs some action in the Manager. There may be cases, however, when you want a plugin to execute every time some object is saved even if there's no user action involved. In that case, you'd want one or both of the inner two events.

There is a similar relationship between the following four events (in order of occurrence):

- **OnBeforeObjectFormDelete**
- **OnObjectBeforeRemove**
- (Object is deleted from the DB at this point)
- **OnObjectBeforeRemove**
- **OnObjectFormDelete**

The first and last events above occur when the user deletes an object in the Manager. The two inner events occur in the class code before and after the object deletes itself from the database.

Because of potential changes, the names in the Quick Reference section below may not be accurate. Go to **System → System Settings** to see what the current names are. No matter how the names change, you can count on two things for events that involve Manager actions:

- Events with the word **Form** in the name will occur in response to user actions in the Manager, and the others will occur in the class code.
- Events with **Before** in the name will occur before the database is altered, and the others will occur after the database is altered.

System Events by Function: Quick Reference

This section is a quick reference guide to MODX system events. The events are organized by function, but the sections used here do not necessarily correspond to the group names used in the grid in the Manager. There are many more groups in the Manager grid because they are broken down by object (e.g., snippets, chunks, plugins, etc.), and there are too many subdivisions to list conveniently. Please be aware that the list may have changed by the time you read this. Event names may have changed, deprecated events may have been dropped, and new events may have been added.

Events are fired with:

```
$modx->invokeEvent('eventName', $params);
```

The $params array contains information that will be available in any plugin that listens for the event as variables. The available variables (if any) are listed at the end of each event below. For many events in MODX Evolution and earlier versions, the variables may not be available. In Evolution, the $id variable is usually available, but most of the others are not.

The $modx object is available in all events, as are the $_POST, $_COOKIE, and $_SESSION arrays. The event's output (if any) is available as:

```
$modx->event->_output;
```

System settings are available with:

```
$setting = $modx->getOption('SettingName');
```

Or, for MODX Evolution:

```
$setting = $modx->config['SettingName']
```

The variables listed in the sections below are the variables available in plugin code triggered by the event. If no variables are listed for an event, none are available in the plugin. Wherever you see the variable $mode, it is to distinguish between creation events and update events. When you create a new object (e.g., user, chunk, snippet, etc.), it is a creation event. When you update an existing object by editing it, it is an update event.

The two possible values for the $mode variable are:

```
modSystemEvent::MODE_NEW
modSystemEvent::MODE_UPD
```

The $cacheFlag variable determines whether the object or objects will be saved in the object cache and for how long. If $cacheFlag is an integer value, the object will be cached for that many seconds. If $cacheFlag === true, the object will be cached indefinitely. If $cacheFlag === false, the object will not be cached. If $cacheFlag is set to 0, the object will be cached indefinitely. The default value of $cacheFlag varies depending on the event.

Remember that the methods and variables in the following list may have changed by the time you read this and that some of the variables listed may not be available in MODX Evolution.

Back-end System Events

These events "fire" during regular activities in the MODX Manager. They have no immediate effect on what the user sees in the front end. If you want to step in and modify things during Manager operations (e.g., modifying a document as it is saved), use a plugin that listens for one or more of these events (see the Plugins section in Chapter 7 for more information). The text following the name of the event describes when it fires.

(R) = Revolution only.
(E) = Evolution only.

Manager Access Events

These events involve managing users and logging in and out of the MODX Manager. Note that MODX Revolution no longer distinguishes between Web and Manager users, but some Web user events remain for compatibility with legacy add-on components, though they may be removed in future versions of MODX.

To return a value from a plugin attached to an event, set the event's $_output variable. For the login events, plugins should set the value to true to pass the user on to the next check and false to fail the user and abort the login. Example:

```
/* user failed the test */
$rt = false;
$modx->event->_output = $rt;
```

OnManagerLoginFormPrerender — Fires after the login form has been loaded, but before it is displayed and before the check to make sure an install is not going on.

OnManagerLoginFormRender — Fires just after it has been determined that an install is not in progress, but before the login form is displayed.

OnBeforeManagerLogin — Fires just before an attempt is made to authenticate a user headed for the mgr (back end) context.

> Variables: $username (entered by user), $password (entered by user), $attributes (array: $rememberme, $logincontext).

OnUserNotFound — Fires just after **OnBeforeWebLogin** or **OnBeforeManagerLogin** only if the user is not found in the database.

> Variables: $user (user object), $username (entered by user), $password (entered by user), $attributes (array: $rememberme, $logincontext).

OnManagerAuthentication — Fires after the user has been found and authenticated and is determined to be headed for the Manager, but before the user has been determined to be authorized to access the Manager context.

> Variables: $user (user object), $password, $rememberme.

OnWebAuthentication — Fires after the user has been found and authenticated and is determined to be headed for the front-end context, but before the user has been determined to be authorized to access that context.

> Variables: $user (user object), $password, $rememberme.

OnManagerLogin —Fires just after the user has been cleared for access to the Manager context (back end).

> Variables: $username (entered by user), $password (entered by user), $attributes (array: $rememberme, $logincontext).

OnBeforeManagerPageInit — Fires just before a Manager page is rendered.

Variables: $action (ID of Manager page), $filename (controller file name).

OnManagerPageInit — Fires at the beginning of any Manager page request, before any page data has been loaded.

Variables: $action (ID of Manager page).

OnBeforeManagerLogout — Fires just before the user is logged out of the Manager context (back end).

Variables: $userid, $username.

OnManagerLogout — Fires just after the user has been logged out of the Manager context.

Variables: $userid, $username.

OnManagerChangePassword (E) — Fires just after a user's password has been changed in the database.

Variables: $username, $userid, $userpassword (new password).

OnUserChangePassword (R) — (Users) Fires just after a user's password has been changed in the database.

Variables: $username, $userid, $userpassword (new password).

OnManagerCreateGroup (E) — Fires just after a new manager user group is saved to the database.

Variables: $groupid, $groupname.

OnUserGroupBeforeSave (R) — (User Groups) Fires just before the user group is saved to the database.

Variables: $mode, $usergroup (usergroup object), $cacheflag.

OnUserGroupSave (R) — (User Groups) Fires just after the user group has been saved to the database.

Variables: $mode, $usergroup (usergroup object), $cacheflag.

OnUserGroupBeforeRemove (R) — (User Groups) Fires just before the user group is removed from the database.

Variables: $usergroup (usergroup object), $ancestors (used internally).

OnUserGroupRemove (R) — (User Groups) Fires just after the user group has been removed from the database.

Variables: $usergroup (usergroup object), $ancestors (used internally).

OnBeforeUserFormSave — Fires after a user's info has been created or updated, but before the user is added to any user groups and before the database has been updated.

Variables: $mode, $id (user's ID), $user (user object).

OnUserBeforeSave (R) — Fires just before the user is saved to the database.

Variables: $mode, $id (user's ID), $user (user object).

OnManagerSaveUser (E)— Fires after the user profile for a new or updated user has been saved to the database, but before the user table has been updated.

Variables: $mode, $user (user object), $userid, $username, $userpassword, $useremail, $userfullname, $userroleid, $oldusername, $newusername, $oldusername, $olduseremail.

OnUserSave (R) — Fires just after the user is saved to the database.

Variables: $mode, $id (user's ID), $user (user object).

OnUserFormSave — Fires after all user data has been written to the database and after any email is sent to new users.

Variables: $mode, $id (user's ID), $user (user object).

OnManagerDeleteUser (E) — Fires just after a user is deleted from the database.

Variables: $user (user object), $userid, $username.

OnBeforeUserFormDelete (R) — Fires just after the command has been issued to delete the user.

Variables: $user (user object), $id (user's ID).

OnUserBeforeRemove (R) — Fires just before the user is actually deleted from the database.

Variables: $user (user object), $ancestors (used internally).

OnUserRemove (R) — Fires just after the user is actually deleted from the database.

Variables: $user (user object), $ancestors (used internally).

OnUserFormDelete (R) — Fires after **OnUserRemove**, but before the action is logged.

Variables: $user (user object), $id (user's ID).

OnFileManagerUpload — Fires just after a file is uploaded to the site in the Manager.

Variables: $files (files array), $directory (target directory).

Document (Resource) Manager Events

Document fields are available in most of these as $resource->get('**fieldname**').

OnDocFormPrerender — For new and about-to-be-edited resources. Executes after the resource object has been created, but before the Create/Edit document form is loaded.

> Variables: $mode, $id, $resource (resource object —available only when $mode == modSystemEvent::MODE_UPD).

OnDocFormRender — For new and about-to-be-edited resources. Executes after the resource object has been created and the Create/Edit document form has been loaded, but before the RTE (if any) is loaded and before the form is displayed.

> Variables: $mode, $id, $resource (resource object — available only when $mode == modSystemEvent::MODE_UPD).

OnBeforeDocFormSave — For new and to-be-updated resources. Executes after the resource object has been created or found and after fields and TVs have been set, but before any publication date checks or user permission checks have been performed and before the resource is saved to the database.

> Variables: $mode (modSystemEvent::MODE_NEW /
> modSystemEvent::MODE_UPD),
> $id (resource's ID), $resource (resource object).

OnDocFormSave — Fires after the resource and parent are saved to the database, but before the action is logged and before the cache is cleared.

> Variables: $mode (modSystemEvent::MODE_NEW /
> modSystemEvent::MODE_UPD),
> $id (resource's ID), $resource (resource object).

OnDocPublished — Fires when a user changes the status of a resource from unpublished to published and saves it. Does not fire when documents reach their publication dates and are published automatically.

> Variables: $id (resource's ID), $resource (resource object). The $docId
> variable is also set to the resource's ID for legacy reasons but is deprecated.

OnDocUnPublished — Fires when a user changes the status of a resource from published to unpublished and saves it. Does not fire when documents reach their unpublish date and are unpublished automatically.

> Variables: $id (resource's ID), $resource (resource object). The $docId
> variable is also set to the resource's ID for legacy reasons but is deprecated.

OnBeforeDocFormDelete — Fires after children have been identified, but before the resource or its children have been deleted from the database.

> Variables: $id (resource's ID), $resource (resource object), $children (array of child IDs).

OnDocFormDelete (R) — Fires just after the children and the resource have been marked as deleted in the database. Note that deleted resources are saved with the deleted field set. They are not actually deleted until the user empties the trash.

> Variables: $id (resource's ID), $resource (resource object), $children (array of child IDs).

OnBeforeDocFormDelete — Fires after children have been identified, but before the resource or its children have been deleted from the database.

> Variables: $id (resource's ID), $resource (resource object), $children (array of child IDs).

OnResourceUndelete (R) — Fires just after the delete field has been cleared for the resource and its children and all have been saved to the database.

> Variables: $id (resource's ID), $resource (resource object).

OnResourceBeforeSort — Fires just before the Resource tree is sorted.

> Variables: $nodes (nodes in the Resource tree).

OnResourceSort — Fires just after the Resource tree is sorted.

> Variables: $nodes (nodes in the Resource tree).

OnResourceDuplicate — Fires just after a resource has been duplicated.

> Variables: $newResource, $OldResource (new and old resource objects).

OnResourceTVFormPrerender — Fires just before the Template Variable tab is rendered in the Create/Edit Resource panel.

> Variables: $id (ID of the resource).

OnResourceTVFormRender — Fires just after the Template Variable tab is rendered in the Create/Edit Resource panel.

> Variables: $categories, $template, $id (ID of the resource).

OnResourceToolbarLoad (R)— Fires just after the Resource toolbar is loaded.

> Variables: $items (toolbar items).

OnCreateDocGroup (E) — Fires just after a new document group has been saved to the database.

> Variables: $groupid, $groupname.

OnResourceGroupBeforeSave — Fires just before a resource group is saved to the database.

Variables: $mode, $resourceGroup (resource group object), $cacheFlag.

OnResourceGroupSave — Fires just after a resource group is saved to the database.

Variables: $mode, $resourceGroup (resource group object), $cacheFlag.

OnBeforeResourceGroupRemove — Fires just before a resource group is removed from the database.

Variables: $resourceGroup (resource group object), $ancestors (used internally).

OnResourceGroupRemove — Fires just after a resource group is removed from the database.

Variables: $resourceGroup (resource group object), $ancestors (used internally).

OnBeforeEmptyTrash — Fires after the user has clicked on the empty trash icon, but before the deleted items have been removed from the database.

Variables: $ids (array of IDs of the resources to be deleted), $resources (array of resource objects to be deleted).

OnEmptyTrash — Fires after the deleted items have been removed from the database.

Variables: $ids (array of IDs of the deleted resources), $resources (array of resource objects deleted), $num_deleted (number of resources deleted).

Chunk Manager Events

OnChunkFormPrerender — For new and about-to-be-edited chunks. Fires after the object has been created, but before the Create/Edit chunk form is loaded.

Variables: $mode, $id (chunk's ID), $chunk (chunk object — empty unless $mode == modSystemEvent::MODE_UPD).

OnChunkFormRender — For new and about-to-be-edited chunks. Executes after the object has been created and the Create/Edit chunk form has been loaded, but before the form is displayed.

Variables: $mode, $id (chunk's ID), $chunk (chunk object — empty unless $mode == modSystemEvent::MODE_UPD).

OnBeforeChunkFormSave — Fires after the user has clicked on save, but before the database has been altered.

Variables: $mode, $id (chunk's ID), $chunk (chunk object), $data (array containing the chunk's fields; available only when $mode == new).

OnChunkBeforeSave (R)— Fires just before the chunk is saved to the database.

Variables: $mode, $id (chunk's ID), $chunk (chunk object).

OnChunkSave (R)— Fires just after the chunk is saved to the database.

Variables: $mode, $id (chunk's ID), $chunk (chunk object).

OnChunkFormSave — Fires just after **OnChunkSave**, before the action has been logged and before the cache is cleared.

Variables: $mode, $id (chunk's ID), $chunk (chunk object).

OnBeforeChunkFormDelete — Fires after the user has clicked to delete the chunk, but before the database has been altered.

Variables: $id (chunk's ID), $chunk (chunk object).

OnChunkBeforeRemove (R) — Fires just before the chunk is removed from the database.

Variables: $chunk (chunk object), $ancestors (used internally).

OnChunkRemove (R) — Fires just after the chunk is removed from the database.

Variables: $chunk (chunk object), $ancestors (used internally).

OnChunkFormDelete — Fires just after **OnChunkRemove**.

Variables: $id (chunk's ID), $chunk (chunk object).

Snippet Manager Events

OnSnipFormPrerender — For new and about-to-be-edited snippets. Executes after the snippet object has been created, but before the Create/Edit snippet form is loaded.

Variables: $mode, $id (snippet's ID), $snippet (snippet object — only when $mode == modSystemEvent::MODE_UPD).

OnSnipFormRender — For new and about-to-be-edited snippets. Executes after the snippet object has been created and the Create/Edit snippet form has been loaded, but before the form is displayed.

Variables: $mode, $id (snippet's ID), $snippet (snippet object — only when $mode == modSystemEvent::MODE_UPD).

OnBeforeSnipFormSave — Fires after the user has clicked on save, but before the database has been altered.

Variables: $mode, $id (snippet's ID), $snippet (snippet object).

OnSnippetBeforeSave (R) — Fires just before the snippet is saved to the database.

Variables: $mode, $snippet (snippet object), $cacheFlag.

OnSnippetSave (R) — Fires just after the snippet is saved to the database.

> Variables: $mode, $snippet (snippet object), $cacheFlag.

OnSnipFormSave — Fires after **OnSnippetSave**, but before the action has been logged and before the cache is cleared.

> Variables: $mode, $id (snippet's ID), $snippet (snippet object).

OnBeforeSnipFormDelete — Fires after the user has clicked to delete the snippet, but before the database has been altered.

> Variables: $id (snippet's ID), $snippet (snippet object).

OnSnippetBeforeRemove (R) — Fires just before the snippet is removed from the database.

> Variables: $snippet (snippet object), $ancestors (used internally).

OnSnippetRemove (R) — Fires just after the snippet is removed from the database.

> Variables: $snippet (snippet object), $ancestors (used internally).

OnSnipFormDelete — Fires just after **OnSnippetRemove**.

> Variables: $id (snippet's ID), $snippet (snippet object).

Plugin Manager Events

OnPluginFormPrerender — For new and about-to-be-edited plugins. Executes after the plugin object has been created, but before the Create/Edit plugin form is loaded.

> Variables: $mode, $id (plugin's ID), $plugin (plugin object — only
> when $mode == modSystemEvent::MODE_UPD).

OnPluginFormRender — For new and about-to-be-edited plugins. Executes after the plugin object has been created and the Create/Edit plugin form has been loaded, but before the form is displayed.

> Variables: $mode, $id (plugin's ID), $plugin (plugin object — only
> when $mode == modSystemEvent::MODE_UPD).

OnBeforePluginFormSave — Fires after the user has clicked on save, but before the database has been altered.

> Variables: $mode, $id (plugin's ID), $plugin (plugin object).

OnPluginBeforeSave (R) — Fires just before the database is altered.

> Variables: $mode, $plugin (plugin object), $cacheFlag.

OnPluginSave (R) — Fires just after the database is altered.

> Variables: $mode, $plugin (plugin object), $cacheFlag.

OnPluginFormSave — Fires after the database has been altered, but before the action has been logged and before the cache is cleared.

Variables: $mode, $id (plugin's ID), $plugin (plugin object).

OnBeforePluginFormDelete — Fires after the user has clicked to delete the plugin, but before the database has been altered.

Variables: $id (plugin's ID), $plugin (plugin object).

OnPluginBeforeRemove (R) — Fires just before the plugin is removed from the database.

Variables: $ plugin (plugin object), $ancestors (used internally).

OnPluginRemove (R) — Fires just after the plugin is removed from the database.

Variables: $ plugin (plugin object), $ancestors (used internally).

OnPluginFormDelete — Fires after the plugin has been deleted from the database.

Variables: $id (plugin's ID), $plugin (plugin object).

OnPluginEventBeforeRemove (R) — Fires just before a plugin event has been removed.

Variables: $pluginEvent (event object), $ancestors (used internally).

OnPluginEventRemove (R) — Fires just after a plugin event has been removed.

Variables: $pluginEvent (event object), $ancestors (used internally).

Template Manager Events

OnTempFormPrerender — For new and about-to-be-edited templates. Executes after the template object has been created, but before the Create/Edit template form is loaded.

Variables: $mode, $id (template's ID), $template (template object — only when $mode == modSystemEvent::MODE_UPD).

OnTempFormRender — For new and about-to-be-edited templates. Executes after the template object has been created and the Create/Edit template form has been loaded, but before the form is displayed.

Variables: $mode, $id (template's ID), $template (template object — only when $mode == modSystemEvent::MODE_UPD).

OnBeforeTempFormSave — Fires after the user has clicked on save, but before the database has been altered.

Variables: $mode, $id (template's ID), $template (template object).

OnTemplateBeforeSave (R) — Fires just before the database is altered.

Variables: $mode, $template (template object), $cacheFlag.

OnTemplateSave (R) — Fires just after the database is altered.

> Variables: $mode, $template (template object), $cacheFlag.

OnTempFormSave — Fires just after **OnTemplateSave**, but before the action has been logged and before the cache is cleared.

> Variables: $mode, $id (template's ID), $template (template object).

OnBeforeTempFormDelete — Fires after the user has clicked to delete the template, but before the database has been altered.

> Variables: $id (template's ID), $template (template object).

OnTemplateBeforeRemove (R) — Fires just before the template is deleted from the database.

> Variables: $template (template object), $ancestors (used internally).

OnTemplateRemove (R) — Fires just after the template is deleted from the database.

> Variables: $template (template object), $ancestors (used internally).

OnTempFormDelete — Fires just after **OnTemplateRemove**, but before the action is logged and before the cache is cleared.

> Variables: $id (template's ID), $template (template object).

Template Variable Manager Events

Note that these events fire when a TV is created or updated with the Create/Edit TV form, not when the TV is edited on the Create/Edit Resource form.

OnTVFormPrerender — For new and about-to-be-edited TVs. Executes after the template variable object has been created, but before the Create/Edit TV form is loaded.

> Variables: $mode, $id (template variable's ID), $tv (template variable object — only when $mode == modSystemEvent::MODE_UPD).

OnTVFormRender — For new and about-to-be-edited template variables. Executes after the template variable object has been created and the Create/Edit TV form has been loaded, but before the form is displayed.

> Variables: $mode, $id (template variable's ID), $tv (template variable object — only when $mode == modSystemEvent::MODE_UPD).

OnBeforeTVFormSave — Fires after the user has clicked on save, but before the database has been altered.

> Variables: $mode, $id (template variable's ID), $tv (template variable object).

OnTemplateVarBeforeSave (R) — Fires just before the TV is saved to the database.

> Variables: $mode, $templateVar (template variable object), $cacheFlag.

OnTemplateVarSave (R) — Fires just after the TV is saved to the database.

Variables: $mode, $templateVar (template variable object), $cacheFlag.

OnTVFormSave — Fires just after **OnTemplateVarSave**, but before the action has been logged and before the cache is cleared.

Variables: $mode, $id (template variable's ID), $tv (template variable object).

OnBeforeTVFormDelete — Fires after the user has clicked to delete the template variable, but before the database has been altered.

Variables: $id (template variable's ID), $tv (template variable object).

OnTemplateVarBeforeRemove (R) — Fires just before the template variable is deleted from the database.

Variables: $tv (template variable object), $ancestors (used internally).

OnTemplateVarRemove (R) — Fires just before the template variable is deleted from the database.

Variables: $tv (template variable object), $ancestors (used internally).

OnTVFormDelete — Fires just after **OnTemplateVarRemove**.

Variables: $id (template variable's ID), $tv (template variable object).

User Manager Events

OnUserFormPrerender — For new and about-to-be-edited users. Executes after the user object has been created, but before the Create/Edit user form is loaded.

Variables: $mode, $id (user's ID), $user (user object — only when $mode == modSystemEvent::MODE_UPD).

OnUserFormRender — For new and about-to-be-edited users. Executes after the user object has been created and the Create/Edit user form has been loaded, but before the form is displayed.

Variables: $mode, $id (user's ID) , $user (user object — only when $mode == modSystemEvent::MODE_UPD).

OnManagerSaveUser (E) — See Manager Access Events above.

OnBeforeUserFormSave (R) — Fires after the database has been altered, but before the action has been logged and before the cache is cleared.

Variables: $mode, $id (user's ID), $user (user object).

OnUserFormSave — Fires just before **OnUserSave** and after the database has been altered, but before the action has been logged and before the cache is cleared.

Variables: $mode, $id (user's ID), $user (user object).

OnUserBeforeSave (R) — Fires just before the user is saved to the database.

Variables: $mode, $user (user object), $cacheFlag.

OnUserSave (R) — Fires just after the user is saved to the database.

Variables: $mode, $user (user object), $cacheFlag.

OnManagerDeleteUser (E) — See Manager Access Events above.

OnBeforeUserFormDelete (R) — Fires just after **OnUserSave**.

Variables: $id (template variable's ID), $user (user object).

OnUserBeforeRemove (R) — fires just before the user is removed from the database.

Variables: $user (user object), $ancestors (used internally).

OnUserRemove (R) — fires just after the user is removed from the database.

Variables: $user (user object), $ancestors (used internally).

OnUserFormDelete (R) — Fires just after **OnUserRemove**.

Variables: $id (user's ID), $user (user object).

OnBeforeUserActivate (R) — Fired by the ConfirmRegister snippet just before the active field is set and before the user is saved to the database.

Variables: $user (user object).

OnUserActivate (R) — Fired by the ConfirmRegister snippet just after the activated user is saved to the database.

Variables: $user (user object).

The following (E) events work just like the ones above but no longer exist in MODX Revolution, which doesn't distinguish between Web and Manager users:

OnWUsrFormPrerender

OnWUsrFormRender

OnBeforeWUsrFormSave

OnWUsrFormSave

OnBeforeWUsrFormDelete

OnWUsrFormDelete

Category Events

OnCategoryBeforeSave (R) — Fires just before a category is saved to the database.

Variables: $mode, $category (category object), $cacheFlag.

OnCategorySave (R) — Fires just after a category is saved to the database.

Variables: $mode, $category (category object), $cacheFlag.

OnCategoryBeforeRemove (R) — Fires just before a category is removed from the database.

Variables: $category (category object), $ancestors (used internally).

OnCategoryRemove (R) — Fires just after a category is removed from the database.

Variables: $category (category object), $ancestors (used internally).

Rich Text Editor Manager Events

OnRichTextEditorRegister — Fires only if RTE is checked, after the RTE has been identified, but before it is loaded.

OnRichTextEditorInit — Fires only if RTE is checked, after the RTE has been loaded.

Variables: $editor (editor name), $elements (array: DOM names of fields for which the RTE is to be used), $id (ID of resource being edited), $mode, $resource (resource object — only when $mode == modSystemEvent::MODE_UPD).

Note: in some cases, only the first two of these are available.

OnRichTextBrowserInit — Fires after the Rich-text file browser JS is injected, but before the browser is launched.

Module Manager Events (E)

Modules no longer exist in MODX Revolution. They are replaced by Custom Manager Pages (CMPs). These events exist only in MODX Evolution and earlier. They operate like the events above, but generally, only the $id variable is available.

OnModFormPrerender

OnModFormRender

OnBeforeModFormDelete

OnModFormDelete

OnBeforeModFormSave

OnModFormSave

System Setting Events

The following events do not exist or are deprecated in MODX Revolution. In MODX Evolution, no variables are set. They fire just after their section of the **Tools → Configuration** page has been rendered, and they can be used to add extra settings:

`OnInterfaceSettingsRender`

`OnSiteSettingsRender`

`OnFriendlyURLSettingsRender`

`OnUserSettingsRender`

`OnMiscSettingsRender`

In MODX Revolution, new system settings can be added easily in the Manager or in transport packages.

Context Manager Events (R)

`OnContextFormPrerender` — Fires just before the Create/Edit Context form is loaded. Fires only on update, not create.

> Variables: $mode, $key (context key), $context (context object).

`OnContextFormRender` — Fires just after the Create/Edit Context form is loaded, but before it is displayed. Fires only on update, not create.

> Variables: $key (context key), $mode, $context (context object).

`OnContextBeforeSave` — Fires just before the context object is saved to the database.

> Variables: $mode, $context (the context object), $cacheflag.

`OnContextSave` — Fires just after the context object is saved to the database.

> Variables: $mode, $context (the context object), $cacheflag.

`OnContextUpdate` — Fires just after an existing context is updated in the grid, but before the event is logged.

> Variables: $context (the context object).

`OnContextBeforeRemove` — Fires just before the context is removed from the database.

> Variables: $context (the context object), $ancestors (used internally).

`OnContextRemove` — Fires just after the context is removed from the database.

> Variables: $context (the context object), $ancestors (used internally).

Front-end System Events

OnBeforeWebLogin — Fires just before an attempt is made to authenticate a user headed for the 'web' (front end) context.

> Variables: $username (entered by user), $password (entered by user), $attributes (array: $rememberme, $lifetime, $logincontext).

OnWebAuthentication — Fires after the user has been found and authenticated and is determined to be headed for the front-end context, but before the user has been determined to be authorized to access that context.

> Variables: $user (user object), $password, $lifetime, $rememberme.

OnWebLogin — Fires just after the user has been cleared for access to the **web** context (front end).

> Variables: $user (user object), $attributes (array: $rememberme, $lifetime, $logincontext).

OnWebSaveUser (E) — See **OnManagerSaveUser**.

OnWebDeleteUser (E) — See **OnManagerDeleteUser**.

OnWebChangePassword (E)— See **OnManagerChangePassword**.

OnWebCreateGroup (E) — Fires just after a new web user group is saved to the database.

OnHandleRequest — Fires when any request for a resource is received in the front end.

OnWebPageInit — Fires after determination that the site is online and the requested resource is located.

OnLoadWebDocument — Fires after the requested resource is loaded, but before it is parsed.

OnParseDocument — Fires just before the MODX tags are processed.

OnWebPagePrerender — Fires just before a completed web page in the front end is sent to the browser, after all tags have been processed.

OnWebPageComplete — Fires just after a web page has been sent to the browser and the processed resource is saved to the cache.

OnPageUnauthorized — Fires whenever a user requests a page he or she is not authorized to view. Fires before the user is redirected to the Unauthorized page.

Variables:

$response_code — Defaults to unauthorized_page_header system setting or 'HTTP/1.1 401 Unauthorized' if setting is empty.
$error_type — Defaults to '401'.
$error_header — Default is the same as $response_code.
$error_pagetitle — Defaults to unauthorized_page_pagetitle system setting or 'Error 401: Unauthorized' if setting is empty.
$error_message — Defaults to unauthorized_page_message system setting or '<h1>Unauthorized</h1><p>You are not authorized to view the requested content.</p>' if setting is empty.

OnPageNotFound — Fires whenever a user requests a page that MODX is unable to find. Fires before the user is redirected to the error (page not found) page.

Variables: Same as **OnPageUnauthorized**.

OnBeforeWebLogout — Fires just before the user is logged out of the web context (front end).

Variables: $userid, $username, $user (user object).

OnWebLogout — Fires just after the user is logged out of the web context (front end).

Variables: $userid, $username, $user (user object).

OnLogPageHit (E) — Fires when a front-end page is visited, but only if visitor tracking is on.

Cache Events

These may relate to the back end as well.

OnBeforeCacheUpdate — Fires just before the clearCache() method is called.

OnCacheUpdate — Fires in clearCache() method just after the **sitepublishing.idx. php** file is written.

Variables: $results, $paths, $options.

OnLoadWebPageCache — Fires just before a resource is retrieved from the cache.

OnBeforeSaveWebPageCache — Fires after a resource is sent to the browser and just before the cache is updated (for cacheable resources).

OnSiteRefresh — Fires just after clearCache() is called.

Variables: $results (array of objects deleted from the cache).

Index

getting in code, 312, 318, 327-328
getting parent information, 359
getting TV values for, 331, 376, 378
getting TV values in code, 376
in Evolution, 307
publisher, 389
related objects, 387-389
toArray() method, 328, 356
users related to, 387-389

current user, 16, 318, 327, 381-383, 384, 469, 485, 492-493, 592-593
currently logged-in users, 111
custom database table schemas, 409-411
custom database tables, 409-411
custom hooks
for FormIt, 588-594
variables available for FormIt, 590

custom manager page tutorial, 523-533
custom manager pages in Evolution, 533
custom menus, 513
Custom output modifiers, 174-176
custom permissions, 510-512
creating, 486-487

custom preHooks for FormIt, 591-593
custom Top Menu items, 508-509
custom validator properties for FormIt, 578-579
custom validators for FormIt, 578-579
customizing the Create/Edit Resource panel with form customization, 513-523
customizing the MODX Manager, 501-533

D

data storage in chunks, 238-241
database
adding custom tables to, 409-411
deleting objects in code, 344
dumping, 65-66
exporting, 65-66
getting chunks from, 311
getting related objects, 359-361
getting resources from, 311
getting system settings from, 380
getting template variables from, 377-379
getting user extended fields from, 397
getting user groups from, 406-408

getting user profiles from, 382-383
getting users from, 311, 392-393
host, 42
importing, 65-66
location of properties, 250
location of property sets, 250
modifying MODX objects in code, 338-344
modx_actions table, 506
name, 42
password, 40
queries, 631-632, 635-638
removing objects in code, 344
sharing between sites, 425
site_content table, 137
table prefix, 425
username, 40
users table, 479

database tables
adding to database, 409-411
custom, 409-411
overhead, 121
site_snippets, 250

date (output modifier), 172
date and time functions in PHP, 679
date template variables
formatting codes, 215
input type, 210
output type, 214-215

date() PHP function, 679
DayErrorPage resource, 303
DBAPI in Evolution, 416
debugging PHP code, 686-690
decr (output modifier), 172
decrement (output modifier), 172
default
collation, 63
database, 42
lexicon file, 348
permissions, 442
security settings, 442
template variable output type, 215

default (output modifier), 172, 567
default properties, 249-255
creating, 253
editing, 251
elements, 249-255
in Evolution, 306
of snippets, 276-277
overriding, 256
removing, 255
uses for, 255
using with plugins, 293-295

versus property sets, 249-251
working with, 249-251

Default Value TV field, 207
default.inc.php lexicon file, 348
default_template context setting, 429, 432
defined constants (transport packages), 605-607
deletedby (Deleted By) resource field, 153
DeletedBy related object, 390
deletedon (Deleted On) resource field, 153
deleting
(see also: removing)
branches (Git), 82
categories, 106
default properties, 255
directories, 109
files, 109
MODX objects in code, 344
property sets, 260
resources, 102-103, 182
resources from resource groups, 448
resources from resource groups in code, 332
users from user groups, 447-448
users from user groups in code, 332

delimiter template variable output type, 216
description resource field, 142
description TV field, 205
design philosophy of MODX, xi
develop branch (Git), 71
development version of Evolution, 97
development version of Revolution, 70-89
build.config.php file, 87
building, 87-88
cloning, 73-75
transport.core.php file, 87
updating, 88-89

dialogs
Add Category, 117, 462
Add Permission to Template, 486-487
Add Resource Group, 458, 483
Add User Group dialog (form customization), 518
Add User to Group, 447-448, 472
Chmod directory, 108
Create Access Policy, 471

resource objects, 339
user objects, 404, 651
save_chunk permission, 449, 453
save_document permission, 453, 465
save_element permission, 443
save_tv permission, 514
schema file (MODX), 318-319
schema for custom database files, 410-411
scheme argument for `makeUrl()`, 646
scheme property for link tags, 163
scriptProperties (see: `$scriptProperties`)
Search Locally for Packages, 53, 123, 537, 610
searchable resource field, 149
searching MODX forums, 127-128
searching the site, 112
security
Access Control Lists, 441, 449-454
access policies, 440, 443-445
adding users to user groups, 447-448
Administrator policy, 444-445
authority numbers, 440
context access ACL entries, 449-451
context access policy, 444-445
creating ACL entries, 449-454
creating context access ACL entries, 456-457
creating resource group access ACL entries, 458-459
creating roles, 446
creating user groups, 447, 448
default settings, 442
editing object policies, 465-466
element category access policy, 444-445
Element policy, 444-445
elements, 442-453
`hasPermission()` method, 485
hiding elements tutorial, 461-463
hiding pages with a snippet tutorial, 468-470
hiding resources in the Manager tutorial, 454-460
hiding resources with ACL entries tutorial, 470-474
hiding resources with custom permissions tutorial, 485-488
hiding template variables in the front end tutorial, 484-485
hiding template variables in the

Manager with ACLs tutorials, 481-484
in Evolution, 497-498
limiting permissions in the Manager tutorial, 464-467
manager action policies, 444-445
member pages with `tree_root_id` tutorial, 489-496
MemberPages plugin, 492-493
MemberPages snippet, 490-491
minimum role, 450-453, 456-459
minimum role for context access ACL entries, 449
minimum role for element category access ACL entries, 453
minimum role for resource group access ACL entries, 452, 458-459
object policies, 444-445
overview, 438-441
permissions, 440, 443
permissions for contexts, 433
policies for context access ACL entries, 450-451
policies for element category access ACL entries, 453
policies for resource group access ACL entries, 452, 458-459
protected categories, 453
protected resources, 451-453
protection, 438-439
removing roles, 446
reorganizing site for, 420-423
resource group access policies, 444-445
Resource policy, 444-445
Revolution versus Evolution, 440
roles in, 449
RSS feed, 110
system, 437-496
Top Menu, 113-117
user roles, 448
working with, 454-496
Security menu
Access Controls, 115
Flush All Sessions, 117
Flush Permissions, 117
Manage Users, 114
select (output modifier), 168
`sendEmail()` method, 651
`sendError()` method, 648
`sendErrorPage()` method, 469, 648
`sendForward()` method, 302, 648
`sendRedirect()` method, 488, 648

`sendUnauthorizedPage()` method, 469, 490, 648
SEO-friendly URLs, 55-61
seOnChunkBeforeRemove, 706
server 500 error, 46
server requirements
browsers, 36-37
database, 36-37
for MODX, 36-37
operating system, 36-37
PHP, 36-37
web servers, 36-37
`set()` method, 340, 397, 399, 404, 639
`set()` method (transport packages), 606
`setAttribute()` method, 636
`setContent()` method, 340, 399, 400, 651
`setContent()` method (transport packages), 606
`setDebug()` method, 636, 648
`setLogLevel()` method, 636
`setLogLevel()` method (transport packages), 625
`setLogTarget()` method, 636
`setLogTarget()` method (transport packages), 625
`setLogTarget()` method options, 636
`setOption()` method, 637
setPackageAttributes array (transport packages), 610
`setPackageAttributes()` method (transport packages), 615
`setPlaceholder()` method, 344-347, 591, 593, 648-649
`setPlaceholders()` method, 346-347, 649
sets in form customization, 516
`setService()` method, 643
setting
directory permissions, 108, 108
field default values with form customization tutorial, 523
field labels with form customization tutorial, 523
file and directory permissions, 69
file permissions, 108
package attributes for transport packages, 615
placeholders in code, 344-347, 383-384